Middle School 2-1
학교시험 완벽대비

1학기 전과정

적중 100 plus

영어 기출문제집

중 2
동아 | 이병민

Best Collection

구성과 특징

교과서의 주요 학습 내용을 중심으로 학습 영역별 특성에 맞춰 단계별로 다양한 학습 기회를 제공하여
단원별 학습능력 평가는 물론 중간 및 기말고사 시험 등에 완벽하게 대비할 수 있도록 내용을 구성

Words & Expressions

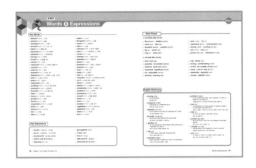

Step1   Key Words 단원별 핵심 단어 설명 및 풀이
          Key Expression 단원별 핵심 숙어 및 관용어 설명
          Word Power 반대 또는 비슷한 뜻 단어 배우기
          English Dictionary 영어로 배우는 영어 단어

Step2   실력평가 단원별 수시평가 대비 주관식, 객관식 문제풀이

Step3   서술형 대비 학업성취도 및 수행능력평가 대비 서술형 문제풀이

Conversation

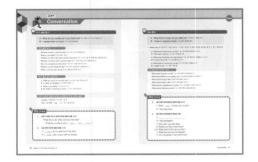

Step1   핵심 의사소통 소통에 필요한 주요 표현 방법 요약
          핵심 Check 기본적인 표현 방법 및 활용능력 확인

Step2   대화문 익히기 교과서 대화문 심층 분석 및 확인

Step3   교과서 확인학습 빈칸 채우기를 통한 문장 완성 능력 확인

Step4   기본평가 시험대비 기초 학습 능력 평가

Step5   실력평가 단원별 수시평가 대비 주관식, 객관식 문제풀이

Step6   서술형 대비 학업성취도 및 수행능력평가 대비 서술형 문제풀이

Grammar

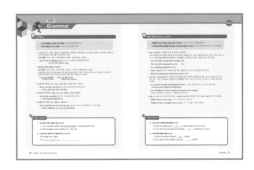

Step1   주요 문법 단원별 주요 문법 사항과 예문을 알기 쉽게 설명
          핵심 Check 기본 문법사항에 대한 이해 여부 확인

Step2   기본평가 시험대비 기초 학습 능력 평가

Step3   실력평가 단원별 수시평가 대비 주관식, 객관식 문제풀이

Step4   서술형 대비 학업성취도 및 수행능력평가 대비 서술형 문제풀이

Reading

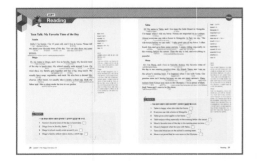

Step1   구문 분석 단원별로 제시된 문장에 대한 구문별 분석과 내용 설명
          확인문제 문장에 대한 기본적인 이해와 인지능력 확인

Step2   확인학습A 빈칸 채우기를 통한 문장 완성 능력 확인

Step3   확인학습B 제시된 우리말을 영어로 완성하여 작문 능력 키우기

Step4   실력평가 단원별 수시평가 대비 주관식, 객관식 문제풀이

Step5   서술형 대비 학업성취도 및 수행능력평가 대비 서술형 문제풀이
          교과서 구석구석 교과서에 나오는 기타 문장까지 완벽 학습

Composition

|영역별 핵심문제|

단어 및 어휘, 대화문, 문법, 독해 등 각 영역별 기출문제의 출제 유형을 분석하여 실전에 대비하고 연습할 수 있도록 문제를 배열

|단원별 예상문제|

기출문제를 분석한 후 새로운 시험 출제 경향을 더하여 새롭게 출제될 수 있는 문제를 포함하여 시험에 완벽하게 대비할 수 있도록 준비

|서술형 실전 및 창의사고력 문제|

학교 시험에서 점차 늘어나는 서술형 시험에 집중 대비하고 고득점을 취득하는데 만전을 기하기 위한 학습 코너

|단원별 모의고사|

영역별, 단계별 학습을 모두 마친 후 실전 연습을 위한 모의고사

on the textbook

교과서 파헤치기

- **단어Test1~3** 영어 단어 우리말 쓰기, 우리말을 영어 단어로 쓰기, 영영풀이에 해당하는 단어와 우리말 쓰기
- **대화문Test1~2** 대화문 빈칸 완성 및 전체 대화문 쓰기
- **본문Test1~5** 빈칸 완성, 우리말 쓰기, 문장 배열연습, 영어 작문하기 복습 등 단계별 반복 학습을 통해 교과서 지문에 대한 완벽한 습득
- **구석구석지문Test1~2** 지문 빈칸 완성 및 전문 영어로 쓰기

이책의 차례 **Contents**

Can We Talk?

🎤 의사소통 기능

- 조언 구하기

  A: What can I do to sleep better?

  B: You can drink warm milk before bed.

- 제안하기

  A: How about going to the bookstore?

  B: Great idea!

🎤 언어 형식

- to부정사의 형용사적 용법

  Give the other person a chance **to talk**.

- 명령문 + and / or

  Change the topic, **or** your partner will fall asleep.

교과서

Words & Expressions

Key Words

- **active** [ǽktiv] 형 적극적인, 능동적인
- **ad** [aed] 명 광고 (= advertisement)
- **angry** [ǽŋgri] 형 화난
- **app** [æp] 명 앱, 응용프로그램
- **asleep** [əslíːp] 형 잠이 든
- **attention** [əténʃən] 명 주의
- **boots** [buːts] 명 장화, 부츠
- **bulletin board** 게시판
- **capital** [kǽpətl] 명 대문자, 수도
- **chance** [tʃæns] 명 기회
- **character** [kǽriktər] 명 글자, 특성, 성격
- **club** [klʌb] 명 동아리, 동호회
- **conversation** [kànvərséiʃən] 명 대화
- **direction** [dirékʃən] 명 방향
- **feedback** [fíːdbæk] 명 반응, 피드백
- **foreigner** [fɔ́ːrənər] 명 외국인
- **gladly** [glǽdli] 부 기꺼이, 즐거이, 기쁘게
- **healthily** [hélθili] 부 건강하게
- **improve** [imprúːv] 동 향상시키다, 개선하다
- **information** [ìnfərméiʃən] 명 정보
- **interest** [íntərəst] 명 관심사, 흥미
- **join** [dʒɔin] 동 ~에 들다, ~에 가입하다
- **keep** [kiːp] 동 유지하다
- **leave** [liːv] 동 떠나다
- **mad** [mæd] 형 성난
- **magic** [mǽdʒik] 형 마법의 명 마법, 마술

- **manage** [mǽnidʒ] 동 관리하다
- **manner** [mǽnər] 명 예절, 예의
- **mean** [miːn] 동 의미하다
- **nervous** [nɔ́ːrvəs] 형 긴장한
- **nod** [nɑd] 동 (고개를) 끄덕이다
- **opinion** [əpínjən] 명 의견, 견해
- **poor** [puər] 형 잘 못하는, 형편없는
- **post** [poust] 동 올리다, 게시하다
- **practice** [prǽktis] 동 연습하다
- **president** [prézədənt] 명 장, 회장
- **probably** [prάbəbli] 부 아마 (= perhaps)
- **quickly** [kwíkli] 부 급히, 빠르게
- **recycle** [riːsáikl] 동 재활용하다
- **rude** [ruːd] 형 무례한 (↔ polite)
- **respect** [rispékt] 동 존중하다 명 존경
- **respond** [rispánd] 동 대답하다, 응답하다
- **save** [seiv] 동 구하다, 건지다
- **share** [ʃɛər] 동 나누다, 공유하다, 분배하다
- **shout** [ʃaut] 동 외치다, 소리치다
- **sometimes** [sʌ́mtàimz] 부 때때로, 이따금
- **terrible** [térəbl] 형 끔찍한
- **text message** 문자 메시지
- **trouble** [trʌ́bl] 명 문제, 곤란, 어려움
- **useful** [júːsfəl] 형 유용한 (↔ useless)
- **waste** [weist] 동 낭비하다
- **wet** [wet] 형 젖은 (↔ dry)

Key Expressions

- **be mad at** ~에게 화나다
- **fall asleep** 잠들다
- **have ~ in common** ~을 공통적으로 지니다
- **keep -ing** 계속 ~하다
- **make up with** ~와 화해하다
- **no wonder** ~하는 것도 당연하다, ~할 만도 하다

- **on time** 정각에
- **pay attention to** ~에 주의를 기울이다
- **put ~ first** ~을 우선시하다
- **put on** ~을 신다, 입다, 쓰다
- **run into** ~을 우연히 만나다
- **space out** 딴생각하다

Word Power

※ 서로 반대되는 뜻을 가진 단어

☐ **useful** (유용한) ↔ **useless** (쓸모없는)

☐ **common** (공통의, 흔한) ↔ **rare** (드문)

☐ **active** (활동적인) ↔ **passive** (수동적인)

☐ **quickly** (빠르게) ↔ **slowly** (느리게)

☐ **low** (낮은) ↔ **high** (높은)

☐ **rude** (무례한) ↔ **polite** (예의바른)

☐ **listener** (듣는 사람) ↔ **speaker** (말하는 사람)

☐ **wet** (젖은) ↔ **dry** (건조한)

☐ **nervous** (불안해하는) ↔ **calm** (침착한)

☐ **ask** (묻다) ↔ **reply** (대답하다)

English Dictionary

☐ **attention** 주의
→ the act of listening to, looking at, or thinking about something or someone carefully
어떤 것이나 어떤 사람을 주의 깊게 듣고, 보고, 생각하는 행위

☐ **capital** 대문자
→ a letter of the form and size that is used at the beginning of a sentence or a name
문장이나 이름의 시작에서 사용되는 형태와 크기의 글자

☐ **chance** 기회, 가망
→ a possibility of something happening, especially something that you want
무언가 특히 당신이 원하는 무언가가 일어날 가능성

☐ **common** 흔한, 공통의
→ happening often and to many people or in many places
자주 그리고 많은 사람들에게 혹은 많은 장소에서 일어나는

☐ **conversation** 대화
→ an informal talk involving a small group of people or only two
소그룹의 사람들 또는 두 사람을 포함하는 비공식적인 담화

☐ **improve** 향상시키다
→ to make something better than before
어떤 것을 전보다 더 나아지게 하다

☐ **mad** 성난
→ very angry
매우 화가 난

☐ **manner** 태도
→ the way that somebody behaves towards other people
어떤 사람이 다른 사람들을 향해 행동하는 방식

☐ **nod** 끄덕이다
→ to move your head up and down to show agreement, understanding
동의나 이해를 보여주기 위해 머리를 위 아래로 움직이다

☐ **recycle** 재활용하다
→ to treat things that have already been used so that they can be used again
이미 사용되었던 것을 다시 사용할 수 있도록 처리하다

☐ **respond** 대답하다, 응답하다
→ to give a spoken or written answer to somebody or something
누군가 또는 무언가에 구두나 서면 답변을 주다

☐ **rude** 무례한, 버릇없는
→ having or showing a lack of respect for other people and their feelings
다른 사람들과 그들의 감정에 대한 존중이 부족함을 보여주는

☐ **save** 구하다
→ to keep someone or something safe from death, harm, loss, etc.
누군가나 뭔가를 죽음, 해악, 상실로부터 안전하게 지키다

☐ **share** 공유하다, 함께 쓰다
→ to have something, use it, or occupy it with another person
어떤 것을 다른 사람과 함께 가지거나 사용하거나 점유하다

☐ **shout** 외치다, 소리치다
→ to say something very loudly
어떤 것을 아주 큰 소리로 말하다

☐ **terrible** 끔찍한
→ making you feel very unhappy, upset or frightened
기분이 매우 나쁘거나, 화나거나, 깜짝 놀라게 만드는

서답형

01 다음 짝지어진 단어의 관계가 같도록 빈칸에 알맞은 말을 쓰시오.

rich : poor = _____ : dry

02 다음 문장의 밑줄 친 단어와 같은 의미로 쓰인 것은?

You should not be <u>poor</u> listeners.

① I practiced a lot not to be a <u>poor</u> speaker.
② They moved from a <u>poor</u> country.
③ My <u>poor</u> puppy have starved for a few days.
④ I want to help <u>poor</u> children in my hometown.
⑤ They are too <u>poor</u> to buy a piece of bread.

03 다음 중 밑줄 친 부분의 뜻풀이가 바르지 않은 것은?

① He <u>nodded</u>, showing that he understood.
　고개를 끄덕였다
② Let's <u>recycle</u> paper to save the earth.
　재활용하다
③ Why don't you share <u>common</u> interest?
　공통의
④ You need to <u>respect</u> others' opinions.
　존중하다
⑤ What is today's <u>topic</u> of discussion?
　목적

[04~05] 다음 중 밑줄 친 어휘와 바꾸어 쓸 수 있는 것을 <u>모두</u> 고르시오.

04

I have a <u>trouble</u> sleeping at night.

① problem　　　② trial
③ danger　　　④ pay
⑤ difficulty

05

We had no <u>chance</u> to talk about it.

① opportunity　　② play
③ fortune　　　④ dancer
⑤ space

서답형

[06~07] 다음 영영풀이에 해당하는 말을 쓰시오.

06

a board for putting notices on

➡ _____

07

a person who talks in a particular way or who talks a lot

➡ _____

서답형

08 다음 우리말에 맞게 빈칸에 알맞은 말을 쓰시오.

네가 잘못된 방향으로 가고 있는 거 같아.
➡ I'm afraid you are going in the wrong
_____.

01 다음 빈칸에 들어갈 말을 〈보기〉에서 찾아 쓰시오.

┌── 보기 ├──
have   put   pay   keep

(1) _____ going straight ahead until you find a library.
(2) What do you and your sister _____ in common?
(3) If you want to improve your grade, you should _____ attention to classes.
(4) Doctors _____ the patients first.

02 다음 빈칸에 들어갈 말을 순서대로 쓰시오.

- My teacher called me when I spaced (A)_____ during the class.
- Successful people have many things (B)_____ common.
- I was nervous when they paid attention (C)_____ me.

(A) _____ (B) _____ (C) _____

03 다음 우리말과 일치하도록 주어진 단어를 배열하시오.

(1) 청중들은 잠들어 버릴 것이다.
(fall / the / audience / will / asleep)
➡ _____

(2) Jane은 나에게 화가 났다.
(me / is / at / mad / Jane)
➡ _____

(3) 우리의 영어 실력을 향상시키기 위해 우리는 무엇을 할 수 있을까?
(English / can / do / improve / what / our / we / to)
➡ _____

04 다음 우리말에 맞게 빈칸에 알맞은 말을 쓰시오. (주어진 말을 이용할 것.)

나는 도서관에 가는 길에 우연히 한 외국인을 만났다. (run)
➡ On the way to the library, I _____ _____ a foreigner.

05 다음 문장의 빈칸에 들어갈 말을 〈보기〉에서 찾아 쓰시오.

┌── 보기 ├──
respect capital ignore useful useless

(1) You should _____ others' opinions.
(2) You should post _____ information.
(3) You should not use only _____ letters.

06 다음 대화의 밑줄 친 우리말을 주어진 단어를 사용하여 영어로 쓰시오.

A: Minsu, let's do something together on Thursday.
B: Sounds great! What do you want to do?
A: 병원에서 자원봉사하는 게 어때?
(how / volunteer)
B: Great idea!

➡ _____

교과서 Conversation

1 조언 구하기

> **A** What can I do to sleep better? 잠을 잘 자기 위해 무엇을 해야 할까?
>
> **B** You can drink warm milk before bed. 자기 전에 따뜻한 우유를 마셔.

■ 'What can I do to ~?'는 조언을 구할 때 쓰는 표현으로, 이에 대한 대답으로 You can ~., I think you should ~., You'd better ~. 등의 표현을 사용하여 대답할 수 있다.

- A: What can I do to manage my time better? 나의 시간을 더 잘 관리하기 위해 무엇을 할 수 있을까?
  B: I think you should make a weekly plan. 나는 네가 주간 계획을 만들어야 한다고 생각해.

조언 구하기 표현

- What can I do to ~? 내가 ~하기 위해 무엇을 할 수 있을까?
- What should I do to ~? 내가 ~하기 위해 무엇을 해야 할까?
- Is there anything I can do to ~? 내가 ~하기 위해 할 수 있는 게 있을까?

- A: What can I do to improve my English? 나의 영어 실력을 향상시키기 위해 무엇을 할 수 있을까?
  B: You can read English books. 너는 영어 책을 읽을 수 있어.

- A: What should I do to stay healthy? 건강을 유지하기 위해 무엇을 해야 할까?
  B: I think you should eat lots of vegetables. 나는 네가 채소를 많이 먹어야 한다고 생각해.

핵심 Check

1. 다음 우리말과 일치하도록 빈칸에 알맞은 말을 쓰시오.

   (1) A: What can I do to _____ _____ _____ _____ _____?
      (많은 친구들을 사귀기 위해 무엇을 할 수 있을까?)

      B: _____ _____ _____ a sports club. (너는 스포츠 동아리에 가입할 수 있어.)

   (2) A: What should I do to lose my weight? (살을 빼기 위해 무엇을 해야 할까?)

      B: You should _____ _____. (너는 운동을 규칙적으로 해야 해.)

② 제안하기

> **A** How about going to the bookstore? 서점에 가는 게 어때?
> **B** Great idea! 좋은 생각이다!

■ 'How about ~?'은 '~하는 게 어때?'라는 의미로 무언가를 제안할 때 쓰는 표현이다. 이에 대해 제안을 받아들일 때는 Great idea! / Sounds good. / That's a good idea. 등으로 대답할 수 있다. 반면에 제안을 받아들이지 않을 때는 I'm sorry but I can't. / I don't feel like ~. 등으로 거절할 수 있다.

제안하기

- How about ~? ~하는 게 어때?
- What about ~? ~하는 게 어때?
- Why don't you[we] ~? ~하는 게 어때?
- Let's ~. ~ 하자.

- A: What about going to the movies? 영화 보러 가는 게 어때?
  B: That's a great idea! 좋은 생각이야!

- A: Why don't we volunteer at the hospital? 병원에서 자원봉사하는 게 어때?
  B: Sounds good. 좋은 생각이야.

핵심 Check

2. 다음 우리말과 일치하도록 빈칸에 알맞은 말을 쓰시오.

(1) A: How about ＿＿＿＿ ＿＿＿＿ ＿＿＿＿ ＿＿＿＿? (서점에 가는 게 어때?)
    B: Great idea! (좋은 생각이야.)

(2) A: Why don't you ＿＿＿＿ ＿＿＿＿ ＿＿＿＿? (이 상자를 재활용하는 게 어때?)
    B: That's a good idea. (좋은 생각이야.)

A. Listen and Speak 1-A

B: I'm so ❶excited about the new school year.

G: Me, too. It's going to be great!

B: ❷What can I do to make a lot of new friends?

G: You can ❸join a sports club.

B: That's a great idea.

B: 나는 새 학년이 되어 아주 신나.
G: 나도. 정말 좋을 것 같아!
B: 새 친구를 많이 사귀려면 어떻게 해야 할까?
G: 스포츠 동아리에 가입해.
B: 그거 좋은 생각이다.

❶ excited: 신이 난, 들뜬, 흥분한
❷ 'What can I do to ~?'는 '~하려면 어떻게 해야 할까요?'라는 뜻으로 조언을 구할 때 사용하는 표현이다. make a friend: 친구를 사귀다, a lot of: 많은
❸ join: 가입하다

Check(√) True or False

(1) The boy wants to make many new friends.　　　　　T ☐ F ☐

(2) The girl is worried about the new school year.　　　T ☐ F ☐

B. Listen and Speak 1-B

Jenny: Mike, did you join any clubs?

Mike: Yes, I joined the singing club.

Jenny: Oh, I see.

Mike: ❶What's wrong, Jenny?

Jenny: I'm the ❷president of the magic club. ❸But I only have two members.

Mike: Oh, no. ❹That's terrible.

Jenny: What can I do to get more members?

Mike: ❺Why don't you post an ad on the school bulletin board?

Jenny: That's a good idea. ❻I'll do it right away.

Jenny: Mike, 동아리에 가입했니?
Mike: 응. 노래 동아리에 가입했어.
Jenny: 아, 알겠어.
Mike: 무슨 일이니, Jenny?
Jenny: 나는 마술 동아리의 회장이야. 그런데 회원이 두 명뿐이야.
Mike: 아, 저런. 큰일이네.
Jenny: 더 많은 회원을 모으려면 어떻게 해야 할까?
Mike: 학교 게시판에 광고를 붙이는 게 어떠니?
Jenny: 그거 좋은 생각이다. 당장 붙여야겠어.

❶ What's wrong?: 무슨 안 좋은 일이 있니?(= What's the matter?)
❷ president: 회장
❸ member: 회원
❹ That's terrible.: (그거) 큰일이네.
❺ 'Why don't you ~?'는 '~하는 게 어떠니?'라는 조언을 나타낸다.
❻ right away: 즉시, 당장

Check(√) True or False

(3) There are a lot of members in the magic club.　　　　　　　　　T ☐ F ☐

(4) Jenny will post an ad about the magic club on the school bulletin board.　T ☐ F ☐

Listen and Speak 1-C

A: ❶What can I do to sleep better?

B: ❷You can drink warm milk ❸before bed.

A: That's a good idea. ❹I'll do that.

❶ 'What can I do to ~?'는 '~하기 위해 어떻게 해야 할까요?'라는 뜻으로 조언을 구할 때 사용하는 표현이다. sleep better: 잠을 더 잘 자다

❷ 'You can ~'을 사용해 조언을 할 수 있다.

❸ before bed: 취침 전에

❹ do that = drink warm milk before bed

Listen and Speak 2-A

Brian: ❶Amy, what does this Chinese character mean?

Amy: Hmm... ❷I have no idea. ❸How about asking your teacher?

Brian: Okay, I will.

❶ character: 글자, Chinese character: 한자

❷ I have no idea.: 전혀 모르겠다.

❸ 'How about ~?'은 '~하는 게 어떠니?'라는 뜻으로 어떤 일을 제안할 때 사용하는 표현이다.

Listen and Speak 2-B

Sue: Minsu, why are you so late?

Minsu: Oh, I'm sorry. ❶On the way, I ran into a foreigner.

Sue: Yes, and?

Minsu: ❷I had to take him to the subway station.

Sue: ❸Why didn't you just tell him the directions?

Minsu: He didn't speak English very well.

Sue: Hmm... ❹How about using the *Talk Smart* app next time?

Minsu: *Talk Smart*? ❺What kind of app is it?

Sue: It changes one language to another. It's really helpful.

Minsu: Really? ❻I'll try it next time.

❶ on the way: 도중에

❷ had to: ~해야 했다

❸ tell A the directions: A에게 방향을 말해 주다

❹ app: 응용프로그램(application의 약자)

❺ What kind of: 무슨 종류의

❻ it = the *Talk Smart* app

Listen and Speak 2-C

A: ❶Minsu, let's do something together on Thursday.

B: Sounds great! ❷What do you want to do?

A: ❸How about going to the bookstore?

B: Great idea!

❶ 'Let's+동사원형'은 '~하자.'라는 뜻으로 제안할 때 사용하는 표현이다.

❷ 'What do you want to do?'는 무엇을 하고 싶은지 묻는 표현이다.

❸ 'How about ~?'은 '~하는 게 어떠니?'라는 뜻으로 어떤 일을 제안할 때 사용하는 표현이다.

Real Life Talk

Brian: Hey, Mina, what's wrong?

Mina: ❶My best friend, Kate, is mad at me.

Brian: That's terrible. What happened?

Mina: ❷I said her new hairstyle was cute just like my dog's.

Brian: ❸No wonder she's mad at you.

Mina: Right. ❹She won't talk to me.

Brian: Yeah, She's probably really angry.

Mina: ❺What can I do to make up with her?

Brian: ❻How about sending her a text?

Mina: That's a good idea. ❼I'll do that.

❶ be mad at: ~에게 화가 나다

❷ just like ~: 꼭 ~처럼, my dog's = my dog's hairstyle

❸ No wonder: ~이 놀랍지 않다[당연하다] (= It is no wonder that ~)

❹ won't = will not: ~하려고 하지 않는다

❺ make up with: ~와 화해하다

❻ text: (휴대 전화로 보내는) 문자 메시지

❼ do that = send her a text

● 다음 우리말과 일치하도록 빈칸에 알맞은 말을 쓰시오.

Listen & Speak 1 A

B: I'm so _____ about the new school year.

G: Me, _____. It's _____ to be great!

B: What can I do to make a lot of _____ _____?

G: You can _____ _____ _____ _____.

B: That's a great _____.

B: 나는 새 학년이 되어 아주 신나.
G: 나도. 정말 좋을 것 같아!
B: 새 친구를 많이 사귀려면 어떻게 해야 할까?
G: 스포츠 동아리에 가입해.
B: 그거 좋은 생각이다.

Listen & Speak 1 B

Jenny: Mike, did you _____ any clubs?

Mike: Yes, I joined _____ _____ _____.

Jenny: Oh, I _____.

Mike: What's _____, Jenny?

Jenny: I'm the _____ of the magic club. But I only have _____ _____.

Mike: Oh, no. That's _____.

Jenny: What can I do to _____ _____ _____?

Mike: Why don't you post an ad on the _____ _____ _____?

Jenny: That's a good _____. I'll do it _____ _____.

Jenny: Mike, 동아리에 가입했니?
Mike: 응, 노래 동아리에 가입했어.
Jenny: 아, 알겠어.
Mike: 무슨 일이니, Jenny?
Jenny: 나는 마술 동아리의 회장이야. 그런데 회원이 두 명 뿐이야.
Mike: 아, 저런. 큰일이네.
Jenny: 더 많은 회원을 모으려면 어떻게 해야 할까?
Mike: 학교 게시판에 광고를 붙이는 게 어떠니?
Jenny: 그거 좋은 생각이다. 당장 붙여야겠어.

Listen & Speak 1 C

A: What can I do to _____ _____?

B: You can drink _____ _____ before bed.

A: That's _____ _____ _____. I'll do that.

A: 잠을 더 잘 자기 위해 무엇을 해야 할까?
B: 취침 전에 따뜻한 우유를 마셔.
A: 그거 좋은 생각이다. 그렇게 할게.

Listen & Speak 2 A

Brian: Amy, what does this Chinese character _____?

Amy: Hmm... I have no _____. _____ _____ _____ your teacher?

Brian: Okay, I will.

B: Amy, 이 한자가 무슨 뜻이니?
A: 음... 잘 모르겠어. 너희 선생님께 물어보는 게 어떠니?
B: 응, 그렇게 할게.

Listen & Talk 2 B

Sue: Minsu, _____ are you so late?

Minsu: Oh, I'm sorry. On the way, I _____ _____ a _____.

Sue: Yes, and?

Minsu: I had to take him to the _____ _____.

Sue: Why didn't you just _____ him the _____?

Minsu: He didn't speak English very well.

Sue: Hmm... How _____ _____ the *Talk Smart* app next time?

Minsu: *Talk Smart*? What _____ _____ app is it?

Sue: It _____ one language to another. It's really _____.

Minsu: Really? I'll try it _____ _____.

Listen & Talk 2 C

A: Minsu, let's do _____ _____ on Thursday.

B: Sounds great! What do you _____ _____ _____?

A: How about going to the _____?

B: _____ idea!

Real Life Talk

Brian: Hey, Mina, what's _____?

Mina: My _____ friend, Kate, is _____ _____ me.

Brian: That's _____. What _____?

Mina: I _____ her new hairstyle was cute _____ _____ my dog's.

Brian: _____ _____ she's mad _____ you.

Mina: Right. She _____ _____ to me.

Brian: Yeah. She's _____ really angry.

Mina: What can I do to _____ _____ _____ her?

Brian: How _____ _____ her a text?

Mina: That's a good _____. I'll _____ that.

Sue: 민수야, 왜 이렇게 늦었니?
Minsu: 아, 미안해. 길에서 외국인을 만났어.
Sue: 응, 그래서?
Minsu: 내가 그를 지하철역까지 데려다 줘야 했어.
Sue: 그에게 그냥 방향만 말해 주지 않았니?
Minsu: 그는 영어를 잘하지 못했어.
Sue: 음... 다음에는 'Talk Smart' 앱을 사용하는 게 어떠니?
Minsu: 'Talk Smart'라고? 그게 어떤 종류의 앱이니?
Sue: 그것은 한 언어를 다른 언어로 바꿔 줘. 아주 도움이 돼.
Minsu: 정말? 다음에는 그것을 사용해 봐야겠다.

A: 민수야, 목요일에 함께 무언가를 하자.
B: 좋아! 너는 무엇을 하고 싶니?
A: 서점에 가는 게 어때?
B: 좋은 생각이야!

Brian: 얘, 미나야, 무슨 일 있니?
미나: 내 가장 친한 친구인 Kate가 나에게 화가 났어.
Brian: 큰일이다. 무슨 일 있었니?
미나: 내가 그녀의 새로 한 머리 모양이 꼭 우리 개의 머리 모양처럼 귀엽다고 말했어.
Brian: 그녀가 너에게 화내는 게 당연해.
미나: 맞아. 그녀는 나와 말하지 않을 거야.
Brian: 그래. 그녀는 아마도 정말 화났을 거야.
미나: 그녀와 화해하려면 어떻게 해야 할까?
Brian: 그녀에게 문자를 보내는 게 어떠니?
미나: 그거 좋은 생각이다. 그렇게 할게.

01 다음 대화의 빈칸에 들어갈 말로 적절한 것은?

> A: What can we do to _____?
> B: How about reading an English book every month?
> C: Sounds great! We can also speak only in English during class.
> D: That's a good idea!

① improve our English ② make a lot of new friends
③ manage our time better ④ have fun with classmates
⑤ stay healthy

02 다음 대화의 빈칸에 들어갈 말로 <u>어색한</u> 것은?

> A: What can I do to sleep better?
> B: _____

① How about drinking warm milk before bed?
② You can drink warm milk before bed.
③ You'd better drink warm milk before bed.
④ Why don't you drink warm milk before bed?
⑤ I'm sure you can drink warm milk before bed.

[03~04] 다음 대화를 읽고, 물음에 답하시오.

> B: I'm so excited about the new school year.
> G: Me, too. It's going to be great!
> B: What can I do to make a lot of new friends?
> G: You can join a sports club.
> B: (A)That's a great idea.

03 위 대화의 밑줄 친 (A)와 바꾸어 쓸 수 <u>없는</u> 것은?

① Sounds good. ② Good idea. ③ All right.
④ That's great. ⑤ I'm afraid I can't.

04 What did the girl suggest to the boy?

➡ _____

01 다음 대화의 빈칸에 들어갈 말로 가장 적절한 것은?

> A: What can I do to sleep better?
> B: You can _____.
> A: That's a great idea.

① drink warm milk before bed
② recycle paper
③ drink lots of coffee
④ volunteer at the hospital
⑤ go to the movies

[02~03] 다음 대화를 읽고, 물음에 답하시오.

> B: I'm so excited about the new school year.
> G: Me, too. It's going to be great!
> B: What can I do to make a lot of new friends?
> G: You can join a sports club.
> B: That's a great idea.

02 위 대화의 밑줄 친 표현과 바꾸어 쓸 수 있는 것은?

① What about making a lot of new friends?
② Why don't you make a lot of new friends?
③ Are you able to make a lot of new friends?
④ How did you make a lot of new friends?
⑤ What should I do to make a lot of new friends?

03 위 대화의 내용과 일치하지 <u>않는</u> 것은?

① B는 새 학기에 대해 걱정하고 있다.
② B는 G에게 새로운 친구들을 사귀는 법에 대한 조언을 구하였다.
③ G는 새 학기가 매우 좋을 것이라고 예상하였다.
④ G는 B에게 새로운 친구들을 사귀기 위해 스포츠 동아리 가입을 제안하였다.
⑤ B는 스포츠 동아리에 가입하는 것은 좋은 생각이라고 여긴다.

[04~05] 다음 대화를 읽고, 물음에 답하시오.

> Brian: Hey, Mina, what's wrong?
> Mina: My best friend, Kate, is mad at me.
> Brian: That's terrible. What happened?
> Mina: I said her new hairstyle was cute just like my dog's.
> Brian: <u>그녀가 너에게 화내는 게 당연해.</u>
> Mina: Right. She won't talk to me.
> Brian: Yeah. She's probably really angry.
> Mina: What can I do to make up with her?
> Brian: How about sending her a text?
> Mina: That's a good idea. I'll do that.

서답형

04 위 대화의 밑줄 친 우리말을 주어진 단어를 알맞게 배열하여 영어로 쓰시오.

> you / she / is / wonder/ mad / no / at

➡ _____

05 위 대화의 내용과 일치하는 것은?

① Kate was very upset because of Mina's dog.
② Mina didn't like Brian's new hairstyle.
③ Mina made Kate happy with her praise.
④ Mina accepted Brian's advice to make up with Kate.
⑤ Brian didn't understand why Kate would not talk to Mina.

[06~08] 다음 대화를 읽고, 물음에 답하시오.

Jenny: Mike, did you join any clubs?

Mike: Yes, I joined the singing club.

Jenny: Oh, I see.

Mike: What's wrong, Jenny?

Jenny: I'm the president of the magic club. But I only have two members.

Mike: Oh, no. That's (A)[terrific / terrible].

Jenny: What can I do to (B)[leave / gather] more members?

Mike: Why don't you post an ad on the school (C)[bulletin / bullet] board?

Jenny: That's a good idea. I'll do ⓐit right away.

06 위 대화의 (A)~(C)의 괄호 안에 들어갈 말로 바르게 짝지어진 것은?

① terrific – leave – bulletin

② terrific – gather – bullet

③ terrible – gather – bulletin

④ terrible – gather – bullet

⑤ terrible – leave – bulletin

07 위 대화에서 Jenny의 심경 변화로 적절한 것은?

① sad → worried

② lonely → disappointed

③ worried → relieved

④ happy → nervous

⑤ disappointed → nervous

서답형
08 위 대화의 밑줄 친 ⓐit이 가리키는 것을 찾아 우리말 20자 내외로 쓰시오.

➡ _____

[09~12] 다음 대화를 읽고, 물음에 답하시오.

Sue: Minsu, why are you so late?

Minsu: Oh, I'm sorry. On the way, I __ⓐ__ a foreigner.

Sue: Yes, and?

Minsu: I had to take him to the subway station.

Sue: Why didn't you just tell him the directions?

Minsu: He didn't speak English very well.

Sue: Hmm... _____ⓑ_____

Minsu: *Talk Smart*? What kind of app is it?

Sue: It ⓒchanges one language into another. It's really helpful.

Minsu: Really? I'll try it next time.

서답형
09 위 대화의 빈칸 ⓐ에 주어진 영영풀이에 해당하는 말을 시제를 고려하여 주어진 글자로 시작하여 쓰시오.

to meet somebody by chance

➡ r_____

서답형
10 위 대화의 빈칸 ⓑ에 주어진 어구를 배열하여 영어로 쓰시오.

the *Talk Smart* app / about / next time / what / using

➡ _____

중요
11 위 대화의 밑줄 친 ⓒ 대신 바꾸어 쓸 수 있는 것은?

① translates ② keeps

③ remains ④ spreads

⑤ expands

서답형
12 Why is the *Talk Smart* app helpful when Minsu meets a foreigner by chance?

➡ _____

[01~02] 다음 대화의 밑줄 친 우리말을 괄호 안의 단어를 이용하여 영작하시오.

01

A: 잠을 잘 자기 위해 무엇을 해야 할까? (better, can)

B: You can drink warm milk before bed.

➡ _____

02 중요

A: 서점에 가는 게 어때? (bookstore, how)

B: Great idea!

➡ _____

[03~05] 다음 대화를 읽고, 물음에 답하시오.

B: (A)I'm so exciting about the new school year.

G: (B)Me, too. It's going to be great!

B: (C)_____?

G: You can join a sports club.

B: That's a great idea.

03 위 대화의 밑줄 친 (A)에서 어법상 틀린 것을 찾아 고쳐 쓰시오.

➡ _____

04 중요

위 대화의 밑줄 친 표현 (B)와 바꾸어 쓸 수 있는 표현을 주어진 단어로 시작하는 말로 쓰시오.

So _____.

05 위 대화의 빈칸 (C)에 〈보기〉에 주어진 어구를 배열하여 문장을 완성하시오.

┌─ 보기 ─┐

do / a lot of / friends / I / what / new / can / to make

➡ _____

[06~07] 다음 대화를 읽고, 물음에 답하시오.

Jenny: Mike, did you join any clubs?

Mike: Yes, I joined the singing club.

Jenny: Oh, I see.

Mike: What's wrong, Jenny?

Jenny: I'm the _____ of the magic club. But I only have two members.

Mike: Oh, no. That's terrible.

Jenny: What can I do to get more members?

Mike: Why don't you post an ad on the school bulletin board?

Jenny: That's a good idea. I'll do it right away.

06 위 대화의 빈칸에 다음 영영풀이에 해당하는 단어를 쓰시오.

a head of an organization

➡ _____

07 What will Jenny do to get more members in her club?

➡ _____

Grammar

① to부정사의 형용사적 용법

> • Give the other person a chance **to talk**. 다른 사람에게 말할 기회를 줘라.
>
> • I have a lot of homework **to finish** today. 나는 오늘 끝낼 많은 숙제가 있다.

■ to부정사는 'to+동사원형'의 형태로 명사, 형용사, 부사로 사용될 수 있다.

  • **To sing** a song is my favorite hobby. [명사적 용법] 노래를 부르는 것은 내가 가장 좋아하는 취미이다.

  • Is there anything **to read**? [형용사적 용법] 읽을 것이 있나요?

  • He went to the market **to buy** some groceries. [부사적 용법] 그는 식료품을 사기 위해 시장으로 갔다.

■ to부정사가 형용사로 사용될 때는 바로 앞에 위치한 명사나 대명사를 꾸며준다.

  • He has a large family **to support**. 그에게는 부양해야 할 대가족이 있다.

  • I have something **to tell** you. 나는 너에게 할 말이 있어.

■ to부정사가 형용사로 사용될 때 전치사로 끝나는 경우를 주의하자. 수식받는 명사가 본래 전치사의 목적어로 사용되었기 때문에, 수식받는 명사를 to부정사 뒤에 넣어 보아 전치사가 필요한지 여부를 확인하는 것이 좋다.

  • I have many friends **to play with**. (play with friends (○))
    I have many friends to play. (play friends (×))

  • I need a chair **to sit on**. (sit on a chair(○))
    I need a chair to sit. (sit a chair (×))

■ 형용사와 to부정사가 -thing, -body, -one으로 끝나는 부정대명사를 동시에 수식할 때는 '대명사+형용사+to부정사'의 어순을 따른다.

  • Can you give me anything **cold to drink**?

핵심 Check

1. 다음 우리말과 같도록 빈칸에 알맞은 말을 쓰시오.

   (1) 나는 만날 친구가 있다.
      ➡ I have a friend _____ _____.

   (2) 그는 그 말을 한 최초의 남자였다.
      ➡ He was the first man _____ _____ the word.

   (3) 너는 쓸 펜을 가지고 있니?
      ➡ Do you have a pen _____ _____ _____?

2 명령문 + and / or

> • **Change** the topic, **or** your partner will fall asleep.
> 화제를 바꿔라, 그렇지 않으면 너의 파트너가 잠들 것이다.
>
> • **Practice** hard, **and** you can improve your English.
> 열심히 연습해라, 그러면 너는 영어 실력을 향상시킬 수 있다.

■ 동사원형으로 시작하는 명령문 뒤에 'and'로 문장을 이어주면 '~해라, 그러면'이라는 의미가 된다. If절이 이끄는 조건문으로 바꿀 수 있다.

• **Plan** your day, **and** you will be able to manage your time better.
하루를 계획해라, 그러면 너의 시간을 더 잘 관리할 수 있을 것이다.

(= If you plan your day, you will be able to manage your time better.)

• **Press** the button, **and** the door will open.
그 버튼을 눌러라, 그러면 문이 열릴 것이다.

(= If you press the button, the door will open.)

■ 명령문 뒤에 'or'로 문장을 이어주면 '~해라, 그렇지 않으면'이라는 의미가 된다. Unless 혹은 'If ~ not'이 이끄는 조건문으로 바꿀 수 있다.

• **Get** up early, **or** you can't get there on time.
일찍 일어나라, 그렇지 않으면 너는 제시간에 그곳에 도착할 수 없다.

(= If you don't get up early, you can't get there on time.)
(= Unless you get up early, you can't get there on time.)

• **Work** hard, **or** you will fail. 열심히 일해라, 그렇지 않으면 너는 실패할 것이다.

(= If you don't work hard, you will fail.)
(= Unless you work hard, you will fail.)

핵심 Check

2. 다음 우리말과 같도록 빈칸에 알맞은 말을 쓰시오.

(1) 그 주소를 적어 두어라, 그렇지 않으면 잊어버릴 것이다.

➡ _____ down the address, _____ you will forget.

➡ _____ _____ _____ down the address, you will forget.

(2) 그 친구를 도와라, 그러면 그가 고마워할 것이다.

➡ _____ the friend, _____ he will be thankful to you.

➡ _____ you _____ the friend, he will be thankful to you.

01 다음 문장에서 어법상 <u>어색한</u> 부분을 바르게 고쳐 쓰시오.

>> hand in ~을 제출하다

(1) She has much homework to handing in.

_____ ➡ _____

(2) There are many options choose.

_____ ➡ _____

(3) Keep in mind the goal to achieved.

_____ ➡ _____

(4) Can I have a spoon to eat?

_____ ➡ _____

02 'and'나 'or'를 이용하여 다음 문장을 완성하시오.

(1) Don't tell anybody the secret, _____ you will be in trouble.

(2) Go straight, _____ you can find it.

(3) Finish your meal first, _____ you can't have your dessert.

(4) Hurry up, _____ you will miss the train.

(5) Practice hard, _____ you can do it successfully.

03 다음 우리말에 맞게 주어진 단어를 바르게 배열하시오. (필요하면 어형을 바꿀 것.)

(1) 나는 먹을 것을 원해요.

(want / eat / I / something)

➡ _____

(2) 우리에겐 계획할 파티가 있어.

(we / party / have / plan / the)

➡ _____

(3) 일찍 자라, 그러면 내일 피곤하지 않을 것이다.

(sleep / be / won't / you / tired / early / tomorrow / and)

➡ _____

(4) 옷을 갈아입어라, 그렇지 않으면 감기에 걸릴 것이다.

(will / change / catch / your / a / you / or / clothes / cold)

➡ _____

서답형

01 다음 빈칸에 들어갈 말이 다른 하나를 고르시오.

① Read lots of books, _____ you will be smart.
② Turn off the light, _____ you can save energy.
③ Open your mind, _____ you will miss many precious things.
④ Listen to her carefully, _____ you will understand her.
⑤ Don't rush, _____ you won't make any mistakes.

02 다음 빈칸에 알맞은 것은?

> I have no time _____.

① to see   ② to touch
③ to waste   ④ to sit in
⑤ playing

중요

03 다음 빈칸에 and가 들어가기에 어색한 것은?

① Keep going, _____ you can see her at the corner.
② Both his mother _____ his sister welcomed me.
③ Miss another class, _____ you will be in serious trouble.
④ Five _____ five makes ten.
⑤ It's too loud. Turn the radio down, _____ she will be upset.

04 다음 빈칸에 알맞은 말이 바르게 짝지어진 것은?

> • He has a little sister _____.
> • Actually, they have many questions _____.

① to take care – to ask about
② to take care – to ask
③ to take care of – to ask about
④ to take care of – to ask
⑤ taking care of – to ask

서답형

05 다음 문장에서 어법상 틀린 부분을 찾아 바르게 고쳐 쓰시오.

> Put on your coat, or it will warm you up.

_____ ➡ _____

중요

06 다음 빈칸에 들어갈 말로 적절하지 않은 것은?

> She has many friends _____.

① to play with   ② to help her
③ to talk to   ④ to hang out
⑤ to meet

07 다음 밑줄 친 부분 중 용법이 다른 하나는?

① She bought a house to live in.
② I have a lot of letters to write.
③ We need some food to eat.
④ He went out to see the scenery.
⑤ They have a problem to solve.

08 다음 문장과 같은 의미의 문장은?

> Don't use only capital letters, or you will sound like you're shouting.

① If you don't use only capital letters, you will sound like you're shouting.

② If you use only capital letters, you won't sound like you're shouting.

③ If you use only capital letters, you will sound like you're shouting.

④ Unless you use capital letters so much, people will shout to you.

⑤ Unless you use only capital letters, you will sound like you're shouting.

중요

09 다음 빈칸에 공통으로 들어갈 말은?

> • Take a hot bath, _____ you'll be really tired.
> • Apologize to me, _____ I'll never speak to you again.
> • Let me know if you will come _____ not.

① and ② so ③ or
④ nor ⑤ for

10 다음 중 어법상 옳은 문장은?

① Did you reserve a hotel room to stay?
② I bought a notebook to write.
③ There is no water to drink on.
④ She wrote many guidelines to follow.
⑤ He always has interesting things to talk.

11 다음 문장을 같은 의미의 명령문으로 쓰시오.

> If you don't tell me the truth, I won't help you.

➡ _____

_____

중요

12 다음 주어진 말을 바르게 배열한 것은?

> 나는 흥미로운 볼거리를 원해.
> ➡ I want _____.

① interesting something to see
② to see interesting something
③ something interesting to see
④ something to see interesting
⑤ interesting to see something

13 다음 빈칸에 알맞은 말을 쓰시오.

> • Do your best, _____ you will lose the game.
> • Do your best, _____ you will win the game.

14 다음 우리말과 같도록 주어진 어구를 바르게 배열하여 문장을 완성하시오.

> 지금 떠나라, 그러면 너는 정시에 그곳에 도착할 것이다.
> (on time / now / you / leave / get / will / and / there)

➡ _____

15 다음 빈칸에 알맞은 것은?

> It's time _____ to school.

① go   ② going   ③ went
④ to going   ⑤ to go

16 중요 다음 중 어법상 올바르지 <u>않은</u> 것은?

> She ①has to ②prepare delicious ③dessert ④for serve the picky ⑤guest.

①   ②   ③   ④   ⑤

17 다음 빈칸에 공통으로 들어갈 말로 알맞은 것은? (대 · 소문자 무시)

> • _____ kind to people, and you'll be happy.
> • She will _____ surprised to hear the news.
> • I hope to _____ stronger than now.

① do   ② stay   ③ be
④ don't   ⑤ make

18 서답형 다음 문장에서 어법상 <u>어색한</u> 부분을 찾아 바르게 고쳐 쓰시오.

> On her birthday, I will give her a nice pen to write.

_____ ➡ _____

19 다음 빈칸에 알맞지 <u>않은</u> 것은?

> _____, and you will be healthier.

① Have more vegetables
② Exercise regularly
③ Eat more snacks
④ Stop eating soda
⑤ Think positively

20 중요 다음 중 어법상 올바르지 <u>않은</u> 것은?

① Do you have a book to read?
② There is no one to help you.
③ Julian has a project to finish.
④ Is there to use a computer?
⑤ I would like to have something warm to drink.

21 서답형 다음 두 문장의 의미가 같도록 빈칸에 알맞은 말을 쓰시오.

> Unless you respond quickly, you can hurt others' feelings.
> = _____ _____, _____ you can hurt others' feelings.

22 서답형 다음 우리말과 같도록 주어진 어구를 바르게 배열하시오.

> 나는 그녀에게 줄 선물을 사러 백화점으로 가는 중이야.
> (her / am / give / to / I / the department store / a present / going / to / buy / to)

➡ _____

_____

01 다음 빈칸에 괄호 안에 주어진 단어의 올바른 형태를 쓰시오.

(1) Give her a book _____ _____. (read)

(2) There are many things _____ _____ for this exam. (study)

(3) There is nothing _____ _____ _____. (worry about)

02 다음 우리말과 뜻이 같도록 빈칸에 알맞은 말을 쓰시오.

(1) 흥미로운 할 일들이 많이 있어.
➡ There are many interesting things _____ _____.

(2) 마실 것을 주시겠어요?
➡ Can you give me something _____ _____ ?

(3) 그녀는 들을 노래를 많이 가지고 있어.
➡ She has many songs _____ _____.

(4) 나는 앉을 의자가 필요해.
➡ I need a chair _____ _____ _____.

(5) 우리는 그것을 살 돈이 없어.
➡ We don't have money _____ _____ it.

03 다음 주어진 단어를 어법에 맞게 배열하시오.

Do you want (something / eat / sweet / to)?

➡ _____

04 다음 주어진 문장과 같은 의미의 문장을 쓰시오.

Speak slowly, or I can't understand you.

➡ _____

➡ _____

05 다음 문장에서 어법상 어색한 부분을 찾아 바르게 고쳐 쓰시오.

(1) Eat slowly, and you will have a stomachache.
_____ ➡ _____

(2) We bought a house to live on together.
_____ ➡ _____

06 우리말의 의미에 맞도록 주어진 단어를 바르게 배열하시오.

너는 조부모님을 방문할 시간이 충분히 있니?
(grandparents / enough / do / to / you / your / have / visit / time)?

➡ _____

07 주어진 문장과 의미가 같도록 빈칸에 알맞은 말을 쓰시오.

> Unless you tell lies, I will trust you.

➡ _____, and I will trust you.

08 Andy에게 해줄 수 있는 적절한 조언을 주어진 단어를 이용하여 명령문 형태로 쓰시오.

> **Andy:** I want to get a good grade on an English exam. What should I do?
> **You:** _____

➡ _____, and _____
_____.

09 두 문장을 연결하여 자연스러운 문장이 되도록 명령문을 만드시오.

> You should be careful with the cup.
> You must respect others' opinions.
> You should try new things.

> You can discover a new world.
> You will make many friends.
> You will break it.

➡ _____
➡ _____
➡ _____

10 주어진 단어를 이용하여 다음 대화의 빈칸에 알맞은 말을 쓰시오.

> **Jason:** You look thirsty. Is there anything I can do for you?
> **Kelly:** Yes. _____?
> (can / bring / cold / drink)

➡ _____

11 다음 상황을 읽고 and와 or를 이용한 명령문으로 친구에게 해 줄 알맞은 조언을 쓰시오.

> You have a friend who keeps forgetting something. You think it will be helpful for her to write down what she must remember. In this situation, what can you say to her?

➡ _____
➡ _____
_____

12 주어진 단어를 활용하여 빈칸에 알맞은 말을 쓰시오.

> **A:** You look really tired these days. What's up?
> **B:** _____. It makes me exhausted. (have / lots of / do)
> **A:** _____ work too hard, _____ you will ruin your health.

➡ _____
➡ _____

Talk Your Best!

The new school year is here! Are you nervous about talking to
other students? Do you have trouble starting conversations? What
about keeping conversations going? Don't worry. Here are five tips to
become a better talker.

1. Start by asking interesting questions.

Most people love to talk about themselves. So give them the
chance. When you ask questions about people, they will answer
gladly.

2. Be a good listener.

Many people are poor listeners. So how can you be a good listener?
Look people in the eye. Listen carefully to their words. Don't look
at your cell phone or space out!

---

nervous 긴장한, 불안해하는
other 다른
have trouble (in) -ing
~하는 데 어려움을 겪다
keep A going A를 지속시키다
tip 조언
by -ing ~함으로써
chance 기회
question 질문
answer 답하다
gladly 기쁘게
poor 형편없는
look 사람 in the eye(s)
~의 눈을 똑바로 쳐다보다
listen to ~을 듣다
space out 딴생각하다

📎 확인문제

● 다음 문장이 본문의 내용과 일치하면 T, 일치하지 않으면 F를 쓰시오.

1   There are some students who feel nervous about talking to other students. ☐

2   The passage is about how to be a good talker. ☐

3   Listening to other people well isn't helpful to become a good talker. ☐

4   It is not a good idea to look at your cell phone while your friend is talking. ☐

3. Give feedback.

Be an active listener. Nod your head from time to time. You can say
= Listen actively

little things like, "Wow!" or "Cool." You can also say something
~와 같은(전치사)   또한(부사)

like, "That's interesting. Tell me more." Giving feedback shows that
동명사 주어   접속사, 생략 가능

you're listening.

4. Share common interests.

You can't have a conversation by just listening. What do you and
대화를 나누다   단지, 그저(부사)

your partner have in common? Do you both like sports? Then talk
둘 다(대명사)   그렇다면(부사)

about your favorite baseball team.

5. Pay attention to the listener.

Sometimes people may not be interested in your topic. Don't say,
빈도부사   ~일지도 모른다(조동사)

"Hey, wake up!" or "Why aren't you listening to me?" Change
listen to: ~을 듣다 (listen: 자동사)

the topic, or your partner will fall asleep. Give the other person a
명령문 ..., or ~(=If ~ not= Unless ~): ...해라, 그렇지 않으면 ~   수여동사   간접목적어

chance to talk.
직접목적어

Practice these tips, and you will soon be a great talker. Put others first,
명령문 ..., and ~: ...해라, 그러면 ~   = talk well

and everyone will want to talk with you.

---

feedback 반응, 피드백

active 능동적인, 적극적인

nod (고개를) 끄덕이다

from time to time 가끔, 이따금

interesting 흥미로운

share 공유하다

have a conversation 대화하다

have in common (관심사나 생각 등을) 공통적으로 지니다

both 둘 다

pay attention to ~에 주의를 기울이다

be interested in ~에 흥미를 느끼다

fall asleep 잠들다

the other (둘 중에서) 다른 하나

soon 곧

확인문제

● 다음 문장이 본문의 내용과 일치하면 T, 일치하지 않으면 F를 쓰시오.

1 Active listeners sometimes nod their head. ☐

2 By only listening, you can keep conversations going well. ☐

3 One of the five tips to become a better talker is sharing common interests. ☐

4 If your topic is boring, your partner will fall asleep. ☐

5 You should pay attention to your partner while you are talking. ☐

6 You can't be a great talker by just practicing the tips. ☐

● 우리말을 참고하여 빈칸에 알맞은 말을 쓰시오.

1 The new _____ _____ is _____!

2 _____ you _____ about _____ to _____ students?

3 Do you _____ _____ _____ conversations?

4 What about _____ conversations _____?

5 _____ worry.

6 Here _____ five _____ to _____ a better talker.

7 _____ by _____ _____ questions.

8 Most people _____ _____ _____ about _____.

9 So give _____ _____ _____.

10 When you _____ _____ _____ people, they will _____ _____.

11 _____ a good listener.

12 Many people _____ _____ _____.

13 So _____ _____ you _____ a good listener?

14 _____ people _____ the eye.

15 _____ carefully _____ _____ _____.

16 _____ _____ _____ your cell phone _____ space out!

17 _____ _____.

1	새 학년이 시작되었다!
2	당신은 다른 학생들과 대화하는 것이 긴장되는가?
3	당신은 대화를 시작하는 데 어려움이 있는가?
4	대화를 계속 이어가는 것은 어떤가?
5	걱정마라.
6	여기 더욱 대화를 잘하는 사람이 되기 위한 다섯 가지 조언이 있다.
7	흥미로운 질문을 하는 것으로 시작해라.
8	대부분의 사람들은 그들 자신에 관해 말하는 것을 좋아한다.
9	그러니 그들에게 기회를 줘라.
10	당신이 사람들에 관해 질문하면, 그들은 기쁘게 대답할 것이다.
11	잘 듣는 사람이 되어라.
12	많은 사람들이 잘 듣지 못한다.
13	그러면 어떻게 잘 듣는 사람이 될 수 있을까?
14	사람들의 눈을 봐라.
15	그들의 말을 주의 깊게 들어라.
16	당신의 휴대 전화를 보거나 딴 생각하지 마라!
17	반응을 보여 줘라.

18 _____ an _____ listener.

19 _____ your head _____ _____ _____ _____.

20 You can _____ _____ _____ like, "Wow!" or "Cool."

21 You can _____ _____ something _____, "That's _____.
_____ _____ more."

22 _____ feedback _____ _____ you're listening.

23 _____ _____ _____.

24 You can't _____ _____ _____ _____ just _____.

25 What do you and your partner _____ _____ _____?

26 _____ you _____ _____ sports?

27 Then _____ about _____ _____ baseball team.

28 _____ _____ _____ the listener.

29 Sometimes people may not _____ _____ _____ your topic.

30 _____ say, "Hey, wake up!" or "Why _____ you _____
_____ me?"

31 _____ the topic, _____ your partner _____ fall _____.

32 Give _____ _____ person a chance _____ _____.

33 _____ these tips, _____ you will _____ _____ a good talker.

34 _____ _____ first, and everyone will _____ _____
_____ with you.

18 능동적으로 듣는 사람이 되어라.

19 가끔 당신의 고개를 끄덕여라.

20 "와!" 또는 "멋지다."와 같은 간단한 것들을 말해도 좋다.

21 또한 "흥미롭다. 더 이야기해 봐."와 같은 것을 말해도 좋다.

22 반응을 보여 주는 것은 당신이 듣고 있다는 것을 보여 준다.

23 공통의 관심사를 나눠라.

24 당신은 그저 듣는 것만으로 대화할 수는 없다.

25 당신과 상대편은 어떤 공통점을 가지고 있는가?

26 둘 다 스포츠를 좋아하는가?

27 그렇다면 당신이 가장 좋아하는 야구팀에 관해 대화해라.

28 듣는 사람에게 주의를 기울여라.

29 때때로 사람들은 당신의 화제에 관심이 없을지도 모른다.

30 "이봐, 잠 깨!" 또는 "왜 내 말을 안 듣는 거니?"라고 말하지 마라.

31 화제를 바꿔라, 그렇지 않으면 상대편은 잠이 들 것이다.

32 다른 사람에게 말할 기회를 줘라.

33 이 조언들을 연습해라, 그러면 당신은 곧 대화를 잘하는 사람이 될 것이다.

34 다른 사람을 먼저 생각해라, 그러면 모든 사람이 당신과 대화하고 싶어 할 것이다.

● 우리말을 참고하여 본문을 영작하시오.

1 새 학년이 시작되었다!
➡ _____

2 당신은 다른 학생들과 대화하는 것이 긴장되는가?
➡ _____

3 당신은 대화를 시작하는 데 어려움이 있는가?
➡ _____

4 대화를 계속 이어가는 것은 어떤가?
➡ _____

5 걱정마라.
➡ _____

6 여기 더욱 대화를 잘하는 사람이 되기 위한 다섯 가지 조언이 있다.
➡ _____

7 흥미로운 질문을 하는 것으로 시작해라.
➡ _____

8 대부분의 사람들은 그들 자신에 관해 말하는 것을 좋아한다.
➡ _____

9 그러니 그들에게 기회를 줘라.
➡ _____

10 당신이 사람들에 관해 질문하면, 그들은 기쁘게 대답할 것이다.
➡ _____

11 잘 듣는 사람이 되어라.
➡ _____

12 많은 사람들이 잘 듣지 못한다.
➡ _____

13 그러면 어떻게 잘 듣는 사람이 될 수 있을까?
➡ _____

14 사람들의 눈을 봐라.
➡ _____

15 그들의 말을 주의 깊게 들어라.
➡ _____

16 당신의 휴대 전화를 보거나 딴생각하지 마라!
➡ _____

17 반응을 보여 줘라.
➡ _____

18 능동적으로 듣는 사람이 되어라.

➡ _____

19 가끔 당신의 고개를 끄덕여라.

➡ _____

20 "와!" 또는 "멋지다."와 같은 간단한 것들을 말해도 좋다.

➡ _____

21 또한 "흥미롭다, 더 이야기해 봐."와 같은 것을 말해도 좋다.

➡ _____

22 반응을 보여 주는 것은 당신이 듣고 있다는 것을 보여 준다.

➡ _____

23 공통의 관심사를 나눠라.

➡ _____

24 당신은 그저 듣는 것만으로 대화할 수는 없다.

➡ _____

25 당신과 상대편은 어떤 공통점을 가지고 있는가?

➡ _____

26 둘 다 스포츠를 좋아하는가?

➡ _____

27 그렇다면 당신이 가장 좋아하는 야구팀에 관해 대화해라.

➡ _____

28 듣는 사람에게 주의를 기울여라.

➡ _____

29 때때로 사람들은 당신의 화제에 관심이 없을지도 모른다.

➡ _____

30 "이봐, 잠 깨!" 또는 "왜 내 말을 안 듣는 거니?"라고 말하지 마라.

➡ _____

31 화제를 바꿔라, 그렇지 않으면 상대편은 잠이 들 것이다.

➡ _____

32 다른 사람에게 말할 기회를 줘라.

➡ _____

33 이 조언들을 연습해라, 그러면 당신은 곧 대화를 잘하는 사람이 될 것이다.

➡ _____

34 다른 사람을 먼저 생각해라, 그러면 모든 사람이 당신과 대화하고 싶어 할 것이다.

➡ _____

[01~03] 다음 글을 읽고, 물음에 답하시오.

The new school year is here! Are you nervous about ⓐtalk to other students? Do you have trouble ⓑstart _____ ⓒ ? What about keeping _____ ⓒ going? Don't worry. Here are five tips to become a better talker.

서답형

01 위 글의 밑줄 친 ⓐ와 ⓑ를 알맞은 형태로 고쳐 쓰시오.

ⓐ _____ ⓑ _____

서답형

02 다음 영영풀이에 해당하는 단어를 빈칸 ⓒ에 어법에 맞게 쓰시오.

> a talk with someone usually in an informal situation

➡ _____

03 위 글에 이어질 내용으로 가장 적절한 것은?

① some tips to be a nice student
② some ways to start the new school year
③ some tips to avoid embarrassing situations
④ some hints to be a student keeping secrets better
⑤ some hints to be a student who talks better

[04~08] 다음 글을 읽고, 물음에 답하시오.

Here are some tips to become a better talker.
1. Start by asking interesting questions.
 Most people love to talk about themselves. So give them (A)the chance. When you ask questions _____ ⓐ people, they will answer gladly.
2. _____ **(B)** _____
 Many people are poor listeners. So how can you be a good listener? Look people in the eye. Listen carefully _____ ⓑ their words. Don't look _____ ⓒ your cell phone or space out!

중요

04 위 글의 빈칸 ⓐ~ⓒ에 들어갈 말이 순서대로 바르게 짝지어진 것은?

① about – on – in
② about – to – at
③ at – on – by
④ at – about – with
⑤ with – at – in

서답형

05 to부정사를 이용하여 밑줄 친 (A)의 구체적인 의미를 쓰시오.

➡ the chance _____

서답형

06 위 글의 빈칸 (B)에 알맞은 조언을 위 글에서 찾아 쓰시오.

➡ _____

서답형

07 다음과 같이 풀이할 수 있는 단어를 위 글에서 찾아 쓰시오.

> a useful piece of advice

➡ _____

08 위 글을 읽고 답할 수 없는 질문은?

① What do most people love to do?

② What should we do to talk to people?

③ How will people respond to our questions about them?

④ Are many people good at listening?

⑤ What should we do in order not to space out?

[09~14] 다음 글을 읽고, 물음에 답하시오.

Here are some tips to become a better talker.

1. Start by asking interesting questions.

Most people ⓐlove to talk about themselves. So (A)그들에게 말할 기회를 주어라. When you ask questions about people, they will answer ⓑgladly.

2. Be a good listener.

Many people are ⓒpoor listeners. So how can you be a good listener? Look people in the eye. Listen carefully to their words. Don't look at your cell phone or ⓓspace out!

3. Give feedback.

Be an ⓔinactive listener. Nod your head from time to time. You can say little things (B)like, "Wow!" or "Cool." You can also say something like, "That's interesting. Tell me more." Giving feedback shows that you're listening.

09 What is the passage mainly talking about?

① being a good listener

② becoming a better speaker

③ criticizing a poor listener

④ listening intentively in class

⑤ becoming a modest student

10 위 글의 밑줄 친 ⓐ~ⓔ 중 글의 흐름상 알맞지 않은 것은?

① ⓐ   ② ⓑ   ③ ⓒ   ④ ⓓ   ⑤ ⓔ

11 명령문과 to부정사를 활용하여 밑줄 친 우리말 (A)를 영어로 쓰시오.

➡ _____

12 위 글의 내용과 일치하지 않는 것을 고르시오.

① 대부분의 사람들은 자신에 관한 질문에 기꺼이 답하려고 한다.

② 사람들은 그들 자신에 관하여 말하는 것을 좋아한다.

③ 말하는 사람의 눈을 바라보는 것은 좋은 청자의 자세이다.

④ 상대방의 말에 항상 고개를 끄덕이는 것이 좋다.

⑤ 상대방의 말을 듣고 있다는 신호를 보내는 것이 중요하다.

13 Choose an incorrect feature of a good talker.

① Asking questions about the partner

② Listening attentively to what the partner is saying

③ Not looking at his or her cell phone

④ Keeping eye contact with the partner

⑤ Giving feedback about the mistakes the partner made

14 위 글의 밑줄 친 (B)와 쓰임이 같은 것은?

① They like riding bicycles together.
② He is very like his father.
③ I am into novels like '1984.'
④ She likes to eat vegetables.
⑤ My parents treat me like a baby.

[15~19] 다음 글을 읽고, 물음에 답하시오.

Share common interests.

You can't have a conversation by just listening. What do you and your partner have in common? Do you both like sports? Then talk about your favorite baseball team. ⓐ듣는 사람에게 주의를 기울여라.

Sometimes people may not be interested in your topic. Don't say, "Hey, wake up!" or "Why aren't you listening to me?" ⓑUnless you change the topic, your partner will fall asleep. Give the other person a chance ⓒto talk.

Practice these tips, and you will soon be a great talker. Put others first, and everyone will want to talk with you.

서답형

15 다음 영영풀이에 해당하는 단어를 위 글에서 찾아 쓰시오.

liked more than others of the same kind

➡ _____

서답형

16 위 글의 밑줄 친 우리말 ⓐ를 영어로 쓰시오.

➡ _____

서답형

17 위 글의 밑줄 친 문장 ⓑ를 같은 의미의 명령문으로 바꿔 쓰시오.

➡ _____

중요

18 위 글의 밑줄 친 ⓒ와 같은 용법으로 쓰인 것은?

① The subject is difficult to talk about.
② I have something to tell you.
③ The man wanted to be a doctor.
④ The river is dangerous to swim in.
⑤ It is necessary to discuss the problem.

19 위 글의 내용과 일치하지 않는 것은?

① 대화하는 사람과 공통점을 갖고 있는 것은 도움이 된다.
② 듣는 사람에게 집중하는 것이 좋다.
③ 상대방에게 발언할 기회를 주는 것이 중요하다.
④ 대화 중 상대방이 잠들면 깨워 주어야 한다.
⑤ 대화할 때 상대방을 우선시하는 것이 좋다.

[20~23] 다음 글을 읽고, 물음에 답하시오.

The new school year is here! Are you nervous about talking to other students? Do you have trouble starting conversations? What about ____ⓐ____ conversations ____ⓑ____? Don't worry. Here are five tips ____ⓒ____ a better talker.
Start by ____ⓓ____ interesting questions.
Most people love to talk about ____ⓔ____. So (A)give them the chance. When you ask questions about people, they will answer ____ⓕ____.

서답형

20 주어진 단어를 문맥이나 어법에 맞게 빈칸 ⓐ~ⓓ에 쓰시오.

ask / go / keep / become

ⓐ_____ ⓑ_____

ⓒ_____ ⓓ_____

서답형

21 위 글의 빈칸 ⓔ에 알맞은 대명사를 쓰시오.

➡ _____

22 위 글의 밑줄 친 (A)의 의미로 가장 적절한 것은?

① give them interesting stories
② let them talk about themselves
③ make them talk in public
④ ask them what they want to answer
⑤ answer them with a smile

중요

23 위 글의 빈칸 ⓕ에 들어갈 말로 어색한 것은?

① willingly   ② readily
③ reluctantly   ④ gladly
⑤ without hesitation

[24~27] 다음 글을 읽고, 물음에 답하시오.

Here are some tips to become a better talker.
_____ ⓐ _____

Many people are poor listeners. (①) So how can you be a good listener? Look people in the eye. (②) Don't look at your cell phone or space out!
_____ ⓑ _____

Be an active listener. (③) Nod your head

from time to time. You can say little things like, "Wow!" or "Cool." You can also say something like, "That's interesting. Tell me more." It shows that you're listening. (④)
_____ ⓒ _____

You can't have a conversation by just listening. (⑤) What do you and your partner have in common? Do you both like sports? Then talk about _____ ⓓ _____.

24 위 글의 ①~⑤ 중 다음 주어진 문장이 들어갈 알맞은 곳은?

Listen carefully to their words.

①   ②   ③   ④   ⑤

서답형

25 위 글의 빈칸 ⓐ~ⓒ에 알맞은 것을 다음에서 골라 쓰시오.

Give feedback. / Be a good listener. / Share common interests.

ⓐ_____ ⓑ_____

ⓒ_____

중요

26 위 글의 빈칸 ⓓ에 들어갈 말로 가장 적절한 것은?

① going to a college
② your favorite computer game
③ a basketball team you like most
④ songs you heard from the radio
⑤ what your partner likes most

서답형

27 According to the passage, how can we be an active listener? Answer in Korean.

➡ _____

_____

[01~04] 다음 글을 읽고, 물음에 답하시오.

Talk Your Best!

The new school year is here! Are you nervous about talking to other students? Do you have trouble starting conversations? ⓐ대화를 계속 이어가는 것은 어떤가? Don't worry. Here are five tips to become a better talker.

Start by asking interesting questions.

Most people love to talk about themselves. So give them the chance. When you ask questions about people, they will answer ⓑglad.

01 주어진 단어를 어법에 맞게 변형하여 밑줄 친 우리말 ⓐ를 영어로 쓰시오.

keep / go

➡ _____

02 위 글의 밑줄 친 ⓑ를 알맞은 형으로 고치시오.

➡ _____

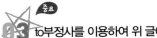

03 to부정사를 이용하여 위 글에 맞도록 다음 문장을 완성하시오.

The writer wants to give students some advice _____.

04 According to the passage, how can we start a conversation?

We can start _____.

[05~08] 다음 글을 읽고, 물음에 답하시오.

4. Share common ⓐinterest.

You can't have a conversation by just listening. What do you and your partner have in common? Do you both like sports? Then talk about your favorite baseball team.

5. Pay attention to the listener.

Sometimes people may not be ⓑinterest in your topic. Don't say, "Hey, wake up!" or "Why aren't you listening to me?" (A)화제를 바꾸어라, 그렇지 않으면 상대편은 잠들 것이다. Give the other person a chance to talk. Practice these tips, and you will soon be a great talker. _____(B)_____

05 위 글의 밑줄 친 ⓐ와 ⓑ에 주어진 단어를 어법에 맞게 쓰시오.

ⓐ_____ ⓑ_____

06 명령문을 이용하여 밑줄 친 우리말 (A)를 영어로 쓰시오.

➡ _____

07 위 글의 내용에 맞도록 다음 문장을 완성하시오.

If you want to be a great talker, you must _____ that the writer said.

08 위 글의 빈칸 (B)에 다음 문장과 같은 의미의 명령문을 and를 이용하여 쓰시오.

If you don't put others first, everyone won't want to talk with you.

➡ _____
_____

[09~12] 다음 글을 읽고, 물음에 답하시오.

Here are some tips to become a better talker. Be a good listener.

Many people are poor listeners. So how can you be a good listener? Look people in the eye. Listen carefully to their words. Don't look at your cell phone or space out!

Give feedback.

Be an active listener. Nod your head from time to time. You can say little things like, "Wow!" or "Cool." You can also say something like, "That's interesting. Tell me more." Giving feedback shows that you're listening.

Share common interests.

You can't ___ⓐ___ a conversation by just listening. What do you and your partner ___ⓑ___ in common? Do you both like sports? Then talk about your favorite baseball team.

09 위 글의 빈칸 ⓐ와 ⓑ에 공통으로 들어갈 알맞은 말을 쓰시오.

➡ _____

10 위 글을 읽고 'Do's'와 'Don'ts'로 구분하여 좋은 청자의 자세를 두 가지씩 쓰시오.

Do's

➡ _____

_____

Don'ts

➡ _____

_____

11 To be an active listener, what should we do?

➡ _____

12 위 글을 읽고 다음 대화에서 적용된 conversation tip을 모두 쓰시오.

A: I visited my uncle in Jeju-do.
B: Cool! Tell me more.
A: I saw many beautiful flowers and ate delicious food. How about you? Have you been to Jeju-do?
B: Yes, I have. My family spends a vacation in Jeju-do every year.

➡ _____

[13~15] 다음 글을 읽고, 물음에 답하시오.

A: I want to be a better talker. What should I do?
B: Here ___ⓐ___ some tips. ___ⓑ___ a good listener. Look into your partner's eyes and listen carefully. Also give feedback. (A) 가끔 당신의 고개를 끄덕여라 and ___ⓒ___ an active listener. Lastly, when you talk, pay attention to your partner.

13 대·소문자에 유의하여 be동사의 알맞은 형태를 빈칸 ⓐ~ⓒ에 쓰시오.

ⓐ _____ ⓑ _____ ⓒ _____

14 주어진 단어를 활용하여 우리말 (A)를 영어로 쓰시오.

(from / to)

➡ _____

15 주어진 단어를 활용하여 지문의 내용에 맞도록 빈칸을 채우시오.

_____, and you will become a better talker. (attention)

➡ _____

Project Culture

A: Do your best! Fighting! (→ Go for it!)

B: How about going eye (→ window) shopping?

C: Your one-piece (→ dress) is beautiful.

구문해설 · Go for it: '힘내!'라는 의미로 응원할 때 쓰는 표현이다 · window shopping: 한국어로 '아이 쇼핑'이라 하는 것을 영어로 window shopping이라고 한다. · dress: 한국어로 '원피스'라고 하는 옷 을 영어로 dress라고 한다.

해석

A: 최선을 다해! 힘내!

B: 윈도쇼핑 가는 게 어때?

C: 당신의 원피스가 아름다 워요.

Think and Write

Facelook Manners

Respect others' opinions, and you will make many friends. Post useful
그러면

information, or you will waste others' time. Don't use only capital letters,
그렇지 않으면   오직

or you will sound like you're shouting. Don't use rude language, or you will
~처럼 들리다

make others angry.
동사+목적어+목적격보어

구문해설 · manners: 예절 · respect: 존중하다 · opinion: 의견 · useful: 유용한 · waste: 낭비하다 · capital: 대문자의 · letter: 글자 · rude: 무례한

Facelook 예절

타인의 의견을 존중해라, 그러면 당신은 많은 친구를 사귈 것이다. 유용한 정보를 게시해라, 그렇지 않으면 당신은 타인의 시간을 낭비할 것이다. 대문자만을 사용하지 마라, 그렇지 않으면 당신은 소리치고 있는 것처럼 들릴 것이다. 무례한 언어를 사용하지 마라, 그렇지 않으면 당신은 타인을 화나게 만들 것이다.

Read and Write

Jason: I want to be a better talker. What should I do?
조언 구하기

Janet: Here are some tips. Be a good listener. Look into your partner's eyes
여기 ~이 있다

and listen carefully. Also give feedback. Nod your head from time to
이따금씩

time and be an active listener. Lastly, when you talk, pay attention to
능동적인

your partner.

구문해설 · look into: ~을 들여다보다 · carefully: 주의 깊게 · nod: (고개를) 끄덕이다 · lastly: 마지막으로 · pay attention to ~: ~에 주의를 기울이다

Jason: 나는 말을 더 잘하는 사람이 되고 싶어. 어떻게 해야 좋을까?

Janet: 여기 몇 가지 조언이 있어. 말을 잘 들어주는 사람이 되렴. 상대편의 눈을 바라보고 주의 깊게 들어줘. 또 반응을 보여줘. 가끔씩 머리를 끄덕이고 능동적으로 듣는 사람이 되렴. 마지막으로, 네가 이야기할 때, 상대편에게 집중해.

Words & Expressions

01 다음 짝지어진 단어의 관계가 같도록 빈칸에 알맞은 말을 쓰시오.

early : late =_____ : passive

[02~03] 다음 영영풀이에 해당하는 단어를 고르시오.

02
to move your head up and down to show agreement or understanding

① fall   ② nod
③ shake   ④ respond
⑤ respect

03
an informal talk involving a small group of people or only two

① discussion   ② diary
③ conversation   ④ opinion
⑤ information

[04~06] 다음 우리말에 맞게 빈칸에 알맞은 말을 쓰시오.

04
제가 하는 말에 주의를 기울여 주세요.
➡ _____ _____ _____ what I'm saying, please.

05
휴대폰을 보거나 딴생각하지 마세요.
➡ Don't look at your cell phone or _____ _____.

06
노래를 들으며 아기는 잠들었다.
➡ Listening to music, the baby _____ _____.

Conversation

07 다음 대화의 빈칸에 들어갈 말로 어색한 것은?

Brian: Amy, what does this Chinese character mean?
Amy: Hmm... I have no idea. _____
Brian: Okay, I will.

① Why don't you look for it in the dictionary?
② How about asking your teacher?
③ I suggest you should repeat it many times.
④ What about searching the Internet?
⑤ You'd better use a dictionary app.

08 다음 대화의 빈칸에 들어갈 말로 가장 적절한 것은?

> B: I'm so excited about the new school year.
> G: Me, too. It's going to be great!
> B: What can I do to make a lot of new friends?
> G: _____
> B: That's a great idea.

① How about reading an English book every month?
② You can join a sports club.
③ Why don't you make a weekly plan?
④ You can eat lots of vegetables.
⑤ What about drinking warm milk before bed?

09 다음 빈칸에 들어갈 말로 나머지와 의미가 <u>다른</u> 것은?

> A: Minsu, _____
> B: Sounds great! what do you want to do?
> A: How about going to the bookstore?
> B: Great idea!

① let's do something together on Thursday.
② what about doing something together on Thursday?
③ why don't we do something together on Thursday?
④ what do you think about doing something together on Thursday?
⑤ we are supposed to do something together on Thursday.

[10~12] 다음 대화를 읽고, 물음에 답하시오.

> Brian: Hey, Mina, what's wrong?
> Mina: My best friend, Kate, (A)[is / are] mad at me.
> Brian: That's terrible. What happened?
> Mina: I said her new hairstyle was cute just like my dog's.
> Brian: No (B)[wondering / wonder] she's mad at you.
> Mina: Right. She won't talk to me.
> Brian: Yeah. She's probably really angry.
> Mina: What can I do to (C)[make up with / make up] her?
> Brian: <u>그녀에게 문자를 보내는 게 어떠니?</u> (text, how)
> Mina: That's a good idea. I'll do that.

10 위 대화에 나타난 Mina의 심정으로 적절한 것은?

① nervous   ② sorry
③ surprised   ④ joyful
⑤ upset

11 위 대화의 (A)~(C)에 들어갈 말이 바르게 짝지어진 것은?

① is – wondering – make up with
② is – wonder – make up
③ is – wonder – make up with
④ are – wonder – make up
⑤ are – wondering – make up with

12 위 대화의 밑줄 친 우리말을 주어진 단어를 사용하여 영어로 쓰시오. (6 단어)

➡ _____

Grammar

13 다음 문장의 빈칸에 알맞은 전치사는?

> Do you have many friends to play _____?

① in　　　② about　　　③ on
④ with　　　⑤ by

14 다음 중 주어진 문장의 to부정사와 쓰임이 같은 것은?

> We didn't have any money to spend at that time.

① We will be happy to see you again.
② I decided to become a lawyer.
③ It is important to be honest with your friend.
④ Do you have a friend to trust?
⑤ Margo wants him to come back to her.

15 다음 중 어법상 바르지 않은 것은?

① Go along the street, and you'll find the building.
② He wants something to drink cold.
③ He promised not to be late again.
④ Tell me the truth, or I will hate you.
⑤ Jessica had nothing to eat in the refrigerator.

16 주어진 어구를 활용하여 다음 우리말을 영어로 쓰시오.

> 손을 씻어라, 그렇지 않으면 감기에 걸릴 것이다.
> (wash / catch / a cold)
>
> ➡ _____

17 다음 문장에서 어색한 곳을 찾아 바르게 고치시오.

> They have many children to take care.

_____ ➡ _____

18 주어진 단어를 바르게 배열하여 빈칸을 채우시오.

> It is a little cold. Can you give me _____.
> (on / warm / something / put / to)

➡ _____

19 다음 대화의 빈칸에 들어갈 말로 가장 적절한 것은?

> A: You are driving too fast. _____, or you will have a car accident.
> B: Oh, okay. I'll pay more attention to the speed.

① Gather speed　　　② Try harder
③ Slow down　　　④ Stay calm
⑤ Don't bother

20 다음 중 어법상 바르지 않은 것은?

① She has many students to teach.
② Can you give me a pen to write with?
③ She got a chair to sit on.
④ There are many problems to discuss about.
⑤ We have lots of things to do tomorrow.

21 주어진 단어를 활용하여 다음 우리말을 영어로 쓰시오.

> 읽을 책을 가져와라, 그렇지 않으면 너는 지루할 것이다. (bring / bore)

➡ _____

22 다음 중 to부정사의 용법이 주어진 문장과 같은 것은?

> There are strict rules to follow.

① Mago came to Korea to study Korean.
② The citizens were glad to hear the news.
③ He has only one person to rely on.
④ My dream is to be a billionaire.
⑤ She hoped to bring home the bacon.

23 다음 빈칸에 가장 적절한 것은?

> Leave right now, or you will miss the bus.
> = _____ you leave right now, you will miss the bus.

① Because   ② When   ③ Although
④ If   ⑤ Unless

24 다음 빈칸에 들어갈 말과 같은 말이 들어가는 것을 모두 고르시오.

> Be careful, _____ you will be dangerous.

① Take this medicine, _____ you will get better.
② It was still painful, _____ I went to see a doctor.
③ We listened carefully, _____ he brought news of her.
④ Are you coming _____ not?
⑤ Don't be late again, _____ I'll punish you.

[25~27] 다음 글을 읽고, 물음에 답하시오.

> The new school year is here! Are you nervous ⓐ _____ talking to other students? (A) 당신은 대화를 시작하는 데에 어려움이 있는가? What _____ ⓑ keeping conversations going? Don't worry. Here are five tips to become a better talker.

25 위 글의 빈칸 ⓐ와 ⓑ에 공통으로 들어갈 말로 알맞은 것은?

① in   ② on   ③ about
④ at   ⑤ by

26 위 글의 밑줄 친 (A)의 우리말을 주어진 단어를 이용하여 영작하시오.

> (trouble / start)

➡ _____

27 위 글의 내용으로 알 수 없는 것을 고르시오.

① The passage is helpful to students who start the new school year.
② It is difficult for some students to talk to other students.
③ The writer is going to give students some tips to solve the problem.
④ The passage will teach students how to talk with their parents.
⑤ With five hints, students can become a better talker.

[28~31] 다음 글을 읽고, 물음에 답하시오.

1. Start by asking (A)interest questions.

Most people love ⓐtalking about themselves. So give ⓑthem the chance. When you ⓒwill ask questions about people, they will answer gladly.

2. Be a good listener.

Many people are poor listeners. So how can you be a good listener? Look people in the eye. Listen ⓓcarefully to their words. Don't look at your cell phone or space out!

3. Give feedback.

Be an active listener. Nod your head from time to time. You can say ⓔlittle things like, "Wow!" or "Cool." You can also say something like, "That's (B)interest. Tell me more." Giving feedback shows that you're listening.

28 위 글의 ⓐ~ⓔ 중 어법상 바르지 <u>않은</u> 것을 고르시오.

① ⓐ 　② ⓑ 　③ ⓒ 　④ ⓓ 　⑤ ⓔ

29 위 글의 밑줄 친 (A)와 (B)를 어법에 맞게 고쳐 쓰시오.

(A) _____ (B) _____

30 위 글의 내용과 일치하지 <u>않는</u> 것은?

① People usually like to talk about themselves.

② It is good to give people the chance to talk about themselves.

③ Most people are not good at listening.

④ Nodding your head shows that you are listening.

⑤ It is rude to say "Wow!" in the middle of listening.

31 위 글의 내용을 토대로 한 다음 문장을 알맞게 채우시오.

> ____ ____ ____ ____, ____ people will know that you are listening to their words.

[32~33] 다음 글을 읽고, 물음에 답하시오.

Share common ⓐinterests. You can't have a conversation by just listening. What do you and your partner have (A)[in / about] common? Do you both like sports? Then talk about your favorite baseball team. Pay attention (B)[on / to] the listener. Sometimes people may not be interested in your topic. Don't say, "Hey, wake up!" or "Why aren't you listening to me?" Change the topic, or your partner will fall asleep. Give the other person a chance to talk. Practice these tips, and you will soon be a great talker. Put others first, and everyone will want to talk (C)[with / by] you.

32 위 글의 밑줄 친 ⓐ에 대한 풀이로 알맞은 것은?

① games such as football and basketball

② activities or subjects that you enjoy

③ particular subjects that you discuss or write about

④ opportunities to do something

⑤ some useful pieces of advice

33 위 글 (A)~(C)에서 어법상 적절한 것으로 짝지은 것은?

① in – on – with　② in – to – with

③ in – to – by　④ about – to – with

⑤ about – on – by

단원별 예상문제

[01~02] 다음 영영풀이에 해당하는 말을 고르시오.

출제율 90%

01

advice, criticism or information about how good or useful something or somebody's work is

① shouting   ② attention

③ conversation   ④ trouble

⑤ feedback

출제율 90%

02

from time to time

① sometimes   ② anytime

③ overtime   ④ sometime

⑤ daytime

출제율 95%

03 다음 빈칸에 공통으로 들어갈 말로 적절한 것은?

• I was so _____ because of the interview.

• Before the performance, I felt _____.

① nervous   ② attention

③ space   ④ fall

⑤ common

출제율 100%

04 다음 중 밑줄 친 부분의 뜻풀이가 바르지 <u>않은</u> 것은?

① I have <u>trouble</u> sleeping at night.
　　　　 어려움

② She is a very <u>active</u> student.
　　　　　 활발한

③ I will <u>gladly</u> help you when you need a help. 기꺼이

④ <u>Sometimes</u>, we need to take a rest.
　　　 언젠가

⑤ I was glad to have a <u>conversation</u> with her. 대화

[05~06] 다음 대화를 읽고, 물음에 답하시오.

Sue: Minsu, why are you so late?

Minsu: Oh, I'm sorry. On the way, I ⓐ<u>ran into</u> a foreigner.

Sue: Yes, and?

Minsu: I ⓑ<u>had to</u> take him to the subway station.

Sue: Why didn't you just ⓒ<u>tell</u> him the directions?

Minsu: He didn't speak English very well.

Sue: Hmm… How about ⓓ<u>using</u> the *Talk Smart* app next time?

Minsu: *Talk Smart*? What kind of app is it?

Sue: It changes one language to ⓔ<u>other</u>. It's really helpful.

Minsu: Really? I'll try it next time.

출제율 95%

05 위 대화의 ⓐ~ⓔ 중 어법상 어색한 것을 찾아 바르게 고치시오.

➡ _____

출제율 90%

06 위 대화의 내용과 일치하는 것은?

① Minsu와 Sue는 지하철역에서 만났다.

② Minsu와 Sue는 함께 외국인을 만났다.

③ 외국인은 영어에 유창했다.

④ *Talk Smart* 앱은 번역 앱의 일종이다.

⑤ Minsu는 *Talk Smart* 앱을 사용해서 외국인에게 방향을 설명해 주었다.

Brian: Hey, Mina, what's wrong?

Mina: My best friend, Kate, is mad at me.

Brian: That's terrible. What happened?

Mina: I said her new hairstyle was cute just like my dog's.

Brian: No wonder she's mad at you.

Mina: Right. She won't talk to me.

Brian: Yeah. She's probably really angry.

Mina: What can I do to make up with her?

Brian: (A)How about sending her a text?

Mina: That's a good idea. I'll do that.

출제율 95%

07 위 대화의 흐름상 밑줄 친 (A)와 바꾸어 쓸 수 있는 것은?

① Why don't you write a letter of apology to her?

② I think you should praise her dog.

③ I'm sure many people are choosing texting rather than calling.

④ You'd better keep your friend's secrets.

⑤ I suggest that you should not blame yourself.

출제율 85%

08 위 대화를 읽고 대답할 수 없는 질문은?

① Why was Kate so upset?

② What did Mina say about Kate's new hairstyle?

③ Why did Mina compare Kate's hairstyle to her dog's?

④ What did Brian advise to Mina?

⑤ What will Mina do to make up with Kate?

Jenny: Mike, did you join any clubs?

Mike: Yes, I joined the singing club.

Jenny: Oh, I see.

Mike: What's wrong, Jenny? (A)

Jenny: I'm the president of the magic club. (B)

Mike: Oh, no. That's terrible. (C)

Jenny: What can I do to get more members? (D)

Mike: Why don't you post an ad on the school bulletin board? (E)

Jenny: That's a good idea. I'll do it right away.

출제율 90%

09 위 대화의 (A)~(E) 중 주어진 문장이 들어가기에 가장 적절한 곳은?

> But I only have two members.

① (A)   ② (B)   ③ (C)   ④ (D)   ⑤ (E)

출제율 95%

10 위 대화의 내용과 일치하는 것은?

① Mike and Jenny joined the same club.

② Mike was interested in the magic club.

③ The singing club had only two members.

④ Mike advised Jenny to advertise her club.

⑤ Jenny was going to post an ad about her school on SNS.

출제율 100%

11 다음 중 어법상 바르지 않은 것은?

① Give me the letter to send.

② Go now, and you will be able to meet her.

③ There is nothing to eat.

④ Exercise regularly, or you will look good.

⑤ Do you have a message to leave?

12 다음 빈칸에 들어갈 말로 어법상 적절하지 <u>않은</u> 것은?

> Chris has many friends _____.

① to meet ② to talk to
③ to play ④ to call
⑤ to help

13 주어진 문장을 or를 이용하여 9단어로 이루어진 명령문으로 만드시오.

> If you don't post useful information, there is a chance that you will waste others' time.

➡ _____

14 다음 중 빈칸에 들어갈 말을 바르게 배열한 것은?

> Mom, I have _____.

① something about important to talk
② something to talk about important
③ something important to talk about
④ to talk about important something
⑤ to talk something important about

15 다음 문장에서 어법상 틀린 것을 골라 바르게 고치시오.

> The house has a pool to swim.

_____ ➡ _____

16 다음 문장을 두 가지 형태의 명령문으로 고치시오.

> If you don't wash your hands, germs will invade your body.

➡ _____

➡ _____

17 다음 우리말에 맞도록 빈칸에 알맞은 말을 쓰시오.

> 우리에게 읽을 책 한 권과 마실 물, 사용할 쿠션, 앉을 의자 하나를 주세요.
> ➡ Please give us a book _____, water _____, a cushion _____, a chair _____.

[18~19] 다음 글을 읽고, 물음에 답하시오.

> The new school year is here! Are you nervous about (A)talking to other students? Do you have (B)trouble (C)starting conversations? What about keeping conversations (D)go? ⓐDon't worry. Here (E)are five tips to become a better talker.

18 위 글의 밑줄 친 (A)~(E) 중 어법상 바르지 <u>않은</u> 것을 고르시오.

① (A) ② (B) ③ (C) ④ (D) ⑤ (E)

19 다음은 글쓴이가 밑줄 친 ⓐ와 같이 말한 이유이다. 빈칸에 알맞은 말을 위 글에서 찾아 쓰시오.

> He tells students not to worry because he will give them some hints _____.

➡ _____

[20~23] 다음 글을 읽고, 물음에 답하시오.

Talk Your Best!

The new school year is here! Are you nervous about talking to other students? Do you have trouble starting conversations? What about keeping conversations going? Don't worry. Here are five tips ⓐto become a better talker.

1. _____ ⓑ _____

Most people love to talk about themselves. So give them the chance. When you ask questions about people, they will answer gladly.

2. Be a good listener.

Many people are poor listener. So how can you be a good listener? Look people in the eye. Listen carefully to their words. Don't look at your cell phone or space out!

출제율 85%

20 다음 영영풀이에 해당하는 단어를 위 글에서 찾아 쓰시오.

> to be unable to think clearly, or not aware of what is happening around you

➡ _____

출제율 90%

21 위 글의 밑줄 친 ⓐ와 같은 용법으로 쓰인 것은?

① My hobby is to collect valuable stamps.
② It is important to protect the earth.
③ He says he came here to see me.
④ This book is interesting to read.
⑤ I have an errand to run.

출제율 90%

22 다음 주어진 단어를 바르게 배열하여 빈칸 ⓑ에 알맞은 말을 쓰시오.

> questions / by / start / interesting / asking

➡ _____

출제율 90%

23 위 글의 내용과 일치하는 것은?

① The writer doesn't have any clues about being a better talker.
② This passage will be helpful to students at the end of school year.
③ Listening carefully to what people say is important to be a good listener.
④ When people say something, you shouldn't see their eyes.
⑤ Using your cell phone is polite behavior when listening to someone.

[24~25] 다음 글을 읽고, 물음에 답하시오.

4. ____ ⓐ ____ common interests.

You can't have a conversation by just listening. What do you and your partner have in common? Do you both like sports? Then talk about your favorite baseball team.

5. ____ ⓑ ____ attention to the listener.

Sometimes people may not be (A)[interesting / interested] in your topic. Don't say, "Hey, wake up!" or "Why aren't you listening to me?" Change the topic, or your partner will fall asleep. ____ⓒ____ the other person a chance (B)[to talk / to talk with].

____ⓓ____ these tips, and you will soon be a great talker. Put others first, and everyone will want to talk (C)[with / about] you.

출제율 95%

24 주어진 단어를 글의 흐름에 맞게 빈칸 ⓐ~ⓓ에 쓰시오.

> pay / give / share / practice

ⓐ_____ ⓑ_____ ⓒ_____ ⓓ_____

출제율 100%

25 위 글의 괄호 (A)~(C)에서 옳은 것을 고르시오.

(A)_____ (B)_____ (C)_____

[01~02] 다음 대화를 읽고, 물음에 답하시오.

> A: What can I do to sleep better?
> B: (A)You can drink warm milk before bed.
> A: That's a good idea. I'll (B)do that.

01 위 대화의 밑줄 친 (A)와 바꿔 쓸 때 빈칸에 알맞은 말을 쓰시오.

_____ _____ _____ drink warm milk before bed?

➡ _____

02 위 대화의 밑줄 친 (B)가 가리키는 내용을 우리말로 쓰시오.

➡ _____

03 다음 주어진 단어를 활용하여 우리말을 영어로 쓰시오.

함께 대화할 많은 친구를 만들어라, 그러면 외롭지 않을 것이다. (many / talk / lonely)

➡ _____
_____

04 and를 사용하여 다음 문장을 명령문으로 만드시오.

Unless you open the window, you won't breathe in fresh air.

➡ _____
_____

05 다음 문장을 어법에 맞게 고쳐 쓰시오.

(1) Susan had nothing to gave up.

➡ _____

(2) There is too much trash to pick.

➡ _____

06 주어진 어구를 활용하여 Jessica에게 해줄 조언을 명령문으로 쓰시오.

> Jessica: I want to improve my English. What should I do?
> You: _____
> (every month / an / read / book / English / and / your English)

➡ _____
_____

07 다음 <조건>에 맞게 괄호 안의 단어들을 이용하여 우리말을 바르게 영작하시오.

┤ 조건 ├
1. 주어진 단어들을 모두 이용할 것.
2. 필요시 어형을 바꾸거나 단어를 추가할 것.
3. 주어와 동사를 갖춘 완전한 문장으로 쓸 것.
4. 대·소문자 및 구두점에 유의할 것.

(1) 나는 운전할 자동차가 필요해. (need / drive)

➡ _____

(2) 침착함을 유지해라, 그렇지 않으면 실수할 것이다. (stay / make / some)

➡ _____

Here are some tips to become a better talker.

Start by asking interesting questions.

Most people love to talk about themselves. So give them the chance. When you ask questions about people, (A)they will answer gladly.

Be a good listener.

Many people are poor listeners. So how can you be a good listener? Look people in the eye. Listen carefully to their words. (B)_____ or space out!

08 Write the reason why the writer is saying like (A). Answer in English.

➡ _____

09 다음 문장을 읽고 빈칸 (B)에 들어갈 알맞은 말을 6단어로 쓰시오.

> If you look at your cell phone, your partner will think you are not listening.

➡ _____

Share common interests.

You can't have a conversation by just listening. (A)당신과 상대편은 어떤 공통점을 가지고 있는가? Do you both like sports? Then talk about your favorite baseball team.

Pay attention to the listener.

Sometimes people may not be interested in your topic. Don't say, "Hey, wake up!" or "Why aren't you listening to me?" Change the topic, or your partner will fall asleep.

Give the other person a chance to talk.

Practice these tips, and you will soon be a great talker. Put others first, and everyone will want to talk with you.

10 다음 주어진 단어를 활용하여 밑줄 친 우리말 (A)를 영어로 쓰시오.

> (what / common)

➡ _____

11 위 글에서 적절한 표현을 찾아 글의 제목을 완성하시오.

> How to _____

12 What should you do if your partner fall asleep while you are talking?

➡ _____

01 다음 주간 계획표를 보고 대화를 완성하시오.

Mon	Tue	Wed	Thu	Fri	Sat	Sun
volunteer at the nursing home		have a walk with my pet		study English	go to the library	go to the movies

A: Let's do something together on (1)_____.
B: Sounds great! (2)_____ together?
A: That's a good idea.

02 다음 장소에서 지키면 좋을 것들을 〈보기〉와 같이 써 보시오.

┌─── 보기 ───────────────────────────────────────
• In class, pay attention to the teacher's words, and you will get good grades.
• In the library, be quiet, or you will disturb other people.
• In the park, don't throw the garbage, or you can make other people feel bad.
• In the car, fasten your seat belt, and you will be safe.
└──

(1) _____
(2) _____
(3) _____
(4) _____

03 다음 〈보기〉의 명사들을 이용하여 to부정사의 형용사적 용법을 활용한 문장을 쓰시오.

┌─── 보기 ───────────────────────────────────────
friends   things   water   books   plants
└──

(1) _____
(2) _____
(3) _____

단원별 모의고사

01 다음 대화가 자연스럽게 이어지도록 순서대로 배열하시오.

> (A) That's a great idea.
> (B) Me, too. It's going to be great!
> (C) I'm so excited about the new school year.
> (D) What can I do to make a lot of new friends?
> (E) You can join a sports club.

➡ _____ → _____ → _____ → _____ → _____

02 다음 대화가 자연스럽게 짝지어지지 <u>않은</u> 것은?

① A: What can I do to sleep better?
  B: You can drink warm milk before bed.
② A: What can I do to improve my English?
  B: Why don't you read English books?
③ A: Is there anything I can do to save the Earth?
  B: How about recycling paper?
④ A: What should I do to eat healthily?
  B: You'd better eat lots of vegetables.
⑤ A: What should I do to stay healthy?
  B: Sounds great! What do you want to do?

03 다음 밑줄 친 말과 바꾸어 쓸 수 있는 것은?

> A: Minsu, let's do something together on Thursday.
> B: Sounds great! <u>What do you want to do?</u>
> A: How about going to the bookstore?
> B: Great idea!

① Is there something you want to do?
② Will you do me a favor?
③ Can I give you a hand?
④ How did you find it?
⑤ Do you want me to do it?

[04~05] 다음 대화를 읽고, 물음에 답하시오.

> Jenny: Mike, did you join (A)<u>any</u> clubs?
> Mike: Yes, I joined the singing club.
> Jenny: Oh, I see.
> Mike: What's wrong, Jenny?
> Jenny: I'm the president of the magic club. But I only have two members.
> Mike: Oh, no. That's (B)<u>terrible</u>.
> Jenny: What can I do (C)<u>to getting</u> more members?
> Mike: Why don't you (D)<u>post</u> an ad on the school bulletin board?
> Jenny: That's a good idea. I'll do it (E)<u>right</u> away.

04 위 대화의 (A)~(E) 중 어법상 <u>틀린</u> 것을 골라 바르게 고치시오.

➡ _____

05 위 대화의 내용과 일치하지 <u>않는</u> 것은?

① Jenny는 마술 동아리의 회장이다.
② 마술 동아리에는 오직 두 명의 회원만 있다.
③ Mike는 마술 동아리에 가입하였다.
④ Jenny는 더 많은 동아리 회원을 모집하기 위해 조언을 구하였다.
⑤ Mike는 Jenny에게 학교 게시판에 마술 동아리 광고를 게시해 볼 것을 제안하였다.

06 다음 대화의 빈칸에 들어갈 말로 적절한 것은?

> A: _____ can I do to sleep better?
> B: You can drink warm milk before bed.

① Why   ② What   ③ How
④ Who   ⑤ Which

07 다음 대화의 밑줄 친 부분과 바꾸어 쓸 수 있는 것은?

> A: How about going to the bookstore?
> B: Great idea!

① Which   ② What   ③ Why
④ When   ⑤ Where

[08~09] 다음 대화를 읽고, 물음에 답하시오.

> Sue: Minsu, why are you so late?
> Minsu: Oh, I'm sorry. _____ the way, I ran into a foreigner.
> Sue: Yes, and?
> Minsu: I had to take him to the subway station.
> Sue: Why didn't you just tell him the directions?
> Minsu: He didn't speak English very well.
> Sue: Hmm... How about using the *Talk Smart* app next time?
> Minsu: *Talk Smart*? What kind of app is it?
> Sue: It changes one language to another. It's really helpful.
> Minsu: Really? I'll try it next time.

08 위 대화의 빈칸에 들어갈 말로 알맞은 것은?

① In   ② On   ③ By
④ From   ⑤ Under

09 위 대화를 읽고 대답할 수 <u>없는</u> 질문은?

① Who did Minsu run into when he was coming to meet Sue?
② What did Minsu do for a foreigner?
③ What kind of app is *Talk Smart*?
④ When did Sue use the *Talk Smart*?
⑤ Why did Minsu take the foreigner to the subway station?

[10~12] 다음 대화를 읽고, 물음에 답하시오.

> Brian: Hey, Mina, what's wrong?
> Mina: My best friend, Kate, is (A)mad at me.
> Brian: That's terrible. (B)What happened?
> Mina: I said her new hairstyle was cute just like my dog's.
> Brian: No wonder she's mad at you.
> Mina: Right. She won't talk to me.
> Brian: Yeah. She's probably really angry.
> Mina: What can I do to make up with her?
> Brian: How about sending her a text?
> Mina: That's a good idea. I'll do that.

10 위 대화의 밑줄 친 (A)와 바꾸어 쓸 수 있는 것은?

① bored   ② angry
③ afraid   ④ worried
⑤ anxious

11 위 대화의 밑줄 친 (B)와 바꾸어 쓸 수 있는 것은?

① Why are you so happy?
② What's the matter with you?
③ What makes you feel good?
④ How's everything going?
⑤ What are you looking forward to?

12 위 대화의 내용과 일치하지 <u>않는</u> 것은?

① Kate는 Mina에게 화가 많이 났다.

② Mina는 Kate의 새로운 머리 스타일에 대해 부적절한 말을 하였다.

③ Brian은 Kate가 화를 내는 것이 당연하다고 생각한다.

④ Mina는 Kate와 화해하기 위해 문자를 보낼 것이다.

⑤ Kate는 화가 나서 Brian과 이야기를 하지 않을 것이다.

13 다음 중 어법상 바르지 <u>않은</u> 것을 <u>모두</u> 고르시오.

① Hurry up, or you will be late for the meeting.

② I'm looking for a handyman to fixing this.

③ Tom is used to living in this town.

④ You need to buy something useful to use.

⑤ Drink enough water, and your skin will be dry.

14 다음 표를 보고 수요일 날씨에 관하여 해줄 수 있는 조언을 주어진 단어를 이용하여 명령문으로 쓰시오.

MON	TUE	WED	THU	FRI
Sunny	Sunny	Rainy	Cloudy	Sunny

(take / get all wet)

➡ _____

15 다음 중 어법상 바르지 <u>않은</u> 것은?

Don't <u>make fun of</u> <u>other</u> people, <u>and</u> you
     ①   ②   ③

<u>will</u> hurt <u>their</u> feelings.
 ④   ⑤

16 다음 괄호 안의 단어를 어법에 맞게 각각 쓰시오.

I have trouble (make) friends, so I don't have a friend (depend on).

➡ _____

17 다음 중 빈칸에 들어갈 말로 가장 적절한 것은?

Turn down the radio, and you will understand what I'm saying.

= _____ you don't turn down the radio, you will not understand what I'm saying.

① Unless   ② If   ③ As

④ Though   ⑤ As soon as

[18~21] 다음 글을 읽고, 물음에 답하시오.

(A)여기 더 나은 화자가 되기 위한 몇 가지 조언이 있다.

1. Start by ⓐasking interesting questions.

Most people love to talk about themselves. So give them the chance. When you ask questions about people, they will answer gladly.

2. Be a good listener.

Many people are poor listeners. So how can you be a good listener? Look people in the eye. Listen carefully to their words. Don't look at your cell phone or space out!

3. Give feedback.

Be an active listener. Nod your head from time to time. You can say little things like, "Wow!" or "Cool." You can also say something like, "That's interesting. Tell me more." ⓑ_____ feedback shows that you're listening.

18 밑줄 친 우리말 (A)를 주어진 단어를 어법에 맞게 변형하여 영어로 옮기시오.

> talker / to / tips / better / some / a / here / be / become

➡ _____

19 밑줄 친 ⓐ와 쓰임이 같은 것은?

① She is writing something down.
② My brother is sitting next to the dog.
③ You were dancing on the stage.
④ What I like most is talking in front of people.
⑤ Her sister was running to chase the rabbit.

20 빈칸 ⓑ에 들어갈 말을 위 글에서 찾아 어법에 맞게 쓰시오.

➡ _____

21 위 글을 읽고, 대화하고 싶은 상대에 해당하지 않는 사람을 고르시오.

① Amy: I give others a chance to talk.
② Julian: I love to talk about myself.
③ Jamie: I look people in the eye when they talk.
④ Emma: I usually space out when someone talks.
⑤ Nick: I sometimes nod to let them know I am listening.

[22~25] 다음 글을 읽고, 물음에 답하시오.

4. Share common interests.
  You can't have a conversation by just ⓐlisten. What do you and your partner have in common? Do you both like sports? Then talk about your favorite baseball team.

5. Pay attention to the listener.
  Sometimes people may not be interested in your topic. Don't say, "Hey, wake up!" or "Why aren't you listening to me?" Change the topic, ___ⓑ___ your partner will fall asleep. Give the other person a chance ⓒtalk.

  (A)Practice these tips, and you will soon be a great talker. Put others first, ___ⓓ___ everyone will want to talk with you.

22 밑줄 친 ⓐ와 ⓒ를 어법에 맞게 각각 쓰시오.

ⓐ _____   ⓒ _____

23 빈칸 ⓑ와 ⓓ에 알맞은 접속사를 각각 쓰시오.

ⓑ _____   ⓓ _____

24 위 글의 내용과 일치하지 않는 것은?

① Just listening makes it hard to keep a conversation going.
② It is good for you and your partner to have something in common.
③ In order to have a conversation, you must like baseball.
④ Sharing common interests is good in having a conversation.
⑤ Putting others first makes everyone want to talk with you.

25 접속사 if를 이용하여 밑줄 친 (A)와 같은 의미의 문장을 쓰시오.

➡ _____
  _____

Lesson 2

Close to You

의사소통 기능

- 확신 말하기
  A: Sam plays the guitar really well.
  B: I'm sure he will get first place in the contest.

- 성격 묘사하기
  A: What is she like?
  B: She is active and outgoing

언어 형식

- 현재완료
  My father **has been** invisible since last night.

- to부정사를 목적격보어로 취하는 동사
  We **asked** the doctor **to help** us.

Words & Expressions

Key Words

- **active** [ǽktiv] 형 적극적인, 능동적인 (↔ passive)
- **arrive** [əráiv] 동 도착하다 (↔ leave)
- **awful** [ɔ́ːfəl] 형 끔찍한, 무시무시한
- **badminton** [bǽdmintn] 명 배드민턴
- **banker** [bǽŋkər] 명 은행원, 은행업자
- **beautifully** [bjúːtəfəli] 부 아름답게
- **caring** [kέəriŋ] 형 배려하는, 보살피는
- **charity** [tʃǽrəti] 명 자선 단체
- **classmate** [klǽsmeit] 명 급우, 동급생
- **cleaner** [klíːnər] 명 깨끗이 하는 사람, 세제
- **coach** [koutʃ] 명 코치
- **comedian** [kəmíːdiən] 명 희극배우, 코미디언
- **contest** [kántest] 명 경기, 경연
- **crazy** [kréizi] 형 말도 안 되는, 미친
- **creative** [kriéitiv] 형 창조적인, 창의적인
- **disappear** [dìsəpíər] 동 사라지다, 모습을 감추다
- **donate** [dóuneit] 동 기부하다
- **feed** [fiːd] 동 (음식을) 주다, 먹이다
- **friendly** [fréndli] 형 친절한, 상냥한
- **funny** [fʌ́ni] 형 재미있는, 익살맞은
- **hard-working** [hɑːrdwərkiŋ] 형 근면한, 열심히 일하는
- **helpful** [hélpfəl] 형 도움이 되는
- **hug** [hʌg] 동 껴안다

- **humorous** [hjúːmərəs] 형 재미있는, 익살스러운
- **insect** [ínsekt] 명 곤충, 벌레
- **intelligent** [intélədʒənt] 형 똑똑한, 영리한
- **invisible** [invízəbl] 형 눈에 보이지 않는 (↔ visible)
- **joke** [dʒouk] 명 농담
- **leave** [liːv] 동 떠나다, (뒤에) 남기다
- **normal** [nɔ́ːrməl] 형 평범한, 정상적인
- **outgoing** [áutgouiŋ] 형 외향적인, 사교적인
- **pass** [pæs] 동 건네주다, 통과하다, 지나가다
- **patient** [péiʃənt] 형 참을성이 있는 (↔ impatient)
- **personality** [pɜ̀ːrsənǽləti] 명 개성, 성격
- **pianist** [piǽnist] 명 피아니스트, 피아노 연주자
- **promise** [prámis] 동 약속하다 명 약속
- **recycling** [riːsáikəliŋ] 명 재활용
- **responsible** [rispánsəbl] 형 책임 있는, ~의 원인이 되는
- **secret** [síːkrit] 명 비밀
- **shake** [ʃeik] 동 (고개를) 흔들다
- **shout** [ʃaut] 동 소리치다
- **station** [stéiʃən] 명 정거장, 역
- **thin** [θin] 형 얇은 (↔ thick), 마른 (↔ fat)
- **tidy** [táidi] 형 깔끔한
- **voice** [vɔis] 명 목소리, 음성
- **yell** [jel] 동 소리치다

Key Expressions

- **a sea of** ~ ~의 바다, 다량의 ~
- **at once** 즉시
- **do one's own thing** 자기가 하고 싶은 일을 하다
- **do well** 잘하다
- **far from** ~에서 멀리
- **get the first place** 1등을 하다
- **in front of** ~의 앞쪽에, ~ 앞에(서)

- **in a few moments** 곧
- **invite ~ over** ~을 자기 집으로 초대하다
- **look for** ~을 찾다, 구하다
- **in time** 늦지 않게, 제시간에
- **turn off** (전기, 가스, 수도 등을) 끄다
- **travel abroad** 해외여행을 하다
- **wait for** ~을 기다리다

Word Power

※ 서로 반대되는 뜻을 가진 어휘

- appear (나타나다) → disappear (사라지다)
- arrive (도착하다) → leave (떠나다)
- friendly (친절한, 상냥한) → unfriendly (불친절한)
- send (보내다) → receive (받다)
- intelligent (똑똑한, 영리한) → foolish (어리석은)
- active (적극적인, 능동적인) → passive (소극적인)

- responsible (책임 있는) → irresponsible (책임감이 없는)
- outgoing (외향적인, 사교적인) → shy (소심한, 수줍어하는)
- tidy (깔끔한) → messy (어질러진)
- patient (참을성이 있는) → impatient (참을성이 없는)
- normal (정상적인) → abnormal (보통과 다른, 정상이 아닌)
- turn off (~을 끄다) → turn on (~을 켜다)

English Dictionary

- **banker** 은행원, 은행업자
  → a person who owns a bank or has an important job at a bank
  은행에서 중요한 일을 하거나 은행을 소유한 사람

- **classmate** 급우, 동급생
  → a person who is or was in the same class as you at school or college
  학교 또는 대학에서 당신과 같은 반에 있거나 있었던 사람

- **charity** 자선 단체
  → an organization for helping people in need
  어려움에 처한 사람들을 도와주기 위한 단체

- **cleaner** 깨끗이 하는 사람
  → a person whose job is to clean other people's houses or offices, etc.
  다른 사람들의 집이나 사무실을 청소하는 직업을 갖고 있는 사람

- **comedian** 희극배우, 코미디언
  → an entertainer who makes people laugh by telling jokes or funny stories
  농담이나 재미있는 이야기로 사람들을 웃게 하는 예능인

- **contest** 경연, 경기
  → a competition in which people try to win something
  무언가에 이기기 위해 사람들이 노력하는 경쟁

- **donate** 기부하다
  → to give money, food, clothes, etc. to somebody/something, especially a charity
  돈, 음식, 옷 등을 누군가에게, 또는 어떤 것에, 특히 자선 단체에 주다

- **friendly** 친절한, 상냥한
  → behaving in a kind and pleasant way
  친절하고 기쁜 방식으로 행동하는

- **hug** 껴안다
  → to put your arms around somebody and hold them tightly, especially to show that you like or love them
  특히 당신이 매우 좋아한다는 것을 표현하기 위해 당신의 팔을 다른 누군가에게 올려놓거나 꽉 잡다

- **insect** 곤충
  → any small creature with six legs and a body divided into three parts
  6개의 다리와 3개의 부분으로 나누어진 몸을 갖고 있는 작은 생명체

- **invisible** 보이지 않는
  → unable to be seen
  눈에 보이지 않는

- **joke** 농담
  → something that you say or do to make people laugh
  사람들을 웃게 만들기 위해 당신이 말하거나 행동하는 어떤 것

- **normal** 정상적인
  → typical, usual or ordinary
  전형적인, 일반적인 또는 보통의

- **promise** 약속하다
  → to tell somebody that you will definitely do or not do something
  네가 무언가를 하거나 하지 않을 것이라고 누군가에게 말하다

- **rude** 무례한, 버릇없는
  → showing a lack of respect for other people and their feelings
  다른 사람들과 그들의 감정에 대해 존중이 부족함을 보여주는

- **shout** 소리치다
  → to say something in a loud voice
  큰 소리로 무언가를 말하다

- **tidy** 말끔히 정돈된, 단정한
  → keeping things neat and in order
  무언가를 깔끔하거나 질서 있게 유지하고 있는

서답형

01 다음 짝지어진 단어의 관계가 같도록 빈칸에 알맞은 말을 쓰시오.

> like : dislike = appear : _____

02 다음 빈칸에 들어갈 말 중 의미가 <u>다른</u> 것은?

> She is a very _____ and creative person.

① smart   ② clever
③ intelligent   ④ bright
⑤ ignorant

서답형

03 다음 영영풀이에 해당하는 말을 고르시오.

> to tell somebody that you will definitely do or not do something

➡ _____

서답형

04 다음 괄호 안의 우리말과 같은 뜻이 되도록 주어진 철자로 시작하는 단어로 빈칸을 완성하시오.

> B: Who's that?
> G: He's my new badminton coach.
> B: He's very tall and handsome. What is he like?
> G: He is very f_____ and h_____. I like him a lot. (그는 상냥하고 유머가 풍부하셔.)

➡ f_____, h_____

05 다음 빈칸에 공통으로 들어갈 말로 적절한 것을 고르시오.

> • He will _____ the ball to the captain to score a goal.
> • They are waiting for the typhoon to _____.
> • I was so happy to _____ the exam.

① donate   ② promise
③ join   ④ disappear
⑤ pass

서답형

06 다음 빈칸 (A)~(C)에 들어갈 말을 쓰시오.

> • How about inviting Mike (A)_____ to watch a movie?
> • Jake is looking (B)_____ a bus stop.
> • Many people were crowded in front (C)_____ the school.

(A) _____ (B) _____ (C) _____

중요

07 다음 중 밑줄 친 부분의 뜻풀이가 바르지 <u>않은</u> 것은?

① A few years ago, many people suffered from an <u>awful</u> earthquake.
     무시무시한
② I usually <u>feed</u> my cats in the morning.
     먹이다
③ You should not <u>yell</u> in the aisle.
     소리 지르다
④ Let's <u>shake</u> hands and then sit down.
     외치다
⑤ Have you ever eaten an <u>insect</u>?
     벌레

[01~03] 다음 영영풀이에 해당하는 말을 쓰시오.

01

a person who owns a bank or has an important job at a bank

➡ _____

02

an organization for helping people in need

➡ _____

03

a competition in which people try to win something

➡ _____

04 다음 우리말과 일치하도록 주어진 어구를 배열하여 완성하시오.

(1) 나의 애완견이 죽자마자, 우리 가족은 눈물바다가 되었다.
As soon as my pet dog was dead, (were / of / tears / a sea / my / family).
➡ _____

(2) 그는 방에서 자기가 하고 싶은 일을 하고 있었다.
(room / he / his / own / the / doing / in / was / thing)
➡ _____

05 다음 문장의 빈칸에 들어갈 말을 〈보기〉에서 골라 쓰시오.

┤ 보기 ├
a sea of / turn off / get the first place

(1) 전쟁은 도시를 불바다로 바꿀 수 있다.
➡ The war can turn the city into _____ fire.

(2) 정말 멋진 공연이야! 네가 1등을 할 것이라고 확신해.
➡ What a wonderful performance! I'm sure you'll _____.

(3) 나갈 때, 히터를 꺼주세요.
➡ When you go out, _____ the heater, please.

06 다음 문장의 의미를 고려하여 빈칸에 들어갈 말을 〈보기〉에서 찾아 쓰시오.

┤ 보기 ├
promise, normal, charity, outgoing

• The bazaar will be held to raise money for a local _____.
• What did you _____ your mother before going to the party?
• I like Emma because she is _____ and confident.

07 다음 우리말과 일치하도록 주어진 단어를 사용하여 영어로 쓰시오.

(1) 마법사는 자신을 보이지 않게 만들 수 있다.
(invisible, wizard)
➡ _____

(2) 오늘 당신의 어머니를 안아 드리는 것이 어때요?
(hug, why)
➡ _____

Conversation

① 확신 말하기

> **A** Sam plays the guitar really well. Sam은 기타를 정말 잘 쳐.
> **B** I'm sure he will get first place in the contest. 나는 그가 대회에서 일등을 할 것이라고 확신해.

■ 'I'm sure ~'는 상대방의 이야기에 대해 자신의 확실성을 나타낼 때 쓰는 표현이다.

확신 말하기 표현

- I'm sure (that) ~. 나는 ~을 확신한다.
- I'm certain (that) ~. 나는 ~을 확신한다.
- I have no doubt that ~. 나는 ~에 대해 의심치 않는다.

- A: Jane has a great voice. Jane은 좋은 목소리를 갖고 있어.
  B: I'm certain she will be a great singer. 나는 그녀가 좋은 가수가 될 거라고 확신해.

- A: Jack studies all day. Jack은 하루 종일 공부해.
  B: I have no doubt that he will get a good grade on the test.
  나는 그가 시험에서 좋은 성적을 받을 것이라는 것을 의심치 않아.

핵심 Check

1. 다음 우리말과 일치하도록 빈칸에 알맞은 말을 쓰시오.

   (1) **A:** Amy runs really fast. (Amy는 정말 빨리 달려.)

   B: I'm _____ she will _____ _____ _____.

   (나는 그녀가 경주에서 이길 것이라고 확신해.)

   (2) **A:** The train station isn't very _____ _____ here. (기차역이 여기서 별로 멀지 않아.)

   B: I have _____ _____ that we'll arrive there before 5.

   (나는 우리가 5시 전에 도착할 것이라고 의심하지 않아.)

   (3) **A:** Tomorrow, we're going to Jeju island. I _____ wait.

   (내일 우리는 제주도에 가. 너무 기대된다.)

   B: Me, too. _____ _____ it will be a wonderful trip.

   (나도 그래. 나는 멋진 여행이 될 것이라고 확신해.)

② 성격 묘사하기

A What is she like? 그녀는 성격이 어떠니?
B She is active and outgoing. 그녀는 적극적이고 외향적이야.

■ 인물의 성격이나 특징을 물어 볼 때 'What is he[she] like?'의 표현을 사용할 수 있으며, 이에 대한 대답으로 성격을 묘사하는 형용사를 사용하여 대답할 수 있다.

성격묻기와 성격을 묘사하는 다양한 형용사

• What is she like? 그녀는 성격이 어떠니?

• What is his personality like? 그의 성격은 어때?

• active 활발한, patient 참을성이 있는, outgoing 외향적인. 사교적인, friendly 친절한, responsible 책임감 있는, tidy 깔끔한, honest 정직한, humorous 재미있는. 익살스러운, hard-working 근면한, caring 배려하는. 보살피는, helpful 도움이 되는

• A: What is Jenny like? Jenny는 성격이 어때?
  B: She is patient and friendly. 그녀는 참을성이 있고 친절해.

• A: What is Sam's personality like? Sam의 성격은 어때?
  B: He is kind and active. 그는 상냥하고 활발해.

핵심 Check

2. 다음 우리말과 일치하도록 빈칸에 알맞은 말을 쓰시오.

(1) **A:** What is Emma like? (Emma는 어떤 사람이야?)

   B: She is _____ and _____. (그녀는 책임감 있고 참을성이 있어.)

(2) **A:** What is Jack's _____ like? (Jack의 성격은 어때?)

   B: He is a _____ and _____ person. (그는 근면하고 도움이 되는 사람이야.)

(3) **A:** _____ is the best person to be a class comedian?

   (학급 코미디언으로 누가 가장 적절할까?)

   B: How about Jack? He is _____ and _____.

   (Jack이 어때? 그는 유머가 풍부하고 외향적이야.)

A. Listen and Speak 1-A

G: ❶Can we arrive in time?

B: Of course. The train leaves at 5:10.

G: But, it's already 4:30.

B: ❷The train station isn't very far from here. ❸I'm sure we'll arrive there before 5.

G: 우리가 늦지 않게 도착할 수 있을까?

B: 물론이야. 기차는 5시 10분에 떠나.

G: 하지만 벌써 4시 30분이야.

B: 기차역은 여기서 별로 멀지 않아. 나는 우리가 5시 전에 거기에 도착할 거라고 확신해.

❶ arrive: 도착하다
❷ far: 멀리; 먼
❸ 'I'm sure ～'는 '나는 ～을 확신해.'라는 뜻으로 확신을 말할 때 쓰는 표현이다.

Check(√) True or False

(1) The boy is sure that they can arrive at the train station before 5. T ☐ F ☐

(2) It will take over 30 minutes for them to get to the train station. T ☐ F ☐

A. Listen and Speak 1-B

Jenny: Hey, Minsu. ❶What's up? ❷You look so worried.

Minsu: The English speaking test is this afternoon.

Jenny: Don't worry. ❸You practiced a lot.

Minsu: ❹But I get so nervous when I'm in front of the teacher.

Jenny: Everybody does. ❺I'm sure you'll do well.

Minsu: Do you really think so?

Jenny: Of course. ❻You are a great English speaker.

Minsu: Thanks. ❼I feel much better now.

Jenny: 안녕, 민수야. 무슨 일 있니? 걱정스러워 보여.

Minsu: 영어 말하기 시험이 오늘 오후에 있어.

Jenny: 걱정 마. 너는 연습을 많이 했잖아.

Minsu: 하지만 선생님 앞에 있으면 너무 긴장 돼.

Jenny: 누구나 그래. 나는 네가 잘할 거라고 확신해.

Minsu: 정말 그렇게 생각해?

Jenny: 물론이야. 너는 영어를 잘해.

Minsu: 고마워. 이제 기분이 훨씬 나아졌어.

❶ What's up?은 '무슨 일 있니?'라는 의미로 상대방의 안부를 물을 때 쓰인다.
❷ look+형용사(보어)
❸ a lot: 많이
❹ nervous: 긴장되는, in front of: ～ 앞에(서)
❺ 'I'm sure ～': '나는 ～을 확신해.'
❻ 'You speak English well.'로 바꿔 쓸 수 있다.
❼ much는 비교급을 강조하는 부사이다.

Check(√) True or False

(3) Minsu is worried about the English speaking test. T ☐ F ☐

(4) Jenny isn't certain that Minsu will do well. T ☐ F ☐

Listen and Speak 1-C

A: ❶Sam plays the guitar really well.

B: ❷Yeah, I'm sure he will get first place in the contest.

A: ❸I think so, too.

❶ play the guitar: 기타를 연주하다
❷ I'm sure ~.: '나는 ~을 확신해.'
❸ I think so, too.: '나도 그렇게 생각해.'라는 의미로 상대방의 의견에 동의하는 표현이다.

Listen and Speak 2-A

B: Who's that?

G: ❶He's my new badminton coach.

B: He's very tall and handsome. ❷What is he like?

G: ❸He is very friendly and humorous. I like him a lot.

❶ badminton coach: 배드민턴 코치
❷ 누군가의 성격을 물을 때는 What is he like?(그는 어떤 분이야?)라고 물을 수 있다.
❸ friendly: 친절한, 상냥한, humorous: 유머가 풍부한, 재미있는

Listen and Speak 2-B

Dad: ❶Sue, how do you like your school these days?

Sue: I like it a lot, Dad. ❷I already made two new friends, Rosa and Mike.

Dad: ❸Happy to hear that. How did you become friends?

Sue: ❹We all love English. We are also in the same club.

Dad: That's great. ❺What are they like?

Sue: Rosa is very kind.

Dad: ❻How about Mike?

Sue: He is outgoing.

Dad: ❼Why don't you invite them over for dinner?

Sue: Okay, Dad.

❶ how do you like ~?: ~이 마음에 드니?, these days: 요즘
❷ two new friends와 Rosa and Mike는 동격이다.
❸ Happy to hear that. = I'm happy to hear that.
❹ We와 all은 동격이다.
❺ What are they like?: 그들의 성격은 어떠니?
❻ How about ~?: ~은 어떠니?
❼ Why don't you~: ~하는 게 어떠니?

Listen and Speak 2-C

A: ❶I'm looking for a new member for my dance club.

B: ❷How about Jenny?

A: What is she like?

B: ❸She is active and outgoing.

A: Thanks. I'll ask her.

❶ look for: ~을 찾다, ~을 구하다
❷ How about ~?: ~은 어떠니?
❸ active: 적극적인, outgoing: 외향적인

Real Life Talk

Judy: Hojin, I'm looking for a singer for my school band.

Hojin: How about Junho Kim?

Judy: Junho Kim? Who's that?

Hojin: Oh, he's my classmate. ❶He just moved to our school last week.

Judy: ❷Is he a good singer?

Hojin: Yeah, he sings beautifully. ❸I'm sure he will be perfect for your band.

Judy: ❹Can you tell me more about him? What's he like?

Hojin: Well, he is very outgoing and friendly.

Judy: Great. Can I have his phone number?

Hojin: Sure.

❶ moved to our school: 우리 학교로 전학 왔다
❷ = Does he sing well?
❸ I'm sure ~: '나는 ~을 확신해.'
❹ more는 much의 비교급으로 tell의 직접목적어이다.

● 다음 우리말과 일치하도록 빈칸에 알맞은 말을 쓰시오.

Listen & Speak 1 A

G: Can we _____ in time?

B: Of course. The train _____ at 5:10.

G: But, it's _____ 4:30.

B: The train station isn't very _____ _____ here. I'm sure we'll _____ there before 5.

해석

G: 우리가 늦지 않게 도착할 수 있을까?
B: 물론이야. 기차는 5시 10분에 떠나.
G: 하지만 벌써 4시 30분이야.
B: 기차역은 여기서 별로 멀지 않아. 나는 우리가 5시 전에 거기에 도착할 거라고 확신해.

Listen & Speak 1 B

Jenny: Hey, Minsu. What's up? You look so _____.

Minsu: The _____ _____ _____ is this afternoon.

Jenny: Don't _____. You practiced a lot.

Minsu: But I get so _____ when I'm _____ _____ _____ the teacher.

Jenny: Everybody does. I'm sure you'll _____ _____.

Minsu: Do you really _____ _____?

Jenny: Of course. You are a great English _____.

Minsu: Thanks. I _____ _____ _____ now.

Jenny: 안녕, 민수야. 무슨 일 있니? 걱정스러워 보여.
Minsu: 영어 말하기 시험이 오늘 오후에 있어.
Jenny: 걱정 마. 너는 연습을 많이 했잖아.
Minsu: 하지만 선생님 앞에 있으면 너무 긴장돼.
Jenny: 누구나 그래. 나는 네가 잘할 거라고 확신해.
Minsu: 정말 그렇게 생각해?
Jenny: 물론이야. 너는 정말 영어를 잘해.
Minsu: 고마워. 이제 기분이 훨씬 나아졌어.

Listen & Speak 1 C

A: Sam plays _____ _____ really well.

B: Yeah, I'm sure he will _____ _____ _____ in the contest.

A: I think so, _____.

A: Sam은 기타를 정말 잘 쳐.
B: 응, 나는 그가 대회에서 1등을 할 것이라고 확신해.
B: 나도 그렇게 생각해.

Listen & Speak 2 A

B: Who's that?

G: He's my new badminton _____.

B: He's very _____ and _____. What is he _____?

G: He is very _____ and _____. I like him a lot.

B: 저 사람은 누구니?
G: 저 분은 새로 오신 우리 배드민턴 코치님이셔.
B: 정말 키가 크고 잘생기셨구나. 어떤 분이셔?
G: 코치님은 정말 상냥하고 유머가 풍부하셔. 나는 코치님이 정말 좋아.

Listen & Talk 2 B

Dad: Sue, _____ do you like your school these days?

Sue: I like it a lot, Dad. I _____ made two new friends, Rosa and Mike.

Dad: Happy to _____ that. How did you _____ friends?

Sue: We all love English. We are also _____ _____ _____ _____.

Dad: That's great. What are they _____?

Sue: Rosa is very _____.

Dad: How about Mike?

Sue: He is _____.

Dad: Why don't you _____ _____ _____ for dinner?

Sue: Okay, Dad.

Listen & Talk 2 C

A: I'm _____ _____ a new member for my dance club.

B: How about Jenny?

A: _____ _____ _____ _____?

B: She is _____ and _____.

A: Thanks. I'll _____ her.

Real Life Talk

Judy: Hojin, I'm looking _____ a singer for my school band.

Hojin: How _____ Junho Kim?

Judy: Junho Kim? Who's that?

Hojin: Oh, he's my classmate. He just _____ to our school last week.

Judy: Is he a good _____?

Hojin: Yeah, he _____ beautifully. I'm _____ he will be _____ for your band.

Judy: Can you tell me _____ about him? What's he _____?

Hojin: Well, he is very outgoing and _____.

Judy: Great. Can I _____ his phone _____?

Hojin: Sure.

해석

Dad: Sue, 요즘 학교는 어떠니?

Sue: 정말 좋아요, 아빠. 벌써 Rosa와 Mike라는 새 친구 두 명을 사귀었어요.

Dad: 그 말을 들으니 좋구나. 너희들은 어떻게 친구가 되었니?

Sue: 우리 모두는 영어를 정말 좋아해요. 우리는 같은 동아리에 있기도 해요.

Dad: 좋구나. 그 친구들은 성격이 어떠니?

Sue: Rosa는 아주 상냥해요.

Dad: Mike는 어떠니?

Sue: 그는 외향적이에요.

Dad: 그 친구들을 저녁 식사에 초대하는 게 어떠니?

Sue: 좋아요, 아빠.

A: 나는 우리 댄스 동아리에 새 회원을 찾고 있어.

B: Jenny는 어때?

A: Jenny의 성격이 어떠니?

B: 그녀는 적극적이고 외향적이야.

A: 고마워. 그녀에게 물어볼게.

Judy: 호진아, 나는 우리 학교 밴드에서 노래 부를 사람을 찾고 있어.

Hojin: 김준호는 어때?

Judy: 김준호? 걔가 누구야?

Hojin: 오, 우리 반 친구야. 그는 지난주에 우리 학교에 전학 왔어.

Judy: 그는 노래를 잘하니?

Hojin: 응, 그는 아름답게 노래를 해. 너희 밴드에 꼭 맞을 거라고 확신해.

Judy: 그에 관해 좀 더 말해 줄 수 있니? 그는 어떤 애니?

Hojin: 음, 그는 아주 외향적이고 상냥해.

Judy: 좋네. 그의 전화번호를 알 수 있을까?

Hojin: 그럼.

Conversation 시험대비 기본평가

01 다음 주어진 우리말과 일치하도록 빈칸을 완성하시오.

A: What is she like?
B: She is _____ and _____. (그녀는 활발하고 외향적이야.)

[02~03] 다음 대화를 읽고, 물음에 답하시오.

G: Can we arrive in time?
B: Of course. The train leaves at 5:10.
G: But, it's already 4:30.
B: The train station isn't very far from here. I'm sure we'll arrive (A) there before 5.

02 위 대화의 밑줄 친 (A)there가 가리키는 것을 영어로 쓰시오.

➡ _____

03 위 대화의 내용과 일치하지 <u>않는</u> 것은?

① 지금 시각은 4:30분이다.
② G와 B는 5시 전에 기차역에 도착하려고 한다.
③ 기차는 5시 10분에 떠날 예정이다.
④ 기차역은 멀리 떨어져 있지 않다.
⑤ B는 기차역에 늦을까 봐 불안해하고 있다.

04 다음 밑줄 친 말과 바꾸어 쓸 수 있는 것을 <u>모두</u> 고르시오.

A: Sam plays the guitar really well.
B: <u>I'm sure he will get first place in the contest.</u>

① I'm certain he will get first place in the contest.
② I doubt whether he will get first place in the contest.
③ I don't doubt that he will get first place in the contest.
④ I wonder if he will get first place in the contest.
⑤ I'm curious he will get first place in the contest.

서답형

01 다음 주어진 우리말과 뜻이 일치하도록 빈칸을 완성하시오.

A: Sam plays the guitar really well.
B: 나는 그가 대회에서 1등을 할 것이라고 확신해.

➡ I'm sure he will get _____ _____ in the contest.

[02~03] 다음 대화를 읽고, 물음에 답하시오.

G: Can we arrive _____ _____?
B: Of course. The train leaves at 5:10.
G: But, it's already 4:30.
B: The train station isn't very far from here. I'm sure we'll arrive there before 5.

서답형

02 위 대화의 빈칸에 '늦지 않게'를 나타내는 표현을 두 단어로 완성하시오.

➡ _____

03 위 대화를 읽고 대답할 수 없는 질문은?

① What time is it now?
② Where are they going now?
③ When is the train supposed to leave?
④ What is *B* certain about?
⑤ Which train are they going to take?

[04~07] 다음 대화를 읽고, 물음에 답하시오.

Jane: Hey, Minsu. What's up? You look so (A)worrying.
Minsu: The English speaking test is this afternoon.
Jane: Don't worry. You (B)practiced a lot.
Minsu: But I get so nervous when I'm (C)in front of the teacher.
Jane: Everybody does. I'm sure you'll do (D)well.

Minsu: Do you really think so?
Jane: Of course. You are a great English speaker.
Minsu: Thanks. I feel much (E)better now.

서답형

04 위 대화의 (A)~(E) 중 어법상 어색한 것을 찾아 바르게 고치시오.

➡ _____

05 위 대화에서 민수의 심경 변화로 적절한 것은?

① nervous → relieved
② worried → disappointed
③ surprised → worried
④ excited → nervous
⑤ lonely → relieved

서답형

06 Why does Minsu look so worried?

➡ _____

서답형

07 Even though Minsu practiced a lot for the speaking test, why is he so anxious about it?

➡ _____
_____

중요

08 다음 밑줄 친 표현과 바꾸어 쓸 수 있는 것은?

A: Sam plays the guitar really well.
B: Yeah, I'm sure he will get first place in the contest.
A: I think so, too.

① I agree with you. ② I don't believe so.
③ No, it isn't. ④ That's not correct.
⑤ I'm against it.

09 다음 주어진 문장이 들어가기에 가장 적절한 곳은?

> What is he like?

> B: Who's that? (A)
> G: He's my new badminton coach. (B)
> B: He's very tall and handsome. (C)
> G: He is very friendly and humorous. (D) I like him a lot. (E)

① (A)　② (B)　③ (C)　④ (D)　⑤ (E)

[10~11] 다음 대화를 읽고, 물음에 답하시오.

> Dad: Sue, how do you like your school these days?
> Sue: I like it a lot, Dad. I already made two new friends, Rosa and Mike.
> Dad: Happy to hear that. How did you become friends?
> Sue: We all love English. We are also in the same club.
> Dad: That's great. What are they like?
> Sue: Rosa is very kind.
> Dad: How about Mike?
> Sue: He is outgoing.
> Dad: (A)Why don't you invite them over for dinner? (how)
> Sue: Okay, Dad.

서답형

10 위 대화의 밑줄 친 (A)와 의미가 같도록 주어진 어휘를 사용하여 다시 쓰시오.

➡ _____

11 위 대화의 내용과 일치하지 <u>않는</u> 것은?

① Sue는 요즘 학교생활을 좋아하고 있다.
② Sue는 Rosa와 Mike와 친구가 되었다.
③ Sue, Rosa 그리고 Mike는 영어 동아리에 가입하였다.
④ Rosa는 매우 상냥하고 Mike는 외향적이다.
⑤ 아버지는 Sue에게 Rosa와 Mike를 집에 초대할 것을 제안하였다.

[12~13] 다음 대화를 읽고, 물음에 답하시오.

> Judy: Hojin, I'm looking for a singer for my school band.
> Hojin: How about Junho Kim?
> Judy: Junho Kim? Who's that?
> Hojin: Oh, he's my classmate. He just moved to our school last week.
> Judy: Is he a good singer? (A)
> Hojin: Yea, he sings beautifully. I'm sure he will be perfect for your band. (B)
> Judy: Can you tell me more about him? (C)
> Hojin: Well, he is very outgoing and friendly. (D)
> Judy: Great. Can I have his phone number? (E)
> Hojin: Sure.

12 위 대화의 (A)~(E) 중 주어진 문장이 들어가기에 적절한 곳은?

> What's his personality like?

① (A)　② (B)　③ (C)　④ (D)　⑤ (E)

13 위 대화를 읽고 대답할 수 <u>없는</u> 질문은?

① What is Judy looking for now?
② When did Junho move to Hojin's school?
③ What club does Hojin belong to?
④ What is Junho good at?
⑤ How can Judy get Junho's phone number?

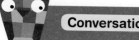

01 다음 밑줄 친 우리말과 뜻이 일치하도록 주어진 단어를 알맞게 배열하시오.

┌ 보기 ┐

sure / the / get / I'm / he / first / contest / in / will / place

A: Sam plays the guitar really well.
B: <u>나는 그가 대회에서 1등을 할 것이라고 확신해.</u>

➡ _____

02 다음 빈칸에 들어갈 말을 보기에 주어진 단어 중 4단어를 사용하여 완성하시오.

┌ 보기 ┐

like / does / how / what / is / he / as

B: Who's that?
G: He's my new badminton coach.
B: He's very tall and handsome.

_____

G: He is very friendly and humorous. I like him a lot.

➡ _____

[03~04] 다음 대화를 읽고, 물음에 답하시오.

G: Can we arrive in time?
B: Of course. The train leaves at 5:10.
G: But, it's already 4:30.
B: The train station isn't very far from here.
<u>나는 우리가 5시 전에 거기에 도착할 거라고 확신해.</u> (we'll, arrive, sure)

03 위 대화의 밑줄 친 우리말을 주어진 단어를 사용하여 영어로 쓰시오.

➡ _____

04 다음 질문에 완전한 문장의 영어로 답하시오.

Q: What are they planning to do after arriving at the train station?

➡ _____

05 다음 대화의 내용과 일치하도록 Jane의 일기에 있는 빈칸을 알맞게 채우시오.

Jane: Hey, Minsu. What's up? You look so worried.
Minsu: The English speaking test is this afternoon.
Jane: Don't worry. You practiced a lot.
Minsu: But I get so nervous when I'm in front of the teacher.
Jane: Everybody does. I'm sure you'll do well.
Minsu: Do you really think so?
Jane: Of course. You are a great English speaker.
Minsu: Thanks. I feel much better now.

April 24, 2019. Sunny
Minsu didn't look so good because of
(1)_____ in the afternoon.
Although he practiced a lot, he was worried because he was usually nervous
(2)_____ the teacher. But I believed (3)_____ because he speaks English very well.

(1) _____
(2) _____
(3) _____

Grammar

1 현재완료

> • I **have** just **mailed** the letter. 나는 지금 막 편지를 부쳤다.
> • **Have** you **seen** the movie before? 너는 전에 그 영화를 본 적이 있니?

■ 현재완료는 과거의 사건이 현재까지 영향을 미칠 때 사용한다. 'have[has]+p.p.'의 형태로, 부정형은 'have not[has not]+p.p.'이며, 의문형은 'Have[Has]+주어+p.p. ~?'로 나타낸다.

  • I **haven't finished** my lunch yet. 나는 아직 점심을 다 먹지 않았다.

  • **Have** you ever **been** to Jeju-do before? 너는 전에 제주도에 가 본 적이 있니?

■ 현재완료는 '완료, 경험, 계속, 결과'의 네 가지 용법으로 쓰인다. 완료 용법은 'just, already, yet'과 같은 부사와 주로 함께 쓰이며, 경험은 'ever, never, once, before' 등과 같은 부사와 함께 쓰인다. 'How long ~?'으로 묻는 질문이나 'for+기간', 'since+특정 시점'은 현재완료의 계속 용법에 속한다. 결과 용법은 특별한 부사와 어울리지 않고 과거에 발생한 사건으로 인하여 현재까지 영향을 미치고 있는 상태를 나타낼 때 결과 용법으로 본다.

  • I **have** already **met** her at the church. [완료] 나는 교회에서 그녀를 이미 만났어.

  • She **has never been** to Busan. [경험] 그녀는 부산에 가 본 적이 없다.

  • My father **has worked** in the company since 2012. [계속] 나의 아버지는 2012년 이래로 그 회사에서 일해 왔다.

  • Jason **has gone** to Spain. [결과] Jason은 스페인에 가고 없다.

■ have[has] been to와 have[has] gone to의 사용에 유의하자. '~에 가 본 적이 있다'는 경험은 have[has] been to로 표현하고, '~에 가고 없다'는 결과는 have[has] gone to로 표현한다.

■ 현재완료는 과거의 일이 현재까지 영향을 미칠 때 쓰는 시제이므로 과거를 나타내는 어구인 yesterday, last year, ~ ago 등과 함께 쓸 수 없다.

  • Kelly met Julian a few minutes ago. Kelly는 몇 분 전에 Julian을 만났다.

  • When did you leave the place? 넌 그 장소를 언제 떠났니?

핵심 Check

1. 다음 우리말과 같도록 빈칸에 알맞은 말을 쓰시오.

  (1) He _____ _____ his room already. (clean)
  (2) Mary _____ _____ to China, so she is not here now. (go)
  (3) _____ you ever _____ badminton? (play)
  (4) How long _____ you _____ in Korea? (live)

② to부정사를 목적격보어로 취하는 동사

- I don't **want** you **to** go yet. 나는 아직 네가 가기를 원하지 않아.
- Mom **persuaded** me **to join** the club. 엄마는 내가 그 클럽에 가입하도록 설득하셨다.

■ '동사+목적어+to V' 형태로 목적어가 to부정사의 주체가 되도록 해석한다.

■ to부정사를 목적격보어로 취하는 동사에는 allow, ask, tell, advise, get, force, require, order, persuade, encourage, enable, cause, want, help, would like, teach, expect 등이 있다.

- Our teacher **encourages** us **to cheer** up. 우리 선생님은 우리에게 힘을 내라고 격려하신다.

- We **would like** you **to introduce** yourself. 우리는 당신이 자신을 소개하길 원해요.

■ to부정사 목적격보어의 부정형은 'not to V'로 표현한다.

- My lawyer **advised** me **not to tell** anything. 나의 변호사는 내게 아무 말도 하지 말라고 충고했다.

- Ted **ordered** her **not to make** any noise. Ted는 그녀에게 어떠한 소음도 내지 말라고 명령했다.

■ make, have, let은 원형부정사를 목적격보어로 취하는 사역동사이다. '목적어가 V하게 하다'로 해석한다.

- She **let** me **go** to the museum. 그녀는 내가 박물관에 가게 허락했다.

- My father **made** me **do** my homework first. 나의 아버지는 내가 먼저 숙제를 하게 하셨다.

핵심 Check

2. 다음 우리말과 같도록 빈칸에 알맞은 말을 쓰시오.

(1) Dan은 나에게 극장에 가도록 설득했다.

➡ Dan _____ me _____ _____ to the cinema.

(2) 나는 그들이 훨씬 더 늦게 도착하리라고 예상한다.

➡ I _____ them _____ _____ much later.

(3) 그 여자는 그녀의 아들에게 뛰지 말라고 말했다.

➡ The woman _____ her son _____ _____ _____.

01 다음 문장에서 어법상 어색한 부분을 바르게 고쳐 쓰시오.

(1) She hasn't gave up the project yet.

_____ ➡ _____

(2) Do you have been to France?

_____ ➡ _____

(3) I want him leaving now.

_____ ➡ _____

(4) Promise me to not tell a lie.

_____ ➡ _____

02 다음 괄호 안의 동사를 어법에 맞게 빈칸에 쓰시오.

(1) She _____ her uncle yesterday. (visit)

(2) Mike asked us _____ _____ quiet. (be)

(3) I _____ _____ anything since yesterday. (not / eat)

(4) He advised me _____ _____ water more often. (drink)

03 다음 우리말에 맞게 주어진 어구를 바르게 배열하시오. (필요하면 단어를 추가할 것)

(1) 나의 부모님은 내가 선생님이 되기를 원하신다.

(parents / be / a teacher / want / me)

➡ _____

(2) 그는 이미 자기 방을 청소했다.

(room / he / clean / already)

➡ _____

(3) 이 신발은 내가 편안하게 걷는 것을 가능하게 해.

(enable / comfortably / me / shoes / walk)

➡ _____

(4) 나는 2년 동안 중국어를 공부해 왔다.

(study / for two years / I / Chinese)

➡ _____

(5) 그 비는 강이 범람하게 하였다.

(cause / overflow / the river / the rain)

➡ _____

서답형

01 다음 문장에서 어법상 틀린 부분을 찾아 바르게 고쳐 쓰시오.

> What time have you gone out last night?

_____ ➡ _____

02 다음 빈칸에 알맞은 것은?

> She asked her friend _____ her some money.

① lend   ② have lent

③ to lend   ④ lending

⑤ lent

03 다음 중 밑줄 친 현재완료의 용법이 다른 하나는?

① Have you ever <u>been</u> to London?

② She <u>has won</u> the race twice.

③ I <u>have played</u> tennis once.

④ We <u>have known</u> her for a long time.

⑤ Tom <u>has never ridden</u> a horse.

04 다음 중 어법상 바르지 않은 것은?

① Cindy has met him before.

② The teacher told her students to draw a picture.

③ Susan and Mike have gone out yesterday.

④ They have worked together since last night.

⑤ The accident caused us to be more careful.

서답형

05 주어진 단어를 이용하여 다음 우리말을 영어로 쓰시오.

> Tom은 4월 이래로 캐나다에서 살고 있다.
> (live / since)

➡ _____

중요
06 다음 빈칸에 적절하지 않은 것은?

> We _____ him to go there.

① want   ② expect   ③ persuaded

④ told   ⑤ make

서답형

07 주어진 동사를 어법에 맞게 빈칸에 쓰시오.

> She _____(allow) me _____(go) to the party yesterday.

➡ _____

08 다음 중 어법상 바르지 않은 것은?

> You ①have played the computer game ② for three hours. I ③won't allow you ④ playing it again if you ⑤don't stop right now.

①   ②   ③   ④   ⑤

서답형

09 다음 두 문장을 하나의 문장으로 쓰시오.

> I lost my passport. I can't find it now.

➡ _____

10 다음 빈칸에 들어갈 말을 바르게 짝지은 것은?

> • Jenny has _____ finished her homework.
> • Jenny hasn't finished her homework _____.

① already – since　　② already – yet
③ yet – just　　④ just – since
⑤ just – already

11 다음 우리말을 영어로 바르게 옮긴 것은?

> 나는 모든 손님들이 일찍 자기를 원해.

① I sleep all the guests with me.
② I would sleep all the guests early.
③ I would like all the guests to sleep early.
④ I would like to sleep early with all the guests.
⑤ I would like you to sleep all the guests early.

12 다음 중 빈칸에 들어갈 말이 <u>다른</u> 하나는?

① The room has been empty _____ 2 o'clock.
② They have been married _____ 20 years.
③ I haven't seen him _____ this morning.
④ We have known each other _____ 2010.
⑤ Bruno has been sick _____ last night.

13 다음 중 어법상 옳은 것은?

① What time have you arrived here?
② He forced me studying abroad.
③ Kelly persuaded me to talking with Jim.
④ We have waited him since two hours.
⑤ She has gone to bed.

서답형
14 주어진 어구를 활용하여 다음 우리말을 영어로 쓰시오.

> 그녀는 내가 그녀의 집에 들러주길 요청했다.
> (me / ask / drop by)

➡ _____

15 다음 빈칸에 들어갈 말이 바르게 짝지어진 것은?

> A: How long have you played golf?
> B: I _____ to play golf at 6, so I _____ it for 20 years.

① have learned – have played
② have learned – play
③ learned – played
④ have learned – played
⑤ learned – have played

16 다음 빈칸에 들어갈 동사 do의 형태가 <u>다른</u> 하나는?

① Dan asked me _____ the dishes.
② Give me some work _____.
③ Can you _____ me a favor?
④ Do you want her _____ it?
⑤ My parents expect me _____ my best.

서답형

17 다음 문장을 읽고 같은 뜻의 현재완료 문장으로 쓰시오.

> Karen plays the violin. She started to play the violin when she was six years old.

➡ _____

_____

18 다음 상황을 영어로 바르게 옮긴 것은?

> Ann had lots of luggage. She said to Jason "Can you help me?"

① Jason can help Ann for the luggage.
② Ann asked Jason to help her.
③ Jason asked Ann to help him.
④ Ann asked Jason to help himself.
⑤ Ann told Jason to move away.

서답형

19 주어진 어구를 바르게 배열하여 다음 우리말을 영어로 쓰시오.

> 내가 설거지하는 것을 네가 도와줘야겠어.
> (want / with the dishes / help / I / you / me / to)

➡ _____

중요

20 다음 빈칸에 알맞은 것이 바르게 짝지어진 것은?

> The teacher encourages students _____ together and wants them _____ well.

① working – get along
② work – to get along
③ to work – get along
④ to work – to get along
⑤ working – getting along

21 다음 빈칸에 가장 적절한 것은?

> Julian has a stomachache. He _____ a stomachache since he got up this morning.

① has   ② had   ③ have had
④ had had   ⑤ has had

22 다음 빈칸에 들어갈 말로 가장 적절한 것은?

> Jim said to me, "Don't use my phone."
> = Jim forbade me _____ his phone.
> = Jim told me _____ his phone.

① use – to use
② to use – not to use
③ to use – to use
④ use – to not use
⑤ not to use – to use

중요

23 다음 빈칸에 적절하지 <u>않은</u> 것은?

> I have met him _____.

① before   ② three times
③ twice   ④ once
⑤ yet

서답형

24 다음 두 문장의 차이를 우리말로 서술하시오.

> (1) George has been to America.
> (2) George has gone to America.

➡ _____

_____

_____

01 주어진 단어를 활용하여 다음 빈칸에 알맞은 말을 쓰시오.

Please don't be upset. I don't _____ .
(want / be)

➡ _____

02 다음 두 문장을 하나의 문장으로 쓰시오.

- We began to use this computer three years ago.
- We still use it.

➡ _____

03 다음 대화를 읽고 주어진 어구로 시작하는 문장을 완성하시오

Jason: I don't feel well.
Linda: You should see a doctor.

➡ Linda advises _____ .

04 주어진 어구를 바르게 배열하여 다음 우리말을 영어로 쓰시오.

선생님께서 학생들에게 계단에서 뛰지 말라고 말씀하셨다.
(not / the teacher / on the stairs / the students / told / run / to)

➡ _____
_____

05 주어진 단어를 활용하여 Jim의 상태를 현재완료 문장으로 쓰시오.

Jim arrived in Italy three days ago. It's Thursday today.

(1) (be, since를 사용할 것)
➡ _____
(2) (be, for를 사용할 것)
➡ _____

06 다음 대화를 읽고 주어진 단어를 활용하여 Ann에 관하여 영어로 쓰시오.

Jason: Do you play the guitar?
Ann: Yes, my mother taught me.

(teach / Ann)

➡ _____

07 다음 빈칸에 알맞은 형태의 동사를 쓰시오.

Cathy works in a bank. She _____ in the bank for five years.

➡ _____

08 다음 빈칸에 알맞은 말을 각각 쓰시오.

- My parents got married 17 years _____ .
- They have been married _____ 17 years.

➡ _____

09 다음 우리말을 주어진 단어를 활용하여 영어로 옮기시오.

> 그들은 내가 제주도로 여행가는 것을 허락했다.
> (allow / travel)

➡ _____

10 주어진 어휘를 어법에 맞도록 빈칸에 쓰시오.

> A: _____ (you / ever / be) to
> Japan?
> B: Yes, we _____ (go) there a year ago.
> A: _____ (you / have) a good
> time?
> B: Yes, it _____ (be) great.

➡ _____, _____

_____, _____

11 다음 문장을 읽고 빈칸에 알맞은 말을 쓰시오.

> Sarah: I heard you had a big fight with
> Kelly. She wants to apologize to you. I
> think you must accept her apology.

➡ Sarah advises _____.

12 현재완료를 써서 밑줄 친 문장과 같은 의미의 문장을 쓰시오.

> A: Brian is away on holiday.
> B: Oh, where is he now?
> A: I heard he is in Vietnam now.

➡ _____

13 다음 주어진 동사를 문맥과 어법에 맞게 빈칸에 쓰시오.

> do / buy / use / stop / wait

> • She made me _____ playing the
> computer game.
> • Slow music encourages us _____
> _____ more products.
> • Clair had me _____ my job on my
> own.
> • Sue let me _____ her laptop computer
> because mine wasn't working.
> • Would you like me _____ _____
> for you until you get back?

14 주어진 단어를 활용하여 다음 우리말을 영어로 쓰시오.

> 형편없는 관리가 그 질병이 퍼지도록 야기하였다.
> The poor management _____.
> (cause, disease)

➡ _____

15 주어진 어구를 바르게 배열하여 다음 우리말을 영어로 쓰시오.

> 그녀는 그녀의 아이들이 한동안 수영장에서 첨벙
> 거리며 놀게 두었다.
> (for a while / she / her children / around /
> splash / let / in the pool)

➡ _____

_____

Reading

Where Is Dady?

My name is Jimmy. I am in the eighth grade and my sister, Hope, is
in the third grade. My father is a banker and my mother is a teacher.
We have a dog, Smiley. Sounds pretty normal, right? But a crazy thing
happened last week.

My father usually comes home late from work. So, we only see him
on the weekends. Even then, he usually sleeps or watches television.
But last Friday, he came home early for dinner. At the table, we were
all doing our own thing. Hope was giving food to Smiley. My mother
was telling her not to do so. I was texting.

My father said, "Pass me the bread, please." No one heard him, so he
asked again, "Can someone pass me the bread?" I heard him this time,
but I was too busy with my phone. My mother was yelling, "Don't
feed Smiley!" Hope was feeding Smiley. Smiley was jumping up and
down. My father shouted, "Am I invisible? Pass me the bread!"

Then, it happened. Poof! My father disappeared like magic. He
became invisible!

---

banker 은행원
sound ~처럼 들리다
happen 발생하다
usually 주로
late 늦게
early 일찍
one's own 자기 자신의
text 문자를 보내다
pass ~에게 …을 건네다
ask 요청하다
too 너무
yell 소리 지르다
feed ~에게 먹이를 주다
up and down 위아래로
invisible 보이지 않는
disappear 사라지다

📎 확인문제

● 다음 문장이 본문의 내용과 일치하면 T, 일치하지 않으면 F를 쓰시오.

1 The writer is named Jimmy. ☐

2 The writer has a father and a mother and two sisters. ☐

3 Jimmy's father doesn't usually spend time with Jimmy. ☐

4 Jimmy's father had dinner with his family last Friday. ☐

5 Jimmy's father went out to buy some bread. ☐

We could hear him, but we couldn't see him. We asked, "Where are you?" "I'm right in front of you," he replied. We couldn't do anything for him. It was an awful night.

Next morning, we went to the hospital and asked the doctor to help us. I said, "He has been invisible since last night." The doctor shook his head and said, "I can't help you. I've never seen anything like this before."

When we came home, Hope said, "I miss Daddy." She started crying. My mother joined her. In a few moments, we were a sea of tears. "Come back, Dad! I promise to pass you the bread every day!" I cried.

Then, it happened. My father appeared again! He hugged us and said, "Thank you for all the attention. I promise to come home earlier and play with you on the weekends."

hear ~의 말을 듣다
in front of ~ 앞에
reply 대답하다
awful 끔찍한
since ~ 이래로
shake ~을 흔들다
like ~ 같은
miss ~을 그리워하다
join ~와 함께하다
a sea of tears 눈물 바다
promise ~을 약속하다
appear 나타나다
hug 포옹하다
attention 관심

확인문제

● 다음 문장이 본문의 내용과 일치하면 T, 일치하지 않으면 F를 쓰시오.

1 Jimmy couldn't hear or see his dad. ☐

2 Jimmy's family went to the hospital to see a doctor. ☐

3 The doctor doesn't have any experiences like the case. ☐

4 Jimmy wanted his father to promise to pass him the bread. ☐

5 Jimmy's father thanked his family for the attention. ☐

6 Hugging his family members, Jimmy's father said he would play with them on the weekends. ☐

● 우리말을 참고하여 빈칸에 알맞은 말을 쓰시오.

1 _____ _____ is Jimmy.

2 I am _____ _____ _____ _____ and my sister, Hope, is _____ _____ _____ _____ .

3 My father is _____ and my mother is _____ _____ .

4 We have a dog, Smiley. _____ _____ _____ , right?

5 But a crazy thing _____ last week.

6 My father _____ _____ _____ _____ from work.

7 So, we only see him _____ _____ _____ .

8 _____ _____ , he _____ _____ or _____ television.

9 But _____ Friday, he came _____ _____ for dinner.

10 At the table, we _____ all _____ _____ _____ .

11 Hope was _____ _____ _____ Smiley.

12 My mother was _____ _____ _____ _____ so. I was texting.

13 My father said, "Pass _____ _____ _____ , please."

14 No one heard him, so he _____ again, "Can someone _____ _____ _____ _____ ?"

15 I heard him this time, but I was _____ _____ _____ my phone.

16 My mother was _____ , " _____ _____ Smiley!"

17 Hope was _____ Smiley.

1	내 이름은 Jimmy다.
2	나는 8학년이고, 내 여동생 Hope는 3학년이다.
3	우리 아버지는 은행원이시고, 어머니는 선생님이시다.
4	우리에겐 Smiley라는 개가 한 마리 있다. 꽤 평범한 것 같다, 그렇지?
5	그런데 정말 이상한 일이 지난 주에 일어났다.
6	우리 아버지는 보통 회사에서 늦게 집에 오신다.
7	그래서 우리는 주말에만 아버지를 본다.
8	주말에도 아버지는 보통 주무시거나 텔레비전을 보신다.
9	하지만 지난주 금요일에 아버지는 저녁을 드시러 일찍 집에 오셨다.
10	식탁에서 우리는 모두 각자의 일을 하고 있었다.
11	Hope는 Smiley에게 음식을 주고 있었다.
12	어머니는 동생에게 그러지 말라고 말씀하고 계셨다. 나는 문자를 보내고 있었다.
13	아버지가 말씀하셨다. "빵 좀 건네줘요."
14	아무도 그의 말을 듣지 못하자, 아버지는 다시 물으셨다. "누구 나한테 빵 좀 건네 줄래?"
15	이번에 나는 아버지의 말을 들었지만 휴대 전화에 빠져 너무 바빴다.
16	어머니는 소리치고 계셨다. "Smiley한테 음식을 주지 마!"
17	Hope는 Smiley에게 먹이를 주고 있었다.

18 Smiley was _____ up and down.

19 My father _____, "Am I _____? Pass me the bread!"

20 Then, it _____. Poof! My father _____ _____ _____.

21 He _____ _____!

22 We could _____ him, but we couldn't _____ him.

23 We _____, "Where are you?"

24 "I'm _____ _____ _____ _____ you," he _____.

25 We couldn't do _____ for him. It was an _____ night.

26 Next morning, we _____ to the hospital and _____ the doctor _____ _____ us.

27 I said, "He _____ _____ _____ _____ last night."

28 The doctor shook his head and said, "I can't help you. I've _____ _____ _____ _____ this _____."

29 _____ we came home, Hope said, "I _____ Daddy."

30 She _____ _____. My mother _____ her.

31 _____ _____ _____ moments, we were a sea of tears.

32 "Come back, Dad! I _____ _____ _____ you the bread every day!" I cried.

33 Then, it _____. My father _____ again!

34 He hugged us and said, "Thank you for _____ _____ _____. I promise to come home _____ and _____ _____ _____ on the weekends."

18 Smiley는 펄쩍펄쩍 뛰고 있었다.

19 아버지가 소리치셨다. "내가 안 보이는 거야? 빵 좀 건네 줘!"

20 그때 일이 벌어졌다. 뿅! 아버지가 마법처럼 사라지셨다.

21 아버지는 투명 인간이 되셨다!

22 우리는 그의 말을 들을 수는 있었지만 그를 볼 수는 없었다.

23 우리는 물었다. "어디 계세요?"

24 아버지가 대답하셨다. "너희들 바로 앞에 있어."

25 우리는 그를 위해 할 수 있는 게 없었다. 끔찍한 밤이었다.

26 다음 날 아침. 우리는 병원에 가서 의사 선생님에게 도움을 요청했다.

27 내가 말했다. "아버지가 어젯밤부터 안 보여요."

28 의사 선생님은 고개를 저으며 말씀하셨다. "도와 드릴 수가 없네요. 이런 건 본 적이 없어요."

29 집에 왔을 때 Hope가 말했다. "아빠가 보고 싶어요."

30 그녀는 울기 시작했다. 어머니가 같이 우셨다.

31 곧 우리는 눈물바다가 되었다.

32 "돌아오세요, 아빠! 매일 아빠한테 빵을 건네드리겠다고 약속해요!" 내가 외쳤다.

33 그때 일이 일어났다. 아버지가 다시 나타나셨다!

34 아버지가 우리를 안고 말씀하셨다. "관심 가져 줘서 고마워. 집에 더 일찍 오고 주말에는 너희와 함께 놀겠다고 약속하마."

● 우리말을 참고하여 본문을 영작하시오.

1 내 이름은 Jimmy다.

➡ _____

2 나는 8학년이고, 내 여동생 Hope는 3학년이다.

➡ _____

3 우리 아버지는 은행원이시고, 어머니는 선생님이시다.

➡ _____

4 우리에겐 Smiley라는 개가 한 마리 있다. 꽤 평범한 것 같다, 그렇지?

➡ _____

5 그런데 정말 이상한 일이 지난주에 일어났다.

➡ _____

6 우리 아버지는 보통 회사에서 늦게 집에 오신다.

➡ _____

7 그래서 우리는 주말에만 아버지를 본다.

➡ _____

8 주말에도 아버지는 보통 주무시거나 텔레비전을 보신다.

➡ _____

9 하지만 지난주 금요일에 아버지는 저녁을 드시러 일찍 집에 오셨다.

➡ _____

10 식탁에서 우리는 모두 각자의 일을 하고 있었다.

➡ _____

11 Hope는 Smiley에게 음식을 주고 있었다.

➡ _____

12 어머니는 동생에게 그러지 말라고 말씀하고 계셨다. 나는 문자를 보내고 있었다.

➡ _____

13 아버지가 말씀하셨다. "빵 좀 건네줘요."

➡ _____

14 아무도 그의 말을 듣지 못하자, 아버지는 다시 물으셨다. "누구 나한테 빵 좀 건네줄래?"

➡ _____

15 이번에 나는 아버지의 말을 들었지만 휴대 전화에 빠져 너무 바빴다.

➡ _____

16 어머니는 소리치고 계셨다. "Smiley한테 음식을 주지 마!"

➡ _____

17 Hope는 Smiley에게 먹이를 주고 있었다.

➡ _____

18 Smiley는 펄쩍펄쩍 뛰고 있었다.

➡ _____

19 아버지가 소리치셨다. "내가 안 보이는 거야? 빵 좀 건네줘!"

➡ _____

20 그때 일이 벌어졌다. 뿅! 아버지가 마법처럼 사라지셨다.

➡ _____

21 아버지는 투명 인간이 되셨다!

➡ _____

22 우리는 그의 말을 들을 수는 있었지만 그를 볼 수는 없었다.

➡ _____

23 우리는 물었다. "어디 계세요?"

➡ _____

24 아버지가 대답하셨다. "너희들 바로 앞에 있어."

➡ _____

25 우리는 그를 위해 할 수 있는 게 없었다. 끔찍한 밤이었다.

➡ _____

26 다음 날 아침, 우리는 병원에 가서 의사 선생님에게 도움을 요청했다.

➡ _____

27 내가 말했다. "아버지가 어젯밤부터 안 보여요."

➡ _____

28 의사 선생님은 고개를 저으며 말씀하셨다. "도와 드릴 수가 없네요. 이런 건 본 적이 없어요."

➡ _____

29 집에 왔을 때 Hope가 말했다. "아빠가 보고 싶어요."

➡ _____

30 그녀는 울기 시작했다. 어머니가 같이 우셨다.

➡ _____

31 곧 우리는 눈물바다가 되었다.

➡ _____

32 "돌아오세요, 아빠! 매일 아빠한테 빵을 건네드리겠다고 약속해요!" 내가 외쳤다.

➡ _____

33 그때 일이 일어났다. 아버지가 다시 나타나셨다!

➡ _____

34 아버지가 우리를 안고 말씀하셨다. "관심 가져 줘서 고마워. 집에 더 일찍 오고 주말에는 너희와 함께 놀겠다고 약속하마."

➡ _____

_____

[01~03] 다음 글을 읽고, 물음에 답하시오.

My name is Jimmy. I am in the eighth grade and my sister, Hope, is in the third grade. My father is a banker and my mother is a teacher. We have a dog, Smiley. Sounds pretty normal, right? But a crazy thing happened last week.

01 위 글을 읽고 답할 수 <u>없는</u> 질문은?

① How many people are there in Jimmy's family?
② How old is Jimmy?
③ What does Jimmy's father do for a living?
④ What does Jimmy hope to be in the future?
⑤ What is the name of Jimmy's dog?

서답형

02 다음 영영풀이와 같은 의미의 단어를 위 글에서 찾아 쓰시오.

usual and ordinary

➡ _____

중요

03 위 글에 이어질 내용으로 가장 적절한 것은?

① 아버지와 어머니의 첫 만남
② 지난주에 일어난 황당한 일
③ 동생의 진로에 관한 가족 회의
④ 평범한 가족의 하루 일과
⑤ 어제 오전에 학교에서 있었던 일

[04~07] 다음 글을 읽고, 물음에 답하시오.

My father said, "Pass me the bread, please." ⓐNo one heard him, so he asked again, "Can someone pass me the bread?" I heard him this time, but I was too busy with my phone. My mother was yelling, "Don't feed Smiley!" Hope was feeding Smiley. Smiley was jumping up and down. My father shouted, "Am I invisible? Pass me the bread!"
Then, it happened. Poof! My father disappeared ⓑlike magic. He became invisible!

* I = Jimmy

04 위 글의 내용과 일치하지 <u>않는</u> 것은?

① Jimmy's father wanted the bread.
② Jimmy was busy using his phone.
③ Smiley was running across the room.
④ Jimmy's father got angry at last.
⑤ Hope was giving Smiley food.

서답형

05 위 글의 내용에 맞도록 빈칸에 알맞은 말을 쓰시오.

Jimmy's father asked _____ .

➡ _____

중요

06 위 글의 밑줄 친 ⓐ의 이유로 가장 적절한 것은?

① It's because no one wanted him to eat the bread.
② It's because he spoke too quietly.
③ It's because everyone was busy doing something.
④ It's because Smiley made loud noises.
⑤ It's because everyone ignored him.

07 위 글을 밑줄 친 ⓑ와 쓰임이 같은 것은?

① The students <u>like</u> their teacher.
② No one sings the song <u>like</u> she did.
③ She acts <u>like</u> she owns everything.
④ My uncle treats me <u>like</u> a baby.
⑤ Which dress do you <u>like</u> best?

[08~11] 다음 글을 읽고, 물음에 답하시오.

My father usually comes home late from work. ① Even then, he usually sleeps or watches television. ② But last Friday, he came home early for dinner. ③ At the table, ⓐwe were all doing our own thing. ④ Hope was giving food to Smiley. My mother was telling her not to do so. I was texting. ⑤

* I = Jimmy

08 주어진 문장이 들어가기에 알맞은 곳은?

So, we only see him on the weekends.

①　　　②　　　③　　　④　　　⑤

09 위 글의 내용과 일치하는 것은?

① Jimmy's father doesn't like to watch television.
② Jimmy's father likes his job.
③ Jimmy had dinner with his father last Friday.
④ Hope was sitting at a couch.
⑤ Jimmy's mother told Jimmy to stop texting.

10 Why do you think Jimmy's father come home late?

① It's because he doesn't have to sleep much.
② It's because Hope loves only Smiley.
③ It's because there are many things to do at work.
④ It's because he doesn't want to have dinner.
⑤ It's because his mother tells him to do so.

11 위 글의 밑줄 친 ⓐ가 의미하는 것은?

① All the family were having dinner with joy.
② Each of the family was doing the same thing in their own way.
③ All the family wanted to do something together.
④ Each of the family was doing what they wanted to do.
⑤ There were many things to do with the family.

[12~13] 다음 글을 읽고, 물음에 답하시오.

My father usually comes home ⓐ[late / lately] from work. So, we only see him on the weekends. ① Even then, he usually sleeps or watches television. ② But last Friday, he came home early ⓑ[on / for] dinner. ③ At the table, we were all doing our own thing. ④ Hope was giving food to Smiley. ⑤ I was texting.

12 위 글의 ①~⑤ 중 다음에 주어진 문장이 들어갈 위치로 알맞은 곳은?

My mother was telling her not to do so.

①　　　②　　　③　　　④　　　⑤

서답형
13 위 글의 괄호 ⓐ와 ⓑ에서 알맞은 것을 쓰시오.

ⓐ _____ ⓑ _____

[14~17] 다음 글을 읽고, 물음에 답하시오.

My father said, "Pass me the bread, please." No one heard him, so he ⓐasked again, "Can someone pass me the bread?" I heard him this time, but I was too busy with my phone. My mother was yelling, "Don't ⓑfeed Smiley!" Hope was feeding Smiley. Smiley was ⓒjumping up and down. My father shouted, "Am I invisible? Pass me the bread!"

Then, it ⓓhappened. Poof! My father disappeared like magic. He became (A) invisible!

We could ⓔhear him, but we couldn't see him. We asked, "Where are you?" "(B)너희들 바로 앞에 있어," he replied. We couldn't do anything for him. (C)It was an awful night.

14 위 글의 ⓐ~ⓔ 중 단어의 뜻풀이가 바르지 않은 것은?

① ⓐ: tell someone to do something
② ⓑ: give a person or animal food to eat
③ ⓒ: jump in one spot with excitement
④ ⓓ: occur without being planned
⑤ ⓔ: become aware of something with your eyes

서답형
15 위 글의 밑줄 친 (A)를 설명하는 문장을 위 글에서 찾아 쓰시오.

➡ _____

서답형
16 다음 주어진 단어를 바르게 배열하여 밑줄 친 (B)를 영작하시오.

(you / I / of / am / front / right / in)

➡ _____

중요
17 위 글의 밑줄 친 (C)와 쓰임이 다른 것은?

① It's ten past twelve.
② It's Sunday today.
③ It's warm outside.
④ It's good to talk with you.
⑤ It's two miles from here to the mall.

[18~21] 다음 글을 읽고, 물음에 답하시오.

My father disappeared like magic. ①He became invisible!

We could hear him, but we couldn't see ②him. We asked, "Where are you?" "I'm right in front of you," he replied. We couldn't do anything for ③him. ⓐ끔찍한 밤이었다.

Next morning, we went to the hospital and asked the doctor ⓑto help us. I said, "④He has been invisible ⓒ____ last night." The doctor shook ⑤his head and said, "I can't help you. I've never seen anything like this before."

서답형
18 위 글의 밑줄 친 우리말 ⓐ를 영어로 쓰시오.

➡ _____

19 위 글의 ①~⑤ 중 지칭하는 바가 다른 하나는?

①   ②   ③   ④   ⑤

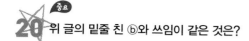

20 위 글의 밑줄 친 ⓑ와 쓰임이 같은 것은?

① We went to the gym to lose some weight.
② There are many things to do tonight.
③ I have some friends to introduce to you.
④ The situation forced me to take the job.
⑤ He visited his teacher to say hello.

서답형

21 위 글의 빈칸 ⓒ에 알맞은 말을 쓰시오.

➡ _____

[22~25] 다음 글을 읽고, 물음에 답하시오.

Then, it happened. Poof! My father disappeared like magic. He became invisible! We ①couldn't hear him, but we couldn't see him. We asked, "Where are you?" "I'm right in front of you," he replied. We could do ② nothing for him. It was an ③awful night.

Next morning, we ④went to the hospital and ⑤begged the doctor to help us. I said, "(A)He has been invisible since last night." The doctor shook his head and said, "I can't help you. I've never seen anything like (B) this before."

22 다음 중 위 글에서 반의어를 찾을 수 <u>없는</u> 단어는?

① appear   ② behind   ③ visible
④ answer   ⑤ shocking

23 위 글의 ①~⑤ 중 글의 흐름상 어색한 것은?

①   ②   ③   ④   ⑤

24 위 글의 밑줄 친 (A)에서 사용된 현재완료와 쓰임이 같은 것은?

① I have traveled abroad many times.
② I have donated my old shoes to charity before.
③ I have never seen a French movie.
④ I have cooked for my family for a year.
⑤ I have never eaten Japanese food.

서답형

25 위 글의 밑줄 친 (B)가 의미하는 바를 우리말로 쓰시오.

➡ _____

[26~27] 다음 글을 읽고, 물음에 답하시오.

Next morning, we ①to the hospital and asked the doctor to help us. I said, "He has been invisible since last night." The doctor shook his head and said, "I can't help you. I've never seen anything like this before."

When we came home, Hope said, "I miss Daddy." She started ②to cry. My mother ③joined with her. In a few moments, we were ④a sea of tears. "Come back, Dad! I promise to pass you the bread every day!" I cried.

Then, it ⑤happened. My father appeared again! He hugged us and said, "Thank you for all the attention. (A)집에 좀 더 일찍 오겠다고 약속하마 and play with you on the weekends."

26 위 글의 ①~⑤ 중 어법상 바르지 <u>않은</u> 것은?

①   ②   ③   ④   ⑤

서답형

27 주어진 어구를 어법에 맞게 활용하여 밑줄 친 우리말 (A)를 영어로 쓰시오.

(come home / early)

➡ _____

[01~02] 다음 글을 읽고, 물음에 답하시오.

My name is Jimmy. I am in the eighth grade and my sister, Hope, is in the third grade. My father is a banker and my mother is a teacher. We have a dog, Smiley. Sounds pretty normal, right? (A)그러나 정말 이상한 일이 지난 주에 일어났다.

01 What do Jimmy's parents do for a living?

➡ _____

02 주어진 단어를 활용하여 밑줄 친 우리말 (A)를 영어로 쓰시오.

(crazy / thing)

➡ _____

[03~05] 다음 글을 읽고, 물음에 답하시오.

My father usually comes home late from work. So, we only see him on the weekends. Even then, he usually sleeps or watches television. But last Friday, he came home early for dinner. At the table, @we were all doing our own thing. Hope was giving food to Smiley. My mother was telling her not to do so. I was texting.

* I = Jimmy

03 위 글을 읽고 Jimmy의 엄마가 Hope에게 할 수 있는 말을 5 단어로 이루어진 명령문으로 쓰시오.

➡ _____

04 What does Jimmy's father usually do on the weekends?

➡ _____

05 위 글의 밑줄 친 @가 가리키는 것을 모두 쓰시오.

➡ _____

[06~08] 다음 글을 읽고, 물음에 답하시오.

My father said, "Pass me the bread, please." No one heard him, so he asked again, "Can someone pass me the bread?" I heard him this time, but I (A)_____ my phone. My mother was yelling, "Don't feed Smiley!" Hope was feeding Smiley. Smiley was jumping up and down. My father shouted, "Am I invisible? Pass me the bread!"

Then, it happened. Poof! (B)아버지가 마법처럼 사라지셨다. He became invisible!

06 위 글의 빈칸 (A)에 '~에 너무 바빴다'는 표현을 쓰시오.

➡ _____

07 위 글을 읽고 주어진 단어를 이용하여 다음 물음에 답하시오.

Q: What did the writer's father want the other family members to do?

A: (he / them / to / to)

➡ _____

08 주어진 단어를 활용하여 밑줄 친 (B)를 영어로 쓰시오.

(disappear)

➡ _____

[09~11] 다음 글을 읽고, 물음에 답하시오.

Then, it happened. Poof! My father disappeared like magic. He became invisible! We could hear him, but we couldn't see him. We asked, "Where are you?" "I'm right in front of you," he replied. We couldn't do anything for him. It was an awful night.

Next morning, we went to the hospital and (A)said to the doctor, "Can you help us?" I said, "(B)He became invisible last night, and we can't still see him." The doctor shook his head and said, "I can't help you. I've never seen anything like this before."

09 주어진 어구를 활용하여 밑줄 친 (A)와 같은 의미의 문장을 쓰시오.

(ask / the doctor)

➡ _____

10 현재완료 시제를 이용하여 밑줄 친 (B)를 한 문장으로 만드시오.

➡ _____

11 위 글에서 적절한 단어를 찾아 빈칸에 그 반의어를 쓰시오.

The family members wanted his father to be _____ .

➡ _____

[12~15] 다음 글을 읽고, 물음에 답하시오.

Then, ⓐit happened. Poof! My father disappeared like magic. He became invisible! We could hear him, but we couldn't see him. We asked, "Where are you?" "I'm right in front of you," he replied. We couldn't do anything for him. (A)It was an awful night.

Next morning, we went to the hospital and asked the doctor to help us. I said, "He has been invisible since last night." The doctor shook his head and said, "I can't help you. I've never seen anything like this before."

When we came home, Hope said, "I miss Daddy." She started crying. My mother joined her. In a few moments, we were a sea of tears. "(B)Come back, Dad! I promise to pass you the bread every day!" I cried.

Then, ⓑit happened. My father appeared again! He hugged us and said, "Thank you for all the attention. I promise to come home earlier and play with you on the weekends."

12 위 글의 밑줄 친 ⓐ와 ⓑ의 의미를 구체적으로 영어로 쓰시오.

ⓐ _____

ⓑ _____

13 위 글의 밑줄 친 (A)와 같이 말한 이유를 우리말로 쓰시오.

➡ _____

14 Write the reason why the doctor said he couldn't help them.

It's because _____ _____ .

15 주어진 단어를 활용하여 밑줄 친 (B)와 같은 의미의 문장을 쓰시오.

Dad, _____! (want / you)

➡ _____

해석

Real Life Talk - Step 2

A: Who is the best person to be the board cleaner?
형용사적 용법

B: How about Minsu?
~은 어때?

A: What is he like?
누군가의 성격을 물을 때 사용할 수 있다.

C: He is responsible and tidy.

D: I'm sure he will be a good board cleaner for our class.
sure 뒤에 접속사 that이 생략된 형태이다.

구문해설 · responsible: 책임감 있는 · tidy: 깔끔한

A: 누가 칠판지우기 담당으로 가장 적합할까요?

B: 민수 어때요?

A: 그의 성격은 어때요?

C: 그는 책임감 있고 깔끔해요.

D: 나는 그가 우리 반을 위해 좋은 칠판지우기 담당이 될 것이라고 확신해요.

Think and Write

My Best Friend, Subin
good의 최상급

My best friend is Subin. I have known her for 3 years. She is humorous.
현재완료 – 계속   for+기간

She tells me many funny jokes. She and I both like movies. So we have
4형식 동사동사+간접목적어+직접목적어   둘 다   현재완료 – 경험

watched many movies together. I'm sure we'll be friends forever.

구문해설 · best: 최고의 · for: ~ 동안 · humorous: 재미있는, 익살스러운 · funny: 재미있는
· both: 둘 다 · forever: 영원히

나의 가장 좋은 친구, 수빈
나의 가장 좋은 친구는 수빈입니다. 나는 수빈이를 3년 동안 알고 지냈습니다. 그녀는 유머가 있습니다. 그녀는 나에게 많은 재미있는 농담을 합니다. 그녀와 나는 둘 다 영화를 좋아합니다. 그래서 우리는 함께 많은 영화를 봤습니다. 나는 우리가 영원히 친구일 것이라고 확신합니다.

Project - Step 3

Dear Mina,
친애하는

I'm happy that you're my secret friend. I like you because you are very kind. I
접속사   부사절을 이끄는 접속사

also like your big smile. I'm sure we'll be good friends this year.
올해

P.S. I've already helped you three times.
현재완료 – 완료

구문해설 · secret: 비밀; 비밀의 · because: 왜냐하면 · smile: 미소 · be sure (that): ~을 확신하다
· P.S: (post script의 약어) 추신 · already: 이미, 벌써 · three times: 세 번

친애하는 미나에게
나는 네가 나의 비밀 친구라서 행복해. 네가 친절하기 때문에 나는 널 좋아해. 나는 또 너의 환한 미소가 좋아. 나는 올해 우리가 좋은 친구가 될 것이라고 확신해.
추신. 나는 벌써 너를 세 번이나 도왔어.

영역별 핵심문제

01 다음 짝지어진 단어의 관계가 같도록 빈칸에 알맞은 말을 쓰시오.

> rich : poor = normal : _____

02 다음 영영풀이가 가리키는 말을 쓰시오.

> to put your arms around somebody and hold them tightly, especially to show that you like or love them

➡ _____

03 다음 중 밑줄 친 부분의 뜻풀이가 바르지 <u>않은</u> 것은?

① I <u>promise</u> you to be on time at the bus stop. 약속하다

② My best friend knows my <u>secret</u>.
비밀

③ My parents <u>donate</u> some clothes to the nursing home every year. 기부하다

④ There are <u>invisible</u> stars in the sky.
보이지 않는

⑤ My younger brother is an <u>outgoing</u> person.
태평한

04 다음 문장의 밑줄 친 의미와 같은 의미로 쓰인 것은?

> The <u>crazy</u> things happened last Sunday.

① I know it sounds <u>crazy</u> but the rumor might be true.

② My brother is <u>crazy</u> about football.

③ The noise from the upper floor is driving me <u>crazy</u>.

④ The crowd went <u>crazy</u> when BTS came on stage.

⑤ I'm not <u>crazy</u> about Italian food.

05 다음 빈칸에 공통으로 들어갈 말로 적절한 것을 고르시오.

> • They usually _____ hands when they meet.
> • She seemed to _____ in a cold weather.
> • His faith began to _____ because of the rumor.

① shout   ② shake
③ yell   ④ feed
⑤ hug

06 다음 우리말에 맞게 빈칸에 알맞은 말을 쓰시오.

> 내 친구들은 모두 자신이 하고 싶은 일을 하고 있었다.
> ➡ My friends were _____.

Conversation

07 다음 빈칸에 우리말과 일치하도록 주어진 단어를 사용하여 질문을 완성하시오.

> A: _____? (like)
>
> (그녀는 어떤 사람인가요?)
>
> B: She is active and outgoing.

➡ _____

08 다음 대화가 자연스럽게 이어지도록 순서대로 배열하시오.

> (A) But, it's already 4:30.
> (B) Of course. The train leaves at 5:10.
> (C) The train station isn't very far from here. I'm sure we'll arrive there before 5.
> (D) Can we arrive in time?

➡ _____

[09~10] 다음 대화를 읽고, 물음에 답하시오.

> Jane: Hey, Minsu. What's up? You look so worried.
> Minsu: The English speaking test is this afternoon.
> Jane: (A)Don't worry. You practiced a lot.
> Minsu: But I get so nervous when I'm in front of the teacher.
> Jane: Everybody does. I'm sure you'll do well.
> Minsu: Do you really think so?
> Jane: Of course. You are a great English speaker.
> Minsu: Thanks. I feel much better now.

09 위 대화의 밑줄 친 (A)와 바꾸어 쓸 수 있는 것은?

① That's a shame. ② Cheer up!
③ What a pity! ④ That's too bad.
⑤ I'm sorry to hear that.

10 위 대화를 읽고 대답할 수 <u>없는</u> 질문은?

① What is Minsu worried about?
② What is Jane certain about?
③ When is the English speaking test scheduled?
④ How has Minsu's feeling changed after talking with Jane?
⑤ What does Jane usually do to overcome the test anxiety?

[11~12] 다음 대화를 읽고, 물음에 답하시오.

> Dad: Sue, how do you like your school these days?
> Sue: I like it a lot, Dad. I already made two new friends, Rosa and Mike.
> Dad: Happy to hear that. ____ⓐ____ did you become friends?
> Sue: We all love English. We are also in the same club.
> Dad: That's great. ____ⓑ____ are they like?
> Sue: Rosa is very kind.
> Dad: ____ⓐ____ about Mike?
> Sue: He is outgoing.
> Dad: ⓒ그 친구들을 저녁 식사에 초대하는 게 어떠니?
> Sue: Okay, Dad.

11 위 대화의 빈칸 ⓐ와 ⓑ에 들어갈 알맞은 말을 쓰시오.

ⓐ _____ ⓑ _____

12 위 대화의 밑줄 친 (C)의 우리말과 일치하도록 주어진 단어를 모두 배열하시오.

> ┌ 보기 ┐
> dinner / don't / them / for / you / why / invite / over

➡ _____

Grammar

13 다음 두 문장을 주어진 단어를 이용하여 하나의 문장으로 쓰시오.

> It began to rain a few minutes ago. It is still raining.(stop / raining)
> ➡ _____

14 다음 빈칸에 들어갈 말로 알맞은 것은?

> He _____ her to wait for him in his office.

① hoped   ② saw   ③ made
④ got   ⑤ had

15 다음 빈칸에 들어갈 동사 talk의 형태가 <u>다른</u> 하나는?

① I want you _____ about it.
② She has many friends _____ with.
③ Don't persuade me _____ to him.
④ I have trouble _____ to someone.
⑤ We helped him _____ about himself.

---

16 다음 상황을 읽고 빈칸에 알맞은 말을 쓰시오.

> Jim: Don't make any noise.
> Kate: Okay. I won't.

➡ Jim told _____.

17 다음 빈칸에 동사 know를 어법에 맞게 쓰시오.

> Karen and I are friends. I _____ her for a long time. I _____ her very well.

➡ _____

18 다음 문장을 읽고 알 수 있는 것을 <u>모두</u> 고르시오.

> Kelly has recovered from her illness.

① Kelly suffered from illness.
② Kelly has trouble recovering from her illness.
③ Kelly has an illness to recover.
④ Kelly is now well again.
⑤ Kelly will not fall ill.

19 다음 중 어법상 바르지 <u>않은</u> 것은?

① The taxi has just arrived.
② He begged me slowing down.
③ How long have you read it?
④ She forced me to give her the bread.
⑤ We have lived in this house since last year.

20 다음 중 주어진 현재완료 문장과 용법이 같은 것은?

> I have never seen a movie by myself.

① How long have you studied English?
② The bus has just left the station.
③ They have traveled together for a year.
④ Have you ever thrown a party?
⑤ She hasn't fixed dinner yet.

21 다음 우리말을 영어로 바르게 옮긴 것은?

① 너는 학교 갈 준비를 했니?
= Do you prepare to go to school?
② Kelly는 일기를 써 본 적이 없다.
= Kelly has kept a diary yet.
③ 나는 스웨덴에 가 본 적이 있다.
= I have gone to Sweden.
④ 중간고사가 막 끝났다.
= The midterm exam has just finished.
⑤ 그는 어제 그녀를 봤다.
= He has seen her yesterday.

22 다음 중 밑줄 친 부분의 쓰임이 다른 하나는?

① Mom expects me to try hard.
② The car enables me to go anywhere.
③ Paul told her not to wait him.
④ Kevin asked me to visit him later.
⑤ It's time for you to go.

23 다음 우리말을 주어진 단어를 써서 영어로 쓰시오.

> 그것은 그 질병이 확산하도록 유발한다.
> (cause / disease / spread)

➡ _____

24 다음 괄호 안에 주어진 동사를 어법에 맞게 쓰시오.

> A: Can I have a look at your newspaper?
> B: No, I (finish) reading it yet.

➡ _____

Reading

[25~26] 다음 글을 읽고, 물음에 답하시오.

> My name is Jimmy. I am in the eighth grade and my sister, Hope, is in the third grade. My father is a banker and my mother is a teacher. We have a dog, Smiley. Sounds pretty normal, right? But a crazy thing happened last week.

25 위 글을 읽고 답할 수 <u>없는</u> 질문은?

① What is the name of Jimmy's sister?
② How old is Jimmy's sister?
③ What is Jimmy's mother doing?
④ Where does Jimmy's father work?
⑤ How many dogs does Jimmy have?

26 다음 질문에 완전한 문장의 영어로 답하시오.

> Q: What is Smiley?
> A: _____

➡ _____

[27~28] 다음 글을 읽고, 물음에 답하시오.

My father usually comes home late from work. So, we only see him on the weekends. Even then, he usually sleeps or watches television. But last Friday, he came home early for dinner. At the table, we were all doing our own thing. Hope was giving food to Smiley. My mother was telling her not to do so. I was texting.   * I = Jimmy

27 위 글의 내용과 일치하지 <u>않는</u> 것은?

① Jimmy의 아버지는 주로 늦게 퇴근한다.

② 지난 금요일에는 Jimmy의 아버지가 저녁시간에 퇴근을 했다.

③ Jimmy의 집에는 아버지, 어머니, Hope, Smiley가 있다.

④ Jimmy와 그의 아버지는 주말에 즐거운 시간을 보낸다.

⑤ Jimmy의 어머니는 Smiley에게 음식을 주지 말라고 Hope에게 말했다.

28 위 글을 읽고 Jimmy의 어머니가 Jimmy에게 할 말의 빈칸을 채우시오.

| _____ texting and _____ down your cell phone. |

[29~31] 다음 글을 읽고, 물음에 답하시오.

But last Friday, he came home early for dinner. At the table, we were all doing our own thing. Hope was giving food to Smiley. My mother was telling her not to do so. I was

texting. My father said, "Pass me the bread, please." No one heard him, so he asked again, "Can someone pass me the bread?" I heard him this time, but I was too busy with my phone. My mother was yelling, "Don't feed Smiley!" Hope was feeding Smiley. Smiley was jumping up and down. My father shouted, "Am I invisible? Pass me the bread!" Then, it happened. Poof! My father disappeared like magic. ⓐHe became invisible!

29 위 글의 내용과 일치하지 <u>않는</u> 것은?

① There was some bread on the table.

② The writer heard what his father said.

③ The writer's mother was yelling at the writer.

④ Smiley was eating food.

⑤ The writer's father had dinner at home last Friday.

30 다음 주어진 단어를 활용하여 엄마가 Hope에게 소리 지른 이유를 쓰시오.

| (didn't want) |

➡ _____

31 위 글의 밑줄 친 ⓐ의 의미로 가장 적절한 것은?

① He ran out of the house.

② He was not seen to his family members.

③ He didn't want to talk with his wife and children.

④ He went out to buy some bread.

⑤ He went into his room.

01 출제율 90%

다음 영영풀이에 해당하는 단어를 쓰시오.

> keeping things neat and in order

➡ _____

02 출제율 90%

다음 우리말에 맞게 빈칸에 알맞은 말을 쓰시오.

> 할아버지가 돌아가셨을 때, 우리 가족은 눈물바다였다.
> ➡ When my grandfather passed away, my family was _____.

03 출제율 90%

다음 빈칸에 들어갈 말로 적절하지 <u>않은</u> 것은?

> A: What is she like?
> B: She is _____ and _____.

① patient   ② outgoing
③ intelligent   ④ creative
⑤ carefully

04 출제율 90%

다음 글을 읽고 문맥상 알맞은 어휘를 고르시오.

> My best friend is Subin. I have known her for 3 years. She is (A)[humor / humorous]. She tells me many (B)[funny / boring] jokes. She and I (C)[both / either] like movies. So we have watched many movies together. I'm sure we'll be friends forever.

(A)_____ (B)_____ (C)_____

[05~07] 다음 대화를 읽고, 물음에 답하시오.

> Dad: Sue, how do you like your school ⓐ ?
> Sue: I like it a lot, Dad. I already made two new friends, Rosa and Mike.
> Dad: Happy to hear that. (A)
> Sue: We all love English. We are also in the same club. (B)
> Dad: That's great. What are they like?
> Sue: Rosa is very kind. (C)
> Dad: How about Mike? (D)
> Sue: He is outgoing. (E)
> Dad: Why don't you invite them over for dinner?
> Sue: Okay, Dad.

05 출제율 90%

위 대화의 빈칸 ⓐ에 '요즘에'를 뜻하는 말을 2 단어로 쓰시오.

➡ _____

06 출제율 100%

위 대화의 (A)~(E) 중 주어진 문장이 들어가기에 가장 적절한 곳은?

> How did you become friends?

① (A)   ② (B)   ③ (C)   ④ (D)   ⑤ (E)

07 출제율 90%

위 대화를 읽고 대답할 수 <u>없는</u> 질문은?

① Is Sue satisfied with her school these days?
② How many friends did Sue make?
③ What club are Sue and Mike in?
④ What is Mike's personality like?
⑤ What did Sue's father suggest to Sue?

Judy: Hojin, I'm looking for a singer for my school band.

Hojin: How about Junho Kim?

Judy: Junho Kim? Who's that?

Hojin: Oh, he's my classmate. He just moved to our school last week.

Judy: Is he a good singer?

Hojin: Yeah, he sings beautifully. I'm sure he will be perfect for your band.

Judy: Can you tell me more about him? What's he like?

Hojin: Well, he is very outgoing and friendly.

Judy: Great. (A)Can I have his phone number?

Hojin: Sure.

출제율 85%

08 What is Junho's personality like?

➡ _____

출제율 95%

09 위 대화의 밑줄 친 (A)와 바꾸어 쓸 수 없는 것은?

① Would you give me his phone number?
② Can I get his phone number?
③ Let me know his phone number, please.
④ Will you tell me his phone number?
⑤ May I hand out his phone number?

출제율 100%

10 다음 빈칸에 들어갈 말로 적절한 것은?

Would you like _____ you a hand?

① to give me   ② me to give
③ to give   ④ me giving
⑤ giving me

출제율 95%

11 다음 중 어법상 바르지 않은 것은?

① Have you worn your new pants?
② Ben went home five minutes ago.
③ I have lost my wallet last week.
④ The weather was not very good yesterday.
⑤ When did you buy your pen?

출제율 95%

12 다음 빈칸에 알맞은 말로 바르게 짝지어진 것은?

• Tom _____ in a hotel for ten years. Everyone likes him, so they want Tom _____ with them for a long time.

① worked – worked
② works – to work
③ has worked – to work
④ has worked – working
⑤ works – work

출제율 95%

13 다음 빈칸에 공통으로 들어갈 수 있는 것을 모두 고르시오.

• We _____ you to come to the party.
• I _____ to have some coffee.

① would like   ② tell
③ cause   ④ want
⑤ enable

출제율 90%

14 주어진 단어를 활용하여 다음 우리말을 영어로 쓰시오.

그 의사는 나의 아빠에게 담배를 피우지 말라고 했다. (advise)

➡ _____

15 다음 빈칸에 알맞은 말을 쓰시오.

> I bought this book two weeks _____.
> I have read this book _____ the first of April.
> I have read this book _____ two weeks.

16 다음 괄호 안에 주어진 단어를 어법에 맞도록 고치시오.

> Rose works in a hospital.
> She (work) there for five months.
> Before that, she (be) a teacher.
> She was unhappy because she had to force her students (do) something.

➡ _____

[17~18] 다음 글을 읽고, 물음에 답하시오.

My father usually comes home late from work. So, we only see him on the weekends. Even ⓐthen, he usually sleeps or watches television. But last Friday, he came home early for dinner. At the table, we were all doing our own thing. Hope was giving food to Smiley. My mother was telling her not to do so. I was texting.

17 위 글의 내용과 일치하지 않는 것은?

① The writer's father usually works till late.
② The writer sees his father only on the weekends.
③ The writer's father came home early last Friday.
④ The writer's mother told Hope to feed the dog.
⑤ The writer was using his smart phone at the table.

18 위 글의 밑줄 친 ⓐ가 의미하는 것을 영어로 쓰시오.

➡ _____

[19~20] 다음 글을 읽고, 물음에 답하시오.

My father said, "Pass me the bread, please." No one heard him, so he asked again, "Can someone pass me the bread?" I ⓐ him this time, but I was too busy with my phone. My mother was ⓑ, "Don't feed Smiley!" Hope was ⓒ Smiley. Smiley was ⓓ up and down. My father shouted, "(A)Am I invisible? Pass me the bread!"

Then, it ⓔ. Poof! My father disappeared like magic. He became invisible!

19 주어진 단어를 어법에 맞게 ⓐ~ⓔ에 각각 쓰시오.

> (yell / feed / hear / jump / happen)

ⓐ_____ ⓑ_____ ⓒ_____
ⓓ_____ ⓔ_____

20 밑줄 친 (A)를 대신할 수 있는 것은?

① Don't I see you?
② Do you want to see me?
③ Are you invisible?
④ Can't you see me?
⑤ What am I seeing?

21 주어진 문장에 이어질 글의 순서를 바르게 연결한 것은?

> Then, it happened. Poof! My father disappeared like magic. He became invisible!

(A) "I'm right in front of you," he replied. We couldn't do anything for him. It was an awful night.

(B) The doctor shook his head and said, "I can't help you. I've never seen anything like this before."

(C) We could hear him, but we couldn't see him. We asked, "Where are you?"

(D) Next morning, we went to the hospital and asked the doctor to help us. I said, "He has been invisible since last night."

① (A) – (C) – (D) – (B)
② (B) – (A) – (C) – (D)
③ (B) – (D) – (A) – (C)
④ (C) – (A) – (D) – (B)
⑤ (D) – (B) – (C) – (A)

[22~24] 다음 글을 읽고, 물음에 답하시오.

> We could hear him, but we couldn't see him. We asked dad, "①Where are you?" "I'm right in front of you," he replied. We couldn't ②do anything for him. It was an awful night.
>
> Next morning, we ③came back from the hospital and asked the doctor to help us. I said, "He ④has been invisible since last night." The doctor ⑤shook his head and said, "I can't help you. ⓐI've never seen anything like this before."

22 위 글의 밑줄 친 ①~⑤ 중 글의 흐름상 어색한 것은?

①   ②   ③   ④   ⑤

23 위 글의 밑줄 친 ⓐ를 답변으로 할 수 있는 질문을 쓰시오.

➡ _____

24 위 글의 내용에 맞게 빈칸에 알맞은 말을 쓰시오.

> The writer's father _____, but the rest of the family could still _____ what he said.

[01~02] 다음 대화를 읽고, 물음에 답하시오.

G: Can we arrive in time?
B: Of course. The train leaves at 5:10.
G: But, it's already 4:30.
B: The train station isn't very far from here. I'm sure we'll arrive there before 5.

01 By when do G and B want to arrive at the train station?

➡ _____

02 중요 Why is B sure that they will not be late?

➡ _____

03 다음 대화의 내용과 일치하도록 빈칸을 완성하시오.

Dad: Sue, how do you like your school these days?
Sue: I like it a lot, Dad. I already made two new friends, Rosa and Mike.
Dad: Happy to hear that. How did you become friends?
Sue: We all love English. We are also in the same club.
Dad: That's great. What are they like?
Sue: Rosa is very kind.
Dad: How about Mike?
Sue: He is outgoing.
Dad: Why don't you invite them over for dinner?
Sue: Okay, Dad.

Sue: Let me introduce my friends, Rosa and Mike. We all love (1)_____ and belong to (2)_____. Rosa is very (3)_____ and Mike is (4)_____. My father recommended me to (5)_____ _____ soon. I'm really looking forward to it.

04 다음 주어진 어휘를 어법에 맞게 각각 쓰시오.

A: (hear, you) of George Washington?
B: Of course. He (be) the first President of the United States.

➡ _____

05 중요 다음 주어진 단어를 어법에 맞게 쓰시오.

A: Is this a new coat?
B: No, (have) this coat for a long time.

➡ _____

06 주어진 단어를 활용하여 다음 문장과 같은 의미의 문장을 쓰시오.

Shall I hand in this paper for you?
(want)

➡ _____

07 다음 주어진 단어를 활용하여 대화를 완성하시오.

A: Would you like something to eat?
B: No, thanks. _____
(just / have / lunch)

➡ _____

08 다음 주어진 단어를 활용하여 빈칸에 알맞은 말을 쓰시오.

> July told me something at the concert. But I didn't hear what she said, so I _____. (ask / repeat / it)

➡ _____

[09~13] 다음 글을 읽고, 물음에 답하시오.

My name is Jimmy. I am in the eighth grade and my sister, Hope, is in the third grade. My father is a banker and my mother is a teacher. We have a dog, Smiley. Sounds pretty normal, right? But ⓐa crazy thing happened last week.

My father usually comes home late from work. So, we only see him on the weekends. Even then, he usually sleeps or watches television. But last Friday, he came home early for dinner. At the table, we were all ⓑ doing our own thing. Hope was giving food to Smiley. My mother was telling her not to do so. I was texting.

My father said, "Pass me the bread, please." No one heard him, so he asked again, "Can someone pass me the bread?" I heard him this time, but I was too busy with my phone. My mother was yelling, "Don't ____ⓒ____!" Hope was ____ⓓ____. Smiley was jumping up and down. My father shouted, "Am I invisible? _____ⓔ_____"

Then, it happened. Poof! My father disappeared like magic.

09 (중요) 주어진 단어를 어법에 맞게 활용하여 밑줄 친 ⓐ가 의미하는 것을 영어로 쓰시오.

> (disappear / and / invisible)

➡ _____

10 위 글을 읽고 주어진 단어를 활용하여 Jimmy와 Hope에게 해줄 조언의 빈칸을 완성하시오.

> • Jimmy, you should _____ (leave) in your room during dinner.
> • Hope, you should _____ (stop) Smiley.

➡ _____

11 (중요) 위 글의 밑줄 친 ⓑ를 우리말로 구체적으로 나열하시오.

➡ _____
_____

12 주어진 어구를 어법에 맞게 빈칸 ⓒ와 ⓓ에 각각 쓰시오.

> (feed Smiley)
>
> ⓒ _____ ⓓ _____

13 위 글의 빈칸 ⓔ에 들어갈 알맞은 말을 어법과 문맥에 맞게 쓰시오.

> I told you _____!

➡ _____

01 다음 대화를 읽고, 대화의 내용과 일치하도록 Judy의 일기를 완성하시오.

> **Judy:** Hojin, I'm looking for a singer for my school band.
>
> **Hojin:** How about Junho Kim?
>
> **Judy:** Junho Kim? Who's that?
>
> **Hojin:** Oh, he's my classmate. He just moved to our school last week.
>
> **Judy:** Is he a good singer?
>
> **Hojin:** Yeah, he sings beautifully. I'm sure he will be perfect for your band.
>
> **Judy:** Can you tell me more about him? What's he like?
>
> **Hojin:** Well, he is very outgoing and friendly.
>
> **Judy:** Great. Can I have his phone number?
>
> **Hojin:** Sure.

> April 30, Tuesday, 2020, Sunny
>
> Today, I got to know about (1)_____. While I was looking for (2)_____
> _____, Hojin recommended him to me. According to Hojin, Junho, who moved
> to our school last week, can (3)_____, so he would be perfect for my band. In
> addition, because he is a very (4)_____ person, I think he can get along with other
> members in my club. I was given (5) _____ by Hojin. Tomorrow, I'll send a text to
> him. I'm really looking forward to meeting him.

02 현재완료의 완료, 계속, 경험, 결과 용법을 이용하여 자신의 이야기를 〈보기〉와 같이 써보시오.

> ┤ 보기 ├
> - I have just finished the marathon.
> - I have studied English for 6 years.
> - I have been to Busan three times.
> - I have lost my glasses.

(1) _____

(2) _____

(3) _____

(4) _____

단원별 모의고사

01 다음 짝지어진 단어의 관계가 같도록 빈칸에 알맞은 말을 쓰시오.

> possible : impossible = visible : _____

➡ _____

02 다음 우리말에 맞게 빈칸에 알맞은 말을 쓰시오.

> 나는 영어 말하기 대회에서 1등을 하고 싶다.
> ➡ I want to _____ _____ _____
> in the English speaking contest.

03 다음 빈칸에 들어갈 말을 〈보기〉에서 찾아 쓰시오.

> ──── 보기 ────
> active / disappear / pass / normal

(1) It's _____ to feel tired after taking the exam.
(2) My friends are _____ in campaigning for the election.
(3) My pens seem to _____ as soon as I buy them.
(4) Would you _____ me the salt, please?

04 다음 우리말을 〈보기〉에 주어진 표현을 사용하여 영어로 쓰시오.

> ──── 보기 ────
> invite over / in front of / move to

(1) 학교 앞에 도서관이 있다.
➡ _____
(2) 나는 오늘 저녁에 너를 초대하고 싶어.
➡ _____
(3) 언제 한국으로 이사했나요?
➡ _____

[05~06] 다음 대화를 읽고, 물음에 답하시오.

> Jane: Hey, Minsu. What's up? You look so worried.
> Minsu: The English speaking test is this afternoon.
> Jane: Don't worry. You practiced a lot.
> Minsu: But I get so nervous when I'm (A)_____ _____ _____ the teacher.
> Jane: Everybody does. I'm sure you'll do well.
> Minsu: Do you really think so?
> Jane: Of course. You are a great English speaker.
> Minsu: Thanks. I feel much better now.

05 위 대화의 빈칸 (A)에 '~ 앞에서'를 뜻하는 표현을 쓰시오.

➡ _____

06 위 대화의 내용과 일치하지 않는 것은?

① Minsu is worried about the English speaking test.
② Minsu practiced a lot for the English speaking test.
③ Minsu is sure that Jane is a fluent speaker.
④ Minsu feels much better because of Jane's encouragement.
⑤ Jane is certain that Minsu will do well on the English speaking test.

07 다음 밑줄 친 우리말을 주어진 단어를 사용하여 영어로 쓰시오.

> A: Jane has a great voice.
> B: Yeah, 나는 그녀가 좋은 가수가 될 것이라고 확신해. (good, sure)
> A: I think so, too.

➡ _____

[08~09] 다음 대화를 읽고, 물음에 답하시오.

Judy: Hojin, I'm looking for a singer for my school band.
Hojin: How about Junho Kim?
Judy: Junho Kim? Who's that?
Hojin: Oh, he's my classmate. He just moved to our school last week.
Judy: Is he a good singer?
Hojin: Yeah, he sings beautifully. (A)나는 그가 너희 밴드에 꼭 맞을 것이라고 확신해.
Judy: Can you tell me more about him? What's he like?
Hojin: Well, he is very outgoing and friendly.
Judy: Great. Can I have his phone number?
Hojin: Sure.

08 Why did Hojin recommend Junho Kim for a singer for his school band?

➡ _____

09 위 대화의 밑줄 친 우리말 (A)에 맞게 주어진 보기에 있는 단어를 모두 배열하시오.

─ 보기 ─
band / be / perfect / I'm / for / he / your / sure / will

➡ _____

10 빈칸 (A)에 주어진 어구를 알맞게 배열하시오.

A: Who is the best person to be the board cleaner?
B: How about Minsu?
A: What is he like?
C: He is responsible and tidy.
D: I'm sure (A)_____.

─ 보기 ─
class / board cleaner / will / for / he / good / a / our / be

➡ _____

11 다음 역할에 어울리는 친구의 성격을 〈보기〉에서 골라 묘사하시오.

A: Who is the best person to be the plant keeper?
B: How about Emma?
A: What is he like?
C: (A)_____.
D: I'm sure she will be a good plant keeper for our class.

─ 보기 ─
active / helpful / honest / hard-working / responsible

➡ _____

[12~13] 다음 대화를 읽고, 물음에 답하시오.

Dad: Sue, (A)what do you like your school these days?
Sue: I like it a lot, Dad. I already made two new friends, Rosa and Mike.
Dad: Happy (B)to hear that. (C)How did you become friends?
Sue: We all love English. We are also in the same club.
Dad: That's great. What are they (D)like?
Sue: Rosa is very kind.
Dad: How about Mike?
Sue: He is outgoing.
Dad: Why don't you invite them (E)over for dinner?
Sue: Okay, Dad.

12 위 대화의 밑줄 친 (A)~(E) 중 대화의 흐름상 어색한 것을 골라 바르게 고치시오.

➡ _____

13 What do Sue, Rosa and Mike have in common?

➡ _____

14 다음 문장의 밑줄 친 부분과 쓰임이 같은 것은?

> Mary reminded me not <u>to be</u> late for the meeting.

① Colin went to the shop <u>to buy</u> a hat.
② Is there something interesting <u>to read</u>?
③ I prefer not <u>to know</u> the secret.
④ Kelly hopes <u>to meet</u> her someday.
⑤ Don't forget to tell Jane <u>to call</u> me.

15 다음 빈칸에 공통으로 들어갈 말은?

> • Can I _____ a favor of you?
> • They _____ us to fill in the blanks.

① help   ② expect   ③ do
④ ask   ⑤ order

16 다음 우리말을 영어로 바르게 옮긴 것은?

① Jane은 아일랜드에 3일 전에 도착했다.
= Jane has arrived in Ireland three days ago.
② 그는 내게 결혼해 달라고 했다.
= He asked me to marry him.
③ 나는 이 신발을 작년에 샀다.
= I bought these shoes since last year.
④ 엄마는 내가 스마트폰을 사용하지 못하게 했다.
= Mom forced me to not use the smart phone.
⑤ 경찰은 그녀에게 운전 중에 조심하라고 조언했다.
= The policeman advised her being careful while driving.

17 다음 상황을 읽고 질문에 답하시오.

> Jane went to the bank, but a few minutes ago she returned.

> Q: Is Jane still at the bank?
> A: No, _____. (come back)

➡ _____

18 괄호 안에 주어진 어휘를 어법에 맞게 쓰시오.

> We (see) each other for a long time. Please stay more. I don't want you (leave) so soon.

➡ _____

[19~20] 다음 글을 읽고, 물음에 답하시오.

> My name is Jimmy. I am in the eighth grade and my sister, Hope, is in the third grade. My father is a banker and ⓐ<u>my mother is a teacher</u>. We have a dog, Smiley. ⓑ<u>Sounds pretty normal</u>, right? But a crazy thing ⓒ <u>happened</u> last week.
>
> ⓓ<u>My father usually comes home late from work</u>. So, we only see him (A)_____ the weekends. Even then, he usually sleeps or watches television. But last Friday, he came home early ⓔ<u>for dinner</u>. (B)_____ the table, we were all doing our own thing. Hope was giving food (C)_____ Smiley. My mother was telling her not to do so. I was texting.

19 밑줄 친 ⓐ~ⓔ를 대신하여 쓸 수 없는 것은?

① ⓐ: my mother teaches students.
② ⓑ: Sounds like something special,
③ ⓒ: took place
④ ⓓ: My father usually works till late at the bank.
⑤ ⓔ: to have dinner

20 빈칸 (A)~(C)에 들어갈 말이 바르게 짝지어진 것은?

① at – On – to   ② to – At – on
③ on – At – to   ④ on – At – for
⑤ in – On – to

[21~24] 다음 글을 읽고, 물음에 답하시오.

My father said, "Pass me the bread, please." No one heard him, so he asked again, "Can someone pass me the bread?" I heard him this time, but I was too busy with my phone. My mother was yelling, "Don't feed Smiley!" Hope was feeding Smiley. Smiley was jumping up and down. My father shouted, "Am I invisible? Pass me the bread!"

Then, it ①happened. Poof! My father disappeared like magic. He became invisible!

We could hear him, but we couldn't see him. We asked, "Where are you?" "I'm right in front of you," he replied. We couldn't do anything for him. ②It was an awful night.

Next morning, we went to the hospital and asked the doctor ③to help us. I said, "He has been invisible ④for last night." The doctor ⑤ shook his head and said, "I can't help you. (A) I've never seen anything like this before."

21 ①~⑤ 중 어법상 바르지 않은 것을 골라 바르게 고치시오.

➡ _____

22 밑줄 친 (A)에서 사용된 현재완료와 그 쓰임이 같은 것은?

① My mom has found the key.
② He has gone to New York.
③ I have eaten the food twice.
④ How long have you lived here?
⑤ We haven't seen each other for a while.

23 위 글의 내용과 일치하는 것은?

① The writer's father used magic to disappear.
② The writer's father couldn't speak while he was invisible.
③ The writer wanted to pass the bread to his father.
④ The writer's mother wanted Hope to stop feeding Smiley.
⑤ The doctor didn't want to help writer's father.

24 위 글의 내용에 맞게 질문에 답하시오.

Q: What did the writer's family do the next morning?
A: _____

➡ _____

[25~26] 다음 글을 읽고, 물음에 답하시오.

Next morning, we went to the hospital and asked the doctor to help us. ① I said, "He has been invisible since last night." The doctor shook his head and said, "I can't help you. I've never seen anything like this before." ②

When we came home, Hope said, "I miss Daddy." She started crying. ③ In a few moments, we were a sea of tears. "Come back, Dad! I promise to pass you the bread every day!" I cried. ④

Then, it happened. ⑤ My father appeared again! He hugged us and said, "Thank you for all the attention. I promise to come home earlier and play with you on the weekends."

25 다음 주어진 문장이 들어가기에 적절한 곳은?

My mother joined her.

①   ②   ③   ④   ⑤

26 다음 빈칸에 들어갈 알맞은 말을 위 글에서 찾아 쓰시오.

The writer went to the hospital and said to the doctor, "We want our father _____. Can you help us?

➡ _____

The Music Goes On

🎙 의사소통 기능

• 선호 말하기

A: Which sport do you like best?

B: I like tennis best.

• 이유 말하기

A: Why do you want to visit Canada?

B: Because I want to see Niagara Falls.

🎙 언어 형식

• 수동태

The Beatles **were loved** by many people.

• If 조건절

If you like today's idols, you will love the original idol.

교과서 Words & Expressions

Key Words

- **amazing** [əméiziŋ] 형 놀라운
- **audience** [ɔ́ːdiəns] 명 청중, 관람객
- **ballet** [bǽlei] 명 발레
- **become** [bikʌ́m] 동 ~이 되다
- **breath** [breθ] 명 숨, 호흡
- **composer** [kəmpóuzər] 명 작곡가
- **concert** [kɑ́ːnsərt] 명 연주회, 음악회, 콘서트
- **creation** [kriéiʃən] 명 창조물, 창작
- **cry** [krai] 동 울다, 외치다
- **definitely** [défənitli] 부 단연, 틀림없이
- **down** [daun] 형 우울한
- **drummer** [drʌ́mər] 명 북 연주자, 드러머
- **even** [íːvən] 부 ~조차
- **face** [feis] 명 얼굴 동 ~을 마주 보다[향하다]
- **fall** [fɔːl] 동 떨어지다
- **fan** [fæn] 명 팬, 부채, 선풍기
- **fantastic** [fæntǽstik] 형 환상적인
- **flea market** 벼룩시장
- **funny** [fʌ́ni] 형 재미있는, 우스운
- **giraffe** [dʒərǽf] 명 기린
- **grape** [greip] 명 포도, 포도나무
- **greeting** [gríːtiŋ] 명 인사
- **hall** [hɔːl] 명 집회장, 홀
- **heal** [hiːl] 동 고치다, 낫게 하다
- **Hungary** [hʌ́ŋɡəri] 명 헝가리
- **idol** [áidl] 명 (많은 사랑을 받는) 우상
- **invent** [invént] 동 발명하다, 창안하다
- **liberty** [líbərti] 명 자유
- **machine** [məʃíːn] 명 기계, 기계장치
- **madly** [mǽdli] 부 미친 듯이, 열렬하게
- **meeting** [míːtiŋ] 명 만남, 모임
- **memory** [méməri] 명 기억, 추억
- **miss** [mis] 동 놓치다, 그리워하다
- **movement** [múːvmənt] 명 움직임
- **novel** [nάvəl] 명 소설
- **note** [nout] 명 음, 음표 동 적어두다, 주목하다
- **original** [ərídʒənl] 형 본래의
- **paper folding** 종이접기
- **performance** [pərfɔ́ːrməns] 명 공연, 연극, 실행
- **pianist** [piǽnist] 명 피아니스트, 피아노 연주자
- **place** [pleis] 명 곳, 장소
- **prepare** [pripɛ́ər] 동 준비하다
- **recent** [ríːsnt] 형 최근의
- **scream** [skriːm] 동 소리치다, 괴성을 지르다
- **seat** [siːt] 명 자리, 좌석
- **sheet music** 악보
- **signature** [sígnəʃər] 명 서명
- **single** [síŋɡl] 형 단 하나의, 혼자의
- **softly** [sɔ́ːftli] 부 부드럽게, 상냥하게
- **strawberry** [strɔ́ːbèri] 명 딸기
- **sunny** [sʌ́ni] 형 화창한
- **throw** [θrou] 동 던지다
- **unlike** [ənláik] 전 ~와는 달리
- **vacation** [veikéiʃən] 명 방학, 휴가
- **wall** [wɔːl] 명 벽, 담
- **zebra** [zíːbrə] 명 얼룩말

Key Expressions

- **at once** 동시에, 한꺼번에
- **because of** ~ 때문에
- **build up** 점점 높이다
- **cheer up** 격려하다, 힘을 북돋우다
- **from memory** 기억해서, 외워서
- **go wild** ~에 열중하다, ~에 열광하다
- **hold one's breath** 숨을 참다, 숨을 죽이다
- **listen to** ~을 듣다
- **in person** 직접
- **press down** 누르다

Word Power

※ 서로 반대되는 뜻을 가진 어휘

- **early** (일찍) ↔ **late** (늦게)
- **strong** (힘 있는, 강한) ↔ **weak** (약한)
- **funny** (재미있는) ↔ **boring** (지루한)
- **like** (좋아하다) ↔ **dislike** (싫어하다)
- **definitely** (단연, 틀림없이) ↔ **indefinitely** (불명확하게)
- **best** (가장 좋은) ↔ **worst** (가장 나쁜)
- **softly** (부드럽게) ↔ **roughly** (거칠게)
- **fold** (접다) ↔ **spread** (펼치다)
- **like** (~와 같이) ↔ **unlike** (~와는 달리)
- **send** (보내다) ↔ **receive** (받다)
- **single** (단 하나의) ↔ **multiple** (다수의)
- **pull** (끌다) ↔ **push** (밀다)

English Dictionary

- **audience** 청중, 관람객
  → the group of people who have gathered to watch or listen to something
  무언가를 보거나 듣기 위해 모인 사람들의 무리

- **ballet** 발레
  → a style of dancing that tells a dramatic story with music but no talking or singing
  이야기하거나 노래하지 않고 음악과 함께 극적인 이야기를 하는 춤

- **breath** 숨, 호흡
  → the air that you take into your lungs and send out again
  당신이 폐로 들이마시고 다시 내뱉는 공기

- **composer** 작곡가
  → a person who writes music
  음악을 쓰는 사람

- **creation** 창조물
  → the act or process of making something that is new, or of causing something to exist that did not exist before
  새롭거나 전에 존재하지 않았던 무언가를 만들어 내는 과정이나 행위

- **fall** 떨어지다
  → to drop down from a higher level to a lower level
  높은 곳에서 낮은 곳으로 떨어지다

- **flea market** 벼룩시장
  → an outdoor market that sells second-hand goods at low prices
  중고 물건들을 낮은 가격에 판매하는 야외 시장

- **hall** 홀, 집회장
  → a space or passage inside the entrance or front door of a building
  건물 정문이나 입구 안의 공간이나 통로

- **heal** 고치다, 낫게 하다
  → to become healthy again; to make something healthy again
  다시 건강하게 되다; 다시 건강하게 만들다

- **idol** 우상
  → a person or thing that is loved and admired very much
  매우 많은 사랑을 받거나 존경받는 사람이나 사물

- **performance** 공연
  → the act of performing a play, concert or some other form of entertainment
  연극, 콘서트 또는 다른 형태의 연회를 공연하는 활동

- **pianist** 피아니스트
  → a person who plays the piano
  피아노를 연주하는 사람

- **prepare** 준비하다
  → to make something or somebody ready to be used or to do something
  사용되거나 또는 무언가 하기 위해 어떤 사물이나 사람을 준비시키다

- **signature** 서명
  → your name as you usually write it, for example, at the end of a letter
  예를 들어, 편지 끝에 당신이 보통 적는 당신의 이름

서답형

01 다음 짝지어진 단어의 관계가 같도록 빈칸에 알맞은 말을 쓰시오.

> early : late = _____ : multiple

서답형

[02~04] 다음 영영풀이에 해당하는 말을 쓰시오.

02

> the air that you take into your lungs and send out again

➡ _____

03

> an outdoor market that sells second-hand goods at low prices

➡ _____

04

> a person who writes music

➡ _____

중요

05 다음 중 밑줄 친 부분의 뜻풀이가 바르지 <u>않은</u> 것은?

① Necessity is the mother of the <u>invention</u>.
(발명)

② It's not easy for me to <u>memorize</u> the musical notes. (기억하다)

③ Please hold your <u>breath</u> for a moment.
(숨, 호흡)

④ This building <u>faces</u> south. (얼굴)

⑤ He'll <u>scream</u> with excitement during the surprise party. (외치다, 소리치다)

06 다음 주어진 문장의 밑줄 친 의미와 같은 의미로 쓰인 것은?

> Some <u>fans</u> screamed madly at concerts.

① Hundreds of football <u>fans</u> were gathered in the stadium.

② The Korean traditional <u>fans</u> are quite popular among foreigners.

③ <u>Fans</u> were used by our ancestors during hot summer.

④ I need the <u>fans</u> to dry my hair.

⑤ People should use <u>fans</u> rather than air conditioners to protect the earth.

중요

07 다음 문장의 빈칸에 공통으로 들어갈 말로 적절한 것은?

> • I need your _____ on the cheque.
> • You should write your _____ on two copies of the contract.
> • He was writing his _____ at the bottom of the paper.

① idol   ② creation

③ sheet   ④ hall

⑤ signature

서답형

08 다음 대화의 밑줄 친 부분을 주어진 단어를 사용하여 의미가 같도록 바꾸어 쓰시오.

> Jack: Which book do you like best?
> Sumin: <u>I like *Charlotte's Web* best.</u> (favorite)

➡ _____

01 다음 짝지어진 단어의 관계가 같도록 빈칸에 알맞은 말을 쓰시오.

| teach : teacher = compose : _____ |

[02~03] 다음 영영풀이에 해당하는 단어를 쓰시오.

02

| the act or process of making something that is new, or of causing something to exist that did not exist before |

➡ _____

03

| the group of people who have gathered to watch or listen to something |

➡ _____

04 다음 문장의 빈칸에 들어갈 말을 〈보기〉에서 골라 쓰시오.

┤ 보기 ├
breath / audience / down

(1) Whenever it rains, I'm usually _____.
(2) Take a deep _____ when you feel nervous.
(3) The _____ was touched by his speech.

05 다음 우리말을 주어진 어구를 모두 배열하여 영작하시오.

(1) 벼룩시장이 공원에서 열릴 것이다.
(market / will / in / held / the park / flea / the / be)
➡ _____

(2) 그녀는 악보 없이 피아노를 연주하였다.
(music / played / she / without / sheet / the / piano)
➡ _____

06 다음 우리말에 맞게 빈칸에 알맞은 말을 쓰시오.

(1) 당신이 문을 열고 싶다면, 버튼을 누르세요.
➡ If you want to open the door, _____ _____ the button please.
(2) 선수들은 결승선을 향해 속도를 점점 높일 것이다.
➡ The players will _____ _____ _____ toward the finish line.
(3) Mike는 한꺼번에 두 가지 일을 다루는 일을 잘한다.
➡ Mike is good at dealing with two things _____ _____.

07 다음 빈칸에 들어갈 말을 순서대로 쓰시오.

| • Jane is a teacher, writer and designer (A)_____ once.
• Because the car is broken down, I can't build (B)_____ speed.
• You have to deliver this document (C)_____ person. |

(A) _____ (B) _____ (C) _____

교과서
Conversation

1 선호 말하기

> **A** Which sport do you like best? 너는 어느 운동을 가장 좋아하니?
> **B** I like tennis best. 나는 테니스를 가장 좋아해.

■ 'Which ~ do you like best[most]?' 또는 'What's your favorite ~?'으로 상대방이 선호하는 것을 물어볼 수 있다.

선호 묻기

- What kind of sports do you like best? 너는 어떤 종류의 운동을 가장 좋아하니?
- Which do you prefer, oranges or apples? 너는 오렌지와 사과 중 어느 것을 더 좋아하니?
- Do you like watching TV more than listening to the radio?
  너는 라디오를 듣는 것보다 TV 보는 것을 더 좋아하니?

선호 말하기

- I like ~ most[best]. 나는 ~을 가장 좋아한다.
- I love ~. 나는 ~을 매우 좋아한다.
- I'm fond of ~. 나는 ~을 좋아한다.
- My favorite ... is ~. 내가 가장 좋아하는 …는 ~이다.
- I enjoy ~ (very much). 나는 ~을 (매우) 즐긴다.

핵심 Check

1. 다음 우리말과 일치하도록 빈칸에 알맞은 말을 쓰시오.

(1) **A:** _____ _____ do you like best? (당신은 어느 동물을 가장 좋아하나요?)

 B: I like cats best. (저는 고양이를 가장 좋아합니다.)

(2) **A:** What is your _____ _____? (당신이 가장 좋아하는 과목은 무엇입니까?)

 B: My favorite subject is English. (제가 가장 좋아하는 과목은 영어입니다.)

(3) **A:** Which flower do you _____? (당신은 어떤 꽃을 아주 좋아합니까?))

 B: I love roses. (저는 장미를 아주 좋아합니다.)

② **이유 말하기**

A Why do you want to visit Canada? 너는 왜 캐나다를 방문하고 싶니?

B Because I want to see Niagara Falls. 왜냐하면 나이아가라 폭포를 보고 싶기 때문이야.

■ 'Why do you ~?', 'Can you tell me the reason why ~?' 또는 'What's the reason why ~?' 등으로 이유를 물어볼 수 있다.

이유 말하기

- Because 주어 + 동사 ~. ~이기 때문이다.
- It is because of+명사(구) ~. 그것은 ~ 때문이다.
- The reason why ~ is because ~. ~한 이유는 ~이다.

핵심 Check

2. 다음 우리말과 일치하도록 빈칸에 알맞은 말을 쓰시오.

(1) **A**: _____ do you want to buy some flowers? (왜 당신은 꽃을 사기를 원하나요?)

B: _____ I want to give them to my mother. (나는 그것들을 어머니에게 주고 싶기 때문이에요.)

(2) **A**: Can you tell me _____ _____ _____ you want to visit the museum?

(당신은 왜 박물관을 방문하고 싶어 하는지 이야기해 줄 수 있나요?)

B: _____ _____ _____ _____ _____ _____ is

because I like history. (제가 그곳에 방문하고 싶은 이유는 제가 역사를 좋아하기 때문입니다.)

(3) **A**: What's _____ _____ _____ _____ _____ _____ _____

to the city? (당신이 그 도시로 이사하고 싶은 이유가 무엇인가요?)

B: The reason why I want to move there is _____ _____ education.

(제가 그곳으로 이사하고 싶은 이유는 교육 때문입니다.)

A. Listen and Speak 1-A

Jack: Hi, Sumin. ❶How's the book club going?

Sumin: It's fun. ❷I read lots of interesting books.

Jack: ❸Which book do you like best?

Sumin: ❹I like *Charlotte's Web* best.

Jack: 안녕, 수민아. 책 동아리는 어때?
Sumin: 재미있어. 나는 흥미로운 책들을 많이 읽어.
Jack: 어떤 책을 가장 좋아하니?
Sumin: 나는 'Charlotte's Web'을 가장 좋아해.

❶ How is ~ going?: ~는 어때?
❷ lots of: 많은 (= a lot of)
❸ Which ~ do you like best?: '너는 어느 ~을 가장 좋아하니?'라는 뜻으로 상대방의 선호를 묻는 표현이다.
❹ 선호를 묻는 질문에 대한 대답으로는 Yes나 No로 답하지 않으며 'I like ~ best.'와 같이 대답할 수 있다.

Check(√) True or False

(1) Sumin read many interesting books in the book club.　　T ☐ F ☐

(2) Sumin likes *Charlotte's Web* best.　　T ☐ F ☐

A. Listen and Speak 1-B

Amy: ❶Jiho, what are you going to do this Saturday?

Jiho: ❷I'm going to Blue Sky's fan meeting with my friends.

Amy: ❸Wow, I'm also a big fan of the band.

Jiho: Really? Which member do you like best, Amy?

Amy: I like Lucy best. She sings really well.

Jiho: ❹I like the drummer, Mike, best. ❺He's fantastic! Do you want to join us?

Amy: Sure, I'd love to. ❻I can't wait!

Amy: 지호야, 이번 주 토요일에 뭐 할 거니?
Jiho: 나는 친구들이랑 Blue Sky 팬 모임에 갈 거야.
Amy: 와, 나도 그 밴드의 열렬한 팬이야.
Jiho: 정말? 너는 어느 멤버를 가장 좋아하니, Amy?
Amy: 나는 Lucy를 가장 좋아해. 그녀는 노래를 정말 잘해.
Jiho: 나는 드러머인 Mike를 가장 좋아해. 그는 환상적이야. 우리와 함께 갈래?
Amy: 물론이지, 너무 좋아. 기대된다!

❶ What are you going to do ~?: 상대방의 계획을 묻는 표현이다.
❷ I'm going to ~ = I'm going to go to ~
❸ big: 열렬한, 매우 좋아하는
❹ the drummer와 Mike는 동격이다.
❺ fantastic: 환상적인
❻ I can't wait!: 기대감을 나타내는 표현으로 I'm looking forward to it!으로 바꾸어 쓸 수 있다.

Check(√) True or False

(3) Lucy and Mike are the members of the band Blue Sky.　　T ☐ F ☐

(4) Amy cannot go to Blue Sky's fan meeting with Jiho.　　T ☐ F ☐

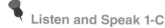 **Listen and Speak 1-C**

A: Do you like sports?

B: Yes, I do.

A: ❶Which sport do you like best?

B: I like tennis best. ❷It's so exciting!

❶ Which ~ do you like best?: '너는 어느 ~을 가장 좋아하니?'라는 뜻으로 상대방의 선호를 묻는 표현이다.

❷ It's so exciting!: 그것은 매우 흥미진진하다!

Listen and Speak 2-A

B: ❶Why do you have all those old clothes?

G: ❷I'm going to sell them at the flea market.

B: Really? I have some old clothes, too.

G: ❸Then why don't you join me this Saturday?

B: Okay.

❶ 'all those+형용사+명사'의 어순이다., clothes: 의류, 옷

❷ them = all those old clothes, flea market: 벼룩 시장

❸ Why don't you ~?: '~하는 게 어때?'라고 제안할 때 쓰는 표현이다.

Listen and Speak 2-B

Sujin: ❶Tom, why do you have so many paper flowers?

Tom: They're for my mom's birthday.

Sujin: They're so beautiful. Where did you get them?

Tom: I made them.

Sujin: Wow, you're really good.

Tom: Thanks. ❷I'm taking a paper folding class these days.

Sujin: They are going to be the perfect gift for your mom.

Tom: ❸I hope so, too.

❶ so many: 그토록 많은

❷ take a class: 수업을 듣다, paper folding: 종이 접기, these days: 요즘

❸ so는 앞 문장의 내용을 받는 지시대명사이다.

Listen and Speak 2-C

A: ❶Which country do you want to visit for your dream vacation?

B: I want to visit Canada.

A: ❷Why do you want to visit Canada?

B: ❸Because I want to see Niagara Falls.

❶ Which country do you want to ~?: '어느 나라를 ~하고 싶니?'라고 의견을 묻고 있다.

❷ '왜 캐나다를 방문하고 싶니?'라는 뜻으로 상대방에게 이유를 묻는 표현이다.

❸ because 뒤에는 '주어+동사'를 포함한 절이 오지만 'because of' 뒤에는 명사(구)가 이어진다. 이때 because를 생략하고 이유만 말할 수 있다.

Real Life Talk

Mina: Good afternoon, friends. I'm Mina with the school radio show. Today Mr. Smith, our English teacher, is here with us. Hi, Mr. Smith.

Mr. Smith: Hello, everyone. I'm happy to be here with you.

Mina: Let's talk about music. Mr. Smith, ❶what's your favorite band?

Mr. Smith: ❷Definitely The Beatles.

Mina: Oh, I like them, too. Which song do you like best?

Mr. Smith: I like most of their songs, but I like *Hey Jude* best.

Mina: Why do you like it?

Mr. Smith: ❸Because the song makes me feel better when I'm down.

Mina: That's great! Let's listen to the song.

❶ What's your favorite ~?: '당신이 가장 좋아하는 ~은 무엇입니까?'라고 선호 표현을 묻는 질문으로 'Which band do you like best?'라고 바꾸어 물어 볼 수 있다.

❷ definitely: 단연, 틀림없이

❸ down: 우울한(= depressed)

• 다음 우리말과 일치하도록 빈칸에 알맞은 말을 쓰시오.

Listen & Speak 1 A

Jack: Hi, Sumin. _____ the book club going?

Sumin: It's fun. I read lots of interesting books.

Jack: _____ _____ do you like best?

Sumin: I like *Charlotte's Web* _____.

Jack: 안녕, 수민아. 책 동아리는 어때?
Sumin: 재미있어. 나는 흥미로운 책들을 많이 읽어.
Jack: 어느 책을 가장 좋아하니?
Sumin: 나는 'Charlotte's Web'을 가장 좋아해.

Listen & Speak 1 B

Amy: Jiho, _____ _____ _____ _____ _____ this Saturday?

Jiho: I'm going to Blue Sky's fan meeting with my friends.

Amy: Wow, I'm also _____ _____ _____ of the band.

Jiho: Really? _____ _____ do you like best, Amy?

Amy: I like Lucy best. She sings really well.

Jiho: I like the _____, Mike, best. He's fantastic! Do you want to join us?

Amy: Sure, I'd love to. _____ _____ _____!

Amy: 지호야, 이번 주 토요일에 뭐 할 거니?
Jiho: 나는 친구들이랑 Blue Sky 팬 모임에 갈 거야.
Amy: 와, 나도 그 밴드의 열렬한 팬이야.
Jiho: 정말? 너는 어느 멤버를 가장 좋아하니, Amy?
Amy: 나는 Lucy를 가장 좋아해. 그녀는 노래를 정말 잘해.
Jiho: 나는 드러머인 Mike를 가장 좋아해. 그는 환상적이야. 우리와 함께 갈래?
Amy: 물론이지, 너무 좋아. 기대된다!

Listen & Speak 1 C

A: Do you like sports?

B: Yes, I do.

A: _____ _____ do you like best?

B: I like _____ best. It's so _____!

A: 운동을 좋아하니?
B: 응, 좋아해.
A: 어느 운동을 가장 좋아하니?
B: 나는 테니스를 가장 좋아해. 그것은 매우 흥미진진해!

Listen & Speak 2 A

B: _____ do you have all those old clothes?

G: I'm going to sell them at the _____ _____.

B: Really? I have some old clothes, too.

G: Then _____ _____ _____ join me this Saturday?

B: Okay.

B: 너는 왜 저 모든 헌 옷들을 가지고 있니?
G: 나는 벼룩시장에 그 옷들을 팔 거야.
B: 정말? 나도 헌 옷들이 좀 있어.
G: 그러면 이번 주 토요일에 나와 함께 팔면 어때?
B: 좋아.

Listen & Speak 2 B

Sujin: Tom, _____ do you have so many paper flowers?

Tom: They're _____ my mom's birthday.

Sujin: They're so beautiful. _____ did you get them?

Tom: I made them.

Sujin: Wow, you're really good.

Tom: Thanks. I'm taking _____ _____ _____ _____ these days.

Sujin: They are going to be _____ _____ _____ for your mom.

Tom: I hope so, too.

Listen & Speak 2 C

A: _____ _____ do you want to visit for your dream vacation?

B: I want to visit Canada.

A: _____ _____ _____ _____ _____ visit Canada?

B: _____ I want to see Niagara Falls.

Real Life Talk

Mina: Good afternoon, friends. I'm Mina _____ _____ _____ _____. Today Mr. Smith, your English teacher, is here with us. Hi, Mr. Smith.

Mr. Smith: Hello, everyone. I'm happy to be here with you.

Mina: Let's talk about music. Mr. Smith, _____ _____ _____?

Mr. Smith: _____ The Beatles.

Mina: Oh, I like them, too. _____ _____ _____ _____ _____?

Mr. Smith: I like most of their songs, but I like *Hey Jude* best.

Mina: _____ _____ _____ _____ _____ _____?

Mr. Smith: _____ the song makes me feel better _____ _____ _____.

Mina: That's great! Let's listen to the song.

해석

Sujin: Tom, 왜 그렇게 많은 종이꽃을 가지고 있니?

Tom: 이 꽃들은 엄마 생신을 위한 거야.

Sujin: 정말 예쁘다. 그 꽃들을 어디서 구했니?

Tom: 내가 만들었어.

Sujin: 와, 너 정말 잘 만든다.

Tom: 고마워. 나 요즘 종이접기 수업을 듣고 있어.

Sujin: 그 꽃들은 너희 엄마에게 완벽한 선물이 될 거야.

Tom: 나도 그러길 바라.

A: 너는 꿈의 휴가로 어느 나라를 방문하고 싶니?

B: 나는 캐나다를 방문하고 싶어.

A: 너는 왜 캐나다를 방문하고 싶니?

B: 나는 나이아가라 폭포를 보고 싶기 때문이야.

Mina: 안녕하세요, 여러분. 저희 학교 라디오 프로그램의 미나입니다. 오늘은 영어 선생님이신 Smith 선생님과 함께하겠습니다. 안녕하세요, Smith 선생님.

Mr. Smith: 안녕하세요, 여러분. 여러분과 함께하게 되어 기쁘군요.

Mina: 음악에 관한 이야기를 나눠 보도록 하죠. Smith 선생님, 어느 밴드를 가장 좋아하시나요?

Mr. Smith: 두말할 것도 없이 The Beatles에요.

Mina: 오, 저도 그들을 좋아해요. 어떤 노래를 가장 좋아하시나요?

Mr. Smith: 그들의 노래 대부분을 좋아하지만 'Hey Jude'를 가장 좋아하죠.

Mina: 왜 그 노래를 좋아하시나요?

Mr. Smith: 그 노래는 내가 우울할 때 기분이 나아지게 해 주기 때문이죠.

Mina: 멋지군요! 그 노래를 함께 들어 보도록 하죠.

Conversation 시험대비 기본평가

01 다음 빈칸에 들어갈 말로 적절하지 <u>않은</u> 것은?

A: Which sport do you like best?
B: _____

① I like tennis best.
② I love baseball.
③ I enjoy badminton very much.
④ My favorite sport is soccer.
⑤ I would like to play basketball.

02 다음 대화의 빈칸에 들어갈 말로 적절한 것은?

A: _____ do you want to visit Canada?
B: Because I want to see Niagara Falls.

① Why   ② When   ③ Which
④ Who   ⑤ What

[03~04] 다음 대화를 읽고, 물음에 답하시오.

Jack: Hi, Sumin. (A)[How's / What's] the book club going?
Sumin: It's fun. I read lots of (B)[interested / interesting] books.
Jack: (C)[Which / Why] book do you like best?
Sumin: I like *Charlotte's Web* best.

03 위 대화의 빈칸 (A)~(C)에 알맞은 말을 쓰시오.

(A) _____ (B) _____ (C) _____

04 위 대화의 내용과 일치하지 <u>않는</u> 것은?

① Sumin is a member of the book club.
② Sumin has fun in the book club.
③ Sumin read many interesting books.
④ Sumin loves *Charlotte's Web*.
⑤ Sumin's book club is *Charlotte's Web*.

서답형

01 다음 대화의 빈칸에 주어진 단어를 사용하여 대답을 완성하시오.

> A: Which sport do you like best?
> B: _____ (tennis, like)

➡ _____

[02~05] 다음 대화를 읽고, 물음에 답하시오.

> Amy: Jiho, _____ ⓐ
> Jiho: I'm going to Blue Sky's fan meeting with my friends.
> Amy: Wow, I'm also a big fan of the band.
> Jiho: Really? Which member do you like best, Amy?
> Amy: I like Lucy best. She sings really well.
> Jiho: I like the ____ⓑ____, Mike, best. He's fantastic! Do you want to join us?
> Amy: Sure, I'd love to. ⓒI can't wait!

02 위 대화의 빈칸 ⓐ에 들어갈 말로 어색한 것은?

① what are you going to do this Saturday?
② what are you planning to do this Saturday?
③ what are you supposed to do this Saturday?
④ what's your plan for this Saturday?
⑤ what are you doing now for this Saturday?

서답형

03 위 대화의 빈칸 ⓑ에 주어진 영영풀이에 해당하는 말을 쓰시오.

> a person who plays a drum or drums

➡ _____

04 위 대화의 밑줄 친 ⓒ와 바꾸어 쓸 수 있는 것은?

① I cannot go with you.
② I'm really looking forward to it.
③ I'm sorry, but I can't.
④ I'm afraid not.
⑤ I have no doubt.

05 위 대화를 읽고 대답할 수 <u>없는</u> 질문은?

① What are Jiho and Amy going to do at Blue Sky's fan meeting?
② Which member of Blue Sky does Jiho like best?
③ Which instrument does Mike play?
④ Which band is Amy a big fan of?
⑤ Who is Amy's favorite member of Blue Sky?

[06~07] 다음 대화를 읽고, 물음에 답하시오.

> B: Why do you have all those old clothes?
> G: I'm going to sell them at the flea market.
> B: Really? I have some old clothes, too.
> G: ⓐ그러면 이번 주 토요일에 나와 함께 팔면 어때?
> (then, join, why)
> B: Okay.

서답형

06 위 대화의 밑줄 친 우리말 ⓐ에 맞게 주어진 단어를 사용하여 영어로 쓰시오.

➡ _____

서답형

07 What is the boy going to bring to the flea market?

➡ _____

[08~09] 다음 대화를 읽고, 물음에 답하시오.

> Sujin: Tom, why do you have so many paper flowers?
> Tom: They're for my mom's birthday. (A)
> Sujin: They're so beautiful. (B)
> Tom: I made them. (C)
> Sujin: Wow, you're really good. (D)
> Tom: Thanks. I'm taking a paper folding class these days. (E)
> Sujin: They are going to be the perfect gift for your mom.
> Tom: I hope so, too.

서답형

08 위 대화의 (A)~(E) 중 주어진 문장이 들어가기에 가장 적절한 곳은?

> Where did you get them?

① (A) ② (B) ③ (C) ④ (D) ⑤ (E)

09 위 대화의 내용과 일치하지 않는 것은?

① Tom made many paper flowers for himself.
② Tom prepared paper flowers as his mom's birthday gift.
③ Tom brought some paper from his class to make paper flowers.
④ Tom learned how to make paper flowers in a paper folding class.
⑤ Sujin is sure that Tom's paper flowers will be the perfect gift for his mom.

[10~12] 다음 대화를 읽고, 물음에 답하시오.

> Mina: Good afternoon, friends. I'm Mina ⓐ<u>with</u> the school radio show. Today Mr. Smith, our English teacher, is here with us. Hi, Mr. Smith.
> Mr. Smith: Hello, everyone. I'm happy ⓑ<u>to be</u> here with you.
> Mina: Let's talk about music. Mr. Smith, what's your favorite band?
> Mr. Smith: ⓒ<u>Definite</u> The Beatles.
> Mina: Oh, I like them, too. ⓓ<u>Which</u> song do you like best?
> Mr. Smith: I like most of their songs, but I like *Hey Jude* best.
> Mina: Why do you like it?
> Mr. Smith: ⓔ<u>Because of</u> the song makes me feel better when I'm down.
> Mina: That's great! Let's listen to (A)the song.

서답형

10 위 대화의 ⓐ~ⓔ 중 어법상 어색한 것을 모두 찾아 바르게 고치시오.

➡ _____

서답형

11 위 대화의 밑줄 친 (A)가 가리키는 것을 찾아 쓰시오.

➡ _____

중요

12 위 대화를 읽고 대답할 수 없는 질문은?

① Who is the guest on the school radio show?
② What does Mr. Smith teach at school?
③ Which band does Mr. Smith like best?
④ Why does Mr. Smith love *Hey Jude*?
⑤ How does Mina feel when listening to *Hey Jude*?

⭐ 중요
01 다음 밑줄 친 우리말을 주어진 단어를 사용하여 영어로 쓰시오.

> **A:** <u>너는 어느 운동을 가장 좋아하니?</u>
> (best, like)
> **B:** I like tennis best.

➡ _____

02 다음 대화의 밑줄 친 우리말을 영어로 쓰시오.

> **A:** Why do you want to visit Canada?
> **B:** <u>왜냐하면 나는 나의 친구를 방문하고 싶기 때문이야.</u>

➡ _____

03 다음 대화를 읽고 대화의 내용과 일치하도록 빈칸을 완성하시오.

> **Mina:** Good afternoon, friends. I'm Mina with the school radio show. Today Mr. Smith, our English teacher, is here with us. Hi, Mr. Smith.
> **Mr. Smith:** Hello, everyone. I'm happy to be here with you.
> **Mina:** Let's talk about music. Mr. Smith, what's your favorite band?
> **Mr. Smith:** Definitely The Beatles.
> **Mina:** Oh, I like them, too. Which song do you like best?
> **Mr. Smith:** I like most of their songs, but I like *Hey Jude* best.
> **Mina:** Why do you like it?
> **Mr. Smith:** Because the song makes me feel better when I'm down.
> **Mina:** That's great! Let's listen to the song.

> Did you hear the school radio show today? There was a special guest on the show. He is (1)_____, our English teacher. Mina and Mr. Smith talked about (2)_____. Mr. Smith said that his favorite band is (3)_____. Among their songs, he liked (4)_____ best, because (5)_____. The song was beautiful. I liked it so much, too.

(1) _____ (2) _____ (3) _____
(4) _____ (5) _____

_____

[04~05] 다음 대화를 읽고, 물음에 답하시오.

> **Sujin:** Tom, why do you have so many paper flowers?
> **Tom:** They're for my mom's birthday.
> **Sujin:** They're so beautiful. Where did you get them?
> **Tom:** I made them.
> **Sujin:** Wow, you're really good.
> **Tom:** Thanks. (A)<u>나 요즘 종이접기 수업을 듣고 있어.</u>
> **Sujin:** They are going to be the perfect gift for your mom.
> **Tom:** I hope so, too.

04 Why did Tom make lots of paper flowers?

➡ _____

⭐ 중요
05 위 대화의 밑줄 친 우리말 (A)에 맞게 〈보기〉에 있는 단어를 모두 배열하시오.

> ┤ 보기 ├
> taking / these / I'm / folding / days /
> a / class / paper

➡ _____

Grammar

① 수동태

> • Tom **built** this house. [능동태] Tom은 이 집을 지었다.
> • This house **was built** by Tom. [수동태] 이 집은 Tom에 의해 지어졌다.

■ 수동태는 능동태의 목적어를 주어로 만들고 동사를 'be+p.p.' 형태로 만든 후, 능동태의 주어를 'by+목적격' 형태로 하여 '주어가 ~되다'라고 해석한다. 능동태 문장의 시제에 따라 수동태 시제를 결정한다.

- • Jane **cleans** the room every day. Jane은 매일 그 방을 청소한다.
- • The room **is cleaned** by Jane every day. 그 방은 Jane에 의해 매일 청소된다.

■ 4형식 문장의 수동태는 두 가지 형태를 갖는다. 직접목적어를 주어로 한 수동태에서는 간접목적어에 특정 전치사를 부여한다. 전치사 to를 쓰는 동사는 'give, tell, teach, show, bring' 등이고, 전치사 for를 쓰는 동사는 'buy, make, cook, get' 등이며, 전치사 of를 쓰는 동사는 'ask'가 있다.

- • English **is taught to** us by Ms. Kim. 영어는 Kim 선생님에 의해서 우리에게 가르쳐진다.
- • Pizza **was cooked for** her yesterday by my mom. 피자는 어제 그녀를 위해 나의 엄마에 의해 만들어졌다.

■ 5형식 문장의 목적격보어가 원형부정사인 경우, 수동태 문장에서는 to부정사로 만들어 준다. 그 외에는 모든 목적격보어를 그대로 쓸 수 있다.

- • He **is called** Smiley by us. 그는 우리에 의해 Smiley라고 불린다.
- • I **was made to do** the job by her. 나는 그녀에 의해 그 일을 하도록 강요받았다.

■ 조동사의 수동태는 '조동사+be+p.p.' 형태를 취한다.

- • A new supermarket **will be built** next year. 새로운 슈퍼마켓이 내년에 지어질 것이다.
- • The chairs **can be replaced** with other ones. 그 의자들은 다른 것들로 교체될 수 있다.

■ by 이외의 전치사를 사용하는 수동태에 유의한다.

- • I **am interested in** reading books. 나는 책 읽는 것에 흥미가 있다.
- • Cheese **is made from** milk. 치즈는 우유로 만들어진다.
- • Jason **was surprised at** the news. Jason은 뉴스에 놀랐다.

핵심 Check

1. 다음 우리말과 같도록 빈칸에 알맞은 말을 쓰시오.

(1) 지구 표면의 대부분이 물로 덮여 있다.

➡ Most of the earth's surface _____ _____ with water.

(2) 그는 나로부터 질문 하나를 받았다.

➡ He _____ _____ a question by me.

❷ If 조건절

> • **If** you watch this movie, you will love it. 네가 만약 이 영화를 본다면, 너는 그것을 좋아할 거야.
>
> • **If** I have time to do this, I will let you know. 내가 이걸 할 시간이 있다면, 너에게 알려 줄게.

- 조건의 부사절에서는 현재시제를 사용하여 미래를 나타내며 '만약 ~라면'이라고 해석한다.

  • **If** we go by bus, it will be comfortable. 우리가 버스를 타고 간다면, 편할 거야.

  • **If** you are hungry, I will make some sandwiches. 네가 배고프다면, 내가 샌드위치를 만들게.

- If절이 명사 역할을 하는 경우도 있다. 명사절 접속사 if와 부사절 접속사 if의 쓰임을 구별하자. 명사절 접속사 if의 경우 '~인지 아닌지'로 해석하며 미래를 나타낼 때에는 미래시제를 써야 한다.

  • **If** he has some rest, he will be much better. 그가 조금 쉰다면, 훨씬 더 좋아질 거야.

  • I wonder **if** you will come or not. 나는 당신이 올지 안 올지가 궁금합니다.

- If ~ not은 '만약 ~하지 않으면'의 의미인 Unless로 쓸 수 있다. unless 역시 조건절이므로 현재시제로 미래를 나타낸다.

  • **If** you **don't** hurry, you will be late for class. 서두르지 않으면, 수업에 늦을 거야.

  • **Unless** you hurry, you will be late for class. 서두르지 않으면, 수업에 늦을 거야.

핵심 Check

2. 다음 우리말과 같도록 빈칸에 알맞은 말을 쓰시오.

(1) 내가 일찍 도착한다면, 너에게 전화할게.

➡ If I _____ early, I _____ _____ you.

(2) 네가 그녀의 파티에 온다면, 그녀는 아주 행복할 거야.

➡ If you _____ to her party, she _____ _____ very happy.

(3) 나는 네가 교회에 갈 건지 알고 싶어.

➡ I want to know _____ you _____ _____ to church.

01 다음 문장에서 어법상 <u>어색한</u> 부분을 바르게 고쳐 쓰시오.

(1) Jimmy born in 2005 in Seoul.

_____ ➡ _____

(2) A letter was sent for her yesterday.

_____ ➡ _____

(3) If you will leave a message, I will give it to Kim.

_____ ➡ _____

(4) I don't know if he visits her this weekend.

_____ ➡ _____

02 주어진 동사를 어법에 맞게 빈칸에 쓰시오.

(1) If you _____ this magazine, I will lend it to you. (want)

(2) Many accidents _____ _____ by careless driving. (cause)

(3) You can _____ the difficult problem. (solve)

(4) I _____ _____ to the party, but I didn't go. (invite)

(5) If you don't hurry, you _____ _____ the train. (miss)

03 다음 우리말에 맞게 주어진 단어를 바르게 배열하시오. (필요하면 어형을 바꿀 것)

(1) 유리는 어떻게 만들어지나요?

(how / be / make / glass)

➡ _____

(2) 나는 이곳에 고용될 거야.

(be / I / here / will / employ)

➡ _____

(3) 네가 달리면, 내가 따라갈게.

(if / follow / you / I / run / will / you)

➡ _____

(4) 네가 약간의 음식을 가지고 올 건지 알려 줘.

(if / you / let / know / me / bring / some / food / will)

➡ _____

01 다음 우리말을 바르게 영작한 것은?

> 그 편지는 일주일 전에 너에게 부쳐졌다.

① The letter is sent you a week ago.
② The letter has been sent to you a week ago.
③ The letter sent to you a week ago.
④ The letter was sent to you a week ago.
⑤ The letter was sent for you a week ago.

02 다음 중 수동태로의 전환이 바르지 <u>않은</u> 것은?

① Did somebody clean the restroom?
　→ Was the restroom cleaned by somebody?
② Ted broke my camera.
　→ My camera was broken by Ted.
③ Jane made me so happy.
　→ I was made so happy by Jane.
④ My grandparents brought me up.
　→ I was brought up my grandparents.
⑤ He showed me some pictures.
　→ I was shown some pictures by him.

03 다음 중 밑줄 친 if의 쓰임이 <u>다른</u> 하나는?

① <u>If</u> anyone calls, I will tell you.
② I will be sad <u>if</u> you leave.
③ I wonder <u>if</u> she liked it or not.
④ He will stay longer <u>if</u> she wants him to.
⑤ <u>If</u> it rains tomorrow, we won't go out.

서답형
04 주어진 단어를 이용하여 다음 우리말을 영어로 쓰시오.

> 네가 그 파티에 초대받는다면 너는 그곳에 갈 거니?
> (invite, will, go)

➡ _____

05 다음 중 어법상 옳은 것은?

① The glass is filled by milk.
② If I make some mistakes, can you help me?
③ I wonder if you meet him tomorrow.
④ He was made do the homework first.
⑤ Some cookies were made to me by Julia.

06 다음 중 어법상 바르지 <u>않은</u> 것은?

> ①<u>Will</u> you call ②<u>me</u> ③<u>if</u> I ④<u>will give</u> you ⑤<u>my phone number</u>?

①　　　②　　　③　　　④　　　⑤

07 다음 빈칸에 공통으로 들어갈 말로 가장 적절한 것은?

> • The mountain is covered _____ snow.
> • She was pleased _____ the news.

① by　　　② at　　　③ with
④ in　　　⑤ from

서답형

08 주어진 어구를 바르게 배열하여 다음 우리말을 영어로 쓰시오.

> 우리가 그 길을 못 찾으면 무엇을 해야 할지 모르겠어.
> (don't know / will / we / I / what / we / don't find / the way / do / if)

➡ _____

09 다음 두 문장이 같은 의미가 되도록 빈칸에 알맞은 말을 고르면?

> He saw the child playing the violin alone.
> = The child _____ the violin alone by him.

① was seen play   ② is seen to play
③ was seen playing   ④ saw playing
⑤ is seen playing

서답형

10 다음 중 if의 쓰임이 같은 것끼리 바르게 묶으시오.

> ⓐ He will come here if he gets up early tomorrow.
> ⓑ If songs are chosen, we can practice together.
> ⓒ I wonder if there is some food to eat.
> ⓓ If you need money, I will lend you some.
> ⓔ She couldn't tell if he said the truth.

➡ _____

서답형

11 다음 두 문장의 의미가 같도록 빈칸에 알맞은 말을 쓰시오.

> If you don't do your best, you will not pass the test.
> = _____ you do your best, you will not pass the test.

12 다음 중 어법상 바르지 않은 것은?

① If you use my computer again, I will punish you.
② Tom was made to fix the radio.
③ Did the building designed by a famous architect?
④ I'm not sure if he wants me to teach him English.
⑤ A present is given to her by her friends.

중요

13 다음 중 빈칸에 들어갈 말이 다른 하나는?

① My mom was disappointed _____ me.
② Jason was satisfied _____ the test result.
③ His clothes are covered _____ dirt.
④ Jessy was worried _____ her dog.
⑤ I filled the bucket _____ various flowers.

서답형

14 주어진 단어를 이용하여 다음 문장을 수동태로 쓰시오.

> Nobody told me about the class meeting.
> (wasn't)

➡ _____

중요

15 다음 빈칸에 적절하지 않은 것은?

> _____ you arrive here, we will start to eat the food.

① If   ② After
③ As soon as   ④ When
⑤ Though

16 다음 밑줄 친 문장을 수동태로 바르게 전환한 것을 <u>모두</u> 고르시오.

> The CEO offered Tom the job, but he refused it.

① The job offered to Tom by the CEO,
② The job was offered to Tom by the CEO,
③ Tom was offered the CEO to the job,
④ Tom was offered the job by the CEO,
⑤ The job was offered for Tom by the CEO,

서답형

17 주어진 단어를 활용하여 다음 우리말을 영어로 쓰시오.

> 너에게 자전거 한 대가 주어진다면, 너는 무엇을 할 거니? (bike / give / to / do)

➡ _____

중요

18 다음 빈칸에 들어갈 말이 <u>다른</u> 하나는?

① Math is taught _____ us by Mr. Henderson.
② A book was given _____ me by John.
③ The ball was thrown _____ him by a boy.
④ A delicious meal was cooked _____ me yesterday.
⑤ Dolls were sold _____ a lot of children at the hospital.

19 다음 빈칸에 들어갈 말이 바르게 짝지어진 것은?

> A: Who took the picture?
> B: The picture _____ Harry.

① was taken to   ② was taken by
③ is taken to   ④ is taken by
⑤ was taken in

20 다음 중 어법상 바르지 <u>않은</u> 것은?

> I ①am worried ②about your health. If I ③make a doctor's appointment, ④do you ⑤go see the doctor?

①   ②   ③   ④   ⑤

서답형

21 주어진 단어를 주어로 하여 다음 물음에 답하시오.

> A: Can you tell me who invented Hangeul?
> B: Hangeul _____.

➡ _____

서답형

22 주어진 어구를 활용하여 다음 우리말을 영어로 쓰시오.

> 내가 당신을 직접 만나게 된다면, 당신에게 많은 질문을 할 거예요.
> (meet / in person / ask / many)

➡ _____

서답형

23 다음 주어진 문장과 같은 의미가 되도록 빈칸에 알맞은 말을 쓰시오.

> Your clothes won't get clean if you don't use soap.
> = If soap _____, your clothes _____.

➡ _____

서답형

24 다음 문장에서 틀린 부분을 찾아 바르게 고치시오.

> If it doesn't rain, the party will hold outside.

_____ ➡ _____

01 주어진 단어를 활용하여 다음 우리말을 영어로 쓰시오.

> 그 기계가 사람들에 의해 사용된다면, 그들은 행복할 거야. (use / be)

➡ _____

02 다음 대화의 빈칸에 알맞은 말을 쓰시오.

> **A:** Who wrote *Romeo and Juliet*?
> **B:** *Romeo and Juliet* _____ Shakespeare.

➡ _____

03 다음 문장을 주어진 단어로 시작하는 문장으로 다시 쓰시오.

> Jimmy's sister made him feel comfortable.

➡ Jimmy _____.

04 주어진 동사를 어법에 맞게 빈칸에 쓰시오.

(1) If you _____ _____ early, please wake me up. (get up)

(2) I'm not sure if Katherine _____ _____ a tree tomorrow. (plant)

(3) Amy _____ _____ by a bee yesterday. (sting)

05 다음 문장을 두 가지 형태의 수동태로 쓰시오.

> Somebody gave the police the important evidence.

➡ _____

➡ _____

06 두 개의 문장을 연결하여 자연스러운 하나의 문장으로 만드시오.

> • You need money.
> • You want those pictures.
> • You are busy now.

> • You can have them.
> • I will call you later.
> • I will lend you some.

➡ _____

➡ _____

➡ _____

07 주어진 문장을 수동태로 쓰시오.

> Liszt's music really moved me.

➡ _____

08 괄호 안에 주어진 단어를 활용하여 빈칸 ⓐ~ⓒ에 알맞은 말을 쓰시오.

A: What will you do if it rains tomorrow?
B: If ⓐ_____(rain) tomorrow, I ⓑ_____(take) my umbrella.
A: Who bought you the umbrella?
B: The umbrella ⓒ_____(be / me) by my dad.

09 주어진 단어를 어법에 맞도록 빈칸에 쓰시오.

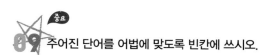

invent / surround / divide / surprise / build

- The electric light bulb _____ by Thomas Edison in 1879.
- I didn't expect Jane to come to the meeting yesterday, but she was there. I _____ to see her.
- An island _____ by water.
- The class was too large last semester, so it _____ into two sections.
- If construction costs aren't high, they _____ a new dormitory.

10 주어진 단어를 활용하여 다음 우리말을 영어로 쓰시오.

- 불이 난다면, 화재경보기가 울릴 거야. (there / a fire / the alarm)
- 내가 너를 도와주길 원한다면, 도와줄게. (want / to / help)
- 내일 몸이 좋지 않으면, 집에 머물 거야. (feel well / stay at)

➡ _____
➡ _____
➡ _____

11 다음 상황을 읽고 주어진 단어를 어법에 맞게 쓰시오.

Next week Mina is going to Paris.
She has a friend, Jimmy, who lives in Paris, but Jimmy is also going away – to New York. So they won't see each other in Paris.
If Jimmy (arrive) in Paris next week, they (see) each other.

➡ _____

12 다음 우리말에 맞도록 빈칸에 알맞은 말을 쓰시오.

- _____ you hurry, you _____ the bus.
  서두르지 않으면, 너는 버스를 놓칠 거야.
- If you win the prize, I _____.
  네가 그 상을 탄다면, 나는 매우 놀랄 거야.
- If the museum _____ many people, I _____ to another museum.
  내일 그 박물관이 많은 사람들로 붐빈다면, 나는 다른 박물관으로 갈 거야.

Reading

The Star of Stars

Do you have a favorite K-pop idol? Many students will answer, "Yes."

These students <u>often</u> show great love for their stars. <u>Some</u> scream
빈도부사(일반 동사 앞에 위치)　　　　　　　　　어떤 학생들은(부정대명사)

madly at concerts. <u>Others</u> wait hours <u>to take</u> pictures of their stars.
다른 어떤 학생들은(부정대명사)　to부정사의 부사적 용법(목적)

Some students <u>even</u> travel to another city <u>to see</u> their favorite stars.
심지어(부사)　　　　　　to부정사의 부사적 용법(목적)

Are idols a recent creation? <u>No way!</u> Did idols begin with The Beatles
절대 아니다!

<u>in the 1960's?</u> <u>They</u> <u>were loved</u> by <u>many</u>, but they were not the first.
1960년대의　=The Beatles　수동태　= many people

<u>How about</u> Elvis Presley in the 1950's? <u>Not</u> even close. To find the
How about+명사 ~?: ~는 어때?　　　　　　　　　Not 앞에 The answer is 생략

answer, <u>let's</u> take a time machine to a concert hall <u>in</u> Vienna <u>in</u> 1845.
let's+동사원형: ~하자　　　　　　　　　　전치사 in: 도시이름, 연도 앞에 사용

<u>All the</u> seats are filled. Unlike other concerts, the side of the piano
All the +복수명사: 모든 ~

<u>faces</u> the audience. <u>This way</u>, the audience can see the handsome
~을 마주본다　　　　이렇게 함으로써

185cm <u>pianist</u> better. He doesn't have any sheet music with him. He
piano에 접미사 -ist 붙인 직업 명사

begins <u>to play</u> from memory.
to부정사의 명사적 용법(begins의 목적어)

favorite 가장 좋아하는	
answer 대답하다	
often 종종	
scream 괴성을 지르다	
madly 미친 듯이, 마구	
concert 콘서트	
even 심지어	
travel 여행하다	
another 또 다른, 또 하나의	
idol 우상	
recent 최근의	
first 첫 번째의; 최초의 인물	
close 가까운	
take ~을 타다	
seat 좌석	
unlike ~와 달리	
audience 청중, 관객	
sheet music 악보	
from memory 기억을 더듬어	

확인문제

- 다음 문장이 본문의 내용과 일치하면 T, 일치하지 <u>않으면</u> F를 쓰시오.

1 Many students have their favorite idols. ☐

2 In order to see the concert, some students are willing to wait hours. ☐

3 There are some students who travel to another city to see their favorite idols. ☐

4 It is hard to say that idols were created recently. ☐

5 In 1845, audience could usually see the side of the piano at all concerts. ☐

He starts <u>slowly</u> by <u>softly</u> touching the keys. <u>All the people</u> hold
　　　　starts를 수식　touching을 수식　　　　　　All the + 복수명사: 모든
their breath <u>because</u> they don't want to miss a single note. He builds
　　　　　　 ~이기 때문에(접속사)
up speed, and his long fingers <u>press down on</u> many keys at once. <u>This</u>
　　　　　　　　　　　　　 ~을 누른다
<u>makes the music very powerful and rich.</u>
5형식: 주어(This)+makes+목적어(the music)+목적격 보어(very powerful and rich)

The audience pays attention to his every little body <u>movement</u>. His
　　　　　　　　　　　　　　　　　　　　 move의 명사형
long beautiful hair flies everywhere. It's <u>like</u> watching a piano and
　　　　　　　　　　　　　　　　 ~와 같은, ~와 비슷한(전치사)
ballet performance <u>at once</u>. Time flies and the concert ends. People
　　　　　　 동시에(= at the same time)
scream and throw flowers and pieces of clothing onto the stage. The
concert hall <u>goes wild</u>!
　　　　 go+형용사: ~하게 되다

Who was this <u>amazing</u> star? His name was Franz Liszt and he was
　　　　 능동의 의미이므로 현재분사 사용
born in 1811 in Hungary. He first started <u>playing</u> the piano when he
　　　　　　　　　　　　　　　　 목적어로 쓰인 동명사
was seven. Liszt later became <u>a great pianist, composer and teacher.</u>
　　　　　　　　　　　셋 이상의 명사의 나열의 경우 마지막 명사 앞에 한 번만 접속사 사용
But many people <u>think of</u> him as the first idol. Why don't you <u>give his</u>
　　　　 think of A as B: A를 B라고 생각하다　　　　　　　　　　그의 음악을 듣다
<u>music a listen</u>? If you like today's idols, you will love the original idol.
　　　　　　 만약 ~라면(조건을 나타내는 접속사)

---

hold one's breath 숨을 죽이다

note (음악) 음, 음표

build up 점점 높이다

key 건반

at once 한꺼번에, 동시에

powerful 강력한

pay attention to ~에 주의를 기울이다

little 작은

movement 움직임

like ~와 같은

performance 공연

throw ~을 던지다

go wild 열광하다

amazing 놀라운

become ~이 되다

think of A as B A를 B라고 여기다

listen 듣다; 듣기

original 원래의, 본래의

확인문제

● 다음 문장이 본문의 내용과 일치하면 T, 일치하지 <u>않으면</u> F를 쓰시오.

1 The pianist starts to play the piano slowly. ☐

2 Pressing down on many keys at once makes the music powerful. ☐

3 The pianist has short beautiful hair. ☐

4 The audience is satisfied with the concert. ☐

5 Franz Liszt was a Hungarian pianist who was born in 1811. ☐

6 Liszt paid attention to only composing music later in life. ☐

● 우리말을 참고하여 빈칸에 알맞은 말을 쓰시오.

1 Do you have _____ _____ K-pop _____? Many students _____ _____, "Yes."

2 These students _____ _____ great love _____ their stars.

3 Some _____ _____ _____ concerts.

4 _____ wait _____ _____ _____ pictures of their stars.

5 Some students _____ _____ _____ another city _____ _____ their favorite stars.

6 Are idols _____ _____ _____? No way!

7 _____ idols _____ The Beatles in the 1960's?

8 They _____ _____ _____ many, but they were not _____ _____.

9 _____ _____ Elvis Presley _____ the 1950's? Not even close.

10 _____ _____ the answer, _____ _____ a time machine _____ a concert hall _____ Vienna _____ 1845.

11 All the seats _____ _____.

12 _____ other concerts, _____ _____ of the piano _____ the audience.

13 This way, the audience _____ _____ the handsome 185cm pianist _____.

14 He doesn't have _____ _____ _____ with him.

15 He begins _____ _____ _____ _____.

16 He starts slowly _____ _____ _____ _____ _____.

1 여러분은 가장 좋아하는 K팝 아이돌이 있는가? 많은 학생들이 "그렇다."라고 답할 것이다.

2 이 학생들은 종종 자신들의 스타를 향해 큰 애정을 보인다.

3 어떤 학생들은 콘서트에서 미친 듯이 괴성을 지른다.

4 어떤 학생들은 스타의 사진을 찍기 위해 몇 시간을 기다린다.

5 어떤 학생들은 심지어 가장 좋아하는 스타를 보기 위해 다른 도시로 여행을 가기까지 한다.

6 아이돌이 최근의 창조물일까? 아니다!

7 아이돌은 1960년대의 The Beatles부터 시작됐을까?

8 그들은 많은 사람들에게 사랑받았지만, 최초는 아니다.

9 1950년대의 Elvis Presley는 어떤가? 완전히 헛짚었다.

10 답을 찾기 위해서 1845년에 빈에 있는 한 콘서트홀로 타임머신을 타고 가 보자.

11 모든 좌석이 꽉 차 있다.

12 다른 연주회와는 달리 피아노의 옆면이 청중을 향해 있다.

13 이렇게 함으로써, 청중은 잘생긴 185cm의 피아니스트를 더 잘 볼 수 있다.

14 그는 어떠한 악보도 가지고 있지 않다.

15 그는 기억으로 연주하기 시작한다.

16 그는 건반을 부드럽게 누르면서 천천히 시작한다.

17 All the people _____ _____ _____ _____ they don't want to miss _____ _____ _____.

18 He _____ _____ speed, and his long fingers _____ _____ _____ many keys _____ _____.

19 This _____ the music very _____ and _____.

20 The audience _____ _____ _____ his every little _____ _____.

21 His _____ _____ _____ _____ everywhere.

22 It's _____ _____ a piano and ballet _____ _____ _____.

23 Time _____ and the concert _____.

24 People scream and _____ _____ and pieces of clothing _____ _____ _____.

25 The concert hall _____ _____!

26 Who was _____ _____ _____?

27 His name _____ Franz Liszt and he _____ _____ _____ 1811 in Hungary.

28 He first started _____ _____ _____ _____ he was seven.

29 Liszt _____ _____ a great pianist, _____ and _____.

30 But many people _____ _____ him _____ the first idol.

31 _____ _____ _____ his music a listen?

32 If you _____ today's idols, you _____ _____ the _____ idol.

17 모든 사람들이 단 하나의 음도 놓치고 싶지 않아서 숨을 죽인다.

18 그는 속도를 점점 올리고, 그의 긴 손가락으로 많은 건반을 한꺼번에 누른다.

19 이것은 음악을 아주 힘 있고 풍성하게 만든다.

20 청중들은 그의 모든 작은 몸짓에 주의를 집중한다.

21 그의 길고 아름다운 머리카락이 사방에 날린다.

22 이것은 마치 피아노와 발레 공연을 동시에 보는 것 같다.

23 시간은 쏜살같이 흐르고 연주회가 끝난다.

24 사람들은 소리를 지르며 꽃과 옷을 무대로 던진다.

25 콘서트홀은 열광의 도가니가 된다!

26 이 놀라운 스타는 누구였을까?

27 그의 이름은 Franz Liszt였고 그는 1811년에 헝가리에서 태어났다.

28 그는 7살에 처음 피아노를 치기 시작했다.

29 Liszt는 나중에 훌륭한 피아니스트이며 작곡가이자 선생님이 되었다.

30 그러나 많은 사람들은 그를 첫 번째 아이돌이라고 생각한다.

31 그의 음악을 한번 들어보는 게 어떤가?

32 만약 당신이 요즘의 아이돌을 좋아한다면, 원래의 아이돌도 좋아할 것이다.

● 우리말을 참고하여 본문을 영작하시오.

1 여러분은 가장 좋아하는 K팝 아이돌이 있는가? 많은 학생들이 "그렇다."라고 답할 것이다.

➡ _____

2 이 학생들은 종종 자신들의 스타를 향해 큰 애정을 보인다.

➡ _____

3 어떤 학생들은 콘서트에서 미친 듯이 괴성을 지른다.

➡ _____

4 어떤 학생들은 스타의 사진을 찍기 위해 몇 시간을 기다린다.

➡ _____

5 어떤 학생들은 심지어 가장 좋아하는 스타를 보기 위해 다른 도시로 여행을 가기까지 한다.

➡ _____

6 아이돌이 최근의 창조물일까? 아니다!

➡ _____

7 아이돌은 1960년대의 The Beatles부터 시작됐을까?

➡ _____

8 그들은 많은 사람들에게 사랑받았지만, 최초는 아니다.

➡ _____

9 1950년대의 Elvis Presley는 어떤가? 완전히 헛짚었다.

➡ _____

10 답을 찾기 위해서 1845년에 빈에 있는 한 콘서트홀로 타임머신을 타고 가 보자.

➡ _____

11 모든 좌석이 꽉 차 있다.

➡ _____

12 다른 연주회와는 달리 피아노의 옆면이 청중을 향해 있다.

➡ _____

13 이렇게 함으로써, 청중은 잘생긴 185cm의 피아니스트를 더 잘 볼 수 있다.

➡ _____

14 그는 어떠한 악보도 가지고 있지 않다.

➡ _____

15 그는 기억으로 연주하기 시작한다.

➡ _____

16 그는 건반을 부드럽게 누르면서 천천히 시작한다.

➡ _____

17 모든 사람들이 단 하나의 음도 놓치고 싶지 않아서 숨을 죽인다.

➡ _____

18 그는 속도를 점점 올리고, 그의 긴 손가락으로 많은 건반을 한꺼번에 누른다.

➡ _____

19 이것은 음악을 아주 힘 있고 풍성하게 만든다.

➡ _____

20 청중들은 그의 모든 작은 몸짓에 주의를 집중한다.

➡ _____

21 그의 길고 아름다운 머리카락이 사방에 날린다.

➡ _____

22 이것은 마치 피아노와 발레 공연을 동시에 보는 것 같다.

➡ _____

23 시간은 쏜살같이 흐르고 연주회가 끝난다.

➡ _____

24 사람들은 소리를 지르며 꽃과 옷을 무대로 던진다.

➡ _____

25 콘서트홀은 열광의 도가니가 된다!

➡ _____

26 이 놀라운 스타는 누구였을까?

➡ _____

27 그의 이름은 Franz Liszt였고 그는 1811년에 헝가리에서 태어났다.

➡ _____

28 그는 7살에 처음 피아노를 치기 시작했다.

➡ _____

29 Liszt는 나중에 훌륭한 피아니스트이며 작곡가이자 선생님이 되었다.

➡ _____

30 그러나 많은 사람들은 그를 첫 번째 아이돌이라고 생각한다.

➡ _____

31 그의 음악을 한번 들어보는 게 어떤가?

➡ _____

32 만약 당신이 요즘의 아이돌을 좋아한다면, 원래의 아이돌도 좋아할 것이다.

➡ _____

[01~03] 다음 글을 읽고, 물음에 답하시오.

Do you have a favorite K-pop idol? Many students will answer, "Yes." These students often show great love for their stars. Some scream madly at concerts. Others wait hours to take pictures of their stars. Some students even travel to another city ⓐto see their favorite stars.

01 위 글의 내용과 일치하지 <u>않는</u> 것은?

① Many students have a favorite K-pop idol.

② The fans of K-pop idols show great love for their stars.

③ Some students go mad when they see K-pop idols.

④ Some students scream at concerts of their favorite stars.

⑤ There are students who wait hours to take pictures of their stars.

02 위 글의 밑줄 친 ⓐ와 쓰임이 같은 것은?

① She wants you <u>to do</u> your best.

② He bought a book <u>to read</u> on the train.

③ Mrs. Peterson went out <u>to see</u> what happened.

④ Sam forced me <u>to do</u> the work.

⑤ The tool enabled water <u>to flow</u> well.

서답형

03 주어진 단어를 어법에 맞게 쓰시오.

If students (ask) whether they have a favorite K-pop idol, they (answer) "Yes."

➡ _____

[04~07] 다음 글을 읽고, 물음에 답하시오.

Are idols a recent creation? No way! Did idols begin with The Beatles in the 1960's? They _____ⓐ_____ many, but they were not the first. ⓑHow about Elvis Presley in the 1950's? Not even close. To find the answer, let's take a time machine to a concert hall in Vienna in 1845.

서답형

04 다음 주어진 동사를 이용하여 빈칸 ⓐ를 완성하시오.

(love)

➡ _____

05 위 글의 밑줄 친 ⓑ의 의미로 가장 적절한 것은?

① Did Elvis Presley like The Beetles in the 1950's?

② Did Elvis Presley begin with The Beetles?

③ Did idols begin with Elvis Presley?

④ Did idols want to be like Elvis Presley?

⑤ Was Elvis Presley the most popular singer in the 1950's?

06 위 글에 이어질 내용으로 가장 적절한 것은?

① the origin of a time machine

② a story about the first idol in the world

③ how to build a concert hall in 1845

④ the reason why idols are a recent creation

⑤ how popular the Beatles and Elvis Presley were

서답형

07 위 글의 내용에 맞게 다음 질문에 완전한 문장으로 답하시오.

> Q: Where does the writer want to go with a time machine?

➡ _____

_____

[08~11] 다음 글을 읽고, 물음에 답하시오.

To find the answer, let's take a time machine to a concert hall in Vienna ⓐ 1845.

All the seats are filled. ① This way, the audience can see the handsome 185cm pianist better. ② He doesn't have any sheet music with him. ⓑ그는 기억으로 연주하기 시작한다.

He starts slowly by softly touching the keys. ③ All the people hold their breath because they don't want to miss a single note. ④ He builds up speed, and his long fingers press down on many keys at once. ⑤ This makes the music very powerful and rich.

중요

08 주어진 문장이 들어가기에 가장 적절한 곳은?

> Unlike other concerts, the side of the piano faces the audience.

①   ②   ③   ④   ⑤

09 위 글의 빈칸 ⓐ에 들어갈 말로 적절한 것은?

① on   ② by   ③ in
④ until   ⑤ to

서답형

10 주어진 단어를 활용하여 밑줄 친 우리말 ⓑ를 영어로 쓰시오.

> (begin / from)

➡ _____

11 위 글을 읽고 답할 수 없는 질문은?

① Where is the concert held?
② How tall is the pianist?
③ How does he start to play the piano?
④ What kind of answer does the writer want to find?
⑤ How does the pianist touch the piano keys?

[12~17] 다음 글을 읽고, 물음에 답하시오.

Are ⓐidols a recent creation? No way! Did idols begin with The Beatles in the 1960's? (A)Many people loved them, but they were not the first. How about Elvis Presley in the 1950's? Not even close. To find (B)the answer, let's take a time machine to a concert hall in Vienna in 1845.

(C)All the seats are taken. Unlike other concerts, the side of the piano faces ⓑthe audience. This way, the audience can see the handsome 185cm pianist better. He doesn't have any ⓒsheet music with him. He begins to play from memory.

He starts slowly by softly touching ⓓthe keys. All the people hold their ⓔbreath because they don't want to miss a single note. He builds up speed, and his long fingers press down on many keys at once. This makes the music very powerful and rich.

12 위 글의 밑줄 친 ⓐ~ⓔ의 영영풀이가 틀린 것은?

① ⓐ: people who are greatly admired or loved by many fans

② ⓑ: the group of people watching or listening to a concert

③ ⓒ: music that is printed on sheets of paper

④ ⓓ: specially shaped pieces of metal that you place in a lock

⑤ ⓔ: the air that you let out through your mouth

서답형

13 위 글의 밑줄 친 (A)를 수동태 문장으로 쓰시오.

➡ _____

14 위 글의 밑줄 친 (B)에 대한 질문으로 가장 적절한 것은?

① When was the first concert held?

② When did the first idol begin?

③ Who wants to be like The Beetles?

④ Who was the first pianist in the world?

⑤ Why weren't idols made recently?

서답형

15 다음 주어진 동사를 이용하여 밑줄 친 (C)와 같은 의미의 문장을 쓰시오.

(fill)

➡ _____

서답형

16 위 글의 내용에 맞도록 아래 질문에 답하시오.

Q: How is the concert different from others?
A: _____

➡ _____

17 위 글의 내용과 일치하지 <u>않는</u> 것은?

① 비틀즈는 1960년대에 활동하였다.

② 피아니스트는 악보 없이 연주했다.

③ 콘서트 연주는 처음부터 끝까지 부드럽게 이어졌다.

④ 청중들에게 피아니스트의 모습이 잘 보였다.

⑤ 청중들은 숨죽여 피아니스트의 연주를 감상하였다.

[18~22] 다음 글을 읽고, 물음에 답하시오.

All the seats are filled. Unlike other concerts, the side of the piano faces the audience. This way, the audience can see the handsome 185cm pianist better. ① He doesn't have any sheet music with him. He begins to play from memory. ②

He starts slowly by softly touching the keys. All the people hold their breath because they don't want to miss a single note. ③ This makes the music very powerful and rich.

The audience pays attention to his every little body movement. ④ His long beautiful hair flies everywhere. ⑤ It's like watching a piano and ballet performance at once. Time flies and the concert ends. People scream and throw flowers and pieces of clothing onto the stage. The concert hall goes ____ⓐ____ !

18 주어진 문장이 들어가기에 가장 알맞은 곳은?

He builds up speed, and his long fingers press down on many keys at once.

① ② ③ ④ ⑤

중요

19 분위기로 미루어 보아 빈칸 ⓐ에 가장 적절한 것은?

① bad ② wild ③ blind

④ deaf ⑤ angry

20 위 글에서 찾아볼 수 없는 것은?

① the concert hall filled with many people
② the handsome pianist playing from memory
③ the audience listening to the music with enthusiasm
④ the audience focusing on a ballet performance
⑤ the pianist who has long hair

21 위 글의 내용과 일치하지 <u>않는</u> 것은?

① The audience wants to hear every single note that the pianist plays.
② The keys are touched softly by the pianist at first.
③ The pianist doesn't have any sheet music.
④ The audience doesn't care about the body movement of the pianist.
⑤ People scream after the concert ends.

서답형
22 위 글의 내용에 맞도록 다음 빈칸에 알맞은 말을 쓰시오.

> Flowers _____ onto the stage by people.

➡ _____

[23~24] 다음 글을 읽고, 물음에 답하시오.

Do you have a favorite K-pop idol? Many students will answer, "Yes." (A)These students often show great love for their stars. Some scream madly at concerts. Others wait hours to take pictures of their stars. Some students even travel to another city to see their favorite stars.

Are idols a recent creation? No way! Did idols begin with The Beatles in the 1960's? They were loved by many, but they were not the first. How about Elvis Presley in the 1950's? Not even close. To find the answer, (B)let's take a time machine to a concert hall in Vienna in 1845.

23 위 글의 밑줄 친 문장 (A)를 수동태로 쓰시오.

➡ _____

_____

24 위 글의 글쓴이가 밑줄 친 (B)와 같이 말한 이유로 가장 적절한 것은?

① to ask some questions about music
② to find the first concert in the world
③ to find out who the first idol is
④ to meet the famous K-pop idol
⑤ to see the concert of Franz Liszt

[01~02] 다음 글을 읽고, 물음에 답하시오.

Do you have a favorite K-pop idol? Many students will answer, "Yes." These students often show great love for their stars. (A)몇몇은 콘서트에서 미친 듯이 괴성을 지른다. Others wait hours to take pictures of their stars. Some students even travel to another city to see their favorite stars.

01 다음 단어를 활용하여 밑줄 친 우리말 (A)를 영어로 쓰시오.

(scream / mad / concerts)

➡ _____

02 다음 주어진 어구를 바르게 배열하여 빈칸에 알맞은 말을 쓰시오.

Some students spend hours _____ _____.
(waiting / to take pictures of / their stars / for / them)

➡ _____

[03~05] 다음 글을 읽고, 물음에 답하시오.

Are idols a recent creation? (A)No way! Did idols begin with The Beatles in the 1960's? They were loved by many, but they were not ⓐthe first. How about Elvis Presley in the 1950's? Not even close. To find the answer, (B)타임 머신을 타고 가보자 to a concert hall in Vienna in 1845.

03 주어진 단어를 활용하여 밑줄 친 (A)와 같은 의미의 문장을 쓰시오.

Idols (not, create) recently.

➡ _____

04 위 글의 밑줄 친 ⓐ를 구체적으로 쓰시오.

➡ _____

05 위 글의 밑줄 친 우리말 (B)를 영어로 쓰시오.

➡ _____

[06~10] 다음 글을 읽고, 물음에 답하시오.

To find the answer, let's take a time machine to a concert hall in Vienna in 1845.

All the seats are filled. Unlike other concerts, the side of the piano faces the audience. (A)This way, the audience can see the handsome 185cm pianist better. He doesn't have any sheet music with him. He begins to play from memory.

He starts slowly by softly touching the keys. All the people hold their breath because they don't want to miss a single note. He builds up speed, and his long fingers press down on many keys at once. (B)이것은 그 음악을 매우 힘있고 풍성하게 만든다.

06 위 글의 밑줄 친 (A)가 의미하는 것을 우리말로 쓰시오.

➡ _____

07 위 글의 내용에 맞도록 대화의 빈칸에 알맞은 말을 쓰시오.

> A: Why are people holding their breath?
> B: It's because _____.

➡ _____

08 How does the pianist play without any sheet music?

➡ _____

09 (중요) 위 글의 밑줄 친 우리말 (B)를 영어로 쓰시오.

➡ _____

10 위 글의 내용에 맞도록 다음 기사의 빈칸에 알맞은 말을 쓰시오.

> The Star of Our Time
> Yesterday Franz Liszt performed his piano concert very successfully in _____.
> This concert was _____ from others. The side of the piano _____ the audience. They could _____ Liszt better this way. He didn't have any sheet music and _____ from _____. His music was so _____ and rich. When the concert ended, the concert hall went wild.

[11~14] 다음 글을 읽고, 물음에 답하시오.

All the seats are filled. Unlike other concerts, the side of the piano faces the audience. This way, the audience can see the handsome 185cm pianist ⓐbetter. He doesn't have any sheet music with him. He begins ⓑ to play from memory.

He starts slowly by softly ___(A)___ the keys. All the people hold their ⓒbreath because they don't want to miss a single note. He builds up speed, and his long fingers press down on many keys at once. This makes the music very powerful and rich.

The audience pays attention to his every little body ⓓmovements. His long beautiful hair flies everywhere. It's like ___(B)___ a piano and ballet performance at once. Time ⓔflies and the concert ends. People scream and throw flowers and pieces of clothing onto the stage. The concert hall ___(C)___ wild!

11 수동태를 사용하여 다음 물음에 완전한 문장으로 답하시오.

> What is thrown onto the stage?

➡ _____

_____

12 위 글의 ⓐ~ⓔ 중에서 어법상 바르지 않은 것의 기호를 쓰고 바르게 고치시오.

➡ _____

13 (중요) 주어진 단어를 어법에 맞게 빈칸 (A)~(C)에 쓰시오.

> go / touch / watch

(A)_____ (B)_____ (C)_____

14 위 글의 내용에 맞도록 다음 대화의 빈칸에 들어갈 말을 쓰시오.

> A: Where is the concert held?
> B: It _____.
> A: How does the music sound?
> B: It _____.

Real Life Talk - Step 2

A: Which singer do you like best?
　　= Who's your favorite singer?

B: I like John Lennon best.

A: Why do you like him?
　　　　　　　John Lennon을 가리킨다.

B: Because he is a great singer.
　　Because+주어+동사

A: Which song do you like best?
　　　　　　　　　　= most

B: I like *Imagine* best. It cheers me up.

구문해설 ・cheer up: 기운 나게 하다

해석

A: 어느 가수를 가장 좋아하니?
B: 나는 John Lennon을 가장 좋아해.
A: 왜 그를 좋아해?
B: 왜냐하면 그는 훌륭한 가수이기 때문이야.
A: 너는 어느 곡을 가장 좋아하니?
B: 나는 Imagine을 가장 좋아해. 그것은 내게 힘을 북돋아 줘.

Think and Write

Dear Sandra,

Hello, my name is Jina and I'm a big fan of you. I watched all of your movies
　　　　　　　　　　　　　　당신의 열렬한 팬
and I love "Into the Sky" best. I think that your acting is so real. How do you
　　　　　　　　　　　　　　　　　명사절 접속사 that
prepare for your roles? If I meet you in person, I will ask you many more
~를 준비하다　　　　　　　조건의 부사절에서 현재시제가 미래를 표현
questions. I hope to see you soon.
　　　　　　hope의 목적어

　　　　　　　　　　　　　　　　　　　　　　　　Love, Jina

구문해설 ・a big fan: 열렬한 팬　・acting: 연기　・real: 진짜의　・prepare: 준비하다　・role: 배역

・in person: 직접　・soon: 곧

Sandra 씨에게,

안녕하세요, 제 이름은 Jina이고 저는 당신의 열렬한 팬이에요. 저는 당신이 출연한 모든 영화를 다 봤고요 "Into the Sky"를 가장 좋아해요. 저는 당신의 연기가 매우 진정성 있다고 생각해요. 당신이 맡은 역할을 어떻게 준비하나요? 제가 당신을 직접 만나게 된다면, 저는 당신에게 더 많은 질문을 할 거예요. 당신을 곧 만나길 바랍니다.
사랑을 담아, Jina

Read and Write

The Star of Our Time
　　　　　　시대

Yesterday Franz Liszt performed his piano concert very successfully in
　　　　　　　　　　　　　　　　　　　　　　　　　범위가 넓은 장소 앞에서 쓰는 전치사
Vienna. This concert was different from others. The side of the piano faced the
　　　　　　　　　　~와는 달랐다　　　= other concerts
audience. They could see Liszt better this way. He didn't have any sheet music
　　　　　　　　　　　　　well의 비교급
and played from memory. His music was so powerful and rich. When the
　　　　　　　　　　　　　　　　　　　　　매우　　　　　　　　~할 때
concert ended, the concert hall went wild.

구문해설 ・perform: 공연하다　・successfully: 성공적으로　・others: 다른 것들　・face: ~을 마주보다

・better: 더 잘　・go wild: 열광하다

우리 시대의 스타
어제 Franz Liszt가 Vienna에서 매우 성공적으로 피아노 연주회를 하였습니다. 이 콘서트는 다른 콘서트들과 달랐습니다. 피아노의 측면이 청중을 향해 있었습니다. 청중들은 이런 식으로 Liszt를 더 잘 볼 수 있었습니다. 그는 어떠한 악보도 가지고 있지 않았고 기억으로 연주했습니다. 그의 음악은 매우 힘 있고 풍성했습니다. 콘서트가 끝날 때, 콘서트홀은 열광의 도가니가 되었습니다.

영역별 핵심문제

01 다음 〈보기〉의 주어진 단어와 관계가 <u>다른</u> 것은?

┌─ 보기 ─┐
recent – recently

① mad – madly
② original – originally
③ definite – definitely
④ careful – carefully
⑤ friend – friendly

02 다음 영영풀이에 해당하는 단어를 쓰시오.

your name as you usually write it, for example at the end of a letter

➡ _____

03 다음 중 밑줄 친 부분의 뜻풀이가 바르지 <u>않은</u> 것은?

① My parents are <u>madly</u> in love with each other. 열렬히
② <u>Unlike</u> his father, he is not good at sports. 싫어하다
③ I need the most <u>recent</u> information. 최신의
④ It's not my <u>original</u> plan to do. 본래의
⑤ One of the biggest mysteries is about the <u>creation</u> of life. 창조

04 다음 문장의 빈칸에 들어갈 말을 〈보기〉에서 골라 쓰시오. (필요하면 어형을 바꿀 것)

┌─ 보기 ─┐
sheet music / go wild / in person

(1) Only ten pieces of _____ _____ existed.
(2) When the singer came on the stage, the fans _____ _____.
(3) You need to bring your letter _____ _____.

05 다음 주어진 문장의 밑줄 친 단어와 같은 의미로 쓰인 것은?

They don't want to <u>miss</u> a single note.

① He completely <u>missed</u> the joke.
② I don't know why she didn't <u>miss</u> her mother so much.
③ What did you <u>miss</u> most when you were in Canada?
④ He must have <u>missed</u> a chance to go abroad.
⑤ After my English teacher left, many students <u>missed</u> her.

06 다음 대화의 밑줄 친 우리말을 영어로 쓰시오. (4 단어)

A: Which song do you like best?
B: I like *Imagine* best.
<u>그것은 내게 힘을 북돋아 줘.</u>

➡ _____

Conversation

07 다음 대화의 밑줄 친 우리말을 영어로 쓰시오.

> Jack: 너는 어느 책을 가장 좋아하니?
> Sumin: I like *Charlotte's Web* best.

➡ _____

[08~09] 다음 대화를 읽고, 물음에 답하시오.

> Amy: Jiho, what are you going to do this Saturday?
> Jiho: I'm going to Blue Sky's fan meeting with my friends. (A)
> Amy: Wow, I'm also a big fan of the band. (B)
> Jiho: Really? Which member do you like best, Amy? (C)
> Amy: I like Lucy best. She sings really well. (D)
> Jiho: I like the drummer, Mike, best. He's fantastic! (E)
> Amy: Sure, I'd love to. I can't wait!

08 위 대화의 (A)~(E) 중 주어진 문장이 들어가기에 적절한 곳은?

> Do you want to join us?

① (A)   ② (B)   ③ (C)   ④ (D)   ⑤ (E)

09 Which instrument does Mike play in Blue Sky band?

➡ _____

[10~11] 다음 대화를 읽고, 물음에 답하시오.

> B: Why do you have all those old clothes?
> G: I'm going to sell them at the ___(A)___.
> B: Really? I have some old clothes, too.
> G: Then why don't you join me this Saturday?
> B: Okay.

10 위 대화의 빈칸 (A)에 '벼룩시장'을 의미하는 말을 영어로 쓰시오.

➡ _____

11 What are they going to do this Saturday together?

➡ _____
_____

[12~13] 다음 대화를 읽고, 물음에 답하시오.

> Mina: Good afternoon, friends. I'm Mina with the school radio show. Today Mr. Smith, our English teacher, is here with us. Hi, Mr. Smith.
> Mr. Smith: Hello, everyone. I'm happy to be here with you.
> Mina: Let's talk about music. Mr. Smith, what's your favorite band?
> Mr. Smith: Definitely The Beatles.
> Mina: Oh, I like them, too. Which song do you like best?
> Mr. Smith: I like most of their songs, but I like *Hey Jude* best.
> Mina: Why do you like it?
> Mr. Smith: Because the song makes me feel better when I'm (A)down.
> Mina: That's great! Let's listen to the song.

12 위 대화의 밑줄 친 (A)와 바꾸어 쓸 수 없는 것은?

① depressed   ② gloomy
③ satisfied   ④ discouraged
⑤ blue

13 위 대화의 내용과 일치하지 않는 것은?

① Mr. Smith is a guest on the school radio show.
② Mr. Smith likes The Beatles best.
③ Mina likes most of The Beatles' songs.
④ They are going to listen to *Hey Jude*.
⑤ *Hey Jude* makes Mr. Smith feel better when he feels down.

14 다음 빈칸에 들어갈 말로 알맞지 <u>않은</u> 것을 <u>모두</u> 고르시오.

> _____ you come back, I won't leave here.

① Unless   ② If   ③ That
④ Until   ⑤ For

15 다음 중 어법상 옳지 <u>않은</u> 것은?

① If you like today's idols, you will love the original idol.
② My camera was disappeared from my classroom.
③ Her father has been told about the work for three hours.
④ The music is played by the most famous pianist.
⑤ I will be a doctor when I grow up.

16 다음 문장의 빈칸에 들어갈 말로 가장 적절한 것은?

> _____ late this evening, I won't wait for you.

① Because you were ② If you are
③ If you will be   ④ When you will be
⑤ Though you are

17 다음 주어진 동사를 어법에 맞게 쓰시오.

> We (play) football yesterday. The match (cancel).

➡ _____

18 다음 중 수동태로의 전환이 바르지 <u>않은</u> 것은?

① A loud noise woke us up.
→ We were woken up by a loud noise.
② How do people learn languages?
→ How are languages learned by people?
③ Somebody recorded our conversation.
→ Our conversation is recorded by somebody.
④ We must do something before it's too late.
→ Something must be done before it's too late.
⑤ I will give you plenty of time to decide.
→ You will be given plenty of time to decide.

19 다음 우리말을 영어로 바르게 옮긴 것은?

> 내 차가 고장 나면, 나는 그것을 수리할 거야.

① If my car broke, I repair it.
② If my car was broken, I will repair it.
③ If my car will be broken, I will repair it.
④ If my car is broken, I will repair it.
⑤ If my car break, I will repair it.

20 다음 문장에서 어법상 옳지 <u>않은</u> 것은?

> Nothing ①<u>has been said</u> ②<u>about</u> the incident ③<u>since</u> it ④<u>was happened</u> ⑤<u>last year</u>.

①   ②   ③   ④   ⑤

21 다음 문장과 같은 의미의 문장을 주어진 어구를 주어로 하여 쓰시오.

> If you take care of your sister, I will be really relieved.
> = If your sister _____, I will be really relieved.

➡ _____

22 다음 중 밑줄 친 부분의 쓰임이 <u>다른</u> 하나는?

① <u>If</u> it is sunny tomorrow, will you go out with me?
② I will go there <u>if</u> you let me go there.
③ I wonder <u>if</u> he is going to join us.
④ You will look good <u>if</u> you wear glasses.
⑤ <u>If</u> you solve this problem, I will admit that you are a genius.

23 다음 우리말을 영어로 <u>잘못</u> 옮긴 것은?

① 그가 너에게 그 사진을 보여주었니?
  → Was the picture shown to you by him?
② 내일 널 만나면, 그걸 줄게.
  → If I see you tomorrow, I will give it to you.
③ 그녀가 그에게 시계 하나를 사 줬어.
  → A watch was bought for him by her.
④ BTS는 아이돌 그룹으로 알려져 있다.
  → BTS is known to an idol group.
⑤ 그는 나로부터 몇 가지 질문을 받았다.
  → He was asked some questions by me.

24 다음 문장을 수동태로 전환하시오.

> My mom didn't allow me to go to the park alone.

➡ _____

Reading

[25~27] 다음 글을 읽고, 물음에 답하시오.

Do you have a favorite K-pop idol? Many students will answer, "Yes." These students often show great love for their stars. Some scream madly at concerts. ___(A)___ wait hours to take pictures of their stars. Some students ⓐeven travel to ___(B)___ city to see their favorite stars.

25 위 글의 내용과 일치하지 <u>않는</u> 것은?

① 많은 학생들이 K-pop 아이돌을 좋아한다.
② 스타를 향한 사랑을 표현하는 방법이 학생들마다 다양하다.
③ 어떤 학생은 콘서트에서 스타를 향해 비명을 지르기도 한다.
④ 콘서트에 입장하기 위해 몇 시간을 기다리는 학생들도 있다.
⑤ 어떤 학생들은 스타를 보기 위해 다른 도시로 여행을 한다.

26 위 글의 밑줄 친 ⓐ와 의미가 같은 것은?

① You need an <u>even</u> surface to work on.
② She spoke in a steady, <u>even</u> voice.
③ You know <u>even</u> less about it than I do.
④ It is unattractive and <u>even</u> ugly.
⑤ That was an <u>even</u> decision.

27 위 글의 빈칸 (A)와 (B)에 들어갈 말로 바르게 짝지어진 것은?

① Some – other
② Another – another
③ Others – the other
④ Others – other
⑤ Others – another

[28~29] 다음 글을 읽고, 물음에 답하시오.

Are idols a recent creation? No way! Did idols begin with The Beatles in the 1960's? They were loved by many, but they were not the first. How about Elvis Presley in the 1950's? Not even close. ⓐTo find the answer, let's take a time machine to a concert hall in Vienna in 1845.

28 위 글의 내용과 일치하는 것은?

① Idols were made lately.
② The Beatles were the first idol in the world.
③ Many people loved The Beatles.
④ Elvis Presley liked The Beatles.
⑤ Idols in the 1960's were very popular.

[30~32] 다음 글을 읽고, 물음에 답하시오.

All the seats are filled. Unlike other concerts, the side of the piano faces the audience. This way, the audience can see the handsome 185cm pianist better. He doesn't have any sheet music with him. He begins to play from memory.

He starts slowly by softly touching the keys. All the people hold their breath because they don't want to miss a single note. He builds up speed, and his long fingers press down on many keys at once. ⓐThis makes the music very powerful and rich.

The audience pays attention to his every little body movement. His long beautiful hair flies everywhere. It's like watching a piano and ballet performance ___ⓑ___ . Time flies and the concert ends. People scream and throw flowers and pieces of clothing onto the stage. The concert hall goes wild!

30 위 글의 밑줄 친 ⓐ가 의미하는 것을 우리말로 쓰시오.

➡ _____

31 위 글의 빈칸 ⓑ에 들어갈 알맞은 말을 위 글에서 찾아 쓰시오.

➡ _____

29 위 글의 밑줄 친 ⓐ와 쓰임이 같은 것은?

① There are many problems to solve.
② He studied hard to become a great teacher.
③ Jason hoped to meet her again.
④ She allowed me to go out with him.
⑤ Karen tried to help her friends.

32 위 글을 읽고 답할 수 없는 질문은?

① How is the concert different from others?
② How tall is the pianist?
③ How does the pianist start to play?
④ How does the pianist move his body?
⑤ Why do people scream?

01 다음 문장의 빈칸에 공통으로 들어갈 말로 적절한 것은?

- The government is going to _____ the same risk.
- There are no eyebrows on the _____ of *Mona Lisa*.
- Why the long _____?

① miss   ② scream   ③ face
④ breath   ⑤ note

02 다음 대화의 밑줄 친 부분을 주어진 단어를 이용하여 다시 쓰시오.

A: Which sport do you like?
B: I like tennis very much. (fond, very)

➡ _____

03 다음 문장의 빈칸에 들어갈 말을 〈보기〉에서 골라 쓰시오.

— 보기 —
paper folding / at once / pay attention to / from memory

(1) You should _____ the teacher in class.
(2) I learned how to make a paper flower in _____ class.
(3) He began to play _____ on the stage.

04 다음 우리말을 주어진 단어를 활용하여 영어로 쓰시오.

(1) 나는 벼룩시장에서 그 신발을 샀다. (flea)
➡ _____
(2) 마지막 주자는 속도를 높이기 시작했다. (build, runner)
➡ _____
(3) 운전자는 브레이크를 밟았다. (pressed, brake, on)
➡ _____

[05~06] 다음 대화를 읽고, 물음에 답하시오.

Mina: Good afternoon, friends. I'm Mina with the school radio show. Today Mr. Smith, our English teacher, is here with us. Hi, Mr. Smith. (A)
Mr. Smith: Hello, everyone. I'm happy to be here with you. (B)
Mina: Let's talk about music. Mr. Smith, what's your favorite band?
Mr. Smith: Definitely The Beatles. (C)
Mina: Oh, I like them, too. (D)
Mr. Smith: I like most of their songs, but I like *Hey Jude* best. (E)
Mina: Why do you like it?
Mr. Smith: Because the song makes me feel better when I'm down.
Mina: That's great! _____ ⓐ

05 위 대화의 (A)~(E) 중 주어진 문장이 들어가기에 가장 적절한 곳은?

Which song do you like best?

① (A)   ② (B)   ③ (C)   ④ (D)   ⑤ (E)

06 위 대화의 빈칸 ⓐ에 들어갈 말로 나머지와 의미가 <u>다른</u> 것은?

① Let's listen to the song.
② How about listening to the song?
③ Why don't we listen to the song?
④ What about listening to the song?
⑤ Why did you listen to the song?

07 다음 대화의 밑줄 친 우리말 (A)를 주어진 단어를 이용하여 영어로 쓰시오.

> **A:** (A)너는 어떤 과일을 가장 좋아하니? (best, which)
>
> **B:** I like apples best.

➡ _____

08 다음 대화가 자연스럽게 이어지도록 순서대로 배열하시오.

> (A) I like Lucy best. She sings really well.
> (B) Wow, I'm also a big fan of the band.
> (C) What are you going to do this Saturday?
> (D) Really? Which member do you like best, Amy?
> (E) I'm going to Blue Sky's fan meeting with my friends.

➡ _____

[09~10] Read the dialogue and answer the questions.

> Jack: Hi, Sumin. How's the book club going?
> Sumin: It's fun. I read lots of interesting books.
> Jack: Which book do you like best?
> Sumin: I like *Charlotte's Web* best.

09 What did Sumin think about her book club?

➡ _____

10 What is Sumin's favorite book?

➡ _____

11 다음 중 어법상 바른 것은?

① The house was painted by he.
② By whom did the bridge constructed?
③ The project can't be finished on time.
④ Karen is locking up in the room.
⑤ My decision will not change by anything.

12 주어진 단어를 어법에 맞게 각각 쓰시오.

> (disappoint)
> If you give up, you _____ me.
> = If you give up, I _____ you.

➡ _____

13 다음 중 어법상 바르지 <u>않은</u> 것은?

> We ①are scheduled ②to go on③a field trip. But if it ④will rain on the day, we ⑤will change the plan.

①   ②   ③   ④   ⑤

14 주어진 단어를 활용하여 다음 우리말을 영어로 쓰시오.

> 눈이 오면 도로가 폐쇄될 거야. (close)

➡ _____

15 다음 중 어법상 바른 문장의 개수는?

> ⓐ Emma can't close the window. It is stuck.
> ⓑ Could you give me directions? I lost.
> ⓒ I will fix your bike if I have a screwdriver.
> ⓓ I love my wife. I am married a wonderful woman.
> ⓔ King Sejong was born in 1397.

① 1개   ② 2개   ③ 3개
④ 4개   ⑤ 5개

16 다음 중 밑줄 친 부분이 어법상 옳은 것은?

① Tim was made <u>clean</u> the window.
② I <u>called</u> Puppy by my dad.
③ <u>Did</u> the lights turned off?
④ Is the book <u>borrowed</u> from the library?
⑤ If they <u>will throw</u> a party, will you go there?

17 주어진 단어를 이용하여 다음 빈칸에 알맞은 말을 쓰시오.

> block / call

A: The water won't go down the drain. The drain _____ with food.
B: Don't worry. I _____ a plumber.

[18~20] 다음 글을 읽고, 물음에 답하시오.

> To find the answer, let's take a time machine to a concert hall in Vienna in 1845.
> All the seats are filled. ⓐUnlike other concerts, the side of the piano faces the audience. This way, the audience can see the handsome 185cm pianist better. He doesn't have any sheet music with him. He begins to play ⓑfrom memory.
> He starts slowly by softly touching the keys. All the people ⓒhold their breath because they ⓓwant to miss a single note. He ⓔbuilds up speed, and his long fingers press down on many keys at once. This (A)makes the music very powerful and rich.

18 위 글의 ⓐ~ⓔ 중 글의 흐름상 어색한 것은?

① ⓐ   ② ⓑ   ③ ⓒ   ④ ⓓ   ⑤ ⓔ

19 위 글의 내용과 일치하지 <u>않는</u> 것은?

① The concert is held in Vienna.
② The pianist is tall and handsome.
③ The pianist memorizes what he has to play.
④ The pianist starts to play fast.
⑤ The performance is getting faster.

20 위 글의 밑줄 친 (A)와 쓰임이 같은 것은?

① He <u>made</u> it by himself.
② The computer <u>makes</u> our work easy.
③ She <u>makes</u> me delicious cookies all the time.
④ My mom <u>makes</u> her own clothes.
⑤ I wanted to <u>make</u> a good impression on you.

[21~24] 다음 글을 읽고, 물음에 답하시오.

All the seats ⓐare filled. Unlike other concerts, the side of the piano faces the audience. This way, the audience can see the handsome 185cm pianist better. He doesn't have ⓑany sheet music with him. He begins to play from memory.

He starts ⓒslowly by softly touching the keys. All the people hold their ⓓbreathe because they don't want to miss a single note. He ⓔbuilds up speed, and his long fingers press down on many keys at once. This makes the music very powerful and rich.

(A)청중들은 그의 모든 작은 몸짓에 주의를 집중한다. His long beautiful hair flies everywhere. It's like watching a piano and ballet performance at once. Time flies and the concert ends. People scream and throw flowers and pieces of clothing onto the stage. The concert hall goes wild!

21 위 글의 밑줄 친 ⓐ~ⓔ 중 바르지 <u>않은</u> 것은?

① ⓐ   ② ⓑ   ③ ⓒ   ④ ⓓ   ⑤ ⓔ

22 주어진 단어를 써서 밑줄 친 우리말 (A)를 영어로 쓰시오.

pay, every, little, movement

➡ _____

_____

23 다음을 읽고 해당하는 단어를 위 글에서 찾아 쓰시오.

This word is used when someone entertains an audience by doing something such as singing, dancing, or playing a musical instrument.

➡ _____

24 위 글의 내용과 일치하는 것은?

① The side of the piano usually faces the audience in the concerts.
② The pianist tries hard to see the sheet music.
③ The pianist presses lots of keys at one time.
④ The audience feels bored with the concerts.
⑤ The concert shows a piano performance with a ballet show.

25 다음 밑줄 친 (A)를 주어진 말로 시작하여 문장을 완성하시오.

The Star of Our Time
 Yesterday Franz Liszt performed his piano concert very successfully in Vienna. (A)This concert was different from others. The side of the piano faced the audience. They could see Liszt better this way. He didn't have any sheet music and played from memory. His music was so powerful and rich. When the concert ended, the concert hall went wild.

(A) Unlike _____

_____.

[01~03] 다음 대화를 읽고, 물음에 답하시오.

> Mina: Good afternoon, friends. I'm Mina with the school radio show. Today Mr. Smith, our English teacher, is here with us. Hi, Mr. Smith.
>
> Mr. Smith: Hello, everyone. I'm happy to be here with you.
>
> Mina: Let's talk about music. Mr. Smith, what's your favorite band?
>
> Mr. Smith: ___(A)___ The Beatles.
>
> Mina: Oh, I like them, too. (B)어느 노래를 가장 좋아하시나요? (which)
>
> Mr. Smith: I like most of their songs, but I like *Hey Jude* best.
>
> Mina: Why do you like it?
>
> Mr. Smith: Because the song makes me feel better when I'm down.
>
> Mina: That's great! Let's listen to the song.

01 위 대화의 빈칸 (A)에 다음 영영풀이에 해당하는 단어를 쓰시오. (D로 시작할 것)

> a way of emphasizing that something is true and that there is no doubt about it

➡ _____

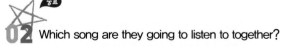

02 Which song are they going to listen to together?

➡ _____

03 위 대화의 우리말 (B)를 주어진 단어를 사용하여 영어로 쓰시오.

➡ _____

04 다음 문장을 수동태로 각각 쓰시오.

> • She made some mistakes.
> • My friend made me lots of cookies.
> • Jason always makes me laugh.

➡ _____

_____

_____

05 다음 괄호 안에 주어진 동사를 어법에 맞게 쓰시오.

> A: I think I left my textbook at your house. Have you seen it?
> B: No, but if I (find) it, I (tell) you.

➡ _____

06 괄호 안에 주어진 어휘를 이용하여 어법에 맞게 쓰시오.

> A: Do you have time to go to a movie?
> B: I don't know yet if there will be homework to do. If I (not / have / any homework / do), I (go / to) with you.

➡ _____

07 다음 우리말 뜻에 맞도록 주어진 단어를 이용하여 빈칸을 채우시오.

> • If _____, _____ an apple pie this afternoon. (enough, bake) (내가 충분한 사과를 가지고 있다면 나는 오늘 오후에 사과파이를 구울 거야.)
> • Vietnam _____ in Southeast Asia. (locate) (베트남은 동남아시아에 위치해 있다.)

08 다음 두 문장이 같은 의미가 되도록 빈칸에 알맞은 말을 쓰시오.

> The teacher didn't write the letters on the table.
> = The letters on the table _____ the teacher.

➡ _____

10 위 글의 밑줄 친 문장 (B)를 수동태로 전환하시오.

➡ _____

11 위 글의 밑줄 친 문장 (C)에서 어법상 바르지 <u>않은</u> 것을 바르게 고치시오.

_____ ➡ _____

[09~11] 다음 글을 읽고, 물음에 답하시오.

The audience pays attention to his every little body movement. His long beautiful hair flies everywhere. (A)<u>이것은 마치 피아노와 발레 공연을 동시에 보는 것 같다.</u> Time flies and the concert ends. People scream and throw flowers and pieces of clothing onto the stage. The concert hall goes wild!

Who was this amazing star? His name was Franz Liszt and he was born in 1811 in Hungary. He first started playing the piano when he was seven. Liszt later became a great pianist, composer and teacher. But (B)<u>many people think of him as the first idol.</u> Why don't you give his music a listen? (C)<u>If you will like today's idols, you will love the original idol.</u>

[12~13] 다음 글을 읽고, 물음에 답하시오.

The Star of Our Time

Yesterday Franz Liszt performed his piano concert very successfully in Vienna. This concert was different from ⓐ<u>others</u>. The side of the piano faced the audience. ⓑ<u>They could see Liszt better this way.</u> He didn't have any sheet music and played from memory. His music was so powerful and rich. When the concert ended, the concert hall went wild.

12 위 글의 밑줄 친 ⓐ를 두 개의 단어로 쓰시오.

➡ _____

09 위 글의 주어진 단어를 활용하여 밑줄 친 우리말 (A)를 영어로 쓰시오.

> (like / performance)

➡ _____

13 다음은 밑줄 친 ⓑ와 같은 의미의 문장이다. 빈칸을 알맞게 채우시오.

> This way, Liszt could _____ .

➡ _____

01 다음 대화의 내용과 일치하도록 Tom의 어머니의 담화에 있는 빈칸을 알맞은 말로 채우시오.

Sujin: Tom, why do you have so many paper flowers?

Tom: They're for my mom's birthday.

Sujin: They're so beautiful. Where did you get them?

Tom: I made them.

Sujin: Wow, you're really good.

Tom: Thanks. I'm taking a paper folding class these days.

Sujin: They are going to be the perfect gift for your mom.

Tom: I hope so, too.

Tom's mother:

Today, I was so happy when I got Tom's present. He made (1)_____ for me. It looked so (2)_____. These days he was taking (3)_____. He seemed to learn (4)_____ to make them in that class. I was proud of him so much.

---

02 다음 주어진 동사를 이용하여 수동태 문장을 만드시오.

보기

bake   read   draw   pass   make

---

(1) _____

(2) _____

(3) _____

(4) _____

(5) _____

03 다음 단어를 이용하여 〈보기〉와 같이 내일 계획을 써 보시오.

보기

sunny   windy   rain   hot

➡ If it is cloudy tomorrow, I will cancel my appointment.

---

(1) _____

(2) _____

(3) _____

(4) _____

단원별 모의고사

01 다음 대화의 밑줄 친 우리말을 영어로 쓰시오.

> **A:** 너는 어느 나라를 방문하고 싶니?
> **B:** I want to visit China because I want to see the Great Wall of China.

➡ _____

02 다음 우리말을 주어진 단어를 배열하여 문장을 완성하시오.

(1) 어느 소설이 가장 인기가 있나요?
(popular / novel / is / the / most / which)

➡ _____

(2) 어떻게 당신의 역할을 준비하였나요?
(you / did / prepare / role / your / how / for)

➡ _____

(3) 왜 세종대왕은 한글을 창조하셨나요?
(Hangeul / why / King Sejong / did / invent)

➡ _____

03 다음 문장의 빈칸에 들어갈 말을 〈보기〉에서 골라 쓰시오. (필요하면 어형을 바꿀 것)

> ┤ 보기 ├
> throw / performance / invent / face

(1) The students were _____ with difficult problems.
(2) I enjoyed ballet _____, *The Nutcracker*.
(3) Don't _____ stones at the animals.
(4) Who _____ the first bicycle?

04 다음 대화의 빈칸 (A)와 (B)에 들어갈 말이 바르게 짝지어진 것은?

> **A:** (A)_____ country do you want to visit for your dream vacation?
> **B:** I want to visit Canada.
> **A:** (B)_____ do you want to visit Canada?
> **B:** Because I want to see Niagara Falls.

	(A)	(B)
①	Which	When
②	Which	Why
③	Where	Why
④	Where	Which
⑤	Why	Which

05 주어진 문장에 이어지는 대화가 자연스럽게 이어지도록 순서대로 배열하시오.

> Which singer do you like best?
> (A) I like *Imagine* best. It cheers me up.
> (B) Why do you like him?
> (C) Which song do you like best?
> (D) I like John Lennon best.
> (E) Because he is a great singer.

➡ _____

06 다음 〈보기〉의 주어진 단어를 모두 배열하여 빈칸을 완성하시오.

> **A:** _____
> **B:** Because I want to see Niagara Falls.
>
> ┤ 보기 ├
> visit / do / why / to / Canada / you / want

➡ _____

[07~08] 다음 대화를 읽고, 물음에 답하시오.

> **Sujin:** Tom, why do you have ⓐso many paper flowers?
> **Tom:** They're ⓑfor my mom's birthday.
> **Sujin:** They're so beautiful. Where did you get them?
> **Tom:** I made them.
> **Sujin:** Wow, you're really ⓒgood.
> **Tom:** Thanks. I'm taking a paper folding class ⓓthose days.
> **Sujin:** They are going to be the perfect (A)gift for your mom.
> **Tom:** I hope ⓔso, too.

07 위 대화의 밑줄 친 ⓐ~ⓔ 중 어색한 것을 골라 바르게 고치시오.

➡ _____

08 위 대화의 밑줄 친 (A)와 의미가 다른 것은?

① I was given a special gift at the event.
② My sister was wrapping a gift in her room.
③ She has a great gift for art.
④ A small gift moved his heart.
⑤ His baseball was the best gift for me.

[09~10] 다음 대화를 읽고, 물음에 답하시오.

Amy: Jiho, what are you going to do this Saturday?
Jiho: I'm going to Blue Sky's fan meeting with my friends.
Amy: Wow, I'm also a big fan of the band.
Jiho: Really? (A)너는 어느 멤버를 가장 좋아하니? (like, which)
Amy: I like Lucy best. She sings really well.
Jiho: I like the drummer, Mike, best. He's fantastic! Do you want to join us?
Amy: Sure, I'd love to. I can't wait!

09 위 대화의 밑줄 친 (A)의 우리말을 주어진 단어를 사용하여 영어로 쓰시오.

➡ _____

10 위 대화의 내용과 일치하지 않는 것은?

① Lucy and Mike are the members of Blue Sky.
② Jiho is planning to go to Blue Sky's fan meeting.
③ Amy's favorite member is Lucy.
④ Mike is the drummer of Blue Sky.
⑤ Amy cannot go with Jiho this Saturday.

11 다음 대화가 자연스럽게 이어지도록 순서대로 배열하시오.

(A) Okay.
(B) Why do you have all those old clothes?
(C) Really? I have some old clothes, too.
(D) I'm going to sell them at the flea market.
(E) Then why don't you join me this Saturday?

➡ _____

[12~13] 다음 대화를 읽고, 물음에 답하시오.

Jack: Hi, Sumin. How's the book club going?
Sumin: It's fun. I read lots of (A)_____ books.
Jack: (B)Which book do you like best?
Sumin: I like *Charlotte's Web* best.

12 위 대화의 빈칸 (A)에 들어갈 말로 어색한 것은?

① useful   ② impressive
③ fascinating   ④ boring
⑤ interesting

13 위 대화의 밑줄 친 (B)와 바꾸어 쓸 수 있는 것은?

① What is your favorite book?
② Why do you like that book?
③ What kind of book do you like?
④ Why don't you read the book?
⑤ Do you like reading books?

14 다음 중 어법상 바르지 않은 것은?

① The blouse is made of cotton.
② We can leave now because the class has just ended.
③ By whom was the door shut?
④ The keys to the house is lost.
⑤ If you are done with your work, you can go out.

15 다음 주어진 단어를 이용하여 대화를 문맥에 맞게 완성하시오.

> back / pay

> **A:** I don't have enough money to buy the ear phone. If _____ _____ _____ ten dollars, _____ _____ _____ you _____ tomorrow.
> **B:** Sure. I can lend you more than that.

➡ _____, _____, _____

16 다음 중 빈칸에 들어갈 말이 다른 하나는?

① Every little movement is paid attention _____ by the audience.

② Jane is married _____ Jack.

③ The star's life is exposed _____ all the people.

④ My grandparents are accustomed _____ reading books with glasses.

⑤ Water is composed _____ oxygen and hydrogen.

17 두 문장이 같은 의미가 되도록 빈칸에 알맞은 말을 쓰시오.

> We saw the car stop.
> = The car _____.

➡ _____

18 다음 중 문장 전환이 올바르지 않은 것은?

① He laughed at me.
  → I was laughed at by him.
② John could see Jane in the mirror.
  → Jane could be seen in the mirror by John.
③ Jina gave Tom some good advice about studying English.
  → Tom was given to some good advice about studying English.
④ If you have a problem, we will discuss it later.
  → If you have a problem, it will be discussed later by us.
⑤ They let me enter the church.
  → I was allowed to enter the church.

[19~21] 다음 글을 읽고, 물음에 답하시오.

Are idols a recent creation? ⓐNo way! Did idols begin with The Beatles in the 1960's? They were loved by many, but they were not the first. How about Elvis Presley in the 1950's? Not even close. ⓑTo find the answer, ⓒlet's take a time machine to a concert hall in Vienna in 1845.

ⓓAll the seats are filled. ① Unlike other concerts, the side of the piano faces the audience. ② He doesn't have any sheet music with him. He begins to play from memory. ③ He starts slowly by softly touching the keys. ④ All the people hold their breath because they don't want to miss a single note. ⑤ He builds up speed, and his long fingers press down on many keys ⓔat once. This makes the music very powerful and rich.

19 주어진 문장이 들어가기에 가장 적절한 곳은?

> This way, the audience can see the handsome 185cm pianist better.

① ② ③ ④ ⑤

20 ⓐ~ⓔ에 관한 설명으로 바르지 <u>않은</u> 것은?

① ⓐ: 'Not at all!'로 바꾸어 쓸 수 있다.
② ⓑ: 'In order to find'의 의미로 쓰였다.
③ ⓒ: 'shall we take a time machine to a concert hall in Vienna in 1845?'와 같은 의미이다.
④ ⓓ: 'All the seats are filled with the audience.'로 바꾸어 쓸 수 있다.
⑤ ⓔ: 'one at a time'과 같은 의미이다.

21 위 글을 참고하여 대화의 빈칸에 알맞은 말을 쓰시오.

> **A:** I don't want to miss a single note of his play. What should I do?
> **B:** If _____ .

➡ _____

[22~25] 다음 글을 읽고, 물음에 답하시오.

The audience ⓐpay attention to his every little body movement. His long beautiful hair flies everywhere. It's like watching a piano and ballet performance ⓑonce. Time ⓒis flown and the concert ends. People scream and throw flowers and pieces of clothing onto the stage. The concert hall goes wild!

Who was this ⓓamazed star? His name was Franz Liszt and he was born in 1811 in Hungary. He first started playing the piano when he was seven. Liszt later became a great pianist, composer and teacher. But many people think of him ⓔto be the first idol. (A) <u>그의 음악을 한 번 들어 보는 것이 어때?</u> If you like today's idols, you will love the original idol.

22 콘서트가 끝난 후 사람들의 반응으로 가장 적절한 것은?

① sad   ② embarrassed
③ upset   ④ excited
⑤ annoyed

23 밑줄 친 ⓐ~ⓔ를 바르게 고치지 <u>않은</u> 것은?

① ⓐ → pays attention to
② ⓑ → at once
③ ⓒ → flies
④ ⓓ → amazing
⑤ ⓔ → about

24 위 글의 내용과 일치하지 <u>않는</u> 것은?

① Franz Liszt's body movement is paid attention to by the audience.
② The audience seems to be satisfied with the concert.
③ Franz Liszt was born in Hungary.
④ Franz Liszt started to play the piano at the age of seven.
⑤ The writer thinks Franz Liszt isn't the original idol.

25 주어진 단어를 활용하여 밑줄 친 우리말 (A)를 영어로 쓰시오.

> why / give / listen

➡ _____

26 다음 빈칸에 알맞은 기사 제목으로 가장 적절한 것은?

> _____
>
> Yesterday Franz Liszt performed his piano concert very successfully in Vienna. This concert was different from others. The side of the piano faced the audience. They could see Liszt better this way. He didn't have any sheet music and played from memory. His music was so powerful and rich. When the concert ended, the concert hall went wild.

① The Worst Piano Concert
② The Star of Our Time
③ Franz Liszt: Who Is He?
④ What You Should Know about Music
⑤ The Most Famous Concert Hall in Vienna

Lesson

4

Go for It!

의사소통 기능

- **여가 활동 말하기**
  A: What do you do in your free time?
  B: I often play table tennis.

- **경험 말하기**
  A: Have you ever ridden a horse?
  B: Yes, I have.

언어 형식

- **최상급**
  The Atacama Desert is **the driest** desert in the world.

- **관계대명사**
  They are the people **who** take part in the 4 Deserts Race.

Words & Expressions

Key Words

- **amazing** [əméiziŋ] 형 놀라운
- **Antarctica** [æntáːrktikə] 명 남극대륙
- **athlete** [ǽθliːt] 명 선수, 육상 경기 선수
- **backpack** [bǽkpæk] 명 배낭
- **bake** [beik] 동 굽다
- **bat** [bæt] 명 배트, 막대기, 박쥐
- **boiling** [bɔ́iliŋ] 형 끓는, 끓어오르는
- **burn** [bəːrn] 동 태우다, 타다
- **desert** [dézərt] 명 사막
- **direction** [dirékʃən] 명 방향
- **dry** [drai] 형 마른, 건조한
- **equipment** [ikwípmənt] 명 장비, 설비
- **expect** [ikspékt] 동 기대하다
- **field** [fiːld] 명 들(판), 경기장
- **finish line** 결승선
- **freeze** [friːz] 동 얼다, 얼어붙다
- **giant** [dʒáiənt] 형 거대한
- **gym** [dʒim] 명 체육관
- **hang** [hæŋ] 동 매달다
- **hit** [hit] 동 치다, 때리다
- **imagine** [imǽdʒin] 동 상상하다
- **jump rope** 줄넘기
- **kick** [kik] 동 차다
- **librarian** [laibréəriən] 명 사서
- **limit** [límit] 명 한계, 제한 동 제한하다

- **marathon** [mǽrəθàn] 명 마라톤
- **mean** [miːn] 동 의미하다
- **ordinary** [ɔ́ːrdənèri] 형 보통의, 평범한
- **participant** [paːrtísəpənt] 명 참가자
- **planet** [plǽnit] 명 행성
- **protect** [prətékt] 동 보호하다
- **punch** [pʌntʃ] 명 타격, 펀치
- **race** [reis] 명 경주, 경쟁
- **reach** [riːtʃ] 동 도달하다, ~에 이르다
- **relay** [ríːlei] 명 계주, 릴레이 경주
- **request** [rikwést] 동 요청하다 명 요구, 요청
- **ride** [raid] 동 타다
- **rock climbing** 암벽 등반
- **sand** [sænd] 명 모래
- **scared** [skɛərd] 형 무서워하는
- **scary** [skɛ́əri] 형 무서운, 두려운
- **temperature** [témpərətʃər] 명 온도
- **throat** [θrout] 명 목구멍
- **throw** [θrou] 동 던지다
- **tough** [tʌf] 형 힘든, 어려운
- **traditional** [trədíʃənl] 형 전통적인
- **train** [trein] 동 훈련하다 명 기차
- **uniform** [júːnəfɔ̀ːrm] 명 제복, 유니폼
- **wet** [wet] 형 젖은, 축축한
- **windy** [wíndi] 형 바람이 (많이) 부는

Key Expressions

- **a series of** 일련의
- **be out of** ~가 떨어지다, 바닥나다
- **for a living** 생계를 위해
- **go on** 계속되다
- **in fact** 사실은, 실제로

- **in the middle of** ~의 한가운데에
- **take care of** ~을 돌보다
- **take part in** ~에 참가하다
- **take place** 일어나다, 개최되다
- **up to** ~까지

Word Power

※ 서로 반대되는 뜻을 가진 어휘

- □ **dry** 건조한 ↔ **wet** 젖은, 축축한
- □ **thin** 마른 ↔ **fat** 살찐
- □ **ordinary** 보통의, 평범한 ↔ **extraordinary** 대단한, 보통이 아닌
- □ **giant** 거인 ↔ **dwarf** 난쟁이
- □ **careful** 주의깊은 ↔ **careless** 부주의한
- □ **ancient** 고대의 ↔ **modern** 현대의

- □ **get on** ~에 타다 ↔ **get off** ~에서 내리다
- □ **freeze** 얼다, 얼어붙다 ↔ **melt** 녹다
- □ **limited** 한정된, 제한된 ↔ **limitless**, **unlimited** 무한의, 무제한의
- □ **arrive** 도착하다 ↔ **depart** 출발하다
- □ **throw** 던지다 ↔ **catch** 잡다
- □ **high** 높은 ↔ **low** 낮은

English Dictionary

- □ **Antarctica** 남극대륙
  → the continent around the South Pole
  남쪽 극지방 주위의 대륙

- □ **athlete** (운동) 선수
  → a person who competes in sports
  스포츠에서 경쟁하는 사람

- □ **backpack** 배낭
  → a piece of equipment that is carried on the back
  등으로 나르는 장비의 하나

- □ **boil** 끓다
  → to be heated to the point where it forms bubbles and turns to steam or vapour
  공기 방울이 형성되거나 수증기 또는 기체로 변하는 지점까지 열을 받다

- □ **desert** 사막
  → a large area of land that has very little water and very few plants growing on it
  물이 거의 없고 이곳에서 자라는 식물도 거의 없는 넓은 땅

- □ **freeze** 얼다, 얼어붙다
  → to become hard, and often turn to ice, as a result of extreme cold
  극도의 추위로 딱딱해지거나 얼음으로 변하다

- □ **gym** 체육관
  → a room or hall with equipment for doing physical exercise
  신체 운동을 하기 위해 장비가 있는 공간 또는 회관

- □ **librarian** 사서
  → a person who is in charge of or works in a library
  도서관을 담당하거나 도서관에서 일을 하는 사람

- □ **marathon** 마라톤
  → a race in which people run a distance of 26 miles, which is about 42 km
  26마일, 즉 약 42km의 거리를 달리는 경주

- □ **participant** 참가자
  → a person who is taking part in an activity or event
  활동 또는 행사에 참가하는 사람

- □ **protect** 보호하다
  → to make sure that somebody/something is not harmed, injured, damaged
  여러 사람 또는 어떤 것이 손상이나 부상 또는 해를 입지 않도록 하다

- □ **race** 경주
  → a competition between people, animals, vehicles, etc. to see which one is faster or the fastest
  누가 더 빠르거나 가장 빠른지 보기 위한 사람, 동물, 수송수단 간의 경쟁

- □ **temperature** 온도
  → the measurement in degrees of how hot or cold a thing or place is
  어떤 물건이나 장소가 얼마나 뜨거운지 또는 차가운지 그 정도의 측정

- □ **traditional** 전통적인
  → being part of the beliefs, customs or way of life of a particular group of people, that have not changed for a long time
  오랫동안 변하지 않은 특정 그룹의 사람들의 삶의 양식, 믿음, 관습의

서답형

01 다음 짝지어진 단어의 관계가 같도록 빈칸에 알맞은 말을 쓰시오.

> heavy : light = _____ : wet

서답형

[02~03] 다음 영영풀이에 해당하는 단어를 쓰시오.

02
> a person who is taking part in an activity or event

➡ _____

03
> a person who is in charge of or works in a library

➡ _____

중요

04 다음 중 밑줄 친 부분의 뜻풀이가 바르지 않은 것은?

① He felt so thirsty in the middle of the desert. 사막
② She always smiled when she was dealing with a tough work. 힘든
③ They went through the desert on a windy day. 바람이 (많이) 부는
④ We attended an ordinary meeting to discuss the issue. 여느 때와 다른
⑤ Tom was an active participant in the discussion. 참가자

05 다음 문장의 밑줄 친 단어와 같은 의미로 쓰인 것은?

> The baseball is played with a bat and a ball.

① The bat was flying in the cave.
② There are lots of different bat species in the world.
③ Would you put the bat down and help me, please?
④ He is as blind as a bat without glasses.
⑤ Do you know how the bat avoids obstacles?

서답형

06 다음 문장의 빈칸에 들어갈 말을 〈보기〉에서 골라 쓰시오.

> ┤ 보기 ├
> tough / burn / frozen / giant

(1) Don't worry. I won't _____ the bread.
(2) I don't know how to deal with this _____ situation.
(3) Minsu slipped on the _____ path.
(4) This balloon looks like a _____ ball.

중요

07 다음 문장의 빈칸에 공통으로 들어갈 말로 적절한 것은?

> • Emma is famous in the _____ of education.
> • John is working on the _____ of wheat.
> • The gold _____ was found in the woods.

① region ② area
③ garden ④ field
⑤ land

01 다음 짝지어진 단어의 관계가 같도록 빈칸에 알맞은 말을 쓰시오.

> dark: bright = freeze : _____

[02~03] 다음 영영풀이에 해당하는 단어를 쓰시오.

02

> being part of the beliefs, customs or way of life of a particular group of people, that have not changed for a long time

➡ _____

03

> a large area of land that has very little water and very few plants growing on it

➡ _____

04 다음 문장의 빈칸에 들어갈 말을 순서대로 쓰시오.

> • (A)_____ fact, today was the busiest day for me.
> • I'm so worried because I'm almost (B)_____ of water.
> • She practiced a lot before taking part (C)_____ the dance contest.

(A) _____ (B) _____ (C) _____

05 다음 문장의 빈칸에 들어갈 말을 〈보기〉에서 골라 알맞은 형태로 쓰시오.

> ┤ 보기 ├
> take place / be out of / go on / in the middle of

(1) I woke up _____ the night.
(2) The fashion show _____ every year.
(3) The event will _____ for a week.
(4) Because we _____ sugar, I have to go to the grocery store.

06 다음 대화의 밑줄 친 우리말을 영어로 쓰시오.

> **A:** Have you ever been to Busan?
> **B:** 아니요, 그곳에 가본 적이 없어요.

➡ _____

07 다음 우리말을 주어진 단어를 모두 배열하여 문장을 완성하시오.

(1) 너는 요가를 해 본 적이 있니?
(yoga / you / tried / ever / have)
➡ _____

(2) 사실, 우리는 소금이 다 떨어졌어.
(of / salt / out / in / we / fact / are)
➡ _____

(3) 나는 암벽 등반 대회에 참가하고 싶어.
(contest / to / rock / in / the / part / I / take / want / climbing)
➡ _____

Conversation

① 여가 활동 말하기

A What do you do in your free time? 너는 여가 시간에 무엇을 하니?

B I often play table tennis. 나는 종종 탁구를 쳐.

■ What do you do in your free time? 또는 What's your favorite free time activity?를 통해 상대방이 여가 시간을 어떻게 보내는지 물어볼 수 있다. free time은 '여가 시간'을 의미하며 leisure time 또는 spare time으로 바꾸어 쓸 수 있다.

여가 활동 묻기

• What's your hobby? 너의 취미가 무엇이니?

• What do you do in your leisure[spare] time? 너는 여가 시간에 무엇을 하니?

• How do you spend your leisure time? 너는 여가 시간을 어떻게 보내니?

• What's your favorite free time activity? 네가 가장 좋아하는 여가 시간 활동은 무엇이니?

• What do you like doing for fun? 너는 재미로 무엇을 하는 것을 좋아하니?

핵심 Check

1. 다음 우리말과 일치하도록 빈칸에 알맞은 말을 쓰시오.

(1) **A:** _____ _____ _____ _____ _____ _____ _____ _____?
   (너는 여가 시간에 무엇을 하니?)

   B: I usually play baseball. (나는 보통 야구를 해.)

(2) **A:** What's your _____ _____ _____ _____?
   (당신이 가장 좋아하는 여가 활동은 무엇인가요?)

   B: I love _____ _____. (나는 요가하는 것을 매우 좋아해요.)

(3) **A:** What do you do in your free time? (너는 여가 시간에 무엇을 하니?)

   B: _____ _____ _____ _____. (나는 종종 쿠키를 구워.)

2 경험 말하기

> **A** Have you ever ridden a horse? 너는 말을 타본 적이 있니?
> **B** Yes, I have. 응, 있어.

■ 'Have you ever+과거분사 ~?'는 경험을 묻는 표현으로 이에 대한 대답으로 긍정일 때는 'Yes, I have.', 부정일 때는 'No, I haven't.'로 대답한다. Have you?는 상대방에게 받은 질문을 다시 상대방에게 묻는 표현으로 반복된 부분은 생략한다.

■ 현재까지의 경험을 물을 때 현재완료 시제를 사용하므로 'Have you ever+과거분사~?' 형태에 유의한다.

■ 경험하지 못한 것으로 '전혀 ~해 본 적이 없다.'라고 강조하기 위해 'No, I've never ~'로 대답할 수 있다.

■ 과거의 경험은 과거시제를 이용한다.

ex) • Did you ever play table tennis? 과거에 탁구를 친 적이 있는지 묻는 표현
    • Have you ever played table tennis? 과거부터 현재까지 탁구를 친 적이 있는지 묻는 표현

핵심 Check

2. 다음 우리말과 일치하도록 빈칸에 알맞은 말을 쓰시오.

(1) **A:** _____ _____ _____ _____ a marathon? (마라톤을 해 본 적이 있나요?)

    B: No, I haven't. (아니요, 해 본 적이 없어요.)

(2) **A:** Have you ever _____ _____? (캐나다에 가 본 적이 있나요?)

    B: _____, _____ _____. _____ _____?

    (예, 가 보았어요. 당신은 가 본 적이 있나요?)

(3) **A:** Have you ever _____ a paper flower? (종이꽃을 만들어 본 적이 있나요?)

    B: No, I've _____ done it. (아니요, 전혀 해 보지 않았어요.)

A. Listen and Speak 1-A

Tony: Bomi, ❶what do you do in your free time?

Bomi: ❷I often bake cookies. ❸How about you, Tony?

Tony: I usually watch movies.

Tony: 보미야, 너는 한가할 때 무엇을 하니?
Bomi: 나는 종종 쿠키를 구워. 너는 어때, Tony?
Tony: 나는 보통 영화를 봐.

❶ what do you do in your free time?은 '너는 여가 시간에 무엇을 하니?'라는 뜻으로 여가 활동에 관해 묻는 표현이다.

❷ 자신의 여가 활동에 대해 말할 때는 'I often/usually ～'의 표현을 사용하여 말할 수 있다.

❸ 'How about you?'는 '너는 어때?'라고 상대방에게 같은 질문을 할 때 사용할 수 있으며 'What about you?'로 바꾸어 쓸 수 있다.

Check(√) True or False

(1) Bomi has never baked cookies.   T ☐ F ☐

(2) Tony usually watches movies in his free time.   T ☐ F ☐

A. Listen and Speak 1-B

Jean: I'm so happy. It's Friday!

Tom: ❶What are you going to do on the weekend, Jean?

Jean: ❷I'm going to play badminton.

Tom: Do you play badminton often?

Jean: Yes, it's my favorite ❸free time activity.

Tom: Who do you usually play with?

Jean: ❹My dad. What do you do in your free time?

Tom: I often go to the Han River and ❺ride my bike.

Jean: 정말 기뻐. 금요일이야!
Tom: 주말에 무엇을 할 거니, Jean?
Jean: 나는 배드민턴을 칠 거야.
Tom: 배드민턴을 자주 치니?
Jean: 응, 그건 내가 가장 좋아하는 여가 활동이야.
Tom: 보통 누구랑 치니?
Jean: 우리 아빠랑. 너는 여가 시간에 무엇을 하니?
Tom: 나는 종종 한강에 가서 자전거를 타.

❶ What are you going to do on the weekend?는 '주말에 무엇을 할 거니?'라는 뜻으로 계획을 묻는 표현이다. 이와 같은 표현으로 'What's your plan for the weekend?'가 있다.

❷ be going to ～: ～할 것이다

❸ free time activity: 여가 활동

❹ 'I usually play with my dad.'를 줄인 표현이다.

❺ ride a bike: 자전거를 타다

Check(√) True or False

(3) Jean loves playing badminton in her free time.   T ☐ F ☐

(4) Tom often goes to the Han River to play badminton with his dad.   T ☐ F ☐

Listen and Speak 1-C

Minsu: Ms. Allen, ❶what do you do for a living?

Allen: I'm a doctor.

Minsu: ❷What do you do in your free time?

Allen: I often play table tennis.

❶ what do you do for a living?는 직업이 무엇인지 묻는 표현이다.
❷ 여가 활동에 관한 질문으로 대답은 often 또는 usually를 이용하여 대답할 수 있다.

Listen and Speak 2-A

Mina: Tom, ❶have you ever been to Jeju-do?

Tom: ❷Yes, I have. I went there last winter vacation. What about you?

Mina: I've never been there, but I'm going there this summer.

Tom: That's great! ❸I'm sure you'll like it a lot.

❶ have you (ever) ~?는 '~해 본 적이 있니?'라는 뜻으로 상대방의 경험 유무를 묻는다.
❷ 경험을 한 경우 'Yes, I have.'로, 경험하지 않은 경우는 'No, I haven't.'로 대답한다.
❸ 'I'm sure ~'는 '~을 확신하다'는 표현으로 확실성을 나타낸다.

Listen and Speak 2-B

Suji: Mike, ❶have you ever heard of flying yoga?

Mike: Yeah! I've seen it on TV. People were ❷ hanging in the air!

Suji: Guess what? I'm learning it these days.

Mike: Really? It looked so ❸scary. Do you like it, Suji?

Suji: ❹At first, I was a little scared, but now I'm enjoying it.

Mike: Sounds great! I think I should exercise ❺ more, too.

Suji: Do you want to join my yoga class?

Mike: No, that's too scary for me. I'll ❻just play basketball.

❶ 'have you (ever) ~?'는 '~해 본 적이 있니?'라는 뜻으로 상대방의 경험 유무를 묻는다.
❷ hang: 매달리다 / in the air: 공중에
❸ scary: 무서운, 두려운
❹ at first: 처음에는
❺ more: 더 (much의 비교급)
❻ just: 그저, 단지

Listen and Speak 2-C

A: Have you ever ❶ridden a horse?

B: ❷Yes, I have.

A: When did you ride a horse?

B: Last summer.

❶ ride a horse: 말을 타다
❷ 경험을 한 경우 'Yes, I have.'로, 경험하지 않은 경우는 'No, I haven't.'로 대답한다.

Real Life Talk

Hojin: Judy, what do you do in your free time?

Judy: I often go ❶rock climbing with my dad.

Hojin: What mountain do you go to?

Judy: No, Hojin. I usually do it at a gym near my house.

Hojin: ❷I see. Have you ever done it on a real mountain?

Judy: ❸Not yet. But I hope to do it someday.

Hojin: That's really cool. Can I come and join you next time?

Judy: Sure. I'm going ❹this Saturday.

Hojin: That sounds great.

Judy: You're going to love it.

❶ rock climbing: 암벽등반
❷ I see.: '알겠어.' 또는 '그렇구나.'를 뜻한다.
❸ Not yet: 아직 없어.
❹ 이번 토요일에

● 다음 우리말과 일치하도록 빈칸에 알맞은 말을 쓰시오.

Listen & Speak 1 A

Tony: Bomi, what do you do _____ _____ _____ _____?

Bomi: I _____ bake cookies. How about you, Tony?

Tony: I _____ _____ _____.

해석

Tony: 보미야, 너는 여가 시간에 무엇을 하니?
Bomi: 나는 종종 쿠키를 구워. 너는 어때, Tony?
Tony: 나는 보통 영화를 봐.

Listen & Speak 1 B

Jean: I'm so happy. It's Friday!

Tom: _____ _____ _____ _____ _____ _____ on the weekend, Jean?

Jean: I'm going to _____ _____.

Tom: Do you play badminton often?

Jean: Yes, it's _____ _____ _____ _____ _____.

Tom: _____ do you usually play with?

Jean: My dad. _____ _____ _____ _____ _____ _____ _____ _____?

Tom: I often go to the Han River and _____ _____ _____.

Jean: 정말 기뻐. 금요일이야!
Tom: 주말에 무엇을 할 거니, Jean?
Jean: 나는 배드민턴을 칠 거야.
Tom: 배드민턴을 자주 치니?
Jean: 응, 그건 내가 가장 좋아하는 여가 활동이야.
Tom: 보통 누구랑 치니?
Jean: 우리 아빠랑. 너는 여가 시간에 무엇을 하니.
Tom: 나는 종종 한강에 가서 자전거를 타.

Listen & Speak 1 C

Minsu: Ms. Allen, what do you do _____ _____ _____?

Allen: I'm a doctor.

Minsu: What do you do in your free time?

Allen: _____ _____ _____ _____ _____ _____.

Minsu: Ms. Allen, 직업이 무언가요?
Allen: 의사입니다.
Minsu: 여가 시간에 무엇을 하나요?
Allen: 나는 종종 탁구를 칩니다.

Listen & Speak 2 A

Mina: Tom, _____ _____ _____ _____ _____ Jeju-do?

Tom: Yes, _____ _____. I went there last winter vacation. What about you?

Mina: _____ _____ _____ _____, but I'm going there this summer.

Tom: That's great! I'm sure you'll like it a lot.

Mina: Tom, 너는 제주도에 가 본 적이 있니?
Tom: 응, 가 봤어. 지난 겨울 방학에 거기에 갔어. 너는?
Mina: 나는 거기에 가 본 적이 없는데, 이번 여름에 갈 거야.
Tom: 잘됐네! 네가 아주 좋아할 거라고 확신해.

Listen & Speak 2 B

Suji: Mike, _____ _____ _____ _____ _____ flying yoga?

Mike: Yeah! _____ _____ it on TV. People were hanging in the air!

Suji: Guess what? I'm learning it _____ _____.

Mike: Really? It looked so _____. Do you like it, Suji?

Suji: At first, I was a little _____, but now I'm enjoying it.

Mike: Sounds great! I think I should _____ more, too.

Suji: Do you want to _____ my yoga class?

Mike: No, that's too _____ for me. I'll just _____ _____.

Listen & Speak 1 C

A: _____ _____ _____ _____ a horse?

B: Yes, I have.

A: _____ did you ride a horse?

B: Last summer.

Real Life Talk

Hojin: Judy, what do you do in your free time?

Judy: I _____ _____ _____ _____ with my dad.

Hojin: _____ _____ do you go to?

Judy: No, Hojin. I usually do it at a _____ near my house.

Hojin: I see. _____ _____ _____ _____ it on a real mountain?

Judy: _____ _____. But I hope to do it someday.

Hojin: That's really cool. Can I _____ _____ _____ you next time?

Judy: Sure. I'm going _____ _____.

Hojin: That _____ great.

Judy: You're _____ _____ love it.

Suji: Mike, 너는 플라잉 요가를 들어본 적이 있니?

Mike: 응! TV에서 본 적이 있어. 사람들이 공중에 매달려 있었어!

Suji: 그거 알아? 내가 요즘 그걸 배우고 있어.

Mike: 정말? 아주 무서워 보였는데. 그걸 좋아하니, 수지야?

Suji: 처음엔 조금 무서웠는데, 지금은 즐기고 있어.

Mike: 좋구나! 나도 운동을 더 해야 할 것 같아.

Suji: 우리 요가 수업을 함께 할래?

Mike: 아니, 그건 내게 너무 무서워. 나는 그냥 농구를 할게.

A: 너는 말을 타 본 적이 있니?

B: 응. 있어.

A: 언제 말을 타 보았니?

B: 지난 여름에.

Hojin: Judy, 너는 여가 시간에 무엇을 하니?

Judy: 나는 종종 아빠와 암벽 등반을 하러 가.

Hojin: 어떤 산에 가니?

Judy: 아니야, 호진아. 나는 보통 집 근처에 있는 체육관에서 그걸 해.

Hojin: 그렇구나. 실제 산에서 해 본 적이 있니?

Judy: 아직 없어. 하지만 언젠가 해 보기를 바라.

Hojin: 그거 정말 멋지다. 다음번에 내가 가서 함께 해도 될까?

Judy: 물론이야. 이번 주 토요일에 갈 거야.

Hojin: 잘됐네.

Judy: 너는 그걸 정말 좋아할 거야.

01 다음 대화의 빈칸에 들어갈 말을 주어진 단어를 모두 배열하여 완성하시오.

> A: Ms. Allen, _____?
>   (do / for / you / a / what / living / do)
> B: I'm a doctor.

➡ _____

02 다음 대화의 우리말을 영작하시오.

> A: <u>너는 말을 타 본 적이 있니?</u>
> B: Yes, I have.

➡ _____

03 다음 빈칸에 들어갈 말로 어색한 것은?

> Tony: Bomi, what do you do in your free time?
> Bomi: I often bake cookies. How about you, Tony?
> Tony: _____

① I usually watch movies.   ② I read books.
③ I am a fire fighter.   ④ I listen to music.
⑤ I draw pictures.

04 다음 대화가 자연스럽게 이어지도록 순서대로 배열하시오.

> (A) That's great! I'm sure you'll like it a lot.
> (B) Have you ever been to Jeju-do?
> (C) I've never been there, but I'm going there this summer.
> (D) Yes, I have. I went there last winter vacation. What about
>   you?

➡ _____

★ 중요

01 다음 빈칸에 들어갈 말로 어색한 것은?

> **A:** _____
>
> **B:** I'm a teacher.

① What kind of job do you have?
② What do you do?
③ What do you do for a living?
④ What is your occupation?
⑤ What are you going to do?

[02~03] 다음 대화를 읽고, 물음에 답하시오.

> **Tony:** Bomi, _____ do you do in your free time?
>
> **Bomi:** I often bake cookies. _____ about you, Tony?
>
> **Tony:** <u>나는 보통 영화를 봐.</u>

02 위 대화의 빈칸에 공통으로 들어갈 말로 적절한 것은? (대·소문자 무시)

① why   ② what   ③ how
④ where   ⑤ who

서답형

03 위 대화의 밑줄 친 우리말을 4단어를 사용하여 영작하시오.

➡ _____

[04~05] 다음 대화를 읽고, 물음에 답하시오.

> **Jean:** I'm so happy. It's Friday!
>
> **Tom:** _____
>
> **Jean:** I'm going to play badminton. (A)
>
> **Tom:** Do you play badminton often? (B)
>
> **Jean:** Yes, it's my favorite free time activity. (C)
>
> **Tom:** Who do you usually play with? (D)

> **Jean:** My dad. (E)
>
> **Tom:** I often go to the Han River and ride my bike.

04 위 대화의 빈칸에 들어갈 말로 어색한 것은?

① What are you going to do on the weekend?
② What are you planning to do on the weekend?
③ What's your plan for the weekend?
④ What will you do on the weekend?
⑤ What do you do for a living?

★ 중요

05 위 대화의 (A)~(E) 중 주어진 문장이 들어가기에 적절한 곳은?

> What do you do in your free time?

① (A)   ② (B)   ③ (C)   ④ (D)   ⑤ (E)

06 다음 대화가 자연스럽게 이어지도록 순서대로 배열하시오.

> Mike, have you ever heard of flying yoga?

> (A) Guess what? I'm learning it these days.
>
> (B) At first, I was a little scared, but now I'm enjoying it.
>
> (C) Really? It looked so scary. Do you like it, Suji?
>
> (D) Sounds great! I think I should exercise more, too.
>
> (E) Yeah! I've seen it on TV. People were hanging in the air!

➡ _____

[07~08] 다음 대화를 읽고 물음에 답하시오.

Suji: Mike, have you ever heard of flying yoga?

Mike: Yeah! I've seen it on TV. People were hanging in the air!

Suji: Guess what? I'm learning it these days.

Mike: Really? It looked so scary. Do you like it, Suji?

Suji: At first, I was a little scared, but now I'm enjoying it.

Mike: Sounds great! I think I should exercise more, too.

Suji: Do you want to join my yoga class?

Mike: No, that's too scary for me. I'll just play basketball.

서답형

07 What does Mike think about flying yoga?

➡ _____

서답형

08 What is Mike going to do instead of joining the yoga class?

➡ _____

09 다음 대화의 내용과 일치하도록 Hojin의 일기를 완성하시오.

Hojin: Judy, what do you do in your free time?

Judy: I often go rock climbing with my dad.

Hojin: What mountain do you go to?

Judy: No, Hojin. I usually do it at a gym near my house.

Hojin: I see. Have you ever done it on a real mountain?

Judy: Not yet. But I hope to do it someday.

Hojin: That's really cool. Can I come and join you next time?

Judy: Sure. I'm going this Saturday.

Hojin: That sounds great.

Judy: You're going to love it.

Mon, June 3th, 2019
Today, I talked about free time activity with Judy. She said (1)_____ in her free time. She usually does it at (2)_____. However, (3)_____ on a real mountain and she hopes to do it someday. I was interested in rock climbing so I asked if (4)_____. We are going to do it this Saturday. I'm really looking forward to it.

(1) _____
(2) _____
(3) _____
(4) _____

서답형

10 다음 대화가 자연스럽게 이어지도록 순서대로 배열하시오.

(A) Last summer.
(B) Yes, I have.
(C) When did you ride a horse?
(D) Have you ever ridden a horse?

➡ _____

01 다음 대화의 밑줄 친 우리말을 주어진 어구를 이용하여 영작하시오.

> Tony: Bomi, 너는 여가 시간에 무엇을 하니? (free time)
>
> Bomi: I often bake cookies. How about you, Tony?
>
> Tony: I usually watch movies.

➡ _____

[02~04] 다음 대화를 읽고, 물음에 답하시오.

> Jean: I'm so happy. It's Friday!
>
> Tom: What are you going to do on the weekend, Jean?
>
> Jean: I'm going to play badminton.
>
> Tom: Do you play badminton often?
>
> Jean: Yes, it's my favorite free time activity.
>
> Tom: Who do you usually play with?
>
> Jean: _____(A)_____ (my dad). What do you do in your free time?
>
> Tom: I often go to the Han River and ride my bike.

02 위 대화의 빈칸 (A)에 들어갈 대답을 주어진 단어를 사용하여 완전한 문장으로 쓰시오.

➡ _____

03 위 대화에서 다음 영영풀이가 나타내는 말을 찾아 쓰시오.

> liked more than others of the same kind

➡ _____

04 위 대화의 내용과 일치하도록 빈칸을 완성하시오.

> In her free time, Jean (1)_____ with her dad, while Tom often (2)_____ _____ and (3)_____.

[05~07] 다음 대화를 읽고, 물음에 답하시오.

> Hojin: Judy, what do you do in your free time?
>
> Judy: (A)나는 종종 아빠와 함께 암벽 등반을 하러 가.
>
> Hojin: What mountain do you go to?
>
> Judy: No, Hojin. I usually do it at a gym near my house.
>
> Hojin: I see. Have you ever done it on a real mountain?
>
> Judy: Not yet. But I hope to do it someday.
>
> Hojin: That's really cool. Can I come and join you next time?
>
> Judy: Sure. I'm going this Saturday.
>
> Hojin: That sounds great.
>
> Judy: You're going to love it.

05 위 대화의 밑줄 친 (A)의 우리말을 8단어를 사용하여 영작하시오.

➡ _____

06 Where does Judy usually do rock climbing?

➡ _____

07 What are Judy and Hojin going to do this Saturday?

➡ _____

Grammar

① 최상급

> • She is **the smartest** girl in our class. 그녀는 우리 반에서 가장 똑똑한 소녀이다.
> • Seoul is **the biggest** city in Korea. 서울은 한국에서 가장 큰 도시이다.

■ 최상급은 셋 이상의 것 중에서 양, 정도, 수에 있어서 가장 많거나 가장 정도가 높은 것을 나타낼 때 쓰는 표현이다. 형용사의 최상급은 정관사 the를 사용하지만, 부사의 최상급에서는 정관사 the를 생략하는 것이 일반적이다. 최상급의 범위를 나타낼 때에는 'of+기간' 혹은 'in+장소, 조직, 사람들의 무리'를 사용하여 '~ 중에서'라는 의미로 쓸 수 있다.

  • James is **the busiest** man in the company. James는 그 회사에서 가장 바쁜 사람이다.

  • Yesterday was **the hottest** day of the year. 어제는 1년 중 가장 더운 날이었다.

■ 최상급은 형용사 어미에 '-est'를 붙여서 만든다. 단, 3음절 이상의 단어와 -ous, -ful, -ive, -less, -ant, -ing 등으로 끝나는 2음절의 단어는 'the most'를 사용하여 최상급을 만든다.

  • It is **the most difficult** problem. 그것은 가장 어려운 문제이다.

  • BTS is **the most famous** K-pop star in America. BTS는 미국에서 가장 유명한 K-pop 스타이다.

■ 불규칙으로 변하는 최상급

  • good, well − best   many, much − most

  • bad, ill − worst   little − least

  • I like math **(the) best of** all subjects. 나는 모든 과목 중에서 수학을 가장 좋아한다.

■ 비교급과 원급을 이용하여 최상급의 의미를 표현할 수 있다.

  • Chris is **the strongest** boy in his class. Chris는 그의 반에서 가장 힘이 센 소년이다.

    = Chris is **stronger than any other** boy in his class. [비교급+than any other+단수명사]
      Chris는 그의 반에서 다른 어떤 소년보다 더 힘이 세다.

    = Chris is **stronger than all the other** boys in his class. [비교급+than all the other+복수명사]
      Chris는 그의 반에서 다른 모든 소년들보다 더 힘이 세다.

    = **No other** boy in his class is **as** strong **as** Chris. [부정주어+so[as] 원급 as]
      그의 반에서 다른 어떤 소년도 Chris만큼 힘이 세지 않다.

    = **No other** boy in his class is **stronger than** Chris. [부정주어+비교급+than]
      그의 반에서 다른 어떤 소년도 Chris보다 더 힘이 세지 않다.

핵심 Check

1. 다음 우리말과 같도록 빈칸에 알맞은 말을 쓰시오.

(1) 그것은 모든 펜 중에서 가장 싼 펜이다.

➡ It is _____ _____ pen of _____.

(2) 이것은 일곱 권 중 가장 흥미로운 책이다.

➡ This is _____ _____ _____ book of the seven books.

② 관계대명사

> • I have a friend **who** makes pumpkin pies well. 내게는 호박파이를 잘 만드는 친구가 있다.
> • The book **whose** cover is red is mine. 표지가 빨간색인 그 책은 내 것이다.

■ 관계대명사는 두 개의 문장을 하나로 이어주는 접속사 역할을 하면서 동시에 대명사 역할을 한다. 본래 문장에서 주격으로 쓰인 명사는 주격 관계대명사로, 소유격으로 쓰인 명사는 소유격 관계대명사로, 목적격으로 쓰인 명사는 목적격 관계대명사로 바꾸어 준다.

- I thanked the woman. She helped me.
  = I thanked the woman **who** helped me.

- The sunglasses were under the sofa. I was looking for them.
  = The sunglasses **which** I was looking for were under the sofa.

■ 선행사에 따라서 사용되는 관계대명사의 종류는 다음과 같으며, 목적격 관계대명사는 생략 가능하다.

	주격	소유격	목적격
사람	who	whose	whom[who]
사물	which	whose / of which	which

- Tell me about the people **who[whom]** you visited when you were in Harvard.
  네가 Harvard에 있을 때 방문했던 사람들에 대해 말해 줘.

- I know a doctor **whose** last name is Peterson. 나는 성이 Peterson인 의사를 안다.

- The movie **which** we saw last night was not so good. 우리가 어젯밤에 본 영화는 그리 좋지 않았다.

■ 관계대명사 that은 who와 which를 대신하여 사용될 수 있으며 소유격은 쓰이지 않는다. 또, 선행사가 '사람+사물[동물]'인 경우에는 반드시 that을 쓰며, 선행사가 'the+최상급', 'the+서수', 'the only', 'the very', 'the same'의 수식을 받거나, 선행사가 '-thing', '-body', '-one'으로 끝나는 경우에는 that을 쓰는 경우가 많다.

- The woman **that[who]** I met yesterday was kind. 내가 어제 만난 여자는 친절했다.

- Jina is the only friend **that[whom]** I can rely on. Jina는 내가 의지할 수 있는 유일한 친구이다.

핵심 Check

2. 다음 우리말과 같도록 빈칸에 알맞은 말을 쓰시오.

(1) 경주에서 이긴 그 소녀는 행복했다.
  ➡ The girl _____ won the race was happy.

(2) 나는 자전거를 도난당한 남자를 안다.
  ➡ I know the man _____ _____ was stolen.

01 관계대명사를 이용하여 다음 두 문장을 하나의 문장으로 만드시오. (that은 쓰지 말 것)

(1) I have a friend. She studies abroad.

➡ _____

(2) We stayed in the hotel. It had a beautiful lounge.

➡ _____

(3) Do you want to see the pictures? The photographer took them.

➡ _____

(4) Jenny took care of the dog. Its leg was hurt. (whose를 이용할 것)

➡ _____

02 주어진 단어를 어법에 맞게 빈칸에 쓰시오.

(1) Summer is _____ _____ season of the year. (hot)

(2) No other boy in the club is _____ _____ Jimmy. (tall)

(3) Look at the girl who _____ playing the violin on the stage. (be)

(4) Parker is _____ _____ _____ boy in his school. (diligent)

03 다음 우리말에 맞게 주어진 단어를 바르게 배열하시오. (필요하면 어형을 바꿀 것)

(1) 내가 너에게 빌려준 책을 읽었니?

(the book / did / to / you / you / read / that / I / lend)

➡ _____

(2) 묻고 싶은 것이 있나요?

(ask / there / to / is / you / anything / that / want)

➡ _____

(3) 세계에서 제일 긴 강을 아니?

(in / do / you / the / long / the / know / world / river)

➡ _____

(4) 시간은 모든 것 중에서 가장 귀중하다.

(all / time / precious / of / the / is / most)

➡ _____

01 다음 중 최상급의 형태가 <u>다른</u> 하나는?

① healthy   ② tired   ③ afraid
④ foolish   ⑤ helpful

02 다음 빈칸에 들어갈 말이 <u>다른</u> 하나는?

① He is the man _____ you can trust.
② You can see many people _____ live and work nearby.
③ There lived a girl _____ fell in love with a king.
④ I know the boy _____ hobby is jumping rope.
⑤ The man _____ invented the telephone was Bell.

03 다음 중 어법상 바르지 <u>않은</u> 것은?

A: Did you ①see the movie ②that I told you about?
B: Yes, I ③did. I think that's ④more boring movie ⑤that I've ever seen.

①   ②   ③   ④   ⑤

서답형

04 적절한 관계사를 이용하여 다음 두 문장을 하나의 문장으로 쓰시오.

• Where is the cheese?
• It was in the refrigerator.

➡ _____

_____

05 다음 빈칸에 알맞은 말이 바르게 짝지어진 것은?

No other hotel room in the world is bigger than this room.
= This room is _____ than any other hotel room in the world.
= This room is _____ hotel room in the world.
= No other hotel room is as _____ as this room.

① bigger – bigger – big
② bigger – the big – bigger
③ bigger – the biggest – big
④ the biggest – the biggest – big
⑤ the biggest – the biggest – bigger

06 다음 빈칸에 적절한 것을 <u>모두</u> 고르시오.

The people _____ I call most often on my cell phone are my mother and my sisters.

① which   ② who   ③ that
④ whose   ⑤ whom

07 다음 빈칸에 알맞지 <u>않은</u> 것은?

돌고래는 세계에서 가장 영리한 동물이다.
= A dolphin is _____ in the world.

① the smartest animal
② smarter than any other animal
③ the smartest of all the animals
④ smarter than all the other animals
⑤ as smart as all the other animals

08 주어진 문장의 밑줄 친 부분과 같은 의미가 되도록 빈칸에 알맞은 말을 쓰시오.

> I prefer this chair to the others. It's the most comfortable.
> = This chair is _____ _____ _____ all the other chairs.

09 다음 중 어법상 바르지 않은 것은?

> Bill Gates ①who ②was born in 1955 is the man ③who established a company ④named Microsoft. He is one of the richest ⑤man in the world.

①   ②   ③   ④   ⑤

10 다음 중 의미가 다른 하나는?

① This is the most valuable painting in the gallery.
② No other painting in the gallery is more valuable than this.
③ This is more valuable than any other painting in the gallery.
④ This is more valuable than all the other paintings in the gallery.
⑤ This is as valuable as all the other paintings in the gallery.

11 다음 질문에 어법에 맞게 답하시오.

> A: What is the tallest building in the world?
> B: Burj Khalifa _____ is in Dubai is _____ any other building in the world.

➡ _____

12 다음 중 어법상 바르지 않은 것은?

① He is the best guitarist that I have ever known.
② Yesterday I ran into an old friend whom I hadn't seen for years.
③ Family is the most important than all the other things.
④ No other singer is as popular as Adele.
⑤ Kyle has a sister whose job is taking care of the elderly.

중요

13 다음 중 어법상 옳은 것을 바르게 묶은 것은?

> ⓐ In our town, there are people don't have a car.
> ⓑ The dress she is wearing is new.
> ⓒ The music that I listened to last night was good.
> ⓓ Helen actually enjoyed the book I told her to read it.
> ⓔ Mr. Kim teaches a subject which I am not interested in.

① ⓐ, ⓑ, ⓓ   ② ⓑ, ⓒ, ⓓ
③ ⓑ, ⓒ, ⓔ   ④ ⓒ, ⓓ, ⓔ
⑤ ⓐ, ⓓ, ⓔ

14 다음 빈칸에 적절한 관계대명사를 쓰시오.

> • The story _____ he told us was hard to believe.
> • I know the girl _____ eyes are brown.
> • Is this the watch _____ Kevin bought last month?

서답형

15 주어진 단어를 활용하여 다음 우리말을 영어로 쓰시오.

> 나와 함께 대화를 나눈 그 여자는 내게 좋은 조언을 해 주었다.
> (speak to / give / advice)

➡ _____

_____

서답형

16 주어진 단어를 활용하여 다음 우리말을 영어로 쓰시오.

> 너희 나라에서 가장 인기 있는 스포츠는 무엇이니? (popular)

➡ _____

중요

17 다음 중 밑줄 친 부분의 쓰임이 다른 하나는?

① Jason will buy a robot <u>that</u> cleans the house.
② Don't you have a dog <u>that</u> has a cute tail?
③ This is the purse <u>that</u> Kelly lost on the street.
④ He knew <u>that</u> he had to do the work.
⑤ I didn't call the man <u>that</u> gave me his phone number.

18 다음 빈칸에 공통으로 들어갈 말은?

> • What is the name of the man _____ car you borrowed?
> • This school is only for children _____ first language is not Korean.

① who   ② that   ③ which
④ whose   ⑤ whom

서답형

19 주어진 단어를 이용하여 빈칸에 알맞은 말을 쓰시오.

> Mr. and Mrs. Brown have three daughters. _____ of their three daughters is 15 years old. (old)

➡ _____

서답형

20 적절한 관계대명사를 이용하여 다음 두 문장을 하나의 문장으로 쓰시오.

> • I liked the woman.
> • I met her at the party last night.

➡ _____

21 다음 문장을 바르게 영작한 것은?

> 그건 내가 저지른 것 중 최악의 실수야.

① It's a bad mistake that I made.
② It's the baddest mistake that I had.
③ It's the worst mistake that I've ever made.
④ It's worse mistake than any other mistakes.
⑤ It's the bad mistake that I've ever done.

중요

22 다음 중 어법상 바르지 않은 것은?

① Did you check everything that you needed?
② It is the most prettiest cat I've ever had.
③ I know the boy whose hands are so cold.
④ Kelly kept the secret that I told her.
⑤ No other flowers are more beautiful than roses.

01 다음 빈칸에 적절한 말을 어법에 맞게 쓰시오.

> • Everest is _____ mountain in the world.
> • Everest is _____ any other mountain in the world.

➡ _____

02 〈보기〉의 문장과 관계대명사를 이용하여 빈칸을 알맞게 채우시오.

> ┤ 보기 ├
> • They were on the wall.
> • They are never on time.
> • It cannot be explained.

(1) A mystery is something _____ _____.

(2) What happened to the pictures _____ _____?

(3) I don't like people _____.

03 다음 주어진 단어를 이용하여 우리말을 영어로 쓰시오.

> 아픈 아이들을 진찰한 그 남자는 이 병원에서 가장 친절한 의사이다.
> (examine / the / kind / in)

➡ _____
_____

04 다음 중 알맞은 것을 골라 최상급을 이용하여 빈칸에 알맞은 말을 쓰시오.

> • Sydney • Jupiter • The Nile

> • long   • large

(1) _____ city in Australia.
(2) _____ any other planet in the solar system.
(3) _____ in the world.

05 주어진 단어를 바르게 배열하여 다음 우리말을 영어로 쓰시오.

> 그는 내가 만나 본 사람 중 가장 지루한 사람이야.
> (the / most / ever / he / have / is / person / met / boring / that / I)

➡ _____

06 다음은 Rope A, B, C, D에 대한 설명이다. 빈칸에 알맞은 말을 쓰시오.

> Rope A _____
> Rope B _____
> Rope C _____
> Rope D _____

(1) Rope B is _____ Rope A.
(2) Rope D is _____ the other ropes.
(3) Rope A is _____ of all.
(4) No other rope is _____ Rope A.

07 다음 중 서로 관련 있는 문장을 연결하여 하나의 문장으로 쓰시오.

> • A customer is someone.
> • The boy is now in the hospital.
> • The bus runs every half hour.
> • A dictionary is a book.
> • I met somebody.

> • It gives you the meanings of words.
> • Her mother is a famous writer.
> • He was injured in the accident.
> • It goes to the airport.
> • The person buys something from a store.

➡ _____
_____

➡ _____
_____

➡ _____
_____

➡ _____
_____

➡ _____
_____

08 우리말과 같은 뜻이 되도록 빈칸에 알맞은 말을 쓰시오.

(1) 나는 나와 함께 일하는 그 사람들을 좋아해.
➡ I like _____ _____ _____ I
work with.

(2) 그들은 그들의 아이들에게 원하는 모든 것을 준다.
➡ They give _____ _____ _____
_____ they want.

(3) 나는 메뉴가 매우 단순한 식당을 안다.
➡ I know a restaurant _____ _____
is very simple.

09 다음 상황을 읽고 빈칸에 알맞은 말을 쓰시오.

> Jason is talking to his friend about Kelly. Kelly is very patient. He has never met a person like Kelly. So Jason tells his friend about Kelly like this.
> **Jason:** She is _____ .

➡ _____

10 〈보기〉와 같이 하나의 문장을 두 개의 문장으로 쓰시오.

> ┤ 보기 ├
> The people who live upstairs talk very loudly in the morning.
> ➡ The people talk very loudly in the morning.
> ➡ They live upstairs.

(1) I know the boy whose bicycle was stolen.
➡ _____
➡ _____

(2) Daisy lectured on a topic which she knew very little about.
➡ _____
➡ _____

11 다음은 주어진 문장과 같은 의미의 문장이다. 빈칸에 알맞은 말을 쓰시오.

> The Mississippi River is longer than any other river in the United States.

(1) _____ _____ _____ in the United States is _____ _____ the Mississippi River.

(2) The Mississippi River is _____ _____ _____ _____ the United States.

Reading

교과서

Too Hot to Run

Imagine you are in the middle of a great desert. The sands go on and
on in every direction. The sun feels like a giant ball of fire. The hot
wind burns your face and throat. You open your backpack to drink
some water. Oh, no! You're almost out of water. You wet your throat
with a drop of water and keep going.

Sounds like a bad dream? Well, this is not a dream for the people who
take part in the 4 Deserts Race. The 4 Deserts Race is a series of four
races across the world's toughest deserts. Each race is 250 kilometers
long and takes seven days.

The first race takes place in the Atacama Desert in Chile. It is the
driest desert in the world. In fact, it hasn't rained in some parts of the
Atacama Desert for 400 years! The next race goes to the Gobi Desert
in China. It is the windiest desert on earth.

The Atacama Desert

imagine 상상하다
desert 사막
in the middle of ~의 한 가운데에
go on 계속되다
burn 태우다
throat 목구멍
be out of 떨어지다, 바닥나다
wet 적시다
keep Ving 계속해서 V하다
take part in ~에 참가하다
(= participate in)
a series of 일련의, 연속된
each 각각의
take ~의 시간이 걸리다
take place 개최되다, 일어나다
dry 건조한
in fact 사실은, 실제로
for+기간 ~ 동안
windy 바람이 (많이) 부는

확인문제

● 다음 문장이 본문의 내용과 일치하면 T, 일치하지 않으면 F를 쓰시오.

1 The sun makes you feel thirsty. ☐

2 Your water is in your backpack. ☐

3 There is enough water to drink. ☐

4 The 4 Deserts Race takes place in the world's toughest deserts. ☐

5 The Gobi Desert is drier than any other place in the world. ☐

The third race heads to the Sahara Desert in Egypt. It is the hottest of
~로 가다[향하다]   = The Sahara Desert
the four deserts. Temperatures can reach up to 50°C. Finally, the race
최상급+of+복수 명사: ~중 에서 가장 ~한   ~에까지 이르다
travels to the coldest desert on earth, Antarctica. If you throw boiling
              the coldest desert on earth와 Antarctica는 동격   할 만약 ~한다면   throw A into B: A를 B로 던지다
water into the air here, it freezes!
              = boiling water

Only the greatest runners on the planet can take part in 4 Deserts Race,
오직   세상에서
right? Not exactly. Many of the participants are ordinary people like
                    Many of+복수명사: 많은 ~   ~와 같은(전치사)
you and me. So why do they do it? Adrianna, a librarian from France,
                                    Adrianna와 a librarian from France는 동격
says, "It's a chance to test your limits and make your own history.
4 Deserts Race   to부정사의 형용사적 용법-a chance를 수식   make 앞에 to가 생략된 형태
Anyone who crosses the finish line can do anything."
주격 관계대명사 (who ~ line이 Anyone을 수식함)

head to ~로 향하다	
temperature 온도	
reach up ~에 도달하다	
boil 끓다. 끓어오르다	
freeze 얼다. 얼어붙다	
planet 행성	
exactly 정확하게	
participant 참가자	
ordinary 평범한. 보통의	
like ~처럼	
librarian 사서	
chance 기회	
limit 한계	
cross 가로지르다	
finish line 결승선	

확인문제

● 다음 문장이 본문의 내용과 일치하면 T, 일치하지 않으면 F를 쓰시오.

1 The Sahara Desert is the last race. ☐

2 We can see the Sahara Desert in Egypt. ☐

3 The temperature of the Sahara Desert is higher than 50°C. ☐

4 The final race takes place in Antarctica. ☐

5 Only expert runners take part in the 4 Deserts Race. ☐

6 Anyone who wants to test his or her limits can take part in the race. ☐

● 우리말을 참고하여 빈칸에 알맞은 말을 쓰시오.

1 _____ you are _____ _____ _____ _____ a great desert.

2 The sands _____ _____ _____ _____ in every direction.

3 The sun _____ _____ a giant ball of _____ .

4 The hot wind _____ _____ _____ and _____ .

5 You open _____ _____ _____ _____ some water.

6 Oh, no! You're almost _____ _____ _____ .

7 You _____ your throat _____ _____ _____ water and _____ _____ .

8 _____ _____ a bad dream?

9 Well, this is not a dream for the people _____ _____ _____ _____ the 4 Deserts Race.

10 The 4 Deserts Race is _____ _____ _____ across the world's _____ _____ .

11 _____ _____ _____ 250 kilometers long and _____ seven days.

12 The first race _____ _____ in the Atacama Desert _____ Chile.

13 It is _____ _____ _____ in the world.

14 In fact, it _____ _____ in some parts of the Atacama Desert _____ 400 years!

15 The next race _____ _____ the Gobi Desert _____ China.

16 It is _____ _____ _____ on earth.

1 당신이 아주 큰 사막의 한 가운데에 있다고 상상해 봐라.

2 모래 벌판이 사면팔방으로 계속 이어진다.

3 태양은 거대한 불덩이 같다.

4 뜨거운 바람이 당신의 얼굴과 목구멍을 태운다.

5 당신은 물을 좀 마시려고 배낭을 연다.

6 오, 이런! 물이 거의 떨어져 간다.

7 당신은 물 한 방울로 목을 적시고 계속 간다.

8 나쁜 꿈인 것 같은가?

9 글쎄, '4 Deserts Race'에 참가하는 사람들에게 이것은 꿈이 아니다.

10 '4 Deserts Race'는 세계에서 가장 험한 사막들을 가로지르는 연속된 4개의 경주이다.

11 각 경주는 250킬로미터이고 7일이 걸린다.

12 첫 번째 경주는 칠레에 있는 아타카마 사막에서 열린다.

13 그곳은 세계에서 가장 건조한 사막이다.

14 실제로 아타카마 사막의 어떤 곳에는 400년간 비가 내리지 않았다!

15 다음 경주는 중국에 있는 고비 사막으로 이어진다.

16 그곳은 세상에서 가장 바람이 많이 부는 사막이다.

17 The third race _____ _____ the Sahara Desert in Egypt.

18 It is _____ _____ of the four deserts.

19 Temperatures can _____ _____ _____ 50℃.

20 Finally, the race _____ _____ _____ _____ _____ on earth, Antarctica.

21 If you throw _____ _____ into the air here, it _____!

22 Only _____ _____ _____ on the planet can _____ _____ _____ 4 Deserts Race, right?

23 Not _____.

24 Many of _____ _____ _____ _____ people like you and me.

25 So why do they _____ _____?

26 Adrianna, _____ _____ _____ France, says,

27 "It's _____ _____ _____ _____ your limits and _____ your own history.

28 Anyone _____ _____ the finish line _____ _____ _____."

---

17 세 번째 경주는 이집트에 있는 사하라 사막으로 향한다.

18 그곳은 네 개의 사막 중 가장 뜨겁다.

19 온도가 섭씨 50도까지 올라갈 수 있다.

20 마지막으로 경주는 세상에서 가장 추운 사막인 남극 대륙으로 향한다.

21 이곳에서 끓는 물을 공중에 던지면, 그것은 얼어버린다!

22 세상에서 가장 훌륭한 달리기 주자들만 '4 Deserts Race'에 참가할 수 있다, 맞는가?

23 꼭 그렇진 않다.

24 많은 참가자들은 당신과 나와 같은 평범한 사람들이다.

25 그러면 그들은 왜 그것을 하는 가?

26 프랑스 출신의 사서인 Adrianna 는 말한다.

27 "그것은 당신의 한계를 시험하고 당신만의 역사를 만들 기회예요.

28 결승선을 넘는 사람은 어떤 것이든 할 수 있어요."

● 우리말을 참고하여 본문을 영작하시오.

1 당신이 아주 큰 사막의 한 가운데에 있다고 상상해 봐라.

➡ _____

2 모래 벌판이 사면팔방으로 계속 이어진다.

➡ _____

3 태양은 거대한 불덩이 같다.

➡ _____

4 뜨거운 바람이 당신의 얼굴과 목구멍을 태운다.

➡ _____

5 당신은 물을 좀 마시려고 배낭을 연다.

➡ _____

6 오, 이런! 물이 거의 떨어져 간다.

➡ _____

7 당신은 물 한 방울로 목을 적시고 계속 간다.

➡ _____

8 나쁜 꿈인 것 같은가?

➡ _____

9 글쎄, '4 Deserts Race'에 참가하는 사람들에게 이것은 꿈이 아니다.

➡ _____

10 '4 Deserts Race'는 세계에서 가장 험한 사막들을 가로지르는 연속된 4개의 경주이다.

➡ _____

11 각 경주는 250킬로미터이고 7일이 걸린다.

➡ _____

12 첫 번째 경주는 칠레에 있는 아타카마 사막에서 열린다.

➡ _____

13 그곳은 세계에서 가장 건조한 사막이다.

➡ _____

14 실제로 아타카마 사막의 어떤 곳에는 400년간 비가 내리지 않았다!

➡ _____

15 다음 경주는 중국에 있는 고비 사막으로 이어진다.

➡ _____

16 그곳은 세상에서 가장 바람이 많이 부는 사막이다.

➡ _____

17 세 번째 경주는 이집트에 있는 사하라 사막으로 향한다.

➡ _____

18 그곳은 네 개의 사막 중 가장 뜨겁다.

➡ _____

19 온도가 섭씨 50도까지 올라갈 수 있다.

➡ _____

20 마지막으로 경주는 세상에서 가장 추운 사막인 남극 대륙으로 향한다.

➡ _____

21 이곳에서 끓는 물을 공중에 던지면, 그것은 얼어버린다!

➡ _____

22 세상에서 가장 훌륭한 달리기 주자들만 '4 Deserts Race'에 참가할 수 있다, 맞는가?

➡ _____

23 꼭 그렇진 않다.

➡ _____

24 많은 참가자들은 당신과 나와 같은 평범한 사람들이다.

➡ _____

25 그러면 그들은 왜 그것을 하는가?

➡ _____

26 프랑스 출신의 사서인 Adrianna는 말한다.

➡ _____

27 "그것은 당신의 한계를 시험하고 당신만의 역사를 만들 기회예요.

➡ _____

28 결승선을 넘는 사람은 어떤 것이든 할 수 있어요."

➡ _____

[01~04] 다음 글을 읽고, 물음에 답하시오.

ⓐ_____ you are in the middle of a great desert. The sands go on and on in every direction. The sun feels like a ⓑgiant ball of fire. The hot wind burns your face and throat. You open your backpack ⓒ_____ some water. Oh, no! You're almost out of water. You wet your throat with a drop of water and keep ⓓ_____ .

서답형

01 다음과 같이 풀이되는 단어를 빈칸 ⓐ에 쓰시오.

> This word is used when you think about something and your mind forms a picture or idea of it.

➡ _____

02 위 글을 읽고 떠올릴 수 없는 것은?

① a person who is standing in the middle of a desert
② a desert which stretches endlessly
③ a burning throat with the hot wind
④ a full bottle of water
⑤ a person who has a backpack

03 위 글의 밑줄 친 ⓑ를 대신하여 쓸 수 있는 것은?

① tiny　　② small　　③ huge
④ round　　⑤ rolling

중요

04 위 글의 빈칸 ⓒ와 ⓓ에 들어갈 말이 적절하게 짝지어진 것은?

① drinking – go　　② drinking – going
③ to drink – to go　　④ drinking – to go
⑤ to drink – going

[05~09] 다음 글을 읽고, 물음에 답하시오.

Imagine you are ⓐin the middle of a great desert. The sands go ⓑon and on in every direction. The sun feels like (A)a giant ball of fire. The hot wind burns your face and throat. You open your backpack (B)to drink some water. Oh, no! You're almost out of water. You wet your throat with a drop of water and keep going.

Sounds like a ⓒbad dream? Well, this is not a dream for (C)'4 Deserts Race'에 참가한 사람들. The 4 Deserts Race is ⓓa series of four races across the world's toughest deserts. Each race is 250 kilometers long and takes seven days.

05 다음 중 밑줄 친 ⓐ~ⓓ를 대신할 수 없는 것은?

① continuously　　② in the heart of
③ a chain of　　④ carry on
⑤ terrible

06 위 글의 밑줄 친 (A)와 같이 표현한 이유로 가장 적절한 것은?

① It's because the sun looks like a ball.
② It's because the sun makes fire.
③ It's because the sun is huge.
④ It's because the sun is too hot.
⑤ It's because the sun is like a monster.

중요

07 위 글의 밑줄 친 (B)와 쓰임이 같은 것은?

① She wants us to become friends.
② Kyle went to the library to study hard.
③ Do you want something to drink?
④ I would like to have some cookies.
⑤ It is good to see you again.

서답형

08 위 글의 밑줄 친 우리말 (C)를 주어진 단어를 이용하여 영어로 쓰시오.

> (take / the 4 Deserts Race)

➡ _____

서답형

09 위 글의 내용에 맞도록 다음 물음에 답하시오.

> A: How long is each of the deserts race?
>
> B: _____

[10~14] 다음 글을 읽고, 물음에 답하시오.

The first race takes place in the Atacama Desert in Chile. It is the driest desert in the world. ⓐ , it hasn't rained in some parts of the Atacama Desert for 400 years! The next race goes to the Gobi Desert in China. ⓑ그곳은 세상에서 가장 바람이 많이 부는 사막이다. The third race heads to the Sahara Desert in Egypt. It is the hottest of the four deserts. Temperatures can reach up to 50℃. Finally, the race travels to the coldest desert on earth, Antarctica. If you throw boiling water into the air here, ⓒit freezes!

10 위 글의 빈칸 ⓐ에 들어갈 말로 가장 적절한 것은?

① However ② In fact

③ Thus ④ For example

⑤ Then

11 '4 Deserts Race'에 관한 위 글을 읽고 답할 수 없는 것은?

① Where does the first race take place?

② What is the next race following the first race?

③ Where is the Atacama Desert?

④ Where is the smallest desert on earth?

⑤ Which desert is hotter than all the other deserts?

12 위 글을 밑줄 친 우리말 ⓑ를 영어로 바르게 옮기지 않은 것은?

① It is windier than any other desert on earth.

② No other desert on earth is windier than it.

③ It is the windiest desert on earth.

④ No other desert on earth is as windy as it.

⑤ It is not windier than all the other deserts on earth.

중요

13 위 글의 밑줄 친 ⓒ가 가리키는 것을 영어로 쓰시오.

➡ _____

중요

14 위 글의 내용에 맞도록 다음 빈칸에 알맞은 말을 쓰시오.

> A: Where is the final destination of the desert race?
>
> B: It is in _____ which _____.

➡ _____

[15~19] 다음 글을 읽고, 물음에 답하시오.

Only the greatest runners on the planet can take part in 4 Deserts Race, right? Not exactly. Many of the participants are ⓐ_____ people like you and me. So why do they ⓑdo it? Adrianna, a librarian from France, says, "It's a chance to test your limits and make your own history. Anyone _____ⓒ crosses the finish line can do anything."

서답형

15 다음과 같이 풀이되는 단어를 위 글에서 찾아 쓰시오.

the greatest amount, extent, or degree of something that is possible

➡ _____

16 위 글의 문맥상 빈칸 ⓐ에 들어갈 말로 가장 적절한 것은?

① special ② traditional
③ ordinary ④ certain
⑤ unusual

서답형

17 위 글의 밑줄 친 ⓑ가 의미하는 것을 위 글에서 찾아 쓰시오.

➡ _____

18 위 글의 빈칸 ⓒ에 적합한 것을 <u>모두</u> 고르시오.

① whom ② whose ③ who
④ that ⑤ which

19 위 글의 주제로 가장 적절한 것은?

① the difficulty of applying for the 4 Deserts Race
② the reason ordinary people participate in the 4 Deserts Race
③ an effort to run through all the deserts
④ the importance of testing one's limits
⑤ the importance of knowing one's history

[20~23] 다음 글을 읽고, 물음에 답하시오.

Reporter: _____(A)_____
Adrianna: I've run through four deserts. They were the Atacama Desert, the Gobi Desert, the Sahara Desert, and Antarctica.
Reporter: (B)Which desert was the toughest for you?
Adrianna: The Sahara Desert. Temperature often reached up to 50℃.
Reporter: What kind of people ran in the race?
Adrianna: Most of them were ordinary people like you and me. I became good friends with them.
Reporter: Why did you take part in the race?
Adrianna: I wanted to test my limits and make my own history. I thought, "If I can (C)finish the race, then I can do anything."

서답형

20 위 글의 빈칸 (A)에 알맞은 질문을 쓰시오.

➡ _____

서답형

21 위 글의 밑줄 친 (B)와 같은 의미의 문장이 되도록 빈칸에 알맞은 말을 쓰시오.

Which desert was _____ _____ all the other _____ for you?

➡ _____

22 위 글의 내용과 일치하지 <u>않는</u> 것은?

① Adrianna has run through the Atacama Desert.
② Adrianna thinks the Sahara Desert is the toughest.
③ Most of the participants were not special people.
④ It was hard for Adrianna to become friends with the participants.
⑤ There were two reasons why Adrianna took part in the race.

서답형
23 다음과 같이 풀이되는 말을 위 글에서 찾아 쓰시오.

> a measure of how hot or cold something is

➡ _____

[24~27] 다음 글을 읽고, 물음에 답하시오.

Sounds like a bad dream? Well, this is not a dream for the people who take part in the 4 Deserts Race. The 4 Deserts Race is a series of four races across the world's toughest deserts. Each race is 250 kilometers long and takes seven days.

The first race takes place in the Atacama Desert in Chile. ⓐIt is the driest desert in the world. ① In fact, it hasn't rained in some parts of the Atacama Desert for 400 years! ② The next race goes to the Gobi Desert in China. It is the windiest desert on earth. ③ The third race heads to the Sahara Desert in Egypt. ④ It is the hottest of the four deserts. Temperatures can reach up to 50℃. ⑤ If you throw boiling water into the air here, it freezes!

서답형
24 다음 주어진 문장이 들어가기에 가장 적합한 곳은?

> Finally, the race travels to the coldest desert on earth, Antarctica.

①　　②　　③　　④　　⑤

25 위 글을 읽고 답할 수 <u>없는</u> 것은?

① How long does it take to run through the Atacama Desert?
② What makes the Atacama Desert the driest place in the world?
③ Where is the Gobi Desert?
④ What makes the Gobi Desert windier than any other place?
⑤ What degrees does the temperature of the Sahara Desert reach up to?

중요
26 위 글의 밑줄 친 ⓐ와 쓰임이 같은 것은?

① It is wise to accept the apology.
② Is it the invitation card from her?
③ It is warm outside.
④ I find it strange that he is not here.
⑤ It is a long time since they left.

서답형
27 위 글의 내용에 맞게 빈칸에 알맞은 말을 쓰시오.

> The participants of the 4 Deserts Race run through four deserts _____ are the world's _____.

➡ _____

[01~03] 다음 글을 읽고 물음에 답하시오.

_____(A)_____ The sands go on and on in every direction. The sun feels like a giant ball of fire. The hot wind burns your face and throat. You open your backpack to drink some water. Oh, no! You're almost out of water. You wet your throat with a drop of water and keep going.

01 주어진 어구를 바르게 배열하여 빈칸 (A)에 들어갈 말을 쓰시오.

(a great desert / imagine / of / in / are / the middle / you / that)

➡ _____

02 What makes your face and throat burn? Answer in English with a full sentence.

➡ _____

03 위 글의 내용에 맞도록 빈칸에 알맞은 말을 쓰시오.

A: Aren't you thirsty? Why did you drink only a drop of water?
B: It's because _____.

➡ _____

[04~06] 다음 글을 읽고, 물음에 답하시오.

Imagine you are in the middle of a great desert. The sands go on and on in every direction. The sun feels like a giant ball of fire. The hot wind burns your face and throat. You open your backpack to drink some water. Oh, no! You're almost out of water. You wet your throat with a drop of water and keep going.

Sounds like a bad dream? _____(A)_____ The 4 Deserts Race is a series of four races across the world's ___(B)___ deserts. Each race is 250 kilometers long and takes seven days.

04 위 글의 내용에 맞도록 빈칸에 알맞은 말을 6단어로 쓰시오.

A: Why do you open your backpack?
B: I open it _____.

➡ _____

05 관계대명사를 이용하여 다음 두 문장을 하나로 이어 빈칸 (A)에 쓰시오.

• Well, this is not a dream for the people.
• They take part in the 4 Deserts Race.

➡ _____

_____

06 위 글의 빈칸 (B)에 주어진 단어를 어법에 맞게 쓰시오.

(tough)

➡ _____

[07~10] 다음 글을 읽고, 물음에 답하시오.

The first race takes place in the Atacama Desert in Chile. It is the driest desert in the world. In fact, it hasn't rained in some parts of the Atacama Desert for 400 years! The next race goes to the Gobi Desert in China. It is the windiest desert on earth. The third race heads to the Sahara Desert in Egypt. It is the hottest of the four deserts. Temperatures can reach up to 50℃. Finally, the race travels to the coldest desert on earth, Antarctica. If you throw boiling water into the air here, it ____ⓐ____ !

07 다음과 같이 풀이되는 단어를 빈칸 ⓐ에 어법에 맞게 쓰시오.

This word is used when something becomes solid because of low temperatures.

➡ _____

08 위 글을 읽고 다음 조건에 맞도록 사하라 사막의 특징을 쓰시오.

- 비교급을 사용할 것
- 단어 all을 사용할 것

➡ _____

_____

09 다음 질문에 완전한 문장의 영어로 답하시오.

Where does the second race take place?

➡ _____

_____

10 위 글의 내용에 맞도록 빈칸에 알맞은 말을 쓰시오.

No other desert on earth is _____ Antarctica.

➡ _____

[11~12] 다음 글을 읽고, 물음에 답하시오.

Only the greatest runners on the planet can take part in 4 Deserts Race, right? Not exactly. Many of the participants are ordinary people like you and me. ⓐSo why do they do it? Adrianna, a librarian from France, says, "It's a chance to test your limits and make your own history. Anyone who crosses the finish line can do anything."

11 다음은 밑줄 친 ⓐ를 다시 쓴 것이다. 같은 의미가 되도록 빈칸에 알맞은 말을 쓰시오.

So why do the people _____ _____ _____ like us do it?

➡ _____

12 관계대명사를 이용하여 다음 빈칸에 알맞은 말을 쓰시오.

Adrianna is a woman _____ _____ .

➡ _____

해석

Real Life Talk - Step 2

G: What do you do in your free time?
　　　　　　　　　여가 시간에

B: I often play sports.

G: Have you ever played table tennis?
　　have + p.p.: 현재완료 (경험)

B: No, I haven't.
부정의 대답에 do가 아닌 have를 써서 답한다.

G: Have you ever played baseball?

B: Yes, I have.
　긍정의 대답에 do 동사가 아닌 have를 써서 답한다.

G: Have you ever hit a home run?
　　　　　　　　홈런을 치다

B: Yes, I have.

구문해설 • free time: 여가 시간 • table tennis: 탁구 • hit: 치다 • home run: 홈런

G: 너는 여가 시간에 무엇을 하니?
B: 나는 종종 운동을 해.
G: 탁구를 쳐 본 적이 있니?
B: 아니, 없어.
G: 야구를 해 본 적이 있니?
B: 응, 있어.
G: 홈런을 쳐 본 적이 있니?
B: 응, 있어.

Think and Write

A Happy Day for Class 3

The school sports day was held on May 14th. It was very exciting. Students
　　　　　　　　　　　　特정 날짜 앞에 쓰는 전치사　　　　감정을 유발할 때 현재분사형
played basketball and did group jump rope. They also ran a relay race and a
　　　　　　　　　　　　　　　　　　　　　　　　릴레이 경주를 했다
100m race. Class 2 won the group jump rope, and Class 1 won the relay race.
Class 3 won the basketball game and the 100m race. They got the highest
　　　　　　　　　　　　　　　　　　　　　　　　　　　　(점수를) 얻었다
score and became the overall winner. All the classes had great fun.
　　　　　 ~이 되었다　　　　　　　　　　　　　 have fun 재미있게 놀다, 흥겨워하다

구문해설 • hold: 개최하다 • exciting: 신나는 • group jump rope: 단체 줄넘기
• relay race: 릴레이 경주 • overall: 전반적인

3반을 위한 행복한 날

학교 운동회는 5월 14일에 개최되었다. 그것은 매우 신났다. 학생들은 농구를 하고 단체 줄넘기를 했다. 그들은 또한 릴레이 경주를 했고 100미터 달리기도 했다. 2반은 단체 줄넘기에서 우승을 했고, 1반은 릴레이 경주에서 우승을 했다. 3반은 농구 경기와 100미터 경주에서 우승을 차지했다. 그들은 가장 높은 점수를 얻어서 전체 우승자가 되었다. 모든 반은 재미있는 시간을 보냈다.

Culture

Taekwondo is a Korean traditional sport that trains one's body and mind. It is
　　　　　　　　　　　　　　　　　　　= which　　　　　 몸과 마음
one of the most popular sports in the world. People who do taekwondo wear
one of the 최상급+복수명사　　　　　　　　　　　　　主격 관계대명사
white uniforms. Taekwondo training includes jumping, punching, kicking and
shouting. It teaches you ways to protect yourself.
　　　　　　　　　　　　　　　　　 to부정사의 형용사 용법

구문해설 • traditional: 전통적인 • train: 단련시키다, 훈련하다 • popular: 인기 있는, 대중적인
• wear: 입다 • include: 포함하다 • protect: 보호하다

태권도는 몸과 마음을 단련하는 한국의 전통 스포츠이다. 그것은 세계에서 가장 인기 있는 스포츠 중 하나이다. 태권도를 하는 사람들은 흰색 유니폼을 입는다. 태권도 훈련은 뛰기, 치기, 차기, 소리치기를 포함한다. 태권도는 너에게 스스로를 보호하는 방법을 가르쳐 준다.

영역별 핵심문제

01 다음 영영풀이가 나타내는 말을 쓰시오.

> a race in which people run a distance of 26 miles, which is about 42 km

➡ _____

02 다음 중 밑줄 친 부분의 뜻풀이가 바르지 <u>않은</u> 것은?

① I took part in the marathon to test my <u>limits</u>. 한계
② I got a <u>punch</u> on my chin during the boxing match. 타격
③ His work is to <u>train</u> dogs to obey their owners. 훈련시키다
④ We need to wear a hat to <u>protect</u> our skin from the sunlight. 보호하다
⑤ I have a sore <u>throat</u> because of the cold. ~을 통하여

03 다음 문장의 빈칸에 들어갈 말을 〈보기〉에서 골라 쓰시오.

> ┤ 보기 ├
> take part in / a series of / for a living

(1) I'm reading _____ _____ _____ magazines about science.
(2) They will _____ _____ _____ the English speaking contest.
(3) She baked bread every day _____ _____ _____ .

04 다음 주어진 문장의 밑줄 친 부분과 같은 의미로 쓰인 것을 고르시오.

> Emily <u>went on</u> working until late at night.

① Let's <u>go on</u> to the next page.
② What's <u>going on</u> here?
③ We should <u>go on</u> a picnic on such a beautiful day.
④ The hot weather will <u>go on</u> for this week.
⑤ You don't have to <u>go on</u> a diet.

05 다음 우리말을 주어진 단어를 활용하여 영작하시오.

(1) 너는 홈런을 쳐 본 적이 있니? (hit)
➡ _____
(2) 나는 종종 여가 시간에 탁구를 쳐. (free)
➡ _____
(3) 그는 어떤 일을 하나요? (living)
➡ _____

[06~08] 다음 대화를 읽고, 물음에 답하시오.

Jean: I'm so happy. It's Friday!
Tom: What are you going to do on the weekend, Jean?
Jean: I'm going to play badminton.
Tom: Do you play badminton often?
Jean: Yes, it's my favorite free time activity.
Tom: _____ (A) _____
Jean: My dad. What do you do in your free time?
Tom: I often go to the Han River and ride my bike.

06 위 대화의 빈칸 (A)에 들어갈 말을 〈보기〉에 주어진 단어를 모두 배열하여 완성하시오.

> ┤ 보기 ├
>
> usually / who / with / you / play / do

➡ _____

07 What does Jean do in her free time?

➡ _____

08 위 대화의 주제로 적절한 것은?

① volunteer activity
② school activity
③ leisure activity
④ club activity
⑤ festival activity

[09~11] 다음 대화를 읽고, 물음에 답하시오.

Suji: Mike, have you ever heard @of flying yoga?

Mike: Yeah! ⓑI've seen it on TV. People were hanging in the air!

Suji: Guess what? I'm learning it these days.

Mike: Really? It looked so scary. Do you like it, Suji?

Suji: At first, I was a little ©scaring, but now I'm enjoying it.

Mike: _____(A)_____ I think I should ⓓexercise more, too.

Suji: Do you want to join my yoga class?

Mike: No, that's too scary ⓔfor me. I'll just play basketball.

09 위 대화의 @~ⓔ 중 어법상 어색한 것을 찾아 바르게 고치시오.

➡ _____

10 위 대화의 빈칸 (A)에 들어갈 말로 어색한 것은?

① Sounds great!
② Good for you.
③ That's really cool.
④ I'm happy to hear that.
⑤ That's all right.

11 위 대화를 읽고 대답할 수 없는 것은?

① Has Mike ever seen flying yoga?
② What is Suji learning these days?
③ What does Mike think he should do?
④ Does Mike want to join Suji's yoga class?
⑤ Why does Suji like doing yoga these days?

[12~14] 다음 대화를 읽고, 물음에 답하시오.

Hojin: Judy, what do you do in your free time?

Judy: I often go rock climbing with my dad.

Hojin: _____(A)_____

Judy: No, Hojin. I usually do it at a gym near my house.

Hojin: I see. Have you ever done it on a real mountain?

Judy: Not yet. But I hope to do it someday.

Hojin: That's really cool. Can I come and join you next time?

Judy: Sure. I'm going this Saturday.

Hojin: That sounds great.

Judy: You're going to love it.

12 위 대화에서 다음 영영풀이가 가리키는 말을 찾아 쓰시오.

> the sport or activity of climbing steep rock surfaces

➡ _____

13 위 대화의 빈칸 (A)에 〈보기〉에 주어진 단어를 모두 배열하여 문장을 완성하시오.

> ┤ 보기 ├
>
> to / what / you / do / mountain / go

➡ _____

14 위 대화의 내용과 일치하지 <u>않는</u> 것은?

① Judy는 여가 시간에 종종 아빠와 함께 암벽 등반을 간다.

② Judy는 주로 집 근처의 체육관에서 암벽 등반을 한다.

③ Judy는 실제 산에서 암벽 등반을 해 본 적이 없다.

④ Judy는 이번 주 토요일에 암벽 등반을 하러 산에 갈 것이다.

⑤ Judy는 Hojin이 암벽 등반을 좋아하게 될 것이라고 생각한다.

15 다음 대화가 자연스럽게 이어지도록 순서대로 배열하시오.

> (A) That's great! I'm sure you'll like it a lot.
>
> (B) Have you ever been to Jeju-do?
>
> (C) I've never been there, but I'm going there this summer.
>
> (D) Yes, I have. I went there last winter vacation. What about you?

➡ _____

Grammar

16 다음 중 밑줄 친 부분의 쓰임이 적절하지 <u>않은</u> 것은?

① He is the man <u>who</u> I really look up to.

② I apologized to the girl <u>whose</u> milk I spilled.

③ Kyle made friends with a boy <u>which</u> is in my class.

④ Harvard is the best university <u>that</u> I have ever visited.

⑤ Did the woman <u>who</u> stepped on your toes apologize to you?

17 주어진 단어를 활용하여 다음 우리말을 영어로 쓰시오.

> 네가 오늘 수영한 호수는 우리나라에서 가장 깊은 호수이다.
>
> (which / swim in / deep)

➡ _____

18 다음 중 의미가 같지 <u>않은</u> 것은?

① This is the longest bridge in our country.

  → This bridge is longer than any other bridge in our country.

② I worked at a company whose employees were really happy.

  → I worked at a company. Its employees were really happy.

③ Jake is the fastest boy in our school.

  → No other boy in our school is faster than Jake.

④ The woman who had found my wallet called me.

  → I called the woman whose wallet I had found.

⑤ The teacher is excellent. I am taking her lessons.

  → The teacher whose lessons I am taking is excellent.

19 다음 중 어법상 바르지 <u>않은</u> 것은?

> The woman ①whose hair ②is blond ③is Taylor Swift. She is ④one of the most famous ⑤singer in America.

①   ②   ③   ④   ⑤

20 다음 중 밑줄 친 부분을 생략할 수 <u>없는</u> 것은?

① The book <u>that</u> you bought yesterday is very interesting.
② The woman <u>who</u> I wanted to meet was on vacation.
③ I wish to get the job <u>which</u> I applied for.
④ The doctor <u>who</u> lives next door is my father's best friend.
⑤ Is this the key <u>that</u> you lost the other day?

[21~22] 다음 글을 읽고 빈칸에 알맞은 답을 쓰시오.

> There are three boxes on the table. They are named box A, box B, and box C. Box A is smaller than any other box on the table. And no other box is as big as box C. However, box C is the lightest of the three boxes and box A is heavier than all the other boxes.

21 Which is the biggest box?

> Box C is _____ _____ _____ _____ box on the table.

22 Which is the heaviest box?

> No other box on the table is _____ _____ _____ box A.

23 다음 문장의 빈칸에 들어갈 말과 같은 것은?

> There were many children _____ made a lot of noise in the library. (that 사용 불가)

① That is the boy _____ mother is a farmer.
② Picasso painted many pictures _____ are now very expensive.
③ I have two sisters _____ I should take care of.
④ Look at the house _____ roof is red.
⑤ I saw a man and a dog _____ were running together.

24 다음 글을 읽고 빈칸에 알맞은 말을 쓰시오.

> Your friend meets a lot of people, and some of them are very famous. So you ask your friend like this, "Who is _____ person _____ you've ever met?"

➡ _____

25 다음 빈칸에 들어갈 말이 바르게 짝지어진 것은?

> • I know a girl _____ dream is to be a singer.
> • They liked the house _____ was very large.

① who – which   ② whom – that
③ whose – that   ④ whose – who
⑤ who – whose

[26~28] 다음 글을 읽고 물음에 답하시오.

Imagine you are ___ⓐ___ a great desert. The sands go on and on in every direction. The sun ___ⓑ___ a giant ball of fire. The hot wind burns your face and throat. You open your backpack to drink some water. Oh, no! You're almost ___ⓒ___ water. You wet your throat with ___ⓓ___ water and keep going.

26 위 글의 빈칸 ⓐ~ⓓ에 적합한 말이 <u>아닌</u> 것은?

① feels like   ② in the middle of

③ out of   ④ full of

⑤ a drop of

27 위 글의 내용과 일치하지 <u>않는</u> 것은? (2개)

① The sands are everywhere.

② The wind is so hot that you are too thirsty.

③ Your water was in your pocket.

④ You have a lot of water.

⑤ You keep walking after drinking a little water.

28 위 글의 내용에 맞게 빈칸에 알맞은 말을 쓰시오.

A: Due to the hot wind, how does your face feel?

B: My face feels _____ due to the hot wind.

➡ _____

[29~31] 다음 글을 읽고, 물음에 답하시오.

Only the greatest runners on the planet can take part in 4 Deserts Race, right? Not exactly. Many of the (A)<u>participants</u> are ordinary people like you and me. So why do they do ⓐ [it / them]? Adrianna, a librarian from France, says, "It's a chance to test your limits and ⓑ [makes / make] your own history. Anyone who ⓒ[crosses / cross] the finish line can do anything."

29 다음은 밑줄 친 (A)를 설명하는 문장이다. 빈칸에 알맞은 말을 위 글에서 찾아 쓰시오.

A participant means a person _____ _____ an event.

➡ _____

30 위 글의 ⓐ~ⓒ에 들어갈 말이 바르게 짝지어진 것은?

① it – makes – crosses

② it – make – crosses

③ it – make – cross

④ them – make – crosses

⑤ them – makes – cross

31 위 글의 내용과 일치하는 것은?

① Only expert runners can be found in the 4 Deserts Race.

② Ordinary people can't participate in the 4 Deserts Race.

③ A German woman took part in the 4 Deserts Race.

④ Adrianna works in the library.

⑤ Adrianna doesn't want to know her limits.

01 출제율 90%

다음 짝지어진 단어의 관계가 같도록 빈칸에 알맞은 말을 쓰시오.

early : late = melt : _____

02 출제율 95%

다음 주어진 문장의 밑줄 친 부분과 같은 의미로 쓰인 것은?

They succeeded in completing the tough project by cooperating with each other.

① He was in charge of the tough work as a leader.
② My mother's tough hands made me so sad.
③ Tom applied the lotion to relieve his tough skin.
④ He had his teeth broken because of the tough meat.
⑤ She became as tough as nails after moving to China.

[03~04] 다음 대화를 읽고, 물음에 답하시오.

Jean: I'm so happy. It's Friday!
Tom: ⓐWhat are you going to do on the weekend, Jean?
Jean: I'm going to play badminton.
Tom: Do you play badminton ⓑoften?
Jean: Yes, it's my favorite free time activity.
Tom: ⓒWhere do you usually play with?
Jean: My dad. ⓓWhat do you do in your free time?
Tom: I often go to the Han River and ⓔride my bike.

03 출제율 100%

위 대화의 밑줄 친 ⓐ~ⓔ 중 어색한 것을 찾아 바르게 고치시오.

➡ _____

04 출제율 85%

위 대화의 내용과 일치하지 않는 것은?

① Jean feels so good because it's Friday.
② Jean is planning to play badminton.
③ Jean loves playing badminton in her free time.
④ Jean usually plays badminton with her father.
⑤ Jean is going to ride a bike with Tom this Saturday.

05 출제율 90%

다음 주어진 단어를 써서 우리말과 일치하도록 영작하시오.

(1) 나는 종종 여가 시간에 그림을 그려요. (draw, free)
➡ _____
(2) 당신은 일본에 가 본 적이 있나요? (ever, to)
➡ _____
(3) 저는 중국에 가 본 적이 없어요. (never)
➡ _____

06 출제율 90%

다음 주어진 단어를 모두 배열하여 빈칸에 들어갈 말을 영작하시오.

Tony: Bomi, _____
(free / do / what / you / do / in / time / your / ?)
Bomi: I often bake cookies.

➡ _____

Mina: Tom, have you ever been to Jeju-do?

Tom: Yes, I have. I went there last winter vacation. What about you?

Mina: (A)<u>나는 거기에 가 본 적이 없어</u>, but I'm going there this summer.

Tom: That's great! I'm (B)<u>sure</u> you'll like it a lot.

✎ 출제율 95%

07 위 대화의 밑줄 친 우리말 (A)를 4단어를 사용하여 영작하시오.

➡ _____

✎ 출제율 100%

08 위 대화의 밑줄 친 (B)와 바꾸어 쓸 수 있는 것은?

① certain   ② doubtful
③ clear   ④ likely
⑤ believable

✎ 출제율 90%

09 Who has been to Jeju-do?

➡ _____

Suji: Mike, ⓐ<u>너는 플라잉 요가에 대해 들어 본 적이 있니</u>? (of, flying yoga)

Mike: Yeah! I've seen it on TV. People were hanging in the air!

Suji: Guess what? I'm learning it these days.

Mike: (A) Really? It looked so scary. Do you like it, Suji?

Suji: (B) At first, I was a little scared, but now I'm enjoying it.

Mike: (C) Sounds great! I think I should exercise more, too.

Suji: (D) Do you want to join my yoga class?

Mike: (E) I'll just play basketball.

✎ 출제율 90%

10 위 대화의 밑줄 친 ⓐ의 우리말을 주어진 단어를 사용하여 영작하시오.

➡ _____

✎ 출제율 95%

11 위 대화의 (A)~(E) 중 주어진 문장이 들어가기 적절한 곳은?

> No, that's too scary for me.

① (A)   ② (B)   ③ (C)   ④ (D)   ⑤ (E)

✎ 출제율 100%

12 다음 빈칸에 공통으로 들어갈 말은?

> • The problem is not _____ difficult.
> • Everything _____ you made for me is beautiful.
> • I think _____ Tom wants you to help him.

① what   ② who   ③ that
④ which   ⑤ whom

✎ 출제율 90%

13 다음 우리말을 바르게 영작한 것을 <u>모두</u> 고르시오.

> 나는 머리가 긴 그 소녀를 안다.

① I know the girl which has long hair.
② I know the girl who is long hair.
③ I know the girl whose hair is long.
④ I know the girl that hair is long.
⑤ I know the girl who has long hair.

14 다음 중 어법상 바르지 않은 것은?

① Is this the oldest building in the country?
② Tom is the funniest boy in the class.
③ You are the latest person I want to talk with.
④ Julia is the most creative and beautiful person I know.
⑤ It is the dirtiest room I've ever seen.

15 다음 중 나머지 넷과 의미가 다른 하나는?

① Honesty is more important than any other thing.
② Nothing is more important than honesty.
③ Honesty is the most important thing of all.
④ Nothing is so important as honesty.
⑤ Nothing is less important than honesty.

16 주어진 단어를 활용하여 다음 우리말을 영어로 쓰시오.

그것은 내 생애에서 가장 고통스러운 순간이었다. (it, painful)

➡ _____

17 다음 두 문장을 관계대명사 whose를 써서 한 문장으로 만드시오.

• Kelly bought a book.
• Its cover looked familiar to him.

➡ _____
_____

18 주어진 단어를 어법에 맞게 각각 쓰시오.

(diligent)

A: What do you think is _____ _____ _____ insect on earth?
B: I think no other insect on earth is _____ _____ _____ bees.

➡ _____

[19~21] 다음 글을 읽고, 물음에 답하시오.

The first race takes place in the Atacama Desert in Chile. It is the driest desert in the world. In fact, it ⓐhasn't rained in some parts of the Atacama Desert for 400 years! ① The next race goes to the Gobi Desert in China. It is the windiest desert on earth. ② The third race heads to the Sahara Desert in Egypt. It is the hottest of the four deserts. ③ Finally, the race travels to the coldest desert on earth, Antartica. ④ If you throw boiling water into the air here, it freezes! ⑤

19 다음 주어진 문장이 들어가기에 가장 적절한 곳은?

Temperatures can reach up to 50℃.

① ② ③ ④ ⑤

20 위 글의 밑줄 친 ⓐ와 쓰임이 같은 것은?

① She has just had dinner with me.
② Have you ever heard about the news?
③ How long have you seen each other?
④ Jimmy has lost his cell phone.
⑤ My mom has gone out.

21 다음 우리말을 관계대명사를 이용하여 영어로 쓰시오.

> 중국에 있는 고비 사막은 지구상에서 가장 바람이 많이 부는 사막이다.

➡ _____

_____

23 다음 ①~⑤ 중 글의 흐름상 어색한 것은?

①   ②   ③   ④   ⑤

24 (A)~(E) 중 글의 내용과 일치하는 것의 개수는?

> (A) The Antarctica Desert race is 250km long.
> (B) The Sahara Desert is in Egypt.
> (C) It takes 14 days to run through two deserts.
> (D) The participants are made up of only ordinary people.
> (E) The last race is held in Antarctica.

① 1개   ② 2개   ③ 3개   ④ 4개   ⑤ 5개

[22~26] 다음 글을 읽고, 물음에 답하시오.

The 4 Deserts Race is a series of four races across the world's ①toughest deserts. Each race is 250 kilometers long and ⓐ ____ seven days.

The first race ⓑ ____ place in the Atacama Desert in Chile. It is the driest desert in the world. In fact, it ②hasn't rained in some parts of the Atacama Desert for 400 years! The next race goes to the Gobi Desert in China. It is ③windier than any other desert on earth. The third race heads to the Sahara Desert in Egypt. It is the hottest of the four deserts. Temperatures can reach ④down to 50℃. Finally, the race travels to the coldest desert on earth, Antarctica. If you throw boiling water into the air here, it ⑤freezes!

Only the greatest runners on the planet can take part in 4 Deserts Race, right? Not exactly. Many of the participants are ordinary people like you and me. So why do they do it? Adrianna, a librarian from France, says, "It's a chance to test your limits and make your own history. ⓒ _____ "

22 위 글의 빈칸 ⓐ, ⓑ에 공통으로 들어갈 말은?

① makes   ② has   ③ takes
④ holds   ⑤ gets

25 위 글의 내용에 맞도록 빈칸에 알맞은 말을 쓰시오.

> Not only ____ ____ ____ but also ____ ____ take part in the 4 Deserts Race.

➡ _____

26 주어진 단어를 바르게 배열하여 빈칸 ⓒ를 알맞게 채우시오.

> (anything / who / do / can / anyone / the finish line / crosses)

➡ _____

[01~03] 다음 대화를 읽고 물음에 답하시오.

> Mina: Tom, (A)너는 제주도에 가 본 적이 있니?
>
> Tom: Yes, I have. I went there last winter vacation. What about you?
>
> Mina: I've never been there, but I'm going there this summer.
>
> Tom: That's great! I'm sure you'll like (B)it a lot.

01 위 대화의 밑줄 친 우리말 (A)를 영작하시오.

➡ _____

02 위 대화의 밑줄 친 (B)가 가리키는 것을 영어로 쓰시오.

➡ _____

03 What is Mina planning to do this summer?

➡ _____

04 다음 우리말을 여러 가지 표현을 이용하여 영어로 쓰시오.

> Kevin은 그의 가족 구성원 중에서 가장 어리다.

➡ _____
➡ _____
➡ _____
➡ _____
➡ _____

05 다음 문장을 하나의 문장으로 만드시오.

> • You are sitting on the chair.
> • Is it comfortable?

➡ _____

06 다음 빈칸에 알맞은 말을 쓰시오.

> The town _____ I grew up in is very small. People in the town is nicer _____ any other people in the world. If you visit there, you will see many people _____ smile is very bright.

➡ _____

07 주어진 조건에 맞도록 다음 우리말을 영어로 쓰시오.

> • 최상급을 한 번 사용할 것
> • laugh를 두 번 사용할 것
> • 관계대명사를 사용할 것

> 마지막에 웃는 사람이 가장 잘 웃는 사람이다.
> (= 마지막에 웃는 사람이 최후의 승자이다.)

➡ He _____.

08 주어진 단어를 바르게 배열하여 문장을 완성하시오.

> A myth _____.
> (traditional / is / expresses / a story / beliefs / which)

➡ _____

[09~11] 다음 글을 읽고, 물음에 답하시오.

> Imagine you are in the middle of a great desert. The sands ⓐ on and on in every direction. The sun feels like a giant ball of fire. The hot wind burns your face and throat. You open your backpack to drink some water. Oh, no! You're almost out of water. You wet your throat with a drop of water and keep ⓑ .

Sounds like a bad dream? Well, this is not a dream for the people who take part in the 4 Deserts Race. The 4 Deserts Race is a series of four races across the world's toughest deserts. Each race is 250 kilometers long and takes seven days.

(A)The first race takes place in the Atacama Desert in Chile. It is the driest desert in the world.   (B)   fact, it hasn't rained in some parts of the Atacama Desert for 400 years! The next race   ⓒ   to the Gobi Desert in China. It is the windiest desert on earth.

09 주어진 동사를 어법에 맞게 빈칸 ⓐ~ⓒ에 쓰시오.

(go)

ⓐ _____ ⓑ _____ ⓒ _____

10 적절한 관계대명사를 이용하여 밑줄 친 (A)를 하나의 문장으로 쓰시오.

➡ _____

_____

11 위 글의 빈칸 (B)에 알맞은 전치사를 쓰시오.

➡ _____

[12~13] 다음 글을 읽고, 물음에 답하시오.

The third race heads to the Sahara Desert in Egypt. It is the hottest of the four deserts. Temperatures can reach up to 50℃. Finally, the race travels to the coldest desert on earth, Antarctica. If you throw boiling water into the air here, it freezes!

Only the greatest runners on the planet can take part in 4 Deserts Race, right? Not exactly. Many of the participants are ordinary people like you and me. So why do they do it? Adrianna, a librarian from France, says, "It's a chance to test your limits and make your own history. Anyone who crosses the finish line can do anything."

12 원급을 이용하여 다음 질문에 답하시오.

Q: Which desert is colder than any other desert on earth?
A: No other desert _____.

➡ _____

13 '4 Deserts Race' 광고에 알맞은 말을 쓰시오.

_____ _____ _____ 4 Deserts
Race _____ offers you a chance
_____ _____ _____ and
_____ _____ _____ _____.
당신의 한계를 시험하고 당신의 역사를 만들 기회를 제공하는 '4 Deserts Race'에 참가하세요.

➡ _____

_____

창의사고력 서술형 문제

01 다음 대화의 내용과 일치하도록 Mike의 일기를 완성하시오.

> **Suji:** Mike, have you ever heard of flying yoga?
>
> **Mike:** Yeah! I've seen it on TV. People were hanging in the air!
>
> **Suji:** Guess what? I'm learning it these days.
>
> **Mike:** Really? It looked so scary. Do you like it, Suji?
>
> **Suji:** At first, I was a little scared, but now I'm enjoying it.
>
> **Mike:** Sounds great! I think I should exercise more, too.
>
> **Suji:** Do you want to join my yoga class?
>
> **Mike:** No, that's too scary for me. I'll just play basketball.

> Today, I talked about (1)_____ with Suji. I have seen it on TV. Surprisingly, she was learning and enjoying it recently. She suggested (2)_____, but it looked so (3)_____ for me. Although I didn't accept her suggestion, I decided to (4)_____.

02 관계대명사를 이용하여 〈보기〉와 같이 직업과 사물을 설명하는 문장을 쓰시오.

> 보기
>
> A coward is a person who is not brave.

(1) English teachers are people _____.

(2) Hair designers are people _____.

(3) A computer is a machine _____.

(4) A car is a vehicle _____.

(5) The Wright Brothers were people _____.

03 다음 〈보기〉에 나오는 형용사를 이용하여 최상급을 나타내는 문장을 쓰시오.

> 보기
>
> beautiful   delicious   spicy   hard   soft

(1) _____

(2) _____

(3) _____

(4) _____

(5) _____

단원별 모의고사

01 다음 영영풀이가 나타내는 말을 쓰시오.

> the measurement in degrees of how hot or cold a thing or place is

➡ _____

02 다음 문장의 빈칸에 들어갈 말을 〈보기〉에서 골라 쓰시오.

┌─ 보기 ─┐
temperature / direction / scary / boiling

(1) I'm afraid you're going in the wrong _____.

(2) I had a nightmare because I saw the _____ movie yesterday.

(3) Be careful! There is lots of _____ water in the pot.

(4) My doctor was measuring my _____.

03 다음 주어진 문장의 밑줄 친 부분과 같은 의미로 쓰인 것은?

> Many tourists <u>head</u> to Jeju-do in Korea.

① You look so tired. Why don't you <u>head</u> to the house?

② Mike shook his <u>head</u> during the meeting.

③ I hit my <u>head</u> on the window.

④ Tony is not the <u>head</u> of our company.

⑤ The <u>head</u> of the department has been changed.

04 다음 우리말을 주어진 어구를 사용하여 영작하시오.

(1) 이 소설은 일련의 역사적 사실에 관해 쓰여졌다. (a series of)

➡ _____

(2) 경주는 매년 봄에 개최된다. (take place)

➡ _____

(3) 고양이가 길 한 가운데에서 발견되었다. (in the middle of, road)

➡ _____

[05~06] 다음 대화를 읽고 물음에 답하시오.

Jean: I'm so happy. It's Friday!

Tom: What are you going to do on the weekend, Jean?

Jean: I'm going to play badminton.

Tom: (A)[Do / Have] you play badminton often?

Jean: Yes, it's my favorite free time activity.

Tom: Who do you usually play (B)[by / with]?

Jean: My dad. What do you do in your free time?

Tom: I often go to the Han River and (C)[ride / riding] my bike.

05 위 대화의 괄호 (A)~(C)에 들어갈 말이 바르게 짝지어진 것은?

	(A)	(B)	(C)
①	Do	by	ride
②	Do	with	riding
③	Do	with	ride
④	Have	with	riding
⑤	Have	by	ride

06 What sport does Jean like best as her free time activity?

➡ _____

[07~09] 다음 대화를 읽고, 물음에 답하시오.

Suji: Mike, have you ever heard of flying yoga?

Mike: Yeah! I've seen ⓐit on TV. People were hanging in the air!

Suji: Guess what? I'm learning ⓑit these days.

Mike: Really? ⓒIt looked so scary. Do you like it, Suji?

Suji: At first, I was a little scared, but now I'm enjoying ⓓit.

Mike: Sounds great! I think ⓔit is necessary for me to exercise more, too.

Suji: Do you want to join my yoga class?

Mike: No, that's too (A)scary for me. I'll just play basketball.

07 위 대화의 ⓐ~ⓔ 중 가리키는 대상이 나머지와 넷과 다른 것은?

① ⓐ   ② ⓑ   ③ ⓒ   ④ ⓓ   ⑤ ⓔ

08 위 대화의 밑줄 친 (A)와 의미가 다른 것은?

① terrifying   ② scaring
③ frightening   ④ fearful
⑤ terrific

09 위 대화의 내용과 일치하지 않는 것은?

① Suji is learning flying yoga these days.
② Mike feels scary about flying yoga.
③ Mike has seen flying yoga on TV.
④ Mike is going to join the yoga class with Suji.
⑤ Mike thinks he needs to exercise more.

[10~11] 다음 대화를 읽고, 물음에 답하시오.

Hojin: Judy, what do you do in your free time?

Judy: I often go rock climbing with my dad.

Hojin: What mountain do you go to?

Judy: No, Hojin. I usually do it at a gym near my house.

Hojin: I see. (A)너는 실제 산에서 그것을 해 본 적이 있니?

Judy: Not yet. But I hope to do it someday.

Hojin: That's really cool. (B)_____

Judy: Sure. I'm going this Saturday.

Hojin: That sounds great.

Judy: You're going to love it.

10 위 대화의 밑줄 친 (A)의 우리말과 일치하도록 〈보기〉에 주어진 단어를 모두 배열하시오.

┌─ 보기 ─┐
ever / mountain / have / done / you / a / real / it / on

➡ _____

11 위 대화의 빈칸 (B)에 들어갈 말로 어색한 것은?

① Can I come and join you next time?
② Do you wonder if I come and join you next time?
③ Is it okay for me to come and join you next time?
④ May I come and join you next time?
⑤ Would it be possible for me to come and join you next time?

12 주어진 문장에 대화가 자연스럽게 이어지도록 순서대로 배열하시오.

┌─────────────────────────────────────┐
│ What are you going to do on the weekend? │
└─────────────────────────────────────┘

┌─────────────────────────────────────┐
│ (A) Who do you usually play with?   │
│ (B) My dad.   │
│ (C) Do you play badminton often?   │
│ (D) Yes, it's my favorite free time activity. │
│ (E) I'm going to play badminton.   │
└─────────────────────────────────────┘

➡ _____

13 다음 중 빈칸에 들어갈 말이 바르게 짝지어진 것은?

> • What is the name of the boy _____ pen you borrowed?
> • What is the name of the boy _____ you lent your pen?

① whom – who
② who – whose
③ whose – whom
④ whom – that
⑤ whose – whose

14 다음 우리말을 영어로 바르게 옮기지 <u>않은</u> 것은?

① 그건 내가 할 수 있는 최소한이야.
→ It's the least I can do.
② 그는 그 소년들 중에서 가장 행복해 보여.
→ He looks happiest of the boys.
③ 그것은 내 인생에서 가장 무서웠던 순간이었어.
→ It was the scariest moment of my life.
④ 이 사탕이 그 슈퍼마켓에서 가장 싼 사탕이야.
→ This candy is cheaper than all the other candies in the supermarket.
⑤ 그것은 그 주에서 가장 좋은 대학이야.
→ It is the best college in the state.

15 다음 빈칸에 적절한 것을 <u>모두</u> 고르시오.

> These are the blue jeans _____ Tom Cruise wore in the movie.

① who
② whose
③ which
④ that
⑤ whom

16 주어진 단어를 바르게 배열하여 다음 문장을 완성하시오.

> August _____
> September.
> (before / that / the / comes / month / is)

➡ _____

17 주어진 단어를 활용하여 다음 우리말을 영어로 쓰시오.

> 그것은 내 생애 최악의 경험들 중 하나야. (bad)

➡ _____

[18~20] 다음 글을 읽고, 물음에 답하시오.

> Imagine you are in the middle of a great desert. The sands go on and on in every direction. The sun feels like a giant ball of ⓐfire. The hot wind ⓑburns your face and throat. You open your backpack to drink some water. Oh, no! You're almost out of water. You wet your throat with ⓒ<u>plenty of</u> water and keep going.
> Sounds like a ⓓbad dream? Well, this is not a dream for the people who take part in the 4 Deserts Race. The 4 Deserts Race is a series of four races across the world's ⓔtoughest deserts. Each race is 250 kilometers long and takes seven days.

18 위 글의 밑줄 친 ⓐ~ⓔ 중 문맥상 어색한 것은?

① ⓐ ② ⓑ ③ ⓒ ④ ⓓ ⑤ ⓔ

19 위 글의 내용과 일치하는 것은?

① You can see the sands only in one direction.
② The hot sun makes the wind cold.
③ You are thirsty because of a long walk.
④ There are people who participate in the 4 Deserts Race.
⑤ The 4 Deserts Race is 250km long.

20 위 글의 내용에 맞게 빈칸에 알맞은 답을 하시오.

> A: How long does it take to finish a race?
> B: _____

➡ _____

[21~23] 다음 글을 읽고, 물음에 답하시오.

The first race takes place ①in the Atacama Desert in Chile. It is the driest desert in the world. In fact, it hasn't rained in some parts of the Atacama Desert ②since 400 years! The next race goes to the Gobi Desert in China. It is ③the windiest desert on earth. The third race heads to the Sahara Desert in Egypt. It is the hottest of the four deserts. Temperatures can reach up ④ to 50℃. Finally, the race travels to the coldest desert on earth, Antarctica. If you throw ⑤ boiling water into the air here, it freezes!

21 위 글의 ①~⑤ 중 어법상 바르지 않은 것은?

①   ②   ③   ④   ⑤

22 위 글의 내용에 맞도록 빈칸에 알맞은 말을 쓰시오.

No other desert on earth is _____ _____ Antarctica.
= No other desert on earth is _____ _____ _____ Antarctica.

➡ _____, _____

23 다음 중 위 글을 읽고 답할 수 없는 것은?

① Where is the Atacama Desert?
② How long hasn't it rained in some parts of the Atacama Desert?
③ Where do the participants go after the first race?
④ Which desert is hotter than any other desert?
⑤ Why do people take part in the desert race?

[24~25] 다음 글을 읽고, 물음에 답하시오.

Only the greatest runners on the planet can take part in 4 Deserts Race, right? Not exactly. Many of the participants are ordinary people like you and me. So why do they do it? Adrianna, a librarian from France, says, "It's a chance to test your limits and make your own history. Anyone who crosses the finish line can do anything."

24 위 글을 읽고 답할 수 있는 것은?

① How many people participate in the 4 Deserts Race?
② Where is the first race held?
③ What is the reason people take part in the race?
④ How many deserts has Adrianna run through?
⑤ Why does Adrianna want to test her limits?

25 다음 우리말에 맞게 빈칸을 채우시오.

Anyone _____ wants to _____ his or her _____ can _____ in 4 Deserts Race.
자신의 한계를 시험하기를 원하는 사람은 누구든 사막 레이스에 참가할 수 있다.

➡ _____

26 주어진 문장에 자연스럽게 연결되도록 (A)~(C)를 바르게 나열하시오.

Imagine you are in the middle of a great desert. The sands go on and on in every direction.

(A) Oh, no! You're almost out of water. You wet your throat with a drop of water and keep going.
(B) Sounds like a bad dream? Well, this is not a dream for the people who take part in the 4 Deserts Race.
(C) The sun feels like a giant ball of fire. The hot wind burns your face and throat. You open your backpack to drink some water.

➡ _____ → _____ → _____

Lesson
Special

Summer on a Stick

Words & Expressions

Key Words

- **about**[əbáut] 부 대략, 약
- **add**[æd] 동 더하다, 추가하다
- **apple juice** 사과 주스
- **blend**[blend] 동 섞다, 혼합하다
- **blender**[bléndər] 명 믹서
- **close**[klouz] 동 (문, 가게를) 닫다, (눈을) 감다
- **cold**[kould] 형 추운, 찬 명 감기
- **cool**[ku:l] 형 시원한, 냉정한, 멋진
- **cut**[kʌt] 동 자르다
- **enjoy**[indʒói] 동 즐기다, (즐겁게) 맛보다
- **excellent**[éksələnt] 형 우수한, 훌륭한
- **finish**[fíniʃ] 동 끝내다, 마치다
- **freezer**[frí:zər] 명 냉동고
- **health**[helθ] 명 건강
- **ice pop** 막대 아이스크림
- **kiwi**[kí:wi] 명 키위
- **maker**[méikər] 명 ~을 만드는 기계(사람, 회사)
- **mix**[miks] 명 혼합(물) 동 섞다, 혼합하다
- **need**[ni:d] 동 필요하다

- **orange**[ɔ́:rindʒ] 명 오렌지
- **own**[oun] 형 자기 자신의, 고유한
- **peel**[pi:l] 동 껍질을 벗기다 명 껍질
- **piece**[pi:s] 명 조각, 일부, 부분
- **pineapple**[painǽpəl] 명 파인애플
- **pour**[pɔ:r] 동 붓다, 따르다
- **pretty**[príti] 형 예쁜, 귀여운 부 꽤, 상당히
- **share**[ʃɛər] 동 나누다, 공유하다
- **slice**[slais] 동 얇게 썰다[베다] 명 얇은 조각
- **smooth**[smu:ð] 형 매끄러운, 부드러운
- **source**[sɔ:rs] 명 원천, 근원
- **stay**[stei] 동 ~인 채로 있다, 남다, 머무르다
- **step**[step] 명 단계
- **stick**[stik] 명 막대기, 지팡이
- **strawberry**[strɔ́:bèri] 명 딸기
- **tip**[tip] 명 조언, 비결
- **try**[trai] 동 시도하다, 해 보다
- **until**[əntíl] 전 ~까지
- **vitamin**[váitəmin] 명 비타민

Key Expressions

- **a cup of** ~ 한 잔[컵]의
- **a half** (= **one half**) 2분의 1
- **cut A into B** A를 B(상태)로 자르다
- **have a cold** 감기에 걸리다

- **mix up** ~을 섞다
- **pour A into B** A를 B에 붓다
- **put A into B** A를 B에 넣다
- **stay cool** 시원함을 유지하다

Word Power

※ 서로 반대되는 뜻을 가진 어휘

☐ **smooth** 매끄러운, 부드러운 ↔ **rough** 거친

☐ **part** 부분 ↔ **whole** 전체, 전부

☐ **cool** 시원한 ↔ **warm** 따뜻한

☐ **close** 닫다 ↔ **open** 열다

☐ **ask** 묻다 ↔ **answer** 대답하다

☐ **add** 더하다 ↔ **subtract** 빼다

☐ **finish** 끝내다 ↔ **begin** 시작하다

☐ **high** 높은 ↔ **low** 낮은

English Dictionary

☐ **add** 더하다
→ to put something together with something else so as to increase the size, number, amount, etc.
크기, 수, 양 등을 증가시키기 위해 무언가에 다른 무언가를 더하다

☐ **blender** 믹서
→ an electric machine for mixing soft food or liquid
부드러운 음식이나 음료를 섞기 위한 전기 기기

☐ **cut** 자르다
→ to divide something into two or more pieces with a knife, etc.
칼 등으로 무언가를 두 개 또는 그 이상의 조각으로 나누다

☐ **excellent** 훌륭한, 우수한
→ extremely good
극히 좋은

☐ **mix** 혼합
→ a combination of things that you need to make something
무언가를 만들기 위해 필요한 것들의 결합

☐ **peel** 껍질을 벗기다
→ to take the outer layer off fruit, vegetables, etc.
과일이나 야채 등의 외면을 벗겨 내다

☐ **pineapple** 파인애플
→ a large tropical fruit with thick rough skin, sweet yellow flesh with a lot of juice and stiff leaves on top
두껍고 거친 표면을 가졌으며 많은 즙이 있는 달콤한 노란색의 과육과 맨 윗부분의 뻣뻣한 나뭇잎을 가진 큰 열대 과일

☐ **pour** 붓다, 따르다
→ to make a liquid or other substance flow from a container in a continuous stream
액체나 다른 물질을 용기로부터 계속 흐르게 만들다

☐ **slice** 얇은 조각
→ a thin flat piece of food that has been cut off a larger piece
큰 조각을 잘라낸 음식의 얇고 평평한 조각

☐ **smooth** 매끄러운
→ completely flat and even, without any lumps, holes or rough areas
어떤 혹, 구멍, 또는 거친 부분이 없이 완전히 평평하고 균일한

☐ **step** 단계
→ one of a series of things that you do in order to achieve something
무언가를 성취하기 위해 당신이 하는 일련의 것들 중 하나

☐ **stick** 막대기
→ a thin piece of wood that has fallen or been broken from a tree
나무로부터 떨어지거나 부서진 나무의 얇은 조각

☐ **tip** 조언, 비결
→ a small piece of advice about something practical
어떤 실제적인 것에 관한 사소한 조언

☐ **vitamin** 비타민
→ a natural substance found in food that is an essential part of what humans and animals eat to help them grow and stay healthy
성장하고 건강을 유지하는 데 도움을 주기 위해 동물이나 사람들이 먹는 것의 필수적인 부분으로 음식에서 발견되는 자연적 물질

Pineapple Ice Pops

The hot days of summer are here. How can we <u>stay cool</u>? Let's make
stay(2형식 동사)+형용사: ~한 상태로 있다

ice pops together!

You need:

1/2 pineapple
분자는 기수로, 분모는 서수로 읽음 = a half 또는 one half

2 kiwis

1 cup of apple juice

ice pop makers

Steps

1. <u>Cut</u> the pineapple <u>into</u> small pieces. 2. Peel the kiwis and slice <u>them</u>.
cut A into B: A를 B(상태)로 자르다   = the kiwis

3. <u>Put</u> the pineapple pieces <u>into</u> the blender. 4. Add the apple juice. 5.
put A into B: A를 B에 넣다

Blend <u>until</u> the mix is smooth. 6. Pour <u>the mix</u> into the ice pop makers.
~할 때까지(접속사)   혼합물(명사)

7. Add the kiwi slices. 8. Close the ice pop makers. 9. Put <u>them</u> in the
= the ice pop makers

<u>freezer for</u> about three hours.
~동안 (전치사)

Finished!

Enjoy your summer on a stick!

---

stay cool 시원함을 유지하다

let's ~ ~하자

ice pop 막대 아이스크림

maker 만드는 기계

peel 껍질을 벗기다

slice 얇게 썰다

blender 믹서기, 분쇄기

add ~을 첨가하다

blend ~을 섞다

smooth (덩어리 없이) 고루 잘 섞인

pour ~을 붓다

freezer 냉동고

about 대략

📎 **확인문제**

● 다음 문장이 본문의 내용과 일치하면 T, 일치하지 <u>않으면</u> F를 쓰시오.

1   It is a recipe for pineapple ice pops. ☐

2   You don't need apple juice to make pineapple ice pops. ☐

3   The first step is cutting pineapples. ☐

4   You don't have to peel the kiwis. ☐

5   What you need to put into the blender first is kiwis. ☐

Health Tips

Pineapples are an excellent source of vitamin C. They have more
vitamin C than oranges. So when you have a cold, try pineapples.

Share Your Ideas!

How will you make your own ice pops? Share your ideas!

Jinsu

I will use kiwis and strawberries. I will cut them into big pieces. I will
put them into the ice pop makers with apple juice. I think my ice pops
will be pretty.

---

tip 조언	
excellent 탁월한, 훌륭한	
source 원천	
vitamin 비타민	
have a cold 감기에 걸리다	
share 공유하다	
own 자신의	
cut A into B A를 B로 자르다	
pretty 예쁜	

확인문제

● 다음 문장이 본문의 내용과 일치하면 T, 일치하지 않으면 F를 쓰시오.

1 Pineapples are good for us when we have a cold. ☐

2 Oranges have more vitamin C than pineapples. ☐

3 There is only one way to make ice pops. ☐

4 You don't need to cut strawberries to make ice pops. ☐

5 Ice pops are made from kiwis, strawberries and apple juice. ☐

● 우리말을 참고하여 빈칸에 알맞은 말을 쓰시오.

1 The _____ _____ of summer _____ here.

2 How can we _____ _____?

3 Let's _____ ice pops together!

4 You need:

1/2 _____

2 _____

1 _____ of apple juice

ice pop _____

5 _____

6 _____ the pineapple _____ _____ _____.

7 _____ the kiwis and _____ _____.

8 _____ the pineapple _____ _____ the blender.

9 _____ the apple juice.

10 _____ _____ the mix is _____.

11 _____ the mix _____ the ice pop makers.

12 _____ the kiwi _____.

13 _____ the ice pop makers.

14 _____ _____ in the freezer _____ _____ three hours.

1	더운 여름날이 왔어요.
2	우리는 어떻게 시원하게 지낼 수 있을까요?
3	막대 아이스크림을 함께 만들어 봐요!
4	여러분은 필요해요:
	파인애플 1/2개
	키위 2개
	사과 주스 1컵
	막대 아이스크림 틀
5	단계
6	파인애플을 작은 조각으로 자르세요.
7	키위의 껍질을 벗기고 얇게 자르세요.
8	파인애플 조각들을 믹서에 넣으세요.
9	사과 주스를 첨가하세요.
10	혼합물이 덩어리 없이 골고루 잘 섞일 때까지 섞으세요.
11	혼합물을 막대 아이스크림 틀에 부으세요.
12	키위 조각을 추가하세요.
13	막대 아이스크림 틀을 닫으세요.
14	약 세 시간 동안 그것들을 냉동고에 넣으세요.

15 _____ !

16 _____ your summer _____ _____ _____ !

17 Health _____

18 Pineapples _____ _____ _____ _____ _____ vitamin C.

19 They have _____ _____ _____ _____ oranges.

20 So _____ you have _____ _____ , _____ pineapples.

21 _____ Your Ideas!

22 How will you _____ _____ _____ ice pops?

23 _____ your ideas!

24 I will _____ kiwis and strawberries.

25 I will _____ _____ _____ big pieces.

26 I will _____ _____ _____ the ice pop makers _____ apple juice.

27 I think my ice pops _____ _____ _____ .

15	끝났어요!
16	막대 위의 여름을 맛보세요!
17	건강 조언들
18	파인애플은 비타민 C의 훌륭한 원천이에요.
19	파인애플에는 비타민 C가 오렌지보다 더 많이 들어 있어요.
20	그러니 감기에 걸리면 파인애플을 먹어 보세요.
21	여러분의 생각을 나누세요!
22	여러분은 어떻게 막대 아이스크림을 만들 건가요?
23	여러분의 생각을 나누세요!
24	저는 키위와 딸기를 사용할 거예요.
25	저는 그것들을 크게 자를 거예요.
26	그것들을 사과 주스와 함께 막대 아이스크림 틀에 넣을 거예요.
27	제 막대 아이스크림은 예쁠 것 같아요.

● 우리말을 참고하여 본문을 영작하시오.

1 더운 여름날이 왔어요.

➡ _____

2 우리는 어떻게 시원하게 지낼 수 있을까요?

➡ _____

3 막대 아이스크림을 함께 만들어 봐요!

➡ _____

4 여러분은 필요해요: 파인애플 1/2개, 키위 2개, 사과 주스 1컵, 막대 아이스크림 틀

➡ _____

5 단계

➡ _____

6 파인애플을 작은 조각으로 자르세요.

➡ _____

7 키위의 껍질을 벗기고 얇게 자르세요.

➡ _____

8 파인애플 조각들을 믹서에 넣으세요.

➡ _____

9 사과 주스를 첨가하세요.

➡ _____

10 혼합물이 덩어리 없이 골고루 잘 섞일 때까지 섞으세요.

➡ _____

11 혼합물을 막대 아이스크림 틀에 부으세요.

➡ _____

12 키위 조각을 추가하세요.

➡ _____

13 막대 아이스크림 틀을 닫으세요.

➡ _____

14 약 세 시간 동안 그것들을 냉동고에 넣으세요.

➡ _____

15 끝났어요!

➡ _____

16 막대 위의 여름을 맛보세요!

➡ _____

17 건강 조언들

➡ _____

18 파인애플은 비타민 C의 훌륭한 원천이에요.

➡ _____

19 파인애플에는 비타민 C가 오렌지보다 더 많이 들어 있어요.

➡ _____

20 그러니 감기에 걸리면 파인애플을 먹어 보세요.

➡ _____

21 여러분의 생각을 나누세요!

➡ _____

22 여러분은 어떻게 막대 아이스크림을 만들 건가요?

➡ _____

23 여러분의 생각을 나누세요!

➡ _____

24 저는 키위와 딸기를 사용할 거예요.

➡ _____

25 저는 그것들을 크게 자를 거예요.

➡ _____

26 그것들을 사과 주스와 함께 막대 아이스크림 틀에 넣을 거예요.

➡ _____

27 제 막대 아이스크림은 예쁠 것 같아요.

➡ _____

01 다음 빈칸에 알맞은 말을 〈보기〉에서 골라 쓰시오.

┤ 보기 ├
slice / freezer / source / pour

(1) My sister hid the chocolates in the _____, but I found them.
(2) I put some peanut butter on a _____ of bread.
(3) _____ the milk, banana and honey into a blender.
(4) Pineapples are a good _____ of vitamin C.

[02~03] 다음 영영풀이에 해당하는 단어를 쓰시오.

02

an electric machine for mixing soft food or liquid

➡ _____

03

a large tropical fruit with thick rough skin, sweet yellow flesh with a lot of juice and stiff leaves on top

➡ _____

04 주어진 단어를 바르게 배열하여 우리말 의미에 맞는 문장을 완성하시오.

(1) 그 쓰레기를 휴지통에 넣어라.
(the garbage / can / put / the trash / into)
➡ _____

(2) 물속으로 다이빙해서 그녀와 함께 수영하여라.
(her / dive / with / into / swim / the water / and)
➡ _____

05 대·소문자에 유의하여 빈칸에 알맞은 말을 〈보기〉에서 골라 쓰시오.

┤ 보기 ├
until / when / and

(1) What do you usually do _____ you are at home on the weekend?
(2) Let's wait _____ the rain stops.
(3) Stay focused, _____ you will understand it better.

06 다음 주어진 단어를 이용하여 우리말을 영어로 옮기시오.

(1) 당근을 작은 조각으로 잘라라. (cut, a carrot)
➡ _____

(2) 나는 그 책이 매우 유용할 것이라고 생각해. (think, useful)
➡ _____

[07~11] 다음 글을 읽고, 물음에 답하시오.

The hot days of summer are here. How can we stay cool? Let's make ice pops together!

Steps
1. Cut the pineapple into small ⓐ _____ .
2. Peel the kiwis and slice them.
3. Put the pineapple ⓑ _____ into the blender.
4. Add the apple juice.
5. Blend until the mix is smooth.
6. Pour the mix into the ice pop makers.
7. Add the kiwi slices.
8. Close the ice pop makers.
9. Put ⓒthem in the freezer for about three hours.
Finished!
Enjoy your summer on a stick!

07 위 글의 빈칸 @와 ⓑ에 공통으로 들어갈 말을 쓰시오.

➡ _____

08 ⭐(중요) 다음 설명에 해당하는 단어를 위 글에서 찾아 쓰시오.

> You use this word when you remove skins of something.

➡ _____

09 Where do we have to pour the apple juice? Answer in English.

➡ _____

10 ⭐(중요) 위 글의 밑줄 친 ⓒ가 가리키는 것을 영어로 쓰시오.

➡ _____

11 위 글의 내용에 맞게 빈칸에 알맞은 말을 쓰시오.

> Jina: How long do I have to blend?
> Kelly: If it looks _____, then you can stop _____ it.

➡ _____

[12~15] 다음 글을 읽고, 물음에 답하시오.

Health Tips

Pineapples are an excellent source of vitamin C. They have more vitamin C than oranges. So when you have a cold, try pineapples.

Share Your Ideas!

Kyle: How will you make your own ice pops? Share your ideas!

Jinsu: I will use kiwis and strawberries. I will cut them into big pieces. I will put them into the ice pop makers with apple juice. I think ___@___ my ice pops will be pretty.

12 ⭐(중요) 위 글의 내용에 맞게 빈칸에 알맞은 말을 쓰시오.

> Pineapples are rich in _____.

➡ _____

13 What kind of fruit will Jinsu use to make his own ice pops? Answer in English.

➡ _____

14 위 글의 빈칸 @에 들어갈 알맞은 접속사를 쓰시오.

➡ _____

15 진수의 막대 아이스크림을 본 친구의 반응을 영어로 쓰시오.

> 진수야, 그것은 예뻐 보인다!

➡ _____

단원별 예상문제

[01~02] 다음 영영풀이에 해당하는 단어를 쓰시오.

출제율 90%

01

> to take the outer layer off fruit, vegetables, etc.

➡ _____

출제율 90%

02

> a thin flat piece of food that has been cut off a larger piece

➡ _____

출제율 85%

03 다음 짝지어진 두 단어의 관계가 같도록 빈칸에 알맞은 말을 쓰시오.

> close : open = _____ : rough

출제율 95%

04 다음 중 밑줄 친 부분의 뜻풀이가 바르지 <u>않은</u> 것은?

① I ate a <u>piece</u> of cake. 조각
② Would you <u>add</u> some salt to the boiling water? 더하다
③ <u>Pour</u> some water into the pot. 휘젓다
④ It took an hour for me to <u>peel</u> these onions. 껍질을 벗기다
⑤ You need to <u>blend</u> eggs with the flour. 섞다

출제율 90%

05 다음 주어진 문장의 밑줄 친 부분과 같은 의미로 쓰인 것은?

> <u>Close</u> ice pop makers.

① Would you mind <u>closing</u> the window?
② Brian, the police officer, is my <u>close</u> friend.
③ I want to live <u>close</u> to the river.
④ Can you sit <u>close</u> to Mike?
⑤ Jake is one of my <u>close</u> friends.

출제율 100%

06 다음 문장의 빈칸에 들어갈 말을 〈보기〉에서 골라 쓰시오.

> ┌─ 보기 ─┐
> stay / mix / cut / put

(1) First, _____ sweet potatoes into small pieces.
(2) My mother _____ the ice cream in the freezer.
(3) Let's _____ the brown sugar, honey and butter.
(4) What is the best way to _____ cool in summer?

출제율 95%

07 다음 문장의 빈칸에 공통으로 들어갈 말로 적절한 것은?

> • This color does not _____ with the white wall.
> • My daughters _____ in well with the new classmates.
> • Will you _____ milk and flour together?

① add
② stay
③ blend
④ finish
⑤ try

08 다음 중 쓰임이 다른 하나는?

① I have enough money <u>to buy</u> a car.

② Julia went to the hospital <u>to see</u> a doctor.

③ He came here <u>to meet</u> me.

④ <u>To keep</u> the promise, Dan studied hard.

⑤ You had better bring a book not <u>to be</u> bored.

09 다음 우리말을 조건에 맞도록 주어진 단어를 이용하여 영어로 쓰시오.

> 그 방을 깨끗하게 치우지 않으면, 너희 엄마가 화내실 거야. (upset)

(1) 명령문으로

➡ _____

(2) Unless를 사용하여

➡ _____

10 다음 중 〈보기〉의 밑줄 친 부분과 쓰임이 같은 것은?

> ─ 보기 ─
> I <u>haven't seen</u> her for a while.

① She <u>has lost</u> her wallet.

② Jimmy <u>has lived</u> in Seoul since he was seven.

③ <u>Have</u> you ever <u>used</u> the machine?

④ I <u>have been</u> to the place three times.

⑤ Danny <u>has</u> already <u>finished</u> his homework.

11 같은 의미의 문장이 되도록 빈칸에 알맞은 말을 쓰시오.

(1) The doctor advised that I should eat regularly.

➡ The doctor advised _____ _____

_____ _____ .

(2) Jenny told me that I had better make more friends.

➡ Jenny told _____ _____

_____ _____ .

12 다음 문장의 빈칸에 알맞은 것은?

> 사람들은 Brady에 대해 좋게 말해.
> ➡ Brady is _____ people.

① spoken

② spoken by

③ spoken well

④ spoken well of

⑤ spoken well of by

13 다음 문장을 수동태로 전환하시오.

> People around the world look up to Mother Theresa.

➡ _____

_____

14 다음 빈칸에 공통으로 들어갈 말은?

> • Tom is the last man _____ tells a lie.
> • Mike, _____ do you think is the most intelligent?
> • Frank is the boy _____ Linda fell in love with.

① that

② whom

③ who

④ which

⑤ whose

15 괄호 안에 주어진 어휘를 어법에 맞게 쓰시오.

> • If I (be) not busy tomorrow, I (call) on you.
> • I don't know if they (take part in) the contest tomorrow.

➡ _____

_____

[16~20] 다음 대화를 읽고, 물음에 답하시오.

Pineapple Ice Pops

The hot days of summer ①are here. How can we stay ②cool? Let's make ice pops together!

You need:
1/2 pineapple
2 kiwis
1 cup of apple juice
ice pop makers

Steps
1. Cut the pineapple into small ③pieces.
2. Peel the kiwis and slice them.
3. Put the pineapple pieces into the blender.
4. Add the apple juice.
5. Blend until the mix is ④smoothly.
6. Pour the mix into the ice pop makers.
7. Add the kiwi slices.
8. Close the ice pop makers.
9. Put ⑤them in the freezer for about three hours.
Finished!
Enjoy your summer on a stick!

16 다음과 같이 풀이되는 단어를 위 글에서 찾아 쓰시오.

> You find pleasure and satisfaction in doing something or experiencing something.

➡ _____

17 위 글의 내용과 일치하지 <u>않는</u> 것은?

① Ice pops help us stay cool.
② We need half of a pineapple to make the ice pops.
③ Ice pop makers are needed.
④ We need pineapple juice.
⑤ Two kiwis are used to make the ice pops.

18 위 글의 ①~⑤ 중 어법상 바르지 <u>않은</u> 것은?

① ② ③ ④ ⑤

19 What do you have to do with kiwis before you slice them? Answer in English.

➡ _____

20 Where do we put the closed ice pop makers? Answer in English.

➡ _____

[21~24] 다음 글을 읽고 물음에 답하시오.

Health Tips

Pineapples are an excellent source of vitamin C. They have more vitamin C than oranges. So when you have a cold, try pineapples.
Share Your Ideas!

Kyle: ____ⓐ____ will you make your own ice pops? Share your ideas!

Jinsu: I will use kiwis and strawberries. I will cut ⓑthem into big pieces. I will put them into the ice pop makers with apple juice. I think my ice pops will be pretty.

21 위 글의 빈칸 ⓐ에 들어갈 말로 가장 적절한 것은?

① When　② What　③ Who
④ How　⑤ Where

22 위 글을 읽고 답할 수 <u>없는</u> 것은?

① What can you try when you have a cold?
② What do pineapples have more than oranges?
③ What will Jinsu use to make his own ice pops?
④ Why will Jinsu use apple juice?
⑤ What kind of ideas does Kyle want to share?

출제율 85%

23 밑줄 친 ⓑ가 가리키는 것을 영어로 쓰시오.

➡ _____

출제율 90%

24 Write the reason why the writer advises us to try pineapples when we have a cold. Answer in Korean.

➡ _____

[25~29] 다음 설명을 읽고 빈칸에 알맞은 답을 쓰시오.

Pineapple Ice Pops

The hot days of summer are here. How can we stay cool? Let's make ice pops together!

You need:

1/2 pineapple

2 kiwis

1 cup of apple juice

ice pop makers

Steps

1. Cut the pineapple into small pieces.

2. Peel the kiwis and slice them.

(A) Blend until the mix is smooth.

(B) Add the apple juice.

(C) Pour the mix into the ice pop makers.

(D) Put the pineapple pieces into the blender.

7. Add the kiwi slices.

8. Close the ice pop makers.

9. Put them in the freezer ⓐfor about three hours.

ⓑFinished!

Enjoy your summer on a stick!

출제율 95%

25 위 글을 읽고 답할 수 <u>없는</u> 것은?

① How many pineapples do we need?

② How much apple juice do we need?

③ How many ice pop makers do we need?

④ What do we first do with the pineapple?

⑤ What do we do after peeling the kiwis?

출제율 100%

26 위 글의 (A)~(D)의 순서를 바르게 배열한 것은?

① (B) – (A) – (C) – (D)

② (B) – (D) – (A) – (C)

③ (C) – (B) – (A) – (D)

④ (D) – (A) – (B) – (C)

⑤ (D) – (B) – (A) – (C)

출제율 95%

27 위 글의 밑줄 친 ⓐ와 쓰임이 같은 것은?

① They are anxious for his safety.

② What can I do for you?

③ She is working for Google.

④ I'm for you.

⑤ I'm going away for a few days.

출제율 90%

28 After adding the kiwi slices, what do we do next? Answer in English.

➡ _____

출제율 85%

29 주어진 단어를 활용하여 밑줄 친 ⓑ의 의미를 완성하시오.

(you, make)

➡ _____

[30~33] 다음 글을 읽고 물음에 답하시오.

Health Tips

Pineapples are an excellent source of vitamin C. ⓐThey have more vitamin C than oranges. So ⓑ감기에 걸리면, 파인애플을 먹어 보세요.

Share Your Ideas!

Kyle: How will you make your own ice pops? Share your ideas!

Jinsu: I will use kiwis and strawberries. I will cut them into big pieces. I will put ⓒ them into the ice pop makers with apple juice. I think my ice pops will be pretty.

30 다음 중 밑줄 친 ⓐ와 같은 의미의 문장은?

① Pineapples have as much vitamin C as oranges.

② Pineapples don't have as much vitamin C as oranges.

③ Oranges have less vitamin C than pineapples.

④ Oranges don't have much vitamin C.

⑤ No other fruit on earth has more vitamin C than pineapples.

31 주어진 단어를 활용하여 밑줄 친 우리말 ⓑ를 영어로 쓰시오.

have / try

➡ _____

32 다음은 밑줄 친 ⓒ가 가리키는 말이다. 빈칸에 알맞은 말을 쓰시오.

_____ _____ of _____ _____ _____

➡ _____

33 위 글의 내용과 일치하지 <u>않는</u> 것은?

① Pineapples are rich in vitamin C.

② Kyle wants to share ideas about making ice pops.

③ There will be strawberries in Jinsu's ice pops.

④ Jinsu thinks his ice pops will be delicious.

⑤ Jinsu's strawberries and kiwis will be cut into big pieces.

[34~36] 다음 글을 읽고, 물음에 답하시오.

Pineapple Ice Pops

The hot days of summer are here. ①How can we stay cool? Let's make ice pops together!

You need: 1/2 pineapple, 2 ②kiwis, 1 cup of apple juice, ice pop makers

Steps

1. Cut the pineapple into small pieces.
2. Peel the kiwis and slice ③it.
3. Put the pineapple pieces into the blender.
4. Add the apple juice.
5. Blend ④until the mix is smooth.
6. Pour the mix into the ice pop makers.
7. Add the kiwi slices.
8. Close the ice pop makers.
9. Put ⑤them in the freezer for about three hours.

Finished!

Enjoy your summer on a stick!

34 위 글의 내용과 일치하는 것은?

① We need three kinds of fruits to make ice pops.

② A bottle of apple juice will be used.

③ A blender is needed to mix the fruit.

④ We don't need to peel the kiwis.

⑤ We need to cut the pineapple as big as possible.

35 위 글의 ①~⑤ 중 어법상 바르지 <u>않은</u> 것은?

① ② ③ ④ ⑤

36 How long do we put the ice pop makers in the freezer? Answer in English.

➡ _____

중간 + 기말

적중100 plus

영어 기출문제집

영어 중 2

동아 | 이병민

Best Collection

내용문의 중등영어발전소 적중100 편집부 TEL 070-7707-0457
인터넷 서비스 www.jj100.co.kr

INSIGHT
on the textbook

교과서 파헤치기

영어 기출 문제집

적중 100 plus
1학기 전과정

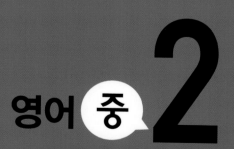

영어 중 2

동아 | 이병민

INSIGHT
on the textbook
교과서 파헤치기

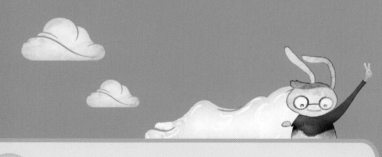

※ 다음 영어를 우리말로 쓰시오.

01 wet		22 rude
02 share		23 terrible
03 probably		24 waste
04 boot		25 chance
05 capital		26 recycle
06 president		27 respond
07 direction		28 foreigner
08 respect		29 post
09 healthily		30 opinion
10 ad		31 improve
11 trouble		32 information
12 active		33 conversation
13 keep		34 useful
14 mad		35 no wonder
15 leave		36 have ~ in common
16 magic		37 fall asleep
17 nervous		38 pay attention to
18 nod		39 keep -ing
19 poor		40 run into
20 quickly		41 put on
21 interest		42 make up with
		43 be mad at

※ 다음 우리말을 영어로 쓰시오.

01	올리다, 게시하다	
02	관리하다	
03	잠이 든	
04	외치다, 소리치다	
05	문자 메시지	
06	게시판	
07	외국인	
08	기꺼이, 기쁘게	
09	향상시키다, 개선하다	
10	대화	
11	정보	
12	~에 가입하다	
13	반응, 피드백	
14	대답하다, 응답하다	
15	때때로, 이따금	
16	화난	
17	동아리, 동호회	
18	의견, 견해	
19	의미하다	
20	재활용하다	
21	특성, 성격, 글자	

22	유용한	
23	예절, 예의	
24	긴장한	
25	존중하다; 존경	
26	대문자, 수도	
27	끔찍한	
28	방향	
29	건강하게	
30	문제, 곤란, 어려움	
31	무례한	
32	관심사, 흥미	
33	성난	
34	(고개를) 끄덕이다	
35	아마	
36	~에게 화나다	
37	~와 화해하다	
38	정각에	
39	계속 ~하다	
40	잠들다	
41	~을 우연히 만나다	
42	~에 주의를 기울이다	
43	~을 신다, 입다	

※ 다음 영영풀이에 알맞은 단어를 <보기>에서 골라 쓴 후, 우리말 뜻을 쓰시오.

1 _____ : very angry: _____

2 _____ : to have something, use it, or occupy it with another person: _____

3 _____ : to keep someone or something safe from death, harm, loss, etc.: _____

4 _____ : the act of listening to, looking at, or thinking about something or someone carefully: _____

5 _____ : happening often and to many people or in many places: _____

6 _____ : making you feel very unhappy, upset or frightened: _____

7 _____ : to move your head up and down to show agreement, understanding: _____

8 _____ : the way that somebody behaves towards other people: _____

9 _____ : an informal talk involving a small group of people or only two: _____

10 _____ : our feelings or thoughts about somebody/something, rather than a fact: _____

11 _____ : having or showing a lack of respect for other people and their feelings: _____

12 _____ : a possibility of something happening, especially something that you want: _____

13 _____ : to give a spoken or written answer to somebody or something: _____

14 _____ : a letter of the form and size that is used at the beginning of a sentence or a name: _____

15 _____ : to make something better: _____

16 _____ : to treat things that have already been used so that they can be used again: _____

보기			
common	opinion	mad	respond
chance	attention	terrible	capital
nod	improve	conversation	share
recycle	save	rude	manner

※ 다음 우리말과 일치하도록 빈칸에 알맞은 말을 쓰시오.

Listen & Speak 1 A

B: I'm so _____ about the new _____ _____.

G: Me, _____. It's _____ _____ be great!

B: _____ can I do to _____ a lot of _____ _____?

G: You can _____ _____ _____ _____.

B: That's a great _____.

B: 나는 새 학년이 되어 아주 신나.
G: 나도. 정말 좋을 것 같아!
B: 새 친구를 많이 사귀려면 어떻게 해야 할까?
G: 스포츠 동아리에 가입해.
B: 그거 좋은 생각이다.

Listen & Speak 1 B

Jenny: Mike, did you _____ any _____?

Mike: Yes, I _____ _____ _____ _____.

Jenny: Oh, I _____.

Mike: _____ _____, Jenny?

Jenny: I'm the _____ of the _____ _____. But I only have _____ _____ _____.

Mike: Oh, no. That's _____.

Jenny: _____ can I do to _____ _____ _____?

Mike: _____ _____ you post an ad on the _____ _____ _____?

Jenny: That's a good _____. I'll do it _____ _____.

Jenny: Mike, 동아리에 가입했니?
Mike: 응, 노래 동아리에 가입했어.
Jenny: 아, 알겠어.
Mike: 무슨 일이니, Jenny?
Jenny: 나는 마술 동아리의 회장이야. 그런데 회원이 두 명 뿐이야.
Mike: 아, 저런. 큰일이네.
Jenny: 더 많은 회원을 모으려면 어떻게 해야 할까?
Mike: 학교 게시판에 광고를 붙이는 게 어떠니?
Jenny: 그거 좋은 생각이다. 당장 붙여야겠어.

Listen & Speak 1 C

A: _____ can I do _____ _____ _____?

B: You can _____ _____ _____ before bed.

A: That's _____ _____ _____. I'll _____ that.

A: 잠을 더 잘 자기 위해 무엇을 해야 할까?
B: 취침 전에 따뜻한 우유를 마셔.
A: 그거 좋은 생각이다. 그렇게 할게.

Listen & Speak 2 A

Brian: Amy, what does this _____ _____ _____?

Amy: Hmm... I have no _____. _____ _____ _____ your teacher?

Brian: Okay, _____ _____.

B: Amy, 이 한자가 무슨 뜻이니?
A: 음... 잘 모르겠어. 너희 선생님께 물어보는 게 어떠니?
B: 응, 그렇게 할게.

Listen & Talk 2 B

Sue: Minsu, _____ are you _____ _____?

Minsu: Oh, I'm sorry. _____ the way, I _____ _____ a foreigner.

Sue: Yes, and?

Minsu: I _____ _____ _____ him to the _____ _____.

Sue: Why _____ you just _____ him the _____?

Minsu: He _____ _____ English very well.

Sue: Hmm... How _____ _____ the *Talk Smart* app _____ _____?

Minsu: *Talk Smart*? _____ _____ _____ app is it?

Sue: It _____ one language _____ _____. It's really _____.

Minsu: Really? I'll _____ it _____ _____.

Listen & Talk 2 C

A: Minsu, _____ do _____ _____ on Thursday.

B: Sounds great! What do you _____ _____ _____?

A: _____ _____ _____ to the _____?

B: _____ idea!

Real Life Talk

Brian: Hey, Mina, _____ _____?

Mina: My _____ friend, Kate, is _____ _____ me.

Brian: That's _____. What _____?

Mina: I _____ her _____ _____ was cute _____ _____ my dog's.

Brian: _____ _____ she's _____ _____ you.

Mina: Right. She _____ _____ to me.

Brian: Yeah. She's _____ really _____.

Mina: _____ can I do to _____ _____ _____ her?

Brian: _____ _____ _____ her a text?

Mina: That's a _____ . I'll _____ that.

Sue: 민수야, 왜 이렇게 늦었니?
Minsu: 아, 미안해. 길에서 외국인을 만났어.
Sue: 응, 그래서?
Minsu: 내가 그를 지하철역까지 데려다 줘야 했어.
Sue: 그에게 그냥 방향만 말해 주지 않았니?
Minsu: 그는 영어를 잘하지 못했어.
Sue: 음... 다음에는 'Talk Smart' 앱을 사용하는 게 어떠니?
Minsu: 'Talk Smart'라고? 그게 어떤 종류의 앱이니?
Sue: 그것은 한 언어를 다른 언어로 바꿔 줘. 아주 도움이 돼.
Minsu: 정말? 다음에는 그것을 사용해 봐야겠다.

A: 민수야, 목요일에 함께 무언가를 하자.
B: 좋아! 너는 무엇을 하고 싶니?
A: 서점에 가는 게 어때?
B: 좋은 생각이야!

Brian: 얘, 미나야, 무슨 일 있니?
미나: 내 가장 친한 친구인 Kate가 나에게 화가 났어.
Brian: 큰일이다. 무슨 일 있었니?
미나: 내가 그녀의 새로 한 머리 모양이 꼭 우리 개의 머리 모양처럼 귀엽다고 말했어.
Brian: 그녀가 너에게 화내는 게 당연해.
미나: 맞아. 그녀는 나와 말하지 않을 거야.
Brian: 그래. 그녀는 아마도 정말 화났을 거야.
미나: 그녀와 화해하려면 어떻게 해야 할까?
Brian: 그녀에게 문자를 보내는 게 어떠니?
미나: 그거 좋은 생각이다. 그렇게 할게.

※ 다음 우리말에 맞도록 대화를 영어로 쓰시오.

Listen & Speak 1 A

B: _____

G: _____

B: _____

G: _____

B: _____

B: 나는 새 학년이 되어 아주 신나.
G: 나도. 정말 좋을 것 같아!
B: 새 친구를 많이 사귀려면 어떻게 해야 할까?
G: 스포츠 동아리에 가입해.
B: 그거 좋은 생각이다.

Listen & Speak 1 B

Jenny: _____

Mike: _____

Jenny: _____

Mike: _____

Jenny: _____

Mike: _____

Jenny: _____

Mike: _____

Jenny: _____

Jenny: Mike, 동아리에 가입했니?
Mike: 응, 노래 동아리에 가입했어.
Jenny: 아, 알겠어.
Mike: 무슨 일이니, Jenny?
Jenny: 나는 마술 동아리의 회장이야. 그런데 회원이 두 명 뿐이야.
Mike: 아, 저런. 큰일이네.
Jenny: 더 많은 회원을 모으려면 어떻게 해야 할까?
Mike: 학교 게시판에 광고를 붙이는 게 어떠니?
Jenny: 그거 좋은 생각이다. 당장 붙여야겠어.

Listen & Speak 1 C

A: _____

B: _____

A: _____

A: 잠을 더 잘 자기 위해 무엇을 해야 할까?
B: 취침 전에 따뜻한 우유를 마셔.
A: 그거 좋은 생각이다. 그렇게 할게.

Listen & Speak 2 A

Brian: _____

Amy: _____

Brian: _____

B: Amy, 이 한자가 무슨 뜻이니?
A: 음... 잘 모르겠어. 너희 선생님께 물어보는 게 어떠니?
B: 응, 그렇게 할게.

Listen & Talk 2 B

Sue: _____

Minsu: _____

Sue: _____

Minsu: _____

Sue: _____

Minsu: _____

Sue: _____

Minsu: _____

Sue: _____

Minsu: _____

Sue: 민수야, 왜 이렇게 늦었니?
Minsu: 아, 미안해. 길에서 외국인을 만났어.
Sue: 응, 그래서?
Minsu: 내가 그를 지하철역까지 데려다 줘야 했어.
Sue: 그에게 그냥 방향만 말해 주지 않았니?
Minsu: 그는 영어를 잘하지 못했어.
Sue: 음... 다음에는 'Talk Smart' 앱을 사용하는 게 어떠니?
Minsu: 'Talk Smart'라고? 그게 어떤 종류의 앱이니?
Sue: 그것은 한 언어를 다른 언어로 바꿔줘. 아주 도움이 돼.
Minsu: 정말? 다음에는 그것을 사용해 봐야겠다.

Listen & Talk 2 C

A: _____
B: _____
A: _____
B: _____

A: 민수야, 목요일에 함께 무언가를 하자.
B: 좋아! 너는 무엇을 하고 싶니?
A: 서점에 가는 게 어때?
B: 좋은 생각이야!

Real Life Talk

Brian: _____
Mina: _____
Brian: _____
Mina: _____
Brian: _____
Mina: _____
Brian: _____
Mina: _____
Brian: _____
Mina: _____

Brian: 얘, 미나야, 무슨 일 있니?
미나: 내 가장 친한 친구인 Kate가 나에게 화가 났어.
Brian: 큰일이다. 무슨 일 있었니?
미나: 내가 그녀의 새로 한 머리 모양이 꼭 우리 개의 머리 모양처럼 귀엽다고 말했어.
Brian: 그녀가 너에게 화내는 게 당연해.
미나: 맞아. 그녀는 나와 말하지 않을 거야.
Brian: 그래. 그녀는 아마도 정말 화났을 거야.
미나: 그녀와 화해하려면 어떻게 해야 할까?
Brian: 그녀에게 문자를 보내는 게 어떠니?
미나: 그거 좋은 생각이다. 그렇게 할게.

※ 다음 우리말과 일치하도록 빈칸에 알맞은 것을 골라 쓰시오.

1 The _____ school _____ is here!
A. year   B. new

2 Are you _____ about _____ to _____ students?
A. other   B. talking   C. nervous

3 Do you have _____ _____ conversations?
A. starting   B. trouble

4 What about _____ conversations _____ ?
A. going   B. keeping

5 _____ _____ .
A. worry   B. don't

6 Here _____ five _____ to _____ a better talker.
A. become   B. tips   C. are

7 _____ by _____ interesting questions.
A. asking   B. start

8 _____ people _____ to talk about _____ .
A. love   B. most   C. themselves

9 So give _____ the _____ .
A. chance   B. them

10 When you _____ questions about people, they will _____ _____ .
A. gladly   B. answer   C. ask

11 _____ a good _____ .
A. listener   B. be

12 _____ people are _____ listeners.
A. poor   B. many

13 So _____ _____ you _____ a good listener?
A. be   B. can   C. how

14 _____ people _____ the eye.
A. in   B. look

15 _____ carefully _____ their _____ .
A. words   B. to   C. listen

16 Don't look _____ your cell phone _____ space _____ !
A. out   B. or   C. at

17 _____ _____ .
A. feedback   B. give

1 새 학년이 시작되었다!

2 당신은 다른 학생들과 대화하는 것이 긴장되는가?

3 당신은 대화를 시작하는 데 어려움이 있는가?

4 대화를 계속 이어가는 것은 어떤가?

5 걱정마라.

6 여기 더욱 대화를 잘하는 사람이 되기 위한 다섯 가지 조언이 있다.

7 흥미로운 질문을 하는 것으로 시작해라.

8 대부분의 사람들은 그들 자신에 관해 말하는 것을 좋아한다.

9 그러니 그들에게 기회를 줘라.

10 당신이 사람들에 관해 질문하면, 그들은 기쁘게 대답할 것이다.

11 잘 듣는 사람이 되어라.

12 많은 사람들이 잘 듣지 못한다.

13 그러면 어떻게 잘 듣는 사람이 될 수 있을까?

14 사람들의 눈을 봐라.

15 그들의 말을 주의 깊게 들어라.

16 당신의 휴대 전화를 보거나 딴 생각하지 마라!

17 반응을 보여 줘라.

18 _____ an _____ listener.
　A. active　　　　B. be

19 _____ your head _____ time _____ time.
　A. to　　　　B. from　　　　C. nod

20 You _____ say _____ things like, "Wow!" _____ "Cool."
　A. little　　　　B. or　　　　C. can

21 You can _____ say something _____, "That's interesting.
Tell me _____."
　A. more　　　　B. like　　　　C. also

22 _____ feedback _____ _____ you're listening.
　A. that　　　　B. giving　　　　C. shows

23 _____ common _____.
　A. interests　　　　B. share

24 You can't _____ a conversation _____ just _____.
　A. by　　　　B. have　　　　C. listening

25 What do you and _____ partner _____ in _____?
　A. common　　　　B. your　　　　C. have

26 Do you _____ _____ sports?
　A. like　　　　B. both

27 Then _____ about _____ _____ baseball team.
　A. favorite　　　　B. your　　　　C. talk

28 _____ attention _____ the listener.
　A. to　　　　B. pay

29 _____ people _____ not be interested _____ your topic.
　A. in　　　　B. sometimes　　　C. may

30 _____ say, "Hey, wake _____!" or "Why _____ you
listening _____ me?"
　A. to　　　　B. up　　　　C. don't　　　　D. aren't

31 _____ the topic, _____ your partner will _____ asleep.
　A. fall　　　　B. or　　　　C. change

32 Give the _____ person a _____ to _____.
　A. talk　　　　B. chance　　　　C. other

33 _____ these tips, _____ you will soon _____ a good
talker.
　A. be　　　　B. and　　　　C. practice

34 _____ _____ first, and everyone _____ want to talk
_____ you.
　A. with　　　　B. others　　　　C. will　　　　D. put

18 능동적으로 듣는 사람이 되어라.

19 가끔 당신의 고개를 끄덕여라.

20 "와!" 또는 "멋지다."와 같은 간단한 것들을 말해도 좋다.

21 또한 "흥미롭다. 더 이야기해봐."와 같은 것을 말해도 좋다.

22 반응을 보여 주는 것은 당신이 듣고 있다는 것을 보여 준다.

23 공통의 관심사를 나눠라.

24 당신은 그저 듣는 것만으로 대화할 수는 없다.

25 당신과 상대편은 어떤 공통점을 가지고 있는가?

26 둘 다 스포츠를 좋아하는가?

27 그렇다면 당신이 가장 좋아하는 야구팀에 관해 대화해라.

28 듣는 사람에게 주의를 기울여라.

29 때때로 사람들은 당신의 화제에 관심이 없을지도 모른다.

30 "이봐, 잠 깨!" 또는 "왜 내 말을 안 듣는 거니?"라고 말하지 마라.

31 화제를 바꿔라. 그렇지 않으면 상대편은 잠이 들 것이다.

32 다른 사람에게 말할 기회를 줘라.

33 이 조언들을 연습해라. 그러면 당신은 곧 대화를 잘하는 사람이 될 것이다.

34 다른 사람을 먼저 생각해라. 그러면 모든 사람이 당신과 대화하고 싶어 할 것이다.

Step2

※ 다음 우리말과 일치하도록 빈칸에 알맞은 말을 쓰시오.

1 The new _____ _____ is here!

2 Are you _____ _____ _____ to _____ students?

3 Do you _____ _____ _____ conversations?

4 What _____ _____ conversations _____ ?

5 _____ _____ .

6 Here _____ five tips to _____ a _____ _____ .

7 _____ by _____ _____ questions.

8 _____ people _____ _____ _____ _____ about _____ .

9 So _____ _____ _____ _____ _____ .

10 _____ you _____ _____ about people, they will _____ _____ .

11 _____ a _____ _____ .

12 Many people are _____ _____ .

13 So _____ _____ you _____ a good listener?

14 _____ people _____ the _____ .

15 _____ carefully _____ their words.

16 _____ _____ _____ your cell phone or _____ _____ !

17 _____ _____ .

1 새 학년이 시작되었다!

2 당신은 다른 학생들과 대화하는 것이 긴장되는가?

3 당신은 대화를 시작하는 데 어려움이 있는가?

4 대화를 계속 이어가는 것은 어떤가?

5 걱정마라.

6 여기 더욱 대화를 잘하는 사람이 되기 위한 다섯 가지 조언이 있다.

7 흥미로운 질문을 하는 것으로 시작해라.

8 대부분의 사람들은 그들 자신에 관해 말하는 것을 좋아한다.

9 그러니 그들에게 기회를 줘라.

10 당신이 사람들에 관해 질문하면, 그들은 기쁘게 대답할 것이다.

11 잘 듣는 사람이 되어라.

12 많은 사람들이 잘 듣지 못한다.

13 그러면 어떻게 잘 듣는 사람이 될 수 있을까?

14 사람들의 눈을 봐라.

15 그들의 말을 주의 깊게 들어라.

16 당신의 휴대 전화를 보거나 딴 생각하지 마라!

17 반응을 보여 줘라.

18 _____ an _____ _____.

19 _____ your head _____ time _____ time.

20 You can _____ _____ things _____, "Wow!" or "Cool."

21 You can _____ _____ something _____, "That's _____. _____ me more."

22 _____ feedback _____ that you're _____.

23 _____ common _____.

24 You _____ _____ a conversation _____ just _____.

25 _____ do you and your partner _____ _____ _____?

26 Do you _____ _____ sports?

27 Then _____ _____ _____ _____ _____ baseball team.

28 _____ _____ _____ the listener.

29 Sometimes people _____ _____ _____ _____ _____ your topic.

30 _____ say, "Hey, _____ _____!" or "Why _____ you _____ _____ me?"

31 _____ the topic, _____ your partner _____ fall _____.

32 Give the _____ person a _____ _____ _____.

33 _____ these tips, _____ you _____ _____ _____ a good talker.

34 _____ _____ first, and everyone will _____ _____ _____ _____ you.

18	능동적으로 듣는 사람이 되어라.
19	가끔 당신의 고개를 끄덕여라.
20	"와!" 또는 "멋지다."와 같은 간단한 것들을 말해도 좋다.
21	또한 "흥미롭다. 더 이야기해봐."와 같은 것을 말해도 좋다.
22	반응을 보여 주는 것은 당신이 듣고 있다는 것을 보여 준다.
23	공통의 관심사를 나눠라.
24	당신은 그저 듣는 것만으로 대화할 수는 없다.
25	당신과 상대편은 어떤 공통점을 가지고 있는가?
26	둘 다 스포츠를 좋아하는가?
27	그렇다면 당신이 가장 좋아하는 야구팀에 관해 대화해라.
28	듣는 사람에게 주의를 기울여라.
29	때때로 사람들은 당신의 화제에 관심이 없을지도 모른다.
30	"이봐, 잠 깨!" 또는 "왜 내 말을 안 듣는 거니?"라고 말하지 마라.
31	화제를 바꿔라. 그렇지 않으면 상대편은 잠이 들 것이다.
32	다른 사람에게 말할 기회를 줘라.
33	이 조언들을 연습해라. 그러면 당신은 곧 대화를 잘하는 사람이 될 것이다.
34	다른 사람을 먼저 생각해라. 그러면 모든 사람이 당신과 대화하고 싶어 할 것이다.

※ 다음 문장을 우리말로 쓰시오.

1 The new school year is here!

➡ _____

2 Are you nervous about talking to other students?

➡ _____

3 Do you have trouble starting conversations?

➡ _____

4 What about keeping conversations going?

➡ _____

5 Don't worry.

➡ _____

6 Here are five tips to become a better talker.

➡ _____

7 Start by asking interesting questions.

➡ _____

8 Most people love to talk about themselves.

➡ _____

9 So give them the chance.

➡ _____

10 When you ask questions about people, they will answer gladly.

➡ _____

11 Be a good listener.

➡ _____

12 Many people are poor listeners.

➡ _____

13 So how can you be a good listener?

➡ _____

14 Look people in the eye.

➡ _____

15 Listen carefully to their words.

➡ _____

16 Don't look at your cell phone or space out!

➡ _____

17 Give feedback.

➡ _____

18 ⏵ Be an active listener.

➡ _____

19 ⏵ Nod your head from time to time.

➡ _____

20 ⏵ You can say little things like, "Wow!" or "Cool."

➡ _____

21 ⏵ You can also say something like, "That's interesting. Tell me more."

➡ _____

22 ⏵ Giving feedback shows that you're listening.

➡ _____

23 ⏵ Share common interests.

➡ _____

24 ⏵ You can't have a conversation by just listening.

➡ _____

25 ⏵ What do you and your partner have in common?

➡ _____

26 ⏵ Do you both like sports?

➡ _____

27 ⏵ Then talk about your favorite baseball team.

➡ _____

28 ⏵ Pay attention to the listener.

➡ _____

29 ⏵ Sometimes people may not be interested in your topic.

➡ _____

30 ⏵ Don't say, "Hey, wake up!" or "Why aren't you listening to me?"

➡ _____

31 ⏵ Change the topic, or your partner will fall asleep.

➡ _____

32 ⏵ Give the other person a chance to talk.

➡ _____

33 ⏵ Practice these tips, and you will soon be a great talker.

➡ _____

34 ⏵ Put others first, and everyone will want to talk with you.

➡ _____

※ 다음 괄호 안의 단어들을 우리말에 맞도록 바르게 배열하시오.

1 (new / the / year / school / here! / is)
➡ _____

2 (you / are / about / nervous / to / talking / students? / other)
➡ _____

3 (have / you / do / trouble / conversations? / starting)
➡ _____

4 (about / what / going? / conversations / keeping)
➡ _____

5 (worry. / don't)
➡ _____

6 (five / are / here / tips / become / to / talker. / better / a)
➡ _____

7 (by / start / interesting / asking / questions.)
➡ _____

8 (most / love / people / talk / to / themselves. / about)
➡ _____

9 (give / so / chance. / the / them)
➡ _____

10 (when / ask / you / about / questions / people, / will / they / gladly. / answer)
➡ _____

11 (good / a / be / listener.)
➡ _____

12 (people / are / many / listeners. / poor)
➡ _____

13 (how / so / you / can / be / listener? / good / a)
➡ _____

14 (people / look / in / eye. / the)
➡ _____

15 (carefully / listen / their / to / words.)
➡ _____

16 (your / don't / at / look / phone / or / cell / out! / space)
➡ _____

17 (feedback. / give)
➡ _____

1 새 학년이 시작되었다!

2 당신은 다른 학생들과 대화하는 것이 긴장되는가?

3 당신은 대화를 시작하는 데 어려움이 있는가?

4 대화를 계속 이어가는 것은 어떤가?

5 걱정마라.

6 여기 더욱 대화를 잘하는 사람이 되기 위한 다섯 가지 조언이 있다.

7 흥미로운 질문을 하는 것으로 시작해라.

8 대부분의 사람들은 그들 자신에 관해 말하는 것을 좋아한다.

9 그러니 그들에게 기회를 줘라.

10 당신이 사람들에 관해 질문하면, 그들은 기쁘게 대답할 것이다.

11 잘 듣는 사람이 되어라.

12 많은 사람들이 잘 듣지 못한다.

13 그러면 어떻게 잘 듣는 사람이 될 수 있을까?

14 사람들의 눈을 봐라.

15 그들의 말을 주의 깊게 들어라.

16 당신의 휴대 전화를 보거나 딴 생각하지 마라!

17 반응을 보여 줘라.

18 (active / be / listener. / an)

➡ _____

19 (your / nod / from / head / time. / to / time)

➡ _____

20 (can / you / say / things / little / like, / "Cool." / or / "Wow!")

➡ _____

21 (can / you / say / also / like, / something / interesting. / "that's / more." / me / tell)

➡ _____

22 (feedback / giving / shows / you're / listening. / that)

➡ _____

23 (interests. / common / share)

➡ _____

24 (can't / you / a / have / by / conversation / listening. / just)

➡ _____

25 (do / what / you / and / partner / your / common? / in / have)

➡ _____

26 (you / do / like / both / sports?)

➡ _____

27 (talk / then / about / favorite / your / team. / baseball)

➡ _____

28 (attention / pay / listener. / the / to)

➡ _____

29 (people / sometimes / not / may / interested / be / topic / in / your)

➡ _____

30 (say, / don't / "hey, / up!" / wake / or / aren't / "why / listening / you / me?" / to)

➡ _____

31 (the / change / topic, / or / partner / your / will / asleep. / fall)

➡ _____

32 (the / give / person / other / chance / a / talk. / to)

➡ _____

33 (these / practice / tips, / and / will / you / be / soon / talker. / great / a)

➡ _____

34 (first, / others / put / and / everyone / want / will / you. / to / with / talk)

➡ _____

18 능동적으로 듣는 사람이 되어라.

19 가끔 당신의 고개를 끄덕여라.

20 "와!" 또는 "멋지다."와 같은 간단한 것들을 말해도 좋다.

21 또한 "흥미롭다. 더 이야기해 봐."와 같은 것을 말해도 좋다.

22 반응을 보여 주는 것은 당신이 듣고 있다는 것을 보여 준다.

23 공통의 관심사를 나눠라.

24 당신은 그저 듣는 것만으로 대화할 수는 없다.

25 당신과 상대편은 어떤 공통점을 가지고 있는가?

26 둘 다 스포츠를 좋아하는가?

27 그렇다면 당신이 가장 좋아하는 야구팀에 관해 대화해라.

28 듣는 사람에게 주의를 기울여라.

29 때때로 사람들은 당신의 화제에 관심이 없을지도 모른다.

30 "이봐, 잠 깨!" 또는 "왜 내 말을 안 듣는 거니?"라고 말하지 마라.

31 화제를 바꿔라, 그렇지 않으면 상대편은 잠이 들 것이다.

32 다른 사람에게 말할 기회를 줘라.

33 이 조언들을 연습해라, 그러면 당신은 곧 대화를 잘하는 사람이 될 것이다.

34 다른 사람을 먼저 생각해라, 그러면 모든 사람이 당신과 대화하고 싶어 할 것이다.

※ 다음 우리말을 영어로 쓰시오.

1 새 학년이 시작되었다!

➡ _____

2 당신은 다른 학생들과 대화하는 것이 긴장되는가?

➡ _____

3 당신은 대화를 시작하는 데 어려움이 있는가?

➡ _____

4 대화를 계속 이어가는 것은 어떤가?

➡ _____

5 걱정마라.

➡ _____

6 여기 더욱 대화를 잘하는 사람이 되기 위한 다섯 가지 조언이 있다.

➡ _____

7 흥미로운 질문을 하는 것으로 시작해라.

➡ _____

8 대부분의 사람들은 그들 자신에 관해 말하는 것을 좋아한다.

➡ _____

9 그러니 그들에게 기회를 줘라.

➡ _____

10 당신이 사람들에 관해 질문하면, 그들은 기쁘게 대답할 것이다.

➡ _____

11 잘 듣는 사람이 되어라.

➡ _____

12 많은 사람들이 잘 듣지 못한다.

➡ _____

13 그러면 어떻게 잘 듣는 사람이 될 수 있을까?

➡ _____

14 사람들의 눈을 봐라.

➡ _____

15 그들의 말을 주의 깊게 들어라.

➡ _____

16 당신의 휴대 전화를 보거나 딴생각하지 마라!

➡ _____

17 반응을 보여 줘라.

➡ _____

18 능동적으로 듣는 사람이 되어라.

➡ _____

19 가끔 당신의 고개를 끄덕여라.

➡ _____

20 "와!" 또는 "멋지다."와 같은 간단한 것들을 말해도 좋다.

➡ _____

21 또한 "흥미롭다. 더 이야기해 봐."와 같은 것을 말해도 좋다.

➡ _____

22 반응을 보여 주는 것은 당신이 듣고 있다는 것을 보여 준다.

➡ _____

23 공통의 관심사를 나눠라.

➡ _____

24 당신은 그저 듣는 것만으로 대화할 수는 없다.

➡ _____

25 당신과 상대편은 어떤 공통점을 가지고 있는가?

➡ _____

26 둘 다 스포츠를 좋아하는가?

➡ _____

27 그렇다면 당신이 가장 좋아하는 야구팀에 관해 대화해라.

➡ _____

28 듣는 사람에게 주의를 기울여라.

➡ _____

29 때때로 사람들은 당신의 화제에 관심이 없을지도 모른다.

➡ _____

30 "이봐, 잠 깨!" 또는 "왜 내 말을 안 듣는 거니?"라고 말하지 마라.

➡ _____

31 화제를 바꿔라, 그렇지 않으면 상대편은 잠이 들 것이다.

➡ _____

32 다른 사람에게 말할 기회를 줘라.

➡ _____

33 이 조언들을 연습해라, 그러면 당신은 곧 대화를 잘하는 사람이 될 것이다.

➡ _____

34 다른 사람을 먼저 생각해라, 그러면 모든 사람이 당신과 대화하고 싶어 할 것이다.

➡ _____

※ 다음 우리말과 일치하도록 빈칸에 알맞은 말을 쓰시오.

Project Culture

1. A: _____ your _____! Go for it!

2. B: _____ _____ going window shopping?

3. C: Your _____ is _____.

1. A: 최선을 다해! 힘내!
2. B: 윈도쇼핑 가는 게 어때?
3. C: 당신의 원피스가 아름다워요.

Think and Write

1. Facelook _____

2. Respect _____ _____, _____ you will make many friends.

3. _____ useful information, or you will _____ others' time.

4. Don't use _____ _____ letters, or you will _____ _____ you're shouting.

5. _____ _____ rude language, or you will _____ _____ _____.

1. Facelook 예절
2. 타인의 의견을 존중해라. 그러면 당신은 많은 친구를 사귈 것이다.
3. 유용한 정보를 게시해라, 그렇지 않으면 당신은 타인의 시간을 낭비할 것이다.
4. 대문자만을 사용하지 말아라, 그렇지 않으면 당신은 소리치고 있는 것처럼 들릴 것이다.
5. 무례한 언어를 사용하지 마라, 그렇지 않으면 당신은 타인을 화나게 만들 것이다.

Read and Write

1. Jason: I want to be a _____ talker.

2. _____ _____ I do?

3. Janet: Here _____ some _____.

4. Be a good _____.

5. _____ _____ your partner's eyes and listen _____.

6. Also _____ _____.

7. _____ your head _____ time _____ time and be an _____ listener.

8. _____, when you talk, _____ _____ _____ your partner.

1. Jason: 나는 말을 좀 더 잘하는 사람이 되고 싶어.
2. 어떻게 해야 좋을까?
3. Janet: 여기 몇 가지 조언이 있어.
4. 말을 잘 들어주는 사람이 되렴.
5. 상대편의 눈을 바라보고 주의 깊게 들어줘.
6. 또 반응을 보여줘.
7. 가끔씩 머리를 끄덕이고 능동적으로 듣는 사람이 되렴.
8. 마지막으로, 네가 이야기할 때, 상대편에 집중해.

구석구석 지문 Test

※ 다음 우리말을 영어로 쓰시오.

Project Culture

1. A: 최선을 다해! 힘내!

  ➡ _____

2. B: 윈도쇼핑 가는 게 어때?

  ➡ _____

3. C: 당신의 원피스가 아름다워요.

  ➡ _____

Think and Write

1. Facelook 예절

  ➡ _____

2. 타인의 의견을 존중해라, 그러면 당신은 많은 친구를 사귈 것이다.

  ➡ _____

3. 유용한 정보를 게시해라, 그렇지 않으면 당신은 타인의 시간을 낭비할 것이다.

  ➡ _____

4. 대문자만을 사용하지 말아라, 그렇지 않으면 당신은 소리치고 있는 것처럼 들릴 것이다.

  ➡ _____

5. 무례한 언어를 사용하지 마라, 그렇지 않으면 당신은 타인을 화나게 만들 것이다.

  ➡ _____

Read and Write

1. Jason: 나는 말을 좀 더 잘하는 사람이 되고 싶어.

  ➡ _____

2. 어떻게 해야 좋을까?

  ➡ _____

3. Janet: 여기 몇 가지 조언이 있어.

  ➡ _____

4. 말을 잘 들어주는 사람이 되렴.

  ➡ _____

5. 상대편의 눈을 바라보고 주의 깊게 들어줘.

  ➡ _____

6. 또 반응을 보여줘.

  ➡ _____

7. 가끔씩 머리를 끄덕이고 능동적으로 듣는 사람이 되렴.

  ➡ _____

8. 마지막으로, 네가 이야기할 때, 상대편에 집중해.

  ➡ _____

※ 다음 영어를 우리말로 쓰시오.

01 intelligent

02 awful

03 promise

04 caring

05 hug

06 shout

07 funny

08 personality

09 responsible

10 feed

11 yell

12 contest

13 hard-working

14 helpful

15 humorous

16 disappear

17 joke

18 friendly

19 outgoing

20 cleaner

21 tidy

22 classmate

23 charity

24 station

25 patient

26 donate

27 beautifully

28 recycling

29 arrive

30 normal

31 insect

32 secret

33 creative

34 thin

35 in front of

36 do one's own thing

37 far from

38 turn off

39 a sea of ~

40 in a few moments

41 travel abroad

42 invite ~ over

43 wait for

※ 다음 우리말을 영어로 쓰시오.

01	건네주다, 통과하다	
02	은행원	
03	재활용	
04	아름답게	
05	말도 안 되는, 미친	
06	창조적인, 창의적인	
07	코치	
08	희극배우, 코미디언	
09	기부하다	
10	비밀	
11	적극적인, 능동적인	
12	도착하다	
13	(고개를) 흔들다	
14	참을성이 있는	
15	곤충, 벌레	
16	배드민턴	
17	떠나다, (뒤에) 남기다	
18	평범한, 정상적인	
19	피아노 연주자	
20	정거장, 역	
21	마른, 얇은	

22	목소리, 음성	
23	보이지 않는	
24	친절한, 상냥한	
25	사라지다	
26	소리치다	
27	도움이 되는	
28	자선 단체	
29	개성, 성격	
30	외향적인, 사교적인	
31	주다, 먹이다	
32	약속하다, 약속	
33	깔끔한	
34	익살스러운	
35	~을 찾다, 구하다	
36	이사하다	
37	잘하다	
38	~을 기다리다	
39	즉시	
40	(전기, 가스, 수도 등을) 끄다	
41	늦지 않게	
42	~에서 멀리	
43	~의 앞쪽에, ~ 앞에(서)	

※ 다음 영영풀이에 알맞은 단어를 <보기>에서 골라 쓴 후, 우리말 뜻을 쓰시오.

1 _____ : a person who owns a bank or has an important job at a bank: _____

2 _____ : to tell somebody that you will definitely do or not do something: _____

3 _____ : an organization for helping people in need: _____

4 _____ : to put your arms around somebody and hold them tightly, especially to show that you like or love them: _____

5 _____ : keeping things neat and in order: _____

6 _____ : having or showing a lack of respect for other people and their feelings: _____

7 _____ : a person who is or was in the same class as you at school or college: _____

8 _____ : an entertainer who makes people laugh by telling jokes or funny stories: _____

9 _____ : unable to be seen: _____

10 _____ : to give money, food, clothes, etc. to somebody/something, especially a charity: _____

11 _____ : behaving in a kind and pleasant way: _____

12 _____ : any small creature with six legs and a body divided into three parts: _____

13 _____ : something that you say or do to make people laugh: _____

14 _____ : to say something in a loud voice: _____

15 _____ : a competition in which people try to win something: _____

16 _____ : a person whose job is to clean other people's houses or offices, etc: _____

※ 다음 우리말과 일치하도록 빈칸에 알맞은 말을 쓰시오.

Listen & Speak 1 A

G: Can we _____ _____ _____?
B: Of _____. The train _____ _____ 5:10.
G: But, it's _____ 4:30.
B: The _____ _____ isn't very _____ _____ here. _____
   _____ we'll _____ there _____ 5.

Listen & Speak 1 B

Jenny: Hey, Minsu. What's _____? You _____ so _____.
Minsu: The _____ _____ is this afternoon.
Jenny: Don't _____. You _____ a _____.
Minsu: But I get so _____ when I'm _____ _____ _____ the
       teacher.
Jenny: Everybody _____. I'm _____ you'll _____ _____.
Minsu: Do you _____ _____ _____?
Jenny: _____. You are a great _____ _____.
Minsu: Thanks. I _____ _____ _____ now.

Listen & Speak 1 C

A: Sam _____ _____ _____ really _____.
B: Yeah, _____ he will _____ _____ _____ in the
   contest.
A: I _____ _____, _____.

Listen & Speak 2 A

B: Who's _____?
G: He's _____ _____ badminton _____.
B: He's very _____ and _____. _____ is he _____?
G: He is very _____ and _____. I like him _____ _____.

Listen & Talk 2 B

Dad: Sue, _____ do you _____ your school _____ _____?

Sue: I like it _____ _____, Dad. I _____ _____ two new _____, Rosa and Mike.

Dad: _____ to _____ that. _____ did you _____ _____?

Sue: We _____ _____ English. We are also _____ _____ _____ _____.

Dad: That's _____. _____ are they _____?

Sue: Rosa is very _____.

Dad: _____ _____ Mike?

Sue: He is _____.

Dad: _____ _____ you _____ _____ _____ for dinner?

Sue: Okay, Dad.

Dad: Sue, 요즘 학교는 어떠니?
Sue: 정말 좋아요, 아빠. 벌써 Rosa와 Mike라는 새 친구 두 명을 사귀었어요.
Dad: 그 말을 들으니 좋구나. 너희들은 어떻게 친구가 되었니?
Sue: 우리 모두는 영어를 정말 좋아해요. 우리는 같은 동아리에 있기도 해요.
Dad: 좋구나. 그 친구들은 성격이 어떠니?
Sue: Rosa는 아주 상냥해요.
Dad: Mike는 어떠니?
Sue: 그는 외향적이에요.
Dad: 그 친구들을 저녁 식사에 초대하는 게 어떠니?
Sue: 좋아요, 아빠.

Listen & Talk 2 C

A: I'm _____ _____ a new member for my _____ _____.

B: _____ _____ Jenny?

A: _____ _____ _____ _____ _____?

B: She is _____ and _____.

A: Thanks. I'll _____ _____.

A: 나는 우리 댄스 동아리에 새 회원을 찾고 있어.
B: Jenny는 어때?
A: Jenny의 성격이 어떠니?
B: 그녀는 적극적이고 외향적이야.
A: 고마워. 그녀에게 물어볼게.

Real Life Talk

Judy: Hojin, I'm _____ _____ a singer _____ my school band.

Hojin: _____ _____ Junho Kim?

Judy: Junho Kim? _____ that?

Hojin: Oh, he's _____ _____. He just _____ to our school _____ _____.

Judy: Is he a _____?

Hojin: Yeah, he _____ _____. I'm _____ he will be _____ your band.

Judy: Can you _____ me _____ him? What's he _____?

Hojin: Well, he is very _____ and _____.

Judy: Great. Can I _____ his phone _____?

Hojin: _____.

Judy: 호진아, 나는 우리 학교 밴드에서 노래 부를 사람을 찾고 있어.
Hojin: 김준호는 어때?
Judy: 김준호? 걔가 누구야?
Hojin: 오, 우리 반 친구야. 그는 지난주에 우리 학교에 전학 왔어.
Judy: 그는 노래를 잘하니?
Hojin: 응, 그는 아름답게 노래를 해. 너희 밴드에 꼭 맞을 거라고 확신해.
Judy: 그에 관해 좀 더 말해 줄 수 있니? 그는 어떤 애니?
Hojin: 음, 그는 아주 외향적이고 상냥해.
Judy: 좋네. 그의 전화번호를 알 수 있을까?
Hojin: 그럼.

※ 다음 우리말에 맞도록 대화를 영어로 쓰시오.

Listen & Speak 1 A

G: _____

B: _____

G: _____

B: _____

해석

G: 우리가 늦지 않게 도착할 수 있을까?
B: 물론이야. 기차는 5시 10분에 떠나.
G: 하지만 벌써 4시 30분이야.
B: 기차역은 여기서 별로 멀지 않아. 나는 우리가 5시 전에 거기에 도착할 거라고 확신해.

Listen & Speak 1 B

Jenny: _____

Minsu: _____

Jenny: _____

Minsu: _____

Jenny: _____

Minsu: _____

Jenny: _____

Minsu: _____

Jenny: 안녕, 민수야. 무슨 일 있니? 걱정스러워 보여.
Minsu: 영어 말하기 시험이 오늘 오후에 있어.
Jenny: 걱정 마. 너는 연습을 많이 했잖아.
Minsu: 하지만 선생님 앞에 있으면 너무 긴장돼.
Jenny: 누구나 그래. 나는 네가 잘할 거라고 확신해.
Minsu: 정말 그렇게 생각해?
Jenny: 물론이야. 너는 정말 영어를 잘해.
Minsu: 고마워. 이제 기분이 훨씬 나아졌어.

Listen & Speak 1 C

A: _____

B: _____

A: _____

A: Sam은 기타를 정말 잘 쳐.
B: 응, 나는 그가 대회에서 1등을 할 것이라고 확신해.
B: 나도 그렇게 생각해.

Listen & Speak 2 A

B: _____

G: _____

B: _____

G: _____

B: 저 사람은 누구니?
G: 저 분은 새로 오신 우리 배드민턴 코치님이셔.
B: 정말 키가 크고 잘생기셨구나. 어떤 분이셔?
G: 코치님은 정말 상냥하고 유머가 풍부하셔. 나는 코치님이 정말 좋아.

Listen & Talk 2 B

Dad: _____

Sue: _____

Dad: _____

Sue: _____

Dad: _____

Sue: _____

Dad: _____

Sue: _____

Dad: _____

Sue: _____

Dad: Sue, 요즘 학교는 어떠니?

Sue: 정말 좋아요, 아빠. 벌써 Rosa와 Mike라는 새 친구 두 명을 사귀었어요.

Dad: 그 말을 들으니 좋구나. 너희들은 어떻게 친구가 되었니?

Sue: 우리 모두는 영어를 정말 좋아해요. 우리는 같은 동아리에 있기도 해요.

Dad: 좋구나. 그 친구들은 성격이 어떠니?

Sue: Rosa는 아주 상냥해요.

Dad: Mike는 어떠니?

Sue: 그는 외향적이에요.

Dad: 그 친구들을 저녁 식사에 초대하는 게 어떠니?

Sue: 좋아요, 아빠.

Listen & Talk 2 C

A: _____

B: _____

A: _____

B: _____

A: _____

A: 나는 우리 댄스 동아리에 새 회원을 찾고 있어.

B: Jenny는 어때?

A: Jenny의 성격이 어떠니?

B: 그녀는 적극적이고 외향적이야.

A: 고마워. 그녀에게 물어볼게.

Real Life Talk

Judy: _____

Hojin: _____

Judy: _____

Hojin: _____

Judy: _____

Hojin: _____

Judy: _____

Hojin: _____

Judy: _____

Hojin: _____

Judy: 호진아, 나는 우리 학교 밴드에서 노래 부를 사람을 찾고 있어.

Hojin: 김준호는 어때?

Judy: 김준호? 걔가 누구야?

Hojin: 오, 우리 반 친구야. 그는 지난주에 우리 학교에 전학 왔어.

Judy: 그는 노래를 잘하니?

Hojin: 응, 그는 아름답게 노래를 해. 너희 밴드에 꼭 맞을 거라고 확신해.

Judy: 그에 관해 좀 더 말해 줄 수 있니? 그는 어떤 애니?

Hojin: 음, 그는 아주 외향적이고 상냥해.

Judy: 좋네. 그의 전화번호를 알 수 있을까?

Hojin: 그럼.

※ 다음 우리말과 일치하도록 빈칸에 알맞은 것을 골라 쓰시오.

1 _____ _____ is Jimmy.
    A. name   B. my

2 I am _____ the _____ grade and my sister, Hope, is in the _____ grade.
    A. third   B. eighth   C. in

3 My father is a _____ and my mother is a _____.
    A. teacher   B. banker

4 We _____ a dog, Smiley. _____ pretty _____, right?
    A. normal   B. sounds   C. have

5 But a _____ thing _____ _____ week.
    A. last   B. happened   C. crazy

6 My father _____ comes _____ _____ from work.
    A. late   B. home   C. usually

7 _____, we _____ see him _____ the weekends.
    A. on   B. only   C. so

8 _____ then, he _____ sleeps or _____ television.
    A. watches   B. usually   C. even

9 But _____ Friday, he came _____ _____ for dinner.
    A. early   B. home   C. last

10 At the table, we _____ all _____ our _____ thing.
    A. own   B. doing   C. were

11 Hope was _____ _____ _____ Smiley.
    A. to   B. food   C. giving

12 My mother was _____ her _____ to do so. I was _____.
    A. not   B. texting   C. telling

13 My father _____, "_____ _____ the bread, please."
    A. said   B. me   C. pass

14 No _____ heard him, so he _____ again, "Can someone _____ me the bread?"
    A. pass   B. one   C. asked

15 I _____ him this time, but I was _____ busy _____ my phone.
    A. with   B. too   C. heard

16 My mother was _____, "_____ _____ Smiley!"
    A. don't   B. yelling   C. feed

17 Hope _____ _____ Smiley.
    A. feeding   B. was

1 내 이름은 Jimmy다.

2 나는 8학년이고, 내 여동생 Hope는 3학년이다.

3 우리 아버지는 은행원이시고, 어머니는 선생님이시다.

4 우리에겐 Smiley라는 개가 한 마리 있다. 꽤 평범한 것 같다. 그렇지?

5 그런데 정말 이상한 일이 지난 주에 일어났다.

6 우리 아버지는 보통 회사에서 늦게 집에 오신다.

7 그래서 우리는 주말에만 아버지를 본다.

8 주말에도 아버지는 보통 주무시거나 텔레비전을 보신다.

9 하지만 지난주 금요일에 아버지는 저녁을 드시러 일찍 집에 오셨다.

10 식탁에서 우리는 모두 각자의 일을 하고 있었다.

11 Hope는 Smiley에게 음식을 주고 있었다.

12 어머니는 동생에게 그러지 말라고 말씀하고 계셨다. 나는 문자를 보내고 있었다.

13 아버지가 말씀하셨다. "빵 좀 건네 줘요."

14 아무도 그의 말을 듣지 못하자, 아버지는 다시 물으셨다. "누구 나한테 빵 좀 건네 줄래?"

15 이번에 나는 아버지의 말을 들었지만 휴대 전화에 빠져 너무 바빴다.

16 어머니는 소리치고 계셨다. "Smiley한테 음식을 주지 마!"

17 Hope는 Smiley에게 먹이를 주고 있었다.

18 Smiley was _____ _____ and _____.

    A. down   B. up   C. jumping

19 My father _____, "Am I _____? _____ me the bread!"

    A. pass   B. invisible   C. shouted

20 Then, it _____. Poof! My father _____ _____ magic.

    A. disappeared   B. happened   C. like

21 He _____ _____!

    A. invisible   B. became

22 We could _____ him, but we _____ _____ him.

    A. couldn't   B. hear   C. see

23 We _____, "_____ are you?"

    A. where   B. asked

24 "I'm _____ in _____ of you," he _____.

    A. replied   B. front   C. right

25 We _____ do _____ for him. It was an _____ night.

    A. awful   B. anything   C. couldn't

26 Next morning, we _____ to the hospital and _____ the doctor _____ us.

    A. help   B. went   C. to   D. asked

27 I said, "He has _____ _____ last night."

    A. since   B. invisible   C. been

28 The doctor _____ his head and said, "I can't help you. I've _____ _____ anything _____ this before."

    A. like   B. never   C. seen   D. shook

29 _____ we came _____, Hope said, "I _____ Daddy."

    A. miss   B. home   C. when

30 She _____ _____. My mother _____ her.

    A. joined   B. crying   C. started

31 _____ a few _____, we were a sea of _____.

    A. tears   B. moments   C. in

32 "Come _____, Dad! I _____ to pass you the bread every day!" I _____.

    A. promise   B. cried   C. back

33 Then, it _____. My father _____ again!

    A. appeared   B. happened

34 He _____ us and said, "Thank you for all the _____. I promise to come home _____ and play with you _____ the weekends."

    A. earlier   B. on   C. attention   D. hugged

18 Smiley는 펄쩍펄쩍 뛰고 있었다.

19 아버지가 소리치셨다. "내가 안 보이는 거야? 빵 좀 건네 줘!"

20 그때 일이 벌어졌다. 뿅! 아버지가 마법처럼 사라지셨다.

21 아버지는 투명 인간이 되셨다!

22 우리는 그의 말을 들을 수는 있었지만 그를 볼 수는 없었다.

23 우리는 물었다. "어디 계세요?"

24 아버지가 대답하셨다. "너희들 바로 앞에 있어."

25 우리는 그를 위해 할 수 있는 게 없었다. 끔찍한 밤이었다.

26 다음 날 아침. 우리는 병원에 가서 의사 선생님에게 도움을 요청했다.

27 내가 말했다. "아버지가 어젯밤부터 안 보여요."

28 의사 선생님은 고개를 저으며 말씀하셨다. "도와 드릴 수가 없네요. 이런 건 본 적이 없어요."

29 집에 왔을 때 Hope가 말했다. "아빠가 보고 싶어요."

30 그녀는 울기 시작했다. 어머니가 같이 우셨다.

31 곧 우리는 눈물바다가 되었다.

32 "돌아오세요, 아빠! 매일 아빠한테 빵을 건네드리겠다고 약속해요!" 내가 외쳤다.

33 그때 일이 일어났다. 아버지가 다시 나타나셨다!

34 아버지가 우리를 안고 말씀하셨다. "관심 가져 줘서 고마워. 집에 더 일찍 오고 주말에는 너희와 함께 놀겠다고 약속하마."

※ 다음 우리말과 일치하도록 빈칸에 알맞은 말을 쓰시오.

1 _____ _____ is Jimmy.

2 I am _____ _____ _____ _____ and my sister, Hope, is in the _____ _____.

3 My father is _____ _____ and _____ _____ is a teacher.

4 We _____ a dog, Smiley. _____ _____ _____, right?

5 But a _____ thing _____ last week.

6 My father _____ _____ _____ _____ from work.

7 So, we _____ _____ him _____ _____ _____.

8 _____ then, he _____ _____ or _____ television.

9 But _____ Friday, he came _____ _____ for dinner.

10 At the table, we _____ all _____ _____ _____ _____ _____.

11 Hope was _____ _____ _____ Smiley.

12 My mother was _____ her _____ _____ _____ so. I _____ _____.

13 My father said, "_____ _____ _____ _____, please."

14 No one _____ him, so he asked again, "Can someone _____ _____ _____ _____?"

15 I _____ _____ this time, but I was _____ _____ _____ my phone.

16 My mother _____ _____, "_____ _____ Smiley!"

17 Hope _____ _____ Smiley.

1 내 이름은 Jimmy다.

2 나는 8학년이고, 내 여동생 Hope는 3학년이다.

3 우리 아버지는 은행원이시고, 어머니는 선생님이시다.

4 우리에겐 Smiley라는 개가 한 마리 있다. 꽤 평범한 것 같다, 그렇지?

5 그런데 정말 이상한 일이 지난 주에 일어났다.

6 우리 아버지는 보통 회사에서 늦게 집에 오신다.

7 그래서 우리는 주말에만 아버지를 본다.

8 주말에도 아버지는 보통 주무시거나 텔레비전을 보신다.

9 하지만 지난주 금요일에 아버지는 저녁을 드시러 일찍 집에 오셨다.

10 식탁에서 우리는 모두 각자의 일을 하고 있었다.

11 Hope는 Smiley에게 음식을 주고 있었다.

12 어머니는 동생에게 그러지 말라고 말씀하고 계셨다. 나는 문자를 보내고 있었다.

13 아버지가 말씀하셨다. "빵 좀 건네 줘요."

14 아무도 그의 말을 듣지 못하자, 아버지는 다시 물으셨다. "누구 나한테 빵 좀 건네 줄래?"

15 이번에 나는 아버지의 말을 들었지만 휴대 전화에 빠져 너무 바빴다.

16 어머니는 소리치고 계셨다. "Smiley한테 음식을 주지 마!"

17 Hope는 Smiley에게 먹이를 주고 있었다.

18 Smiley was _____ _____ and _____.

19 My father _____, "Am I _____? _____ me the bread!"

20 Then, it _____. Poof! My father _____ _____ _____ _____.

21 He _____ _____!

22 We _____ _____ _____ him, but we _____ _____ _____ him.

23 We _____, "_____ _____ _____ you?"

24 "I'm _____ _____ _____ _____ _____ you," he _____.

25 We _____ do _____ for him. It was an _____ night.

26 _____ morning, we _____ _____ the hospital and _____ the doctor _____ _____ us.

27 I said, "He _____ _____ _____ _____ last night."

28 The doctor _____ his head and said, "I _____ _____ you. I've _____ _____ _____ like this before."

29 _____ we _____ _____ _____, Hope said, "I _____ Daddy."

30 She _____ _____. My mother _____ her.

31 _____ _____ _____ moments, we were _____ _____ _____ tears.

32 "_____ _____, Dad! I _____ _____ _____ you the bread every day!" I _____.

33 Then, it _____. My father _____ again!

34 He _____ _____ and said, "Thank you for _____ _____. I promise to come home _____ and play with you _____ _____ _____."

18 Smiley는 펄쩍펄쩍 뛰고 있었다.

19 아버지가 소리치셨다. "내가 안 보이는 거야? 빵 좀 건네 줘!"

20 그때 일이 벌어졌다. 뿅! 아버지 가 마법처럼 사라지셨다.

21 아버지는 투명 인간이 되셨다!

22 우리는 그의 말을 들을 수는 있 었지만 그를 볼 수는 없었다.

23 우리는 물었다. "어디 계세요?"

24 아버지가 대답하셨다. "너희들 바로 앞에 있어."

25 우리는 그를 위해 할 수 있는 게 없었다. 끔찍한 밤이었다.

26 다음 날 아침, 우리는 병원에 가 서 의사 선생님에게 도움을 요 청했다.

27 내가 말했다. "아버지가 어젯밤 부터 안 보여요."

28 의사 선생님은 고개를 저으며 말씀하셨다. "도와 드릴 수가 없 네요. 이런 건 본 적이 없어요."

29 집에 왔을 때 Hope가 말했다. "아빠가 보고 싶어요."

30 그녀는 울기 시작했다. 어머니 가 같이 우셨다.

31 곧 우리는 눈물바다가 되었다.

32 "돌아오세요. 아빠! 매일 아빠한 테 빵을 건네드리겠다고 약속해 요!" 내가 외쳤다.

33 그때 일이 일어났다. 아버지가 다시 나타나셨다!

34 아버지가 우리를 안고 말씀하셨 다. "관심 가져 줘서 고마워. 집 에 더 일찍 오고 주말에는 너희 와 함께 놀겠다고 약속하마."

※ 다음 문장을 우리말로 쓰시오.

1 My name is Jimmy.
➡ _____

2 I am in the eighth and my sister, Hope, is in the third grade.
➡ _____

3 My father is a banker and my mother is a teacher.
➡ _____

4 We have a dog, Smiley. Sounds pretty normal, right?
➡ _____

5 But a crazy thing happened last week.
➡ _____

6 My father usually comes home late from work.
➡ _____

7 So, we only see him on the weekends.
➡ _____

8 Even then, he usually sleeps or watches television.
➡ _____

9 But last Friday, he came home early for dinner.
➡ _____

10 At the table, we were all doing our own thing.
➡ _____

11 Hope was giving food to Smiley.
➡ _____

12 My mother was telling her not to do so. I was texting.
➡ _____

13 My father said, "Pass me the bread, please."
➡ _____

14 No one heard him, so he asked again, "Can someone pass me the bread?"
➡ _____

15 I heard him this time, but I was too busy with my phone.
➡ _____

16 My mother was yelling, "Don't feed Smiley!"
➡ _____

17 Hope was feeding Smiley.
➡ _____

18 Smiley was jumping up and down.

➡ _____

19 My father shouted, "Am I invisible? Pass me the bread!"

➡ _____

20 Then, it happened. Poof! My father disappeared like magic.

➡ _____

21 He became invisible!

➡ _____

22 We could hear him, but we couldn't see him.

➡ _____

23 We asked, "Where are you?"

➡ _____

24 "I'm right in front of you," he replied.

➡ _____

25 We couldn't do anything for him. It was an awful night.

➡ _____

26 Next morning, we went to the hospital and asked the doctor to help us.

➡ _____

27 I said, "He has been invisible since last night."

➡ _____

28 The doctor shook his head and said, "I can't help you. I've never seen anything like this before."

➡ _____

29 When we came home, Hope said, "I miss Daddy."

➡ _____

30 She started crying. My mother joined her.

➡ _____

31 In a few moments, we were a sea of tears.

➡ _____

32 "Come back, Dad! I promise to pass you the bread every day!" I cried.

➡ _____

33 Then, it happened. My father appeared again!

➡ _____

34 He hugged us and said, "Thank you for all the attention. I promise to come home earlier and play with you on the weekends."

➡ _____

※ 다음 괄호 안의 단어들을 우리말에 맞도록 바르게 배열하시오.

1 (is / my / Jimmy. / name)
➡ _____

2 (am / in / I / eighth / the / and / sister, / my / Hope, / in / grade. / is / third / the)
➡ _____

3 (father / is / my / baker / a / and / mother / is / my / teacher. / a)
➡ _____

4 (we / a / have / Smiley. / dog, / pretty / sounds / right? / normal,)
➡ _____

5 (but / thing / crazy / a / week. / last / happened)
➡ _____

6 (father / usually / my / comes / late / home / work. / from)
➡ _____

7 (so, / only / we / see / on / him / weekends. / the)
➡ _____

8 (then, / even / usually / he / sleeps / television. / watches / or)
➡ _____

9 (but / Friday, / last / came / he / early / home / dinner. / for)
➡ _____

10 (table, / the / at / were / we / doing / all / thing. / own / our)
➡ _____

11 (was / Hope / food / Similey. / to / giving)
➡ _____

12 (mother / my / telling / was / not / her / to / so. / do // was / I / texting.)
➡ _____

13 (father / said, / my / "pass / the / bread, / me / please.")
➡ _____

14 (one / no / him, / heard / so / asked / he / again, / "can / pass / someone / bread?" / the / me)
➡ _____

15 (heard / I / this / him / time, / but / was / I / busy / too / phone. / my / with)
➡ _____

16 (mother / was / my / yelling, / "don't / Smiley!" / feed)
➡ _____

17 (feeding / Hope / was / Smiley.)
➡ _____

1 내 이름은 Jimmy다.

2 나는 8학년이고, 내 여동생 Hope는 3학년이다.

3 우리 아버지는 은행원이시고, 어머니는 선생님이시다.

4 우리에겐 Smiley라는 개가 한 마리 있다. 꽤 평범한 것 같다. 그렇지?

5 그런데 정말 이상한 일이 지난 주에 일어났다.

6 우리 아버지는 보통 회사에서 늦게 집에 오신다.

7 그래서 우리는 주말에만 아버지를 본다.

8 주말에도 아버지는 보통 주무시거나 텔레비전을 보신다.

9 하지만 지난주 금요일에 아버지는 저녁을 드시러 일찍 집에 오셨다.

10 식탁에서 우리는 모두 각자의 일을 하고 있었다.

11 Hope는 Smiley에게 음식을 주고 있었다.

12 어머니는 동생에게 그러지 말라고 말씀하고 계셨다. 나는 문자를 보내고 있었다.

13 아버지가 말씀하셨다. "빵 좀 건네 줘요."

14 아무도 그의 말을 듣지 못하자, 아버지는 다시 물으셨다. "누구 나한테 빵 좀 건네 줄래?"

15 이번에 나는 아버지의 말을 들었지만 휴대 전화에 빠져 너무 바빴다.

16 어머니는 소리치고 계셨다. "Smiley한테 음식을 주지 마!"

17 Hope는 Smiley에게 먹이를 주고 있었다.

18 (was / Smiley / jumping / down. / and / up)

➡ _____

19 (shouted, / father / my / I / "am / invisible? / me / bread!" / pass / the)

➡ _____

20 (it / then, / happened. / poof! / father / like / my / magic. / disappeared)

➡ _____

21 (became / invisible! / he)

➡ _____

22 (could / we / hear / him, / but / we / him. / see / couldn't)

➡ _____

23 (asked, / we / you?" / are / "where)

➡ _____

24 (right / "I'm / of / front / in / you," / replied. / he)

➡ _____

25 (we / couldn't / anything / do / him. / for / it / was / night. / an / awful)

➡ _____

26 (morning, / next / went / we / to / the / hospital / and / the / asked / doctor / us. / help / to)

➡ _____

27 (said, / I / "he / been / has / since / invisible / night." / last)

➡ _____

28 (doctor / the / shook / head / his / and / said, / "I / help / you. / can't // I've / seen / never / anything / before." / this / like)

➡ _____

29 (we / when / home, / came / Hope / said, / Daddy." / "I / miss)

➡ _____

30 (started / she / crying. / mother / my / her. / joined)

➡ _____

31 (a / in / moments, / few / we / sea / were / a / tears. / of)

➡ _____

32 (back, / "come / Dad! / I / pass / to / promise / you / bread / the / day!" / every / cried. / I)

➡ _____

33 (it / then, / happened. / father / my / again! / appeared)

➡ _____

34 (hugged / he / said, / us / and / "thank / for / you / the / all / attention. / I / come / to / promise / earlier / home / and / you / play / with / weekends." / the / on)

➡ _____
_____

18 Smiley는 펄쩍펄쩍 뛰고 있었다.

19 아버지가 소리치셨다. "내가 안 보이는 거야? 빵 좀 건네 줘!"

20 그때 일이 벌어졌다. 뽕! 아버지가 마법처럼 사라지셨다.

21 아버지는 투명 인간이 되셨다!

22 우리는 그의 말을 들을 수는 있었지만 그를 볼 수는 없었다.

23 우리는 물었다. "어디 계세요?"

24 아버지가 대답하셨다. "너희들 바로 앞에 있어."

25 우리는 그를 위해 할 수 있는 게 없었다. 끔찍한 밤이었다.

26 다음 날 아침, 우리는 병원에 가서 의사 선생님에게 도움을 요청했다.

27 내가 말했다. "아버지가 어젯밤부터 안 보여요."

28 의사 선생님은 고개를 저으며 말씀하셨다. "도와 드릴 수가 없네요. 이런 건 본 적이 없어요."

29 집에 왔을 때 Hope가 말했다. "아빠가 보고 싶어요."

30 그녀는 울기 시작했다. 어머니가 같이 우셨다.

31 곧 우리는 눈물바다가 되었다.

32 "돌아오세요, 아빠! 매일 아빠한테 빵을 건네드리겠다고 약속해요!" 내가 외쳤다.

33 그때 일이 일어났다. 아버지가 다시 나타나셨다!

34 아버지가 우리를 안고 말씀하셨다. "관심 가져 줘서 고마워. 집에 더 일찍 오고 주말에는 너희와 함께 놀겠다고 약속하마."

※ 다음 우리말을 영어로 쓰시오.

1 내 이름은 Jimmy다.

➡ _____

2 나는 8학년이고, 내 여동생 Hope는 3학년이다.

➡ _____

3 우리 아버지는 은행원이시고, 어머니는 선생님이시다.

➡ _____

4 우리에겐 Smiley라는 개가 한 마리 있다. 꽤 평범한 것 같다, 그렇지?

➡ _____

5 그런데 정말 이상한 일이 지난주에 일어났다.

➡ _____

6 우리 아버지는 보통 회사에서 늦게 집에 오신다.

➡ _____

7 그래서 우리는 주말에만 아버지를 본다.

➡ _____

8 주말에도 아버지는 보통 주무시거나 텔레비전을 보신다.

➡ _____

9 하지만 지난주 금요일에 아버지는 저녁을 드시러 일찍 집에 오셨다.

➡ _____

10 식탁에서 우리는 모두 각자의 일을 하고 있었다.

➡ _____

11 Hope는 Smiley에게 음식을 주고 있었다.

➡ _____

12 어머니는 동생에게 그러지 말라고 말씀하고 계셨다. 나는 문자를 보내고 있었다.

➡ _____

13 아버지가 말씀하셨다. "빵 좀 건네줘요."

➡ _____

14 아무도 그의 말을 듣지 못하자, 아버지는 다시 물으셨다. "누구 나한테 빵 좀 건네줄래?"

➡ _____

15 이번에 나는 아버지의 말을 들었지만 휴대 전화에 빠져 너무 바빴다.

➡ _____

16 어머니는 소리치고 계셨다. "Smiley한테 음식을 주지 마!"

➡ _____

17 Hope는 Smiley에게 먹이를 주고 있었다.

➡ _____

18 Smiley는 펄쩍펄쩍 뛰고 있었다.

➡ _____

19 아버지가 소리치셨다. "내가 안 보이는 거야? 빵 좀 건네줘!"

➡ _____

20 그때 일이 벌어졌다. 뿅! 아버지가 마법처럼 사라지셨다.

➡ _____

21 아버지는 투명 인간이 되셨다!

➡ _____

22 우리는 그의 말을 들을 수는 있었지만 그를 볼 수는 없었다.

➡ _____

23 우리는 물었다. "어디 계세요?"

➡ _____

24 아버지가 대답하셨다. "너희들 바로 앞에 있어."

➡ _____

25 우리는 그를 위해 할 수 있는 게 없었다. 끔찍한 밤이었다.

➡ _____

26 다음 날 아침, 우리는 병원에 가서 의사 선생님에게 도움을 요청했다.

➡ _____

27 내가 말했다. "아버지가 어젯밤부터 안 보여요."

➡ _____

28 의사 선생님은 고개를 저으며 말씀하셨다. "도와 드릴 수가 없네요. 이런 건 본 적이 없어요."

➡ _____

29 집에 왔을 때 Hope가 말했다. "아빠가 보고 싶어요."

➡ _____

30 그녀는 울기 시작했다. 어머니가 같이 우셨다.

➡ _____

31 곧 우리는 눈물바다가 되었다.

➡ _____

32 "돌아오세요, 아빠! 매일 아빠한테 빵을 건네드리겠다고 약속해요!" 내가 외쳤다.

➡ _____

33 그때 일이 일어났다. 아버지가 다시 나타나셨다!

➡ _____

34 아버지가 우리를 안고 말씀하셨다. "관심 가져 줘서 고마워. 집에 더 일찍 오고 주말에는 너희와 함께 놀겠다고 약속하마."

➡ _____

_____

※ 다음 우리말과 일치하도록 빈칸에 알맞은 말을 쓰시오.

Real Life Talk - Step 2

1. A: Who is _____ _____ person _____ _____ the board cleaner?

2. B: _____ _____ Minsu?

3. A: _____ is he _____?

4. C: He is _____ and _____.

5. D: _____ _____ he will be a good _____ _____ for our class.

1. A: 누가 칠판지우기 담당으로 가장 적합할까요?
2. B: 민수 어때요?
3. A: 그의 성격은 어때요?
4. C: 그는 책임감 있고 깔끔해요.
5. D: 나는 그가 우리 반을 위해 좋은 칠판지우기 담당이 될 것이라고 확신해요.

Think and Write

1. _____ Best Friend, Subin

2. _____ _____ _____ is Subin.

3. I _____ _____ her _____ 3 years.

4. She is _____.

5. She tells me many _____ _____.

6. She and I _____ like movies.

7. So we _____ _____ many movies _____.

8. I'm _____ we'll be friends _____.

1. 나의 가장 좋은 친구, 수빈
2. 나의 가장 좋은 친구는 수빈입니다.
3. 나는 수빈이를 3년 동안 알고 지냈습니다.
4. 그녀는 유머가 있습니다.
5. 그녀는 나에게 많은 재미있는 농담을 합니다.
6. 그녀와 나는 둘 다 영화를 좋아합니다.
7. 그래서 우리는 함께 많은 영화를 봤습니다.
8. 나는 우리가 영원히 친구일 것이라고 확신합니다.

Project - Step 3

1. _____ Mina,

2. I'm happy _____ you're my _____ friend.

3. I like you _____ you are very _____.

4. I also _____ your _____ _____.

5. _____ _____ we'll be good friends _____ _____.

6. P.S. I've _____ _____ you _____ _____.

1. 친애하는 미나에게,
2. 나는 네가 나의 비밀친구라서 행복해.
3. 네가 친절하기 때문에 나는 널 좋아해.
4. 나는 또 너의 환한 미소가 좋아.
5. 나는 올해 우리가 좋은 친구가 될 것이라고 확신해.
6. 추신. 나는 벌써 너를 세 번이나 도왔어.

Step2

※ 다음 우리말을 영어로 쓰시오.

Real Life Talk - Step 2

1. A: 누가 칠판지우기 담당으로 가장 적합할까요?
   ➡ _____

2. B: 민수 어때요?
   ➡ _____

3. A: 그의 성격은 어때요?
   ➡ _____

4. C: 그는 책임감 있고 깔끔해요.
   ➡ _____

5. D: 나는 그가 우리 반을 위해 좋은 칠판지우기 담당이 될 것이라고 확신해요.
   ➡ _____

Think and Write

1. 나의 가장 좋은 친구, 수빈
   ➡ _____

2. 나의 가장 좋은 친구는 수빈입니다.
   ➡ _____

3. 나는 수빈이를 3년 동안 알고 지냈습니다.
   ➡ _____

4. 그녀는 유머가 있습니다.
   ➡ _____

5. 그녀는 나에게 많은 재미있는 농담을 합니다.
   ➡ _____

6. 그녀와 나는 둘 다 영화를 좋아합니다.
   ➡ _____

7. 그래서 우리는 함께 많은 영화를 봤습니다.
   ➡ _____

8. 나는 우리가 영원히 친구일 것이라고 확신합니다.
   ➡ _____

Project - Step 3

1. 친애하는 미나에게.
   ➡ _____

2. 나는 네가 나의 비밀친구라서 행복해.
   ➡ _____

3. 네가 친절하기 때문에 나는 널 좋아해.
   ➡ _____

4. 나는 또 너의 환한 미소가 좋아.
   ➡ _____

5. 나는 올해 우리가 좋은 친구가 될 것이라고 확신해.
   ➡ _____

6. 추신. 나는 벌써 너를 세 번이나 도왔어.
   ➡ _____

※ 다음 영어를 우리말로 쓰시오.

01	madly	_____
02	throw	_____
03	definitely	_____
04	audience	_____
05	funny	_____
06	giraffe	_____
07	wall	_____
08	hall	_____
09	pianist	_____
10	heal	_____
11	meeting	_____
12	Hungary	_____
13	machine	_____
14	idol	_____
15	miss	_____
16	fantastic	_____
17	seat	_____
18	liberty	_____
19	badminton	_____
20	invent	_____
21	original	_____
22	flea market	_____
23	scream	_____
24	zebra	_____
25	signature	_____
26	greeting	_____
27	creation	_____
28	composer	_____
29	prepare	_____
30	movement	_____
31	performance	_____
32	recent	_____
33	face	_____
34	unlike	_____
35	strawberry	_____
36	sheet music	_____
37	paper folding	_____
38	build up	_____
39	cheer up	_____
40	at once	_____
41	press down	_____
42	from memory	_____
43	go wild	_____

※ 다음 우리말을 영어로 쓰시오.

01	부드럽게, 상냥하게	
02	놀라운	
03	팬; 부채, 선풍기	
04	서명	
05	포도, 포도나무	
06	방학, 휴가	
07	인사	
08	북 연주자, 드러머	
09	단 하나의, 혼자의	
10	떨어지다	
11	딸기	
12	연주회, 음악회	
13	준비하다	
14	숨, 호흡	
15	작곡가	
16	움직임	
17	발레	
18	음, 음표	
19	공연	
20	최근의	
21	소설	

22	창조물, 창작	
23	~와는 달리	
24	얼굴; ~을 향하다	
25	놓치다, 그리워하다	
26	자유	
27	소리치다, 괴성을 지르다	
28	발명하다, 창안하다	
29	고치다, 낫게 하다	
30	기계, 기계장치	
31	단연, 틀림없이	
32	미친 듯이, 열렬하게	
33	벼룩시장	
34	본래의	
35	악보	
36	청중, 관람객	
37	환상적인	
38	격려하다, 힘을 북돋우다	
39	숨을 참다, 숨을 죽이다	
40	한꺼번에	
41	누르다	
42	점점 높이다	
43	직접	

※ 다음 영영풀이에 알맞은 단어를 <보기>에서 골라 쓴 후, 우리말 뜻을 쓰시오.

1 _____ : a public performance of music: _____

2 _____ : a person who writes music: _____

3 _____ : the air that you take into your lungs and send out again: _____

4 _____ : a person who plays the piano: _____

5 _____ : an outdoor market that sells second-hand goods at low prices: _____

6 _____ : to drop down from a higher level to a lower level: _____

7 _____ : your name as you usually write it, for example at the end of a letter: _____

8 _____ : a person or thing that is loved and admired very much: _____

9 _____ : the act of performing a play, concert or some other form of entertainment: _____

10 _____ : a space or passage inside the entrance or front door of a building: _____

11 _____ : to become healthy again; to make something healthy again: _____

12 _____ : existing at the beginning of a particular period, process or activity: _____

13 _____ : to make something or somebody ready to be used or to do something: _____

14 _____ : the group of people who have gathered to watch or listen to something: _____

15 _____ : a style of dancing that tells a dramatic story with music but no talking or singing: _____

16 _____ : the act or process of making something that is new, or of causing something to exist that did not exist before: _____

보기			
performance	hall	signature	audience
creation	ballet	idol	original
composer	flea market	breath	prepare
heal	fall	pianist	concert

※ 다음 우리말과 일치하도록 빈칸에 알맞은 말을 쓰시오.

Listen & Speak 1 A

Jack: Hi, Sumin. _____ the book club _____?

Sumin: It's _____. I _____ _____ _____ interesting books.

Jack: _____ _____ do you _____ _____?

Sumin: I _____ *Charlotte's Web* _____.

Jack: 안녕, 수민아. 책 동아리는 어때?
Sumin: 재미있어. 나는 흥미로운 책들을 많이 읽어.
Jack: 어느 책을 가장 좋아하니?
Sumin: 나는 'Charlotte's Web'을 가장 좋아해.

Listen & Speak 1 B

Amy: Jiho, _____ _____ you _____ _____ do _____ _____?

Jiho: _____ _____ _____ Blue Sky's _____ _____ with my friends.

Amy: Wow, I'm also _____ _____ _____ of the band.

Jiho: Really? _____ _____ do you _____ _____, Amy?

Amy: I _____ Lucy _____. She _____ really _____.

Jiho: I like the _____, Mike, best. He's _____! Do you _____ _____ us?

Amy: Sure, I'd _____ _____. I _____ _____!

Amy: 지호야, 이번 주 토요일에 뭐 할 거니?
Jiho: 나는 친구들이랑 Blue Sky 팬 모임에 갈 거야.
Amy: 와, 나도 그 밴드의 열렬한 팬이야.
Jiho: 정말? 너는 어느 멤버를 가장 좋아하니, Amy?
Amy: 나는 Lucy를 가장 좋아해. 그녀는 노래를 정말 잘해.
Jiho: 나는 드러머인 Mike를 가장 좋아해. 그는 환상적이야. 우리와 함께 갈래?
Amy: 물론이지, 너무 좋아. 기대된다!

Listen & Speak 1 C

A: Do you _____ _____?

B: _____, I _____.

A: _____ _____ do you _____ _____?

B: I like _____ _____. It's so _____!

A: 운동을 좋아하니?
B: 응, 좋아해.
A: 어느 운동을 가장 좋아하니?
B: 나는 테니스를 가장 좋아해. 그것은 매우 흥미진진해!

Listen & Speak 2 A

B: _____ do you have _____ _____ old clothes?

G: I'm _____ _____ _____ them at the _____ _____.

B: Really? I have some _____ _____, _____.

G: Then _____ _____ _____ _____ me this Saturday?

B: Okay.

B: 너는 왜 저 모든 헌 옷들을 가지고 있니?
G: 나는 벼룩시장에 그 옷들을 팔 거야.
B: 정말? 나도 헌 옷들이 좀 있어.
G: 그러면 이번 주 토요일에 나와 함께 팔면 어때?
B: 좋아.

Listen & Speak 2 B

Sujin: Tom, _____ do you have so _____ _____ _____?

Tom: They're _____ my _____ _____.

Sujin: They're so _____. _____ did you _____ them?

Tom: I _____ them.

Sujin: Wow, you're really _____.

Tom: Thanks. I'm _____ _____ _____ _____ _____ these days.

Sujin: They are _____ to be _____ _____ _____ for your mom.

Tom: I _____ so, _____.

Listen & Speak 2 C

A: _____ _____ do you _____ _____ _____ for your dream vacation?

B: I want _____ _____ _____.

A: _____ _____ _____ _____ _____ visit Canada?

B: _____ I _____ _____ _____ Niagara Falls.

Real Life Talk

Mina: Good afternoon, friends. I'm Mina _____ _____ _____ _____ _____. Today Mr. Smith, _____ _____ _____, is here _____ us. Hi, Mr. Smith.

Mr. Smith: Hello, _____. I'm _____ _____ _____ here with you.

Mina: _____ _____ about music. Mr. Smith, _____ _____ _____ _____ _____?

Mr. Smith: _____ The Beatles.

Mina: Oh, I _____ them, _____. _____ _____ _____ do you _____ _____?

Mr. Smith: I like _____ _____ their songs, but I _____ *Hey Jude* _____.

Mina: _____ _____ _____ _____ _____ _____ _____?

Mr. Smith: _____ the song _____ me _____ _____ when I'm _____.

Mina: That's great! _____ _____ _____ the song.

Sujin: Tom, 왜 그렇게 많은 종이꽃을 가지고 있니?

Tom: 이 꽃들은 엄마 생신을 위한 거야.

Sujin: 정말 예쁘다. 그 꽃들을 어디서 구했니?

Tom: 내가 만들었어.

Sujin: 와, 너 정말 잘 만든다.

Tom: 고마워. 나 요즘 종이접기 수업을 듣고 있어.

Sujin: 그 꽃들은 너희 엄마에게 완벽한 선물이 될 거야.

Tom: 나도 그러길 바라.

A: 너는 꿈의 휴가로 어느 나라를 방문하고 싶니?

B: 나는 캐나다를 방문하고 싶어.

A: 너는 왜 캐나다를 방문하고 싶니?

B: 나는 나이아가라 폭포를 보고 싶기 때문이야.

Mina: 안녕하세요, 여러분. 저희 학교 라디오 프로그램의 미나입니다. 오늘은 영어 선생님이신 Smith 선생님과 함께 하겠습니다. 안녕하세요, Smith 선생님.

Mr. Smith: 안녕하세요, 여러분. 여러분과 함께하게 되어 기쁘군요.

Mina: 음악에 관한 이야기를 나눠 보도록 하죠. Smith 선생님, 어느 밴드를 가장 좋아하시나요?

Mr. Smith: 두말할 것도 없이 The Beatles에요.

Mina: 오, 저도 그들을 좋아해요. 어떤 노래를 가장 좋아하시나요?

Mr. Smith: 그들의 노래 대부분을 좋아하지만 'Hey Jude'를 가장 좋아하죠.

Mina: 왜 그 노래를 좋아하시나요?

Mr. Smith: 그 노래는 내가 우울할 때 기분이 나아지게 해 주기 때문이죠.

Mina: 멋지군요! 그 노래를 함께 들어보도록 하죠.

Step2

※ 다음 우리말에 맞도록 대화를 영어로 쓰시오.

Listen & Speak 1 A

Jack: _____

Sumin: _____

Jack: _____

Sumin: _____

Jack: 안녕, 수민아. 책 동아리는 어때?
Sumin: 재미있어. 나는 흥미로운 책들을 많이 읽어.
Jack: 어느 책을 가장 좋아하니?
Sumin: 나는 'Charlotte's Web'을 가장 좋아해.

Listen & Speak 1 B

Amy: _____

Jiho: _____

Amy: _____

Jiho: _____

Amy: _____

Jiho: _____

Amy: _____

Amy: 지호야, 이번 주 토요일에 뭐 할 거니?
Jiho: 나는 친구들이랑 Blue Sky 팬 모임에 갈 거야.
Amy: 와, 나도 그 밴드의 열렬한 팬이야.
Jiho: 정말? 너는 어느 멤버를 가장 좋아하니, Amy?
Amy: 나는 Lucy를 가장 좋아해. 그녀는 노래를 정말 잘해.
Jiho: 나는 드러머인 Mike를 가장 좋아해. 그는 환상적이야. 우리와 함께 갈래?
Amy: 물론이지, 너무 좋아. 기대된다!

Listen & Speak 1 C

A: _____

B: _____

A: _____

B: _____

A: 운동을 좋아하니?
B: 응, 좋아해.
A: 어느 운동을 가장 좋아하니?
B: 나는 테니스를 가장 좋아해. 그것은 매우 흥미진진해!

Listen & Speak 2 A

B: _____

G: _____

B: _____

G: _____

B: _____

B: 너는 왜 저 모든 헌 옷들을 가지고 있니?
G: 나는 벼룩시장에 그 옷들을 팔 거야.
B: 정말? 나도 헌 옷들이 좀 있어.
G: 그러면 이번 주 토요일에 나와 함께 팔면 어때?
B: 좋아.

Listen & Speak 2 B

Sujin: _____

Tom: _____

Sujin: _____

Tom: _____

Sujin: _____

Tom: _____

Sujin: _____

Tom: _____

Sujin: Tom, 왜 그렇게 많은 종이꽃을 가지고 있니?
Tom: 이 꽃들은 엄마 생신을 위한 거야.
Sujin: 정말 예쁘다. 그 꽃들을 어디서 구했니?
Tom: 내가 만들었어.
Sujin: 와, 너 정말 잘 만든다.
Tom: 고마워. 나 요즘 종이접기 수업을 듣고 있어.
Sujin: 그 꽃들은 너희 엄마에게 완벽한 선물이 될 거야.
Tom: 나도 그러길 바라.

Listen & Speak 1 C

A: _____

B: _____

A: _____

B: _____

A: 너는 꿈의 휴가로 어느 나라를 방문하고 싶니?
B: 나는 캐나다를 방문하고 싶어.
A: 너는 왜 캐나다를 방문하고 싶니?
B: 나는 나이아가라 폭포를 보고 싶기 때문이야.

Real Life Talk

Mina: _____
      _____

Mr. Smith: _____

Mina: _____

Mr. Smith: _____

Mina: _____

Mr. Smith: _____

Mina: _____

Mr. Smith: _____

Mina: _____

Mina: 안녕하세요, 여러분. 저희 학교 라디오 프로그램의 미나입니다. 오늘은 영어 선생님이신 Smith 선생님과 함께 하겠습니다. 안녕하세요, Smith 선생님.
Mr. Smith: 안녕하세요, 여러분. 여러분과 함께하게 되어 기쁘군요.
Mina: 음악에 관한 이야기를 나눠 보도록 하죠. Smith 선생님, 어느 밴드를 가장 좋아하시나요?
Mr. Smith: 두말할 것도 없이 The Beatles예요.
Mina: 오, 저도 그들을 좋아해요. 어떤 노래를 가장 좋아하시나요?
Mr. Smith: 그들의 노래 대부분을 좋아하지만 'Hey Jude'를 가장 좋아하죠.
Mina: 왜 그 노래를 좋아하시나요?
Mr. Smith: 그 노래는 내가 우울할 때 기분이 나아지게 해 주기 때문이죠.
Mina: 멋지군요! 그 노래를 함께 들어 보도록 하죠.

※ 다음 우리말과 일치하도록 빈칸에 알맞은 것을 골라 쓰시오.

1 Do you have a _____ K-pop _____? Many students _____ _____, "Yes."

   A. answer   B. idol   C. will   D. favorite

2 These students _____ _____ great love _____ their stars.

   A. for   B. show   C. often

3 Some _____ _____ at concerts.

   A. madly   B. scream

4 _____ wait _____ to _____ pictures of their stars.

   A. take   B. hours   C. others

5 _____ students _____ travel to _____ city to see their favorite star.

   A. another   B. even   C. some

6 Are idols a _____ _____? No _____!

   A. way   B. creation   C. recent

7 Did idols _____ _____ The Beatles _____ the 1960's?

   A. in   B. with   C. begin

8 They were _____ _____ many, but they were not the _____.

   A. first   B. by   C. loved

9 How _____ Elvis Presley _____ the 1950's? Not even _____.

   A. lose   B. in   C. about

10 To _____ the answer, _____ _____ a time machine to a concert hall in Vienna _____ 1845.

   A. in   B. let's   C. find   D. take

11 _____ the seats _____ _____.

   A. are   B. all   C. filled

12 _____ other concerts, the _____ of the piano _____ the audience.

   A. faces   B. side   C. unlike

13 This _____, the audience _____ see the _____ 185cm pianist _____.

   A. handsome   B. better   C. can   D. way

14 He doesn't have any _____ _____ with him.

   A. music   B. sheet

15 He begins to _____ from _____.

   A. memory   B. play

16 He starts _____ _____ softly _____ the keys.

   A. touching   B. slowly   C. by

1 여러분은 가장 좋아하는 K팝 아이돌이 있는가? 많은 학생들이 "그렇다."라고 답할 것이다.

2 이 학생들은 종종 자신들의 스타를 향해 큰 애정을 보인다.

3 어떤 학생들은 콘서트에서 미친 듯이 괴성을 지른다.

4 어떤 학생들은 스타의 사진을 찍기 위해 몇 시간을 기다린다.

5 어떤 학생들은 심지어 가장 좋아하는 스타를 보기 위해 다른 도시로 여행을 가기까지 한다.

6 아이돌이 최근의 창조물일까? 아니다!

7 아이돌은 1960년대의 The Beatles부터 시작됐을까?

8 그들은 많은 사람들에게 사랑받았지만, 최초는 아니다.

9 1950년대의 Elvis Presley는 어떤가? 완전히 헛짚었다.

10 답을 찾기 위해서 1845년에 빈에 있는 한 콘서트홀로 타임머신을 타고 가 보자.

11 모든 좌석이 꽉 차 있다.

12 다른 연주회와는 달리 피아노의 옆면이 청중을 향해 있다.

13 이렇게 함으로써, 청중은 잘생긴 185cm의 피아니스트를 더 잘 볼 수 있다.

14 그는 어떠한 악보도 가지고 있지 않다.

15 그는 기억으로 연주하기 시작한다.

16 그는 건반을 부드럽게 누르면서 천천히 시작한다.

17 All the people _____ their _____ because they don't want to _____ a single _____.

    A. note   B. breath   C. miss   D. hold

18 He builds _____ speed, and his long fingers press _____ on many keys _____ once.

    A. down   B. up   C. at

19 This _____ the music very _____ and _____.

    A. rich   B. makes   C. powerful

20 The audience _____ _____ to his every little body _____.

    A. movement   B. attention   C. pays

21 His _____ _____ hair _____ everywhere.

    A. flies   B. beautiful   C. long

22 It's _____ _____ a piano and ballet performance _____ _____.

    A. once   B. watching   C. at   D. like

23 Time _____ and the concert _____.

    A. ends   B. flies

24 People _____ and _____ flowers and pieces of _____ onto the _____.

    A. stage   B. throw   C. clothing   D. scream

25 The concert hall _____ _____!

    A. wild   B. goes

26 Who was this _____ _____?

    A. star   B. amazing

27 _____ name was Franz Liszt and he was _____ _____ 1811 in Hungary.

    A. in   B. his   C. born

28 He _____ started _____ the piano _____ he was seven.

    A. when   B. playing   C. first

29 Liszt _____ _____ a great pianist, _____ and teacher.

    A. composer   B. became   C. later

30 But many people _____ _____ him _____ the first idol.

    A. as   B. of   C. think

31 Why _____ you _____ his music a _____?

    A. listen   B. give   C. don't

32 _____ you like _____ idols, you _____ love the _____ idol.

    A. original   B. today's   C. will   D. if

17 모든 사람들이 단 하나의 음도 놓치고 싶지 않아서 숨을 죽인다.

18 그는 속도를 점점 올리고, 그의 긴 손가락으로 많은 건반을 한 꺼번에 누른다.

19 이것은 음악을 아주 힘 있고 풍성하게 만든다.

20 청중들은 그의 모든 작은 몸짓에 주의를 집중한다.

21 그의 길고 아름다운 머리카락이 사방에 날린다.

22 이것은 마치 피아노와 발레 공연을 동시에 보는 것 같다.

23 시간은 쏜살같이 흐르고 연주회가 끝난다.

24 사람들은 소리를 지르며 꽃과 옷을 무대로 던진다.

25 콘서트홀은 열광의 도가니가 된다!

26 이 놀라운 스타는 누구였을까?

27 그의 이름은 Franz Liszt였고 그는 1811년에 헝가리에서 태어났다.

28 그는 7살에 처음 피아노를 치기 시작했다.

29 Liszt는 나중에 훌륭한 피아니스트이며 작곡가이자 선생님이 되었다.

30 그러나 많은 사람들은 그를 첫 번째 아이돌이라고 생각한다.

31 그의 음악을 한번 들어보는 게 어떤가?

32 만약 당신이 요즘의 아이돌을 좋아한다면, 원래의 아이돌도 좋아할 것이다.

※ **다음 우리말과 일치하도록 빈칸에 알맞은 말을 쓰시오.**

1 Do you have a _____ K-pop _____? _____ students _____ answer, "Yes."

2 These students _____ _____ great _____ for their stars.

3 Some _____ _____ _____ concerts.

4 _____ wait hours to _____ _____ _____ their stars.

5 Some students even _____ _____ another city _____ _____ their _____ _____.

6 Are idols a _____ _____? No _____!

7 Did idols _____ _____ The Beatles _____ the 1960's?

8 They were _____ _____ many, but they were _____ _____ _____.

9 _____ _____ Elvis Presley _____ the 1950's? _____ even close.

10 _____ _____ _____ the answer, _____ _____ a time machine to a concert hall _____ Vienna in 1845.

11 _____ the seats _____ _____ _____.

12 _____ _____ _____, the side of the piano _____ the _____.

13 This _____, the audience _____ _____ the _____ 185cm pianist _____.

14 He _____ have _____ _____ _____ with him.

15 He _____ _____ play _____ _____.

16 He starts _____ _____ _____ _____ the keys.

1 여러분은 가장 좋아하는 K팝 아이돌이 있는가? 많은 학생들이 "그렇다."라고 답할 것이다.

2 이 학생들은 종종 자신들의 스타를 향해 큰 애정을 보인다.

3 어떤 학생들은 콘서트에서 미친 듯이 괴성을 지른다.

4 어떤 학생들은 스타의 사진을 찍기 위해 몇 시간을 기다린다.

5 어떤 학생들은 심지어 가장 좋아하는 스타를 보기 위해 다른 도시로 여행을 가기까지 한다.

6 아이돌이 최근의 창조물일까? 아니다!

7 아이돌은 1960년대의 The Beatles부터 시작됐을까?

8 그들은 많은 사람들에게 사랑받았지만, 최초는 아니다.

9 1950년대의 Elvis Presley는 어떤가? 완전히 헛짚었다.

10 답을 찾기 위해서 1845년에 빈에 있는 한 콘서트홀로 타임머신을 타고 가 보자.

11 모든 좌석이 꽉 차 있다.

12 다른 연주회와는 달리 피아노의 옆면이 청중을 향해 있다.

13 이렇게 함으로써, 청중은 잘생긴 185cm의 피아니스트를 더 잘 볼 수 있다.

14 그는 어떠한 악보도 가지고 있지 않다.

15 그는 기억으로 연주하기 시작한다.

16 그는 건반을 부드럽게 누르면서 천천히 시작한다.

17 All the people _____ _____ _____ because they don't want _____ _____ _____ _____ _____.

18 He _____ _____ speed, and his long fingers _____ _____ on many keys _____ _____.

19 This _____ the music very _____ and _____.

20 The audience _____ _____ _____ his every little _____ _____.

21 His _____ _____ hair _____ everywhere.

22 It's _____ _____ a piano and ballet performance _____ _____.

23 Time _____ and the concert _____.

24 People _____ and _____ flowers and pieces of _____ _____ _____ _____.

25 The concert hall _____ _____!

26 _____ was this _____ _____?

27 His name _____ Franz Liszt and he _____ _____ _____ 1811 in Hungary.

28 He first _____ _____ the piano _____ _____ _____.

29 Liszt _____ _____ a great pianist, _____ and teacher.

30 But many people _____ _____ him _____ the first idol.

31 _____ _____ you give his music a _____?

32 _____ you _____ today's _____, you _____ _____ the _____ _____.

17 모든 사람들이 단 하나의 음도 놓치고 싶지 않아서 숨을 죽인다.

18 그는 속도를 점점 올리고, 그의 긴 손가락으로 많은 건반을 한 꺼번에 누른다.

19 이것은 음악을 아주 힘 있고 풍 성하게 만든다.

20 청중들은 그의 모든 작은 몸짓 에 주의를 집중한다.

21 그의 길고 아름다운 머리카락이 사방에 날린다.

22 이것은 마치 피아노와 발레 공 연을 동시에 보는 것 같다.

23 시간은 쏜살같이 흐르고 연주회 가 끝난다.

24 사람들은 소리를 지르며 꽃과 옷을 무대로 던진다.

25 콘서트홀은 열광의 도가니가 된다!

26 이 놀라운 스타는 누구였을까?

27 그의 이름은 Franz Liszt였고 그는 1811년에 헝가리에서 태어났다.

28 그는 7살에 처음 피아노를 치기 시작했다.

29 Liszt는 나중에 훌륭한 피아니스 트이며 작곡가이자 선생님이 되 었다.

30 그러나 많은 사람들은 그를 첫 번째 아이돌이라고 생각한다.

31 그의 음악을 한번 들어보는 게 어떤가?

32 만약 당신이 요즘의 아이돌을 좋아한다면, 원래의 아이돌도 좋아할 것이다.

※ 다음 문장을 우리말로 쓰시오.

1 Do you have a favorite K-pop idol? Many students will answer, "Yes."
➡ _____

2 These students often show great love for their stars.
➡ _____

3 Some scream madly at concerts.
➡ _____

4 Others wait hours to take pictures of their stars.
➡ _____

5 Some students even travel to another city to see their favorite stars.
➡ _____

6 Are idols a recent creation? No way!
➡ _____

7 Did idols begin with The Beatles in the 1960's?
➡ _____

8 They were loved by many, but they were not the first.
➡ _____

9 How about Elvis Presley in the 1950's? Not even close.
➡ _____

10 To find the answer, let's take a time machine to a concert hall in Vienna in 1845.
➡ _____

11 All the seats are filled.
➡ _____

12 Unlike other concerts, the side of the piano faces the audience.
➡ _____

13 This way, the audience can see the handsome 185cm pianist better.
➡ _____

14 He doesn't have any sheet music with him.
➡ _____

15 He begins to play from memory.
➡ _____

16 He starts slowly by softly touching the keys.
➡ _____

17 All the people hold their breath because they don't want to miss a single note.

➡ _____

18 He builds up speed, and his long fingers press down on many keys at once.

➡ _____

19 This makes the music very powerful and rich.

➡ _____

20 The audience pays attention to his every little body movement.

➡ _____

21 His long beautiful hair flies everywhere.

➡ _____

22 It's like watching a piano and ballet performance at once.

➡ _____

23 Time flies and the concert ends.

➡ _____

24 People scream and throw flowers and pieces of clothing onto the stage.

➡ _____

25 The concert hall goes wild!

➡ _____

26 Who was this amazing star?

➡ _____

27 His name was Franz Liszt and he was born in 1811 in Hungary.

➡ _____

28 He first started playing the piano when he was seven.

➡ _____

29 Liszt later became a great pianist, composer and teacher.

➡ _____

30 But many people think of him as the first idol.

➡ _____

31 Why don't you give his music a listen?

➡ _____

32 If you like today's idols, you will love the original idol.

➡ _____

본문 Test

Step4

※ 다음 괄호 안의 단어들을 우리말에 맞도록 바르게 배열하시오.

1 (you / do / a / have / K-pop / favorite / idol? // students / will / many / answer, / “Yes.”)
➡ ________________________________

2 (students / show / these / often / love / great / stars. / their / for)
➡ ________________________________

3 (scream / at / some / concerts. / madly)
➡ ________________________________

4 (wait / others / to / hours / pictures / take / of / stars. / their)
➡ ________________________________

5 (some / even / students / travel / another / to / city / see / to / their / stars. / favorite)
➡ ________________________________

6 (idols / are / recent / a / creation? / way! / no)
➡ ________________________________

7 (idols / did / with / begin / Beatles / The / in / 1960's? / the)
➡ ________________________________

8 (were / they / by / loved / many, / but / were / they / first. / the / not)
➡ ________________________________

9 (Elvis / Presley / about / how / the / in / 1950's? // even / close. / not)
➡ ________________________________

10 (find / answer, / to / the / let's / take / machine / a / time / to / concert / a / Vienna / in / hall / 1845. / in)
➡ ________________________________
____

11 (the / seats / all / filled. / are)
➡ ________________________________

12 (other / unlike / concerts, / the / of / side / the / piano / audience. / the / faces)
➡ ________________________________

13 (way, / this / the / audience / see / can / handsome / the / better. / pianist / 185cm)
➡ ________________________________

14 (he / have / doesn't / sheet / any / with / him. / music)
➡ ________________________________

15 (he / play / to / begins / memory. / from)
➡ ________________________________

16 (starts / he / slowly / touching / by / keys. / the / softly)
➡ ________________________________

1 여러분은 가장 좋아하는 K팝 아이돌이 있는가? 많은 학생들이 “그렇다.”라고 답할 것이다.

2 이 학생들은 종종 자신들의 스타를 향해 큰 애정을 보인다.

3 어떤 학생들은 콘서트에서 미친 듯이 괴성을 지른다.

4 어떤 학생들은 스타의 사진을 찍기 위해 몇 시간을 기다린다.

5 어떤 학생들은 심지어 가장 좋아하는 스타를 보기 위해 다른 도시로 여행을 가기까지 한다.

6 아이돌이 최근의 창조물일까? 아니다!

7 아이돌은 1960년대의 The Beatles부터 시작됐을까?

8 그들은 많은 사람들에게 사랑받았지만, 최초는 아니다.

9 1950년대의 Elvis Presley는 어떤가? 완전히 헛짚었다.

10 답을 찾기 위해서 1845년에 빈에 있는 한 콘서트홀로 타임머신을 타고 가 보자.

11 모든 좌석이 꽉 차 있다.

12 다른 연주회와는 달리 피아노의 옆면이 청중을 향해 있다.

13 이렇게 함으로써, 청중은 잘생긴 185cm의 피아니스트를 더 잘 볼 수 있다.

14 그는 어떠한 악보도 가지고 있지 않다.

15 그는 기억으로 연주하기 시작한다.

16 그는 건반을 부드럽게 누르면서 천천히 시작한다.

17 (the / all / hold / people / breath / their / because / don't / they / to / want / miss / a / note. / single)

➡ _____

18 (builds / he / speed, / up / and / long / his / fingers / down / press / many / on / once. / at / keys)

➡ _____

19 (the / music / makes / this / very / rich. / and / powerful)

➡ _____

20 (audience / the / pays / to / attention / every / his / little / movement. / body)

➡ _____

21 (long / beautiful / his / everywhere. / hair / flies)

➡ _____

22 (like / it's / a / watching / piano / and / performance / once. / at / ballet)

➡ _____

23 (flies / time / and / concert / ends. / the)

➡ _____

24 (scream / people / and / flowers / throw / and / pieces / clothing / of / stage. / the / onto)

➡ _____

25 (concert / the / hall / wild! / goes)

➡ _____

26 (was / who / star? / this / amazing)

➡ _____

27 (name / his / Franz / was / Liszt / and / was / born / in / he / in / Hungary. / 1811)

➡ _____

28 (first / he / playing / started / piano / the / when / seven. / was / he)

➡ _____

29 (later / Liszt / became / pianist, / great / a / and / teacher. / composer)

➡ _____

30 (many / but / think / people / of / him / idol. / as / first / the)

➡ _____

31 (don't / why / give / you / music / his / listen? / a)

➡ _____

32 (you / like / if / idols, / today's / will / you / love / original / the / idol.)

➡ _____

17 모든 사람들이 단 하나의 음도 놓치고 싶지 않아서 숨을 죽인다.

18 그는 속도를 점점 올리고, 그의 긴 손가락으로 많은 건반을 한 꺼번에 누른다.

19 이것은 음악을 아주 힘 있고 풍 성하게 만든다.

20 청중들은 그의 모든 작은 몸짓 에 주의를 집중한다.

21 그의 길고 아름다운 머리카락이 사방에 날린다.

22 이것은 마치 피아노와 발레 공 연을 동시에 보는 것 같다.

23 시간은 쏜살같이 흐르고 연주회 가 끝난다.

24 사람들은 소리를 지르며 꽃과 옷을 무대로 던진다.

25 콘서트홀은 열광의 도가니가 된다!

26 이 놀라운 스타는 누구였을까?

27 그의 이름은 Franz Liszt였고 그는 1811년에 헝가리에서 태어났다.

28 그는 7살에 처음 피아노를 치기 시작했다.

29 Liszt는 나중에 훌륭한 피아니스 트이며 작곡가이자 선생님이 되 었다.

30 그러나 많은 사람들은 그를 첫 번째 아이돌이라고 생각한다.

31 그의 음악을 한번 들어보는 게 어떤가?

32 만약 당신이 요즘의 아이돌을 좋아한다면, 원래의 아이돌도 좋아할 것이다.

※ 다음 우리말을 영어로 쓰시오.

1 여러분은 가장 좋아하는 K팝 아이돌이 있는가? 많은 학생들이 "그렇다."라고 답할 것이다.

➡ _____

2 이 학생들은 종종 자신들의 스타를 향해 큰 애정을 보인다.

➡ _____

3 어떤 학생들은 콘서트에서 미친 듯이 괴성을 지른다.

➡ _____

4 어떤 학생들은 스타의 사진을 찍기 위해 몇 시간을 기다린다.

➡ _____

5 어떤 학생들은 심지어 가장 좋아하는 스타를 보기 위해 다른 도시로 여행을 가기까지 한다.

➡ _____

6 아이돌이 최근의 창조물일까? 아니다!

➡ _____

7 아이돌은 1960년대의 The Beatles부터 시작됐을까?

➡ _____

8 그들은 많은 사람들에게 사랑받았지만, 최초는 아니다.

➡ _____

9 1950년대의 Elvis Presley는 어떤가? 완전히 헛짚었다.

➡ _____

10 답을 찾기 위해서 1845년에 빈에 있는 한 콘서트홀로 타임머신을 타고 가 보자.

➡ _____

11 모든 좌석이 꽉 차 있다.

➡ _____

12 다른 연주회와는 달리 피아노의 옆면이 청중을 향해 있다.

➡ _____

13 이렇게 함으로써, 청중은 잘생긴 185cm의 피아니스트를 더 잘 볼 수 있다.

➡ _____

14 그는 어떠한 악보도 가지고 있지 않다.

➡ _____

15 그는 기억으로 연주하기 시작한다.

➡ _____

16 그는 건반을 부드럽게 누르면서 천천히 시작한다.

➡ _____

17 모든 사람들이 단 하나의 음도 놓치고 싶지 않아서 숨을 죽인다.

➡ _____

18 그는 속도를 점점 올리고, 그의 긴 손가락으로 많은 건반을 한꺼번에 누른다.

➡ _____

19 이것은 음악을 아주 힘 있고 풍성하게 만든다.

➡ _____

20 청중들은 그의 모든 작은 몸짓에 주의를 집중한다.

➡ _____

21 그의 길고 아름다운 머리카락이 사방에 날린다.

➡ _____

22 이것은 마치 피아노와 발레 공연을 동시에 보는 것 같다.

➡ _____

23 시간은 쏜살같이 흐르고 연주회가 끝난다.

➡ _____

24 사람들은 소리를 지르며 꽃과 옷을 무대로 던진다.

➡ _____

25 콘서트홀은 열광의 도가니가 된다!

➡ _____

26 이 놀라운 스타는 누구였을까?

➡ _____

27 그의 이름은 Franz Liszt였고 그는 1811년에 헝가리에서 태어났다.

➡ _____

28 그는 7살에 처음 피아노를 치기 시작했다.

➡ _____

29 Liszt는 나중에 훌륭한 피아니스트이며 작곡가이자 선생님이 되었다.

➡ _____

30 그러나 많은 사람들은 그를 첫 번째 아이돌이라고 생각한다.

➡ _____

31 그의 음악을 한번 들어보는 게 어떤가?

➡ _____

32 만약 당신이 요즘의 아이돌을 좋아한다면, 원래의 아이돌도 좋아할 것이다.

➡ _____

※ 다음 우리말과 일치하도록 빈칸에 알맞은 말을 쓰시오.

Real Life Talk - Step 2

A: _____ singer do you _____ best?

B: I _____ John Lennon _____ .

A: _____ do you _____ him?

B: _____ he is a _____ singer.

A: _____ _____ do you like _____ ?

B: I like Imagine best. It _____ _____ _____ .

A: 어느 가수를 가장 좋아하니?
B: 나는 John Lennon을 가장 좋아해.
A: 왜 그를 좋아해?
B: 왜냐면 그는 훌륭한 가수이기 때문이야.
A: 너는 어느 곡을 가장 좋아하니?
B: 나는 Imagine을 가장 좋아해. 이것은 내게 힘을 북돋아 줘.

Think and Write

1. _____ Sandra,

2. Hello, _____ name is Jina and I'm a _____ _____ _____ you.

3. I watched _____ _____ your movies and I _____ "Into the Sky" _____ .

4. I think _____ your _____ is so _____ .

5. _____ do you _____ _____ your roles?

6. If I meet you _____ _____ , I _____ _____ you many _____ _____ .

7. I _____ _____ see you soon.

8. _____ , Jina

1. Sandra 씨에게,
2. 안녕하세요, 제 이름은 Jina이고 저는 당신의 열렬한 팬이에요.
3. 저는 당신이 출연한 모든 영화를 다 봤고 "Into the Sky"를 가장 좋아해요.
4. 저는 당신의 연기가 매우 진정성 있다고 생각해요.
5. 당신이 맡은 역할을 어떻게 준비하나요?
6. 제가 당신을 직접 만나게 된다면, 저는 당신에게 더 많은 질문을 할 거예요.
7. 당신을 곧 만나길 바랍니다.
8. 사랑을 담아, Jina

Read And Write

1. The Star of _____ _____

2. Yesterday Franz Liszt _____ his piano concert very _____ in Vienna.

3. This concert _____ _____ _____ others.

4. The _____ of the piano _____ the _____ .

5. They _____ _____ Liszt better _____ _____ .

6. He didn't have any _____ _____ and played _____ .

7. His music was so _____ and _____ .

8. When the concert _____ , the concert hall _____ _____ .

1. 우리 시대의 스타
2. 어제 Franz Liszt가 Vienna에서 매우 성공적으로 피아노 연주회를 하였습니다.
3. 이 콘서트는 다른 콘서트들과 달랐습니다.
4. 피아노의 측면이 청중을 향해 있었습니다.
5. 청중들은 이런 식으로 Liszt를 더 잘 볼 수 있었습니다.
6. 그는 어떠한 악보도 필요치 않았고 기억해서 연주했습니다.
7. 그의 음악은 매우 힘 있고 풍성했습니다.
8. 콘서트가 끝날 때, 콘서트홀은 열광의 도가니가 되었습니다

구석구석 지문 Test

※ 다음 우리말을 영어로 쓰시오.

Real Life Talk - Step 2

1. A: 어느 가수를 가장 좋아하니?
➡ _____

2. B: 나는 John Lennon을 가장 좋아해.
➡ _____

3. A: 왜 그를 좋아해?
➡ _____

4. B: 왜냐면 그는 훌륭한 가수이기 때문이야.
➡ _____

5. A: 너는 어느 곡을 가장 좋아하니?
➡ _____

6. B: 나는 Imagine을 가장 좋아해. 이것은 내게 힘을 북돋아 줘.
➡ _____

Think and Write

1. Sandra 씨에게,
➡ _____

2. 안녕하세요, 제 이름은 Jina이고 저는 당신의 열렬한 팬이에요.
➡ _____

3. 저는 당신이 출연한 모든 영화를 다 봤고 "Into the Sky"를 가장 좋아해요.
➡ _____

4. 저는 당신의 연기가 매우 진정성 있다고 생각해요.
➡ _____

5. 당신이 맡은 역할을 어떻게 준비하나요?
➡ _____

6. 제가 당신을 직접 만나게 된다면, 저는 당신에게 더 많은 질문을 할 거예요.
➡ _____

7. 당신을 곧 만나길 바랍니다.
➡ _____

8. 사랑을 담아, Jina
➡ _____

Read and Write

1. 우리 시대의 스타
➡ _____

2. 어제 Franz Liszt가 Vienna에서 매우 성공적으로 피아노 연주회를 하였습니다.
➡ _____

3. 이 콘서트는 다른 콘서트들과 달랐습니다.
➡ _____

4. 피아노의 측면이 청중을 향해 있었습니다.
➡ _____

5. 청중들은 이런 식으로 Liszt를 더 잘 볼 수 있었습니다.
➡ _____

6. 그는 어떠한 악보도 필요치 않았고 기억해서 연주했습니다.
➡ _____

7. 그의 음악은 매우 힘 있고 풍성했습니다.
➡ _____

8. 콘서트가 끝날 때, 콘서트홀은 열광의 도가니가 되었습니다.
➡ _____

※ 다음 영어를 우리말로 쓰시오.

01	athlete
02	reach
03	equipment
04	expect
05	temperature
06	scared
07	amazing
08	scary
09	participant
10	wet
11	throat
12	freeze
13	limit
14	burn
15	request
16	protect
17	windy
18	hit
19	imagine
20	jump rope
21	librarian

22	bake
23	race
24	rock climbing
25	train
26	boiling
27	planet
28	traditional
29	ordinary
30	punch
31	tough
32	backpack
33	throw
34	hang
35	go on
36	take part in
37	up to
38	in fact
39	for a living
40	a series of
41	take place
42	be out of
43	take care of

※ 다음 우리말을 영어로 쓰시오.

01	사막	
02	방향	
03	전통적인	
04	결승선	
05	끓는, 끓어오르는	
06	남극대륙	
07	배낭	
08	들(판), 경기장	
09	던지다	
10	계주, 릴레이 경주	
11	마른, 건조한	
12	마라톤	
13	행성	
14	의미하다	
15	매달다	
16	힘든, 어려운	
17	배트, 막대기, 박쥐	
18	타다	
19	체육관	
20	차다	
21	보통의, 평범한	

22	타격	
23	거대한	
24	모래	
25	제복, 유니폼	
26	온도	
27	장비, 설비	
28	얼다, 얼어붙다	
29	보호하다	
30	참가자	
31	선수, 육상 경기 선수	
32	한계, 제한; 제한하다	
33	목구멍	
34	젖은, 축축한	
35	~에 참가하다	
36	~의 한가운데에	
37	일련의	
38	일어나다, 개최되다	
39	~가 떨어지다, 바닥나다	
40	계속되다	
41	~을 돌보다	
42	~까지	
43	사실은, 실제로	

※ 다음 영영풀이에 알맞은 단어를 <보기>에서 골라 쓴 후, 우리말 뜻을 쓰시오.

1 _____ : much larger or more powerful than normal: _____

2 _____ : the continent around the South Pole: _____

3 _____ : a person who is taking part in an activity or event: _____

4 _____ : a person who is in charge of or works in a library: _____

5 _____ : a person who competes in sports: _____

6 _____ : the measurement in degrees of how hot or cold a thing or place is: _____

7 _____ : a room or hall with equipment for doing physical exercise: _____

8 _____ : to become hard, and often turn to ice, as a result of extreme cold: _____

9 _____ : to be heated to the point where it forms bubbles and turns to steam or vapour: _____

10 _____ : a race in which people run a distance of 26 miles, which is about 42 km: _____

11 _____ : being part of the beliefs, customs or way of life of a particular group of people, that have not changed for a long time: _____

12 _____ : to make sure that somebody/something is not harmed, injured, damaged: _____

13 _____ : a competition between people, animals, vehicles, etc. to see which one is the faster or fastest: _____

14 _____ : a large area of land that has very little water and very few plants growing on it: _____

15 _____ : a passage in the neck through which food and air pass on their way into the body; the front part of the neck: _____

16 _____ : to try to make yourself stronger, faster, or better at doing something before competing in an event or competition: _____

보기			
race	boil	librarian	traditional
freeze	throat	protect	Antarctica
train	desert	participant	giant
marathon	gym	athlete	temperature

대화문 Test

※ 다음 우리말과 일치하도록 빈칸에 알맞은 말을 쓰시오.

Listen & Speak 1 A

Tony: Bomi, what do you do _____ _____ _____ _____?

Bomi: I _____ _____ cookies. _____ _____ you, Tony?

Tony: I _____ _____ _____.

Tony: 보미야, 너는 여가 시간에 무엇을 하니?
Bomi: 나는 종종 쿠키를 구워. 너는 어때, Tony?
Tony: 나는 보통 영화를 봐.

Listen & Speak 1 B

Jean: I'm so _____. _____ Friday!

Tom: _____ _____ _____ _____ _____ _____ on the weekend, Jean?

Jean: I'm _____ _____ _____ _____.

Tom: Do you _____ badminton _____?

Jean: Yes, it's _____ _____ _____ _____ _____.

Tom: _____ do you _____ _____ _____?

Jean: My dad. _____ _____ _____ _____ _____ _____ _____?

Tom: I _____ _____ to the Han River and _____ _____ _____.

Jean: 정말 기뻐. 금요일이야!
Tom: 주말에 무엇을 할 거니, Jean?
Jean: 나는 배드민턴을 칠 거야.
Tom: 배드민턴을 자주 치니?
Jean: 응, 그건 내가 가장 좋아하는 여가 활동이야.
Tom: 보통 누구랑 치니?
Jean: 우리 아빠랑. 너는 여가 시간에 무엇을 하니?
Tom: 나는 종종 한강에 가서 자전거를 타.

Listen & Speak 1 C

Minsu: Ms. Allen, _____ do you do _____ _____ _____?

Allen: I'm a doctor.

Minsu: What do you do _____ _____ _____ _____?

Allen: _____ _____ _____ _____ _____.

Minsu: Ms. Allen, 직업이 무언가요?
Allen: 의사입니다.
Minsu: 여가 시간에 무엇을 하나요?
Allen: 나는 종종 탁구를 칩니다.

Listen & Speak 2 A

Mina: Tom, _____ _____ _____ _____ _____ Jeju-do?

Tom: Yes, _____ _____. I _____ there last winter vacation. _____ _____ you?

Mina: _____ _____ _____ _____ _____, but I'm _____ there this summer

Tom: That's great! _____ _____ you'll like it _____ _____.

Mina: Tom, 너는 제주도에 가 본 적이 있니?
Tom: 응, 가 봤어. 지난 겨울 방학에 거기에 갔어. 너는?
Mina: 나는 거기에 가 본 적이 없는데, 이번 여름에 갈 거야.
Tom: 잘됐네! 네가 아주 좋아할 거라고 확신해.

Listen & Speak 2 B

Suji: Mike, _____ _____ _____ _____ _____ flying yoga?

Mike: Yeah! _____ _____ it on TV. People _____ _____ in the air!

Suji: _____ what? I'm _____ it _____ _____.

Mike: Really? It _____ _____ _____. Do you like it, Suji?

Suji: At first, I was _____ _____ _____, but now I'm _____ it.

Mike: Sounds great! I _____ I _____ _____ more, _____.

Suji: Do you _____ _____ _____ my yoga class?

Mike: No, that's too _____ _____ me. I'll just _____ _____.

Suji: Mike, 너는 플라잉 요가를 들어본 적이 있니?

Mike: 응! TV에서 본 적이 있어. 사람들이 공중에 매달려 있었어!

Suji: 그거 알아? 내가 요즘 그걸 배우고 있어.

Mike: 정말? 아주 무서워 보였는데. 그걸 좋아하니, 수지야?

Suji: 처음엔 조금 무서웠는데, 지금은 즐기고 있어.

Mike: 좋구나! 나도 운동을 더 해야 할 것 같아.

Suji: 우리 요가 수업을 함께 할래?

Mike: 아니, 그건 내게 너무 무서워. 나는 그냥 농구를 할게.

Listen & Speak 2 C

A: _____ _____ _____ _____ a horse?

B: Yes, _____ _____.

A: _____ did you _____ _____ _____?

B: _____ _____.

A: 너는 말을 타 본 적이 있니?
B: 응. 있어.
A: 언제 말을 타 보았니?
B: 지난 여름에.

Real Life Talk

Hojin: Judy, what do you do _____ _____ _____ _____?

Judy: I _____ _____ _____ _____ with my dad.

Hojin: _____ _____ do you _____ _____?

Judy: No, Hojin. I _____ _____ it at a _____ _____ my house.

Hojin: I see. _____ _____ _____ _____ it on a real mountain?

Judy: _____ _____. But I _____ _____ _____ _____ it someday.

Hojin: That's _____ _____. Can I _____ _____ _____ you next time?

Judy: Sure. I'm _____ _____ _____.

Hojin: That _____ _____.

Judy: You're _____ _____ _____ it.

Hojin: Judy, 너는 여가 시간에 무엇을 하니?
Judy: 나는 종종 아빠와 암벽 등반을 하러 가.
Hojin: 어떤 산에 가니?
Judy: 아니야, 호진아. 나는 보통 집 근처에 있는 체육관에서 그걸 해.
Hojin: 그렇구나. 실제 산에서 해 본 적이 있니?
Judy: 아직 없어. 하지만 언젠가 해 보기를 바라.
Hojin: 그거 정말 멋지다. 다음번에 내가 가서 함께 해도 될까?
Judy: 물론이야. 이번 주 토요일에 갈 거야.
Hojin: 잘됐네.
Judy: 너는 그걸 정말 좋아할 거야.

※ 다음 우리말에 맞도록 대화를 영어로 쓰시오.

Listen & Speak 1 A

Tony: _____

Bomi: _____

Tony: _____

Tony: 보미야, 너는 여가 시간에 무엇을 하니?
Bomi: 나는 종종 쿠키를 구워. 너는 어때, Tony?
Tony: 나는 보통 영화를 봐.

Listen & Speak 1 B

Jean: _____

Tom: _____

Jean: _____

Tom: _____

Jean: _____

Tom: _____

Jean: _____

Tom: _____

Jean: 정말 기뻐. 금요일이야!
Tom: 주말에 무엇을 할 거니, Jean?
Jean: 나는 배드민턴을 칠 거야.
Tom: 배드민턴을 자주 치니?
Jean: 응, 그건 내가 가장 좋아하는 여가 활동이야.
Tom: 보통 누구랑 치니?
Jean: 우리 아빠랑. 너는 여가 시간에 무엇을 하니?
Tom: 나는 종종 한강에 가서 자전거를 타.

Listen & Speak 1 C

Minsu: _____

Allen: _____

Minsu: _____

Allen: _____

Minsu: Ms. Allen, 직업이 무언가요?
Allen: 의사입니다.
Minsu: 여가 시간에 무엇을 하나요?
Allen: 나는 종종 탁구를 칩니다.

Listen & Speak 2 A

Mina: _____

Tom: _____

Mina: _____

Tom: _____

Mina: Tom, 너는 제주도에 가 본 적이 있니?
Tom: 응, 가 봤어. 지난 겨울 방학에 거기에 갔어. 너는?
Mina: 나는 거기에 가 본 적이 없는데, 이번 여름에 갈 거야.
Tom: 잘됐네! 네가 아주 좋아할 거라고 확신해.

Listen & Speak 2 B

Suji: _____

Mike: _____

Suji: _____

Mike: _____

Suji: _____

Mike: _____

Suji: _____

Mike: _____

Listen & Speak 2 C

A: _____

B: _____

A: _____

B: _____

Real Life Talk

Hojin: _____

Judy: _____

Hojin: _____

Judy: _____

Hojin: _____

Judy: _____

Hojin: _____

Judy: _____

Hojin: _____

Judy: _____

Suji: Mike, 너는 플라잉 요가를 들어본 적이 있니?

Mike: 응! TV에서 본 적이 있어. 사람들이 공중에 매달려 있었어!

Suji: 그거 알아? 내가 요즘 그걸 배우고 있어.

Mike: 정말? 아주 무서워 보였는데. 그걸 좋아하니, 수지야?

Suji: 처음엔 조금 무서웠는데, 지금은 즐기고 있어.

Mike: 좋구나! 나도 운동을 더 해야 할 것 같아.

Suji: 우리 요가 수업을 함께 할래?

Mike: 아니, 그건 내게 너무 무서워. 나는 그냥 농구를 할게.

A: 너는 말을 타 본 적이 있니?

B: 응. 있어.

A: 언제 말을 타 보았니?

B: 지난 여름에.

Hojin: Judy, 너는 여가 시간에 무엇을 하니?

Judy: 나는 종종 아빠와 암벽 등반을 하러 가.

Hojin: 어떤 산에 가니?

Judy: 아니야, 호진아. 나는 보통 집 근처에 있는 체육관에서 그걸 해.

Hojin: 그렇구나. 실제 산에서 해 본 적이 있니?

Judy: 아직 없어. 하지만 언젠가 해 보기를 바라.

Hojin: 그거 정말 멋지다. 다음번에 내가 가서 함께 해도 될까?

Judy: 물론이야. 이번 주 토요일에 갈 거야.

Hojin: 잘됐네.

Judy: 너는 그걸 정말 좋아할 거야.

※ 다음 우리말과 일치하도록 빈칸에 알맞은 것을 골라 쓰시오.

1 _____ you are in the _____ of a _____ desert.
    A. middle   B. imagine   C. great

2 The sands go _____ and on in _____ _____.
    A. direction   B. on   C. every

3 The sun _____ _____ a giant ball of _____.
    A. fire   B. like   C. feels

4 The hot wind _____ your _____ and _____.
    A. throat   B. face   C. burns

5 You _____ your _____ to _____ some water.
    A. open   B. drink   C. backpack

6 Oh, no! You're _____ _____ _____ water.
    A. of   B. almost   C. out

7 You _____ your throat with a _____ of water and _____ _____.
    A. going   B. drop   C. wet   D. keep

8 _____ _____ a bad dream?
    A. like   B. sounds

9 Well, this is not a _____ for the people who _____ _____ in the 4 Deserts Race.
    A. part   B. take   C. dream

10 The 4 Deserts Race is a _____ of four _____ _____ the world's _____ deserts.
    A. races   B. toughest   C. series   D. across

11 _____ _____ is 250 kilometers _____ and _____ seven days.
    A. takes   B. race   C. each   D. long

12 The first race _____ _____ in the Atacama Desert _____ Chile.
    A. in   B. place   C. takes

13 It is _____ _____ desert _____ the world.
    A. in   B. driest   C. the

14 In _____, it _____ _____ in some parts of the Atacama Desert _____ 400 years!
    A. for   B. hasn't   C. fact   D. rained

15 The next race _____ _____ the Gobi Desert _____ China.
    A. to   B. in   C. goes

16 It is _____ _____ _____ on earth.
    A. desert   B. windiest   C. the

---

1 당신이 아주 큰 사막의 한 가운데에 있다고 상상해 봐라.

2 모래 벌판이 사면팔방으로 계속 이어진다.

3 태양은 거대한 불덩이 같다.

4 뜨거운 바람이 당신의 얼굴과 목구멍을 태운다.

5 당신은 물을 좀 마시려고 배낭을 연다.

6 오, 이런! 물이 거의 떨어져 간다.

7 당신은 물 한 방울로 목을 적시고 계속 간다.

8 나쁜 꿈인 것 같은가?

9 글쎄, '4 Deserts Race'에 참가하는 사람들에게 이것은 꿈이 아니다.

10 '4 Deserts Race'는 세계에서 가장 험한 사막들을 가로지르는 연속된 4개의 경주이다.

11 각 경주는 250킬로미터이고 7일이 걸린다.

12 첫 번째 경주는 칠레에 있는 아타카마 사막에서 열린다.

13 그곳은 세계에서 가장 건조한 사막이다.

14 실제로 아타카마 사막의 어떤 곳에는 400년간 비가 내리지 않았다!

15 다음 경주는 중국에 있는 고비 사막으로 이어진다.

16 그곳은 세상에서 가장 바람이 많이 부는 사막이다.

17 The _____ race _____ _____ the Sahara Desert _____ Egypt.

    A. in   B. to   C. heads   D. third

18 It is _____ _____ of the four _____.

    A. hottest   B. deserts   C. the

19 Temperatures can _____ _____ _____ 50°C.

    A. reach   B. to   C. up

20 Finally, the race _____ to the _____ desert on _____, Antarctica.

    A. coldest   B. earth   C. travels

21 If you _____ _____ water into the air here, it _____!

    A. freezes   B. boiling   C. throw

22 Only _____ _____ runners on the planet can _____ _____ in 4 Deserts Race, right?

    A. part   B. greatest   C. take   D. the

23 _____ _____.

    A. exactly   B. not

24 Many of the _____ are _____ people _____ you and me.

    A. like   B. ordinary   C. participants

25 _____ _____ do they _____ it?

    A. why   B. do   C. so

26 Adrianna, a _____ _____ France, _____,

    A. from   B. librarian   C. says

27 "It's a _____ to test your _____ and make your _____ history.

    A. own   B. chance   C. limits

28 _____e who _____ the finish line can do _____."

    A. anything   B. crosses   C. anyone

---

17 세 번째 경주는 이집트에 있는 사하라 사막으로 향한다.

18 그곳은 네 개의 사막 중 가장 뜨겁다.

19 온도가 섭씨 50도까지 올라갈 수 있다.

20 마지막으로 경주는 세상에서 가장 추운 사막인 남극 대륙으로 향한다.

21 이곳에서 끓는 물을 공중에 던지면, 그것은 얼어버린다!

22 세상에서 가장 훌륭한 달리기 주자들만 '4 Deserts Race'에 참가할 수 있다, 맞는가?

23 꼭 그렇진 않다.

24 많은 참가자들은 당신과 나와 같은 평범한 사람들이다.

25 그러면 그들은 왜 그것을 하는가?

26 프랑스 출신의 사서인 Adrianna는 말한다.

27 "그것은 당신의 한계를 시험하고 당신만의 역사를 만들 기회예요.

28 결승선을 넘는 사람은 어떤 것이든 할 수 있어요."

※ 다음 우리말과 일치하도록 빈칸에 알맞은 말을 쓰시오.

1   _____ you are _____ _____ _____ _____ a great
    desert.

2   The sands _____ _____ _____ _____ in every direction.

3   The sun _____ _____ a _____ ball of _____.

4   The hot wind _____ _____ _____ and _____.

5   You _____ _____ _____ _____ _____ some water.

6   Oh, no! You're _____ _____ _____ _____.

7   You _____ your throat _____ _____ _____ _____
    water and _____ _____.

8   _____ _____ a _____ _____?

9   Well, this is not a dream for the people _____ _____ _____
    _____ the 4 Deserts Race.

10 The 4 Deserts Race is _____ _____ _____ _____
    _____ _____ the world's _____ _____.

11 _____ _____ _____ 250 kilometers _____ and _____
    seven days.

12 The first race _____ _____ in the Atacama Desert _____
    Chile.

13 It is _____ _____ desert in the world.

14 _____ _____, it _____ _____ in some parts of the
    Atacama Desert _____ 400 years!

15 The next race _____ _____ the Gobi Desert _____ China.

16 It is _____ _____ _____ _____ _____ _____.

1   당신이 아주 큰 사막의 한 가운데에 있다고 상상해 봐라.

2   모래 벌판이 사면팔방으로 계속 이어진다.

3   태양은 거대한 불덩이 같다.

4   뜨거운 바람이 당신의 얼굴과 목구멍을 태운다.

5   당신은 물을 좀 마시려고 배낭을 연다.

6   오, 이런! 물이 거의 떨어져 간다.

7   당신은 물 한 방울로 목을 적시고 계속 간다.

8   나쁜 꿈인 것 같은가?

9   글쎄, '4 Deserts Race'에 참가하는 사람들에게 이것은 꿈이 아니다.

10 '4 Deserts Race'는 세계에서 가장 험한 사막들을 가로지르는 연속된 4개의 경주이다.

11 각 경주는 250킬로미터이고 7일이 걸린다.

12 첫 번째 경주는 칠레에 있는 아타카마 사막에서 열린다.

13 그곳은 세계에서 가장 건조한 사막이다.

14 실제로 아타카마 사막의 어떤 곳에는 400년간 비가 내리지 않았다!

15 다음 경주는 중국에 있는 고비 사막으로 이어진다.

16 그곳은 세상에서 가장 바람이 많이 부는 사막이다.

17 The third race _____ _____ the Sahara Desert in Egypt.

18 It is _____ _____ _____ the _____ _____ .

19 Temperatures can _____ _____ _____ 50℃.

20 _____, the race _____ _____ _____ _____ _____ _____ on earth, Antarctica.

21 If you _____ _____ _____ _____ _____ _____ the air here, it _____ !

22 Only _____ _____ _____ on the planet can _____ _____ _____ 4 Deserts Race, _____?

23 _____ _____ .

24 Many of _____ _____ _____ _____ people _____ _____ you and me.

25 So _____ do they _____ _____ ?

26 Adrianna, _____ _____ _____ _____ _____ , says,

27 "It's _____ _____ _____ _____ _____ _____ and _____ your own history.

28 Anyone _____ _____ the finish line _____ _____ _____ ."

17 세 번째 경주는 이집트에 있는 사하라 사막으로 향한다.

18 그곳은 네 개의 사막 중 가장 뜨겁다.

19 온도가 섭씨 50도까지 올라갈 수 있다.

20 마지막으로 경주는 세상에서 가장 추운 사막인 남극 대륙으로 향한다.

21 이곳에서 끓는 물을 공중에 던지면, 그것은 얼어버린다!

22 세상에서 가장 훌륭한 달리기 주자들만 '4 Deserts Race'에 참가할 수 있다. 맞는가?

23 꼭 그렇진 않다.

24 많은 참가자들은 당신과 나와 같은 평범한 사람들이다.

25 그러면 그들은 왜 그것을 하는가?

26 프랑스 출신의 사서인 Adrianna는 말한다.

27 "그것은 당신의 한계를 시험하고 당신만의 역사를 만들 기회예요.

28 결승선을 넘는 사람은 어떤 것이든 할 수 있어요."

※ 다음 문장을 우리말로 쓰시오.

1 Imagine you are in the middle of a great desert.

➡ _____

2 The sands go on and on in every direction.

➡ _____

3 The sun feels like a giant ball of fire.

➡ _____

4 The hot wind burns your face and throat.

➡ _____

5 You open your backpack to drink some water.

➡ _____

6 Oh, no! You're almost out of water.

➡ _____

7 You wet your throat with a drop of water and keep going.

➡ _____

8 Sounds like a bad dream?

➡ _____

9 Well, this is not a dream for the people who take part in the 4 Deserts Race.

➡ _____

10 The 4 Deserts Race is a series of four races across the world's toughest deserts.

➡ _____

11 Each race is 250 kilometers long and takes seven days.

➡ _____

12 The first race takes place in the Atacama Desert in Chile.

➡ _____

13 It is the driest desert in the world.

➡ _____

14 In fact, it hasn't rained in some parts of the Atacama Desert for 400 years!

➡ _____

15 The next race goes to the Gobi Desert in China.

➡ _____

16 It is the windiest desert on earth.

➡ _____

17 The third race heads to the Sahara Desert in Egypt.

➡ _____

18 It is the hottest of the four deserts.

➡ _____

19 Temperatures can reach up to 50℃.

➡ _____

20 Finally, the race travels to the coldest desert on earth, Antarctica.

➡ _____

21 If you throw boiling water into the air here, it freezes!

➡ _____

22 Only the greatest runners on the planet can take part in 4 Deserts Race, right?

➡ _____

23 Not exactly.

➡ _____

24 Many of the participants are ordinary people like you and me.

➡ _____

25 So why do they do it?

➡ _____

26 Adrianna, a librarian from France, says,

➡ _____

27 "It's a chance to test your limits and make your own history.

➡ _____

28 Anyone who crosses the finish line can do anything."

➡ _____

※ 다음 괄호 안의 단어들을 우리말에 맞도록 바르게 배열하시오.

1 (you / imagine / in / are / middle / the / of / desert. / great / a)
➡ _____

2 (sands / the / on / go / and / on / in / direction. / every)
➡ _____

3 (sun / the / feels / like / giant / a / fire. / of / ball)
➡ _____

4 (hot / the / wind / your / burns / throat. / and / face)
➡ _____

5 (open / you / backpack / your / drink / to / water. / some)
➡ _____

6 (no! / oh, / almost / you're / water. / of / out)
➡ _____

7 (wet / you / throat / with / your / a / of / drop / and / going. / keep / water)
➡ _____

8 (like / bad / sounds / dream? / a)
➡ _____

9 (well, / is / this / not / dream / a / for / people / the / take / who / in / part / the / Race. / Deserts / 4)
➡ _____

10 (the / Race / 4 / Deserts / is / series / of / a / four / across / races / world's / the / deserts. / toughest)
➡ _____
_____

11 (race / each / 250 / is / long / kilometers / takes / and / days. / seven)
➡ _____

12 (first / the / race / place / takes / the / in / Desert / Chile. / in / Atacama)
➡ _____

13 (is / the / it / driest / world. / the / in / desert)
➡ _____

14 (fact, / in / hasn't / it / rained / some / in / parts / the / of / Desert / Atacama / year! / 400 / for)
➡ _____

15 (next / the / goes / race / to / Gobi / the / China. / Desert / in)
➡ _____

16 (is / it / the / desert / earth. / on / windiest)
➡ _____

1 당신이 아주 큰 사막의 한 가운데에 있다고 상상해 봐라.

2 모래 벌판이 사면팔방으로 계속 이어진다.

3 태양은 거대한 불덩이 같다.

4 뜨거운 바람이 당신의 얼굴과 목구멍을 태운다.

5 당신은 물을 좀 마시려고 배낭을 연다.

6 오, 이런! 물이 거의 떨어져 간다.

7 당신은 물 한 방울로 목을 적시고 계속 간다.

8 나쁜 꿈인 것 같은가?

9 글쎄, '4 Deserts Race'에 참가하는 사람들에게 이것은 꿈이 아니다.

10 '4 Deserts Race'는 세계에서 가장 험한 사막들을 가로지르는 연속된 4개의 경주이다.

11 각 경주는 250킬로미터이고 7일이 걸린다.

12 첫 번째 경주는 칠레에 있는 아타카마 사막에서 열린다.

13 그곳은 세계에서 가장 건조한 사막이다.

14 실제로 아타카마 사막의 어떤 곳에는 400년간 비가 내리지 않았다!

15 다음 경주는 중국에 있는 고비 사막으로 이어진다.

16 그곳은 세상에서 가장 바람이 많이 부는 사막이다.

17 (third / the / heads / race / the / to / in / Desert / Egypt. / Sahara)

➡ _____

18 (is / the / it / of / hottest / the / deserts. / four)

➡ _____

19 (can / reach / temperatures / 50℃ / to / up)

➡ _____

20 (finally, / race / the / to / travels / coldest / the / on / desert / Antarctica. / earth,)

➡ _____

21 (you / if / boiling / throw / into / water / air / the / here, / freezes! / it)

➡ _____

22 (the / only / runners / greatest / on / planet / the / take / can / in / part / Deserts / 4 / right? / Race,)

➡ _____

_____

23 (exactly. / not)

➡ _____

24 (of / many / participants / the / ordinary / are / like / people / me. / and / you)

➡ _____

25 (why / so / do / they / it? / do)

➡ _____

26 (a / Adrianna, / from / librarian / say, / France,)

➡ _____

27 (a / "It's / to / chance / your / test / limits / and / your / history. / own / make)

➡ _____

28 (who / anyone / crosses / finish / the / can / line / anything." / do)

➡ _____

---

17 세 번째 경주는 이집트에 있는 사하라 사막으로 향한다.

18 그곳은 네 개의 사막 중 가장 뜨겁다.

19 온도가 섭씨 50도까지 올라갈 수 있다.

20 마지막으로 경주는 세상에서 가장 추운 사막인 남극 대륙으로 향한다.

21 이곳에서 끓는 물을 공중에 던지면, 그것은 얼어버린다!

22 세상에서 가장 훌륭한 달리기 주자들만 '4 Deserts Race'에 참가할 수 있다. 맞는가?

23 꼭 그렇진 않다.

24 많은 참가자들은 당신과 나와 같은 평범한 사람들이다.

25 그러면 그들은 왜 그것을 하는가?

26 프랑스 출신의 사서인 Adrianna는 말한다.

27 "그것은 당신의 한계를 시험하고 당신만의 역사를 만들 기회예요.

28 결승선을 넘는 사람은 어떤 것이든 할 수 있어요."

※ 다음 우리말을 영어로 쓰시오.

1 당신이 아주 큰 사막의 한 가운데에 있다고 상상해 봐라.

➡ _____

2 모래 벌판이 사면팔방으로 계속 이어진다.

➡ _____

3 태양은 거대한 불덩이 같다.

➡ _____

4 뜨거운 바람이 당신의 얼굴과 목구멍을 태운다.

➡ _____

5 당신은 물을 좀 마시려고 배낭을 연다.

➡ _____

6 오, 이런! 물이 거의 떨어져 간다.

➡ _____

7 당신은 물 한 방울로 목을 적시고 계속 간다.

➡ _____

8 나쁜 꿈인 것 같은가?

➡ _____

9 글쎄, '4 Deserts Race'에 참가하는 사람들에게 이것은 꿈이 아니다.

➡ _____

10 '4 Deserts Race'는 세계에서 가장 험한 사막들을 가로지르는 연속된 4개의 경주이다.

➡ _____

11 각 경주는 250킬로미터이고 7일이 걸린다.

➡ _____

12 첫 번째 경주는 칠레에 있는 아타카마 사막에서 열린다.

➡ _____

13 그곳은 세계에서 가장 건조한 사막이다.

➡ _____

14 실제로 아타카마 사막의 어떤 곳에는 400년간 비가 내리지 않았다!

➡ _____

15 다음 경주는 중국에 있는 고비 사막으로 이어진다.

➡ _____

16 그곳은 세상에서 가장 바람이 많이 부는 사막이다.

➡ _____

17 세 번째 경주는 이집트에 있는 사하라 사막으로 향한다.

➡ _____

18 그곳은 네 개의 사막 중 가장 뜨겁다.

➡ _____

19 온도가 섭씨 50도까지 올라갈 수 있다.

➡ _____

20 마지막으로 경주는 세상에서 가장 추운 사막인 남극 대륙으로 향한다.

➡ _____

21 이곳에서 끓는 물을 공중에 던지면, 그것은 얼어버린다!

➡ _____

22 세상에서 가장 훌륭한 달리기 주자들만 '4 Deserts Race'에 참가할 수 있다, 맞는가?

➡ _____

23 꼭 그렇진 않다.

➡ _____

24 많은 참가자들은 당신과 나와 같은 평범한 사람들이다.

➡ _____

25 그러면 그들은 왜 그것을 하는가?

➡ _____

26 프랑스 출신의 사서인 Adrianna는 말한다.

➡ _____

27 "그것은 당신의 한계를 시험하고 당신만의 역사를 만들 기회예요.

➡ _____

28 결승선을 넘는 사람은 어떤 것이든 할 수 있어요."

➡ _____

※ 다음 우리말과 일치하도록 빈칸에 알맞은 말을 쓰시오.

Real Life Talk - Step 2

1. G: What do you do _____ _____ _____ _____?

2. B: I _____ _____ sports.

3. G: _____ you ever _____ table tennis?

4. B: No, I _____.

5. G: _____ you ever _____ baseball?

6. B: _____, _____ _____.

7. G: Have you ever _____ _____ _____ _____?

8. B: Yes, I _____.

1. G: 너는 여가 시간에 무엇을 하니?
2. B: 나는 종종 운동을 해.
3. G: 탁구를 쳐 본 적이 있니?
4. B: 아니, 없어.
5. G: 야구를 해 본 적이 있니?
6. B: 응, 있어.
7. G: 홈런을 쳐 본 적이 있니?
8. B: 응, 있어.

Think and Write

1. A Happy _____ for _____ 3

2. The school sports day _____ _____ _____ May 14th.

3. It was very _____.

4. Students _____ _____ and did group _____ _____.

5. They also _____ _____ _____ _____ and a 100m race.

6. Class 2 won the group _____ _____, and Class 1 won the _____ _____.

7. Class 3 _____ the basketball game and the _____ _____.

8. They _____ the _____ _____ and _____ the _____ winner.

9. _____ _____ _____ had great fun.

1. 3반을 위한 행복한 날
2. 학교 운동회는 5월 14일에 개최되었다.
3. 그것은 매우 신났다.
4. 학생들은 농구를 하고 단체 줄넘기를 했다.
5. 그들은 또한 릴레이 경주를 했고 100미터 달리기도 했다.
6. 2반은 단체 줄넘기에서 우승을 했고, 1반은 릴레이 경주에서 우승을 했다.
7. 3반은 농구 경기와 100미터 경주에서 우승을 차지했다.
8. 그들은 가장 높은 점수를 얻어서 전체 우승자가 되었다.
9. 모든 반은 재미있는 시간을 보냈다.

※ 다음 우리말을 영어로 쓰시오.

Real Life Talk - Step 2

1. G: 너는 여가 시간에 무엇을 하니?
   ➡ _____

2. B: 나는 종종 운동을 해.
   ➡ _____

3. G: 탁구를 쳐 본 적이 있니?
   ➡ _____

4. B: 아니, 없어.
   ➡ _____

5. G: 야구를 해 본 적이 있니?
   ➡ _____

6. B: 응, 있어.
   ➡ _____

7. G: 홈런을 쳐 본 적이 있니?
   ➡ _____

8. B: 응, 있어.
   ➡ _____

Think and Write

1. 3반을 위한 행복한 날
   ➡ _____

2. 학교 운동회는 5월 14일에 개최되었다.
   ➡ _____

3. 그것은 매우 신났다.
   ➡ _____

4. 학생들은 농구를 하고 단체 줄넘기를 했다.
   ➡ _____

5. 그들은 또한 릴레이 경주를 했고 100미터 달리기도 했다.
   ➡ _____

6. 2반은 단체 줄넘기에서 우승을 했고, 1반은 릴레이 경주에서 우승을 했다.
   ➡ _____

7. 3반은 농구 경기와 100미터 경주에서 우승을 차지했다.
   ➡ _____

8. 그들은 가장 높은 점수를 얻어서 전체 우승자가 되었다.
   ➡ _____

9. 모든 반은 재미있는 시간을 보냈다.
   ➡ _____

※ 다음 영어를 우리말로 쓰시오.

01	piece		22	mix
02	cool		23	excellent
03	cold		24	pour
04	cut		25	finish
05	step		26	strawberry
06	pineapple		27	until
07	peel		28	stick
08	blender		29	need
09	freezer		30	maker
10	source		31	pretty
11	about		32	own
12	tip		33	close
13	smooth		34	ice pop
14	blend		35	apple juice
15	stay		36	stay cool
16	try		37	have a cold
17	add		38	put A into B
18	slice		39	a half(=one half)
19	vitamin		40	cut A into B
20	share		41	mix up
21	health		42	pour A into B
			43	a cup of ~

※ 다음 우리말을 영어로 쓰시오.

01 사과 주스 _____

02 나누다, 공유하다 _____

03 딸기 _____

04 즐기다 _____

05 우수한, 훌륭한 _____

06 끝내다 _____

07 (문, 가게를) 닫다 _____

08 막대기, 지팡이 _____

09 건강 _____

10 혼합(물); 섞다 _____

11 막대 아이스크림 _____

12 키위 _____

13 ~을 만드는 기계(사람) _____

14 필요하다 _____

15 붓다, 따르다 _____

16 오렌지 _____

17 예쁜; 꽤 _____

18 ~까지 _____

19 자기 자신의 _____

20 껍질을 벗기다; 껍질 _____

21 냉동고 _____

22 얇게 썰다; 얇은 조각 _____

23 매끄러운, 부드러운 _____

24 섞다, 혼합하다 _____

25 조각, 일부, 부분 _____

26 더하다, 추가하다 _____

27 원천, 근원 _____

28 믹서 _____

29 조언, 비결 _____

30 자르다 _____

31 시도하다, 해보다 _____

32 ~인 채로 있다, 머무르다 _____

33 시원한, 냉정한 _____

34 파인애플 _____

35 단계 _____

36 조각, 일부, 부분 _____

37 A를 B에 붓다 _____

38 2분의 1 _____

39 시원함을 유지하다 _____

40 A를 B(상태)로 자르다 _____

41 감기에 걸리다 _____

42 ~을 섞다 _____

43 A를 B에 넣다 _____

※ 다음 영영풀이에 알맞은 단어를 <보기>에서 골라 쓴 후, 우리말 뜻을 쓰시오.

1 _____ : extremely good: _____

2 _____ : to have or use something with others: _____

3 _____ : to take the outer layer off fruit, vegetables, etc.: _____

4 _____ : an electric machine for mixing soft food or liquid: _____

5 _____ : completely flat and even, without any lumps, holes or rough areas:
_____

6 _____ : a thin piece of wood that has fallen or been broken from a tree:
_____

7 _____ : one of a series of things that you do in order to achieve something:
_____

8 _____ : a small piece of advice about something practical: _____

9 _____ : to divide something into two or more pieces with a knife, etc.: _____

10 _____ : a thin flat piece of food that has been cut off a larger piece: _____

11 _____ : a combination of things that you need to make something: _____

12 _____ : a natural substance found in food that is an essential part of what humans
and animals eat to help them grow and stay healthy: _____

13 _____ : a large tropical fruit with thick rough skin, sweet yellow flesh with a lot
of juice and stiff leaves on top: _____

14 _____ : to make a liquid or other substance flow from a container in a continuous
stream: _____

15 _____ : to put something together with something else so as to increase the size,
number, amount, etc.: _____

16 _____ : a soft red fruit with very small yellow seeds on the surface, that grows
on a low plant: _____

보기			
peel	cut	mix	add
tip	step	share	vitamin
pour	slice	excellent	stick
strawberry	pineapple	blender	smooth

※ 다음 우리말과 일치하도록 빈칸에 알맞은 것을 골라 쓰시오.

1 The _____ _____ of summer _____ here.
  A. hot   B. are   C. days

2 How _____ we _____ _____?
  A. stay   B. can   C. cool

3 _____ _____ ice pops _____!
  A. together   B. make   C. let's

4 You _____: 1/2 pineapple, 2 kiwis, 1 cup _____ apple juice, ice pop _____
  A. of   B. need   C. makers

5 Steps: _____ the pineapple _____ small _____.
  A. into   B. cut   C. pieces

6 _____ the kiwis and _____ _____.
  A. them   B. slice   C. peel

7 _____ the pineapple _____ _____ the blender.
  A. pieces   B. into   C. put

8 _____ the apple _____.
  A. juice   B. add

9 _____ _____ the mix is _____.
  A. until   B. smooth   C. blend

10 _____ the mix _____ the ice pop _____.
  A. makers   B. pour   C. into

11 _____ the kiwi _____.
  A. slices   B. add

12 _____ the ice _____ makers.
  A. pop   B. close

13 _____ them _____ the freezer _____ _____ three hours.
  A. in   B. about   C. put   D. for

---

1 더운 여름날이 왔어요.

2 우리는 어떻게 시원하게 지낼 수 있을까요?

3 막대 아이스크림을 함께 만들어 봐요!

4 여러분은 필요해요: 파인애플 1/2개, 키위 2개, 사과 주스 1컵, 막대 아이스크림 틀

5 단계: 파인애플을 작은 조각으로 자르세요.

6 키위의 껍질을 벗기고 얇게 자르세요.

7 파인애플 조각들을 믹서에 넣으세요.

8 사과 주스를 첨가하세요.

9 혼합물이 덩어리 없이 골고루 잘 섞일 때까지 섞으세요.

10 혼합물을 막대 아이스크림 틀에 부으세요.

11 키위 조각을 추가하세요.

12 막대 아이스크림 틀을 닫으세요.

13 약 세 시간 동안 그것들을 냉동고에 넣으세요.

14 _____! _____ your summer _____ a _____!

A. stick   B. enjoy   C. on   D. finished

15 _____ _____

A. Tips   B. Health

16 Pineapples are an _____ _____ of _____ C.

A. source   B. excellent   B. vitamin

17 They have _____ _____ C _____ oranges.

A. vitamin   B. than   C. more

18 So _____ you have a _____, _____ pineapples.

A. try   B. when   C. cold

19 _____ Your _____!

A. Ideas   B. Share

20 How _____ you make _____ _____ ice pops?

A. own   B. your   C. will

21 _____ _____ ideas!

A. your   B. share

22 I _____ _____ kiwis and _____.

A. use   B. strawberries   C. will

23 I will _____ them _____ big _____.

A. into   B. cut   C. pieces

24 I will _____ them _____ the ice pop makers _____ apple juice.

A. into   B. with   C. put

25 I _____ my ice pops _____ _____ pretty.

A. be   B. think   C. will

14 끝났어요! 막대 위의 여름을 맛보세요!

15 건강 조언들

16 파인애플은 비타민 C의 훌륭한 원천이에요.

17 파인애플에는 비타민 C가 오렌지보다 더 많이 들어 있어요.

18 그러니 감기에 걸리면 파인애플을 먹어 보세요.

19 여러분의 생각을 나누세요!

20 여러분은 어떻게 막대 아이스크림을 만들 건가요?

21 여러분의 생각을 나누세요!

22 저는 키위와 딸기를 사용할 거예요.

23 저는 그것들을 크게 자를 거예요.

24 그것들을 사과 주스와 함께 막대 아이스크림 틀에 넣을 거예요.

25 제 막대 아이스크림은 예쁠 것 같아요.

※ 다음 우리말과 일치하도록 빈칸에 알맞은 말을 쓰시오.

1 The _____ _____ _____ summer _____ here.

2 _____ _____ we _____ _____?

3 _____ _____ ice pops _____!

4 You _____:

1/2 _____

2 _____

1 _____ of apple juice

ice pop _____

5 _____

6 _____ the pineapple _____ _____ _____.

7 _____ the kiwis and _____ _____.

8 _____ the pineapple _____ _____ _____ _____.

9 _____ the _____ _____.

10 _____ _____ the mix is _____.

11 _____ the mix _____ the _____ _____ _____.

12 _____ the kiwi _____.

13 _____ the _____ _____ _____.

14 _____ _____ in the freezer _____ _____ three hours.

1 더운 여름날이 왔어요.

2 우리는 어떻게 시원하게 지낼 수 있을까요?

3 막대 아이스크림을 함께 만들어 봐요!

4 여러분은 필요해요:

파인애플 1/2개

키위 2개

사과 주스 1컵

막대 아이스크림 틀

5 단계

6 파인애플을 작은 조각으로 자르세요.

7 키위의 껍질을 벗기고 얇게 자르세요.

8 파인애플 조각들을 믹서에 넣으세요.

9 사과 주스를 첨가하세요.

10 혼합물이 덩어리 없이 골고루 잘 섞일 때까지 섞으세요.

11 혼합물을 막대 아이스크림 틀에 부으세요.

12 키위 조각을 추가하세요.

13 막대 아이스크림 틀을 닫으세요.

14 약 세 시간 동안 그것들을 냉동고에 넣으세요.

15 _____!

16 _____ your summer _____ _____ _____!

17 _____ _____

18 Pineapples _____ _____ _____ _____ _____ _____ C.

19 They have _____ _____ _____ _____ _____ _____.

20 So _____ you _____ _____ _____, _____ pineapples.

21 _____ Your _____!

22 _____ _____ you _____ _____ _____ ice pops?

23 _____ _____ _____!

24 I will _____ kiwis and _____.

25 I will _____ _____ _____ _____ _____.

26 I will _____ _____ _____ the ice pop makers _____ _____ _____.

27 _____ _____ my ice pops _____ _____ _____.

15 끝났어요!

16 막대 위의 여름을 맛보세요!

17 건강 조언들

18 파인애플은 비타민 C의 **훌륭**한 원천이에요.

19 파인애플에는 비타민 C가 오렌지보다 더 많이 들어 있어요.

20 그러니 감기에 걸리면 파인애플을 먹어 보세요.

21 여러분의 생각을 나누세요!

22 여러분은 어떻게 막대 아이스크림을 만들 건가요?

23 여러분의 생각을 나누세요!

24 저는 키위와 딸기를 사용할 거예요.

25 저는 그것들을 크게 자를 거예요.

26 그것들을 사과 주스와 함께 막대 아이스크림 틀에 넣을 거예요.

27 제 막대 아이스크림은 예쁠 것 같아요.

Step3

※ 다음 문장을 우리말로 쓰시오.

1 The hot days of summer are here.

➡ _____

2 How can we stay cool?

➡ _____

3 Let's make ice pops together!

➡ _____

4 You need: 1/2 pineapple, 2 kiwis, 1 cup of apple juice, ice pop makers

➡ _____

5 Steps

➡ _____

6 Cut the pineapple into small pieces.

➡ _____

7 Peel the kiwis and slice them.

➡ _____

8 Put the pineapple pieces into the blender.

➡ _____

9 Add the apple juice.

➡ _____

10 Blend until the mix is smooth.

➡ _____

11 Pour the mix into the ice pop makers.

➡ _____

12 Add the kiwi slices.

➡ _____

13 Close the ice pop makers.

➡ _____

14 Put them in the freezer for about three hours.

➡ _____

15 Finished!

➡ _____

16 Enjoy your summer on a stick!

➡ _____

17 Health Tips

➡ _____

18 Pineapples are an excellent source of vitamin C.

➡ _____

19 They have more vitamin C than oranges.

➡ _____

20 So when you have a cold, try pineapples.

➡ _____

21 Share Your Ideas!

➡ _____

22 How will you make your own ice pops?

➡ _____

23 Share your ideas!

➡ _____

24 I will use kiwis and strawberries.

➡ _____

25 I will cut them into big pieces.

➡ _____

26 I will put them into the ice pop makers with apple juice.

➡ _____

27 I think my ice pops will be pretty.

➡ _____

Step4

※ 다음 괄호 안의 단어들을 우리말에 맞도록 바르게 배열하시오.

1 (hot / the / of / days / here. / are / summer)

➡ _____

2 (can / how / cool? / stay / we)

➡ _____

3 (make / let's / pops / together! / ice)

➡ _____

4 (need: / you / pineapple, / 1/2 / kiwis, / 2 / of / cup / 1 / juice, / apple / makers / pop / ice)

➡ _____

5 (steps: / the / cut / into / pineapple / pieces. / small)

➡ _____

6 (the / peel / and / kiwis / them. / slice)

➡ _____

7 (the / put / pieces / pineapple / blender. / the / into)

➡ _____

8 (the / juice. / apple / add)

➡ _____

9 (the / until / blend / mix / smooth. / is)

➡ _____

10 (the / pour / into / mix / ice / the / makers. / pop)

➡ _____

11 (the / add / slices. / kiwi)

➡ _____

12 (the / close / pop / makers. / ice)

➡ _____

13 (them / put / the / in / freezer / about / for / hours. / three)

➡ _____

1 더운 여름날이 왔어요.

2 우리는 어떻게 시원하게 지낼 수 있을까요?

3 막대 아이스크림을 함께 만들어 봐요!

4 여러분은 필요해요: 파인애플 1/2개, 키위 2개, 사과 주스 1컵, 막대 아이스크림 틀

5 단계: 파인애플을 작은 조각으로 자르세요.

6 키위의 껍질을 벗기고 얇게 자르세요.

7 파인애플 조각들을 믹서에 넣으세요.

8 사과 주스를 첨가하세요.

9 혼합물이 덩어리 없이 골고루 잘 섞일 때까지 섞으세요.

10 혼합물을 막대 아이스크림 틀에 부으세요.

11 키위 조각을 추가하세요.

12 막대 아이스크림 틀을 닫으세요.

13 약 세 시간 동안 그것들을 냉동고에 넣으세요.

14 (finished! // your / enjoy / on / summer / stick! / a)

➡ _____

15 (Tips / Health)

➡ _____

16 (are / pineapples / excellent / an / source / C. / of / vitamin)

➡ _____

17 (have / they / vitamin / more / oranges. / than / C)

➡ _____

18 (when / so / have / you / cold, / a / pineapples. / try)

➡ _____

19 (Ideas! / Your / Share)

➡ _____

20 (will / how / you / make / own / your / pops? / ice)

➡ _____

21 (your / share / ideas!)

➡ _____

22 (will / I / use / kiwis / strawberries. / and)

➡ _____

23 (will / I / cut / into / them / pieces. / big)

➡ _____

24 (will / I / them / put / the / into / pop / ice / with / makers / juice. / apple)

➡ _____

25 (think / I / ice / my / pops / pretty. / be / will)

➡ _____

14 끝났어요! 막대 위의 여름을 맛보세요!

15 건강 조언들

16 파인애플은 비타민 C의 훌륭한 원천이에요.

17 파인애플에는 비타민 C가 오렌지보다 더 많이 들어 있어요.

18 그러니 감기에 걸리면 파인애플을 먹어 보세요.

19 여러분의 생각을 나누세요!

20 여러분은 어떻게 막대 아이스크림을 만들 건가요?

21 여러분의 생각을 나누세요!

22 저는 키위와 딸기를 사용할 거예요.

23 저는 그것들을 크게 자를 거예요.

24 그것들을 사과 주스와 함께 막대 아이스크림 틀에 넣을 거예요.

25 제 막대 아이스크림은 예쁠 것 같아요.

※ 다음 우리말을 영어로 쓰시오.

1 더운 여름날이 왔어요.

➡ _____

2 우리는 어떻게 시원하게 지낼 수 있을까요?

➡ _____

3 막대 아이스크림을 함께 만들어 봐요!

➡ _____

4 여러분은 필요해요: 파인애플 1/2개, 키위 2개, 사과 주스 1컵, 막대 아이스크림 틀

➡ _____

5 단계: 파인애플을 작은 조각으로 자르세요.

➡ _____

6 키위의 껍질을 벗기고 얇게 자르세요.

➡ _____

7 파인애플 조각들을 믹서에 넣으세요.

➡ _____

8 사과 주스를 첨가하세요.

➡ _____

9 혼합물이 덩어리 없이 골고루 잘 섞일 때까지 섞으세요.

➡ _____

10 혼합물을 막대 아이스크림 틀에 부으세요.

➡ _____

11 키위 조각을 추가하세요.

➡ _____

12 막대 아이스크림 틀을 닫으세요.

➡ _____

13 약 세 시간 동안 그것들을 냉동고에 넣으세요.

➡ _____

14 끝났어요! 막대 위의 여름을 맛보세요!

➡ _____

15 건강 조언들

➡ _____

16 파인애플은 비타민 C의 훌륭한 원천이에요.

➡ _____

17 파인애플에는 비타민 C가 오렌지보다 더 많이 들어 있어요.

➡ _____

18 그러니 감기에 걸리면 파인애플을 먹어 보세요.

➡ _____

19 여러분의 생각을 나누세요!

➡ _____

20 여러분은 어떻게 막대 아이스크림을 만들 건가요?

➡ _____

21 여러분의 생각을 나누세요!

➡ _____

22 저는 키위와 딸기를 사용할 거예요.

➡ _____

23 저는 그것들을 크게 자를 거예요.

➡ _____

24 그것들을 사과 주스와 함께 막대 아이스크림 틀에 넣을 거예요.

➡ _____

25 제 막대 아이스크림은 예쁠 것 같아요.

➡ _____

MEMO

MEMO

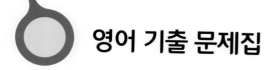

영어 기출 문제집

적중100

1학기

정답 및 해설

동아 | 이병민

중 2

적중100

Lesson 1

Can We Talk?

improve: 향상시키다

04 run into: ~을 우연히 만나다(= come across)

05 respect(존중하다), capital(대문자), ignore(무시하다), useful(유용한), useless(쓸모없는)

06 How about -ing ~?: ~하는 게 어때?, volunteer: 자원 봉사하다

01 wet	02 ①	03 ⑤	04 ①, ⑤
05 ①	06 bulletin board		07 talker
08 direction			

01 주어진 단어의 관계는 반의어로 dry(건조한)의 반의어는 wet(젖은, 축축한)이다.

02 주어진 문장과 ①번의 poor는 '서투른'을 의미한다. ②, ④, ⑤는 '가난한', ③은 '가엾은'을 의미한다.

03 topic: 화제

04 주어진 문장은 '나는 밤에 잠을 자는 데 어려움이 있다.'라는 의미로 trouble과 바꾸어 쓸 수 있는 말로 problem(문제), difficulty(어려움)가 있다. ② trial(시험), ③ danger(위험), ④ pay(보수)

05 주어진 문장에서 chance는 기회를 의미하므로 opportunity와 바꾸어 쓸 수 있다.

06 게시물을 붙이기 위한 판을 가리키는 말은 게시판으로 bulletin board이다.

07 특정한 방식으로 말하거나 또는 말을 많이 하는 사람을 나타내는 말은 talker(이야기하는 사람)이다.

08 direction: 방향

01 (1) Keep　(2) have　(3) pay　(4) put

02 (A) out　(2) in　(3) to

03 (1) The audience will fall asleep.
　(2) Jane is mad at me.
　(3) What can we do to improve our English?

04 ran into

05 (1) respect　(2) useful　(3) capital

06 How about volunteering at the hospital?

01 keep -ing: 계속 ~하다 have ~ in common: ~을 공통으로 가지다 pay attention to: ~에 주의를 기울이다 put ~ first: ~을 우선시하다

02 space out: 딴생각하다 have in common: ~을 공통으로 가지다 pay attention to: ~에 주의를 기울이다

03 (1) fall asleep: 잠들다 (2) be mad at: ~에게 화나다 (3)

1 (1) mae a lot of friends / You can join
　(2) exercise regularly
2 (1) going to the bookstore
　(2) recycle this box

1 T　2 F　3 F　4 T

Listen & Speak 1 A

excited / too, going / new friends / join a sports club / idea

Listen & Speak 1 B

join / the singing club / see / wrong / president, two members / terrible / get more members / school bulletin board / idea, right away

Listen & Speak 1 C

sleep better / warm milk / a good idea

Listen & Speak 2 A

mean / idea, How about asking

Listen & Speak 2 B

why / ran into, foreigner / subway station / tell, directions / about using / kind of / changes, helpful / next time

Listen & Speak 2 C

something together / want to do / bookstore / Great

wrong / best, mad at / terrible, happend / said, just
like / No wonder, at / won't talk / probably / make up
with / about sending / idea, do

시험대비 기본평가
p.16

01 ①   02 ⑤   03 ⑤

04 The girl suggested joining a sports club.

01 B와 C 모두 영어 실력을 향상시키기 위한 방법에 대해 이야기
하고 있다. ③ manage: 관리하다

02 나머지는 모두 조언을 하는 표현이지만 ⑤는 확신을 나타내는
표현이다.

03 (A)는 제안에 동의하는 표현이지만 ⑤는 제안에 거절하는 표현
이다.

04 소녀가 소년에게 제안한 것은 스포츠 동아리에 가입하는 것이다.

시험대비 실력평가
p.17~18

01 ①   02 ⑤   03 ①   04 No
wonder she is mad at you.   05 ④   06 ③
07 ③   08 학교 게시판에 동아리 광고를 게시하는 것
09 (r)an into   10 What about using the *Talk Smart*
app next time?   11 ①
12 Because it can change one language into
    another.

01 잠을 더 잘 잘 수 있는 방법으로 자기 전에 따뜻한 우유를 마시
는 것이 적절하다.

02 밑줄 친 표현은 조언을 구하는 표현으로 What should I do to
~?를 사용하여 조언을 구할 수 있다.

03 ① B는 새 학기에 대해 매우 신이 나 있다.

04 No wonder: ~이 놀랍지도 않다[당연하다]

05 ④ Mina가 Kate와 화해하기 위해 Brian의 충고를 받아들였다
는 설명이 대화의 내용과 일치한다.

06 terrible(심한, 혹독한) - terrific(아주 멋진), gather(모으다)
- leave(떠나다), bullet(총알) - bulletin(게시)

07 worried(걱정스러운) → relieved(안도한)

09 '누군가를 우연히 만나다'라는 의미를 나타내는 run into를 과거
시제로 나타내야 하므로 ran into가 적절하다.

11 translate(번역하다), keep(지키다), remain(유지하다),
spread(퍼지다, 번지다), expand(넓히다)

12 민수가 우연히 외국인을 만났을 때 Talk Smart 앱이 유용한 이
유는 그것이 한 언어를 다른 언어로 바꾸어 줄 수 있기 때문이다.

서술형 시험대비
p.19

01 What can I do to sleep better?

02 How about going to the bookstore?

03 excited

04 am I

05 What can I do to make a lot of new friends?

06 president

07 She will post an ad on the school bulletin board.

01 What can I do to+동사원형 ~?: ~하려면 어떻게 해야 할까?

02 How about+동명사 ~?: ~하는 게 어때?

03 '나는 매우 흥분된다.'를 의미하는 과거분사 excited가 알맞다.
exciting은 현재분사로 '흥분시키는'을 의미한다.

04 '나도 그래.'라는 표현으로 'So am I.'가 적절하다.

06 조직의 장: president(장, 회장)

07 Jenny는 동아리 회원을 더 모으기 위해 학교 게시판에 광고를
게시할 것이다.

교과서
Grammar

핵심 Check
p.20~21

1 (1) to meet   (2) to say   (3) to write with
2 (1) Write, or / Unless you write
  (2) Help, and / If, help

시험대비 기본평가
p.22

01 (1) handing in → hand in
   (2) choose → to choose
   (3) to achieved → to achieve
   (4) to eat → to eat with
02 (1) or (2) and (3) or (4) or (5) and
03 (1) I want something to eat.
   (2) We have the party to plan.
   (3) Sleep early, and you won't be tired tomorrow.
   (4) Change your clothes, or you will catch a cold.

01 (1) to부정사의 형태는 'to+동사원형'이다. (2) to부정사는 형
용사로 쓰여 명사를 꾸밀 수 있으므로, to choose가 options를
수식하도록 to부정사 형태로 만드는 것이 옳다. (3) to+동사원
형 (4) 스푼을 먹는 것이 아니라 스푼으로 먹는 것(eat with a
spoon)이므로 전치사 with를 써야 한다.

02 '명령문+and'는 '~해라, 그러면'이라는 의미이고, '명령문+or'
는 '~해라, 그렇지 않으면'이란 의미이다.

03 (1) '먹을 것'이라고 하였으므로 to eat이 something을 수식하도록 문장을 만든다. (2) '계획할 파티'이므로 to plan이 the party를 수식하도록 문장을 만든다. (3) '~해라, 그러면'이므로 '명령문+and'로 문장을 만든다. (4) '~해라, 그렇지 않으면'이므로 '명령문+or'로 문장을 쓴다.

01 ③   02 ③   03 ⑤   04 ④
05 or → and   06 ④   07 ④   08 ③
09 ③   10 ④   11 Tell me the truth, or I won't help you. [Tell me the truth, and I will help you.]
12 ③   13 or, and   14 Leave now, and you will get there on time.   15 ⑤   16 ④
17 ③   18 write → write with   19 ③
20 ④   21 Respond quickly, or   22 I am going to the department store to buy a present to give her.

01 빈칸에 모두 and가 들어가지만, ③번은 '마음을 열어라, 그렇지 않으면 많은 귀중한 것들을 놓칠 것이다.'의 의미가 되므로 or가 들어간다.

02 '낭비할 시간이 없다'는 의미이므로 to부정사를 사용하여 명사 time을 수식하는 것이 옳다.

03 ①, ③은 각각 명령문으로 '~해라. 그러면 …할 것이다'의 의미로 사용되어 and가 들어가는 것이 옳다. ② 'both A and B'는 'A와 B 둘 다'라는 의미이다. ④ 'plus'의 의미로 쓰인 and이다. ⑤는 or가 들어간다.

04 'take care of a little sister', 'ask many questions'라고 표현하므로 ④번이 옳다.

05 '그러면'이라는 의미의 and가 오는 것이 적합하다.

06 '~와 함께 시간을 보내다'는 표현은 'hang out with'이다.

07 모두 to부정사가 형용사로 사용되고 있으나 ④번은 목적을 나타내는 부사로 사용되었다.

08 주어진 문장의 의미는 '대문자만 사용하지 마라, 그렇지 않으면 네가 소리 지르고 있는 것처럼 들릴 것이다.'이므로 '대문자만 사용한다면 네가 소리 지르고 있는 것처럼 들릴 것이다.'인 ③번이 옳다.

09 '명령문 ~, or' 구문이다., 'if ~ or not'은 '~인지 아닌지'를 의미한다.

10 ① 호텔 방에 머무는 것이므로 'to stay in[at]', ② 공책 위에 쓰는 것이므로 'write on a notebook'으로 표현한다. 따라서 전치사 on을 붙여주는 것이 옳다. ③ 'drink water'이므로 전치사 on을 빼는 것이 옳다. ⑤ 'talk about interesting things'라고 표현하므로, 전치사 about을 붙여야 한다.

11 '명령문 ~+or'는 'Unless ~' 혹은 'If ~ not'으로 바꾸어 쓸 수 있다.

12 -thing으로 끝나는 부정대명사는 형용사의 수식을 뒤에서 받으며, to부정사와 형용사가 동시에 명사를 수식할 때에는 '대명사+형용사+to부정사'의 어순을 따른다. 따라서 ③번이 옳다.

13 명령문 ~, or...: ~해라, 그렇지 않으면 …할 것이다 / 명령문 ~, and...: ~해라, 그러면 …할 것이다

14 on time: 정시에

15 학교에 갈 시간이라는 의미로 쓰려면 to부정사가 time을 수식하도록 해야 한다.

16 '까다로운 손님에게 대접할 디저트'이므로 디저트를 수식하면서 동시에 동사원형 serve를 받아주기 위해서는 전치사 for가 아니라 to부정사를 쓰는 것이 옳다. picky 까다로운

17 형용사 kind, stronger와 분사 surprised를 받아줄 수 있는 동사는 be동사이다.

18 write with a pen이 옳은 표현이므로 전치사 with를 써준다.

19 ③ 더 건강해지기 위해서는 간식을 더 먹어서는 안 된다.

20 '사용할 컴퓨터'라는 의미이므로 'Is there a computer to use?'라고 쓰는 것이 옳다.

21 빨리 답하지 않으면 다른 사람의 감정을 상하게 할 수 있다는 의미이므로 '명령문 ~, or ...'로 표현하는 것이 옳다.

22 the department store: 백화점

01 (1) to read   (2) to study   (3) to worry about
02 (1) to do   (2) to drink   (3) to listen to
    (4) to sit on[in]   (5) to buy
03 something sweet to eat
04 Unless you speak slowly, I can't understand you. If you don't speak slowly, I can't understand you.
05 (1) and → or
    (2) on → in
06 Do you have enough time to visit your grandparents?
07 Don't tell lies
08 Study hard, you will get a good grade on an English exam
09 Try new things, and you can discover a new world. / Respect others' opinions, and you will make many friends. / Be careful with the cup, or you will break it.
10 Can you bring me something cold to drink?
11 Write down what you must remember, and you won't forget it. / Write down what you must remember, or you will forget it.
12 I have lots of work to do. / Don't, or

01 (1) a book을 수식하는 to부정사가 와야 한다. (2) 공부할 많은 것들'을 의미하므로 to부정사를 쓰는 것이 옳다. (3) '~에 관하여 걱정하다'는 'worry about something'이므로 전치사 about을 써야 한다.

02 (1) many interesting things를 수식하는 to부정사 가 와야 하며, '흥미로운 일들을 하다'는 'do interesting things'로 쓰므로 to do가 오는 것이 옳다. (2) '마실 것'이 므로 something을 수식하는 'to drink'를 쓰는 것이 옳다. (3) '~을 듣다'는 표현은 'listen to'이다. (4) sit on[in] a chair가 된다. (5) '살 돈'이므로 to부정사를 써서 money 를 수식해야 한다.

03 -thing으로 끝나는 부정대명사는 '-thing+형용사+to부정사'의 어순을 따른다.

04 '명령문+or ~'는 'Unless ~' 혹은 'If ~ not ...'으로 바꾸어 쓸 수 있다.

05 (1) 천천히 먹지 않으면 배가 아플 것이다. (2) 집 안에서 사는 것이므로 live in a house로 표현한다.

06 '방문할 시간'이므로 'time to visit'이다.

07 거짓말을 하지 않으면 믿어주겠다는 의미이므로 '부정명령문+and ~'를 쓰는 것이 옳다.

08 영어 시험에서 좋은 성적을 받기를 원한다며 조언을 구하고 있다. 이런 경우 '공부를 열심히 하면 좋은 성적을 얻을 수 있다'고 조언하는 것이 옳다.

09 discover: 발견하다 opinion: 의견

10 -thing으로 끝나는 부정대명사는 '-thing+형용사+to부정사'의 어순을 따른다.

11 계속해서 무언가를 잊어버리는 친구에게 기억해야만 하는 것을 적어두라는 조언을 쓰는 문제이다

12 exhausted: 지친 ruin: 해치다

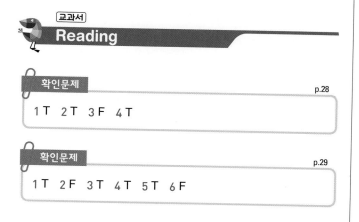

교과서 Reading

확인문제 p.28

1 T 2 T 3 F 4 T

확인문제 p.29

1 T 2 F 3 T 4 T 5 T 6 F

교과서 확인학습 A p.30~31

01 school year, here
02 Are, nervous, talking, other

03 have trouble starting
04 keeping, going   05 Don't
06 are, tips, become
07 Start, asking interesting
08 love to talk, themselves
09 them the chance
10 ask questions about, answer gladly
11 Be   12 are, poor listeners
13 how can, be   14 Look, in
15 Listen, to their words
16 Don't look at, or   17 Give feedback
18 Be, active   19 Nod, from time to time
20 say little things
21 also say, like, interesting, Tell me
22 Giving, shows that
23 Share common interests
24 have a conversation by, listening
25 have in common   26 Do, both like
27 talk, your favorite
28 Pay attention to
29 be interested in
30 Don't, aren't, listening to
31 Change, or, will, asleep
32 the other, to talk
33 Practice, and, soon be
34 Put others, want to talk

교과서 확인학습 B p.32~33

1 The new school year is here!
2 Are you nervous about talking to other students?
3 Do you have trouble starting conversations?
4 What about keeping conversations going?
5 Don't worry.
6 Here are five tips to become a better talker.
7 Start by asking interesting questions.
8 Most people love to talk about themselves.
9 So give them the chance.
10 When you ask questions about people, they will answer gladly.
11 Be a good listener.
12 Many people are poor listeners.
13 So how can you be a good listener?
14 Look people in the eye.
15 Listen carefully to their words.
16 Don't look at your cell phone or space out!
17 Give feedback.

18 Be an active listener.

19 Nod your head from time to time.

20 You can say little things like, "Wow!" or "Cool."

21 You can also say something like, "That's interesting. Tell me more."

22 Giving feedback shows that you're listening.

23 Share common interests.

24 You can't have a conversation by just listening.

25 What do you and your partner have in common?

26 Do you both like sports?

27 Then talk about your favorite baseball team.

28 Pay attention to the listener.

29 Sometimes people may not be interested in your topic.

30 Don't say, "Hey, wake up!" or "Why aren't you listening to me?"

31 Change the topic, or your partner will fall asleep.

32 Give the other person a chance to talk.

33 Practice these tips, and you will soon be a great talker.

34 Put others first, and everyone will want to talk with you.

시험대비 실력평가
p.34~37

01 ⓐ talking ⓑ starting   02 conversations

03 ⑤   04 ②   05 to talk about themselves

06 Be a good listener.   07 tip   08 ⑤

09 ②   10 ⑤   11 give them the chance to talk   12 ④   13 ⑤   14 ③

15 favorite   16 Pay attention to the listener.

17 Change the topic, or your partner will fall asleep.

18 ②   19 ④   20 ⓐ keeping ⓑ going ⓒ to become ⓓ asking   21 themselves   22 ②

23 ③   24 ②   25 ⓐ Be a good listener. ⓑ Give feedback. ⓒ Share common interests.

26 ③   27 이따금씩 고개를 끄덕이고, 'Wow', 'Cool', 'That's interesting.' 같은 간단한 말로 피드백을 준다.

01 ⓐ 전치사의 목적어로 동명사를 써야 하며, ⓑ '~하는 데 어려움이 있다'는 have trouble -ing로 표현한다.

02 주로 비형식적인 상황에서 어떤 사람과 이야기를 나누는 것은 '대화'이다.

03 여기 더 말을 잘하는 학생이 될 수 있는 다섯 가지 조언이 있다고 했으므로 ⑤번이 옳다.

04 '사람들에 관한 질문'이므로 ⓐ는 'about', '~을 듣다'는 'listen

to'이므로 ⓑ는 to, '~을 보다'는 'look at'이므로 ⓒ는 at을 쓰는 것이 옳다.

05 그들 자신에 관해 말할 기회를 주라는 것이다.

06 빈칸이 이끄는 글은 좋은 청자가 되는 방법에 관한 것이므로 Be a good listener.를 쓰면 된다.

07 하나의 유용한 충고

08 딴생각하지 않기 위해서 해야 하는 것은 글에 나와 있지 않다.

09 위 글은 말을 더 잘할 수 있는 방법에 관한 글이다.

10 상대가 말하는 동안 고개를 끄덕이고 추임새를 넣는 것은 능동적인 청자의 자세이므로 active가 옳다.

11 '말할 기회'라고 하였으므로 to talk가 the chance를 수식하도록 문장을 만든다.

12 'from time to time'은 '가끔, 이따금씩'이라는 표현이므로 ④번은 옳지 않다.

13 위 글에 따르면 좋은 화자는 듣고 있다는 신호로써의 피드백을 주는 것이 좋다고 하였으므로 ⑤번은 옳지 않다.

14 ①과 ④ '좋아하다'라는 의미의 동사, ② '~와 비슷한'이란 의미로 전치사이며, ⑤ '~처럼'이란 의미의 전치사이다. 밑줄 친 (B)는 예를 들 때 사용하는 전치사로 '~와 같은'이란 의미로 ③번이 옳다.

15 '같은 종류의 다른 것들보다 더 좋아하는'

16 'pay attention to'는 '주의를 기울이다'는 표현이다.

17 'Unless ~'는 '명령문+or'로 바꾸어 쓸 수 있다.

18 ①, ④번은 to부정사의 부사적 용법으로 앞의 형용사를 수식하고 있다. ③번은 명사적 용법 중 목적어로 쓰인 경우이며, ⑤번은 명사적 용법 중 진주어로 사용되었다. 위 글의 to부정사는 a chance를 수식하는 형용사로 사용되었으므로 ② 번이 옳다.

19 깨우거나 다그치기보다는 대화 주제를 바꾸는 것이 좋다고 하였다.

20 keep A -ing: A가 계속 ~하게 하다

21 주어와 목적어가 같을 때에는 목적어로 재귀대명사를 쓴다.

22 그들에게 기회를 주자는 것은 자신들에 관하여 말할 기회를 주자는 의미이므로 ②번이 옳다.

23 대부분의 사람들은 자신에 관하여 이야기하는 것을 좋아한다고 하였으므로, 질문에 기꺼이 대답할 것이라고 보는 것이 옳다. ③ 마지못해, 꺼려하여

24 주어진 문장은 듣는 방법에 관한 것이며, 대명사 their가 가리키는 복수 명사 뒤에 위치해야 하므로 ②번이 옳다. their는 people을 가리키고 있다.

26 공통 관심사가 스포츠라면 스포츠 이야기를 하는 것이 대화를 이끌어나가는 방법이다.

서술형 시험대비
p.38~39

01 What about keeping conversations going?

02 gladly   03 to become a better talker

04 by asking interesting questions

05 ⓐ interests ⓑ interested
06 Change the topic, or your partner will fall asleep.
07 practice the tips
08 Put others first, and everyone will want to talk with you.
09 have
10 Look people in the eye. Listen carefully to people's words. / Don't look at your cell phone. Don't space out.
11 We should give feedback to be an active listener.
12 giving feedback, sharing common interests
13 ⓐ are ⓑ Be ⓒ be
14 Nod your head from time to time
15 Pay attention to your partner

01 keep something going: ~을 이어나가다
02 glad: 기쁜 / gladly: 기쁘게
03 글쓴이는 학생들에게 말을 더 잘하는 사람이 되기 위한 조언을 하기를 원한다.
04 흥미로운 질문을 함으로써 대화를 시작하기를 권하고 있다.
05 interest는 명사와 동사로 사용되며, 'be interested in'은 '~에 흥미가 있다'는 의미이다.
06 명령문 ~+or ...'의 의미는 '~해라, 그렇지 않으면 ...'이다.
07 글쓴이가 제시한 팁을 연습하면 훌륭한 화자가 될 수 있을 것이라고 말하고 있다.
08 다른 사람을 우선하지 않으면, 모두가 너와 대화하기를 원치 않을 것이라고 했으므로, '다른 사람을 우선시해라, 그러면 모두가 너와 대화하기를 원할 것이다'로 쓰는 것이 옳다.
09 have ~ in common ~을 공통으로 가지다
11 능동적인 청자가 되기 위해서는 피드백을 주어야 한다.
12 제주도 삼촌 댁을 방문했다는 말에 '좀 더 이야기 해줘'라는 말로 feedback을 주었고, 제주도에 가 본 적이 있느냐는 질문으로 공통 관심사를 통해 대화를 이어가려 하였다.
13 ⓐ 'some tips'가 주어이므로 are를 쓴다.

영역별 핵심문제   p.41~45

01 active attention to 02 ② 03 ③ 04 Pay
05 space out 06 fell asleep 07 ③
08 ② 09 ⑤ 10 ② 11 ③
12 How about sending her a text? 13 ④
14 ④ 15 ② 16 Wash your hands, or you will catch a cold. 17 take care → take care of
18 something warm to put on 19 ③
20 ④ 21 Bring a book to read, or you will be bored. 22 ③ 23 ⑤ 24 ④, ⑤
25 ③ 26 Do you have trouble (in) starting conversations? 27 ④ 28 ③
29 (A) interesting (B) interesting 30 ⑤
31 Be an active listener, and 32 ②
33 ②

01 반의어 관계이다. passive(수동적인)의 반의어는 active(활발한, 활기찬)이다.
02 동의나 이해를 표현하기 위해 당신의 머리를 위아래로 움직이다: nod(끄덕이다)
03 사람들의 작은 모임 또는 오직 두 사람을 포함하는 비공식적인 담화: conversation(대화)
04 pay attention to: ~에 주의를 기울이다
05 space out: 딴생각하다
06 fall asleep: 잠들다
07 한자어를 모를 때 여러 번 반복해야 한다는 조언은 적절하지 않다.
08 많은 친구들을 사귈 수 있는 방법을 묻고 있으므로 ② 스포츠 동아리에 가입할 수 있다는 조언이 적절하다.
09 나머지는 모두 제안을 나타내지만 ⑤번은 목요일에 함께 무언가를 하기로 되어 있다는 예정을 나타낸다.
10 Mina는 자기 때문에 화가 난 Kate에게 미안해 하고 있다. ① 긴장한, ③ 놀란, ④ 즐거운, ⑤ 화가 난
11 (A) 주어는 'My best friend'로 단수이므로 is가 적절하다. (B) No wonder: ~가 당연하다. (C) make up with: ~ 와 화해하다, make up: 화장하다
12 How about ~?: '~하는 게 어때?'
13 '함께 놀 친구'라는 의미이므로 전치사 with를 쓰는 것이 옳다.
14 주어진 문장은 형용사로 쓰인 to부정사이다. ① 감정의 원인을 나타내는 부사적 용법, ② 동사의 목적어로 쓰인 명사적 용법, ③ 진주어로 쓰인 명사적 용법, ⑤ 목적격 보어로 쓰인 명사적 용법이며 ④ 앞서 나오는 명사 a friend를 수식하고 있으므로 쓰임이 같다.
15 -thing으로 끝나는 부정대명사는 '대명사+형용사+to부정사'의 어순을 따르므로 something cold to drink로 쓰는 것이 옳다.
17 '돌볼 아이들'이라는 의미로 '~를 돌보다'는 'take care of'이다.
18 -thing으로 끝나는 부정대명사는 형용사의 수식을 먼저 받고 to부정사의 수식을 받는다.
19 너무 빠른 속도로 운전하고 있으므로 속도를 늦추지 않으면 사고를 낼 것이라고 말하는 것이 가장 적절하다.
20 discuss는 타동사로 전치사 없이 목적어를 받아준다. 따라서 전치사 about을 생략하는 것이 옳다.
22 주어진 문장의 to부정사는 rules를 수식하는 형용사로 사용되었다. bring home the bacon: 생활비를 벌다
23 지금 떠나지 않으면 버스를 놓칠 것이라고 하였으므로 'If ~ not'으로 쓰이는 'Unless'가 옳다.
24 ④ 접속사로 사용된 or로 '또는, 혹은, 아니면'의 의미이다. ⑤ 명령문 ~, or ... 구문이다. ① and, ② so, ③ for

25 'be nervous about'은 '~에 긴장하다'라는 의미이며 'What about ~?'은 의견을 묻는 표현이다.

26 have trouble (in) -ing: ~하는 데에 어려움이 있다

27 주어진 글은 새 학기에 친구들과 대화를 나눌 수 있는 방법을 소개하려는 것이므로 ④번은 옳지 않다.

28 시간이나 조건의 부사절에서 현재가 미래를 대신하므로 현재시제 ask로 쓰는 것이 옳다.

29 '흥미를 유발하는'은 interesting으로 쓴다. 반면 '흥미를 느끼는'은 interested를 쓴다.

30 "Wow"라고 말하는 것은 당신이 상대의 말을 듣고 있다는 피드백이 될 수 있으므로 무례하다고 볼 수 없다.

32 밑줄 친 ⓐ는 '관심사'를 의미한다. 따라서 '네가 즐기는 활동이나 대상'인 ②번이 옳다. ① sport ③ subject ④ chance ⑤ tip을 의미한다.

33 have ~ in common' ~을 공통으로 가지다, 'pay attention to' ~에 주의를 기울이다, 'talk with' ~와 이야기하다

단원별 예상문제 p.46~49

01 ⑤	02 ①	03 ①	04 ④
05 ⓔ → another		06 ④	07 ①
08 ③	09 ②	10 ④	11 ④

12 ③   13 Post useful information, or you will waste others' time.   14 ③   15 swim → swim in   16 Wash your hands, or germs will invade your body. / Wash your hands, and germs won't invade your body.   17 to read, to drink, to use, to sit on[in]   18 ④   19 to become a better talker   20 space out   21 ⑤   22 Start by asking interesting questions.   23 ③
24 ⓐ Share ⓑ Pay ⓒ Give ⓓ Practice
25 (A) interested   (B) to talk   (C) with

01 어떤 일 또는 누군가의 일에 관해 얼마나 잘했는지 또는 유용한지에 대한 조언, 비판 또는 정보: feedback(피드백)

02 sometimes(때때로), anytime(언제든지), overtime(초과근무), sometime(언젠가), daytime(낮)

03 나는 인터뷰 때문에 매우 긴장했다. 공연 전에, 나는 긴장을 느꼈다. nervous(긴장한)

04 sometimes: 때때로, 가끔

05 뒤에 language가 생략되어 있는 형태로 단수 명사를 받는 another가 알맞다.

06 Talk Smart는 언어를 다른 언어로 바꾸어 주므로 번역 앱의 한 종류라고 볼 수 있다.

07 Kate와 화해하기 위해 사과 편지를 쓰라는 조언이 적절하다.

08 Mina가 왜 Kate의 헤어스타일을 그녀의 캐의 헤어스타일에 비유했는지는 알 수 없다.

09 이어지는 Mike의 '오, 그거 참 안됐구나.'라는 대화를 통해 주어진 문장은 (B)에 들어가는 것이 적절하다.

10 Mike는 Jenny에게 그녀의 동아리를 홍보할 것을 조언하였다.

11 운동을 규칙적으로 하면 좋아 보일 것이라고 말하는 것이 옳다. 따라서 or를 and로 고쳐야 한다.

12 ③ '함께 놀 친구'이므로 전치사 with와 함께 써야 한다.

13 유용한 정보를 게시하지 않으면, 타인의 시간을 낭비할 가능성이 있다.

14 -thing으로 끝나는 부정대명사의 수식은 '형용사+to부정사' 어순이므로 ③번이 옳다.

15 swim in a pool이므로 전치사 in을 쓰는 것이 옳다.

16 '손을 씻지 않으면, 세균이 당신의 몸에 침투할 것이다.'라는 의미이므로, '손을 씻어라, 그렇지 않으면 세균이 당신의 몸에 침투할 것이다.' 혹은 '손을 씻어라, 그러면 세균이 당신의 몸에 침투하지 않을 것이다.'라고 쓰면 된다.

17 to부정사의 형용사 용법을 활용하여 빈칸을 채울 수 있다.

18 '~을 지속시키다'는 표현은 'keep A -ing'이다. 따라서 going으로 고치는 것이 옳다.

20 '분명하게 생각할 수 없거나 당신 주변에서 무슨 일이 일어나고 있는지를 인식하지 못하다'는 space out의 뜻풀이이다.

21 ⑤ 'run an errand'는 '심부름하다'는 표현이다. to부정사가 명사 'an errand'를 수식하고 있으므로 형용사로 사용되었다.

23 좋은 청자의 자세로 상대방의 말을 귀 기울여 듣는 것을 언급하고 있으므로 ③번이 옳다.

25 (A) 흥미를 '느낄' 때에는 과거분사형을 써야 하며, (B) '말할 기회'라는 의미로 전치사를 필요로 하지 않는다. (C) 너에 '관하여' 이야기하는 것이 아니라 너와 '함께' 이야기하기를 원한다는 내용이 옳다.

서술형 실전문제 p.50~51

01 Why don't you
02 잠들기 전에 따뜻한 우유를 마신다.
03 Make many friends to talk with, and you will not be lonely.
04 Open the window, and you will breathe in fresh air.
05 (1) Susan had nothing to give up.
   (2) There is too much trash to pick up.
06 Read an English book every month, and you will improve your English.
07 (1) I need a car to drive.
   (2) Stay calm, or you will make some mistakes.
08 Because most people love to talk about themselves.

09 Don't look at your cell phone
10 What do you and your partner have in common?
11 be a great talker
12 We should change the topic.

01 제안을 할 때 'Why don't you ~?(~하는 게 어때?)'라는 표현을 쓸 수 있다.

03 lonely: 외로운

04 breathe: 호흡하다

05 to부정사의 형태는 'to+동사원형'이며, pick은 '(꽃)을 꺾다', '(과일)을 따다', '~을 고르다'는 의미이다. '~을 줍다'라는 의미로 사용될 때에는 반드시 pick up으로 표현한다.

08 사람들이 기쁘게 대답할 것이라고 말한 이유는 대부분의 사람들이 스스로에 대해 말하는 것을 좋아하기 때문이다.

09 당신이 휴대전화를 보고 있으면 상대편이 당신이 듣고 있지 않다고 생각할 것이므로, 휴대전화를 보지 말라는 명령문을 만들어 준다.

10 have ~ in common: ~을 공통으로 가지다

11 글의 내용은 훌륭한 화자가 되는 방법에 관한 것이다.

12 당신이 말하고 있는 도중에 상대방이 잠에 빠져든다면 대화 주제를 바꿀 것을 권하고 있다.

창의사고력 서술형 문제
p.52

|모범답안|

01 (1) Monday (2) How about volunteering at the nursing home / (1) Wednesday (2) Why don't we have a walk with my pet / (1) Friday (2) What about studying English / (1) Saturday (2) How about going to the library / (1) Sunday (2) Why don't we go to the movies

02 (1) don't talk with your friend, or your teacher will mad at you.
(2) put books in the right places, and other people can find them easily.
(3) be polite to the elderly, and they will be happy.
(4) sit still, or you can disturb the driver.

03 (1) I have many friends to play with. / There are many things to see.
(2) Do you have some water to drink? / I have some books to read.
(3) She has some plants to take care of.

단원별 모의고사
p.53~56

01 (C) → (B) → (D) → (E) → (A)			02 ⑤
03 ①	04 (C) → to get		05 ③
06 ②	07 ②	08 ②	09 ④
10 ②	11 ②	12 ⑤	13 ②, ⑤

14 Take an umbrella (with you), or you will get all wet. 15 ③ 16 making, to depend on 17 ② 18 Here are some tips to become a better talker. 19 ④ 20 Giving 21 ④ 22 ⓐ listening ⓒ to talk 23 ⓑ or ⓓ and 24 ③ 25 If you practice these tips, you will soon be a great talker.

01 (C) 새 학기에 대한 기분 표현 → (B) 동의 및 기대감 표현 → (D) 조언 구하기 → (E) 조언 제공 → (A) 동의 표현

02 ⑤ 건강을 유지하기 위한 조언이 이어져야 한다.

03 밑줄 친 문장은 '무엇을 하길 원하니?'라고 묻는 것으로 '네가 하고 싶어 하는 무언가가 있니?'라고 바꾸어 쓸 수 있다.

04 to부정사로 to get이 알맞다.

05 ③ Mike는 노래 부르기 동아리에 가입한다.

06 잠을 잘 잘 수 있기 위해 무엇을 할 수 있는지를 묻고 있으므로 What이 적절하다.

07 How about ~? 또는 What about ~?은 모두 '~하는 게 어때?'라는 의미이다.

08 In the way (방해가 되어), By the way (그런데), On the way (가는 중에)를 의미하므로 문맥상 On이 자연스럽다.

09 언제 Sue가 Talk Smart 앱을 사용했는지는 알 수 없다.

10 be mad at ~: ~에게 화나다(= be angry at)

11 (B)는 '무슨 일이니?'라고 묻고 있으므로 ②와 바꾸어 쓸 수 있다.

12 Kate는 Mina에게 화가 나서 Mina와 이야기를 하지 않을 것이라고 Mina와 Brian은 생각한다.

13 ② '이것을 고쳐줄 잡역부'라는 의미이므로 to부정사 형태로 a handyman을 수식해야 한다. ⑤ 물을 많이 마시면 피부가 건조해지지 않는다는 의미가 옳으므로 and를 or로 고쳐야 한다.

14 get all wet: 비에 흠뻑 젖다

15 다른 사람들을 놀리지 말아야 하는 이유는 그들의 감정을 다치게 하지 않기 위해서이므로 or를 쓰는 것이 옳다.

16 have trouble (in) -ing '~하는 데 어려움을 겪다' depend on '~에게 의지하다'

17 Unless는 부정어를 이끌 수 없다. 따라서 'If ~ not'으로 문장을 만들어 주어야 한다.

18 here are ~: 여기 ~이 있다

19 밑줄 친 ⓐ는 전치사의 목적어로 사용된 동명사이다. '~하는 것'으로 해석되는 ④번이 옳다.

20 주어 자리이므로 동명사를 사용하는 것이 적절하다.

9

21 대화 중에 해서는 안 되는 것으로 휴대폰 사용과 명하게 있는 것이 언급되어 있다.

22 ⓐ는 전치사의 목적어 자리이므로 동명사를 써야 하며, ⓑ는 '말할 기회'라는 의미로 명사 'a chance'를 수식해야 하므로 to부정사 형태를 쓰는 것이 옳다.

23 '주제를 바꾸어라. 그렇지 않으면 파트너가 잠들 것이다', '타인을 우선시해라. 그러면 모두가 너와 대화하길 원할 것이다'이므로 각각 or와 and를 써야 한다.

24 ③ 공통 관심사에 대한 예로 스포츠 이야기를 했을 뿐, 반드시 스포츠를 좋아해야 하는 것은 아니다.

25 이 팁들을 연습해라. 그러면 당신은 훌륭한 화자가 될 것이다.'이므로 '이 팁들을 연습하면, 당신은 훌륭한 화자가 될 것이다.'라고 쓰면 된다.

Close to You

시험대비 실력평가		p.60
01 disappear	02 ⑤	03 promise
04 (f)riendly, (h)umorous	05 ⑤	
06 (A) over (B) for (C) of		07 ④

01 반의어 관계이다. 좋아하다 : 싫어하다 = 나타나다 : 사라지다

02 ①번 ~ ④번 모두 '명석한, 똑똑한'을 의미하지만 ⑤번은 '무지한'을 뜻한다.

03 당신이 누군가에게 어떠한 것을 반드시 하겠다거나 하지 않을 것이라고 이야기한다는 말은 promise(약속하다)이다.

04 friendly: 친절한, humorous: 재미있는, 익살스러운

05 그는 골을 넣기 위해 주장에게 공을 패스할 것이다. 그들은 태풍이 지나가기를 기다리고 있다. 나는 시험을 통과해서 너무 행복했다.

06 invite ~ over: ~을 집으로 초대하다, look for: ~을 찾다, in front of: ~ 앞에

07 shake: 흔들다, shake hands: 악수하다

서술형 시험대비		p.61
01 banker	02 charity	03 contest
04 (1) my family were a sea of tears		
(2) He was doing his own thing in the room.		
05 (1) a sea of (2) get the first place (3) turn off		
06 charity, promise, outgoing		
07 (1) The wizard can make himself invisible.		
(2) Why don't you hug your mother today?		

01 은행을 소유하였거나 은행에서 중요한 일을 하는 사람은 banker(은행가, 은행원)이다.

02 어려움에 처한 사람들을 도와주는 단체는 charity(자선 단체)이다.

03 무언가에 이기기 위해 사람들이 노력하는 경쟁

04 do one's own thing: 자기가 하고 싶은 일을 하다

05 sea of ~: ~의 바다, get the first place: 1등을 하다, turn off: ~을 끄다

06 promise: 약속하다, normal: 평범한, 정상적인, charity: 자선 단체, outgoing: 활발한

Conversation

p.62~63

핵심 Check

1 (1) sure[certain] / win the race
  (2) far from / no doubt
  (3) can't / I'm sure[certain]
2 (1) responsible, patient
  (2) personality / hard-working, helpful
  (3) Who / humorous, outgoing

교과서 대화문 익히기

Check(√) True or False
p.64

1 T 2 F 3 T 4 F

교과서 확인학습
p.66~67

Listen & Speak 1 A

arrive / leaves / already / far from, arrive

Listen & Speak 1 B

worried / English speaking test / worry / nervous, in front of / do well / think so / speaker / feel much better

Listen & Speak 1 C

the guitar / get first place / too

Listen & Speak 2 A

coach / tall, handsome, like / friendly, humorous

Listen & Speak 2 B

how / already / hear, become / in the same club / like / kind / outgoing / invite them over

Listen & Speak 2 C

looking for / What is she like / active, outgoing / ask

Real Life Talk

for / about / moved / singer / sings, sure, perfect / more, like / friendly / have, number

시험대비 기본평가
p.68

01 active, outgoing   02 at the train station
03 ⑤   04 ①, ③

---

01 active: 활발한, 적극적인, outgoing: 외향적인

02 there는 장소를 가리키는 부사이다.

03 B는 G에게 5시 전에 도착할 것이라고 확신을 표현하고 있다.

04 밑줄 친 말은 확신을 나타내므로 이와 같은 의미를 나타내는 표현으로는 'I'm certain ~' 또는 'I don't doubt ~'가 있다.

시험대비 실력평가
p.69~70

01 first place 02 in time   03 ⑤   04 (A) → worried   05 ①   06 It's because of the English speaking test this afternoon.   07 It's because he gets so nervous when he is in front of the teacher. 08 ①   09 ③   10 How about inviting them over for dinner?   11 ③
12 ③   13 ③

---

01 get first place: 1등을 하다

02 in time: 제때에, 늦지 않게

03 G와 B가 어느 기차를 탈지는 알 수 없다.

04 worrying: 걱정시키는, worried: 걱정하는

05 민수는 영어 말하기 대회로 불안해 했지만 Jane의 응원을 통해 기분이 나아졌다. nervous: 불안해 하는, relieved: 안도하는, lonely: 외로운, disappointed: 실망한

06 민수는 오후에 있을 영어 말하기 시험 때문에 걱정하고 있다.

07 민수는 연습을 많이 했음에도 선생님 앞에서는 매우 긴장하기 때문에 말하기 시험에 대해 걱정하고 있다.

08 A는 B와 같은 생각을 갖고 있으므로 동의 표현인 I agree with you.(나도 너에게 동의해.)와 바꾸어 쓸 수 있다.

09 주어진 질문에 대해 성격을 말하는 대화가 이어져야 하므로 (C)가 적절하다.

10 Why don't you ~?: ~하는 게 어떠니?

11 ③ Sue, Rosa, Mike는 같은 동아리에 가입하였지만 영어 동아리인지는 알 수 없다.

12 이어지는 대답으로 성격을 묘사하는 말이 이어져야 하므로 (C)가 적절하다.

13 Hojin이 어느 동아리에 속해 있는지는 알 수 없다.

서술형 시험대비
p.71

01 I'm sure he will get first place in the contest.

02 What is he like?

03 I'm sure we'll arrive there before 5.

04 They are planning to take the train leaving at 5:10.

05 (1) the English speaking test
  (2) in front of
  (3) he would do well

02 이어지는 대답으로 보아 '그는 어떤 분이셔?'라는 질문이 적절하다.

03 I'm sure: ~을 확신하다.

04 그들은 기차역에 도착한 후 5시 10분에 떠나는 기차를 타려고 계획하고 있다.

05 Minsu는 오후에 영어 말하기 시험 때문에 좋아 보이지 않았다. 비록 그가 많이 연습했지만 그는 그가 항상 선생님 앞에서 긴장하기 때문에 걱정하고 있었다. 그러나 나는 그가 영어 말하기를 잘하기 때문에 잘 해내리라 믿었다.

교과서
Grammar

핵심 Check
p.72~73

1 (1) has cleaned (2) has gone
  (3) Have, played (4) have, lived
2 (1) persuaded, to go (2) expect, to arrive
  (3) told, not to run

시험대비 기본평가
p.74

01 (1) gave → given
   (2) Do you have been → Have you been
   (3) leaving → to leave
   (4) to not → not to
02 (1) visited (2) to be (3) haven't eaten (4) to drink
03 (1) My parents want me to be a teacher.
   (2) He has already cleaned his room.
   (3) These shoes enable me to walk comfortably.
   (4) I have studied Chinese for two years.
   (5) The rain caused the river to overflow.

01 (1) 현재완료의 형태는 'have[has]+p.p.'이다. (2) 현재완료의 의문문은 'Have[Has]+주어 +p.p. ~?'이다. (3) want의 목적격보어는 to부정사이다. (4) to부정사의 부정형은 'not to V' 형태이다.

02 (1) 과거를 나타내는 yesterday가 있으므로 과거동사를 쓰는 것이 적절하다. (2), (4) ask와 advise 는 to부정사를 목적격보어로 취한다. (3) 현재완료의 부정문은 'have not[has not]+p.p.'로 만든다.

03 (1), (3), (5) want, enable, cause는 to부정사를 목적격보어로 취하는 동사이다. (2) 현재완료의 완료 용법을 이용하여 문장을 만든다. (4) 현재완료의 계속 용법을 이용하여 문장을 만든다.

시험대비 실력평가
p.75~77

01 have you gone → did you go   02 ③

03 ④   04 ③   05 Tom has lived in Canada since April.   06 ⑤   07 allowed, to go   08 ④   09 I have lost my passport.   10 ②   11 ③   12 ②   13 ⑤   14 She asked me to drop by her house.   15 ⑤   16 ③   17 Karen has played the violin since she was six years old.   18 ②   19 I want you to help me with the dishes.   20 ④   21 ⑤   22 ②   23 ⑤   24 문장 (1)은 George가 미국을 방문한 적이 있다는 의미이고, 문장 (2)는 George가 미국에 가고 없다는 의미로 현재 그가 미국에 있다는 뜻이다.

01 과거 시제를 나타내는 어구인 last night은 현재완료와 함께 쓸 수 없다.

02 ask는 목적격보어로 to부정사를 사용한다.

03 ①, ②, ③, ⑤번은 현재완료의 용법 중 '경험'에 해당하지만, ④번은 '계속'에 속한다.

04 ③ 과거를 나타내는 yesterday는 현재완료와 함께 쓸 수 없다.

05 4월부터 현재까지 캐나다에서 살고 있는 것이므로 현재완료를 사용하는 것이 적절하다.

06 빈칸에는 to부정사를 목적격보어로 취할 수 있는 동사가 들어가야 한다.

07 allow는 to부정사를 목적격보어로 취하는 동사이다.

08 allow는 to부정사를 목적격보어로 취하는 동사이다. 따라서 to play가 적절하다.

09 여권을 잃어버린 과거의 사건이 현재까지 영향을 미치고 있으므로 현재완료 시제를 써서 하나의 문장으로 만들어줄 수 있다.

10 일반적으로 '이미, 벌써'라고 해석되는 already의 위치는 have 동사와 p.p. 사이이고, '아직'이라고 해석되는 yet은 주로 부정문에서 사용되며 문장 마지막에 놓인다.

11 일찍 자는 주체는 손님이므로 5형식을 사용하고, would like는 to부정사를 목적격보어로 취하므로 ③번이 적절하다.

12 for+기간, since+특정 시점

13 ① what time은 과거를 나타내는 어구이므로 현재완료와 함께 쓸 수 없다. ② force는 to부정사를 목적격보어로 취하는 동사이다. ③ persuade는 'to+동사원형'을 목적격보어로 취한다. ④ since는 특정 시점을 이끌기 때문에 for로 바꾸어 주는 것이 적절하다.

14 ask+목적어+to부정사: 목적어가 V하도록 요청하다

15 현재완료 질문이므로 B는 현재도 골프를 치는 상태임을 알 수 있다. 6살 때 골프를 배운 것은 과거이고, 20년 동안 골프를 쳐 온 것은 현재완료로 표현하는 것이 적절하다.

16 ①, ④, ⑤번의 동사는 to부정사를 목적격보어로 취하는 동사들이며, ②번에는 형용사로 쓰이는 to부정사가 들어간다. ③번은 조동사 뒤에 위치하는 동사원형의 자리이다.

17 Karen은 6살에 바이올린을 배워 현재도 연주하고 있으므로 현재완료 중 계속 용법으로 표현하는 것이 적절하다.

18 많은 짐을 들고 있는 Ann이 Jason에게 도움을 요청하는 상황이므로 ②번이 적절하다.

19 도와주는 주체가 you이므로 want you to help를 써서 5형식 틀을 갖추어야 한다.

20 encourage와 want는 모두 to부정사를 목적격보어로 취하는 동사이므로 빈칸에는 to부정사가 들어가는 것이 적절하다. get along well: 잘 지내다

21 아침에 일어나서부터 지금까지 배가 아픈 것이므로 현재완료형을 쓰는 것이 적절하다.

22 자신의 전화기를 사용하지 말라고 했으므로 forbid는 to use를, told는 not to use를 쓰는 것이 적절하다. forbid: 금지하다

23 yet은 부정문이나 의문문에서 사용된다.

24 현재완료에서 'have[has] been to ~'는 경험을 나타내고 'have[has] gone to ~'는 결과를 나타낸다.

06 teach는 목적격보어로 to부정사를 사용한다.

07 현재완료와 함께 쓰이는 'for+기간'을 통하여 현재완료 시제를 써야 함을 알 수 있다.

08 첫 문장은 과거시제를 사용하고 있으므로 ago, 다음 문장은 결혼해 온 기간을 의미하므로 for를 쓰는 것이 적절하다.

09 allow+목적어+to V: 목적어가 V하도록 허락하다

10 첫 번째 질문은 일본에 가 본 적이 있느냐는 경험을 묻고 있으므로 현재완료형을 쓰는 것이 적절하며, 나머지 질문과 대답은 과거 내용이므로 모두 과거 시제를 써야 한다.

11 accept an apology: 사과를 받아들이다

12 Brian이 어디로 가고 없는지를 묻는 것이므로 has gone을 쓰는 것이 적절하다.

13 목적격보어로 원형부정사와 to부정사를 사용하는 동사를 구분하는 문제이다. 사역동사 make, have, let은 목적격보어로 원형부정사를 취하지만, encourage, would like는 to부정사를 목적격보어로 받는 동사이다.

14 cause+목적어+to V: 목적어가 V하도록 야기하다

15 splash around: 물장구치다, 첨벙거리다

01 want you to be upset
02 We have used this computer for three years.
03 Jason to see a doctor
04 The teacher told the students not to run on the stairs.
05 (1) Jim has been in Italy since Monday.
　(2) Jim has been in Italy for three days.
06 Ann's mother taught Ann to play the guitar.
07 has worked
08 ago, for
09 They allowed me to travel to Jeju-do.
10 Have you ever been, went / Did you have, was
11 me to accept Kelly's apology
12 where has he gone?
13 stop / to buy / do / use / to wait
14 caused the disease to spread
15 She let her children splash around in the pool for a while.

01 want는 목적격보어로 to부정사를 사용한다.

02 3년 전에 구매하여 지금도 쓰고 있으므로 3년 동안 사용해 왔다는 현재완료로 표현하면 된다.

03 advise는 목적격보어로 to부정사를 사용한다.

04 tell은 목적격보어로 to부정사를 사용한다.

05 월요일에 도착하여 현재 목요일이므로 since를 사용하면 '월요일 이래로 이탈리아에 머물고 있다'라고 표현할 수 있으며 for를 사용할 경우 '3일 동안 머물러 왔다'고 표현할 수 있다.

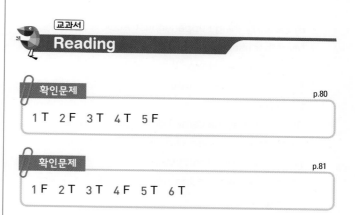

교과서
Reading

1 T   2 F   3 T   4 T   5 F

1 F   2 T   3 T   4 F   5 T   6 T

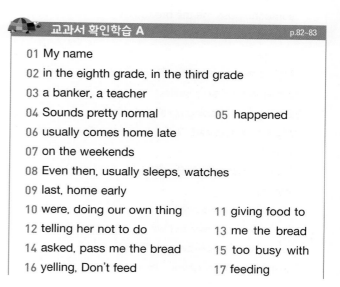

교과서 확인학습 A   p.82~83

01 My name
02 in the eighth grade, in the third grade
03 a banker, a teacher
04 Sounds pretty normal　　　05 happened
06 usually comes home late
07 on the weekends
08 Even then, usually sleeps, watches
09 last, home early
10 were, doing our own thing　　11 giving food to
12 telling her not to do　　13 me the bread
14 asked, pass me the bread　　15 too busy with
16 yelling, Don't feed　　17 feeding

13

18 jumping   19 shouted, invisible

20 happened, disappeared like magic

21 became invisible   22 hear, see

23 asked   24 right in front of, replied

25 anything, awful

26 went, asked, to help

27 has been invisible since

28 never seen anything like, before 29 When, miss

30 started crying, joined   31 In a few

32 promise to pass

33 happened, appeared

34 all the attention, earlier, play with you

교과서 확인학습 B   p.84~85

1 My name is Jimmy.

2 I am in the eighth and my sister, Hope, is in the third grade.

3 My father is a banker and my mother is a teacher.

4 We have a dog, Smiley. Sounds pretty normal, right?

5 But a crazy thing happened last week.

6 My father usually comes home late from work.

7 So, we only see him on the weekends.

8 Even then, he usually sleeps or watches television.

9 But last Friday, he came home early for dinner.

10 At the table, we were all doing our own thing.

11 Hope was giving food to Smiley.

12 My mother was telling her not to do so. I was texting.

13 My father said, "Pass me the bread, please."

14 No one heard him, so he asked again, "Can someone pass me the bread?"

15 I heard him this time, but I was too busy with my phone.

16 My mother was yelling, "Don't feed Smiley!"

17 Hope was feeding Smiley.

18 Smiley was jumping up and down.

19 My father shouted, "Am I invisible? Pass me the bread!"

20 Then, it happened. Poof! My father disappeared like magic.

21 He became invisible!

22 We could hear him, but we couldn't see him.

23 We asked, "Where are you?"

24 "I'm right in front of you," he replied.

---

25 We couldn't do anything for him. It was an awful night.

26 Next morning, we went to the hospital and asked the doctor to help us.

27 I said, "He has been invisible since last night."

28 The doctor shook his head and said, "I can't help you. I've never seen anything like this before."

29 When we came home, Hope said, "I miss Daddy."

30 She started crying. My mother joined her.

31 In a few moments, we were a sea of tears.

32 "Come back, Dad! I promise to pass you the bread every day!" I cried.

33 Then, it happened. My father appeared again!

34 He hugged us and said, "Thank you for all the attention. I promise to come home earlier and play with you on the weekends."

시험대비 실력평가   p.86~89

01 ④	02 normal	03 ②	04 ③
05 someone to pass him the bread			06 ③
07 ④	08 ①	09 ③	10 ③
11 ④	12 ⑤	13 ⓐ late	ⓑ for
14 ⑤	15 We couldn't see him.		16 I am
right in front of you.		17 ④	18 It was
an awful night.		19 ⑤	20 ④
21 since	22 ⑤	23 ①	24 ④
25 사람의 형체가 보이지 않는 것			26 ③
27 I promise to come home earlier			

01 ① Jimmy의 집에는 4명의 식구가 있고, ② Jimmy는 8학년이라고 했으므로 15살이다. ③ 아버지는 은행원이고, ⑤ 개의 이름은 Smiley이다. ④ Jimmy가 미래에 되기를 희망하는 것은 알 수 없다.

02 흔히 있으며 평범한: normal(보통의, 평범한)

03 마지막 문장으로 미루어 보아 ②번이 이어질 내용임을 알 수 있다.

04 Smiley는 펄쩍펄쩍 뛰고 있었다.

06 가족들 모두 자기만의 일에 바빴기 때문에 아빠의 말을 듣지 못했다.

07 ⓑ는 전치사로 '~처럼'이라고 해석된다. ① [동사] 좋아하다, ② [접속사] ~하는 대로[처럼], ③ [접속사] 마치 ~인 것처럼, ④ [전치사] ~처럼, ⑤ [동사] 좋아하다

08 so는 결과를 이끄는 문장으로, 아버지가 주로 늦게 귀가하시기 때문에 그를 주말에만 볼 수 있다는 것이 자연스러운 연결이며, 뒤 문장에서 "Even then'이 주어진 문장의 on the weekends를 받아주는 것이므로 ①이 알맞다.

09 주로 늦게 귀가하시는 아버지가 지난 금요일에는 일찍 오셔서 Jimmy는 아버지와 함께 식사를 할 수 있었다.

10 아버지는 직장에서 늦게 퇴근하는 것이므로 ③번이 가장 적절하다.

11 각자 하고 싶은 일을 하던 중이었다는 의미이므로 ④번이 적절하다.

12 주어진 문장에서 her가 가리키는 것은 Hope이므로 ⑤번에 들어가는 것이 적절하다.

13 lately는 '최근에'라는 의미의 부사이므로 '늦게'의 의미로 쓰이는 late이 적절하다. '저녁식사를 위해서'는 for dinner이다.

14 ⑤번은 see의 의미이다.

15 invisible은 보이지 않는다는 의미이다.

16 in front of: ~ 앞에

17 본문에서 쓰인 it은 비인칭 주어로 요일, 날씨, 거리, 명암 등을 나타낼 때 쓰인다. ④는 to talk with you의 가주어이다.

18 awful: 끔찍한

19 ①~④번은 글쓴이의 아버지를 가리키지만 ⑤번은 의사를 가리킨다.

20 밑줄 친 ⓐ는 목적격보어로 쓰인 to부정사로 목적어가 to V의 주체가 된다. ④번이 적절하다. ①, ⑤는 '~하기 위해서'라고 해석되는 부사적 용법, ②, ③은 각각 many things, some friends를 수식하는 형용사적 용법으로 사용되었다.

21 특정 시점인 last night을 이끄므로 since가 적절하다.

22 shocking은 awful과 동의어이다. 반대되는 의미의 단어는 나와 있지 않다.

23 아버지가 보이지는 않아도 목소리는 들을 수 있었기 때문에 대화를 나눌 수 있었다. 따라서 ①번은 could로 고치는 것이 적절하다.

24 (A)에서 사용된 현재완료는 '계속'의 의미로 쓰였다. ④를 제외한 모든 문장은 '경험'을 나타낸다.

25 사람의 형체가 보이지 않는 경우는 겪어본 적이 없기 때문에 도움을 줄 수 없다는 의미이다.

26 join은 타동사이므로 전치사를 쓰지 않고 목적어를 받아준다. 따라서 with를 없애는 것이 적절하다.

27 promise는 to부정사를 목적어로 취한다.

서술형 시험대비   p.90~91

01 His father is a banker and his mother is a teacher.

02 But a crazy thing happened last week.

03 Don't give food to Smiley.

04 He usually sleeps or watches television.

05 Hope, Jimmy's mother, Jimmy

06 was too busy with

07 He wanted them to pass the bread to him.

08 My father disappeared like magic.

09 asked the doctor to help us.

10 He has been invisible since last night.

11 visible

12 ⓐ my father disappeared.   ⓑ my father appeared.

13 사라진 아빠를 위해 해 줄 수 있는 것이 아무것도 없어서

14 he has never seen anything like this before

15 I want you to come back

01 Jimmy 부모님의 직업을 묻는 문제이다.

02 happen: 발생하다, (일이) 일어나다

03 give를 3형식으로 전환하여야 5단어로 이루어진 문장을 쓸 수 있다.

04 Jimmy의 아버지가 주말마다 주로 하는 것을 묻고 있다.

05 주어진 글에서 알 수 있는 we는 Hope, 엄마, Jimmy이다.

06 be busy with: ~에 바쁘다

07 want는 to부정사를 목적격보어로 취하는 동사이다.

08 disappear: 사라지다

09 ask는 to부정사를 목적격보어로 취하는 동사이다.

10 invisible: 보이지 않는

11 visible: 보이는

12 ⓐ는 아빠가 사라진 일이 발생했음을 의미하며, ⓑ는 아빠가 다시 나타난 것을 의미한다.

13 아빠가 갑자기 사라졌지만 해줄 수 있는 것이 아무것도 없어서 끔찍한 밤이라고 말했다.

14 의사가 왜 그들을 도와줄 수 없다고 말했는지 그 이유를 쓰는 문제이다.

15 want는 to부정사를 목적격보어로 취하는 동사이다.

영역별 핵심문제   p.93~97

01 abnormal   02 hug   03 ⑤   04 ①
05 ②   06 doing their own thing   07 What
is she like   08 (D) → (B) → (A) → (C)   09 ②
10 ⑤   11 ⓐ How   ⓑ What   12 Why
don't you invite them over for dinner?   13 It has
not[hasn't] stopped raining. 14 ④   15 ④
16 Kate not to make any noise   17 have
known, know   18 ①, ④   19 ②
20 ④   21 ④   22 ⑤   23 It
causes the disease to spread.   24 haven't
finished   25 ③   26 It is Jimmy's dog.
27 ④   28 Stop, put 29 ③   30 She
didn't want Hope to feed Smiley.   31 ②

01 반의어 관계이다. 부유한 : 가난한 = 정상적인 : 비정상적인

02 특히 당신이 좋아하거나 사랑한다는 것을 표현하기 위해 당신의

15

팔을 다른 누군가에게 올려놓거나 꽉 잡다: hug(안다)

03 outgoing: 외향적인, 활동적인

04 주어진 문장의 crazy는 '말도 안 되는'을 의미한다. ②, ④, ⑤ 번에서 crazy는 '매우 좋아하는, 열광하는'을 뜻하며 ③번에서 crazy는 '미친 듯이 화가 난'을 뜻한다.

05 그들은 보통 만날 때 악수를 한다. 그녀는 추위에 떠는 것처럼 보였다. 그의 신념이 소문 때문에 흔들리기 시작했다.

06 do one's own thing: 자기가 하고 싶은 일을 하다

08 (D) 제때에 도착 가능한지 질문 → (B) 대답 및 기차 출발 시간 설명 → (A) 현재 시간 진술 → (C) 확신 표현

09 말하기 시험을 앞두고 있는 Minsu에게 할 말로 Cheer up!(힘내!)이 적절하다.

10 위 대화에서 Jane이 시험 불안을 극복하기 위해 무엇을 하는지는 알 수 없다.

12 Why don't you ~?: ~하는 게 어때? / invite ~ over: ~을 자기 집으로 초대하다

13 stop+Ving: V하던 것을 멈추다

14 빈칸에는 to부정사를 목적격보어로 취하는 동사가 들어가는 것이 적절하다.

15 ④ have trouble (in) Ving: ~하는 데에 어려움이 있다 ①, ③, ⑤는 목적격보어로 쓰인 to부정사가 들어가며 ②는 형용사 용법의 to부정사가 들어간다.

16 tell은 to부정사를 목적격 보어로 취한다.

17 그녀를 오랫동안 알아온 것은 과거부터 현재까지 이어지는 일이므로 현재완료를 써야 하며, '그녀를 잘 안다'는 것은 현재 상태를 의미하므로 현재형 동사를 쓰는 것이 적절하다.

18 주어진 문장은 Kelly가 질병으로부터 회복했다는 의미로, 현재완료형으로 표현하고 있기 때문에 Kelly가 과거에 아팠지만 현재 괜찮다는 것을 알 수 있다.

19 beg는 to부정사를 목적격보어로 취하는 동사이다.

20 주어진 문장은 현재완료의 네 가지 용법 중 경험에 해당한다. ①, ③번 계속, ②, ⑤번 완료, ④번은 파티를 열어본 적이 있는지를 묻는 경험에 해당한다.

21 ① Do you prepare → Have you prepared ② has kept a diary yet → has never kept a diary ③ gone → been ⑤ has seen → saw

22 ①~④번은 목적격보어로 쓰인 to부정사이지만, ⑤번은 time을 수식하는 형용사로 사용된 to부정사이다.

23 cause+목적어+to V: 목적어가 V하도록 유발하다

24 아직 읽기를 끝내지 않았다는 의미이므로 현재완료를 쓰는 것이 적절하다.

25 Jimmy의 어머니가 지금 무엇을 하고 있는 중인지는 알 수 없다.

26 Smiley는 무엇인가?

27 Jimmy의 아버지는 주말에 주로 잠을 자거나 텔레비전을 본다고 하였으므로 ④번은 일치하지 않는다.

28 문자 보내는 것을 멈추고 휴대전화기를 내려놓으라고 말할 수 있다.

29 엄마가 소리를 지른 대상은 글쓴이가 아닌 Hope이다.

30 want는 to부정사를 목적격보어로 취하는 동사이다.

31 아버지가 마법처럼 사라져 보이지 않는다고 했으므로 ②가 가장 적절하다.

단원별 예상문제   p.98~101

01 tidy 02 a sea of tears 03 ⑤
04 (A) humorous (B) funny (C) both 05 these
days 06 ① 07 ③ 08 He is
very outgoing and friendly. 09 ⑤ 10 ②
11 ③ 12 ③ 13 ①, ④ 14 The
doctor advised my dad not to smoke. 15 ago,
since, for 16 has worked, was, to do 17 ④
18 on the weekends 19 ⓐ heard ⓑ yelling
ⓒ feeding ⓓ jumping ⓔ happened 20 ④
21 ④ 22 ③ 23 Have you (ever) seen
anything like this (before)? 24 disappeared, hear

01 물건이 정돈되고 제대로 유지되어 있는 상태를 가리키는 말은 tidy(깔끔한)이다.

02 a sea of tears: 눈물바다

03 ①번~④번 모두 사람의 성격을 묘사하는 형용사이지만, ⑤번은 '주의 깊게'라는 부사이다.

04 humor: 유머 humorous: 재미있는, 익살스러운 funny: 재미 있는 boring: 지루한 both: 둘 다 either: 둘 중 하나

05 these days: 요즘에, those days: 그 당시에

06 친구가 될 수 있었던 이유를 설명하는 문장이 이어져야 하므로 (A)가 적절하다.

07 Sue와 Mike가 어떤 동아리에 속해 있는지는 알 수 없다.

08 Junho의 성격은 매우 외향적이고 친절하다.

09 ⑤는 '내가 그의 전화번호를 넘겨도 되니?'라는 의미이므로 (A) 와 바꾸어 쓸 수 없다.

10 '내가 너에게 도움을 주길 원하니?'라는 의미이므로 would like 를 5형식으로 사용하는 것이 적절하다.

11 ③ 과거를 나타내는 어구인 last week와 현재완료를 함께 쓸 수 없다.

12 Tom은 10년 동안 호텔에서 일해 왔고 모두가 그를 좋아해서 함께 오랫동안 일하기를 원한다는 의미이다. 따라서 현재완료형과 want의 목적격보어로 to부정사를 쓰는 것이 적절하다.

13 주어진 문장에는 3형식과 5형식으로 모두 쓰일 수 있으면서, 동시에 to부정사를 목적어와 목적격보어로 취하는 동사를 넣어야 한다. 따라서 ①, ④가 적절하다.

14 담배를 피우지 말 것을 권하였으므로 to부정사의 부정형으로 표

현해야 한다.

15 책을 2주 전에 샀고, 4월 1일부터 계속 책을 읽고 있으며 2주 동안 읽고 있다고 표현하면 된다.

16 현재 병원에서 일하고 있고 그 기간은 5개월이므로 has worked, 선생님이었던 것은 과거 일이므로 was, force는 목적격보어로 to부정사를 취하므로 to do를 쓴다.

17 엄마는 Hope에게 개에게 음식을 주지 말라고 말하는 중이므로 ④가 옳지 않다.

18 주말마다를 의미한다.

19 과거동사와 과거진행형의 자리를 구별하여 적절하게 쓰는 문제이다.

20 '내가 보이지 않니?'이므로 ④번이 가장 적절하다.

21 아버지가 사라지자 (C) 아버지를 볼 수 없던 가족들은 '어디에 있어요?'라고 묻고, 이에 아버지는 (A) 너희들 바로 앞에 있다고 대답한다. 이 끔찍한 밤이 지나고 (D) 다음날 아침 의사를 찾아가지만 (B) 그 의사는 해줄 수 있는 것이 없다고 말한다.

22 병원으로 가서 의사를 만난 것이므로 came back from을 went to로 고쳐야 글의 흐름이 자연스럽다.

23 '이런 경우를 본 적이 있나요?'라고 묻는 것이 적절하다.

24 아버지는 사라졌지만 아버지가 말하는 것은 들을 수 있었다.

은 동아리에 속해 있습니다. Rosa는 매우 상냥하고 Mike는 외향적인 친구입니다. 아빠는 제게 그들을 저녁식사에 초대하도록 권하셨습니다. 저는 이것을 매우 기대하고 있습니다.

04 조지 워싱턴에 관하여 들어본 적이 있는지를 묻는 질문이므로 현재완료를 써서 표현해야 하며, 미국 제1대 대통령이었던 것은 과거의 일이므로 과거동사를 쓰는 것이 적절하다.

05 오랫동안 가지고 있어 온 코트라는 표현이므로 현재완료를 쓰는 것이 적절하다.

06 과제물을 대신 제출해 주기를 원하는지를 묻는 말이므로 'want+목적어+to V'를 써서 표현하면 된다.

07 먹을 것을 거절하는데 그 이유는 '방금 점심을 먹어서'로 볼 수 있다. 따라서 현재완료의 완료 표현을 사용하여 빈칸을 채우면 된다.

08 ask는 목적격 보어로 to부정사를 취하는 동사이다.

09 Jimmy의 아버지가 보이지 않게 된 것을 가리킨다.

10 Jimmy는 휴대전화를 사용 중에 있고 Hope는 개에게 먹을 것을 주고 있으므로 각자에게 적절한 조언으로는 전화기를 사용하지 않으라는 것과 먹을 것을 그만 주라는 것이다.

11 식탁에서 각자 하고 있던 일을 적으면 된다.

12 ⓒ 부정명령문 뒤에 위치하므로 동사 원형을 쓰는 것이 옳다. ⓓ be동사 뒤에 위치하며 Hope가 하는 행동을 설명해야 하므로 진행형을 쓴다.

13 tell은 to부정사를 목적격보어로 취하는 동사이다.

서술형 실전문제
p.102~103

01 They want to arrive at the train station before 5.
02 It's because the train station isn't very far.
03 (1) English (2) the same club (3) kind
   (4) outgoing (5) invite them over for dinner
04 Have you heard, was
05 I have had
06 Do you want me to hand in this paper for you?
07 I have just had lunch.
08 asked her to repeat it
09 Jimmy's father disappeared and he became invisible.
10 leave your phone, stop feeding
11 Hope는 Smiley에게 음식을 주고 있었고, 엄마는 Hope에게 그러지 말라고 말하고 있었고, Jimmy는 문자를 보내고 있었다.
12 ⓒ feed Smiley ⓓ feeding Smiley
13 to pass me the bread

01 G와 B는 5시 전에 기차역에 도착하고 싶어 한다.

02 B는 기차역이 멀리 떨어져 있지 않기 때문에 늦지 않을 것이라고 확신한다.

03 제 친구들을 소개합니다. 우리 모두는 영어를 매우 좋아하고 같

창의사고력 서술형 문제
p.104

|모범답안|

01 (1) Junho Kim (2) a singer for my school band
   (3) sing beautifully (4) outgoing and friendly
   (5) his phone number
02 (1) I have already had my dinner.
   (2) I have lived in Seoul since 2010.
   (3) I have ever cooked a meal for my family.
   (4) I have found my lost dog.

단원별 모의고사
p.105~108

01 invisible 02 get[win] first place
03 (1) normal (2) active (3) disappear (4) pass
04 (1) There is a library in front of the school.
   (2) I want to invite you over this evening.
   (3) When did you move to Korea?
05 in front of 06 ③ 07 I'm sure (that) she will be a good singer. 08 Because he sings beautifully. 09 I'm sure he will be perfect for your band. 10 he will be a good board cleaner for our class 11 She is hard-working and responsible.

01 반의어 관계이다. 가능한 : 불가능한 = 눈에 보이는 : 눈에 보이지 않는

02 get[win] first place: 1등을 하다

03 normal: 정상적인, active: 활발한, disappear: 사라지다, pass: 건네주다

04 (1) 이때의 school은 건물 자체를 가리키므로 the를 붙여야 한다.
(2) invite you over의 어순에 유의한다.

05 in front of: ~ 앞에서

06 ③ Jane은 Minsu가 어를 유창하게 말한다고 확신하고 있다.

07 접속사 that은 생략할 수 있다.

08 Hojin이가 Junho Kim을 학교 밴드의 가수로 추천한 이유는 노래를 아름답게 부르기 때문이다.

09 be perfect for: ~에 꼭 맞다

11 active: 활발한, helpful: 도움이 되는, honest: 정직한, hard-working: 근면한, responsible: 책임감 있는

12 학교생활이 어떠한지 물어보고 있으므로 'how do you like ~?: ~가 어떻습니까?'가 알맞다.

13 Sue, Rosa 그리고 Mike는 모두 어를 좋아하고 같은 동아리라는 공통점을 갖고 있다.

14 주어진 문장의 to부정사는 목적격보어로 쓰으므로 ⑤번이 적절하다. ① to부정사의 부사적 용법으로 '~하기 위해서'라고 해석된다. ② something을 수식하는 형용사로 쓰인 to부정사이다. ③, ④ 각각 prefer 와 hope의 목적어로 쓰인 to부정사이다.

15 5형식으로 쓰일 때에는 to부정사를 목적격보어로 받아줄 수 있는 동사이자, 도움을 요청할 때 쓰이는 동사는 ask이다.

16 ① has arrived → arrived, ③ since 생략, ④ not to use, ⑤ to be careful로 고쳐야 옳은 문장이다.

17 은행에 갔지만 몇 분 전에 돌아왔으므로 '막 돌아왔어'라고 표현하는 것이 적절하다.

18 오랫동안 보아 오지 못한 것이므로 현재완료를 사용해야 하며, want는 to부정사를 목적격보어로 취하는 동사이므로 to leave를 써야 한다.

19 ② pretty normal은 꽤 평범하다는 의미이므로 '특별한 것처럼 들린다'는 의미인 ⓑ 대신 쓸 수 없다

20 (A) weekend 앞에는 전치사 on을 쓰며, (B) 좁은 공간 앞에는 전치사 at을 쓴다. (C) 동사 give를 3형식으로 전환할 때 사용하는 전치사는 to이다.

21 for는 기간을 이끈다. 특정 시점을 이끄는 것은 since이다.

22 주어진 문장은 경험을 나타내는 현재완료이다. ①, ②번은 결과, ④, ⑤번은 계속으로 쓴다.

23 글쓴이의 아버지가 사라지기 위해 마술을 부린 것이 아니고, 보이지 않는 동안 말할 수는 있었다. 또한 아버지가 빵을 건네달라는 말에 누구도 반응을 보이지 않았으며 의사는 아버지를 돕길 원하지 않는 것이 아니라 도울 수 없다고 하였다.

24 글쓴이의 가족은 다음날 아침에 무엇을 했나요?

25 주어진 문장의 대명사 her가 가리키는 문장 뒤에 나와야 하며, 내용상 Hope가 울고 엄마도 함께 울면서 모두 눈물바다를 이루었다고 보는 것이 적절하다.

26 아빠가 다시 나타나기를 원한다고 쓰면 된다.

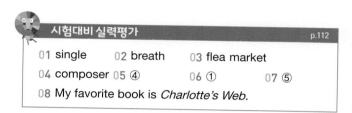

The Music Goes On

시험대비 실력평가
p.112

01 single 02 breath 03 flea market
04 composer 05 ④ 06 ① 07 ⑤
08 My favorite book is *Charlotte's Web*.

01 주어진 단어는 반의어 관계를 나타낸다. multiple: 다수의,
single: 단 하나의
02 당신이 폐로 들이마시고 다시 내뱉는 공기를 가리키는 말은
breath(숨, 호흡)이다.
03 중고 물건들을 낮은 가격에 판매하는 야외 시장을 가리키는 말
은 flea market(벼룩시장)이다.
04 곡을 쓰는 사람을 가리키는 말은 composer(작곡가)이다.
05 ④번의 face는 동사로 '~을 향하다'를 의미한다.
06 주어진 문장에서 fan은 '팬, 열렬한 애호가'를 가리킨다. ②, ③
번의 fan은 '부채', ④, ⑤번은 '선풍기'를 의미한다.
07 • 나는 수표에 당신의 서명이 필요합니다. • 당신은 계약서 두 장
에 당신의 서명을 적어야 합니다. • 그는 종이 밑에 그의 서명을
하고 있었다.
08 favorite: 가장 좋아하는

서술형 시험대비
p.113

01 composer 02 creation 03 audience
04 (1) down (2) breath (3) audience
05 (1) The flea market will be held in the park.
  (2) She played the piano without sheet music
06 (1) press down (2) build up speed (3) at once
06 (A) at (B) up (C) in

01 teach: 가르치다, teacher: 교사, compose: 작곡하다,
composer: 작곡가
02 새롭거나 전에 존재하지 않았던 무언가를 만들어 내는 과정이나
행위를 가리키는 말은 creation(창조)이다.
03 무언가를 보거나 듣기 위해 모인 사람들의 무리를 가리키는 말은
audience(관객, 청중)이다.
04 down: 우울한, breath: 숨, 호흡, audience: 관객, 청중
06 press down: ~을 누르다, build up speed: 속도를 높이다,

at once: 한꺼번에
07 at once: 한꺼번에, build up: 점점 높이다, in person: 직접

Conversation
교과서

핵심 Check
p.114~115

1 (1) Which animal (2) favorite subject (3) love
2 (1) Why / Because
 (2) the reason why / The reason I want to visit it
 (3) the reason why you want to move / because of

교과서 대화문 익히기

Check(√) True or False
p.116

1 T 2 T 3 T 4 F

교과서 확인학습
p.118~119

Listen & Speak 1 A
How's / Which book / best

Listen & Speak 1 B
what are you going to do / a big fan / Which member
/ drummer / I can't wait

Listen & Speak 1 C
Which sport / tennis, exciting

Listen & Speak 2 A
Why / flea market / why don't you

Listen & Speak 2 B
why / for / Where / a paper folding class / the
perfect gift

Listen & Speak 2 C
Which country / Why do you want to / Because

Real Life Talk
with the school radio show / what's your favorite
band / Definitely / Which song do you like best /
Why do you like it / Because, when I'm down

19

01 ⑤　　　　　　02 ①
03 (A) How's　(B) interesting　(C) Which　04 ⑤

01 ①번~④번 모두 선호하는 것을 나타내지만, ⑤번의 'I would like to ~'는 '~하고 싶다'는 의미 를 나타낸다.

02 이어지는 대답으로 이유를 설명하고 있으므로 'Why'가 적절하다.

03 (A) '독서 동아리는 어때?'라고 안부를 묻는 질문으로 How가 적절하다. (B) interested: 흥 미를 갖고 있는, interesting: 흥미로운, (C) 가장 좋아하는 책이 어느 것인지를 묻고 있으므로 Which가 적절하다.

04 *Charlotte's Web* 은 Sumin이 가장 좋아하는 책의 이름이다.

01 I like tennis best.　　　　02 ⑤
03 drummer　04 ②　　05 ①　　06 Then why don't you join me this Saturday?　07 He is going to bring some old clothes to the flea market.
08 ②　　09 ③　　10 ⓒ → Definitely, ⓔ → Because　11 Hey Jude　12 ⑤

01 어느 스포츠를 가장 좋아하는지 질문하고 있으므로 이에 대한 대답으로 테니스를 가장 좋아한다는 답변이 이어져야 한다.

02 ⑤번을 제외한 나머지는 이번 주 토요일 계획에 대해 질문하는 표현이다.

03 드럼을 연주하는 사람을 가리키는 말은 drummer이다.

04 ⓒ는 기대감을 표현하고 있으므로 ②와 바꾸어 쓸 수 있다. look forward to: ~을 고대하다, 기대하다

05 ① Jiho와 Amy가 Blue Sky의 팬 모임에서 무엇을 할지는 알 수 없다.

07 소년은 벼룩시장에 그의 헌옷들을 가져올 것이다.

08 주어진 문장 다음에 이어지는 말로 종이꽃을 직접 만들었다는 말이 와야 자연스러우므로 (B)가 적절하다.

09 ③ Tom이 꽃을 만들기 위해 교실에서 종이를 가져왔다는 설명은 바르지 않다.

10 ⓒ는 '단연, 틀림없이'를 의미하는 부사 Definitely가 적절하다. ⓔ는 뒤에 절이 이어지므로 Because가 적절하다.

11 Mina와 Mr. Smith는 Hey Jude를 들을 것이다.

12 Mina가 Hey Jude 를 들을 때 어떻게 느끼는지는 알 수 없다.

01 Which sport do you like best?
02 Because I want to visit my friend.

03 (1) Mr. Smith　(2) music
　(3) The Beatles　(4) *Hey Jude*
　(5) it makes him feel better when he is down
04 He made them for his mom's birthday
05 I'm taking a paper folding class these days.

03 오늘 라디오 쇼를 들었니? 라디오 쇼에 특별한 손님이 있었다. 그는 우리 영어 선생님인 Mr. Smith였다. Mina와 Mr. Smith는 음악에 대해 이야기했다. Mr. Smith는 그가 가장 좋아하는 밴드는 The Beatles라고 하셨다. 그들의 노래들 중, 그는 Hey Jude 를 가장 좋아했다. 왜냐하면 기분이 안 좋을 때 기분을 좋게 만들어주기 때문이다. 그 노래는 아름다웠다. 나도 그 노래가 매우 좋았다.

04 Tom은 그의 어머니의 생일을 위해서 많은 종이 꽃을 만들었다.

Grammar

1 (1) is covered　(2) was asked
2 (1) arrive, will call　(2) come, will be　(3) if, will go

01 (1) born → was born
　(2) for her → to her
　(3) will leave → leave
　(4) visits → will visit
02 (1) want　(2) are caused　(3) solve
　(4) was invited　(5) will miss
03 (1) How is glass made?
　(2) I will be employed here.
　(3) If you run, I will follow you.
　(4) Let me know if you will bring some food.

01 (1) 태어나다는 'be born'으로 표현한다. (2) 직접목적어를 주어로 한 4형식 수동태는 간접목적어에 특정 전치사를 부여한다. send는 전치사 to를 사용한다. (3) 조건의 부사절에서 현재시제로 미래를 표현한다. (4) if가 명사절을 이끌고 있으므로 내용에 맞게 시제를 바꾸어 주는 것이 옳다.

02 (1) 조건절에서는 현재형으로 미래를 나타낸다. (2) 사고는 유발되는 것이므로 수동태를 쓰는 것이 옳다. (3) 문제를 해결하는 주체가 You이므로 능동태를 쓴다. (4) 파티에 초대되었지만 가지 않았다는 의미이므로 수동태가 옳다. (5) 조건절은 현재형

으로 미래를 나타내지만 주절은 미래를 나타낼 경우 미래시제를 써야 한다.

03 (1) is made: 만들어지다 (2) employ: 고용하다 (3) follow: 따라가다 (4) let+목적어+원형부정사: 목적어가 ~하게 하다

01 ④   02 ④   03 ③   04 If you are invited to the party, will you go there? 05 ②
06 ④   07 ③   08 I don't know what we will do if we don't find the way.   09 ③
10 ⓐⓑⓓ, ⓒⓔ   11 Unless   12 ③
13 ④   14 I wasn't told about the class meeting by anybody.   15 ⑤   16 ②, ④
17 If a bike is given to you, what will you do?
18 ④   19 ②   20 ④   21 was invented by King Sejong   22 If I meet you in person, I will ask you many questions.   23 is not[isn't] used (by you), will not get clean   24 will hold → will be held

01 지난주에 부쳐진 것이므로 과거시제 수동태를 쓰는 것이 옳다.
02 ④ 구동사의 수동태에서 'by+행위자'를 생략하기 쉬우므로 이에 유의한다. brought up by my grandparents라고 써야 한다.
03 ③번은 '~인지 아닌지'로 해석되는 명사절을 이끄는 접속사 if이다. 나머지는 모두 조건절을 이끄는 if이다.
04 초대받는다는 것을 조건으로 하는 문장이므로 if절은 현재시제로 쓰고, 주절은 미래시제를 사용한다.
05 ① be filled with: ~으로 가득 차 있다 ③ 내일 계획이 있는지를 묻는 명사절이므로 내용과 시제를 일치시켜 will meet으로 써야 한다. ④ 5형식 동사의 목적격보어가 원형부정사인 경우 수동태를 만들 때 to부정사로 쓴다. 따라서 made to do가 옳다. ⑤ make는 직접목적어를 주어로 한 수동태에서 간접목적어에 전치사 for를 쓰는 동사이므로 for me로 쓰는 것이 옳다.
06 ④ 현재시제로 미래를 표현하는 조건의 부사절이므로 give를 쓰는 것이 옳다.
07 by 이외에 다른 전치사를 쓰는 수동태 문제이다. be covered with: ~로 덮이다 be pleased with: ~에 기뻐하다
08 부사절 if는 현재시제로 미래를 표현한다.
09 주어진 문장을 수동태로 만드는 문제이다. The child는 단수 주어이고, 본 문장의 시제가 과거형 saw이므로 수동태를 만들 때 was seen으로 쓰고, 목적격보어 playing은 그대로 써주면 된다.
10 ⓐ, ⓑ, ⓓ는 부사절을 이끄는 if이고 ⓒ, ⓔ는 명사절을 이끄는 if이다.
11 if ... not은 unless와 같다.

12 ③ 건물이 디자인된 것이냐고 묻고 있으므로 수동태를 써야 한다. 따라서 Did가 아닌 Was를 쓰는 것이 옳다.
13 ④번의 빈칸에는 about이 들어가고, 나머지는 모두 with가 공통으로 들어간다. ⑤ fill A with B: A를 B로 채우다
14 주어진 문장의 의미는 '누구도 나에게 학급회의에 관하여 말하지 않았다'이므로 '나는 학급회의에 관하여 듣지 못했다'로 쓰면 된다.
15 빈칸이 이끄는 절은 현재형이지만, 주절은 미래이므로 빈칸에는 시간이나 조건의 부사절이 들어가야 한다. 따라서 양보절 접속사인 ⑤번은 적절하지 않다.
16 밑줄 친 offer는 4형식 동사로 직접목적어를 주어로 한 수동태에서는 간접목적어에 전치사 to를 부여하는 동사이다. 따라서 ②, ④번이 옳다.
17 전치사 to를 활용해야 하므로 직접목적어를 주어로 한 수동태를 써야 한다.
18 직접목적어를 주어로 할 때 간접목적어에 전치사 for를 부여하는 동사는 ④번이다. 나머지 동사들은 모두 to를 사용한다.
19 Harry에 의하여 사진이 찍힌 것이므로 ②번이 옳다.
20 ④ 시간이나 조건의 부사절에서는 현재시제가 미래를 대신하지만, 주절에서는 미래시제로 표현하는 것이 옳다. 따라서 do가 아닌 will이 옳다. ⑤ go (and) see 또는 go (to) see
21 한글을 누가 발명했는지 말해달라고 하였으므로 한글은 세종대왕에 의해 발명되었다고 답하면 된다.
22 in person: 직접, 몸소
23 조건절을 수동태로 만드는 문제이다. soap은 단수 주어이고, 조건절은 현재가 미래를 대신하므로 is not used를 쓰는 것이 내용과 일치한다.
24 파티는 개최되는 것이므로 수동태를 써야 옳다.

01 If the machine is used by people, they will be happy.
02 was written by
03 was made to feel comfortable by his sister
04 (1) get up (2) will plant (3) was stung
05 The police were given the important evidence. / The important evidence was given to the police.
06 If you need money, I will lend you some. / If you want those pictures, you can have them. / If you are busy now, I will call you later.
07 I was really moved by Liszt's music.
08 ⓐ it rains ⓑ will take ⓒ was brought for me
09 was invented / was surprised / is surrounded / was divided / will build
10 If there is a fire, the alarm will ring. / If you want

21

me to help you, I will help you. / If I don't feel well tomorrow, I will stay at home.

11 arrives, will see

12 Unless, will miss / will be very surprised / is crowded with / will go

01 기계가 사용되는 것이므로 수동태로 쓰는 것이 옳으며, 조건절은 현재시제로, 주절은 미래시제로 표현하면 된다.

02 로미오와 줄리엣은 누가 썼는지에 관한 질문이므로 셰익스피어에 의해 쓰여진 것이라고 답하면 된다.

03 목적어를 주어로 하고 있으므로 수동태로 만들어 준다. 목적격보어가 원형부사사이므로 to부정사가 되는 것을 잊지 말자.

04 (1) 조건절이므로 현재시제 (2) 명사절 접속사 if가 이끄는 절이므로 내용과 시점을 일치시켜 미래시제 (3) 벌에 의해 쏘인 것이므로 수동태를 쓴다.

05 4형식 동사의 수동태를 묻는 문제이다. 동사 give는 직접목적어를 주어로 하는 수동태에서 간접목적어에 전치사 to를 붙인다. the police는 복수 취급하므로 be동사는 were가 된다. by somebody는 생략할 수 있다.

06 네가 돈이 필요하다면 내가 좀 빌려줄게. / 네가 저 그림들을 원한다면, 가져도 좋아. / 네가 지금 바쁘다면 내가 나중에 전화할게.

07 move: 감동을 주다

08 ⓐ 조건절의 동사는 현재시제로 미래를 나타낼 수 있으므로 it rains를 쓰는 것이 옳다. ⓑ 내일 우산을 가지고 갈 것이라는 의미이므로 주절은 미래형을 쓴다. ⓒ 주어가 우산이므로 수동태를 쓰며, 4형식 수동태이므로 간접목적어에 for를 붙인다.

09 전구는 1879년 Thomas Edison에 의해 발명되었다. / 나는 어제 Jane이 회의에 올 것이라고 기대하지 않았지만 그녀가 그곳에 있었다. 나는 그녀를 보고 놀랐다. / 섬은 물에 의해 둘러싸여 있다. / 지난 학기에 그 수업 규모가 너무 커서 수업이 두 개로 나뉘었다. / 건설 비용이 비싸지 않으면 그들은 새 기숙사를 지을 것이다.

10 feel well: 건강하다

11 시간이나 조건의 부사절에서 현재가 미래를 대신하므로 다음 주에 파리에 도착하는 조건은 현재형으로 표현하고, 만나게 될 것이라는 주절은 미래형으로 표현한다.

12 miss: 놓치다 be surprised: 놀라다 be crowded with: ~으로 붐비다

교과서
Reading

🔖 확인문제   p.132

1 T   2 F   3 T   4 T   5 F

📎 확인문제   p.133

1 T   2 T   3 F   4 T   5 T   6 F

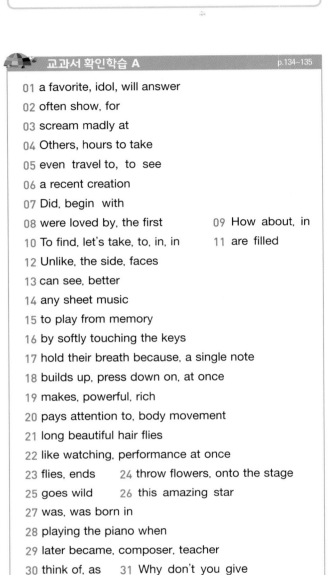

교과서 확인학습 A   p.134~135

01 a favorite, idol, will answer

02 often show, for

03 scream madly at

04 Others, hours to take

05 even travel to, to see

06 a recent creation

07 Did, begin with

08 were loved by, the first   09 How about, in

10 To find, let's take, to, in, in   11 are filled

12 Unlike, the side, faces

13 can see, better

14 any sheet music

15 to play from memory

16 by softly touching the keys

17 hold their breath because, a single note

18 builds up, press down on, at once

19 makes, powerful, rich

20 pays attention to, body movement

21 long beautiful hair flies

22 like watching, performance at once

23 flies, ends   24 throw flowers, onto the stage

25 goes wild   26 this amazing star

27 was, was born in

28 playing the piano when

29 later became, composer, teacher

30 think of, as   31 Why don't you give

32 like, will love, original

교과서 확인학습 B   p.136~137

1 Do you have a favorite K-pop idol? Many students will answer, "Yes."

2 These students often show great love for their stars.

3 Some scream madly at concerts.

4 Others wait hours to take pictures of their stars.

5 Some students even travel to another city to see their favorite stars.

6 Are idols a recent creation? No way!

7 Did idols begin with The Beatles in the 1960's?

8 They were loved by many, but they were not the first.

9 How about Elvis Presley in the 1950's? Not even close.

10 To find the answer, let's take a time machine to a concert hall in Vienna in 1845.

11 All the seats are filled

12 Unlike other concerts, the side of the piano faces the audience.

13 This way, the audience can see the handsome 185cm pianist better.

14 He doesn't have any sheet music with him.

15 He begins to play from memory.

16 He starts slowly by softly touching the keys.

17 All the people hold their breath because they don't want to miss a single note.

18 He builds up speed, and his long fingers press down on many keys at once.

19 This makes the music very powerful and rich.

20 The audience pays attention to his every little body movement.

21 His long beautiful hair flies everywhere.

22 It's like watching a piano and ballet performance at once.

23 Time flies and the concert ends.

24 People scream and throw flowers and pieces of clothing onto the stage.

25 The concert hall goes wild!

26 Who was this amazing star?

27 His name was Franz Liszt and he was born in 1811 in Hungary.

28 He first started playing the piano when he was seven.

29 Liszt later became a great pianist, composer and teacher.

30 But many people think of him as the first idol.

31 Why don't you give his music a listen?

32 If you like today's idols, you will love the original idol.

시험대비 실력평가

p.138~141

01 ③ 02 ③ 03 are asked, will answer 04 were loved by 05 ③
06 ② 07 The writer wants to go to a concert hall in Vienna in 1845. 08 ① 09 ③
10 He begins to play from memory. 11 ④
12 ④ 13 They were loved by many people.
14 ② 15 All the seats are filled. 16 The

---

side of the piano faces the audience. 17 ③
18 ③ 19 ② 20 ④ 21 ④
22 are thrown 23 Great love for their stars is often showed by these students. 24 ③

01 ③ 몇몇 학생들이 콘서트에서 마구 소리를 지르는 것일 뿐, 미치는 것은 아니다.

02 ①, ④, ⑤번은 목적격보어로, ②번은 a book을 수식하는 형용사로 사용된 to부정사이다. 밑줄 친 ⓐ는 '~하기 위해서'로 해석되는 부사로 쓰인 to부정사이므로 ③번이 옳다.

03 학생들이 가장 좋아하는 K-pop 아이돌이 있느냐는 질문을 받으면 "네"라고 대답할 것이다.

04 많은 사람들에게 사랑을 받았던 것이므로 수동태를 쓰는 것이 옳다.

05 최초의 아이돌이 누구인지에 관하여 이야기하고 있다.

06 최초의 아이돌을 알아보기 위하여 타임머신을 타고 가보자고 하였으므로 뒤에 이어질 내용으로는 ②가 옳다.

07 글쓴이는 타임머신을 타고 어디로 가기를 원하나요?

08 ①번 뒤 문장에 이어지는 This way는 주어진 문장을 가리킨다.

09 연도 앞에는 전치사 in을 쓴다.

10 from memory: 외워서, 기억을 더듬어

11 어떤 종류의 대답을 찾기를 원하는지는 알 수 없다.

12 당신이 자물쇠에 꽂는 특수한 모양의 금속 조각은 '열쇠'이다. ⓓ는 '건반'으로 사용된 key이다.

13 수동태로 바꾸기 위해서는 능동태의 목적어인 them을 주격으로 바꾸고, 시제가 과거이므로 were loved로 고친 후, by 이하에 행위자를 넣어 만들면 된다.

14 최초의 아이돌이 언제 시작되었는지에 관한 질문이므로 ②번이 옳다.

15 밑줄 친 문장은 모든 좌석이 찼다는 의미이므로 fill을 수동태로 하여 같은 문장을 만들 수 있다.

16 질문: 콘서트는 다른 콘서트들과 어떻게 다른가요?

17 연주 속도를 점점 올리면서 강력하고 풍부한 음악을 만들었다고 하였으므로 ③번은 옳지 않다.

18 ③번 이후에 나오는 This가 가리키는 것은 피아니스트가 연주 속도를 점점 올리면서 모든 건반을 한 번에 누르는 것을 의미한다. 따라서 ③번에 들어가는 것이 옳다.

19 청중들은 꽃과 옷을 던지며 연주자를 향해 열광하고 있다. '열광하다'는 go wild이다.

20 발레 공연과 피아노 연주를 한 번에 보는 것 같다는 말이 나와 있을 뿐, 발레 공연을 본다는 것은 어디에도 없다.

21 연주자의 사소한 움직임에도 주의를 기울인다고 하였으므로 ④번은 옳지 않다.

22 청중들이 꽃을 던졌다고 했으므로 꽃이 주어로 올 경우 수동태를 쓰는 것이 옳다.

23 목적어인 great love for their stars를 주어로 두고, 이 주어부의 핵심 명사가 great love로 단수이므로 be동사를 is로 하여 수동태를 만들면 된다.

24 최초의 아이돌이 누구인지 알아보기 위해 타임머신을 탈 것을 권하고 있다. 따라서 ③번이 가장 옳다.

서술형 시험대비
p.142~143

01 Some scream madly at concerts. **02** waiting for their stars to take pictures of them **03** Idols were not[weren't] created recently. **04** the first idol **05** let's take a time machine **06** 다른 콘서트들과는 달리 피아노 측면이 청중을 향해 있는 것 **07** they don't want to miss a single note. **08** He plays from memory. **09** This makes the music very powerful and rich. **10** Vienna, different, faced, see, played, memory, powerful **11** Flowers and pieces of clothing are thrown onto the stage. **12** ⓓ → movement **13** (A) touching (B) watching (C) goes **14** is held at the concert hall / sounds powerful and rich

01 madly: 미친 듯이, 마구

02 몇몇 학생들은 그들의 스타 사진을 찍기 위해서 스타를 기다리느라 몇 시간을 소비한다.

03 아이돌은 최근 창작물이 아니라고 하였으므로 create의 수동태를 쓰면 된다.

04 최초의 아이돌이라는 의미이다.

06 다른 콘서트들과는 달리 피아노가 청중을 향해 있는 것을 의미한다.

07 청중들이 숨죽이는 이유는 단 하나의 음도 놓치기를 원치 않아서이다.

08 피아니스트는 악보 없이 어떻게 연주하는가?

09 make를 'make+목적어+목적격보어'로 이루어진 5형식으로 사용하였다.

10 어제 공연에 대한 기사이므로 시제에 유의하여 빈칸을 채운다. face: ~을 마주보다

11 질문은 '무대 위로 무엇이 던져지고 있는가?'이다.

12 every 뒤에는 단수명사가 온다.

13 (A), (B)는 각각 전치사의 목적어로 사용되어야 하므로 동명사 형태로 빈칸을 채우는 것이 옳으며, the concert hall은 단수이므로 (C)는 goes를 쓰는 것이 옳다.

14 피아노 콘서트는 콘서트홀에서 개최되며, 음악은 강력하고 풍부하게 들린다.

영역별 핵심문제
p.145~149

01 ⑤　　**02** signature　　**03** ②　　**04** (1) sheet music (2) went wild (3) in person　　**05** ④
06 It cheers me up.　　**07** Which book do you like best?　　**08** ⑤　　**09** He plays the drums.
10 flea market　　**11** They are going to sell old clothes at the flea market.　　**12** ③
13 ③　　**14** ③, ⑤　　**15** ②　　**16** ②
17 didn't play, was canceled[cancelled]　　**18** ③
19 ④　　**20** ④　　**21** is taken care of by you　　**22** ③　　**23** ④　　**24** I was not allowed to go to the park alone by my mom.
25 ④　　**26** ④　　**27** ⑤　　**28** ③
29 ②　　**30** 연주 속도를 점점 올리고, 많은 건반을 한 번에 누르는 것　　**31** at once　　**32** ④

01 보기와 ① ~ ④번까지의 단어들은 형용사와 부사의 관계를 나타내지만 ⑤번은 명사와 형용사의 관계를 나타낸다.

02 예를 들어, 편지 끝에 당신이 보통 적는 당신의 이름을 가리키는 말은 signature(서명)이다.

03 unlike: ~와 달리

04 sheet music: 악보, go wild: 열광하다, in person: 직접

05 주어진 문장에서 miss는 '놓치다'를 의미하며 이와 같은 의미로 쓰인 것은 ④번이다. ①번은 '이해하지 못하다', ②, ③, ⑤번은 '그리워하다'를 의미한다.

06 cheer up: 힘을 북돋우다

08 주어진 문장은 '우리와 함께 가고 싶니?'라고 질문하고 있으므로 이에 대한 대답이 이어지는 (E)번이 적절하다.

09 Mike는 Blue Sky 밴드에서 드럼을 연주한다.

10 flea market: 벼룩시장

11 그들은 함께 이번 주 토요일에 벼룩시장에서 헌 옷을 팔 예정이다.

12 (A)는 기분이 좋지 않음을 뜻한다. ③ satisfied: 만족스러운

13 The Beatles의 대부분의 노래를 좋아하는 사람은 Mina가 아닌 Mr. Smith이다.

14 빈칸이 이끄는 절은 현재시제이지만 주절은 미래이므로, 빈칸에는 시간이나 조건의 부사절이 들어가야 한다.

15 disappear는 자동사이므로 수동태가 될 수 없다.

16 오늘 밤에 늦게 온다면 기다리지 않을 것이라는 의미로. 조건의 부사절이므로 현재형으로 미래를 나타낼 수 있다. 따라서 ②번이 가장 적절하다.

17 축구를 하는 주체는 we이므로 능동태를 써야 하며, 경기는 취소가 되는 것이므로 수동태를 쓰는 것이 옳다.

18 ③ 능동태 동사의 시제가 과거이므로 was recorded를 쓰는 것이 옳다.

19 be broken: 고장 나다 repair: 수리하다

20 happen은 자동사이므로 수동태로 쓰일 수 없다.

21 relieved: 안도한 take care of: ~을 돌보다

22 ③번은 명사절을 이끄는 접속사 if이다.

23 be known to: ~에게 알려지다 be known as: ~로 알려져 있다

24 엄마는 내가 혼자 공원에 가는 것을 허락하지 않으셨다.

25 스타의 사진을 찍기 위하여 몇 시간을 기다린다고 하였으므로 ④는 옳지 않다.

26 ① (형) 고른, 반반한 ② (형) 차분한 ③ (비교급 강조 부사) 한층, 훨씬 ④ (부) 심지어 ~하기도 ⑤ (형) 공정한, 공평한

27 (A) 앞에서 Some으로 불특정한 학생들을 지칭하였고, 스타 사진을 찍기 위해 몇 시간씩 기다리는 학생들 외에도, 스타를 보기 위해 다른 도시로 이동하는 학생들의 사례도 제시되고 있으므로 the others가 아닌 others를 쓰는 것이 옳다. (B) 단수 명사 city를 수식할 수 있는 것은 another이다.

28 아이돌은 최근에 만들어진 것이 아니고, 비틀즈는 세계 최초의 아이돌이 아니다. 엘비스 프레슬리가 비틀즈를 좋아했는지는 알 수 없으며 1960년대에 아이돌이 매우 인기 있었는지도 알 수 없다.

29 밑줄 친 ⓐ는 to부정사가 부사로 쓰였으며 '~하기 위해서'라는 의미의 목적을 나타낸다. 따라서 ②가 옳다.

30 This는 지시대명사로 앞 문장을 가리킨다.

31 피아노와 발레 공연을 한 번에 보는 것 같았다는 표현이 가장 적절하다.

32 청중들이 연주자의 몸짓에도 집중했다고 나와 있을 뿐, 어떻게 움직였는지는 나와 있지 않다.

단원별 예상문제
p.150~153

01 ③　　02 I'm very fond of tennis.　　03 (1) pay attention to　(2) paper folding　(3) from memory
04 (1) I bought the shoes in the flea market.
　(2) The last runner began to build up the speed.
　(3) The driver pressed down on the brake.
05 ④　　06 ⑤　　07 Which fruit do you like best?　　08 (C) → (E) → (B) → (D) → (A)　09 She thought it was fun.　　10 Her favorite book is *Charlotte's Web*.　　11 ③　　12 will disappoint, will be disappointed with[in, at]
13 ④　　14 If it snows, the roads will be closed.
15 ③　　16 ④　　17 is blocked / will call
18 ④　　19 ④　　20 ②　　21 ④
22 The audience pays attention to his every little body movement.　　23 performance
24 ③　　25 other concerts, the side of the piano faced the audience

01 • 정부는 같은 위험을 마주할 것이다. • 모나리자의 얼굴에는 눈썹이 없다. • 왜 너는 울상이니?

02 be fond of: ~을 좋아하다

03 pay attention to: ~에 주의를 기울이다,
paper folding: 종이 접기,
from memory: 기억해서, 외워서

05 이어지는 대답으로 가장 좋아하는 노래에 대한 설명이 이어져야 하므로 (D)가 적절하다.

06 ⑤번을 제외한 나머지는 모두 노래를 함께 들을 것을 제안하는 표현이다.

08 (C) 이번 주 토요일의 계획 질문 → (E) Blue Sky 팬모임에 갈 계획을 설명 → (B) 반응 및 본인도 팬임을 설명 → (D) 가장 좋아하는 멤버 질문 → (A) 대답

09 Sumin은 독서 동아리에 대해 재미있어 한다.

10 Sumin의 가장 좋아하는 책은 *Charlotte's Web*이다.

11 ① he → him,
② did → was,
④ locking → locked,
⑤ will not change → will not be changed

12 disappoint는 '실망시키다'는 의미로, '네가 포기하면 너는 나를 실망시킬 것이다', '네가 포기하면 나는 너에게 실망할 것이다'로 각각 능동태와 수동태를 활용하여 쓰면 된다.

13 시간 • 조건의 부사절에서 현재시제로 미래를 나타낸다. 따라서 rains로 쓰는 것이 옳다.

15 ⓑ '길을 잃다'는 be lost로 표현한다. ⓓ 누군가와 결혼한 상태임을 표현할 때에는 'be married to'라고 쓰는 것이 옳다.

16 ①번은 목적격보어가 원형부정사인 5형식 동사의 수동태이므로 to clean으로 고쳐야 하며, ②번은 아버지에 의해 강아지라고 불리는 것이므로 수동태 was called, ③번은 불이 꺼졌는지를 물어보는 수동태 의문문이므로 주어 the lights에 맞추어 Were, ⑤ 조건절 시제는 현재형으로 미래를 나타내므로 throw를 쓰는 것이 옳다.

17 block: ~을 막다 drain: 배수관 plumber: 배관공

18 단 하나의 음도 놓치기를 원치 않기 때문에 숨죽이고 있다고 보는 것이 옳다. 따라서 ⓓ는 don't want이다.

19 연주자는 천천히 연주를 시작했다. 따라서 ④번은 옳지 않다.

20 밑줄 친 (A)는 5형식으로 쓰였다. 5형식은 '동사+목적어+ 목적격보어'의 형태로 목적격보어가 목적어를 설명한다. ①, ④, ⑤번은 3형식으로, ③번은 4형식으로 쓰였다.

21 breathe는 '호흡하다'라는 의미의 동사이다. 명사형 breath를 써야 한다.

23 누군가가 노래를 부르거나 춤을 추거나 악기를 연주함으로써 청중을 즐겁게 할 때 사용되는 단어는 '공연'이다.

24 ① 다른 콘서트들과는 달리 피아노 측면이 청중을 향해 있다고 하였다. ② 연주자는 악보 없이 연주하고 있다. ④ 시간이 빠르게 흘러간다고 하였으므로 청중들이 지루함을 느꼈다고 볼 수 없다. ⑤ 발레 공연은 보여주지 않는다.

01 Definitely   02 They are going to listen to *Hey Jude*.
03 Which song do you like best?   04 Some mistakes were made by her. / Lots of cookies were made for me by my friends. / I am always made to laugh by Jason.   05 find, will tell
06 don't have any homework to do, will go to a movie   07 I have enough apples, I wll bake / is located   08 were not written by   09 It's like watching a piano and ballet performance at once.
10 He is thought of as the first idol by many people.
11 will like → like   12 other concerts
13 be seen better by them

01 무언가가 진실이거나 이에 대해 의심이 없다는 것을 강조하는 방식을 가리키는 말은 'definitely(단연, 틀림없이)'이다.

02 그들은 함께 Hey Jude를 들을 것이다.

04 3, 4, 5형식으로 쓰일 수 있는 동사 make를 수동태로 만드는 문제이다. 첫 번째 문장은 3형식 동사로 쓰인 make이고, 두 번째 문장은 4형식 동사로 쓰인 make이다. 직접목적어를 주어로 한 수동태를 만들어 간접목적어에 for를 붙인다. 마지막 문장은 목적격보어로 원형부정사를 취하는 5형식 make로, 수동태를 만들 때 목적격보어를 to부정사화 하는 것을 유의해야 한다.

05 시간 • 조건의 부사절에서 현재시제가 미래를 대신한다는 것에 유의하여 빈칸을 채운다.

06 영화 보러 갈 시간이 있느냐는 물음에 아직 숙제가 있는지 없는지 모른다며, 만약 할 숙제가 없다면 함께 가겠다고 답할 수 있다.

07 be located in: ~에 위치하다

08 수동태의 핵심 주어가 복수명사인 the letters이므로 복수 동사 were를 써서 수동태를 만드는 것에 유의한다.

09 like는 전치사이므로 watch를 동명사 형태로 만들어야 한다.

10 think of A as B: A를 B라고 여기다

11 조건의 부사절에서 현재가 미래를 대신한다.

12 others는 other concerts를 대신하는 대명사이다.

13 조동사의 수동태를 묻고 있다. 조동사 뒤의 be동사는 원형으로 써야 한다.

|모범답안|

01 (1) so many paper flowers   (2) beautiful
    (3) a paper folding class   (4) how
02 (1) The cake was baked by Tom yesterday.
    (2) This book was read by me many times.
    (3) The picture was drawn by my brother three years ago.
    (4) The bread was passed to my dad by me.

    (5) The doll was made for the girl by him.
03 (1) If it is sunny tomorrow, I will go on a picnic.
    (2) If it is windy tomorrow, I'll wear my coat.
    (3) If it rains tomorrow, I will stay at home and watch a movie.
    (4) If it is hot tomorrow, I will have lots of ice cream.

01 오늘 나는 Tom의 선물을 받았을 때 매우 행복했다. 그는 나를 위해 매우 많은 종이꽃을 만들어 주었다. 매우 아름다워 보였다. 요즘 그는 종이접기 수업을 듣고 있다. 그는 수업에서 그것들을 어떻게 만드는지 배운 것 같다. 나는 그가 매우 자랑스러웠다.

01 Which country do you want to visit?
02 (1) Which novel is the most popular?
    (2) How did you prepare for your role?
    (3) Why did King Sejong invent Hangeul?
03 (1) faced   (2) performance   (3) throw   (4) invented
04 ②   05 (D) → (B) → (E) → (C) → (A)
06 Why do you want to visit Canada?   07 ⓓ → these   08 ③   09 Which member do you like best?   10 ⑤   11 (B) → (D) → (C) → (E) → (A)   12 ④   13 ①
14 ④   15 you lend me, I will pay, back
16 ⑤   17 was seen to stop (by us)
18 ③   19 ②   20 ⑤   21 you hold your breath, you won't miss a single note
22 ④   23 ⑤   24 ⑤   25 Why don't you give his music a listen?   26 ②

01 want to~: ~하고 싶다

03 throw: 던지다, performance: 공연, invent: 발명하다, face: 직면하다

04 (A)는 어느 나라를 선호하는지 질문하고 있으므로 which, (B)는 이어지는 대답으로 이유를 설명하고 있으므로 why가 적절하다.

05 (D) 가장 좋아하는 가수 대답 → (B) 이유 질문 → (E) 이유 설명 → (C) 가장 좋아하는 곡 질문 → (A) 가장 좋아하는 곡 대답

06 이어지는 대화가 이유를 설명하고 있으므로 Why로 시작하는 의문문이 적절하다.

07 those days: 그때, 그 당시에, these days: 요즘

08 나머지는 모두 '선물'을 뜻하지만 ③번은 '재능'을 뜻한다.

09 best: 가장

10 ⑤ Jiho와 Amy는 이번 주 Blue Sky의 팬 미팅에 함께 갈 것이다.

11 (B) 헌 옷을 가지고 있는 이유 질문 → (D) 헌 옷을 가지고 있는 이유 설명 → (C) 본인도 헌 옷을 가지고 있음을 설명 → (E) 토요일 계획 제안 → (A) 제안 수락

12 ① 유익한, ② 인상 깊은, ③ 매력적인, ④ 지루한, ⑤ 재미있는

13 가장 선호하는 책이 무엇인지 질문하고 있으므로 ①번과 바꾸어 쓸 수 있다. favorite: 가장 좋아하는

14 주어는 복수명사인 The keys이므로 복수 동사를 쓰는 것이 옳다. 따라서 are이다.

15 pay somebody back: (빌린 돈을) 갚다, 돌려주다

16 by 이외의 다른 전치사를 사용하는 수동태 및 구동사의 수동태를 묻는 문제이다. ① pay attention to: ~에 관심을 기울이다 ② be married to: ~와 결혼한 상태이다 ③ be exposed to: ~에 노출되다 ④ be accustomed to: ~에 익숙하다 ⑤ be composed of: ~으로 구성되어 있다 oxygen: 산소 hydrogen: 수소

17 목적격보어로 원형부정사를 쓰는 동사는 수동태로 전환할 때 목적격보어를 to부정사화 한다.

18 4형식 동사의 수동태에서 간접목적어가 주어로 사용될 경우 직접목적어는 전치사 없이 쓴다. 따라서 'Tom was given some bad advice about studying English.'가 옳다.

19 주어진 문장의 This way가 가리키는 것은 타 콘서트와는 달리 피아노 측면을 청중과 마주보게 하여 청중이 연주자의 모습을 더 잘 볼 수 있게 만든 것을 말한다.

20 at once: 한 번에 one at a time: 차례로, 한 번에 하나씩

21 사람들은 단 하나의 음도 놓치기를 원치 않아서 숨죽이고 있다고 하였다.

22 콘서트가 끝난 후 사람들은 소리를 지르며 꽃을 던지고 있으므로 '흥분한' 반응을 보이고 있다고 하는 것이 옳다.

23 'think of A as B'는 'A를 B로 여기다'라는 의미이다. ⓐ the audience는 집합명사로 단수 취급하며, ⓑ once는 '한 때, 한 번'의 의미로 사용되므로 글에 맞게 고치기 위해서 at once를 쓰는 것이 적절하다. ⓒ 시간은 흘러가는 것이 아니라 저절로 흐르는 것이므로 수동태가 아닌 자동사로써 flies를 쓰는 것이 옳다. ⓓ 놀라움을 유발하는 스타이므로 amazing으로 고치는 것이 맞다.

24 많은 사람들이 Franz Liszt를 최초의 아이돌이라고 여긴다고 하고, 글쓴이 역시 오늘날의 아이돌을 좋아한다면 최초의 아이돌도 좋아하게 될 것이라고 글을 마무리하고 있으므로 ⑤는 옳지 않다.

25 give는 두 개의 목적어를 취하는 4형식 동사이다.

26 Franz Liszt의 콘서트에 관한 기사로 그가 사람들의 환호 속에 성황리에 공연을 마쳤다는 내용이다. 따라서 ②번이 가장 적절하다.

Go for It!

시험대비 실력평가 · p.164

01 dry   02 participant   03 librarian   04 ④

05 ③   06 (1) burn   (2) tough   (3) frozen

(4) giant   07 ④

01 주어진 단어는 반의어 관계를 나타낸다. dry: 마른, 건조한, wet: 젖은

02 어떤 활동이나 행사에 참가하는 사람을 가리키는 말은 participant(참가자)이다.

03 도서관을 담당하거나 도서관에서 일하는 사람을 가리키는 말은 librarian(사서)이다.

04 ordinary: 보통의, 평범한

05 주어진 문장의 bat은 '배트, 막대기'를 의미한다. ③번을 제외한 나머지는 모두 '박쥐'를 뜻한다.

06 tough: 힘든, burn: 태우다, frozen: 얼은, giant: 거대한

07 field: 분야, 들판, 매장지[산지]

서술형 시험대비 · p.165

01 melt   02 traditional

03 desert   04 (A) In (B) out (C) in

05 (1) in the middle of   (2) takes place

(3) go on   (4) are out of

06 No, I've never been there.

07 (1) Have you ever tried yoga?

(2) In fact, we are out of salt.

(3) I want to take part in the rock climbing contest.

01 주어진 단어는 반의어 관계를 나타낸다. freeze: 얼다, melt: 녹다

02 '오랫동안 변하지 않은 특정 그룹의 사람들의 삶의 양식, 믿음, 관습의 일부인' 것은 traditional(전통적인)이다.

03 '물이 거의 없고 이곳에서 자라는 식물도 거의 없는 넓은 땅'은 desert(사막)이다.

04 in fact: 사실은, 실은 be out of: ~이 떨어지다 take part in: ~에 참가하다

05 in the middle of: ~의 한 가운데에 take place: 발생하다, 일어나다 go on: 계속되다 be out of: ~이 바닥나다, ~이 떨어지다

교과서 Conversation

핵심 Check · p.166~167

1 (1) What do you do in your free[leisure] time

(2) favorite free time activity / doing yoga

(3) I often bake cookies

2 (1) Have you ever run

(2) visited Canada / Yes, I have, Have you

(3) made / never

교과서 대화문 익히기

Check(√) True or False · p.168

1 F   2 T   3 T   4 F

교과서 확인학습 · p.170~171

Listen & Speak 1 A

in your free time / often / usually watch movies

Listen & Speak 1 B

What are you going to do / play badminton / my favorite free time activity / Who / What do you do in your free time / ride my bike

Listen & Speak 1 C

for a living / I often play table tennis

Listen & Speak 2 A

have you ever been to / I have / I've never been there

Listen & Speak 2 B

have you ever heard of / I've seen / these days / scary / scared / exercise / join / scary, play basketball

Listen & Speak 1 C

Have you ever ridden / When

Real Life Talk

often go rock climbing / What mountain / gym / Have you ever done / Not yet / come and join / this Saturday / sounds / going to

시험대비 기본평가 · p.172

01 what do you do for a living

02 Have you ever ridden a horse?

03 ③   04 (B) → (D) → (C) → (A)

01 for a living: 생계를 위하여

02 ride - rode - ridden

03 여가 활동을 묻고 있으므로 '나는 소방관이야.'라는 대답은 어색하다.

04 (B) 경험 질문 → (D) 대답 및 상대방에게 경험 질문 → (C) 대답 및 계획 설명 → (A) 반응 및 확신 표현

시험대비 실력평가
p.173~174

01 ⑤ 02 ②

03 I usually watch movies. 04 ⑤ 05 ⑤

06 (E) → (A) → (C) → (B) → (D)

07 He thinks (that) it is too scary for him.

08 He is going to play basketball.

09 (1) she often goes rock climbing with her dad
   (2) a gym near her house
   (3) she has never done it
   (4) I could come and join her next time

10 (D) → (B) → (C) → (A)

01 이어지는 대답으로 보아 빈칸에는 직업을 묻는 질문이 적절하다. occupation: 직업

02 '너는 여가 시간에 무엇을 하니?' '너는 어때?'라고 각각 묻고 있으므로 빈칸에 공통으로 들어가기에 적절한 말은 what이다.

04 ⑤번은 '직업이 무엇인가요?'라는 의미이다.

05 주어진 질문에 대한 대답으로 여가 시간에 무엇을 하는지에 대한 대답이 이어져야 하므로 (E)가 적절하다.

06 (E) 대답 및 추가 설명 → (A) 자신이 플라잉 요가를 배우고 있음을 이야기함 → (C) 놀람 표현 및 선호 여부 질문 → (B) 선호 대답 → (D) 반응 및 다짐

07 Mike는 플라잉 요가가 너무 무섭다고 생각한다.

08 Mike는 요가 수업에 참여하는 대신 농구를 할 것이다.

09 오늘 나는 Judy와 여가 활동에 대해 이야기를 했다. 그녀는 여가 시간에 종종 아빠와 암벽 등반을 간다고 했다. 그녀는 보통 집 근처 체육관에서 그걸 한다. 그러나 그녀는 실제로 산에서는 한 번도 해본 적이 없으며 언젠가는 그렇게 하고 싶어 한다. 나는 암벽 등반에 흥미가 생겨 내가 그녀와 다음에 함께 할 수 있을지 물어 보았다. 우리는 그걸 이번 주 토요일에 할 것이다. 나는 정말 그것이 기대가 된다.

10 (D) 경험 질문 → (B) 경험 여부 대답 → (C) 언제 경험했는지 질문 → (A) 대답

서술형 시험대비
p.175

01 what do you do in your free time?

02 I usually play with my dad.

03 favorite

04 (1) plays badminton (2) goes to the Han River
   (3) ride his bike

05 I often go rock climbing with my dad.

06 She usually does it at a gym near her house.

07 They are going to go rock climbing this Saturday.

02 '보통 누구와 함께 운동하니?'라는 질문에 '나는 보통 아빠와 함께 운동한다.'는 대답이 이어져야 한다.

03 '같은 종류의 다른 것들보다 더 좋아하는'은 favorite(가장 좋아하는)이다.

06 Judy는 주로 집 근처의 체육관에서 암벽 등반을 한다.

07 Judy와 Hojin은 이번 주 토요일에 암벽 등반을 하러 갈 것이다.

교과서
Grammar

핵심 Check
p.176~177

1 (1) the cheapest, all (2) the most interesting
2 (1) who (2) whose bicycle

시험대비 기본평가
p.178

01 (1) I have a friend who studies abroad.
   (2) We stayed in the hotel which had a beautiful lounge.
   (3) Do you want to see the pictures which the photographer took?
   (4) Jenny took care of the dog whose leg was hurt.

02 (1) the hottest (2) taller than
   (3) is (4) the most diligent

03 (1) Did you read the book that I lent to you?
   (2) Is there anything that you want to ask?
   (3) Do you know the longest river in the world?
   (4) Time is the most precious of all.

01 (1) She가 사람이고 주격이므로 주격 관계대명사 who. (2) 선행사가 사물인 the hotel이고, 대명사 It이 주격으로 쓰였으므로 관계대명사 which. (3) them이 목적격으로 쓰인 사물이므로 관계대명사 which. (4) Its가 소유격으로 쓰이고 있고 개를 가리키므로 관계대명사 whose를 쓴다.

02 (1) 내용상 최상급을 쓰는 것이 가장 옳다. (2) 비교급을 이용한 최상급 표현이다. (3) 관계대명사의 수의 일치 문제이다. 선행사에 수의 일치를 시켜야 하므로 the girl에 맞도록 be동사를 쓰

는 것이 옳다. (4) 3음절 이상의 단어이므로 the most를 이용하여 최상급을 만든다.

03 (1) '빌려준 책'이므로 the book을 수식하는 관계절을 만든다. (2) 의문문이나 부정문에서는 anything을 쓴다. (3) long은 -est를 붙여서 최상급을 만든다. (4) precious는 -ous로 끝나는 형용사이므로 the most를 이용하여 최상급을 만든다.

01 ①   02 ④   03 ④   04 Where is the cheese which(또는 that) was in the refrigerator?
05 ③   06 ②, ③, ⑤   07 ⑤   08 more comfortable than   09 ⑤   10 ⑤
11 which(또는 that), higher than   12 ③
13 ③   14 that[which], whose, that[which]
15 The woman who(또는 that 또는 whom) I spoke to gave me good advice.   16 What is the most popular sport in your country?   17 ④
18 ④   19 The eldest daughter   20 I liked the woman whom I met at the party last night.
21 ③   22 ②

01 healthy는 -est를 붙여서 최상급을 만들고 나머지는 모두 the most를 이용해서 최상급을 만드는 형용사이다.

02 모두 주격 혹은 목적격으로 사용되는 관계대명사 who를 쓰지만 ④번은 소유격 관계대명사 whose의 자리이다.

03 의미상 B가 여지껏 본 영화 중 가장 지루한 영화라는 의미가 되어야 하므로 the most boring이라고 쓰는 것이 옳다.

04 냉장고 안에 있던 치즈가 어디 있는지를 묻는 문장으로 쓰면 된다.

05 비교급과 원급으로 최상급의 의미를 표현하는 문장을 찾는 것이다. '비교급+than any other+단수명사', 최상급, 'as 원급 as'를 써서 빈칸을 채운다.

06 목적격 관계대명사 whom의 자리이다. 따라서 who가 가능하며 that이 쓰여도 무방하다.

07 ⑤번은 돌고래가 다른 모든 동물들만큼 영리하다는 의미가 되므로 다른 문장과 의미가 다르다.

08 비교급으로 최상급의 의미를 갖는 표현이다. the+최상급은 '비교급+than all the other+복수명사'와 같다.

09 '가장 ~한 사람들 중 한 사람'이란 표현은 'one of the 최상급+복수명사'를 쓴다. 따라서 men으로 쓰는 것이 옳다.

10 모두 최상급의 의미를 갖지만 ⑤번은 '이것은 다른 모든 그림들만큼 가치 있다.'는 뜻이므로 다른 문장과 의미가 다르다.

11 세계에서 가장 높은 빌딩은 두바이에 있는 Burj Khalifa이다.

12 ③번은 비교급으로 최상급을 나타내는 것으로 the most가 아닌 more로 쓰는 것이 옳다.

13 ⓐ 주격 관계대명사가 빠져 있다. people who don't have a

car로 쓰는 것이 옳다. ⓑ 목적격 관계대명사가 생략되어 있다. ⓒ that은 전치사의 목적어였던 the music을 받는 관계대명사이다. ⓓ 목적격 관계대명사가 생략된 채로 두 문장이 이어지고 있으므로 대명사 it을 빼는 것이 옳다.

14 첫 번째 문장의 빈칸은 목적격 관계대명사 자리이므로 that이나 which를 쓰는 것이 옳다. 두 번째 문장에는 eyes를 받아주는 소유격 관계대명사가 들어가는 것이 옳으며 마지막 문장의 빈칸에는 목적격 관계대명사 that 혹은 which를 쓰면 된다.

15 give someone advice: ~에게 조언을 해 주다

17 ④번은 명사절을 이끄는 접속사 that이다. 명사절을 이끄는 접속사 that은 완전한 문장을 이끌며, 관계대명사 that은 불완전한 문장을 이끈다.

18 빈칸 뒤에 명사가 나오므로 소유격 관계대명사가 오는 것이 옳다.

19 서열상 가장 연장자를 나타낼 때에는 the eldest로 표현한다.

20 whom을 대신하여 who, that을 써도 무방하다.

21 bad의 최상급으로 the worst를 써야 하며 내가 저질러온 실수 중에서 최악이라고 하였으므로 ③번이 옳다.

22 ② the prettiest로 쓰는 것이 옳다. the most와 최상급은 함께 쓰지 않는다.

01 the highest, higher than
02 (1) that cannot be explained
   (2) which(또는 that) were on the wall
   (3) who are never on time
03 The man who[that] examined the sick children is the kindest doctor in this hospital.
04 (1) Sydney is the largest
   (2) Jupiter is larger than
   (3) The Nile is the longest river
05 He is the most boring person that I have ever met.
06 (1) shorter than   (2) shorter than all
   (3) the longest   (4) longer than
07 A customer is someone who buys something from a store. / The boy who was injured in the accident is now in the hospital. / The bus which goes to the airport runs every half hour. / A dictionary is a book which gives you the meanings of words. / I met somebody whose mother is a famous writer.
08 (1) the people whom
   (2) their children everything that
   (3) whose menu
09 the most patient person that I have ever met
10 (1) I know the boy. / His bicycle was stolen.
   (2) Daisy lectured on a topic. /

She knew very little about the topic.

11 (1) No other river / longer than
   (2) the longest river in

01 에베레스트 산은 세계에서 가장 높은 산이다. 산의 높이는 high 를 써서 나타낸다.

02 (1) 선행사가 something이므로 관계대명사 that이나 which 를 쓰는 것이 옳다. (2) 선행사가 사물이므로 which나 that을 써서 문장을 하나로 만든다. (3) 사람이 선행사이므로 관계대명사 who나 that을 이용한다.

03 examine: 검사하다, 진찰하다

04 시드니는 호주에서 가장 큰 도시이며, 목성은 태양계에서 가장 큰 행성이다. 나일 강은 세계에서 가장 긴 강이다.

05 지루함을 유발하는 사람에게는 boring을 쓴다.

06 밧줄의 길이를 비교하는 문제이다. 밧줄 D는 다른 모든 밧줄 중에서 가장 짧고 밧줄 A는 가장 긴 밧줄이다. 문장의 형태를 살펴가며 빈칸을 채우는 것이 좋다.

07 customer: 고객 be injured: 부상을 입다

08 (1) who나 that을 써도 무방하다.

09 Jason은 이제껏 만나본 사람 중에서 Kelly가 가장 인내심 있다고 말하는 것이 적절하다.

10 lecture: 강의하다 topic: 주제 little: 그다지[별로] ~하지 않다

11 비교급을 이용하여 최상급의 의미를 나타내는 표현들이다. the Mississippi River: 미시시피 강

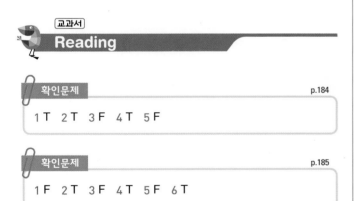

교과서
Reading

확인문제   p.184

1 T   2 T   3 F   4 T   5 F

확인문제   p.185

1 F   2 T   3 F   4 T   5 F   6 T

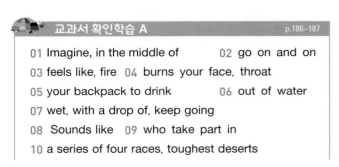

교과서 확인학습 A   p.186~187

01 Imagine, in the middle of   02 go on and on
03 feels like, fire   04 burns your face, throat
05 your backpack to drink   06 out of water
07 wet, with a drop of, keep going
08 Sounds like   09 who take part in
10 a series of four races, toughest deserts

11 Each race is, takes   12 takes place, in
13 the driest desert
14 hasn't rained, for   15 goes to, in
16 the windiest desert   17 heads to
18 the hottest   19 reach up to
20 travels to the coldest desert
21 boiling water, freezes
22 the greatest runners, take part in
23 exactly   24 the participants are ordinary
25 do it   26 a librarian from
27 a chance to test, make
28 who crosses, can do anything

교과서 확인학습 B   p.188~189

1 Imagine you are in the middle of a great desert.
2 The sands go on and on in every direction.
3 The sun feels like a giant ball of fire.
4 The hot wind burns your face and throat.
5 You open your backpack to drink some water.
6 Oh, no! You're almost out of water.
7 You wet your throat with a drop of water and keep going.
8 Sounds like a bad dream?
9 Well, this is not a dream for the people who take part in the 4 Deserts Race.
10 The 4 Deserts Race is a series of four races across the world's toughest deserts.
11 Each race is 250 kilometers long and takes seven days.
12 The first race takes place in the Atacama Desert in Chile.
13 It is the driest desert in the world.
14 In fact, it hasn't rained in some parts of the Atacama Desert for 400 years!
15 The next race goes to the Gobi Desert in China.
16 It is the windiest desert on earth.
17 The third race heads to the Sahara Desert in Egypt.
18 It is the hottest of the four deserts.
19 Temperatures can reach up to 50℃.
20 Finally, the race travels to the coldest desert on earth, Antarctica.
21 If you throw boiling water into the air here, it freezes!
22 Only the greatest runners on the planet can take part in 4 Deserts Race, right?

23 Not exactly.

24 Many of the participants are ordinary people like you and me.

25 So why do they do it?

26 Adrianna, a librarian from France, says,

27 "It's a chance to test your limits and make your own history.

28 Anyone who crosses the finish line can do anything."

시험대비 실력평가
p.190~193

01 Imagine 02 ④ 03 ③ 04 ⑤
05 ④ 06 ④ 07 ② 08 the people who take part in the 4 Deserts Race
09 Each race is 250km long. 10 ② 11 ④
12 ⑤ 13 boiling water
14 Antarctica, is the coldest on earth 15 limit
16 ③ 17 take part in 4 Deserts Race
18 ③, ④ 19 ② 20 How many deserts have you run through? 21 tougher than, deserts
22 ④ 23 temperature 24 ⑤
25 ④ 26 ② 27 which(혹은 that), toughest deserts

01 당신이 무언가에 관하여 생각할 때 마음속에서 그것에 관한 그림이나 아이디어를 형성할 경우 이 단어가 사용된다.

02 물이 거의 떨어져 간다고 하였으므로 ④번은 옳지 않다.

03 '거대한'이라는 의미이므로 ③번이 옳다.

04 ⓒ '물을 마시기 위해서'라는 의미가 적합하므로 to부정사를 이용하여 부사를 만들어 준다. ⓓ keep+Ving: 계속해서 V하다

05 carry on은 '계속해서 ~하다, 계속 가다'는 의미이다. in the middle of는 in the heart of를, on and on은 continuously를, bad는 terrible을, a series of는 a chain of로 대신하여 쓸 수 있다.

06 태양이 거대한 불의 공 같다는 것은 매우 뜨겁다는 의미이다.

07 밑줄 친 (B)는 부사로 쓰인 to부정사로 목적을 나타내며 '~하기 위해서'라는 의미로 해석된다. ① 목적격 보어로 쓰인 to부정사 ③ 형용사로 쓰인 to부정사 ④ would like의 목적어로 쓰인 to부정사 ⑤ 진주어로 쓰인 to부정사

08 take part in: ~에 참가하다

09 각 사막 경주의 길이를 묻고 있다. 각각 250km씩이라고 하였다.

10 Atacama 사막이 세계에서 가장 건조한 곳이라고 말하며 400년 동안 비가 내리지 않은 곳도 있다는 말로 앞 문장을 강조하는 말이 들어가는 것이 옳다.

11 지구상에서 가장 작은 사막이 어디에 있는지는 알 수 없다.

12 ⑤번은 최상급을 나타내는 문장이 아니다.

13 끓는 물을 던지면 언다고 하였다.

14 사막 레이스의 최종 목적지는 지구상에서 가장 추운 남극이다.

15 '가능한 최대의 양, 범위 혹은 정도'는 한계(limit)이다.

16 특별한 사람만이 참가하는 것이 아니라 너와 나 같은 평범한 사람들이라고 말하는 것이 글의 흐름에 맞다.

17 4 Deserts Race에 참가하는 것을 가리킨다.

18 빈칸은 주격 관계대명사의 자리이며 선행사가 사람이므로 who 혹은 that을 쓰는 것이 옳다.

19 위 글은 평범한 사람들이 '4 Deserts Race'에 참가하는 이유이다.

20 답변으로 미루어 보아 얼마나 많은 사막을 뛰었는지를 묻는 질문이 들어가는 것이 옳다.

21 '비교급 than all the other+복수명사'는 최상급의 의미를 갖는다.

22 ④ 참가자들과 좋은 친구가 되었다고 하였으므로 ④번은 옳지 않다.

23 어떤 것이 얼마나 뜨거운지 혹은 얼마나 차가운지에 대한 척도

24 가장 추운 사막이므로 끓는 물을 던지면 언다고 볼 수 있다. 따라서 ⑤번에 들어가는 것이 가장 적합하다.

25 다른 지역보다 고비 사막에 바람이 더 많이 부는 이유는 위 글을 읽고 알 수 없다.

26 ⓐ는 인칭대명사 it으로 ②번이 그 쓰임과 같다. ① 가주어 it, ③, ⑤ 날씨, 날짜, 거리, 명암 등을 말할 때 쓰는 비인칭 주어 it, ④ 가목적어 it으로 각각 쓰였다.

27 선행사가 사물인 four deserts이며 동사를 이끌고 있으므로 주격 관계대명사를 써야 옳다.

서술형 시험대비
p.194~195

01 Imagine that you are in the middle of a great desert.

02 The hot wind makes my face and throat burn.

03 I'm almost out of water

04 in order to drink some water (혹은 so as to drink some water)

05 Well, this is not a dream for the people who[that] take part in the 4 Deserts Race.

06 toughest 07 freezes

08 The Sahara Desert is hotter than all the other deserts.

09 The second race takes place in the Gobi Desert in China.

10 colder than 11 who[that] are ordinary

12 who[that] is a librarian from France

01 '네가 거대한 사막의 한 가운데에 있다고 상상해 보아라.'는 의미이다.

02 얼굴을 뜨겁게 하고 목이 마르게 만드는 것은 뜨거운 바람이다.

03 왜 물을 조금만 마시는지를 묻고 있으므로 물이 거의 떨어져서라고 답하면 된다.

04 부사 중에서 목적을 나타내는 to부정사는 in order to나 so as to로 쓸 수 있다.

06 문맥상 가장 힘든 사막이라는 의미이다.

07 낮은 온도로 인하여 어떤 것이 고체화되는 것을 '얼다'라고 한다. 따라서 수의 일치에 유의하여 freezes를 빈칸에 쓴다.

08 비교급을 이용하여 최상급의 의미를 표현하는 문제이다.

09 두 번째 경주는 어디에서 열리나요?

10 남극이 가장 춥다. 비교급을 이용한 최상급 표현이다.

11 they는 평범한 사람들을 가리키는 말이므로 관계대명사를 이용하여 '우리와 같은 평범한 사람들'이라는 의미의 문장을 만들어 주면 된다.

12 Adrianna는 프랑스에서 온 사서이다.

영역별 핵심문제   p.197~201

01 marathon   **02** ⑤   **03** (1) a series of
(2) take part in   (3) for a living   **04** ④
05 (1) Have you ever hit a home run?
(2) I often play table tennis in my free time.
(3) What does he do for a living?
06 Who do you usually play with?
07 She plays badminton with her dad.   **08** ③
09 ⓒ scaring → scared   **10** ⑤   **11** ⑤
12 rock climbing
13 What mountain do you go to?
14 ④   **15** (B) → (D) → (C) → (A)   **16** ③
17 The lake which you swam in today is the deepest lake in our country.   **18** ④   **19** ⑤
20 ④   **21** bigger than any other   **22** as heavy as   **23** ③   **24** the most famous, that   **25** ③   **26** ④   **27** ③, ④
28 burning   **29** who[that] takes part in   **30** ②
31 ④

01 26마일, 약 42km의 거리를 달리는 경주를 나타내는 말은 marathon(마라톤)이다.

02 throat: 목구멍

03 a series of: 일련의, take part in: ~에 참가하다, for a living: 생계를 위해

04 주어진 문장에서 go on은 '계속하다'라는 의미를 나타내므로 이와 같이 쓰인 것은 ④번이다. ①번은 '넘어가다' ②번은 '일어나다, 발생하다' ③ go on a picnic: 소풍가다, ⑤ go on a diet:

식이요법을 하다

07 Jean은 여가 시간에 아빠와 함께 배드민턴을 친다.

08 두 사람은 여가 활동(leisure activity)에 대해 이야기하고 있다.

09 scaring: 위협하는, scared: 무서운, 겁먹은

10 나머지는 상대방의 말에 대한 만족감을 나타내지만, ⑤는 '괜찮아요.'라고 격려할 때 쓰는 말이다.

11 왜 Suji가 요즘 요가하는 것을 좋아하는지는 알 수 없다.

12 가파른 바위 표면을 오르는 활동이나 스포츠를 가리키는 말은 rock climbing(암벽 등반)이다.

14 ④ Judy는 언젠가 실제 산에서 암벽 등반을 하기를 희망하지만 이번 주 토요일에 암벽 등반을 하러 산에 간다는 설명은 바르지 않다.

15 (B) 경험 질문 → (D) 대답 및 상대방에게 경험 질문 → (C) 대답 및 계획 설명 → (A) 반응 및 확신 표현

16 ③번은 선행사가 사람이므로 who를 쓰는 것이 옳다.

17 swim in: ~에서 수영하다

18 ④번의 위 문장은 '내 지갑을 발견한 여자가 나에게 전화했다.'이고 아래 문장은 '내가 발견한 지갑의 주인에게 내가 전화를 걸었다.'는 의미이다.

19 one of the 최상급+복수명사: 가장 ~한 사람들 중 하나

20 ④번은 주격 관계대명사로 생략이 불가능하다. 생략 가능한 관계대명사는 목적격 관계대명사이다.

21~22 박스 A, B, C 중에서 A의 크기가 가장 작지만 무게는 가장 무거우며, C의 크기가 가장 크지만 무게는 가장 가볍다. 따라서 가장 큰 박스와 가장 무거운 박스를 묻는 질문에 조건에 맞도록 답하면 된다.

23 주어진 문장의 빈칸에는 주격 관계대명사 who가 들어간다. ③번에는 목적격 관계대명사 whom이 들어가야 하며 whom을 대신하여 who를 써도 무방하다. ① whose ② which ④ whose ⑤ that

24 선행사에 최상급이 있으므로 that을 쓰는 것이 보통이지만 who[whom]를 쓰기도 한다.

25 첫 번째 문장은 소녀의 꿈이 가수가 되는 것이므로 소유격 관계대명사가 들어가는 자리이다. 두 번째 문장의 빈칸은 동사를 이끌고 있으므로 주격 관계대명사 자리이다.

26 full of가 들어갈 곳은 없다. ⓐ in the middle of ⓑ feels like ⓒ out of ⓓ a drop of

27 ③ 물은 호주머니가 아닌 배낭에 있었다. ④ 물은 거의 떨어졌다.

28 뜨거운 바람이 얼굴을 태운다고 하였다.

29 참가자는 행사에 참가하는 사람을 의미한다.

30 ⓐ 사막 레이스에 참가하는 것을 가리키므로 복수명사를 지칭하는 them이 아니라 it, ⓑ 내용상 to test와 연결되는 것이므로 make, ⓒ anyone은 단수 취급하는 부정대명사이므로 crosses가 옳다.

31 Adrianna는 프랑스에서 온 사서라고 하였다. 따라서 도서관에서 일한다고 말한 ④번이 옳다.

01 freeze   02 ①

03 ⓒ → Who[Whom]   04 ⑤

05 (1) I often draw pictures in my free time.

    (2) Have you ever been to Japan?

    (3) I've never been to China.

06 what do you do in your free time?

07 I've never been there.   08 ①

09 Tom has been to Jeju-do.

10 have you ever heard of flying yoga?

11 ⑤   12 ③   13 ③, ⑤   14 ③

15 ⑤   16 It was the most painful moment of my life.   17 Kelly bought a book whose cover looked familiar to him.   18 the most diligent, as[so] diligent as (혹은 more diligent than) 19 ③

20 ③   21 The Gobi Desert which[that] is in China is the windiest desert on earth.   22 ③

23 ④   24 ④   25 the greatest runners, ordinary people   26 Anyone who crosses the finish line can do anything.

01 주어진 단어는 반의어 관계를 나타낸다. melt: 녹다, freeze: 얼다

02 주어진 문장과 ①번에서는 '힘든', ②와 ③번에서는 '거친', ④번에서는 '질긴', ⑤번에서는 '건강한'을 의미한다.

03 이어지는 대화에서 '아빠'와 함께 배드민턴을 친다는 것으로 보아 'Who[Whom]'가 적절하다.

04 Jean이 이번 주 토요일에 Tom과 자전거를 탈 것이라는 설명은 바르지 않다.

08 확신을 표현하는 말로 certain(확신하는, 자신하는)과 바꾸어 쓸 수 있다.

09 제주도에 가 본 사람은 Tom이다.

11 No라는 대답으로 보아 (E)가 적절하다.

12 각각 지시부사, 관계대명사, 접속사 that이 들어가야 한다.

13 'She has long hair.' 혹은 'Her hair is long.'으로 머리가 길다는 표현을 할 수 있다.

14 late은 순서상 나중을 나타내는 의미로 사용될 때 최상급으로 last를 쓴다. You are the last person I want to talk with. '너는 내가 가장 대화하고 싶지 않은 사람이야.'라는 의미이다.

15 ⑤번은 '정직보다 덜 중요한 것은 아무것도 없다.'는 의미로 정직이 가장 중요하다는 의미의 다른 문장과 의미가 다르다.

16 painful: 고통스러운

17 look familiar to ~: ~에게 익숙해 보이다

18 diligent: 부지런한, 근면한

19 온도가 50도까지 올라가므로 가장 더운 곳과 어울리는 문장이다.

20 밑줄 친 ⓐ는 현재완료의 계속적 용법이다. ① 완료, ② 경험, ④, ⑤ 결과적 용법으로 쓰였다. 따라서 계속을 나타내는 ③번이 옳다.

21 관계대명사를 적절하게 이용하여 문장을 만든다. '중국에 있는 고비사막'이므로 The Gobi Desert를 which[that] is in China가 수식하도록 한다.

22 take: ~만큼의 시간이 걸리다, take place: 개최되다

23 down이 아닌 up이라고 쓰는 것이 옳다.

24 (D) 평범한 사람들로만 이루어진 것은 아니다.

25 '4 Deserts Race'에 참가하는 사람들은 최고의 경주자들이 아니다.

26 cross the finish line: 결승선을 통과하다

01 have you ever been to Jeju-do?

02 Jeju-do

03 She is planning to go to Jeju-do this summer.

04 Kevin is the youngest of his family members. / Kevin is younger than any other family member. / Kevin is younger than all the other family members. / No other family member is younger than Kevin. / No other family member is as[so] young as Kevin.

05 Is the chair which you are sitting on comfortable?

06 which(혹은 that), than, whose

07 who laughs last laughs best

08 is a story which expresses traditional beliefs

09 ⓐ go ⓑ going ⓒ goes

10 The first race takes place in the Atacama Desert in Chile which is the driest desert in the world.

11 In   12 on earth is as[so] cold as Antarctica

13 Take part in, which(혹은 that), to test your limits, make your own history

03 Mina는 이번 여름에 제주도를 방문할 계획이다.

04 young은 1음절 형용사이므로 -est를 붙여 최상급을 만든다.

05 which 뿐만 아니라 that도 가능하다.

06 첫 번째 빈칸은 선행사가 사물인 the town이므로 관계대명사 which 혹은 that을 쓰는 것이 옳으며, 마지막 빈칸은 이어서 나오는 명사 smile이 있으므로 소유격 관계대명사를 쓰는 것이 옳다.

07 best는 well의 최상급이다.

08 신화란 전통적인 믿음을 표현하는 이야기이다.

09 ⓐ 주어가 복수이므로 go ⓑ keep+Ving: 계속해서 V하다 ⓒ 주어가 단수이므로 goes

10 사물이 선행사이므로 which를 대신하여 that을 사용하여도 무관하다.

11 in fact: 사실

12 질문: 어떤 사막이 지구에서 가장 추운가? 답: 지구에 있는 어떤 사막도 남극만큼 춥지 않다.

13 4 Deserts Race가 사물이므로 관계대명사 which 혹은 that을 사용한다.

|모범답안|

01 (1) flying yoga　(2) joining her yoga class

　　(3) scary　(4) exercise more

02 (1) who teach English to students

　　(2) who cut other people's hair

　　(3) that deals with large amounts of information

　　(4) which operates with an engine

　　(5) who invented the first airplane

03 (1) Roses are the most beautiful flowers on earth.

　　(2) Cheese cake is the most delicious food in the world.

　　(3) No other food is spicier than curry to me.

　　(4) This metal is the hardest material in the world.

　　(5) This sofa is softer than any other sofa in the hall.

01 오늘 나는 Suji와 플라잉 요가에 대해 이야기를 나누었다. 나는 그것을 TV에서 본 적이 있다. 놀랍게도 그녀는 최근에 그것을 배우며 즐기고 있었다. 그녀는 그녀의 요가 수업에 가입할 것을 제안하였지만 그것은 내게 너무 두려워 보였다. 비록 나는 그녀의 제안을 받아들이지 않았지만 운동을 더 할 것을 결심했다.

01 temperature　　02 (1) direction　(2) scary

(3) boiling　(4) temperature　03 ①

04 (1) This novel was written about a series of historical facts.

　　(2) The race takes place every spring.

　　(3) The cat was found in the middle of the road.

05 ③　　　　06 She likes badminton best.

07 ⑤　　08 ⑤　　09 ④　　10 Have you ever done it on a real mountain?　11 ②

12 (E) → (C) → (D) → (A) → (B)　13 ③

14 ②　　15 ③, ④　　16 is the month that comes before　　17 It is one of the worst experiences of my life.　18 ③　　19 ④

20 It takes seven days to finish a race.　21 ②

22 colder than, as[so] cold as　23 ⑤

24 ③　　25 who[that], test, limits, take part

26 (C) → (A) → (B)

01 어떤 물건이나 장소가 얼마나 뜨거운지 또는 차가운지의 정도의 측정을 나타내는 말은 temperature(온도)이다.

02 direction: 방향 scary: 무서운, 두려운 boiling: 끓는 temperature: 온도, 체온

03 주어진 문장에서 head는 '~를 향해서 가다'라는 의미로 사용되었으므로 이와 같이 쓰인 것은 ①번이다. ②번과 ③번은 '머리', ④번과 ⑤번은 '책임자'라는 의미로 쓰였다.

05 (A) 뒤에 동사원형 play가 이어지므로 'Do', (B) '누구와 함께 주로 운동하니?'라고 묻고 있으므로 'with' (C) and 뒤에 동사가 이어져야 하므로 'ride'가 적절하다.

06 Jean이 여가 시간 활동으로 가장 좋아하는 운동은 배드민턴이다.

07 나머지는 모두 flying yoga를 가리키지만 ⓔ는 가주어 it을 나타낸다.

08 (A)와 나머지는 모두 '무서운'을 의미하지만 ⑤번은 '멋진, 아주 좋은'을 의미한다.

09 ④ Mike가 Suji와 함께 요가 수업을 받을 것이라는 진술은 바르지 않다.

12 (E) 주말 계획 설명 → (C) 자주 배드민턴을 치는지 질문 → (D) 대답 및 가장 좋아하는 여가 활동 설명 → (A) 누구와 함께 운동하는지 질문 → (B) 대답

13 위 문장은 'You borrowed his pen.'에서 온 것이고, 아래 문장은 'You lent him your pen.'에서 왔다. 따라서 각각 소유격 관계대명사와 목적격 관계대명사를 쓰면 된다.

14 형용사의 최상급은 정관사 the와 함께 쓴다.

15 선행사가 사물이며 관계대명사가 이끄는 절에 목적어가 빠져 있으므로, 목적격 관계대명사 which 혹은 that을 쓸 수 있다.

16 8월은 9월 앞에 오는 달이다.

17 bad의 최상급은 worst이다.

18 물이 떨어져 간다고 했으므로 충분히 물을 마셨다는 것은 어색하다.

19 ① 모래는 사방으로 뻗어 있고, ② 뜨거운 태양 때문에 바람도 뜨겁다고 하였으며, ③ 목이 마른 이유가 오랜 시간 걸어서인지 더운 바람 때문인지 알 수 없고, ⑤ 사막 레이스는 총 1000km 경주이다.

20 하나의 경주를 완주하는 데에 일주일이 걸린다고 하였다.

21 기간을 나타내고 있으므로 전치사 for를 쓰는 것이 옳다.

22 남극에 있는 사막은 지구상에서 가장 추운 곳이라고 하였다. 비교급과 원급을 이용한 최상급 표현으로 빈칸에 알맞은 말을 쓴다.

23 사람들이 사막 레이스에 참가하는 이유는 알 수 없다.

24 사람들이 경주에 참가하는 이유는 자신의 한계를 시험하고 자신만의 역사를 만들 기회가 되기 때문이다. 글을 읽고 나머지 질문에는 답할 수 없다.

25 anyone은 사람을 가리키며 동사 want를 바로 받아주므로 주격관계대명사를 쓰는 것이 옳다.

26 사막에 있다는 상상을 하는 주어진 문장 → (C) 사막이 뜨거워 물을 마시려고 배낭을 여는 내용 → (A) 물이 거의 없음을 확인하고 한 방울만 마신 채 계속 걷는 내용 → (B) 앞서 나온 모든 상황이 나쁜 꿈같지만 사막 레이스에 참가하는 사람들에게는 꿈이 아니라는 마무리로 이어지는 것이 자연스럽다.

Summer on a Stick

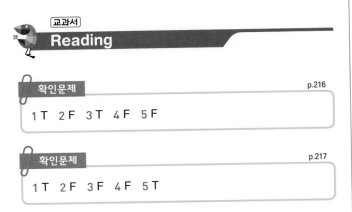

Reading

확인문제	p.216

1 T 2 F 3 T 4 F 5 F

확인문제	p.217

1 T 2 F 3 F 4 F 5 T

교과서 확인학습 A — p.218~219

01 hot days, are 02 stay cool 03 make
04 pineapple, kiwis, cup, makers 05 Steps
06 Cut, into small pieces 07 Peel, slice them
08 Put, pieces into 09 Add
10 Blend until, smooth 11 Pour, into
12 Add, slices 13 Close
14 Put them, for about 15 Finished
16 Enjoy, on a stick 17 Tips
18 are an excellent source of
19 more vitamin C than
20 when, a cold, try 21 Share
22 make your own 23 Share
24 use 25 cut them into
26 put them into, with 27 will be pretty

교과서 확인학습 B — p.220~221

1 The hot days of summer are here.
2 How can we stay cool?
3 Let's make ice pops together!
4 You need: 1/2 pineapple, 2 kiwis, 1 cup of apple juice, ice pop makers
5 Steps
6 Cut the pineapple into small pieces.
7 Peel the kiwis and slice them.
8 Put the pineapple pieces into the blender.

9 Add the apple juice.
10 Blend until the mix is smooth.
11 Pour the mix into the ice pop makers.
12 Add the kiwi slices.
13 Close the ice pop makers.
14 Put them in the freezer for about three hours.
15 Finished!
16 Enjoy your summer on a stick!
17 Health Tips
18 Pineapples are an excellent source of vitamin C.
19 They have more vitamin C than oranges.
20 So when you have a cold, try pineapples.
21 Share Your Ideas!
22 How will you make your own ice pops?
23 Share Your Ideas!
24 I will use kiwis and strawberries.
25 I will cut them into big pieces.
26 I will put them into the ice pop makers with apple juice.
27 I think my ice pops will be pretty.

서술형 실전문제 — p.222~223

01 (1) freezer (2) slice (3) Pour (4) source
02 blender 03 pineapple
04 (1) Put the garbage into the trash can.
   (2) Dive into the water and swim with her.
05 (1) when (2) until (3) and
06 (1) Cut a carrot into small pieces.
   (2) I think (that) the book will be very useful.
07 pieces 08 peel
09 We have to pour the apple juice into the blender.
10 the ice pop makers
11 smooth, blending
12 vitamin C
13 He will use kiwis and strawberries to make his own ice pops.
14 that 15 Jinsu, it looks pretty!

01 slice: 얇은 조각, freezer: 냉동고, source: 원천, pour: 붓다, 따르다
02 부드러운 음식이나 음료를 섞기 위한 전기 기기: blender(믹서)
03 두껍고 거친 표면을 가졌으며 많은 즙이 있는 달콤한 노란색의 과육과 맨 윗부분의 뻣뻣한 나뭇잎을 가진 큰 열대 과일
04 garbage: 쓰레기 trash can: 쓰레기통 dive into: ~로 다이빙하다

05 (1) 주말에 집에 있을 때 주로 무엇을 하니? (2) 비가 그칠 때까지 기다리자. (3) 집중해라. 그러면 너는 그것을 더 잘 이해할 것이다.

06 cut something into pieces: ~을 잘게 자르다 useful: 유용한

07 작은 조각으로 잘라 자른 조각들을 믹서기에 넣는 것이다.

08 무언가의 껍질을 제거하는 것은 '벗기다'이다.

09 질문: 우리는 사과 주스를 어디에 부어야 하나요?

10 막대 아이스크림 틀을 냉동고에 넣는 것이다.

11 얼마나 오래 섞어야 하는지에 대한 질문에, 부드러워 보이면 섞는 것을 멈춰도 좋다고 대답한다. stop Ving: V하는 것을 멈추다

12 파인애플은 비타민 C가 풍부하다.

13 진수는 막대 아이스크림을 만들기 위해서 키위와 딸기를 사용할 것이라고 하였다.

14 완전한 문장을 이끌면서 동사 think의 목적어 역할을 하므로 명사절을 이끄는 접속사 that이 들어가는 것이 옳다.

단원별 예상문제
p.224~228

01 peel **02** slice **03** smooth **04** ③

05 ① **06** (1) cut (2) put (3) mix (4) stay

07 ③ **08** ①

09 (1) Clean the room, or your mom will be upset.
(2) Unless you clean the room, your mom will be upset.

10 ② **11** (1) me to eat regularly (2) me to make more friends. **12** ⑤ **13** Mother Theresa is looked up to by people around the world.

14 ③ **15** am, will call, will take part in

16 enjoy **17** ④ **18** ④ **19** We have to peel the kiwis. **20** We put the ice pop makers in the freezer. **21** ④ **22** ④

23 kiwis and strawberries **24** 파인애플에 비타민 C가 풍부해서 감기에 도움이 되므로 **25** ③ **26** ⑤

27 ⑤ **28** We close the ice pop makers.

29 You finished making ice pops. **30** ③

31 When you have a cold, try pineapples. **32** big pieces, kiwis and strawberries **33** ④

34 ③ **35** ③ **36** We put them in the freezer for about three hours.

01 과일이나 야채 등의 외면을 벗겨내는 것은 peel(껍질을 벗기다)이다.

02 더 큰 조각에서 잘라낸 음식의 얇고 평평한 조각을 나타내는 말은 slice(얇은 조각)이다.

03 주어진 단어는 반의어 관계를 나타낸다. smooth: 부드러운, rough: 거친

04 pour: 쏟다, 붓다

05 보기의 close는 '닫다'라는 동사로 이처럼 쓰인 것은 ①번이다.

②, ⑤는 '친한'을 의미하며 ③, ④번은 '가까이'를 의미한다.

06 stay: 유지하다, mix: 섞다, cut A into B: A를 B(상태)로 자르다, put A into B: A를 B에 넣다

07 blend: 조화되다, 어울리다, 섞다

08 ①번은 to부정사의 형용사적 용법이고, 나머지는 모두 to부정사의 부사적 용법 중 목적을 나타낸다.

09 (1) 명령문+or ~는 '~해라, 그렇지 않으면'이라는 의미이다.
(2) Unless는 접속사로 '~하지 않으면'이라는 의미로 사용된다.

10 보기와 ②에서 사용된 현재완료는 '계속'이다. ① 결과, ③, ④ 경험, ⑤ 완료로 쓰였다.

11 advise와 tell은 모두 to부정사를 목적격 보어로 취하는 동사이다.

12 speak well of: ~에 대해 좋게 말하다

13 look up to: ~을 존경하다

14 첫 번째 빈칸에는 주격 관계대명사, 세 번째 빈칸에는 목적격 관계대명사의 자리이다. 각각 사람 선행사이므로 who를 쓸 수 있으며, 두 번째 빈칸에는 의문사 who가 들어가는 것이 옳다. 사람이고 주격이므로 관계대명사 who가 들어가야 알맞다

15 조건의 부사절에서 현재시제로 미래를 나타내지만, 명사절 접속사 if는 미래를 의미하기 위해서 미래시제를 사용해야 한다.

16 어떤 것을 경험할 때 만족과 즐거움을 발견하는 것은 '즐기다'이다.

17 파인애플 주스가 아닌 사과 주스가 필요하다.

18 부사는 주격보어가 될 수 없다. 따라서 smooth가 옳다.

19 질문: 키위를 자르기 전에 무엇을 해야 하나요?

20 질문: 우리는 막대 아이스크림 틀을 어디에 두나요?

21 이어지는 답변이 막대 아이스크림을 만드는 방법에 관한 것이므로 how가 옳다.

22 진수가 사과 주스를 사용하는 이유는 알 수 없다.

23 키위와 딸기를 가리키는 말이다.

24 감기에 걸렸을 때 파인애플을 먹어 보기를 권하는 이유는 파인애플에 비타민 C가 풍부해서이다.

25 몇 개의 아이스크림 제조기가 필요한지는 알 수 없다.

26 파인애플을 믹서에 넣고 사과 주스를 추가한 후 부드러워질 때까지 섞은 후에 막대 아이스크림에 혼합물을 넣어주는 순서가 옳다.

27 밑줄 친 for는 기간을 나타내는 전치사로 '~ 동안'이라는 의미로 사용된다. ① ~에 대해, ② [~을 돕기] 위해, ③ [고용 되어] ~을 위해[~에서], ④ ~에 찬성[지지]하는

28 질문: 키위 슬라이스를 추가한 다음에 무엇을 하나요?

29 아이스크림을 만드는 것을 끝냈다는 의미이다.

30 파인애플은 오렌지보다 더 많은 비타민 C를 가지고 있다. 따라서 오렌지는 파인애플보다 비타민 C를 덜 가지고 있는 것이다.

31 have a cold: 감기에 걸리다

32 밑줄 친 ⓒ는 큰 조각의 키위와 딸기를 의미한다.

33 진수는 자신의 막대 아이스크림이 예쁠 것이라고 하였지만 맛있을 것이라고 언급하지는 않았다.

34 과일들을 섞기 위하여 믹서가 필요하다.

35 복수명사를 지칭하므로 them이라고 쓰는 것이 옳다.

36 질문: 막대 아이스크림 틀을 냉동실에 얼마나 오랫동안 두어야 하나요?

34 nod 35 probably 36 be mad at
37 make up with 38 on time 39 keep -ing
40 fall asleep 41 run into
42 pay attention to 43 put on

교과서 파헤치기

Lesson
1

01 젖은 02 나누다, 공유하다, 분배하다
03 아마 04 장화, 부츠 05 대문자, 수도
06 장, 회장 07 방향 08 존중하다; 존경
09 건강하게 10 광고
11 문제, 곤란, 어려움
12 적극적인, 능동적인 13 유지하다
14 성난 15 떠나다
16 마법의; 마법, 마술 17 긴장한
18 (고개를) 끄덕이다
19 잘못하는, 형편없는 20 급히, 빠르게
21 관심사, 흥미 22 무례한 23 끔찍한
24 낭비하다 25 기회 26 재활용하다
27 대답하다, 응답하다 28 외국인
29 올리다, 게시하다 30 의견, 견해 31 향상시키다,
개선하다 32 정보 33 대화
34 유용한 35 ~할만도 하다,
~하는 것도 당연하다
36 ~을 공통적으로 지니다 37 잠들다
38 ~에 주의를 기울이다 39 계속 ~하다
40 ~을 우연히 만나다
41 ~을 신다, 입다, 쓰다 42 ~와 화해하다
43 ~에게 화나다

01 post 02 manage 03 asleep
04 shout 05 text message 06 bulletin board
07 foreigner 08 gladly 09 improve
10 conversation 11 information 12 join
13 feedback 14 respond 15 sometimes
16 angry 17 club 18 opinion
19 mean 20 recycle 21 character
22 useful 23 manner 24 nervous
25 respect 26 capital 27 terrible
28 direction 29 healthily 30 trouble
31 rude 32 interest 33 mad

1 mad, 성난 2 share, 공유하다, 함께 쓰다
3 save, 구하다 4 attention, 주의
5 common, 흔한, 공통의 6 terrible, 끔찍한
7 nod, 끄덕이다 8 manner, 태도
9 conversation, 대화 10 opinion, 의견
11 rude, 무례한, 버릇없는 12 chance, 기회, 가망
13 respond, 대답하다, 응답하다 14 capital, 대문자
15 improve, 향상시키다, 개선하다 16 recycle, 재활용하다

Listen & Speak 1 A
excited, school year / too, going to / What, make,
new friends / join a sports club / idea

Listen & Speak 1 B
join, clubs / joined the singing club / see / What's
wrong / president, magic club, two members /
terrible / What, get more members / Why don't,
school bulletin board / idea, right away

Listen & Speak 1 C
What, to sleep better / drink warm milk / a good idea,
do

Listen & Speak 2 A
Chinese character mean / idea, How about asking / I
will

Listen & Speak 2 B
why, so late / Oh, ran into / had to take, subway
station / didn't, tell, directions / didn't speak /about
using, next time / What kind of / changes, to
another, helpful / try, next time

Listen & Speak 2 C
let's, something together / want to do / How about
going, bookstore / Great

Real Life Talk
what's wrong / best, mad at / terrible, happend / said,
new hairstyle, just like / No wonder, mad at / won't
talk / probably, angry / What, make up with / How
about sending / good idea, do

Listen & Speak 1 A

B: I'm so excited about the new school year.

G: Me, too . It's going to be great!

B: What can I do to make a lot of new friends?

G: You can join a sports club.

B: That's a great idea.

Listen & Speak 1 B

Jenny: Mike, did you join any clubs?

Mike: Yes, I joined the singing club.

Jenny: Oh, I see.

Mike: What's wrong , Jenny?

Jenny: I'm the president of the magic club . But I only have two members.

Mike: Oh, no. That's terrible.

Jenny: What can I do to get more members?

Mike: Why don't you post an ad on the school bulletin board?

Jenny: That's a good idea . I'll do it right away.

Listen & Speak 1 C

A: What can I do to sleep better?

B: You can drink warm milk before bed.

A: That's a good idea . I'll do that.

Listen & Speak 2 A

Brian: Amy, what does this Chinese character mean?

Amy: Hmm... I have no idea . How about asking your teacher?

Brian: Okay, I will .

Listen & Speak 2 B

Sue: Minsu, why are you so late?

Minsu: Oh, I'm sorry. On the way, I ran into a foreigner.

Sue: Yes, and?

Minsu: I had to take him to the subway station.

Sue: Why didn't you just tell him the directions?

Minsu: He didn't speak English very well.

Sue: Hmm... How about using the Talk Smart app next time?

Minsu: Talk Smart? What kind of app is it?

Sue: It changes one language to another . It's really helpful.

Minsu: Really? I'll try it next time .

Listen & Speak 2 C

A: Minsu, let's do something together on Thursday.

B: Sounds great! What do you want to do?

A: How about going to the bookstore?

B: Great idea!

Real Life Talk

Brian: Hey, Mina, what's wrong?

Mina: My best friend, Kate, is mad at me.

Brian: That's terrible . What happend?

Mina: I said her new hairstyle was cute just like my dog's.

Brian: No wonder she's mad at you.

Mina: Right. She won't talk to me.

Brian: Yeah, She's probably really angry.

Mina: What can I do to make up with her?

Brian: How about sending her a text?

Mina: That's a good idea . I'll do that.

본문 TEST Step 1   p.09~10

01 new, year   02 nervous, talking, other

03 trouble starting

04 keeping, going   05 Don't worry

06 are, tips, become   07 Start, asking

08 Most, love, themselves   09 them, chance

10 ask, answer gladly   11 Be, listener

12 Many, poor   13 how can, be   14 Look, in

15 Listen, to, words   16 at, or, out

17 Give feedback 18 Be, active   19 Nod, from, to

20 can, little, or   21 also, like, more

22 Giving, shows that

23 Share, interests

24 have, by, listening

25 your, have, common   26 both like

27 talk, your favorite   28 Pay,to

29 Sometimes, may, in

30 Don't, up, aren't, to

31 Change, or, fall

32 other, chance, talk

33 Practice, and, be

34 Put others, will, with

본문 TEST Step 2   p.11~12

01 school year   02 nervous about talking, other

03 have trouble starting

04 about keeping, going   05 Don't worry

06 are, become, better talker

07 Start, asking interesting

08 Most, love to talk, themselves

09 give them the chance

10 When ask questions, answer gladly
11 Be, good listener
12 poor listeners
13 how can, be
14 Look, in, eye
15 Listen, to
16 Don't look at, space out
17 Give feedback
18 Be, active listener
19 Nod, from, to
20 say little, like
21 also say, like, interesting, Tell
22 Giving, shows, listening
23 Share, interests
24 can't have, by, listening
25 What, have in common
26 both like
27 talk about your favorite
28 Pay attention to
29 may not be interested in
30 Don't, wake up, aren't, listening to
31 Change, or, will, asleep
32 other, chance to talk
33 Practice, and, will soon be
34 Put others, want to talk with

1 새 학년이 시작되었다!
2 당신은 다른 학생들과 대화하는 것이 긴장되는가?
3 당신은 대화를 시작하는 데 어려움이 있는가?
4 대화를 계속 이어가는 것은 어떤가?
5 걱정마라.
6 여기 더욱 대화를 잘하는 사람이 되기 위한 다섯 가지 조언이 있다.
7 흥미로운 질문을 하는 것으로 시작해라.
8 대부분의 사람들은 그들 자신에 관해 말하는 것을 좋아한다.
9 그러니 그들에게 기회를 줘라.
10 당신이 사람들에 관해 질문하면, 그들은 기쁘게 대답할 것이다.
11 잘 듣는 사람이 되어라.
12 많은 사람들이 잘 듣지 못한다.
13 그러면 어떻게 잘 듣는 사람이 될 수 있을까?
14 사람들의 눈을 봐라.
15 그들의 말을 주의 깊게 들어라.
16 당신의 휴대 전화를 보거나 딴생각하지 마라!
17 반응을 보여 줘라.
18 능동적으로 듣는 사람이 되어라.
19 가끔 당신의 고개를 끄덕여라.
20 "왜!" 또는 "멋지다."와 같은 간단한 것들을 말해도 좋다.
21 또한 "흥미롭다, 더 이야기해 봐."와 같은 것을 말해도 좋다.
22 반응을 보여 주는 것은 당신이 듣고 있다는 것을 보여 준다.
23 공통의 관심사를 나눠라.
24 당신은 그저 듣는 것만으로 대화할 수는 없다.
25 당신과 상대편은 어떤 공통점을 가지고 있는가?

26 둘 다 스포츠를 좋아하는가?
27 그렇다면 당신이 가장 좋아하는 야구팀에 관해 대화해라.
28 듣는 사람에게 주의를 기울여라.
29 때때로 사람들은 당신의 화제에 관심이 없을지도 모른다.
30 "이봐, 잠 깨!" 또는 "왜 내 말을 안 듣는 거니?"라고 말하지 마라.
31 화제를 바꿔라, 그렇지 않으면 상대편은 잠이 들 것이다.
32 다른 사람에게 말할 기회를 줘라
33 이 조언들을 연습해라, 그러면 당신은 곧 대화를 잘하는 사람이 될 것이다.
34 다른 사람을 먼저 생각해라, 그러면 모든 사람이 당신과 대화하고 싶어 할 것이다.

1 The new school year is here!
2 Are you nervous about talking to other students?
3 Do you have trouble starting conversations?
4 What about keeping conversations going?
5 Don't worry.
6 Here are five tips to become a better talker.
7 Start by asking interesting questions.
8 Most people love to talk about themselves.
9 So give them the chance.
10 When you ask questions about people, they will answer gladly.
11 Be a good listener.
12 Many people are poor listeners.
13 So how can you be a good listener?
14 Look people in the eye.
15 Listen carefully to their words.
16 Don't look at your cell phone or space out!
17 Give feedback.
18 Be an active listener.
19 Nod your head from time to time.
20 You can say little things like, "Wow!" or "Cool."
21 You can also say something like, "That's interesting. Tell me more."
22 Giving feedback shows that you're listening.
23 Share common interests.
24 You can't have a conversation by just listening.
25 What do you and your partner have in common?
26 Do you both like sports?
27 Then talk about your favorite baseball team.
28 Pay attention to the listener.
29 Sometimes people may not be interested in your topic.

30 Don't say, "Hey, wake up!" or "Why aren't you listening to me?"

31 Change the topic, or your partner will fall asleep.

32 Give the other person a chance to talk.

33 Practice these tips, and you will soon be a great talker.

34 Put others first, and everyone will want to talk with you.

구석구석지문 TEST Step 1

p.19

Project Culture

1. Do, best
2. How about
3. dress, beautiful

Think and Write

1. Manners
2. others' opinions, and
3. Post, waste
4. only capital, sound like
5. Don't use, make others angry

Read and Write

1. better
2. What should
3. are, tips
4. listener
5. Look into, carefully
6. give feedback
7. Nod, from, to, active
8. Lastly, pay attention to

구석구석지문 TEST Step 2

p.20

Project Culture

1. A: Do your best! Go for it!
2. B: How about going window shopping?
3. C: Your dress is beautiful.

Think and Write

1. Facelook Manners
2. Respect others' opinions , and you will make many friends.
3. Post useful information, or you will waste others' time.
4. Don't use only capital letters, or you will sound like you're shouting.
5. Don't use rude language, or you will make others

angry.

Read and Write

1. Jason: I want to be a better talker.
2. What should I do?
3. Janet: Here are some tips.
4. Look into your partner's eyes and listen carefully.
5. Look into, carefully
6. Also give feedback.
7. Nod your head from time to time and be an active listener.
8. Lastly , when you talk, pay attention to your partner.

단어 TEST Step 1 p.21

01 똑똑한, 영리한　02 끔찍한, 무시무시한
03 약속하다; 약속　04 배려하는, 보살피는
05 껴안다　06 소리치다
07 재미있는, 익살맞은　08 개성, 성격
09 책임 있는, ~의 원인이 되는
10 (음식을) 주다, 먹이다　11 소리치다
12 경기, 경연　13 근면한, 열심히 일하는
14 도움이 되는　15 재미있는, 익살스러운
16 사라지다, 모습을 감추다　17 농담
18 친절한, 상냥한　19 외향적인, 사교적인
20 깨끗이 하는 사람, 세제　21 깔끔한
22 급우, 동급생　23 자선 단체　24 정거장, 역
25 참을성이 있는　26 기부하다　27 아름답게
28 재활용　29 도착하다　30 평범한, 정상적인
31 곤충, 벌레　32 비밀
33 창조적인, 창의적인　34 마른, 얇은
35 ~의 앞쪽에, ~ 앞에(서)
36 자기가 하고 싶은 일을 하다　37 ~에서 멀리
38 (전기, 가스, 수도 등을) 끄다
39 ~의 바다, 다량의 ~　40 곧
41 해외여행을 하다　42 ~을 자기 집으로 초대하다
43 ~을 기다리다

단어 TEST Step 2 p.22

01 pass	02 banker	03 recycling
04 beautifully	05 crazy	06 creative
07 coach	08 comedian	09 donate
10 secret	11 active	12 arrive
13 shake	14 patient	15 insect
16 badminton	17 leave	18 normal
19 pianist	20 station	21 thin
22 voice	23 invisible	24 friendly
25 disappear	26 yell	27 helpful
28 charity	29 personality	30 outgoing
31 feed	32 promise	33 tidy
34 humorous	35 look for	36 move to
37 do well	38 wait for	39 at once
40 turn off	41 in time	42 far from
43 in front of		

단어 TEST Step 3 p.23

1 banker, 은행원, 은행업자　2 promise, 약속하다
3 charity, 자선 단체　4 hug, 껴안다
5 tidy, 말끔히 정돈된, 단정한　6 rude, 무례한, 버릇없는
7 classmate, 급우, 동급생　8 comedian, 희극 배우, 코미디언
9 invisible, 보이지 않는　10 donate, 기부하다
11 friendly, 친절한, 상냥한　12 insect, 곤충
13 joke, 농담　14 shout, 소리치다　15 contest, 경기, 경연
16 cleaner, 깨끗이 하는 사람

대화문 TEST Step 1 p.24~25

Listen & Speak 1 A

arrive, in time / course, leaves at / already / train station, far from, I'm sure, arrive, before

Listen & Speak 1 B

up, look, worried / English speaking test / worry, practiced, lot / nervous, in front of / does, sure, do well / really think so / Of course, English speaker / feel much better

Listen & Speak 1 C

plays the guitar, well / I'm sure, get first place / think so too

Listen & Speak 2 A

that / my new coach / tall, handsome, What, like / friendly, humorous, a lot

Listen & Speak 2 B

how, like, these days / a lot, already made, friends / Happy, hear, How, become friends / all love, in the same club / great, What, like / kind / How about / outgoing / Why don't, invite them over

Listen & Speak 2 C

looking for, dance club / How about / What is she like / active, outgoing / ask her

Real Life Talk

looking for, for / How about / Who's / my classmate, moved, last week / good singer / sings beautifully, sure, perfect for / tell, more about, like / outgoing, friendly / have, number, Sure

대화문 TEST Step 2 p.26~27

Listen & Speak 1 A

G: Can we arrive in time ?
B: Of course . The train leaves at 5:10.
G: But, it's already 4:30.

B: The train station isn't very far from here. I'm sure we'll arrive there before 5.

Listen & Speak 1 B

Jenny: Hey, Minsu. What's up ? You look so worried.

Minsu: The English speaking test is this afternoon.

Jenny: Don't worry . You practiced a lot.

Minsu: But I get so nervous when I'm in front of the teacher.

Jenny: Everybody does . I'm sure you'll do well.

Minsu: Do you really think so?

Jenny: Of course . You are a great English speaker.

Minsu: Thanks. I feel much better now.

Listen & Speak 1 C

A: Sam plays the guitar really well.

B: Yeah, I'm sure he will get first place in the contest.

A: I think so , too.

Listen & Speak 2 A

B: Who's that?

G: He's my new badminton coach.

B: He's very tall and handsome. What is he like?

G: He is very friendly and humorous. I like him a lot.

Listen & Speak 2 B

Dad: Sue, how do you like your school these days?

Sue: I like it a lot, Dad. I already made two new friends, Rosa and Mike.

Dad: Happy to hear that. How did you become friends?

Sue: We all love English. We are also in the same club.

Dad: That's great . What are they like?

Sue: Rosa is very kind.

Dad: How about Mike?

Sue: He is outgoing.

Dad: Why don't you invite them over for dinner?

Sue: Okay, Dad.

Listen & Speak 2 C

A: I'm looking for a new member for my dance club.

B: How about Jenny?

A: What is she like?

B: She is active and outgoing . A: Thanks. I'll ask her.

Real Life Talk

Judy: Hojin, I'm looking for a singer for my school band.

Hojin: How about Junho Kim?

Judy: Junho Kim? Who's that?

Hojin: Oh, he's my classmate. He just moved to our school last week.

Judy: Is he a good singer?

Hojin: Yeah, he sings beautifully. I'm sure he will be perfect for your band.

Judy: Can you tell me more about him? What's he like?

Hojin: Well, he is very outgoing and friendly.

Judy: Great. Can I have his phone number?

Hojin: Sure.

본문 TEST Step 1   p.28~29

01 My name   02 in, eighth, third
03 banker, teacher
04 have, Sounds, normal
05 crazy, happened last
06 usually, home late   07 So, only, on
08 Even, usually, watches
09 last, home early
10 were, doing, own   11 giving food to
12 telling, not, texting   13 said, pass me
14 one, asked, pass   15 heard, too,with
16 yelling, Don't feed   17 was feeding
18 jumping up, down
19 shouted, invisible, Pass
20 happened, disappeared like
21 became invisible
22 hear, couldn't see   23 asked, Where
24 right, from, replied
25 couldn't, anything, awful
26 went, asked, to help
27 been invisible since
28 shook, never, like
29 When, home, miss
30 started crying, joined
31 In moments, tears
32 back, promise, cried
33 happened, appeared
34 hugged, attention, earlier, on

본문 TEST Step 2   p.30~31

01 My name
02 in the eighth grade, in the third grade
03 a banker, my mother
04 have, Sounds pretty normal
05 crazy, happened
06 usually comes home late

07 only see, on the weekends
08 Even, usually sleeps, watches
09 last, home early
10 were, doing our own thing   11 giving food to
12 telling, not to do, was texting
13 Pass me the bread
14 heard, pass me the bread
15 heard him, too busy with
16 was yelling, Don't feed   17 was feeding
18 jumping up, down
19 shouted, invisible, Pass
20 happened, disappeared like magic
21 became invisible
22 could hear, couldn't see
23 asked, Where are
24 right in front of, replied
25 couldn't, anything, awful
26 Next, went to, asked, to help
27 has been invisible since
28 shook, can't help, never seen anything
29 When, came home, miss
30 started crying, joined
31 In a few, a sea of
32 Come back, promise to pass, cried
33 happened, appeared
34 hugged us, all the attention, earlier, on the
   weekends

"누구 나한테 빵 좀 건네줄래?"
15 이번에 나는 아버지의 말을 들었지만 휴대 전화에 빠져 너무
   바빴다.
16 어머니는 소리치고 계셨다. "Smiley한테 음식을 주지 마!"
17 Hope는 Smiley에게 먹이를 주고 있었다.
18 Smiley는 펄쩍펄쩍 뛰고 있었다.
19 아버지가 소리치셨다. "내가 안 보이는 거야? 빵 좀
   건네줘!"
20 그때 일이 벌어졌다. 뿅! 아버지가 마법처럼 사라지셨다.
21 아버지는 투명 인간이 되셨다!
22 우리는 그의 말을 들을 수는 있었지만 그를 볼 수는 없었다.
23 우리는 물었다. "어디 계세요?"
24 아버지가 대답하셨다. "너희들 바로 앞에 있어."
25 우리는 그를 위해 할 수 있는 게 없었다. 끔찍한 밤이었다.
26 다음 날 아침, 우리는 병원에 가서 의사 선생님에게 도움을
   요청했다.
27 내가 말했다. "아버지가 어젯밤부터 안 보여요."
28 의사 선생님은 고개를 저으며 말씀하셨다. "도와 드릴 수가
   없네요. 이런 건 본 적이 없어요."
29 집에 왔을 때 Hope가 말했다. "아빠가 보고 싶어요."
30 그녀는 울기 시작했다. 어머니가 같이 우셨다.
31 곧 우리는 눈물바다가 되었다.
32 "돌아오세요, 아빠! 매일 아빠한테 빵을 건네드리겠다고
   약속해요!" 내가 외쳤다.
33 그때 일이 일어났다. 아버지가 다시 나타나셨다!
34 아버지가 우리를 안고 말씀하셨다. "관심 가져 줘서 고마워.
   집에 더 일찍 오고 주말에는 너희와 함께 놀겠다고 약속하마."

본문 TEST Step 3 p.32~33

1 내 이름은 Jimmy다.
2 나는 8학년이고, 내 여동생 Hope는 3학년이다.
3 우리 아버지는 은행원이시고, 어머니는 선생님이시다.
4 우리에겐 Smiley라는 개가 한 마리 있다. 꽤 평범한 것
  같다, 그렇지?
5 그런데 정말 이상한 일이 지난주에 일어났다.
6 우리 아버지는 보통 회사에서 늦게 집에 오신다.
7 그래서 우리는 주말에만 아버지를 본다.
8 주말에도 아버지는 보통 주무시거나 텔레비전을 보신다.
9 하지만 지난주 금요일에 아버지는 저녁을 드시러 일찍 집에
  오셨다.
10 식탁에서 우리는 모두 각자의 일을 하고 있었다.
11 Hope는 Smiley에게 음식을 주고 있었다.
12 어머니는 동생에게 그러지 말라고 말씀하고 계셨다. 나는
   문자를 보내고 있었다.
13 아버지가 말씀하셨다. "빵 좀 건네줘요."
14 아무도 그의 말을 듣지 못하자, 아버지는 다시 물으셨다.

본문 TEST Step 4-Step 5 p.34~37

1 My name is Jimmy.
2 I am in the eighth and my sister, Hope, is in the
  third grade.
3 My father is a banker and my mother is a teacher.
4 We have a dog, Smiley. Sounds pretty normal,
  right?
5 But a crazy thing happened last week.
6 My father usually comes home late from work.
7 So, we only see him on the weekends.
8 Even then, he usually sleeps or watches television.
9 But last Friday, he came home early for dinner.
10 At the table, we were all doing our own thing.
11 Hope was giving food to Smiley.
12 My mother was telling her not to do so. I was
   texting.
13 My father said, "Pass me the bread, please."
14 No one heard him, so he asked again, "Can

someone pass me the bread?"

15 I heard him this time, but I was too busy with my phone.

16 My mother was yelling, "Don't feed Smiley!"

17 Hope was feeding Smiley.

18 Smiley was jumping up and down.

19 My father shouted, "Am I invisible? Pass me the bread!"

20 Then, it happened. Poof! My father disappeared like magic.

21 He became invisible!

22 We could hear him, but we couldn't see him.

23 We asked, "Where are you?"

24 "I'm right in front of you," he replied.

25 We couldn't do anything for him. It was an awful night.

26 Next morning, we went to the hospital and asked the doctor to help us.

27 I said, "He has been invisible since last night."

28 The doctor shook his head and said, "I can't help you. I've never seen anything like this before."

29 When we came home, Hope said, "I miss Daddy."

30 She started crying. My mother joined her.

31 In a few moments, we were a sea of tears.

32 "Come back, Dad! I promise to pass you the bread every day!" I cried.

33 Then, it happened. My father appeared again!

34 He hugged us and said, "Thank you for all the attention. I promise to come home earlier and play with you on the weekends."

구석구석지문 TEST Step 1 p.38

Real Life Talk - Step 2

1. the best, to be
2. How about
3. What, like
4. responsible, tidy
5. I'm sure, board cleaner

Think and Write

1. My
2. My best friend
3. have known, for
4. humorous
5. funny jokes
6. both
7. have watched, together

8. sure, forever

Project - Step 3

1. Dear
2. that, secret
3. because, kind
4. like, big smile
5. I'm sure, this year
6. already helped, three times

구석구석지문 TEST Step 2 p.39

Real Life Talk - Step 2

1. A: Who is the best person to be the board cleaner?
2. B: How about Minsu?
3. A: What is he like?
4. C: He is responsible and tidy.
5. D: I'm sure he will be a good board cleaner for our class.

Think and Write

1. My Best Friend, Subin
2. My best friend is Subin.
3. I have known her for 3 years.
4. She is humorous.
5. She tells me many funny jokes.
6. She and I both like movies.
7. So we have watched many movies together.
8. I'm sure we'll be friends forever.

Project - Step 3

1. Dear Mina,
2. I'm happy that you're my secret friend.
3. I like you because you are very kind.
4. I also like your big smile.
5. I'm sure we'll be good friends this year.
6. P.S. I've already helped you three times.

단어 TEST Step 1 — p.40

01 미친 듯이, 열렬하게	02 던지다
03 단연, 틀림없이	04 청중, 관람객	05 재미있는, 우스운
06 기린	07 벽, 담	08 집회장, 홀
09 피아니스트, 피아노 연주자	
10 고치다, 낫게 하다	11 만남, 모임
12 헝가리	13 기계, 기계장치
14 (많은 사랑을 받는) 우상	
15 놓치다, 그리워하다	16 환상적인
17 자리, 좌석	18 자유	19 배드민턴
20 발명하다, 창안하다	21 본래의
22 벼룩시장	23 소리치다, 괴성을 지르다
24 얼룩말	25 서명	26 인사
27 창조물, 창작	28 작곡가	29 준비하다
30 움직임	31 공연, 연극, 실행	32 최근의
33 얼굴; ~을 마주 보다[향하다]	34 ~와는 달리
35 딸기	36 악보	37 종이접기
38 점점 높이다	39 격려하다, 힘을 북돋우다
40 동시에, 한꺼번에	41 누르다	42 기억해서, 외워서
43 ~에 열중하다, ~에 열광하다	

단어 TEST Step 2 — p.41

01 softly	02 amazing	03 fan
04 signature	05 grape	06 vacation
07 greeting	08 drummer	09 single
10 fall	11 strawberry	12 concert
13 prepare	14 breath	15 composer
16 movement	17 ballet	18 note
19 performance	20 recent	21 novel
22 creation	23 unlike	24 face
25 miss	26 liberty	27 scream
28 invent	29 heal	30 machine
31 definitely	32 madly	33 flea market
34 original	35 sheet music	36 audience
37 fantastic	38 cheer up	
39 hold one's breath		40 at once
41 press down	42 build up	43 in person

단어 TEST Step 3 — p.42

1 concert, 연주회, 음악회   2 composer, 작곡가
3 breath, 숨, 호흡   4 pianist, 피아니스트
5 flea market, 벼룩시장   6 fall, 떨어지다
7 signature, 서명   8 idol, 우상   9 performance, 공연
10 hall, 홀, 집회장   11 heal, 고치다, 낫게 하다
12 original, 본래의   13 prepare, 준비하다
14 audience, 청중, 관람객   15 ballet, 발레
16 creation, 창조물

대화문 TEST Step 1 — p.43~44

Listen & Speak 1 A

How's, going / fun, read lots, of / Which book, like best / like, best

Listen & Speak 1 B

what are, going to, this Saturday / I'm going to, fan meeting / a big fan / Which member, like best / like, best, sing, well / drummer, fantastic, want to join / love to, can't wait

Listen & Speak 1 C

like sports / Yes, do / Which sport, like best / tennis best, exciting

Listen & Speak 2 A

Why, all those / going to sell, flea market / old clothes, too / why don't you join

Listen & Speak 2 B

why, many paper flowers / for, mom's birthday / beautiful, Where, get / made / good / taking a paper folding class / going, the perfect gift / hope, too

Listen & Speak 2 C

Which country, want to visit / to visit Canada / Why do you want to / Because, want to see

Real Life Talk

with the school radio show, your English teacher, with / everyone, happy to be / Let's talk, what's your favorite band / Definitely / like, too, Which song, like best / most of, like, best / Why do you like it / Because, makes, feel better, down, Let's listen to

대화문 TEST Step 2 — p.45~46

Listen & Speak 1 A

Jack: Hi, Sumin. How's the book club going?
Sumin: It's fun . I read lots of interesting books.
Jack: Which book do you like best?
Sumin: I like Charlotte's Web best.

Amy: Jiho, what are you going to do this Saturday?

Jiho: I'm going to Blue Sky's fan meeting with my friends.

Amy: Wow, I'm also a big fan of the band.

Jiho: Really? Which member do you like best, Amy?

Amy: I like Lucy best. She sings really well.

Jiho: I like the drummer, Mike, best. He's fantastic! Do you want to join us?

Amy: Sure, I'd love to. I can't wait!

Listen & Speak 1 C

A: Do you like sports?

B: Yes, I do.

A: Which sport do you like best?

B: I like tennis best. It's so exciting!

Listen & Speak 2 A

B: Why do you have all those old clothes?

G: I'm going to sell them at the flea market.

B: Really? I have some old clothes, too.

G: Then why don't you join me this Saturday?

B: Okay.

Listen & Speak 2 B

Sujin: Tom, why do you have so many paper flowers?

Tom: They're for my mom's birthday.

Sujin: They're so beautiful. Where did you get them?

Tom: I made them.

Sujin: Wow, you're really good.

Tom: Thanks. I'm taking a paper folding class these days.

Sujin: They are going to be the perfect gift for your mom.

Tom: I hope so, too.

Listen & Speak 2 C

A: Which country do you want to visit for your dream vacation?

B: I want to visit Canada.

A: Why do you want to visit Canada?

B: Because I want to see Niagara Falls.

Real Life Talk

Mina: Good afternoon, friends. I'm Mina with the school radio show. Today Mr. Smith, your English teacher, is here with us. Hi, Mr. Smith.

Mr. Smith: Hello, everyone. I'm happy to be here with you.

Mina: Let's talk about music. Mr. Smith, what's your favorite band?

Mr. Smith: Definitely The Beatles.

Mina: Oh, I like them, too. Which song do you like best?

Mr. Smith: I like most of their songs, but I like Hey Jude best.

Mina: Why do you like it?

Mr. Smith: Because the song makes me feel better when I'm down.

Mina: That's great! Let's listen to the song.

본문 TEST Step 1   p.47~48

01 favorite, idol, will answer

02 often show, for   03 scream madly

04 Others, hours, take

05 some, even, another

06 recent creation, way   07 begin with, in

08 loved by, first 09 about, in, close

10 find, let's take, in   11 All, are filled

12 Unlike, side, faces

13 way, can, handsome, better   14 sheet music

15 play, memory

16 slowly by, touching

17 hold, breath, miss, note   18 up, down, at,

19 makes, powerful, rich

20 pays attention, movement

21 long beautiful, flies

22 like watching, at once   23 flies, ends

24 scream, throw, clothing, stage

25 goes wild   26 amazing star 27 His, born in

28 first, playing, when

29 later became, composer   30 think of, as

31 don't, give, listen

32 If, today's, will, original

본문 TEST Step 2   p.49~50

01 favorite, idol, Many, will

02 often show, love

03 scream madly at

04 Others, take pictures of

05 travel to, to see, favorite star

06 recent creation, way

07 begin with, in

08 loved by, not the first

09 How about, in, Not

10 To find, let's take, in   11 All, are filled

12 Unlike other concerts , faces, audience

13 way, can see, handsome, better

14 doesn't, any sheet music

15 begins to, from memory

16 slowly by softly touching

17 hold their breath, to miss a single note

18 builds up, press down, at once

19 makes, powerful, rich

20 pays attention to, body movement

21 long beautiful, flies

22 like watching, at once   23 flies, ends

24 scream, throw, clothing, onto the stage

25 goes wild   26 Who, amazing star

27 was, was born in

28 started playing, when he was seven

29 later became, composer   30 think of, as

31 Why don't, listen

32 If, like, idols, will love, original idol

---

19 이것은 음악을 아주 힘 있고 풍성하게 만든다.

20 청중들은 그의 모든 작은 몸짓에 주의를 집중한다.

21 그의 길고 아름다운 머리카락이 사방에 날린다.

22 이것은 마치 피아노와 발레 공연을 동시에 보는 것 같다.

23 시간은 쏜살같이 흐르고 연주회가 끝난다.

24 사람들은 소리를 지르며 꽃과 옷을 무대로 던진다.

25 콘서트홀은 열광의 도가니가 된다!

26 이 놀라운 스타는 누구였을까?

27 그의 이름은 Franz Liszt였고 그는 1811년에 헝가리에서 태어났다.

28 그는 7살에 처음 피아노를 치기 시작했다.

29 Liszt는 나중에 훌륭한 피아니스트이며 작곡가이자 선생님이 되었다.

30 그러나 많은 사람들은 그를 첫 번째 아이돌이라고 생각한다.

31 그의 음악을 한번 들어보는 게 어떤가?

32 만약 당신이 요즘의 아이돌을 좋아한다면, 원래의 아이돌도 좋아할 것이다.

---

1 여러분은 가장 좋아하는 K팝 아이돌이 있는가? 많은 학생들이 "그렇다."라고 답할 것이다.

2 이 학생들은 종종 자신들의 스타를 향해 큰 애정을 보인다.

3 어떤 학생들은 콘서트에서 미친 듯이 괴성을 지른다.

4 어떤 학생들은 스타의 사진을 찍기 위해 몇 시간을 기다린다.

5 어떤 학생들은 심지어 가장 좋아하는 스타를 보기 위해 다른 도시로 여행을 가기까지 한다.

6 아이돌이 최근의 창조물일까? 아니다!

7 아이돌은 1960년대의 The Beatles부터 시작됐을까?

8 그들은 많은 사람들에게 사랑받았지만, 최초는 아니다.

9 1950년대의 Elvis Presley는 어떤가? 완전히 헛짚었다.

10 답을 찾기 위해서 1845년에 빈에 있는 한 콘서트홀로 타임머신을 타고 가 보자.

11 모든 좌석이 꽉 차 있다.

12 다른 연주회와는 달리 피아노의 옆면이 청중을 향해 있다.

13 이렇게 함으로써, 청중은 잘생긴 185cm의 피아니스트를 더 잘 볼 수 있다.

14 그는 어떠한 악보도 가지고 있지 않다.

15 그는 기억으로 연주하기 시작한다.

16 그는 건반을 부드럽게 누르면서 천천히 시작한다.

17 모든 사람들이 단 하나의 음도 놓치고 싶지 않아서 숨을 죽인다.

18 그는 속도를 점점 올리고, 그의 긴 손가락으로 많은 건반을 한꺼번에 누른다.

---

1 Do you have a favorite K-pop idol? Many students will answer, "Yes."

2 These students often show great love for their stars.

3 Some scream madly at concerts.

4 Others wait hours to take pictures of their stars.

5 Some students even travel to another city to see their favorite stars.

6 Are idols a recent creation? No way!

7 Did idols begin with The Beatles in the 1960's?

8 They were loved by many, but they were not the first.

9 How about Elvis Presley in the 1950's? Not even close.

10 To find the answer, let's take a time machine to a concert hall in Vienna in 1845.

11 All the seats are filled

12 Unlike other concerts, the side of the piano faces the audience.

13 This way, the audience can see the handsome 185cm pianist better.

14 He doesn't have any sheet music with him.

15 He begins to play from memory.

16 He starts slowly by softly touching the keys.

17 All the people hold their breath because they don't want to miss a single note.

18 He builds up speed, and his long fingers press down on many keys at once.

19 This makes the music very powerful and rich.

20 The audience pays attention to his every little body movement.

21 His long beautiful hair flies everywhere.

22 It's like watching a piano and ballet performance at once.

23 Time flies and the concert ends.

24 People scream and throw flowers and pieces of clothing onto the stage.

25 The concert hall goes wild!

26 Who was this amazing star?

27 His name was Franz Liszt and he was born in 1811 in Hungary.

28 He first started playing the piano when he was seven.

29 Liszt later became a great pianist, composer and teacher.

30 But many people think of him as the first idol.

31 Why don't you give his music a listen?

32 If you like today's idols, you will love the original idol.

7. powerful, rich

8. ended, went wild

Real Life Talk - Step 2

A: Which, like

B: like, best

A: Why, like

B: Because, great

A: Which song, best

B: cheers me up

Think and Write

1. Dear

2. my, big fan of

3. all of, love, best.

4. that, acting, real

5. How, prepare for

6. in person, will ask, more questions

7. hope to

8. Love

Read And Write

1. Our Time

2. performed, successfully

3. was different from

4. side, faced, audience

5. could see, this way.

6. sheet music, from memory.

Real Life Talk - Step 2

1. A: Which singer do you like best?

2. B: I like John Lennon best.

3. A: Why do you like him?

4. B: Because he is a great singer.

5. A: Which song do you like best?

6. B: I like Imagine best. It cheers me up.

Think and Write

1. Dear Sandra,

2. Hello, my name is Jina and I'm a big fan of you.

3. I watched all of your movies and I love "Into the Sky" best.

4. I think that your acting is so real.

5. How do you prepare for your roles?

6. If I meet you in person, I will ask you many more questions.

7. I hope to see you soon.

8. Love , Jina

Read And Write

1. The Star of Our Time

2. Yesterday Franz Liszt performed his piano concert very successfully in Vienna.

3. This concert was different from others.

4. The side of the piano faced the audience.

5. They could see Liszt better this way.

6. He didn't have any sheet music and played from memory.

7. His music was so powerful and rich.

8. When the concert ended , the concert hall went wild .

10 marathon, 마라톤　11 traditional, 전통적인

12 protect, 보호하다　13 race, 경주　14 desert, 사막

15 throat, 목구멍　16 train, 훈련하다

단어 TEST Step 1　　　　　　　　　　p.59

01 선수, 육상 경기 선수	02 도달하다, ~에 이르다
03 장비, 설비	04 기대하다　05 온도
06 무서워하는	07 놀라운　08 무서운, 두려운
09 참가자	10 젖은, 축축한　11 목구멍
12 얼다, 얼어붙다	13 한계, 제한; 제한하다
14 태우다, 타다	15 요청하다; 요구, 요청
16 보호하다	17 바람이 (많이) 부는　18 치다, 때리다
19 상상하다	20 줄넘기　21 사서
22 굽다	23 경주, 경쟁　24 암벽 등반
25 훈련하다; 기차	26 끓는, 끓어오르는　27 행성
28 전통적인	29 보통의, 평범한　30 타격, 펀치
31 힘든, 어려운	32 배낭　33 던지다
34 매달다	35 계속되다　36 ~에 참가하다
37 ~까지	38 사실은, 실제로　39 생계를 위해
40 일련의	41 일어나다, 개최되다
42 ~가 떨어지다, 바닥나다	43 ~을 돌보다

단어 TEST Step 2　　　　　　　　　　p.60

01 desert	02 direction	03 traditional
04 finish line	05 boiling	06 Antarctica
07 backpack	08 field	09 throw
10 relay	11 dry	12 marathon
13 planet	14 mean	15 hang
16 tough	17 bat	18 ride
19 gym	20 kick	21 ordinary
22 punch	23 giant	24 sand
25 uniform	26 temperature	27 equipment
28 freeze	29 protect	30 participant
31 athlete	32 limit	33 throat
34 wet	35 take part in	36 in the middle of
37 a series of	38 take place	39 be out of
40 go on	41 take care of	42 up to
43 in fact		

단어 TEST Step 3　　　　　　　　　　p.61

1 giant, 거대한　2 Antarctica, 남극대륙

3 participant, 참가자　4 librarian, 사서

5 athlete, (운동) 선수　6 temperature, 온도

7 gym, 체육관　8 freeze, 얼다, 얼어붙다　9 boil, 끓다

대화문 TEST Step 1　　　　　　　　　　p.62~63

Listen & Speak 1 A

in your free time / often bake, How about / usually watch movies

Listen & Speak 1 B

happy, It's / What are you going to do / going to play badminton / play, often / my favorite free time activity / Who, usually play with / What do you do in your free time / often go, ride my bike

Listen & Speak 1 C

what, for a living / doctor / in your free time / I often play table tennis

Listen & Speak 2 A

have you ever been to / I have, went, What about / I've never been there, going / I'm sure, a lot

Listen & Speak 2 B

have you ever heard of / I've seen, were hanging / Guess, learning, these days / looked so scary / a little scared, enjoying / I think, should exercise, too / want to join / scary for, play basketball

Listen & Speak 2 C

Have you ever ridden / I have / When, ride a horse / Last summer

Real Life Talk

in your free time / often go rock climbing / What mountain, go to / usually do, gym near / Have you ever done / Not yet, hope to do / really cool, come and join / going this Saturday / sounds great / going to love

대화문 TEST Step 2　　　　　　　　　　p.64~65

Listen & Speak 1 A

Tony: Bomi, what do you do in your free time?

Bomi: I often bake cookies. How about you, Tony?

Tony: I usually watch movies.

Listen & Speak 1 B

Jean: I'm so happy. It's Friday!

Tom: What are you going to do on the weekend, Jean?

Jean: I'm going to play badminton.

Tom: Do you play badminton often?

Jean: Yes, it's my favorite free time activity.

Tom: Who do you usually play with?

Jean: My dad. What do you do in your free time?

Tom: I often go to the Han River and ride my bike.

Listen & Speak 1 C

Minsu: Ms. Allen, what do you do for a living?

Allen: I'm a doctor.

Minsu: What do you do in your free time?

Allen: I often play table tennis .

Listen & Speak 2 A

Mina: Tom, have you ever been to Jeju-do?

Tom: Yes, I have. I went there last winter vacation. What about you?

Mina: I've never been there, but I'm going there this summer.

Tom: That's great! I'm sure you'll like it a lot.

Listen & Speak 2 B

Suji: Mike, have you ever heard of flying yoga?

Mike: Yeah! I've seen it on TV. People were hanging in the air!

Suji: Guess what? I'm learning it these days.

Mike: Really? It looked so scary. Do you like it, Suji?

Suji: At first, I was a little scared, but now I'm enjoying it.

Mike: Sounds great! I think I should exercise more, too.

Suji: Do you want to join my yoga class?

Mike: No, that's too scary for me. I'll just play basketball.

Listen & Speak 2 C

A: Have you ever ridden a horse?

B: Yes, I have.

A: When did you ride a horse ?

B: Last summer .

Real Life Talk

Hojin: Judy, what do you do in your free time?

Judy: I often go rock climbing with my dad.

Hojin: What mountain do you go to?

Judy: No, Hojin. I usually do it at a gym near my house.

Hojin: I see. Have you ever done it on a real mountain?

Judy: Not yet. But I hope to do it someday.

Hojin: That's really cool. Can I come and join you next time?

Judy: Sure. I'm going this Saturday.

Hojin: That sounds great.

Judy: You're going to love it.

01 Imagine, middle, great

02 on, every direction

03 feels like, fire   04 burns, face, throat

05 open, backpack, drink   06 almost, out of

07 wet, drop, keep going

08 Sounds like   09 dream, take part

10 series, races across, toughest

11 Each race, long, takes   12 takes place, in

13 the driest, in

14 fact, hasn't rained, for   15 goes to, in

16 the windiest desert

17 third, heads to, in

18 the hottest, deserts   19 reach up to

20 travels, coldest, earth

21 throw boiling, freezes

22 the greatest, take part   23 Not, exactly

24 participants, ordinary, like   25 So why, do

26 librarian from, says

27 chance, limits, own

28 Anyone, crosses, anything

01 Imagine, in the middle of

02 go on and on   03 feels like, giant, fire

04 burns your face, throat

05 open your backpack to drink

06 almost, out of water

07 wet, with a drop of, keep going

08 Sounds like, bad dream

09 who take part in

10 a series of four races across, toughest deserts

11 Each race is, long, takes   12 takes place, in

13 the driest   14 In fact, hasn't rained, for

15 goes to, in   16 the windiest desert on earth

17 heads to   18 the hottest of, four deserts

19 reach up to

20 Finally, travels to the coldest desert

21 throw boiling water into freezes

22 the greatest runnners, take part in, right

23 Not, exactly   24 the participants are ordinary, like

25 why, do it   26 a librarian from France

27 a chance to test your limits, make

28 who crosses, can do anything

1 당신이 아주 큰 사막의 한 가운데에 있다고 상상해 봐라.

2 모래 벌판이 사면팔방으로 계속 이어진다.

3 태양은 거대한 불덩이 같다.

4 뜨거운 바람이 당신의 얼굴과 목구멍을 태운다.

5 당신은 물을 좀 마시려고 배낭을 연다.

6 오, 이런! 물이 거의 떨어져 간다.

7 당신은 물 한 방울로 목을 적시고 계속 간다.

8 나쁜 꿈인 것 같은가?

9 글쎄, '4 Deserts Race'에 참가하는 사람들에게 이것은 꿈이 아니다.

10 '4 Deserts Race'는 세계에서 가장 험한 사막들을 가로지르는 연속된 4개의 경주이다.

11 각 경주는 250킬로미터이고 7일이 걸린다.

12 첫 번째 경주는 칠레에 있는 아타카마 사막에서 열린다.

13 그곳은 세계에서 가장 건조한 사막이다.

14 실제로 아타카마 사막의 어떤 곳에는 400년간 비가 내리지 않았다!

15 다음 경주는 중국에 있는 고비 사막으로 이어진다.

16 그곳은 세상에서 가장 바람이 많이 부는 사막이다.

17 세 번째 경주는 이집트에 있는 사하라 사막으로 향한다.

18 그곳은 네 개의 사막 중 가장 뜨겁다.

19 온도가 섭씨 50도까지 올라갈 수 있다.

20 마지막으로 경주는 세상에서 가장 추운 사막인 남극 대륙으로 향한다.

21 이곳에서 끓는 물을 공중에 던지면, 그것은 얼어버린다!

22 세상에서 가장 훌륭한 달리기 주자들만 '4 Deserts Race'에 참가할 수 있다, 맞는가?

23 꼭 그렇진 않다.

24 많은 참가자들은 당신과 나와 같은 평범한 사람들이다.

25 그러면 그들은 왜 그것을 하는가?

26 프랑스 출신의 사서인 Adrianna는 말한다.

27 "그것은 당신의 한계를 시험하고 당신만의 역사를 만들 기회예요.

28 결승선을 넘는 사람은 어떤 것이든 할 수 있어요."

본문 TEST Step 3 - Step 4   p.72~75

1 Imagine you are in the middle of a great desert.

2 The sands go on and on in every direction.

3 The sun feels like a giant ball of fire.

4 The hot wind burns your face and throat.

5 You open your backpack to drink some water.

6 Oh, no! You're almost out of water.

7 You wet your throat with a drop of water and keep going.

8 Sounds like a bad dream?

9 Well, this is not a dream for the people who take part in the 4 Deserts Race.

10 The 4 Deserts Race is a series of four races across the world's toughest deserts.

11 Each race is 250 kilometers long and takes seven days.

12 The first race takes place in the Atacama Desert in Chile.

13 It is the driest desert in the world.

14 In fact, it hasn't rained in some parts of the Atacama Desert for 400 years!

15 The next race goes to the Gobi Desert in China.

16 It is the windiest desert on earth.

17 The third race heads to the Sahara Desert in Egypt.

18 It is the hottest of the four deserts.

19 Temperatures can reach up to 50℃.

20 Finally, the race travels to the coldest desert on earth, Antarctica.

21 If you throw boiling water into the air here, it freezes!

22 Only the greatest runners on the planet can take part in 4 Deserts Race, right?

23 Not exactly.

24 Many of the participants are ordinary people like you and me.

25 So why do they do it?

26 Adrianna, a librarian from France, says,

27 "It's a chance to test your limits and make your own history.

28 Anyone who crosses the finish line can do anything."

구석구석지문 TEST Step 1   p.76

Real Life Talk - Step 2

1. in your free time
2. often play
3. Have, played
4. haven't
5. Have, played
6. Yes, I have
7. hit a home run
8. have

Think and Write

1. Day, class
2. was held on
3. exciting
4. played basketball, jump rope
5. ran a relay race

6. jump rope, relay race

7. won, 100m race

8. got, highest score, became, overall

9. All the classes

단어 TEST Step 1 — p.78

01 조각, 일부, 부분	02 시원한, 냉정한, 멋진
03 추운, 찬; 감기	04 자르다 05 단계
06 파인애플	07 껍질을 벗기다; 껍질 08 믹서
09 냉동고	10 원천, 근원 11 대략, 약
12 조언, 비결	13 매끄러운, 부드러운
14 섞다, 혼합하다	15 ~인 채로 있다, 남다, 머무르다
16 시도하다, 해보다 17 더하다, 추가하다	
18 얇게 썰다(베다); 얇은 조각	19 비타민
20 나누다, 공유하다 21 건강	
22 혼합(물); 섞다, 혼합하다	23 우수한, 훌륭한
24 붓다, 따르다 25 끝내다, 마치다	26 딸기
27 ~까지 28 막대기, 지팡이	29 필요하다
30 ~을 만드는 기계(사람, 회사)	
31 예쁜, 귀여운; 꽤, 상당히	32 자기 자신의, 고유한
33 (문, 가게를) 닫다, (눈을) 감다	34 막대 아이스크림
35 사과 주스 36 시원함을 유지하다	37 감기에 걸리다
38 A를 B에 넣다 39 2분의 1	
40 A를 B(상태)로 자르다	41 ~을 섞다
42 A를 B에 붓다 43 한 잔(컵)의 ~	

구석구석지문 TEST Step 2 — p.77

Real Life Talk - Step 2

1. G: What do you do in your free time?

2. B: I often play sports.

3. G: Have you ever played table tennis?

4. B: No, I haven't.

5. G: Have you ever played baseball?

6. B: Yes, I have.

7. G: Have you ever hit a home run?

8. B: Yes, I have.

Think and Write

1. A Happy Day for Class 3

2. The school sports day was held on May 14th.

3. It was very exciting.

4. Students played basketball and did group jump rope.

5. They also ran a relay race and a 100m race.

6. Class 2 won the group jump rope, and Class 1 won the relay race.

7. Class 3 won the basketball game and the 100m race.

8. They got the highest score and became the overall winner.

9. All the classes had great fun.

단어 TEST Step 2 — p.79

01 apple juice	02 share	03 strawberry
04 enjoy	05 excellent	06 finish
07 close	08 stick	09 health
10 mix	11 ice pop	12 kiwi
13 maker	14 need	15 pour
16 orange	17 pretty	18 until
19 own	20 peel	21 freezer
22 slice	23 smooth	24 blend
25 piece	26 add	27 source
28 blender	29 tip	30 cut
31 try	32 stay	33 cool
34 pineapple	35 step	36 piece
37 pour A into B	38 a half(=one half)	
39 stay cool	40 cut A into B	41 have a cold
42 mix up	43 put A into B	

단어 TEST Step 3 — p.80

1 excellent, 훌륭한, 우수한   2 share, 공유하다

3 peel, 껍질을 벗기다　4 blender, 믹서
5 smooth, 매끄러운　6 stick, 막대기　7 step, 단계
8 tip, 조언, 비결　9 cut, 자르다　10 slice, 얇은 조각
11 mix, 혼합　12 vitamin, 비타민
13 pineapple, 파인애플　14 pour, 붓다, 따르다
15 add, 더하다　16 strawberry, 딸기

본문 TEST Step 1　　　　　　　　　　p.81~82

01 hot days, are　02 can, stay cool
03 Let's make, together
04 need, of, makers
05 Cut, into, pieces
06 Peel, slice them
07 Put, pieces into　　　　08 Add, juice
09 Blend until, smooth
10 Pour, into, makers　　　11 Add, slices
12 Close, pop　13 Put in, for about
14 Finished, Enjoy, on, stick　15 Health Tips
16 excellent source, vitamin
17 more vitamin, than
18 when, cold, try　　　　19 Share, Ideas
20 will, your own　21 Share your
22 will use, strawberries
23 cut, into, pieces　　　24 put into, with
27 think, will be

본문 TEST Step 2　　　　　　　　　　p.83~84

01 hot days of, are
02 How can, stay cool
03 Let's make, together
04 need, pineapple, kiwis, cup, makers
05 Steps　　　06 Cut, into small pieces
07 Peel, slice them
08 Put, pieces into the blender
09 Add, apple juice
10 Blend until, smooth
11 Pour, into, ice pop makers　12 Add, slices
13 Close, ice pop makers
14 Put them, for about　　15 Finished
16 Enjoy, on a stick　　　17 Health Tips
18 are an excellent source of vitamin
19 more vitamin C than oranges
20 when, have a cold, try
21 Share, Ideas　22 How will, make your own

23 Share your Ideas
24 use, strawberries.
25 cut them into big pieces
26 put them into, with apple juice
27 I think, will be pretty

본문 TEST Step 3　　　　　　　　　　p.85~86

1 더운 여름날이 왔어요.
2 우리는 어떻게 시원하게 지낼 수 있을까요?
3 막대 아이스크림을 함께 만들어 봐요!
4 여러분은 필요해요: 파인애플 1/2개, 키위 2개, 사과 주스 1컵,
　막대 아이스크림 틀
5 단계
6 파인애플을 작은 조각으로 자르세요.
7 키위의 껍질을 벗기고 얇게 자르세요.
8 파인애플 조각들을 믹서에 넣으세요.
9 사과 주스를 첨가하세요.
10 혼합물이 덩어리 없이 골고루 잘 섞일 때까지 섞으세요.
11 혼합물을 막대 아이스크림 틀에 부으세요.
12 키위 조각을 추가하세요.
13 막대 아이스크림 틀을 닫으세요.
14 약 세 시간 동안 그것들을 냉동고에 넣으세요.
15 끝났어요!
16 막대 위의 여름을 맛보세요!
17 건강 조언들
18 파인애플은 비타민 C의 훌륭한 원천이에요
19 파인애플에는 비타민 C가 오렌지보다 더 많이 들어 있어요
20 그러니 감기에 걸리면 파인애플을 먹어 보세요.
21 여러분의 생각을 나누세요!
22 여러분은 어떻게 막대 아이스크림을 만들 건가요?
23 여러분의 생각을 나누세요!
24 저는 키위와 딸기를 사용할 거예요.
25 저는 그것들을 크게 자를 거예요.
26 그것들을 사과 주스와 함께 막대 아이스크림 틀에 넣을 거예요.
27 제 막대 아이스크림은 예쁠 것 같아요.

본문 TEST Step 3-Step 4　　　　　　　p.87~90

1 The hot days of summer are here.
2 How can we stay cool?
3 Let's make ice pops together!
4 You need: 1/2 pineapple, 2 kiwis, 1 cup of apple
　juice, ice pop makers
5 Steps: Cut the pineapple into small pieces.
6 Peel the kiwis and slice them.

7 Put the pineapple pieces into the blender.

8 Add the apple juice.

9 Blend until the mix is smooth.

10 Pour the mix into the ice pop makers.

11 Add the kiwi slices.

12 Close the ice pop makers.

13 Put them in the freezer for about three hours.

14 Finished! Enjoy your summer on a stick!

15 Health Tips

16 Pineapples are an excellent source of vitamin C.

17 They have more vitamin C than oranges.

18 So when you have a cold, try pineapples.

19 Share Your Ideas!

20 How will you make your own ice pops?

21 Share Your Ideas!

22 I will use kiwis and strawberries.

23 I will cut them into big pieces.

24 I will put them into the ice pop makers with apple juice.

25 I think my ice pops will be pretty.

MEMO

적중**100**plus

1학기 전과정

영어 기출 문제집

정답 및 해설

동아 | 이병민

적중 1**○○** + 특별부록

Plan B

우리학교
최신기출

동아 · 이병민 교과서를 배우는

학교 시험문제 분석 · 모음 · 해설집

전국단위 학교 시험문제 수집 및 분석
출제 빈도가 높은 문제 위주로 선별
문제 풀이에 필요한 상세한 해설

중2-1
영어

동아 · 이병민

◎ 선택형 문항의 답안은 컴퓨터용 수정 싸인펜을 사용하여 OMR 답안지에 바르게 표기하시오.
◎ 서술형 문제는 답을 답안지에 반드시 검정 볼펜으로 쓰시오.
◎ 총 31문항 100점 만점입니다. 문항별 배점은 각 문항에 표시되어 있습니다.

[울산 ○○중]

1. 다음 단어의 관계가 나머지와 <u>다른</u> 것은?   (2점)

① careful – carefully
② friend – friendly
③ glad – gladly
④ healthy – healthily
⑤ nice – nicely

[경기 ○○중]

3. 다음 중 어법상 옳은 문장의 총 개수는?   (3점)

• Not let's go outside.
• Do you have a pen to write?
• I have several things to buy.
• I want cold something to drink.
• She has some homework to finish it.

① 1개   ② 2개   ③ 3개
④ 4개   ⑤ 5개

[부산 ○○중]

2. 빈칸에 들어갈 말을 순서대로 바르게 나열한 것은?
     (3점)

• The Internet is _____ for finding information quickly.
• You need to _____ your time wisely.
• I'm _____ at math.
• My mom has a good sense of _____.

① use – manage – poor – direct
② use – manner – attention – direct
③ useful – manage – poor – direction
④ useful – manner – poor – direction
⑤ useful – manage – attention – direct

[서울 서초구 ○○중]

4. ( )에 각각 들어갈 말로 알맞지 <u>않은</u> 것은?   (2점)

• What does this Chinese character (   )?
• I'm the (   ) of the sports club.
• How (   ) going to the bookstore?
• What are you (   ) to do this school year?

① about   ② mean
③ improve   ④ planning
⑤ president

5. 여자의 고민에 대한 응답으로 <u>어색한</u> 것은? (2점)

> A: I'm overweight. What can I do to be healthier?
>
> B: _____

① You can drink less soda.

② Why don't you drink more water?

③ Why don't you exercise every day?

④ You can eat more fruits and vegetables.

⑤ You can invite your friends over for dinner.

[6-8] 다음 대화를 읽고 물음에 답하시오.

> Sumi: Minsu, why are you so late?
>
> Minsu: Oh, I'm sorry. On the way, I ran into a foreigner.
>
> Sumi: Yes, and?
>
> Minsu: I had to take him to the subway station.
>
> Sumi: Why didn't you just tell him the directions?
>
> Minsu: He didn't speak English very well.
>
> Sumi: Hmm... How about using the *Talk Smart* app next time?
>
> Minsu: *Talk Smart*? What kind of app is it?
>
> Sumi: It changes one language to another. It's really helpful.
>
> Minsu: Really? I'll try it next time.
>
> *Person A : Sumi / Person B : Minsu

6. If this dialogue is made for a video clip, which one is appropriate? (3점)

① It is an advertisement of a subway map.

② It is a public campaign for being on time all the time.

③ It is a scenario of a movie, which is about citizens' busy life.

④ It is a script of a commercial film. It advertises the *Talk Smart* app.

⑤ Speaking English fluently is important in our everyday life, so it advertises English education.

7. 위 대화의 내용과 일치하는 것은? (4점)

① Minsu had an accident on his way.

② Minsu does not speak English at all.

③ Minsu showed up for the appointment on time.

④ Minsu had the kindness to show Sumi the way.

⑤ Minsu has no experience with the *Talk Smart* app.

8. What is the relationship between person A and person B in this dialogue? (3점)

① mother – son

② student – student

③ doctor – patient

④ teacher – student

⑤ friend – friend

9. 문장 (a)와 (b)가 〈보기〉와 같은 관계가 되도록 빈칸을
채워 문장을 완성하시오. (축약형을 쓰지 않음)   (4점)

보기

Leave now, and you will get there on time.
= If you leave now, you will get there on
time.

(a) Don't say bad words to your friends, or
    they will not like you.

(b) = _____ _____ _____

    _____ words to your friends,

    _____ _____ _____

    _____ _____ .

10 위 글의 내용과 일치하는 것은?   (3점)

① A conversation is just listening.

② Finding common interests is helpful during
   the talk.

③ Every person likes to listen to others' topic.

④ If you give others a chance to talk, they'll
   fall asleep.

⑤ Practicing the tips above cannot make you
   a great talker.

[10~11] 다음 글을 읽고 물음에 답하시오.

• Share common interests.

You can't have a conversation by just
listening. What do you and your partner have
in common? Do you both like sports? Then
talk about your favorite baseball team.

• Pay attention to the listener.

Sometimes people may not be interested in
your topic. Don't say, "Hey, wake up!" or
"Why aren't you listening to me?" Change
the topic, or your partner will fall asleep.
Give the other person a chance ⓐto talk.

Practice these tips, and you will soon be a
great talker. Put others first, and everyone
will want to talk with you.

11. 위 글의 밑줄 친 ⓐ와 용법이 같은 것을 있는 대로 고른
것은?   (4점)

• ⓑTo bake cookies is not that difficult.

• This is a good place ⓒto watch the sunset.

• This book is good ⓓto study English
  grammar.

• My hobby is ⓔto sing happy songs in a
  loud voice.

• A pencil ⓕto write with and a book are all
  you need.

① ⓑ   ② ⓑ, ⓒ

③ ⓒ, ⓔ   ④ ⓒ, ⓕ

⑤ ⓓ, ⓔ, ⓕ

12. 다음 대화의 내용과 일치하는 것은? (3점)

Jenny: Mike, did you join any clubs?
Mike: Yes, I joined the singing club.
Jenny: Oh, I see.
Mike: What's wrong, Jenny?
Jenny: I'm the president of the magic club. But I only have two members.
Mike: Oh, no. That's terrible.
Jenny: What can I do to get more members?
Mike: Why don't you post an ad on the school bulletin board?

① Jenny는 노래 동아리에 가입했다.
② Mike는 마술 동아리의 회장이다.
③ 마술 동아리에는 4명이 가입했다.
④ Mike는 학교 게시판 꾸미기가 취미이다.
⑤ Jenny는 더 많은 동아리 회원들을 모집하고 싶어 한다.

13. 다음 대화의 빈 곳에 가장 알맞은 것은? (3점)

A: _____
B: You can join a club.
A: Good idea. I'll do that.

① What's wrong?
② What club did you join?
③ How did you become friends?
④ What can I do to make new friends?
⑤ What do you want to do this school year?

14. 다음 대화의 밑줄 친 부분과 바꿔 쓸 수 있는 것은? (3점)

B: Amy, what does this Chinese character mean?
G: Hmm... I have no idea. How about asking your teacher?
B: Okay, I will.

① How can you ask your teacher?
② Why don't you ask your teacher?
③ What can I do to ask your teacher?
④ What will you do to ask your teacher?
⑤ What should I do to ask your teacher?

[15-17] 다음 글을 읽고 물음에 답하시오.

1. You can't have a conversation by just listening. What do you and your partner have (A)_____ common? Do you both like sports? Then talk about your favorite baseball team.

2. People may not be interested (B)_____ your topic. Don't say, "Hey, wake up!" or "Why aren't you listening to me?" Change the topic, or your partner will fall asleep. Give the other person a chance ⓐto talk.

Practice these tips, and you will soon be a great talker. Put others first, and everyone will want to talk with you.

15. 위 글의 (A)와 (B)에 공통으로 들어갈 단어는? (2점)

① in   ② on   ③ to

④ up   ⑤ for

16. 위 글의 밑줄 친 ⓐ와 쓰임이 같은 것을 〈보기〉에서 있는 대로 고른 것은?   (3점)

보기

ⓐ I have lots of things <u>to do</u>.

ⓑ There are no chairs <u>to sit on</u>.

ⓒ She wants <u>to buy</u> some clothes.

ⓓ His dream is <u>to become</u> a doctor.

ⓔ I have some pictures <u>to show</u> you.

① ⓐ, ⓓ   ② ⓑ, ⓒ

③ ⓒ, ⓓ   ④ ⓐ, ⓑ, ⓔ

⑤ ⓑ, ⓓ, ⓔ

17. 위 글 첫 문단에서 글쓴이가 말하고자 하는 것은?

(3점)

① Respond quickly.

② Put yourself first.

③ Be a good listener.

④ Talk about baseball.

⑤ Share common interests.

[18–20] 다음 대화를 읽고 물음에 답하시오.

B: Hey, Mina, what's wrong?

(A) Right. She won't talk to me.

(B) That's terrible. What happened?

(C) My best friend, Kate, is mad at me.

(D) No wonder she's mad at you.

(E) I said her new hairstyle was cute just like my dog's.

M: Yeah. She's probably really angry.

B: What can I do to make up with her?

M: (a)_____

B: That's a good idea. I'll do that.

*B: Brian

18. 위 대화가 자연스럽게 이어지도록 (A)~(E)가 바르게 배열된 것은?   (4점)

① (D) - (E) - (B) - (A) - (C)

② (C) - (B) - (E) - (D) - (A)

③ (E) - (B) - (C) - (D) - (A)

④ (C) - (A) - (E) - (B) - (D)

⑤ (E) - (D) - (A) - (C) - (B)

19. Read the conversation and choose the statement that is NOT true.   (3점)

① Kate is made at Mina.

② Kate has a new hairstyle.

③ Brian will send a text to Kate.

④ Kate and Mina are best friends.

⑤ Brian offers a suggestion to Mina.

20. ⓐ에 들어갈 말로 <u>어색한</u> 것은?　　　　(3점)

① How about sending her a text?

② Why don't you say sorry to her?

③ What about writing a letter to her?

④ Maybe you should send her a e-mail.

⑤ I think you should not talk to her anymore.

22 주어진 우리말을 〈조건〉에 맞게 영작하시오.　(4점)

> 조건
> • 'and' 또는 'or'를 사용할 것
> • 축약형을 사용하지 말 것
> • 문장부호에 유의하여 총 9단어로 작성할 것

> • 다른 사람들의 의견들을 존중해라, 그러면 당신은 많은 친구들을 만들 수 있을 것이다.

→ _____

_____

21. 다음 대화의 빈칸 ⓐ에 들어갈 표현으로 적절하지 않은 것은?　　　　(3점)

> B: I'm so excited about the new school year.
> G: Me, too. It's going to be great!
> B: What can I do to make a lot of new friends?
> G: _____
> B: That's a great idea.

① You can join a sports club.

② What about joining a sports club?

③ Let's join a sports club together.

④ You've already joined a sports club.

⑤ Why don't you join a sports club?

23. 밑줄 친 to 부정사의 쓰임이 <u>다른</u> 하나는?　(3점)

① There is a chair <u>to sit</u> on.

② We have lots of things <u>to do</u>.

③ He really likes <u>to play</u> soccer.

④ I have some questions <u>to ask</u>.

⑤ Would you like something <u>to drink</u>?

24. 다음 단어의 영어 풀이가 <u>어색한</u> 것은? (4점)

① improve: to make something/somebody worse than before

② attention: the act of applying the mind to something

③ direction: the path on which something is moving

④ manage: to use your time, money, etc, wisely, without wasting it

⑤ president: a person in charge of an organization

25. 다음 글 뒤에 이어질 내용으로 가장 적절한 것은? (4점)

> The new school year is here! Are you nervous about talking to other students? Do you have trouble starting conversations? What about keeping conversations going? Don't worry. When you practice the following tips, you will soon be a great talker.

① 대화를 할 때 긴장하는 이유

② 좋은 화자가 되기 위한 조언

③ 처음 만난 사람과 친해지는 법

④ 새로운 학교에서 적응하는 방법

⑤ 대화를 이어가지 못하는 사람들의 특징

[26–30] 다음 글을 읽고 물음에 답하시오.

> Here are 3 tips to become a better talker.
>
> 1. Give feedback.
>   Be an active listener. Nod your head (A)<u>from time to time</u>. (ⓐ) You can say little things like, "Wow!" or "Cool." You can also say something like, "That's interesting. Tell me more." (B)<u>피드백을 주는 것은 당신이 듣고 있는 중이라는 것을 보여준다.</u> (ⓑ)
>
> 2. Share common interests.
>   You can't have a conversation by just listening. What do you and your partner have in common? Do you both like sports? Then talk about your favorite baseball team.
>
> 3. Pay attention to the listener.
>   (ⓒ) Sometimes people may not be interested in your topic. Don't say, "Hey, wake up!" or "Why aren't you listening to me?" (ⓓ) Give the other person a chance to talk. Practice these tips, and you will soon be a great talker. Put others first, and everyone will want to talk with you. (ⓔ)

26. 위 글의 ⓐ~ⓔ 중 주어진 문장이 들어갈 알맞은 곳은? (3점)

> Change the topic, or your partner will fall asleep.

① ⓐ   ② ⓑ   ③ ⓒ   ④ ⓓ   ⑤ ⓔ

27. 밑줄 친 (A)from time to time과 같은 의미를 가진 한 단어를 〈조건〉에 맞게 적으시오. (4점)

조건
• s로 시작하는 단어

30. 밑줄 친 (B)를 영작하고자 한다. 아래에 주어진 〈조건〉에 맞게 영작하시오. (5점)

조건
• 동명사 주어를 사용할 것
• give 동사를 사용할 것

→ _____

_____

28. 위 글 속에 나온 단어의 영영풀이가 아닌 것은? (4점)

① the act of applying the mind to something
② someone who comes from a different country
③ the use of speech for informal exchange of views or ideas
④ advice, criticism or information about how good something is
⑤ to move your head up and down as a way of saying "yes"

29. 다음 중 위 글의 내용과 다른 것은? (3점)

① 당신은 그저 듣는 것만으로 대화할 수 있다.
② 와우!, 멋진데! 같은 사소한 말들로 피드백을 줄 수 있다.
③ 당신과 상대편이 어떤 공통점을 가지고 있다면 그 관심사를 나눠라.
④ 때때로 사람들은 당신의 화제에 관심이 없을지도 모른다.
⑤ 다른 사람을 먼저 생각하라. 그러면 모든 사람이 당신과 대화하고 싶어할 것이다.

31. 밑줄 친 ⓐ와 같은 용법인 것은? (3점)

Start by asking interesting questions. Most people love ⓐto talk about themselves. So give them the chance. When you ask questions about people, they will answer gladly.

① I have no money to buy it.
② She didn't want me to sleep.
③ I don't have any chairs to sit on.
④ We need someone to tell the truth.
⑤ I must study hard to pass the exam.

◎ 선택형 문항의 답안은 컴퓨터용 수정 싸인펜을 사용하여 OMR 답안지에 바르게 표기하시오.
◎ 서술형 문제는 답을 답안지에 반드시 검정 볼펜으로 쓰시오.
◎ 총 31문항 100점 만점입니다. 문항별 배점은 각 문항에 표시되어 있습니다.

[대전 ○○중]

1. 다음 중 단어의 영어 뜻으로 가장 알맞은 것은? (3점)

① improve: to make something worse than before

② responsible: putting a lot of effort into something

③ promise: to tell someone that you will do or not do something

④ nod: to move your head from side to side as a way of answering "no"

⑤ active: making an effort and leaving something to happen by itself

[서울 강남구 ○○중]

2. 빈칸에 공통으로 들어갈 단어로 알맞은 것은? (2점)

• Keep these _____s in mind and try to put them into practice.
• In most Western countries, you have to _____ waiters and waitresses at restaurants.

① nod   ② tip   ③ letter
④ point   ⑤ advice

[서울 성북구 ○○중]

3. 다음 중 영영 풀이에 해당하는 단어는? (2점)

always putting lots of effort and care into work

① tidy   ② kind
③ patient   ④ responsible
⑤ hard-working

[경북 ○○중]

4. 다음 문장 중 어법상 옳은 것은? (3점)
① It's time to goes to bed.
② We don't have time to waste.
③ I have some questions ask you.
④ I had a chance talking to her.
⑤ We have no place rested in.

[경기 ○○중]

5. 다음 중 밑줄 친 부분의 용법이 다른 하나는? (3점)
① I need something to eat.
② I think it's going to be great.
③ Love was such an easy game to play.
④ Give the other person a chance to talk.
⑤ I have a lot of homework to finish today.

[6-8] 다음 대화를 읽고 물음에 답하시오.

> Kate: Why are you so late?
> Minsu: I'm sorry. On the way, I ran into a foreigner.
> Kate: Yes, and?
> Minsu: I had to take him to the subway station.
> Kate: Why didn't you just tell him the directions?
> Minsu: He didn't speak English very well.
> Kate: (A)How about using the Talk Smart?
> Minsu: ⓐTalk Smart? What kind of app is it?
> Kate: It changes one language to another. It's really (B)_____.
> Minsu: Really? I'll try it next time.

7. 위 대화의 빈칸 (B)에 들어갈 단어로 알맞은 것은?
(2점)

① awful　　　　② helpful
③ strange　　　④ terrible
⑤ nervous

8. 위 대화의 밑줄 친 ⓐ에 대한 설명으로 옳은 것은?
(3점)

① 발음을 교정해주는 응용프로그램이다.
② 해외여행을 안내해주는 응용프로그램이다.
③ 무료로 외국어를 학습할 수 있는 응용프로그램이다.
④ 한 언어를 다른 언어로 번역해주는 응용프로그램이다.
⑤ 음악을 포함한 사진 동영상을 제작하는 응용프로그램이다.

6. 위 대화의 밑줄 친 부분 (A)와 바꿔 쓸 수 있는 것은?
(4점)

① How do you use the Talk Smart?
② When do you use the Talk Smart?
③ Why don't you use the Talk Smart?
④ What made you use the Talk Smart?
⑤ Why do you want to use Talk Smart?

9. 다음에서 설명하고 있는 영어 단어로 가장 옳은 것은?
(2점)

> a person who is from a country that is not your own country

① foreigner　　② subway
③ helpful　　　④ direction
⑤ language

- 10 -

10. 다음 대화 중 어색한 것은? (3점)

① A: Amy, what does this Chinese character mean?

B: Hmm... I have no idea.

② A: I'm so excited about the new school year.

B: Me, too. It's going to be great!

③ A: What can I do to sleep better?

B: You can drink warm milk before bed.

④ A: Let's do something together on Thursday.

B: Sorry, I can't. What about going to the bookstore?

⑤ A: Why don't you post an ad on the school bulletin board to get more members?

B: That's a good idea. I'll do it right away.

11. 〈보기〉의 밑줄 친 부분과 쓰임이 같은 것은? (3점)

> 보기
> Here comes the bus <u>to take</u>.

① He wants <u>to become</u> a doctor.

② His work is <u>to sweep</u> the floor.

③ The water is not good <u>to drink</u>.

④ They are happy <u>to hear</u> the news.

⑤ I have some pictures <u>to show</u> you.

12. to부정사를 이용하여 "지구를 지키려면 나는 무엇을 할 수 있을까?"를 영작하시오. (5점)

> I: _____
> J: You can recycle paper.
> I: That's a good idea. I'll do that.

[13~14] 다음 글을 읽고 물음에 답하시오.

> ⓐ(from / your / time / head / to / nod / time). You can say little things like, "Wow!" or "Cool." You can also say something like, "That's interesting. Tell me more." ⓑ반응을 보여 주는 것은 당신이 듣고 있다는 것을 보여 준다.

13. 위 글의 ⓐ 안의 단어들을 어법상 순서대로 바르게 배열하여 완성한 문장으로 가장 적절한 것은? (3점)

① Your head nod from time to time.

② Head from time to time your nod.

③ Nod your head from time to time.

④ Nod time to time from your head.

⑤ From nod time to time your head.

14. 위 글의 ⓑ의 우리말을 영어로 바르게 쓴 것은?
(3점)

① To give feedback show you're listening.

② To give feedbacks show that you listen.

③ Give feedback shows that you're listen.

④ Giving feedback show you're listening.

⑤ Giving feedback shows you're listening.

16. 다음 대화문의 (A)에 들어갈 수 있는 것만을 〈보기〉에서 고른 것은?
(4점)

> Tom: Hey, Mina, what's wrong?
>
> Mina: My best friend, Kate, is upset because of me.
>
> Tom: That's too bad. What happened?
>
> Mina: I said her new hairstyle was cute like my dog's.
>
> Tom: No wonder she's mad at you.
>
> Mina: Yeah. Maybe she's really angry.
>
> _____(A)_____
>
> Tom: Why don't you send her a text?
>
> Mina: That's a good idea. I'll do that.

보기

ㄱ. What should I do to make up with her?

ㄴ. What can I do to make her feeling better?

ㄷ. Can you give me some advice how to make her feeling better?

ㄹ. Which one do you like better, my dog's hairstyle or Mina's?

ㅁ. What makes you change your feeling better?

① ㄱ, ㄴ, ㄷ   ② ㄱ, ㄷ, ㄹ

③ ㄴ, ㄷ, ㄹ   ④ ㄴ, ㄷ, ㅁ

⑤ ㄷ, ㄹ, ㅁ

15. 문장 (a)와 (b)가 〈보기〉와 같은 관계가 되도록 빈칸을 채워 문장을 완성하시오. (축약형을 쓰지 않음) (5점)

보기

Leave now, and you will get there on time.
= If you leave now, you will get there on time.

(a) Be quiet, or the baby will wake up.

(b) = _____ _____ _____
_____ quiet, _____ _____
_____ _____ _____.

17. 다음 〈보기〉에서 어법상 쓰임이 알맞은 것을 <u>모두</u> 고른 것은? (3점)

> **보기**
> a. I need friends to play.
> b. That is impolite to say so.
> c. There are no chairs to sit on.
> d. Sam has too much work to do.

① a, b   ② a, d   ③ c, d
④ a, b, c   ⑤ b, c, d

19. 대화가 끝난 후 Jane이 바로 할 일로 적절한 것은? (3점)

① 노래 동아리 가입하기
② 마술 동아리에 가입하기
③ 노래 동아리 포스터 만들기
④ 학교 게시판에 노래 동아리 홍보 안내문 붙이기
⑤ 학교 게시판에 마술 동아리 회원 모집 광고 붙이기

[18-19] 다음 대화를 읽고 물음에 답하시오.

> Jane: Mike, did you join any clubs?
> Mike: Yes, I joined the singing club.
>
> (A) I'm the president of the magic club. But I only have two members.
> (B) What can I do to get more members?
> (C) Oh, I see.
> (D) Why don't you post an ad on the school bulletin board?
> (E) Oh, no. That's terrible.
> (F) What's wrong, Jane?
>
> Jane: That's a good idea. I'll do it right away.

[20-21] 다음 글을 읽고 물음에 답하시오.

> The new school year is here! Are you nervous about talking to other students? Do you have ⓐtrouble starting conversations? What about keeping conversations going? Don't worry. Here are five tips to become a better talker.

18. 위 대화의 순서로 가장 적절한 것은? (3점)
① (C)–(F)–(A)–(B)–(E)–(D)
② (C)–(F)–(A)–(E)–(B)–(D)
③ (C)–(E)–(F)–(B)–(D)–(A)
④ (F)–(A)–(B)–(E)–(C)–(D)
⑤ (B)–(D)–(C)–(E)–(F)–(A)

20. 밑줄 친 ⓐtrouble과 같은 의미를 가진 한 단어를 〈조건〉에 맞게 적으시오. (5점)

> **조건**
> • d로 시작하는 단어
> • 복수형

– 13 –

21. 위 글에 이어질 내용으로 가장 적절한 것은? (3점)

① 친구와 화해하는 방법

② 새 친구를 사귀는 방법

③ 시간 관리를 잘하기 위한 조언

④ 새 학년의 목표 달성을 위한 조언

⑤ 대화를 더 잘하는 사람이 되기 위한 조언

23. 대화의 빈칸에 들어갈 말로 적절하지 <u>않은</u> 것은?

(3점)

> A: What can I do to improve my English?
> B: _____
> A: That's a good idea. I'll do that.

① What about recycling paper?

② You can read many English books.

③ You should sing good English pop songs.

④ How about learning a lot of English words?

⑤ Why don't you listen to the radio in English?

24. Jack이 사용한 대화의 기법으로 가장 적절한 것은?

(3점)

> Jack: What is your favorite hobby?
> Kate: I like reading comic books.
> Jack: So do I. How often do you read comic books?
> Kate: I often read comic books.
> Jack: Which comic book do you read these days?
> Kate: I read "Megahex".
> Jack: Is it interesting? Tell me more.

① 화제를 자주 바꾸기

② 분명한 어조로 말하기

③ 공통의 관심사를 나누기

④ 자신의 강점에 대해 말하기

⑤ 사람들의 눈을 보면서 대화하기

22. 밑줄 친 ⓐ~ⓔ 중 글의 흐름상 적절하지 <u>않은</u> 것은?

(4점)

> Give positive feedback to become a better talker. ⓐ<u>Be an active listener.</u> ⓑ<u>Nod your head from time to time.</u> You can say little things like, ⓒ<u>"Wow!" or "Cool."</u> You can also say something like, ⓓ<u>"That's interesting. Tell me more."</u> ⓔ<u>Giving feedback shows that you're spacing out.</u>

① ⓐ　② ⓑ　③ ⓒ　④ ⓓ　⑤ ⓔ

25. 내용상 어색한 문장은? (3점)

① Take a rest, or you'll feel better.

② Eat breakfast, or you'll get hungry.

③ Be quiet, or the baby will wake up.

④ Push the button, and the door will open.

⑤ Turn off the light, and you can save electricity.

26. 위 글의 밑줄 친 ⓐ~ⓔ 단어의 영영풀이로 옳은 것은? (3점)

① ⓐ active: leaving something to happen by itself

② ⓑ nod: to move your head up and down as a way of answering "yes"

③ ⓒ feedback: the path on which something is moving

④ ⓓ share: to admire someone or something

⑤ ⓔ chance: a talk between people

[26~30] 다음 글을 읽고 물음에 답하시오.

---

3. Give feedback.

 Be an ⓐ<u>active</u> listener. ⓑ<u>Nod</u> your head (A)<u>from time to time</u>. You can say little things like, "Wow!" or "Cool." You can also say something like, "That's interesting. Tell me more." Giving ⓒ<u>feedback</u> shows that you're listening.

4. ⓓ<u>Share</u> common interests.

 You can't have a conversation by just listening. What do you and your partner have in common? Do you both like sports? Then talk about your favorite baseball team.

5. Pay attention to the listener.

 Sometimes people may not be interested in your topic. Don't say, "Hey, wake up!" or "Why aren't you listening to me?" Instead, change the topic. (B)<u>If you don't change the topic, your partner will fall asleep.</u> Give the other person a ⓔ<u>chance</u> to talk.

 Practice these tips, and you will soon be a great talker. Put others first, and everyone will want to talk with you.

---

27. (A)의 의미와 같은 단어로 가장 알맞은 것은? (2점)

① hardly   ② never

③ always   ④ frequently

⑤ sometimes

28. (B)와 일치하도록 접속사 or를 사용하여 문장을 쓰시오. (5점)

→ _____

  _____

29. 다음 질문에 대한 답을 완전한 영어 문장으로 쓰시오.
(3점)

Q: What should you do to make everyone want to talk with you?

A: _____

30 위 글의 조언을 잘 따르고 있는 사람만을 〈보기〉에서 있는 대로 고른 것은?
(3점)

> 보기
> • Lion: When I talk with my friends, I just listen to them.
> • Ally: I change the topic when my friend looks bored during a conversation.
> • Tom: I often say "Cool! Tell me more about it!" when I talk with my friend.
> • Jane: I try to find common interests with my friend and talk about them.
> • Andy: My friend should pay attention to me even when my topic is boring.

① Lion, Ally

② Ally, Tom

③ Ally, Tom, Jane

④ Tom, Jane

⑤ Tom, Jane, Andy

31. 다음 글의 괄호 (A), (B), (C) 안에서 가장 적절한 것끼리 짝지어진 것은?
(4점)

Today at school we got assigned to reading groups. They don't come right out and tell you if you're in the Gifted group or the Easy group, but you can (A)(bring it into / figure it out) right away by looking at the covers of the books they hand out. I was pretty (B)(disappointed / relieved) to find out I got put in the Gifted group, because that just means a lot of extra works. I don't want any extra work!

When they did the screening at the end of last year, I did my best to make sure I got put in the Easy group this year. Mom is real (C)(proud of / tight with) our principal, so I'll bet she stepped in and made sure I got put in the Gifted group again. Mom is always saying I'm a smart kid, but that I just don't "apply" myself.

	(A)	(B)	(C)
①	bring it into	– disappointed	– tight with
②	bring it into	– relieved	– proud of
③	figure it out	– disappointed	– tight with
④	figure it out	– disappointed	– proud of
⑤	figure it out	– relieved	– proud of

◎ 선택형 문항의 답안은 컴퓨터용 수정 싸인펜을
  사용하여 OMR답지에 바르게 표기하시오.
◎ 서술형 문제는 답을 답안지에 반드시 검정볼
  펜으로 쓰시오.
◎ 총 30문항 100점 만점입니다. 문항별 배점
  은 각 문항에 표시되어 있습니다.

[인천 ○○중]

1. 다음 중 단어의 영영풀이가 옳지 않은 것은? (2점)

① honest: always telling the truth

② patient: easily annoyed by things

③ generous: friendly, helpful, and willing to
   think positively

④ humorous: amusing, especially in a clever
   or witty way

⑤ intelligent: having the ability to think,
   understand, and learn things quickly and
   well

[경남 ○○중]

2. (a), (b)에 괄호 안의 우리말 의미와 일치하도록 영어로
문장을 완성하시오. ((a)에 perfect를 사용하여 문장을 완
성할 것.) (5점)

Judy: Is he a good singer?
Hojin: Yeah, he sings beautifully.
    (a)_____ for your
   band.
    (나는 그가 너희 밴드에 꼭 맞을 거라고 확신해.)
Judy: Can you tell me more about him?
    (b)_____?
    (그는 성격이 어때?)
Hojin: Well, he is very outgoing and friendly.

(a) _____ _____ _____
    _____ _____ _____

(b) _____ _____ _____

[경기 ○○중]

3. 다음 글의 흐름상 단어의 쓰임이 옳지 않은 것은?
  (2점)

My name is Jimmy. I am in the ⓐeighth
grade and my ⓑyounger sister, Hope, is in the
third grade. My father works for a bank. So
he is ⓒa baker. My mother is a teacher. We
have a dog, Smiley. Sounds pretty ⓓnormal,
right? But a ⓔcrazy thing happened last week.

① ⓐ   ② ⓑ   ③ ⓒ

④ ⓓ   ⑤ ⓔ

[4-5] 다음 글을 읽고 물음에 답하시오.

Next morning, we went to the hospital and
asked the doctor to help us. I said, (a)"그는 어
젯밤 이후로 보이지 않았어요." The doctor shook
his head and said, "I can't help you. (b)I've
never seen anything like this before."

[서울 노원구 ○○중]

4. 밑줄 친 우리말을 7단어의 영어 문장으로 옮기시오.
  (4점)

조건
반드시 He로 시작하는 현재완료 긍정문으로 쓸 것

→ _____

5. 위 글의 밑줄 친 (b)와 현재완료의 쓰임이 같은 것은?　(3점)

① Junyoung <u>has lost</u> the key.

② Hyeon-gyu <u>has ever eaten</u> an ant.

③ Hanhee <u>hasn't cleaned</u> the room yet.

④ Bunhong and Dahin <u>have just come</u> home.

⑤ Yuna and Sua <u>have known</u> each other since 1980.

[7–10] 다음 대화를 읽고 물음에 답하시오.

> M: Sue, ⓐ_____ do you like your school these days?
> G: I like it a lot, Dad. I already made two new friends, Rosa and Mike.
> M: Happy to hear that. ⓑ_____ did you become friends?
> G: We all love English. We are also in the same club.
> M: That's great. ⓒ_____ are they like?
> G: Rosa is very kind.
> M: ⓓ_____ about Mike?
> G: He is outgoing.
> M: ⓔ_____ about inviting them over for dinner?
> G: Okay, Dad.

7. 위 대화의 밑줄 친 ⓐ~ⓔ에 들어갈 말이 <u>다른</u> 것은?　(2점)

① ⓐ　　　　② ⓑ　　　　③ ⓒ

④ ⓓ　　　　⑤ ⓔ

---

6. 괄호 안에 주어진 단어를 사용하여 현재완료 문장으로 영작하시오.　(5점)

(1) 나는 나의 가족을 위해 요리해 본 적이 없다.
(cook for)

→ _____

_____

(2) 그는 캐나다에서 3년 동안 살고 있다.
(live in Canada)

→ _____

_____

8. 위 대화의 내용과 일치하는 것은?　(3점)

① Sue doesn't like her new school.

② Sue has only one friend, Rosa.

③ Sue is kind and Mike is outgoing.

④ Sue and Rosa are in the same club.

⑤ Dad has met Rosa and Mike before.

9. 위 글을 통해 알 수 없는 것은? (3점)

① 친구들의 성격 ② 친구들의 이름

③ 동아리의 이름 ④ 두 사람의 관계

⑤ 친구가 된 계기

10. 위 대화를 읽고 다음 질문에 영어 문장으로 답하시오. (5점)

(1) What do Sue, Rosa and Mike have in common?

→ _____

_____

(2) What is Mike like?

→ _____

_____

11 다음 대화 중 자연스럽지 않은 것은? (3점)

① A: What can I do to sleep better?

B: You can drink warm milk before bed.

② A: Let's do something together on Thursday.

B: Sounds great! What do you want to do?

③ A: Sam plays the guitar really well.

B: Yeah, I'm sure he will get first place in the contest.

④ A: I'm looking for a new member for my dance club.

B: How about Jenny?

⑤ A: Amy runs really fast.

B: I don't think so. She is patient and kind.

[12-13] 다음 대화를 읽고 물음에 답하시오.

Sujin : Hey, Minsu. What's up? You look so ⓐ(worry/worried).

Minsu : The English speaking test is this afternoon.

Sujin : Don't worry. You (practiced/promised) a lot.

Minsu : But I get so ⓒ(relaxed/nervous) when I'm in front of the teacher.

Sujin : Everybody does. I'm sure you'll do well.

Minsu : Do you really think so?

Sujin : Of course. You are a great English speaker.

Minsu : Thanks. I feel much better now.

12. ⓐ~ⓒ를 알맞게 나열한 것은? (4점)

	ⓐ	ⓑ	ⓒ
①	worried	– practiced	– relaxed
②	worry	– promised	– nervous
③	worried	– promised	– relaxed
④	worry	– practiced	– nervous
⑤	worried	– practiced	– nervous

13. 위 대화를 읽고 알 수 있는 것은? (3점)

① Minsu is cheering up Sujin.

② Minsu looks nervous for the test.

③ Sujin will take a test this afternoon.

④ Sujin practiced a lot for the English speaking test.

⑤ Everybody thinks Minsu is a great English speaker.

14. 다음 대화의 흐름상 밑줄 친 곳에 들어갈 말은? (3점)

A: I'm looking for a new member for my dance club.
B: How about Jenny?
A: Jenny? Who's that?
B: She is my classmate.
A: _____
B: She is active and outgoing.
A: Thanks. I'll ask her.

① How is she?
② What is she like?
③ What does she like?
④ What does she look at?
⑤ How does she look like?

15. 다음 대화에서 (A)에 들어갈 말로 가장 적절한 것은? (3점)

A: Can we arrive at the station in time?
B: Of course. The train leaves at 5:10.
A: But it's already 4:30.
B: The train station isn't very far from here.
_____(A)_____

① I'm sure we'll be late.
② I don't think we'll arrive in time.
③ I'm sure we'll arrive there before 5.
④ I'm not certain we'll arrive there in time.
⑤ I'm sure we can arrive there after 5:10.

16. 다음 중 어법상 올바르지 않은 문장을 두 개 고르면? (3점)

① Has he lost his backpack?
② When have you visited the dentist?
③ I have never been to Busan before.
④ They have left for Jeju an hour ago.
⑤ I have studied English since I entered middle school.

17. 다음 대화의 밑줄 친 Junho에 대한 설명으로 옳은 것은? (4점)

Judy: Hojin, I'm looking for a singer for my school band.
Hojin: How about Junho?
Judy: Junho? Who's that?
Hojin: Oh, he's my classmate. He just moved to our school last week.
Judy: Is he a good singer?
Hojin: Yeah, he sings beautifully. I'm sure he will be perfect for your band.
Judy: Can you tell me more about him? What's he like?
Hojin: Well, he is very outgoing.

① Junho is Judy's classmate.
② Junho cannot sing very well.
③ Junho moved to Hojin's school last year.
④ Hojin is sure Junho will be perfect for Judy's band.
⑤ Hojin doesn't want to give Junho's phone number to Judy.

18. @에 들어갈 말로 알맞은 것은? (3점)

> M: How do you like your school these days?
> G: I like it a lot, I already made two new friends.
> M: That's great. What are they like?
> G: @_____

① They like to play baseball.
② They are Tony and James.
③ They like chicken and bread.
④ They are outgoing and helpful.
⑤ They are both in the singing club.

19. 위 글의 (A)와 의미가 같은 문장은? (3점)

① My father told us to pass me the bread.
② My father wanted to pass me the bread.
③ My father asked us to pass him the bread.
④ My father asked who passed him the bread.
⑤ My father wondered if I wanted to eat the bread.

20. 위 글의 밑줄 친 @~@에서 어법이나 흐름상 알맞은 것은? (4점)

① @   ② ⓑ   ③ ©
④ @   ⑤ @

[19~21] 다음 글을 읽고 물음에 답하시오.

> My father said, (A)"Pass me the bread, please." No one heard him, @for he asked again, "Can someone pass me the bread?" I heard him this time, ⓑbut I was too busy with my phone. My mother was yelling, "Don't feed Smiley!" Hope was feeding Smiley. Smiley ©jumping up and down. My father shouted, "Am I invisible? Pass me the bread!"
>
> Then, it happened. My father @appeared like magic. He became invisible!
>
> We could hear him, but we couldn't see him. We asked, "Where @were you?" "I'm (B)right in front of you," he replied.

21. 위 글의 밑줄 친 (B)와 쓰임이 같은 것은? (3점)

① The film is in color, right?
② He's the right man for the job.
③ Lee was standing right behind her.
④ Keep on the right side of the road.
⑤ I hope we're doing the right thing.

22. 빈칸에 주어진 표현에 맞는 영어 단어를 넣어 문장을 완성하시오. (주의: 'I'm'부터 완전한 문장으로 쓸 것) (5점)

G: Can we arrive in time?
B: Of course. The train leaves at 5:10.
G: But it's already 4:30.
B: The train station isn't very fat from here.
 I'm _____ we'll _____ _____
  _____ 5.
(나는 우리가 5시 전에 거기에 도착할 거라고 확신해.)

[23-24] 다음 글을 읽고 물음에 답하시오.

When we came home, Hope said, "I ⓐmiss Daddy." She started crying. My mother joined her. In a few ⓑmoments, we were a sea of ⓒtears. "Come back, Dad! I ⓓpromise to pass you the bread every day!" I cried.
Then, it happened. My father appeared again! He ⓔhugged us and said, "Thank you for all the attention. I promise to come home earlier and play with you on the weekends."

23. 다음 ⓐ~ⓔ의 의미로 가장 적절한 것은? (3점)

① ⓐ - to tell someone that you are going to do or not to do something
② ⓑ - a quite long period of time
③ ⓒ - a drop of liquid that comes out of your eyes when you cry
④ ⓓ - to put your arms around someone to show love or friendship
⑤ ⓔ - to get to a place that you are going to

24. 위 글의 제목으로 가장 적절한 것은? (3점)

① Father Returning Home
② The Importance of Passing Bread
③ Who Moved My Bread?
④ Why Are Fathers Always Busy?
⑤ How to Play with Kids

25. 다음 대화 중 어색한 것은? (4점)

① A: Can we arrive in time?
   B: Of course. The train leaves at 6:30.
② A: What is she like?
   B: She is friendly and outgoing.
③ A: What does he like?
   B: I like his new haircut.
④ A: Amy runs really fast.
   B: Yeah, I'm sure she will win the race.
⑤ A: How do you like your school these days?
   B: I like it. English teachers are fantastic!

26. 밑줄 친 부분의 쓰임이 나머지와 다른 하나는? (3점)

① I have kept a diary since I was ten.
② He has not tried Indian food.
③ James has been to Paris.
④ I have never seen a Chinese movie.
⑤ I have donated my clothes to charity before.

27. 다음 밑줄 친 부분의 해석이 <u>어색한</u> 것은? (3점)

① They are all <u>doing their own thing</u>.
　(자기가 할 일을 하고 있는)

② He plays with me <u>on the weekends</u>. (주말마
　다)

③ <u>In a few moments</u>, we couldn't see him. (잠
　시 동안)

④ I have <u>kept a diary</u> since I was ten.
　(일기를 쓰다)

⑤ <u>Have you ever been</u> to Jeju Island?
　(갔다온 적이 있니?)

28. 위 글의 (A)와 (B)에 어법상 들어갈 알맞은 말을 차례대로 넣으면? (4점)

	(A)	(B)
①	to help	has been
②	help	has been
③	helping	was
④	to help	have been
⑤	help	was

29. 위 글의 빈칸 (가)에 가장 적절한 것은? (2점)

① since　　② for　　③ during
④ before　　⑤ in

[28–30] 다음 글을 읽고 물음에 답하시오.

> We could hear him, but we couldn't see him. We asked, "Where are you?" "I'm right in front of you," he replied. We couldn't do anything for him. It was an awful night.
> Next morning, we went to the hospital and asked the doctor (A)(help / helping / to help) us. I said, "He (B)(was / has been / have been) invisible ＿＿(가)＿＿ last night." The doctor shook his head and said, "I can't help you. (C)I <u>have never seen</u> anything like this before.

30. 위 글 (C)의 밑줄 친 부분의 용법과 같은 문장은? (3점)

① We <u>have</u> already <u>had</u> lunch.
② James <u>has lost</u> his passport.
③ I <u>have learned</u> English for 10 years.
④ My parents <u>have been</u> to England before.
⑤ He <u>hasn't done</u> his English homework yet.

◎ 선택형 문항의 답안은 컴퓨터용 수정 싸인펜을 사용하여 OMR 답안지에 바르게 표기하시오.
◎ 서술형 문제는 답을 답안지에 반드시 검정 볼펜으로 쓰시오.
◎ 총 30문항 100점 만점입니다. 문항별 배점은 각 문항에 표시되어 있습니다.

[인천 ○○중]

1. 다음 중 영영 풀이의 뜻으로 가장 알맞은 것은? (3점)

① yell: to tell someone that you will definitely do or that something will happen

② tear: a drop of liquid that comes from your eyes especially when you cry

③ shake: to say something very loudly especially because you are angry

④ secret: to move back and forth or up and down with quick movements

⑤ promise: something known to only a few people

[서울 송파구 ○○중]

2. 다음 밑줄 친 부분의 우리말 뜻이 알맞지 <u>않은</u> 것은? (2점)

① She will do it <u>right away</u>. (즉시)

② Can you arrive here <u>on time</u>? (제시간에)

③ I made <u>a lot of</u> new friends. (많은)

④ He is standing <u>in front of</u> the building. (~의 앞에)

⑤ How do you like your school <u>these days</u>? (그날에)

[부산 ○○중]

3. 다음 (a), (b) 두 문장이 한 문장이 되도록 빈칸을 채워 문장을 완성하시오. (3점)

(a) Jane started studying English 6 years ago.
+
(b) She still studies it.
→ Jane _____ _____ _____
_____ 6 _____ .

[경북 ○○중]

4. 다음 대화의 문맥상 빈칸에 들어갈 수 <u>없는</u> 말은? (2점)

A: Who's that?
B: He's my new friend, Mike.
A: What is he like?
B: _____

① He is tall and handsome.

② He is very funny.

③ He is very patient.

④ He is active.

⑤ He is kind.

[부산 ○○중]

5. 다음 문장의 밑줄 친 부분과 쓰임이 <u>다른</u> 것은? (3점)

I <u>have donated</u> my old clothes to charity before.

① I <u>have never seen</u> the movie.

② He <u>has lived</u> here for 10 years.

③ They <u>have traveled</u> abroad twice.

④ <u>Have</u> you ever <u>eaten</u> Chinese food?

⑤ I <u>have cooked</u> *ramyeon* for my family.

[6-9] 다음 대화를 읽고 물음에 답하시오.

Judy: Hojin, I'm looking for a singer for my school band.

Hojin: How about Junho Kim?

Judy: Junho Kim? Who's that?

Hojin: Oh, he's my classmate. He just moved to our school last week.

Judy: Is he a good singer?

Hojin: Yeah, he sings beautifully. I'm sure he will be perfect for your band.

Judy: Can you tell me more about him? (A)_____?

Hojin: Well, he is very outgoing and friendly.

Judy: Great. Can I have his phone number?

Hojin: Sure.

8. Juhho Kim에 대한 설명으로 옳지 <u>않은</u> 것은? (3점)

① He is a good singer.

② He is active and kind.

③ He is Hojin's classmate.

④ He is a member of the school band.

⑤ He moved to Hojin's school last week.

6. 위 대화에서 다음 설명하고 있는 영어 단어로 가장 옳은 것은? (2점)

a place where students go to learn

① singer

② classmate

③ school

④ phone

⑤ number

9. 위 대화의 내용과 일치하지 <u>않는</u> 것은? (4점)

① Judy wants to find a new singer for the band.

② Junho Kim and Hojin are classmates.

③ Hojin moved to Judy's school last week.

④ Judy wants to get Junho Kim's phone number.

⑤ Hojin thinks that Junho Kim is a good singer.

7. 위 대화의 빈칸 (A)에 들어갈 가장 알맞은 말은? (3점)

① What is he like?

② What does he like?

③ What does he look like?

④ What is he going to do?

⑤ What does he like to do?

10. 주어진 우리말과 일치하도록 〈조건〉에 맞는 영어 문장을 쓰시오. (5점)

조건

• know, they, she, a long time을 모두 사용할 것
• 단어의 형태 변형 가능

그녀는 그들을 오랜 시간 동안 알고 지내왔다.
→ _____

[11-12] 다음 대화를 읽고 물음에 답하시오.

G: Hey, Minsu. What's up? ⓐYou look so worried.
B: The English speaking test is this afternoon.
G: ⓑDon't worry. You practiced a lot.
B: But I get so nervous when I'm in front of the teacher.
G: ⓒEveryone doesn't. I'm sure you'll do well.
B: Do you really think so?
G: ⓓOf course. You are a great English speaker.
B: Thanks. ⓔI feel much better now.

[서울 광진구 ○○중]

11. 위 대화의 밑줄 친 ⓐ~ⓔ에서 글의 흐름상 적절하지 않은 것은?   (3점)

① ⓐ   ② ⓑ   ③ ⓒ
④ ⓓ   ⑤ ⓔ

[서울 광진구 ○○중]

12. 위 대화의 내용으로 보아 대답할 수 있는 질문은?   (4점)

① What happened to Minsu?
② What is Minsu sure about?
③ When is the English word test?
④ How does Minsu feel when he's on the stage?
⑤ What should a great English speaker be like?

[서울 마포구 ○○중]

13. 다음 대화 중 자연스럽지 않은 것은?   (4점)

① A: Jack runs really fast.
   B: Yeah, I'm sure he will win the race.
② A: What is Mina like?
   B: She is tall and has brown hair.
③ A: I've been to that restaurant before.
   B: Oh, really? I didn't know that.
④ A: Let's do something together on Thursday.
   B: Good. How about going to the bookstore?
⑤ A: How long have you known Tina?
   B: I have known her for 2 years.

[경기 ○○중]

14. 다음 대화의 빈칸에 들어갈 말로 가장 적절한 것은?   (3점)

A: Jack studies all day.
B: Yeah, _____
A: I think so, too.

① I know he will win the race.
② I think he will feel better soon.
③ I'm afraid he won't pass the test next time.
④ Surely he will get first place in the concert.
⑤ I'm sure he will get a good grade on the test.

[15–18] 다음 대화를 읽고 물음에 답하시오.

M: Sue, (A)요즘 학교는 어떠니?
G: I like it a lot, Dad. I already made two new friends, Rosa and Mike.
M: Happy ⓐto hear that. How did you become friends?

(a): That's great. What ⓑdo they like?
(b): He is outgoing.
(c): Rosa is very kind.
(d): How ⓒabout Mike?
(e): We all love English. We are also ⓓin the same club.

M: Why ⓔdon't you invite them over for dinner?
G: Okay, Dad.

[부산 ○○중]

15. 밑줄 친 ⓐ~ⓔ 중 어법상 옳지 않은 것은? (3점)

① ⓐ to hear
② ⓑ do
③ ⓒ about
④ ⓓ in
⑤ ⓔ don't

[부산 ○○중]

16. (a)~(e)를 자연스러운 대화가 되도록 바르게 배열한 것은? (4점)

① (a)-(b)-(d)-(c)-(e)
② (b)-(e)-(d)-(c)-(a)
③ (c)-(d)-(b)-(e)-(a)
④ (d)-(b)-(c)-(e)-(a)
⑤ (e)-(a)-(c)-(d)-(b)

[부산 ○○중]

17. 위 대화의 (A)의 우리말 의미에 맞는 영어 문장을 아래 주어진 단어들을 모두 사용하여 완전한 문장으로 쓰시오. (3점)

school / days / how / you / like / these / do / your / ?

[경기 ○○중]

18. 위 대화의 내용과 일치하지 않은 것은? (3점)

① Sue는 요즘 학교생활이 대단히 좋다.
② Sue는 학교에서 새로운 친구를 두 명 사귀었다.
③ Sue는 친구들과 영어 동아리에 가입할 예정이다.
④ Sue의 친구 Rosa는 친절하며, Mike는 사교적이다.
⑤ Sue는 새로운 친구들을 저녁식사에 초대할 예정이다.

[19–20] 다음 글을 읽고, 물음에 답하시오.

When we ⓐcome home, Hope said, "I miss Daddy." She started crying. My mother joined her. In a few moments, we were a sea of tears. "Come back, Dad! I promise to pass you the bread every day!" I cried.

Then, it happened. My father ⓑappear again! He ⓒhug us and said, "Thank you for all the attention. I promise to come home earlier and play with you on the weekends."

19. 위 글의 내용으로 알맞지 않은 것은? (3점)

① Mother cried with Hope.

② The children wanted their father back.

③ Father will come home earlier than before.

④ Father promises to pass the bread every day.

⑤ Father will spend time with his children on the weekends.

20. ⓐ~ⓒ 중 어법상 알맞게 나열한 것은? (4점)

① came – appeared – hugged

② came – appeared – has hugged

③ came – has appeared – hugged

④ have came – appeared – hugged

⑤ have came – has appeared – has hugged

21. 다음 대화의 빈 곳에 가장 알맞은 것은? (3점)

A: Can we arrive in time?
B: Of course. The movie starts at 7:30.
A: But it's already 6:40.
B: The movie theater isn't very far from here. _____

① We don't have enough time.

② I am certain that you'll do well.

③ Don't worry. You practiced a lot.

④ I'm sure we'll get there before 7.

⑤ We will be very late for the movie.

[22-23] 다음 글을 읽고 물음에 답하시오.

ⓐMy father usually comes home late from work. So, we only see him on the weekends. ⓑEven then, he usually talks and plays with us on the weekends. But last Friday, he came home early for dinner. ⓒAt the table, we were all doing our own thing. Hope was giving food to Smiley. The food isn't good for Smiley. ⓓMy mother was telling her to do so. ⓔI was texting.

22. 위 글의 흐름상 어색한 것을 모두 고른 것은? (4점)

① ⓐ, ⓒ

② ⓑ, ⓓ

③ ⓒ, ⓓ

④ ⓐ, ⓑ, ⓔ

⑤ ⓐ, ⓒ, ⓔ

23. 위 글을 읽고 답할 수 없는 질문은? (3점)

① Does my father usually come home late from work?

② Did my father come home early last Friday?

③ What was Hope doing at the table?

④ What did my mother want Hope not to do at the table?

⑤ What did my father do at the table?

My name is Jimmy. I am in the eighth grade and my sister, Hope, is in the third grade. My father is a banker and my mother is a teacher. We have a dog, Smiley. Sounds (A)pretty normal, right? But a crazy thing happened last week.

My father usually comes home late from work. So, we only see him on the weekends. Even then, he usually sleeps or watches television. But last Friday, he came home early for dinner. At the table, we were all doing our own thing. Hope was giving food to Smiley. My mother was telling her not to do so. I was texting.

25. 위 글의 (A)pretty와 같은 의미로 쓰인 것을 〈보기〉에서 있는 대로 고른 것은? (4점)

보기
ㄱ. It is pretty windy today.
ㄴ. The math exam was pretty difficult.
ㄷ. A pretty face is very important to a movie star.
ㄹ. The new song of BTS is pretty nice, isn't it?
ㅁ. I'm pretty good at speaking in English but not in Japanese.

① ㄱ, ㄴ, ㄷ

② ㄴ, ㄷ, ㄹ

③ ㄷ, ㄹ, ㅁ

④ ㄱ, ㄴ, ㄹ, ㅁ

⑤ ㄴ, ㄷ, ㄹ, ㅁ

24. 위 글을 읽고 등장인물이 하는 말의 빈칸에 알맞은 말을 쓰시오. (주어진 빈칸에는 단어 하나씩만 쓸 것) (5점)

• Jimmy's father: I work at a ⓐ_____.
• Jimmy's mother: My job is a ⓑ_____.
• Hope: I'm Jimmy's ⓒ_____ sister.
• Jimmy: I'm in the ⓓ_____ grade. I have a ⓔ_____, Smiley.

ⓐ_____

ⓑ_____

ⓒ_____

ⓓ_____

ⓔ_____

26. Which is true according to the passage? (4점)

① Jimmy is eight years old and his sister is third grade in middle school.

② All the family members were at the dinner table last Friday.

③ Jimmy's mother was telling Smiley not to give food to a dog.

④ Jimmy's father works at a bank and usually comes home early for dinner.

⑤ Jimmy was reading his textbook at the dinner table last Friday.

[27-30] 다음 글을 읽고 물음에 답하시오.

My father said, "Pass me the bread, please." No one heard him, so he asked again, "Can someone pass me the bread?" I heard (A)him this time, but I was too busy with my phone. My mother was yelling, "Don't feed Smiley!" Hope was feeding Smiley. Smiley was jumping up and down. My father shouted, "Am I invisible? Pass (B)me the bread!"

Then, it happened. Poof! My father disappeared ⓐlike magic. He became invisible!

We could hear (C)him, but we couldn't see him. We asked, "Where are you?" "I'm right in front of (D)you." he replied. We couldn't do anything for (E)him. It was an awful night.

I : Jimmy

29. 밑줄 친 ⓐlike와 쓰임이 같은 것은? (3점)

① Mom and dad like each other.

② Jimmy's dad doesn't like watching movies.

③ Children are all like sponges in the classroom.

④ People in the office like swimming in the pool.

⑤ Tim would like to say something to his teacher.

27. 위 글의 (A)~(E) 중 가리키는 사람이 다른 것은? (3점)

① (A) ② (B) ③ (C)

④ (D) ⑤ (E)

30. 위 글의 내용과 일치하지 않는 것은? (4점)

① Hope was feeding her dog.

② Jimmy was focusing on his phone.

③ Jimmy's mother was yelling at Hope.

④ Jimmy's father didn't shout at his family.

⑤ Jimmy's father wanted them to pass him the bread.

28. 위 글에서 느껴지는 가정의 분위기는? (3점)

① 산만함 ② 즐거움

③ 신비로움 ④ 고요함

⑤ 따뜻함

◎ 선택형 문항의 답안은 컴퓨터용 수정 싸인펜을
  사용하여 OMR 답안지에 바르게 표기하시오.
◎ 서술형 문제는 답을 답안지에 반드시 검정
  볼펜으로 쓰시오.
◎ 총 30문항 100점 만점입니다. 문항별 배점
  은 각 문항에 표시되어 있습니다.

[경기 ㅇㅇ중]

1. 다음 단어의 우리말 뜻풀이가 옳은 것은?　(2점)

① end : 시작하다　　② pianist : 판매원

③ invent : 파괴하다　④ powerful : 힘없는

⑤ softly : 부드럽게

[부산 ㅇㅇ중]

2. 다음 영어 뜻에 가장 알맞은 단어는?　(3점)

the air that you take into your lungs and send
out again

① audience　　② breath　　③ recent

④ single　　⑤ unlike

[충북 ㅇㅇ중]

3. 다음 글의 빈칸 (A), (B)에 들어갈 말이 순서대로 바르게 연결된 것은?　(3점)

Do you have a favorite K-pop idol? Many
students will answer, "Yes." These students
often show great love for their stars.
(A)_____ scream madly at concerts.
(B)_____ wait hours to take pictures of
their stars.

	(A)	(B)
①	Some	Others
②	One	The other
③	Some	Another
④	Other	Some
⑤	Some	The other

[서울 노원구 ㅇㅇ중]

4. 우리말과 일치하도록 주어진 조건을 반드시 적용하여 영작하시오.　(5점)

　조건
수동태 표현을 이용할 것

만약 그가 그 규칙을 어긴다면 그는 처벌 받을 것이다.

→ _____

[5-6] 다음 대화를 읽고 물음에 답하시오.

G: Tom, (A)_____ do you have so many
   paper flowers?
B: They're for my mom's birthday.
G: They are so beautiful. (B)_____ did
   you get them?
B: I made them.
G: Wow, you're really good.
B: Thanks. I am taking a paper folding class
   these days.
G: They are going to be the perfect gift for
   your mom.
B: I hope so, too.

[경기 ㅇㅇ중]

5. 다음 대화의 빈칸 (A), (B)에 들어갈 낱말을 짝지은 것으로 가장 적절한 것은?　(3점)

	(A)	(B)
①	why	Why
②	why	How
③	when	Where
④	when	How
⑤	what	Where

6. 위 대화를 읽고 답할 수 없는 질문은? (4점)

① What did Tom make?

② What class is Tom taking these days?

③ What does the girl think of paper flowers?

④ Which paper flower does the girl like best?

⑤ Where did Tom learn to make paper flowers?

7. 다음이 자연스러운 대화가 되도록 (A)~(E)를 바르게 배열한 것은? (3점)

(A) Okay.
(B) I'm going to sell them at the flea market.
(C) Why do you have all those old clothes?
(D) Then why don't you join me this Saturday?
(E) Really? I have some old clothes, too.

① (B) - (D) - (C) - (A) - (E)

② (B) - (A) - (C) - (E) - (D)

③ (C) - (B) - (E) - (D) - (A)

④ (C) - (E) - (A) - (B) - (D)

⑤ (E) - (B) - (D) - (C) - (A)

8. 다음 글의 밑줄 친 ⓐ~ⓔ 중 어법상 어색한 것은? (4점)

Who was this amazing star? His name was Franz Liszt and he was born in 1811 ⓐin Hungary. He first started ⓑplaying the piano when he was seven. Liszt later became a great pianist, composer and teacher. But many people think of him ⓒas the first idol. Why don't you ⓓgiving his music a listen? If you ⓔlike today's idols, you will love the original idol.

① ⓐ 　　② ⓑ 　　③ ⓒ

④ ⓓ 　　⑤ ⓔ

[9~10] 다음 대화를 읽고 물음에 답하시오.

Amy: Jiho, what are you going to do this Saturday?

Jiho: I'm going to Blue Sky's fan meeting with my friends.

Amy: Wow, I'm also a big fan of the band.

Jiho: Really? Which member do you like (A)_____, Amy?

Amy: I like Lucy (A)_____. She sings really well.

Jiho: I like the drummer, Mike, (A)_____. He's fantastic! Do you want to join us?

Amy: Sure, I'd love to. I can't wait!

9. 위 대화의 내용과 일치하는 것은? (3점)

① Jiho는 주말에 팬미팅을 다녀왔다.

② Jiho와 Amy는 노래를 잘 부른다.

③ Amy는 Blue Sky라는 밴드를 정말 좋아한다.

④ Jiho는 Blue Sky의 Lucy를 가장 좋아한다.

⑤ Amy는 주말에 드럼을 배우고 싶어 한다.

10. 위 대화의 빈칸 (A)에 공통으로 들어갈 알맞은 것은? (2점)

① good   ② better   ③ well

④ best   ⑤ bad

11. 다음 제시된 우리말을 참고하여 〈조건〉에 맞게 영어 문장을 완성하시오. (4점)

> 조건
> • if를 사용할 것
> • 괄호 안에 주어진 단어를 모두 사용할 것
> • 어법에 맞는 영어 문장을 쓸 것

> 만약 오늘 오후에 비가 온다면 나는 너에게 우산을 가져다 줄 것이다.
> (bring, this afternoon, the umbrella)

→ _____

12. 다음 중 대화의 빈칸 어디에도 들어 갈 수 <u>없는</u> 것은? (4점)

> Mina: Good afternoon, friends. I'm Mina with the school radio show. Today Mr. Smith, our English teacher, is here with us. Hi, Mr. Smith.
> Mr. Smith: Hello, everyone.
> _____
> Mina: Let's talk about music.
> _____
> Mr. Smith: Definitely The Beatles.
> Mina: Oh, I like them, too.
> _____
> Mr. Smith: I like most of their songs, but I like *Hey Jude* best.
> Mina: _____
> Mr. Smith: Because the song makes me feel better when I'm down.
> Mina: That's great! Let's listen to the song.

① Why do you like it?

② What's your favorite band?

③ What are you going to do?

④ Which song do you like best?

⑤ I'm happy to be here with you.

13. 다음 밑줄 친 ①~⑤ 중 어법상 알맞지 않은 것은? (3점)

> I ①<u>like</u> *Frozen* ②<u>best</u> because ③<u>the</u> story is ④<u>very</u> ⑤<u>interested</u>.

[14-17] 다음 글을 읽고 물음에 답하시오.

Do you have a favorite K-pop idol? Many students ⓐwill answer, "Yes." These students often show great love for their stars. Some scream madly at concerts. Others wait hours ⓑto take pictures of their stars. Some students even travel to another city ⓒto see their favorite stars.

Are idols a recent creation? No way! Did idols begin with The Beatles in the 1960's? They ⓓloved by many, but they were not the first. How about Elvis Presley in the 1950's? Not even close. To find the answer, let's ⓔtake a time machine (A)_____ a concert hall (B)_____ Vienna (C)_____ 1845.

14. 위 글의 밑줄 친 부분 중, 어법상 어색한 것은? (3점)

① ⓐ　　　　② ⓑ　　　　③ ⓒ

④ ⓓ　　　　⑤ ⓔ

15. 위 글의 빈칸 (A), (B), (C)에 들어갈 말로 바르게 짝지어진 것은?　　　　　　　　　　　　(3점)

	(A)	(B)	(C)
①	to	to	to
②	to	to	in
③	to	in	in
④	in	to	to
⑤	in	in	in

16. 위 글의 내용과 일치하는 것은?　　　　(4점)

① The Beatles는 많은 사람들에게 사랑을 받지 못했다.

② 많은 학생들은 K-pop 아이돌을 좋아하지 않는다.

③ Elvis Presley는 최초의 아이돌이 아니다.

④ 아이돌은 최근의 창조물이다.

⑤ 아이돌은 1960대의 The Beatles부터 시작되었다.

17. 위 글을 읽고 아래 질문에 대한 답으로 옳은 것을 모두 고르시오. (정답 3개)　　　　　　　　(3점)

Q. How do students show their great love for their stars?

① They scream madly at concerts.

② They wait hours to take pictures of their stars.

③ They write fan letters to their stars.

④ They travel to another city to see their stars.

⑤ They put up celebrity wall posters on the wall.

18. 다음 문장의 빈칸에 가장 알맞은 것은?　　(3점)

> The card was ＿＿＿＿＿ by Eric.
> 그 카드는 Eric에 의해 쓰였다.

① wrote　　② writed　　③ writing

④ writes　　⑤ written

19. 능동문을 수동문으로 바꿔 쓴 문장 중 옳지 <u>않은</u> 것을 고르면?　　(3점)

① James told an amazing story.

　→ An amazing story was told by James.

② Romans built this castle.

　→ This castle was built by Romans.

③ Minsu sells this bag.

　→ This bag is selled by Minsu.

④ Wild penguins attacked Nancy.

　→ Nancy was attacked by wild penguins.

⑤ Mr. Kim was washing the car.

　→ The car was being washed by Mr. Kim.

20. 다음 중 짝지어진 대화가 가장 <u>어색한</u> 것은?　(4점)

① A: How's the book club going?

　B: Take bus number 33.

② A: When did you run a marathon?

　B: Last summer vacation.

③ A: Which sport do you like best?

　B: I like tennis best.

④ A: Do you want to join the band?

　B: Sure, I'd love to. I can't wait.

⑤ A: What do you do in your free time?

　B: I often play table tennis.

[21~24] 다음 글을 읽고 물음에 답하시오.

> Are idols a ＿＿(A)＿＿ creation? No way! Did idols begin with The Beatles in the 1960's? They were loved by many, but they were not the first. How about Elvis Presley in the 1950's? Not even close. (B)To find the answer, let's take a time machine to a concert hall in Vienna in 1845.

21. 위 글의 빈칸 (A)에 들어갈 말을 빈칸에 넣었을 때, 가장 자연스러운 문장은?　　(4점)

① When can you ＿＿＿＿ the work?

② What time will the dance ＿＿＿＿ begin?

③ That dress is the designer's new ＿＿＿＿.

④ Look at the beautiful ＿＿＿＿ of the dancer.

⑤ Let's go to see a ＿＿＿＿ movie tomorrow.

22. 위 글의 (B)To find와 용법이 같은 것은? (2개) (3점)

① I have no time to eat.

② He begins to play the piano.

③ He went to Canada to learn English.

④ I will go to the airport to pick up Jenny.

⑤ I got a chance to meet my favorite star.

23. 위 글의 내용으로 옳은 것은? (3점)

① 아이돌은 최근에 만들어진 것이다.

② The Beatles는 최초의 아이돌이 아니다.

③ 최초의 아이돌은 1960년대의 Elvis Presley이다.

④ 1950년대의 많은 사람들은 The Beatles를 사랑
했다.

⑤ 1845년 Vienna에 있는 한 콘서트 홀에서 타임머
신이 만들어졌다.

24. 위 글 뒤에 이어질 글의 내용으로 가장 적절한 것은?
(3점)

① 최초의 아이돌

② 케이팝의 전망

③ 아이돌에 관심을 갖는 이유

④ 아이돌에 대한 대중의 사랑

⑤ 요즘 인기를 얻고 있는 아이돌

[25-29] 다음 글을 읽고 물음에 답하시오.

All the seats are filled. ⓐThe side of the piano face the audience unlike other concerts. This way, the audience can see the handsome 185cm pianist better. He doesn't have any sheet music with him. He begins to play _____(A)_____.

He starts slowly by softly touching the keys. ⓑAll the people don't want to miss a single note, so they hold their breath. He builds up speed, and his long fingers press down on many keys at once. This makes the music very powerful and rich.

ⓒPeople in the hall pays attention to his every little body movement. His long beautiful hair flies everywhere. It's like watching a piano and ballet performance at once. Time flies and the concert ends. People scream and throw flowers and pieces of clothing onto the stage. (B)콘서트홀은 열광의 도가니가 된다!

Who was this amazing star? ⓓHis name was Franz Liszt and was born in 1811 in Hungary. He first started playing the piano when he was seven. Liszt later became a great pianist, composer and teacher. ⓔBut many people think that he is the first idol. Why don't you give his music a listen now?

25. 위 글의 밑줄 친 ⓐ~ⓔ 중 어법상 바른 것을 모두 고르면? (2개) (3점)

① ⓐ   ② ⓑ   ③ ⓒ

④ ⓓ   ⑤ ⓔ

26. 위 글의 'pianist'에 대한 반응이 <u>어색한</u> 것은?(4점)

① 하니: 어머! 악보를 다 외워서 연주하다니!

② 둘리: 연주를 시작할 때는 건반을 부드럽게 누르는구나.

③ 또치: 긴 손가락으로 건반을 하나씩 따로 누르네.

④ 펭수: 긴 머리카락이 여기저기 흩날리네 이거.

⑤ 범이: 피아니스트가 작곡도 하다니, 정말 대단해.

27. 빈칸 (A)에 들어갈 말로 가장 적절한 표현을 고르시오. (3점)

He begins to play (A)_____. 그는 기억해서 연주하기 시작한다.

① at once

② from memory

③ with a sheet music

④ at the concert

⑤ for his fans

28. 밑줄 친 (B)의 우리말을 영어로 옮기시오. (5점)

조건
5단어로 옮길 것.

(B) 콘서트홀은 열광의 도가니가 된다!

→ _____

29. 위 글을 읽고 난 직후 독자가 할 행동으로 가장 적절한 것은? (3점)

① 피아노 레슨 시작하기

② 자신만의 음악 작곡하기

③ 좋아하는 아이돌 조사하기

④ Franz Liszt의 음악 듣기

⑤ 최초의 작곡가 알아보기

30. 다음 빈칸에 들어갈 말로 알맞은 것은? (3점)

The Amazon River _____ Brazil.

① locates

② is located

③ is locating

④ is located by

⑤ is located in

◎ 선택형 문항의 답안은 컴퓨터용 수정 싸인펜을
사용하여 OMR 답안지에 바르게 표기하시오.
◎ 서술형 문제는 답을 답안지에 반드시 검정
볼펜으로 쓰시오.
◎ 총 30문항 100점 만점입니다. 문항별 배점
은 각 문항에 표시되어 있습니다.

[울산 ○○중]

1. 다음 문장의 빈칸에 들어갈 수 없는 것은?　　(3점)

- This song will _____ you up.
- She took a deep _____ and dived in.
- They won the game by a _____ point.
- We _____ finished the project.
- I've never met the actor in _____.

① creation　　② breath　　③ cheer

④ single　　⑤ person

[서울 ○○중]

2. 다음 빈칸 ⓐ~ⓔ의 어느 곳에도 들어갈 수 없는 단어는? (대·소문자 상관 없음)　　(3점)

ⓐ_____ scream madly at concerts.
ⓑ_____ wait hours ⓒ_____ take pictures of their stars. Some students ⓓ_____ travel to ⓔ_____ city to see their favorite stars.

① to　　② even　　③ other

④ some　　⑤ another

[경기 ○○중]

3. 다음 보기의 빈칸에 들어갈 어휘로 옳은 것은? (2점)

보기
This table was _____ by my mother.

① make　　② made　　③ makes

④ maker　　⑤ making

[경북 ○○중]

4. 다음 중 짝지어진 대화가 자연스럽지 않은 것은? (3점)

① A: How's the book club going?
　B: It's fun. I read lots of interesting books.

② A: Which country do you want to visit?
　B: Because I want to see the Taj Mahal in India.

③ A: What are you going to do this Saturday?
　B: I'm going to sell my old clothes at the flea market.

④ A: Which member do you prefer, the singer or the drummer?
　B: I prefer the singer. She sings really well.

⑤ A: Do you wan to join our movie club?
　B: Sure, I'd love to.

[서울 ○○중]

5. 다음 중 어법상 어색한 것은?　　(3점)

① You will get wet if you go out now.

② If I call your name, answer the question.

③ If I go to Italy, I will eat pizza and spaghetti.

④ Unless it rains tomorrow, we'll go on a picnic.

⑤ They'll go to the sea if it'll be sunny tomorrow.

[6-7] 다음 대화를 읽고 물음에 답하시오.

> Tom, why do you have so many paper flowers?

> ⓐ I hope so, too.
> ⓑ They're for my mom's birthday.
> ⓒ Wow, they're so beautiful. Where did you get them?
> ⓓ They are going to be the perfect gift for your mom.
> ⓔ I made them. I'm taking a paper folding class these days.

[충북 ○○중]

6. 위 대화에서 주어진 글 다음에 이어질 글의 순서로 가장 적절한 것은?　　　　(4점)

① ⓐ-ⓑ-ⓒ-ⓓ-ⓔ
② ⓑ-ⓒ-ⓔ-ⓓ-ⓐ
③ ⓑ-ⓒ-ⓓ-ⓔ-ⓐ
④ ⓒ-ⓔ-ⓑ-ⓓ-ⓐ
⑤ ⓔ-ⓓ-ⓒ-ⓑ-ⓐ

[서울 노원구 ○○중]

7. 위 대화의 내용과 일치하는 것은?　　　　(3점)

① Tom bought lots of paper flowers.
② They are talking about Tom's birthday.
③ Tom hopes that his mom will like his gift.
④ Tom made paper flowers for his girl friend.
⑤ They are going to take a paper folding class together.

[경기 ○○중]

8. 다음 대화의 빈칸에 가장 알맞은 것은?　　　　(3점)

> Mike: Why do you have all those old clothes?
> Amy: I'm going to sell them at the flea market this Saturday.
> Mike: Really? I have some old clothes, too.
> Amy: Then _____
> Mike: Okay.

① why don't you join me?
② do you have those old clothes?
③ when are you going to sell them?
④ why don't we take them to the shopping mall?
⑤ why did you sell the old clothes at the flea market?

[경기 ○○중]

9. 다음 글의 ⓐ와 쓰임이 같은 것은?　　　　(4점)

> All the seats are filled. Unlike other concerts, the side of the piano ⓐfaces the audience. This way, the audience can see the handsome 185cm pianist better. He doesn't have any sheet music with him. He begins to play from memory.

① A cube has six faces.
② I met a new face in my class today.
③ My house faces the south by the lake.
④ He washes his face every morning.
⑤ She always looks at her face on the mirror.

[10-12] 다음 대화를 읽고 물음에 답하시오.

G: Jiho, what are you going to do this Saturday?
B: ⓐI'm going to Blue Sky's fan meeting with my friends.
G: Wow. ⓑI'm sorry to hear that. I'm also a big fan of the band.
B: Really? ⓒWhich member do you like best, Amy?
G: I like Lucy best. She sings really well.
B: I like the drummer, Mike, best. He's fantastic! ⓓDo you want to join us?
G: Sure. I'd love to. ⓔI can't wait!

10. 위 대화의 밑줄 친 ⓐ~ⓔ 중 흐름상 어색한 것은?
(4점)

① ⓐ   ② ⓑ   ③ ⓒ
④ ⓓ   ⑤ ⓔ

11. 위 대화를 읽고 T(true), F(false)의 관계가 올바른 것은?
(3점)

① Lucy sings really well. (F)
② Jiho wants to be a drummer. (T)
③ Amy is going to Blue Sky's fan meeting with Jiho. (F)
④ Amy doesn't like to join Blue Sky's fan meeting. (T)
⑤ Jiho went to Blue Sky's fan meeting with his friends last Saturday. (F)

12. 위 대화에서 알 수 없는 것은?
(3점)

① 주말 계획
② 팬미팅 장소
③ Lucy를 좋아하는 이유
④ 밴드에서 Mike의 역할
⑤ 가장 좋아하는 밴드 멤버

[13-15] 다음을 읽고 물음에 답하시오.

Do you have a favorite K-pop idol? Many students will answer, "Yes." These students often show great love for their stars. Some scream madly at concerts. (A) Others wait hours to take pictures of their stars. (B) Some students even travel to another city to see their favorite stars.

(C) Are idols a recent creation? No way! (D) Many people loved them, but ⓐthey were not the first. (E) How about Elvis Presley in the 1950's? Not even close. (F)정답을 찾기 위해서, 1845년 비엔나의 콘서트장으로 타임머신을 타고 가보자.

13. 위 글의 (A)~(E) 중 다음 문장이 들어가기에 가장 적절한 곳은?
(3점)

Did idols begin with The Beatles in the 1960's?

① (A)   ② (B)   ③ (C)
④ (D)   ⑤ (E)

14. 밑줄 친 ⓐ가 지칭하는 대상을 고르시오. (3점)

① K-pop idols ② students
③ pictures ④ The Beatles
⑤ Elvis Presley

15. 위 글의 밑줄 친 (F)의 우리말을 다음 주어진 단어만을 바르게 배열하여 영작하시오. (대·소문자 및 문장 부호에 유의할 것) (5점)

> a / a / in / in / to / to / the / 1845 / hall / let's / time / find / take / answer / concert / Vienna / machine

정답: _____

[16-17] 다음 대화를 읽고 물음에 답하시오.

> Mina: Good afternoon, friends. I'm Mina with the school radio show. Today Mr. Smith, our English teacher, is here with us. Hi, Mr. Smith.
>
> Mr. Smith: Hello, everyone. I'm happy to be here with you.
>
> Mina: Let's talk about music. Mr. Smith, what's your favorite band?
>
> Mr. Smith: (ⓐ) The Beatles.
>
> Mina: Oh, I like them, too. (ⓑ) song do you like best?
>
> Mr. Smith: I like most of their songs, but I like *Hey Jude* best.
>
> Mina: Why do you like it?
>
> Mr. Smith: Because the song makes me feel better (ⓒ) I'm down.
>
> Mina: That's great! Let's listen to the song.

16. 대화의 흐름에 맞게 빈칸 ⓐ~ⓒ가 맞게 연결된 것은? (4점)

	ⓐ	ⓑ	ⓒ
①	Definite	Which	why
②	Definitely	Which	when
③	Definite	What	why
④	Definitely	What	why
⑤	Definite	Which	when

17. 위 대화의 질문에 대한 답을 본문에서 찾을 수 <u>없는</u> 것은? (3점)

① Who is Mr. Smith?
② How does Mr. Smith feel now?
③ What is the name of the band Mr. Smith likes?
④ Why does Mr. Smith want to listen to *Hey Jude*?
⑤ What are they going to do after this show is over?

18. 다음 문장의 밑줄 친 부분 중 어법상 <u>어색한</u> 것은? (2점)

> ①<u>If</u> it ②<u>won't</u> snow tomorrow, I ③<u>will</u> ④<u>go</u> hiking ⑤<u>with</u> my kids.

[19-21] 다음 글을 읽고 물음에 답하시오.

Do you have a favorite K-pop idol? Many students will answer, "Yes." These students often show great love for their stars. Some scream madly at concerts ⓐto show their love. (A)_____ wait hours ⓑto take pictures of their stars. Some students even travel ⓒto another city to see their favorite stars.

Are idols a recent creation? No way! Did idols begin with The Beatles in the 1960's? They were loved by many, but they were not the first. How about Elvis Presley in the 1950s? Not even close. ⓓTo find the answer, let's take a time machine ⓔto a concert hall in Vienna in 1845.

19. 위 글의 빈칸 (A)에 들어갈 말로 가장 적절한 것은?
(3점)

① Other
② Others
③ Another
④ The other
⑤ The others

20. 위 글의 ⓐ~ⓔ 중 쓰임이 같은 것끼리만 짝지어진 것은?
(3점)

① ⓐ, ⓒ
② ⓑ, ⓒ
③ ⓑ, ⓓ
④ ⓒ, ⓓ
⑤ ⓓ, ⓔ

21. 위 글의 내용과 일치하는 것은?
(4점)

① Idols are a recent creation.
② Students are too young to have their favorite stars.
③ Some students travel far to meet their favorite idols.
④ The first idol was Elvis Presley in 1950's.
⑤ There are many concert halls in Vienna.

[22-25] 다음 글을 읽고 물음에 답하시오.

All the seats (A)(fill). Unlike other concerts, the side of the piano ⓐfaces the audience. This way, the audience can see the handsome 185 cm pianist better. He doesn't have any sheet music with him. He begins to play from memory.

He starts slowly by softly touching the keys. All the people ⓑhold their breath because they don't want (B)(miss) a single note. He ⓒbuilds up speed, and his long fingers press down on many keys at once. This makes the music very powerful and rich.

The audience looks at his every little body movement carefully. His long beautiful hair flies everywhere. It's like (C)(watch) a piano and ballet performance ⓓat once. Time flies and the concert ends. People scream and throw flowers and pieces of clothing onto the stage. The concert hall ⓔgoes wild!

22. 위 글의 밑줄 친 ⓐ~ⓔ의 해석이 적절한 것은? (3점)

① ⓐfaces: 얼굴들

② ⓑhold their breath: 심호흡을 계속하다

③ ⓒbuilds up speed: 속도를 높이다

④ ⓓat once: 한 번, 1회

⑤ ⓔgoes wild: 야생생활로 돌아가다

25. 위 글의 내용과 일치하는 것은? (4점)

① The audience can't see the face of the pianist.

② The pianist presses down on keys one by one.

③ He has a single note that the audience wants.

④ A piano concert and ballet dancing are performed at the same time.

⑤ The audience holds the breath when the pianist starts to touch the keys.

23. 위 글의 괄호 (A)~(C)에 들어갈 말을 바르게 나열한 것은? (4점)

	(A)	(B)	(C)
①	are filled	to miss	watching
②	were filled	to miss	watching
③	fill	to miss	watch
④	filled	missingto	watch
⑤	are filled	miss	watching

[26-29] 다음 글을 읽고 물음에 답하시오.

The audience pays attention to his every little body movement. (A) His long beautiful hair flies everywhere. It's like watching a piano and ballet performance ⓐat once. (B) Time flies and the concert ends. People scream and throw flowers and pieces of clothing onto the stage. The concert hall goes wild!

(C) His name was Franz Liszt and he was born in 1811 in Hungary. (D) He first started playing the piano when he was seven. (E) Liszt later became a great pianist, composer and teacher. But many people think of him as the first idol. Why don't you give his music a listen? 만약 당신이 요즘의 아이돌을 좋아한다면, 원조 아이돌도 좋아할 것이다.

24. 다음 질문에 10단어 이하로 주어와 동사를 갖춘 완전한 문장으로 서술하시오. (5점)

Q: Why did people hold their breath at Liszt's concert?

A: _____

26. 위 글의 흐름으로 보아 주어진 문장이 들어가기에 가장 적절한 곳은? (4점)

Who was this amazing star?

① (A) ② (B) ③ (C)

④ (D) ⑤ (E)

27. 위 글의 내용을 읽고 요약한 것이다. 문맥상 빈칸에 가장 적절한 말은? (3점)

Many people think of Franz Liszt as the first idol because of _____.

① his performance

② his handsome face

③ the scream from the people

④ being a composer and teacher

⑤ the flowers and pieces of his clothing

28. 위 글의 밑줄 친 우리말과 뜻이 같도록 바르게 영작한 것은? (3점)

① If you like today's idols, you will love the original idol.

② If you will like today's idols, you love the original idol.

③ When you like today's idols you will love the original idol.

④ What you like today's idols, you will love the original idol.

⑤ Unless you like today's idols, you love the original idol.

29. 위 글의 밑줄 친 ⓐ와 바꿔 쓸 수 있는 것은? (3점)

① at the same time

② for the first time

③ on time

④ at last

⑤ later

30. 다음 주어진 세 문장의 빈칸에 공통적으로 들어갈 단어로 가장 알맞은 것은? (3점)

• _____ animal do you like best?   • _____ country do you want to visit for your dream vacation?   • _____ book do you like best?

① in ② With ③ Which

④ Within ⑤ Before

◎ 선택형 문항의 답안은 컴퓨터용 수정 싸인펜을
  사용하여 OMR 답안지에 바르게 표기하시오.
◎ 서술형 문제는 답을 답안지에 반드시 검정
  볼펜으로 쓰시오.
◎ 총 31문항 100점 만점입니다. 문항별 배점
  은 각 문항에 표시되어 있습니다.

[경기 ○○중]

1. 다음 단어의 우리말 뜻풀이가 <u>어색한</u> 것은?   (2점)

① tough : 힘든   ② desert : 사막
③ guess : 추측하다   ④ ordinary : 평범한
⑤ temperature : 행성

[서울 노원구 ○○중]

2. 보기의 빈칸 어디에도 들어갈 수 <u>없는</u> 것은?   (3점)

• She had a _____ time last week.
• It's just an _____ computer.
• There is no age _____ for applicants.
• They were active _____ in the project.
• Make sure the iron isn't too hot or you'll
  _____ the shirt

① limit   ② burn   ③ freeze
④ tough   ⑤ participants

[경기 ○○중]

3. 다음 중 문맥상 <u>어색한</u> 문장은?   (2점)

① The rose festival went on for a week.
② We're out of milk, so we don't need to buy
   milk.
③ It was difficult to quit eating sweets for my
   health.
④ My throat really hurts because I have a bad
   cold.
⑤ I need to meet you in person to give you
   this gift.

[서울 광진구 ○○중]

4. 다음 대화에서 빈칸 (A)와 (B)에 들어갈 말이 차례대로
짝지어진 것은?   (3점)

Reporter: Why did you take part in the race?
Sumi: I wanted to test my (A)_____ and
   make my own (B)_____. I thought, "If
   I can finish the race, then I can do
   anything."

① limits – history
② activity – role
③ direction – idol
④ limits – English
⑤ activity – movement

[서울 노원구 ○○중]

5. 다음 대화의 (a)~(c)에 들어갈 단어로 알맞게 짝지어
진 것은?   (3점)

G: Mike, have you ever heard of flying
   yoga?
B: Yeah! I've seen it on TV. People were
   hanging in the air!
G: Guess what? I'm learning it these days.
B: Really? It looked so (a)_____. Do you
   like it, Jessy?
G: At first, I was a little (b)_____, but
   now I'm enjoying it.
B: Sounds great! I think I should exercise
   more, too.
G: Do you want to join my yoga class?
B: No, that's too (c)_____ for me. I'll just
   play basketball.

① scary – scary – scared
② scared – scary – scary
③ scary – scared – scary
④ scary – scared – scared
⑤ scared – scary – scared

[6-7] 다음 대화를 읽고 물음에 답하시오.

Reporter: How many deserts have you run ⓐ through?

Adrianna: Four deserts. They were the Atacama Desert, the Gobi Desert, the Sahara Desert and Antarctica.

Reporter: ⓑWhich desert was the toughest for you?

Adrianna: The Sahara Desert. Temperatures often reached up to 50℃.

Reporter: ⓒWhat kind of people ⓓran in the race?

Adrianna: Most of them ⓔhave been ordinary people like you and me. I became good friends with them.

Reporter: ⓕ당신은 왜 그 경기에 참가했나요?

Adrianna: I wanted to test my limits and make my own history. I thought, "If I can finish the race, then I can do anything."

8. 다음 대화의 빈칸에 들어갈 수 없는 것은? (4점)

Amy: What do you do in your free time?

Minsu: I often get exercise.

Amy: Have you ever _____ in the morning?

Minsu: Yes, I have.

Amy: Have you ever _____ a bike all day long?

Minsu: No, I haven't.

Amy: Have you ever _____ a marathon?

Minsu: Yes, I have.

Amy: Have you ever _____ in the river?

Minsu: No, I haven't.

① grown   ② jogged

③ ridden   ④ run

⑤ swum

6. 위 대화의 밑줄 친 ⓐ~ⓔ 중 어색한 표현은? (3점)

① ⓐ   ② ⓑ   ③ ⓒ

④ ⓓ   ⑤ ⓔ

9. 우리말과 일치하도록 괄호 안의 단어를 바르게 배열한 것은? (2점)

어느 반이 가장 높은 점수를 받았는가?
(class, score, highest, the, got, which)

① The class got highest which score?

② Which score hot the highest class?

③ The highest class got which score?

④ Which class got the highest score?

⑤ Which highest class got the score?

7. 위 대화의 ⓕ를 영작했을 때 5번째 들어갈 단어는? (3점)

① in   ② the   ③ take

④ you   ⑤ part

10. 다음 우리말을 영어로 옮길 때 주어진 단어들을 사용하여 문장을 완성하시오. (5점)

(1) 만약 학생들이 규칙을 어긴다면, 그들은 처벌을 받을 것이다. (break, the rules, punish)

→ If the students _____, they _____.

(2) Yesterday는 비틀즈에 의해 불려졌다. (sing)
→ *Yesterday* _____ the Beatles.

11. 다음 밑줄 친 우리말을 주어진 조건에 맞게 영작하시오. (5점)

조건
1. who/which/whose 중에 하나를 골라 사용하시오.
2. <보기>에서 알맞은 단어를 골라 활용하시오.

보기
sink / lose / save / is / the police / the boys / the man / boat

A: What happened yesterday? Why were the police at the port?
B: 경찰이 그의 배가 가라앉은 남자를 구했어.

→ _____

_____

12. 다음 중 어법상 어색한 것은? (2점)

① I often visit my aunt who lives in Seoul.
② Tony has a friend that is from Australia.
③ I know the boy who is wearing a blue shirt.
④ The man who lives next door is very friendly.
⑤ A desert is a place which are very dry and has little water.

[13–15] 다음 글을 읽고 물음에 답하시오.

The first race takes place in the Atacama Desert in Chile. It is the driest desert in the world. In fact, it hasn't rained in some parts of the Atacama Desert for 400 years! The next race goes to the Gobi Desert in China. It is the windiest desert on earth. The third race heads (A)_____ the Sahara Desert in Egypt. It is the hottest of the four deserts. Temperatures can reach up (B)_____ 50°C. Finally, the race travels (C)_____ the coldest desert on earth, Antarctica. (a)If you throw boiling water into the air here, it freezes.

13. 위 글의 빈칸 (A), (B), (C)에 공통으로 들어갈 말로 옳은 것은? (3점)

① to
② in
③ on
④ with
⑤ as

14. 위 글에 대한 내용 중 옳지 <u>않은</u> 것은? (3점)

① 마지막 네 번째 레이스는 남극에서 열린다.

② 이집트의 사하라 사막은 가장 더운 사막이다.

③ 아타카마 사막은 세계에서 가장 습한 사막이다.

④ 첫 번째 레이스는 칠레의 아타카마 사막에서 열린다.

⑤ 중국의 고비 사막은 가장 바람이 많이 부는 사막이다.

15. 위 글의 (a)가 빈칸에 들어갈 수 <u>없는</u> 문장은? (3점)

① We'll stay at home _____ it rains.

② Plastic will melt _____ it gets too hot.

③ _____ you need money, I can lend you some.

④ You won't get good results _____ you try your best.

⑤ _____ I win the lottery, I will leave my job and go on a trip.

[16-18] 다음 대화를 읽고 물음에 답하시오.

Hojin: Judy, _____

Judy: I often go rock climbing with my dad.

Hojin: What mountain do you go to?

Judy: No, Hojin. I usually do it at a gym near my house.

Hojin: I see. Have you ever done it on a real mountain?

Judy: Not yet. But I hope to do it someday.

Hojin: That's really cool. Can I come and join you next time?

Judy: Sure. I'm going this Saturday.

Hojin: That sounds great.

Judy: You're going to love it!

16. 위 대화의 빈칸에 들어갈 말로 알맞지 <u>않은</u> 것은? (3점)

① how do you spend your free time?

② what do you do when you are free?

③ what do you do in your leisure time?

④ what can I do to enjoy my free time?

⑤ what do you like to do in your spare time?

17. 위 대화의 내용과 일치하지 <u>않은</u> 것은?　　(3점)

① Judy has never gone rock climbing on a real mountain.

② Hojin is going to a gym with Judy this Saturday.

③ Judy doesn't think Hojin will like rock climbing.

④ Judy wants to go rock climbing on a real mountain someday.

⑤ Hojin wants to join Judy this Saturday.

[19~20] 다음 대화를 읽고 물음에 답하시오.

Jessy: <u>너 플라잉 요가를 들어본 적 있어?</u> Mike: Yeah! I've seen it on TV. People were hanging in the air! Jessy: Guess what? I'm learning it these days. Mike: Really? It looked so scary. Do you like it, Jessy? Jessy: At first, I was a little scared, but now I'm enjoying it. Mike: Sounds great! I think I should exercise more, too. Jessy: Do you want to join my yoga class? Mike: No, that's too scary for me. I'll just play basketball.

19. 위 대화의 내용과 일치하는 것은?　　(3점)

① Mike saw flying yoga in the park.

② Jessy was never scared of flying yoga.

③ Jessy is taking a flying yoga class.

④ Jessy and Mike will exercise together.

⑤ Mike will join the yoga class because it sounds fun.

18. 위 대화를 읽고, 다음 질문에 대한 알맞은 답을 쓰시오.　　(4점)

Q: What does Judy do in her free time? A: _____

정답 : _____

20. 위 대화의 밑줄 친 우리말을 다음 〈조건〉에 맞게 영작하시오.　　(5점)

조건
1 : 주어진 단어를 모두 사용하되 필요시 단어의 형태를 바꾸거나 새로운 단어를 추가할 것 2: 7단어로 쓸 것(ever, of, have)

답: _____

[21-23] 다음 글을 읽고 물음에 답하시오.

The first race takes place in the Atacama Desert in Chile. It is the driest desert in the world. (A)_____, it hasn't rained in some parts of the Atacama Desert for 400 years! The second race @heads to the Gobi Desert in China. It is the windiest desert on earth. The next race goes to the Sahara desert in Egypt. It is the hottest of the four deserts. ⓑTemperatures can reach up to 50℃. The last race travels to the coldest desert on earth, Antarctica. If you throw boiling water into the air here, it ⓒfreezes!

Only the greatest runners on the planet can take part in the 4 Deserts Race, right? Not exactly. Many of the participants are ordinary people like you and me. (B)_____ why do they do it? Adrianna, a ⓓlibrary from France, says, "It's a chance to test your limits and make your own history. Anyone who crosses the ⓔfinish line can do anything."

21. 위 글의 빈칸 (A), (B)에 들어갈 말로 가장 적절한 것은? (3점)

	(A)	(B)
①	In fact	So
②	However	Then
③	Actually	In the end
④	As a result	However
⑤	For example	Therefore

22. 위 글의 밑줄 친 @~ⓔ 중 문맥상 잘못 사용된 것은? (3점)

① @   ② ⓑ   ③ ⓒ

④ ⓓ   ⑤ ⓔ

23. 위 글의 내용을 가장 잘 이해한 사람은? (3점)

① 남준: Gobi 사막은 세상에서 가장 건조한 사막이다.

② 태형: Atacama 사막은 세상에서 가장 바람이 많은 사막이다.

③ 정국: 4 Deserts Race의 마지막 경주는 Atacama 사막에서 개최된다.

④ 지민: Adrianna는 자신의 한계를 확인하기 위해 4 Deserts Race에 참여했다.

⑤ 석진: 세상에서 가장 훌륭한 달리기 선수만이 4 Deserts Race에 참여할 수 있다.

[24-25] 다음 대화를 읽고 물음에 답하시오.

Reporter: What kind of people ran in the 4 Deserts Race?

Adrianna: Most of them were ordinary people like you and me. I became good friends with them.

Reporter: (A)당신은 왜 그 경주에 참여했습니까?

Adrianna: I wanted to test my limits and make my own history. I thought, "If I can finish the race, then I can do anything.

24. 위 대화의 밑줄 친 (A)를 영어 문장으로 바꿀 때 필요하지 않은 단어는? (3점)

① take place
② why
③ you
④ the race
⑤ take part in

25. 위 대화를 통해 알 수 없는 것은? (3점)

① Adrianna의 직업은 도서관 사서이다.
② Adrianna는 4대 사막 경주에 참여하였다.
③ 이 대화는 4대 사막 경주에 대한 인터뷰이다.
④ 평범한 사람도 4대 사막 경주에 참여할 수 있다.
⑤ Adrianna는 4대 사막 경주를 통해 자신의 한계를 시험하고 싶었다.

26. 밑줄 친 who의 쓰임이 보기와 같은 것은? (3점)

> 보기
> I have a brother <u>who</u> lives in Canada.

① <u>Who</u> is the smartest of all?
② Did you meet the girl <u>who</u> has blonde hair?
③ <u>Who</u> were you waiting for?
④ Do you know <u>who</u> has the master key?
⑤ <u>Who</u> is that woman?

[27–30] 다음 글을 읽고 물음에 답하시오.

Imagine you are in the middle of a great ⓐ<u>desert</u>. The sands go on and on in every direction. The sun feels like a giant ball of fire. The hot wind ⓑ<u>burns</u> your face and throat. You open your backpack to drink some water. Oh, no! You're almost out of water. You wet your throat with a drop of water and keep (A)[to go / going].

Sounds like a bad dream? Well, this is not a dream for the ⓒ<u>participants</u> (B)[who / which] take part in the 4 Deserts Race. The 4 Deserts Race is a series of four races across the world's ⓔ<u>toughest</u> deserts.

Each race is 250 kilometers long and (C)[take / takes] seven days.

27. 위 글의 밑줄 친 ⓐ~ⓔ의 영영풀이 뜻으로 어색한 것은? (3점)

① desert: a large area of land that is usually very hot and covered with sand
② burn: to destroy something by fire or heat
③ participant: the people who take part in an activity
④ race: a competition to see who is the fastest, for example in running, swimming, or diving
⑤ tough: full of suffering and easy to achieve

28. 위 글의 괄호 (A), (B), (C) 안에서 어법에 맞는 표현으로 가장 적절한 것은? (4점)

	(A)	(B)	(C)
①	to go	who	take
②	going	who	takes
③	to go	which	take
④	going	which	takes
⑤	to go	which	takes

30. 위 글의 제목으로 가장 적절한 것은? (3점)
① The World's Toughest Deserts
② The Introduction of the Four Deserts Race
③ The Special Things about the Four Deserts
④ The Differences between 3 Deserts and Antarctica
⑤ The Interesting Stories about the World Deserts

29. 위 글을 읽고 대답할 수 <u>없는</u> 질문은? (3점)
① How is the desert climate described?
② How many people participate in this race?
③ How many races does the 4 Deserts Race consist of?
④ How many kilometers is each of the 4 Deserts Race?
⑤ How many days does each race take?

31. 우리말과 일치하도록 주어진 조건을 반드시 적용하여 영작하시오. (5점)

조건
최상급 표현을 이용할 것

소금은 세상에서 가장 중요한 것들 중의 하나이다.

→ _____

_____

◎ 선택형 문항의 답안은 컴퓨터용 수정 싸인펜을 사용하여 OMR답안지에 바르게 표기하시오.

◎ 서술형 문제는 답을 답안지에 반드시 검정볼 펜으로 쓰시오.

◎ 총 29문항 100점 만점입니다. 문항별 배점은 각 문항에 표시되어 있습니다.

[경기 ○○중]

1. 다음 중 밑줄 친 단어의 쓰임이 옳은 것은? (3점)

① Water boils at 0℃.

② I felt good because I had a tough time yesterday.

③ I can't walk any more. But I have to go on and on.

④ What a dry day it is! It is raining cats and dogs outside.

⑤ I think I am out of breath. I feel really calm and relaxed.

[광주 ○○중]

2. 다음 중 단어의 설명이 가장 바르지 않은 것은? (3점)

① powerful : having great strength or force; very effective

② original : happening or existing first or at the beginning

③ limit : a point at which something stops being possible

④ boiling : a measure of how hot or cold a place or thing is

⑤ invent : to make, design, or think of a new thing

[서울 강동구 ○○중]

3. 다음 〈보기〉 문장의 밑줄 친 어휘의 영영풀이로 알맞은 것은? (2점)

> **보기**
> My uncle was a professional athlete.

① a person who writes music

② a person who competes in sports

③ a group of listeners or spectators

④ to destroy something by fire or heat

⑤ happening or existing first or at the beginning

[서울 광진구 ○○중]

4. 다음 중 짝지어진 대화가 어색한 것은? (3점)

① A: Who do you usually play soccer with?
  B: My friends.

② A: Do you play badminton often?
  B: Yes, it's my favorite free time activity.

③ A: What does she do for a living?
  B: She is living in Seoul.

④ A: What do you do in your free time?
  B: I often bake cookies.

⑤ A: Why do you have many paper flowers?
  B: They're for my mother's birthday.

[5-7] 다음 대화를 읽고 물음에 답하시오.

Hojin: _____
Judy: I often go rock climbing with my dad.
Hojin: What mountain do you go to?
Judy: No, Hojin. I usually do ⓐit at a gym near my house.
Hojin: I see. Have you ever done ⓑit on a real mountain?
Judy: _____ But I hope to do ⓒit on a real mountain someday.
Hojin: That's really cool. _____
Judy: Sure. I'm going this Saturday. The gym is not that far from here. ⓓIt is located right next to the Central Park.
Hojin: That sounds great. I'm excited to go rock climbing.
Judy: I'm sure you'll love ⓔit!

[경기 ○○중]

7. 위 대화의 빈칸에 들어갈 말을 〈보기〉에서 골라 순서대로 짝지은 것은? (4점)

보기
(A) What did you do last weekend?
(B) Judy, what do you do in your free time?
(C) Yes, I have.
(D) Can I come and join you next time?
(E) Not yet.
(F) When are you going to do it?

① (A) - (C) - (E)
② (A) - (E) - (B)
③ (B) - (C) - (D)
④ (B) - (E) - (D)
⑤ (F) - (C) - (B)

[인천 ○○중]

5. 다음 밑줄 친 ⓐ~ⓔ 중 가리키는 내용이 나머지 넷과 다른 하나는? (3점)

① ⓐ   ② ⓑ   ③ ⓒ
④ ⓓ   ⑤ ⓔ

[경기 ○○중]

6. 위 대화를 읽고 알 수 있는 내용으로 알맞은 것은? (3점)

① Judy의 여가활동 비용
② Judy의 여가활동 횟수
③ Judy의 여가활동 장소
④ Judy가 여가활동을 위해 갔던 산
⑤ Judy가 여가활동을 좋아하는 이유

[부산 ○○중]

8. 다음 우리말을 영어로 바르게 옮긴 것은? (3점)

이것은 아시아에서 가장 큰 백화점이다.

① This is the largest department store in Asia.
② This is most largest department store in Asia.
③ This is largest department store in Asia.
④ This is larger department store in Asia.
⑤ This is the most long department store in Asia.

9. 다음 밑줄 친 우리말을 주어진 조건에 맞게 영작하시오. (5점)

> **조건**
> 1. who/which/whose 중에 하나를 골라 사용하시오.
> 2. <보기>에서 알맞은 단어를 골라 활용하시오.

> **보기**
> by / lose / save / write / the books / I / the man / my mom / are

A: What did you lose?
B: 나는 우리 엄마에 의해서 쓰인 책들을 잃어버렸어.
→ _____
_____

10. 다음 형용사와 그 형용사의 최상급 형태가 바르게 연결된 것의 개수는? (2점)

> · cold – coldest
> · big - biggest
> · good – well
> · large - largest
> · busy - busiest
> · famous - more famous

① 1개   ② 2개   ③ 3개
④ 4개   ⑤ 5개

[11-12] 다음 대화를 읽고 물음에 답하시오.

A: _____(가)_____
B: I often play badminton. How about you?
A: I really like to do _____(나)_____.
B: Where do you usually do it?
A: I usually do it at a gym near my house.

11. 내용상 빈칸 (가)에 들어갈 수 <u>없는</u> 것은? (3점)
① What do you do for fun?
② What do you do for a living?
③ How do you spend your spare time?
④ What do you like to do in your free time?
⑤ What do you enjoy doing in your spare time?

12. 빈칸 (나)에 들어갈 가장 알맞은 말은? (3점)
① computer games
② baduk
③ jogging
④ board games
⑤ rock climbing

13. 다음 중 어법상 알맞지 <u>않은</u> 것은? (4점)

① The man that lives next door is friendly.

② I often visit my uncle who live in Seoul.

③ He is a writer who wrote the book.

④ He works for a company which makes cameras.

⑤ Who ate the apple which was on the table?

14. 알맞은 관계대명사를 이용하여 다음 두 문장을 하나의 문장으로 바꾸어 쓰시오. (4점)

> • I don't like stories.
> • They have unhappy endings.

→ _____

15. 다음 괄호 안에 주어진 단어를 사용하여 예시와 같이 최상급 표현을 이용하여 자동차의 속도를 설명하는 문장을 완성하시오. (5점)

	the gray car	the white car	the black car
model	2008	2015	2019
speed	220km/h	180km/h	150km/h

보기

The gray car is the oldest of the three cars.

→ _____(slow) of

   the three cars.

[16-18] 다음 대화를 읽고 물음에 답하시오.

> Suji: Mike, have you ever heard of flying yoga?
> Mike: Yeah! I've seen it on TV. People were (A)_____ in the air!
> Suji: Guess what? I'm learning it these days.
> Mike: Really? It looked so scary. Do you like it, Suji?
> Suji: At first, I was a little scared, but now I'm enjoying it.
> Mike: Sounds great! I think I should exercise more, too.
> Suji: Do you want to join my yoga class?
> Mike: No, that's too (B)_____ for me. I'll just play basketball.

16. 위 대화의 빈칸 (A)와 (B)에 들어갈 말이 차례대로 짝지어진 것은? (3점)

① hang – scaring

② hanging – scared

③ hung – scared

④ to hang – scary

⑤ hanging – scary

17. 위 대화의 내용과 일치하지 <u>않는</u> 것은? (3점)

① Mike will do flying yoga more for exercise.

② Suji is learning flying yoga these days.

③ Mike has seen flying yoga on TV.

④ Suji was scared of flying yoga at first.

⑤ Suji likes flying yoga and is enjoying it.

18. 위 대화를 읽고 대답할 수 <u>없는</u> 것은? (4점)

① Where is the yoga class?

② What will Mike do for exercise?

③ What is Suji learning these days?

④ What does Mike think he should do?

⑤ Why doesn't Mike want to do flying yoga?

19. 위 글의 밑줄 친 ⓐ~ⓔ 중, 문맥상 표현의 쓰임이 어색한 것은? (4점)

① ⓐ   ② ⓑ   ③ ⓒ

④ ⓓ   ⑤ ⓔ

20. 위 글의 빈칸 (A)에 들어갈 말로 알맞은 것은? (2점)

① clean   ② wet   ③ drink

④ burn   ⑤ wash

[19–23] 다음 글을 읽고 물음에 답하시오.

Imagine you are ⓐ<u>in the middle of</u> a great desert. The sands go on and on ⓑ<u>in every direction</u>. The sun feels like a giant ball of fire. The hot wind burns your face and throat. You open your backpack to drink some water. Oh, no! You're almost ⓒ<u>out of water</u>. You (A)_____ your throat with a drop of water and keep going.

Sounds like a bad dream? Well, this is not a dream for the people who ⓓ<u>take place</u> the 4 Deserts Race. The 4 Deserts Race is ⓔ<u>a series of</u> four races across the world's toughest deserts. (B)각각의 경주는 250킬로미터이고 7일이 걸린다. Participants are given drinking water and a place in a tent each night, but they must carry their own things and food.

21. 위 글에서 대답할 수 <u>없는</u> 질문은? (3점)

① How long is each race?

② What is the 4 Deserts Race?

③ What burns your face and throat?

④ How many days does each race take?

⑤ How many participants are there in the race?

22. 위 글의 목적으로 알맞은 것은? (4점)

① 4 Deserts Race 소개

② 사막 여행의 필요성 홍보

③ 여행할 때 챙겨야 할 물품 안내

④ 4 Deserts Race에서 각 사막의 특징 안내

⑤ 4 Deserts Race를 완주하기 위한 방법 소개

23. 위 글의 밑줄 친 우리말 (B)와 같도록 영어로 쓰시오. (5점)

조건

킬로미터는 줄임 형태로 쓰지 말 것

→ ＿＿＿＿＿＿＿＿＿＿＿＿＿＿＿＿＿＿

24. 다음 ⓐ~ⓔ 중 문맥상 자연스럽지 못한 문장은? (4점)

Sujin: Mike, have you ever heard of flying yoga?

Mike: Yeah! I've seen it on TV. People were hanging in the air!

Sujin: ⓐGuess what? I'm learning it these days.

Mike: ⓑReally? It looked so scary. Do you like it, Sujin?

Sujin: ⓒAt first, I was a little scared, but now I'm enjoying it.

Mike: Sounds great! ⓓI think you should exercise more, too.

Sujin: ⓔDo you want to join my yoga class?

Mike: No, that's too scary for me. I'll just play basketball.

① ⓐ ② ⓑ ③ ⓒ

④ ⓓ ⑤ ⓔ

[25-29] 다음 글을 읽고 물음에 답하시오.

The first race takes place in the Atacama Desert in Chile. (A) It is the ⓐ[driest / most humid] desert in the world. In fact, it hasn't rained in some parts of the Atacama Desert for 400 years! (B) The next race goes to the Gobi Desert in China. (C) It is the windiest desert on earth. (D) The third race heads to the Sahara Desert in Egypt. It is the hottest of the four deserts. (E) Finally, the race travels to the coldest desert on earth, Antarctica. If you throw boiling water into the air here, it ⓑ[freezes / unfreezes]! Even more, your breath turns to ice crystals immediately!

Only the greatest runners on the planet can take part in the 4 Desert Race, right? Not exactly. Many of the participants are ⓒ[ordinary / extraordinary] people like you and me. So why do they do it? Adrianna, a librarian from France, says, ⓓ"It's a chance to test your limits and make your own history. Anyone who crosses the finish line can do anything."

25. 위 글의 흐름으로 보아 주어진 문장이 들어가기에 가장 적절한 곳은? (3점)

Exceeding 50℃ is very common in the area.

① (A) ② (B) ③ (C)

④ (D) ⑤ (E)

26. 위 글의 괄호 ⓐ~ⓒ 안에서 문맥에 맞는 낱말로 가장 적절한 것은? (4점)

	ⓐ	ⓑ	ⓒ
①	driest	freezes	ordinary
②	driest	unfreezes	extraordinary
③	driest	freezes	extraordinary
④	most humid	unfreezes	extraordinary
⑤	most humid	freezes	ordinary

27. 위 글의 밑줄 친 ⓓ에 담긴 4 Deserts Race의 정신으로 옳지 않은 것은? (3점)

① brave

② challenging

③ pessimistic

④ responsible

⑤ goal-oriented

28. 위 글의 주제로 가장 알맞은 것은? (4점)

① 4 Deserts Race

② 4 Toughest Deserts

③ Rain in the Atacama Desert

④ The Length of the Race

⑤ The Temperature of the Race

29. 위 글의 내용을 읽고 친구들이 나눈 대화이다. 친구들이 유추한 내용이 옳은 것은? (4점)

① 김예송: The climate in all deserts is always hot and dry.

② 이예송: But the Atacama Dessert is unusual because it rains a lot throughout the area.

③ 박예송: Because the wind blows a lot in the Gobi Desert, wearing sports goggles will protect your eyes from dust.

④ 최예송: The average temperature of the Antarctica never goes under 30°C.

⑤ 신예송: Only the Olympic gold medalist can participate in and finish the 4 Desert Race.

MEMO

정답 및 해설

Lesson 1 (중간)
1회

> 01 ② 02 ③ 03 ① 04 ③ 05 ⑤ 06 ④ 07 ⑤
> 08 ⑤
> 09 If you say bad (words to your friends), they will not like you.
> 10 ② 11 ④ 12 ⑤ 13 ④ 14 ② 15 ① 16 ④
> 17 ⑤ 18 ② 19 ③ 20 ⑤ 21 ④
> 22 Respect others' opinions, and you will make many friends.
> 23 ③ 24 ① 25 ② 26 ④ 27 sometimes 28 ②
> 29 ①
> 30 Giving feedback shows that you're listening.
> 31 ②

01 ② friend는 친구라는 뜻을 가진 명사, friendly는 다정한이라는 뜻을 가진 형용사이다. 나머지는 모두 형용사-부사 관계이다.

02 useful 유용한 / manage 관리하다 / poor ~를 잘 못하는 / a sense of direction 방향 감각

03 I have several things to buy.를 제외하고 각각 Not let's go → Let's not go / to write → to write with / cold something → something cold / to finish it → to finish로 고쳐야 어법상 적절한 문장이 된다.

04 위에서부터 순서대로 mean, president, about, planning이 들어가야 내용상 적절한 문장이 된다.

05 A가 더 건강해지려면 무엇을 해야 하냐고 묻고 있다. 따라서 이에 대한 B의 대답으로 ⑤ 친구들을 저녁 식사에 초대할 수 있다(You can invite your friends over for dinner.)라는 문장은 대화의 흐름상 어색하다.

06 위의 대화를 영상으로 만들 경우에 적절한 것을 찾는 문제로, 위의 대화는 Talk Smart 응용 프로그램을 광고하는 상업 영상에 쓰이는 것이 대화의 내용상 적절하다.

07 위 대화에 언급되어 있듯이, ⑤ Minsu는 Talk Smart 응용 프로그램을 써 본 적이 없다(Minsu has no experience with the Talk Smart app.).

08 위 대화에서 두 화자의 관계로 가장 적절한 것은 ⑤친구-친구이다.

09 '명령문, and ~'는 '...해라, 그러면 ~'의 뜻으로, If를 사용해 바꿔 쓸 수 있다. '명령문, or ~'는 '...해라, 그렇지 않으면 ~'의 뜻으로, If ~ not (= Unless)을 사용해 바꿔 쓸 수 있다.

10 위 글은 대화를 더 잘 하고 더 좋은 화자가 될 수 있도록 도와주는 조언을 담은 글이다. 따라서 위 글의 내용과 일치하는 것은 맨 첫 문장에 나와 있는 ②공통의 관심사를 찾는 것이 대화에 도움이 된다(Finding common interests is helpful during the talk.)이다.

11 위 글의 ⓐ는 to부정사의 형용사적 용법으로 사용되었다. 따라서 이와 같이 형용사적 용법으로 사용된 것은 ⓒ, ⓕ이다. 나머지는 각각 ⓑ 명사적, ⓓ 부사적, ⓔ명사적 용법으로 사용되었다.

12 위 대화에서 Jenny의 말(What can I do to get more members?)에서 알 수 있듯이 ⑤Jenny는 더 많은 동아리 회원들을 모집하고 싶어 한다.

13 위 대화의 문맥상 조언을 구하는 표현이 들어가는 것이 가장 적절하다. 따라서 ④이 정답이 된다.

14 위 대화에서 "How about ~?"은 상대방에게 제안을 할 때 쓸 수 있는 표현이다. 대체할 수 있는 표현으로는 "What about ~?" 또는 "Why don't you ~?" 등이 있다.

15 have in common ~를 공통으로 갖고 있다
be interested in ~에 관심이 있다

16 위 글의 ⓐ는 to부정사의 형용사적 용법으로 사용되었다. 따라서 이와 같이 형용사적 용법으로 사용된 것은 ④ ⓐ, ⓑ, ⓔ이다. ⓒ, ⓓ는 모두 to부정사의 명사적 용법으로 사용되었다.

17 위 글의 첫 문단에서는 대화에서 그저 듣는 것만 할 수 없으며 서로 공통의 관심사를 찾아 대화해야 한다고 말하고 있다.

18 B가 처음에 Mina에게 무슨 일이 있냐고 물었고 이에 Mina는 친한 친구인 Kate가 자신에게 화가 났다고 말한다. B는 무슨 일이 있었냐고 묻는데, Mina는 Kate에게 자신의 강아지의 머리와 같다고 말했다고 대답한다. 이어서 B는 Kate가 화를 내는게 당연하다고 말하고, Mina는 Kate가 자신과 말을 하지 않을 거라며 걱정하는 순서로 이어지는 것이 대화의 흐름상 자연스럽다.

19 위 대화에서 ③ Brian이 Kate에게 문자를 보낼 것이다(Brian will send a text to Kate.)라는 내용은 언급되지 않았다.

20 위 대화에서 B는 M에게 친구와 화해하려면 어떻게 해야 하는지 묻고 있다. 따라서 이에 대한 대답으로 적절하지 않은 것은 ⑤ 더 이상 친구와 말을 해서는 안 된다(I think you should not talk to her anymore.)이다.

21 위 대화에서 B는 G에게 새 학기에 친구를 많이 사귈 수 있는 방법에 대해서 조언을 구했다. 따라서 이에 대한 대답으로 적절하지 않은 것은 ④ 넌 이미 스포츠 동아리에 가입했잖아.(You've already joined a sports club.)이다.

22 respect 존중하다 / make friends 친구를 만들다

23 ③의 to play는 to부정사의 명사적 용법으로 사용되었다. 나머지는 모두 to부정사의 형용사적 용법으로 사용되었다.

24 어떤 사물이나 사람을 이전보다 더 나쁘게 만들다(to make something/somebody worse than before)라는 영영 풀이는 improve(향상시키다)라는 단어와 의미가 동일하지 않다.

25 위 글의 제일 마지막 문장에서 뒤에 오는 대화를 잘하기 위한 조언들을 연습하면 좋은 화자가 될 수 있다고 말하고 있다(When you practice the following tips, you will soon be a great talker.). 따라서 뒤에 이어질 내용으로는 ② 좋은 화자가 되기 위한 조언이 가장 적절하다.

26 '대화 주제를 바꿔라, 그렇지 않으면 상대방은 잠에 빠질 것이다.'라는 의미의 주어진 문장은 대화 상대방이 지루해하지 않게 그들에게 말할 기회를 주라는 문장에 앞서 위치하는 것이 문맥상 가장 적절하다.

27 from time to time은 '때때로'라는 뜻을 갖고 있으며 sometimes와 바꿔 쓸 수 있다.

28 someone who comes from a different country는 foreigner(외국인)를 가리키는 영어 단어로 위 글에서 언급되어 있지 않다.

29 위 글에서 언급되었듯이, 그저 듣는 것만 하는 것이 아니라 대화 상대방에게 듣고 있다는 것을 나타내 주는 반응을 보여주는 것이 좋은 대화를 할 수 있는 방법이다.

30 동명사 ~ing를 이용해 주어 giving feedback을 만들 수 있다. 또한 주어가 단수이므로 동사는 shows가 된다.

31 밑줄 친 ⓐto talk about themselves는 to부정사의 명사적 용법이다. 따라서 이와 같은 용법으로 사용된 문장은 ② 그녀는 내가 자는 것을 원치 않았다.(She didn't want me to sleep.)는 문장이다.

Lesson 1 (중간)

2회

01 ③	02 ②	03 ⑤	04 ②	05 ②	06 ③	07 ②
08 ④	09 ①	10 ④	11 ⑤			

12 What can I do to save the Earth?　**13** ③　**14** ⑤
15 If you are not (quiet), the baby will wake up

16 ①	17 ③	18 ②	19 ⑤	20 difficulties		
21 ⑤	22 ⑤	23 ①	24 ③	25 ①	26 ②	27 ⑤

28 Change the topic, or your partner will fall asleep
29 I should put others first.　**30** ③　**31** ③

01 미래에 어떤 일을 하거나 하지 않을 것이라고 어떤 사람에게 말하다(to tell someone that you will do or not do something)라는 뜻을 가진 단어는 ③ promise(약속하다)이다.

02 tip이라는 단어는 '조언', '팁을 주다'라는 뜻을 모두 지닌다.

03 '언제나 일에 노력과 주의를 쏟아붓는'이라는 뜻을 가진 영영 풀이가 가리키는 단어는 ⑤ 열심히 일하는 (hard-working)이다.

04 나머지는 모두 ① to goes → to go / ③ ask → to ask / ④ talking → to talk / ⑤ rested → to rest로 고쳐야 어법상 적절한 문장이 된다.

05 ②에서 to be는 to부정사의 명사적 용법으로 사용되었으며 나머지는 모두 to부정사의 형용사적 용법으로 사용되었다.

06 How about ~?은 상대방에게 무언가를 제안하는 표현으로, What about ~?, Why don't you ~? 등으로 바꿔 쓸 수 있다.

07 helpful 유용한, 도움이 되는

08 대화에서 Talk Smart에 대해 Kate가 그것은 한 언어를 다른 언어로 바꿔 준다(It changes one language to another.)고 언급했다.

09 '자신의 나라가 아닌 다른 곳에서 온 사람'이라는 뜻을 가진 단어는 ① 외국인(foreigner)이다.

10 ④에서 A가 목요일에 함께 무엇을 하며 놀자로 제안했는데, 이에 대해 B는 안된다고 대답했지만 서점에 가는 것은 어떠냐고 묻고 있으므로 대화 흐름상 어색하다.

11 <보기>에서 밑줄 친 부분은 to부정사의 형용사적 용법으로 사용되었다. 이와 같이 to부정사의 형용사적 용법으로 쓰인 문장은 ⑤이다. ①, ②는 명사적 용법, ③, ④는 부사적 용법으로 쓰였다.

12 조언을 구하는 표현으로 What can I do to ~? 또는 What should I do to ~?와 같은 표현을 쓸 수 있다. /

save the Earth 지구를 지키다

13 명령문을 이용하여 동사+목적어+부사구 순으로 쓴다.

14 동명사 ~ing를 써서 주어 giving feedback을 만들고 이에 따라 동사는 단수형 shows를 쓴다.

15 명령문, and ~'는 '...해라, 그러면 ~'의 뜻으로, If를 사용해 바꿔 쓸 수 있다. '명령문, or ~'는 '...해라, 그렇지 않으면 ~'의 뜻으로, If ~ not (= Unless)을 사용해 바꿔 쓸 수 있다.

16 위 대화의 내용으로 미루어 볼 때, (A)에는 친구와 화해하려면 어떻게 해야하는지 조언을 구하는 표현이 들어가야 적절하다. 따라서 ① ㄱ, ㄴ, ㄷ이 정답이다.

17 ④ c, d는 모두 to부정사의 형용사적 용법이 쓰인 어법상 옳은 문장이다. a. play → play with b. That → It

18 위 글에서 Mike가 자신은 노래 동아리에 가입했다고 말하자 Jane이 알겠다고 대답하는데, Mike가 무슨 일이냐며 묻는다. 이에 Jane은 자신은 마술 동아리 회장인데 회원이 2명 밖에 없다고 걱정하자 안됐다고 한다. 또한 Jane이 회원을 더 모을 수 있는 방법에 대해 조언을 구하자 Mike는 학교 게시판에 모집 광고를 붙이는 것이 어떠냐고 조언하는 순서로 이어지는 것이 대화 흐름상 가장 자연스럽다.

19 Jane의 마지막 말(That's a good idea. I'll do it right away.)로 미루어 볼 때, Jane은 Mike의 조언을 받아들여 자신이 회장으로 있는 마술 동아리 회원 모집 공고를 학교 게시판에 붙일 것이다.

20 trouble: 문제, 곤란, 골칫거리 / difficulty: 어려움, 곤경

21 위 글의 맨 마지막 문장(Here are five tips to become a better talker.)에서 알 수 있듯이, 더 나은 화자가 될 수 있게 도와주는 조언들이 나올 것이다.

22 ⓔ'상대방의 말에 반응을 하는 등의 피드백을 주는 것이 명하게 있다는 것을 보여준다'는 문장은 위 글의 내용에서 벗어나는 문장이다.

23 A는 B에게 영어 실력을 늘리려면 어떻게 해야 하는지 물었다. 따라서 이에 대한 대답으로 적절하지 않은 것은 ① 종이를 재활용하는 것은 어때?(What about recycling paper?)이다.

24 Jack은 대화 초반에 취미에 대한 질문을 Kate에게 던졌고 그럼으로써 공통의 관심사인 만화책에 대해서 이야기 하는 방향으로 대화가 진행되고 있다. 따라서 ③ 공통의 관심사를 나누기가 정답이다.

25 ① Take a rest, or you'll feel better.에서 or를 and로 고쳐야 내용상 자연스러운 문장이 된다.

26 '동의'를 표현하기 위한 방법으로 머리를 위아래로 움직

이다'라는 영영 풀이가 가리키는 것은 ⓑ nod(끄덕이다)이다.

27 (A) from time to time은 '때때로'라는 뜻으로, sometimes와 바꿔 쓸 수 있다.

28 fall asleep 잠에 빠져 들다

29 조동사 should를 사용해 질문했으므로, I should ~로 대답해야 한다. 또한 위 글에서 맨 마지막 문단에 나와 있듯이, 다른 사람을 나보다 앞에 두면(배려하면) 모두 나와 이야기하고 싶어할 것(Put others first, and everyone will want to talk with you.)이라고 직접적으로 언급되어 있다.

30 친구들이 말할 때 그냥 듣기만 한다는 Lion이나 자신이 말할 때에는 주제가 지루해도 친구들이 자신의 말에 귀를 기울여야 한다는 Andy의 말은 모두 위 글에서 언급된 좋은 화자가 되기 위한 조언들과는 일치하지 않는다.

31 bring into ~에 끌어들이다, figure out 알아채다, 생각해내다 / disappointed 실망한, relieved 안도한 / be proud of ~를 자랑스러워하다, tight with ~에 인색한

Lesson 2 (중간)

01 ②
02 (a) I'm sure he will be perfect (b) What's he like?
03 ③   **04** He has been invisible since last night.
05 ②
06 (1) I have not cooked for my family.
    (2) He has lived in Canada for three years.
07 ③ **08** ④ **09** ③
10 (1) They all love English. (2) He is outgoing.
11 ⑤ **12** ⑤ **13** ② **14** ② **15** ③ **16** ②, ④
17 ④ **18** ④ **19** ② **20** ② **21** ③
22 I'm sure we'll arrive there before 5.
23 ③ **24** ① **25** ③ **26** ① **27** ③ **28** ① **29** ①
30 ④

01 어떤 일에 의해 쉽게 짜증이 난(easily annoyed by things)이라는 영영 풀이는 patient의 반의어인 impatient를 가리킨다.

02 (a) "I'm sure ~"는 어떤 일에 대해 확신할 때 쓸 수 있는 표현이다. (b) "What is he like?"는 어떤 인물의 성격을 물어볼 때 쓸 수 있는 표현이다.

03 아버지는 은행에서 일하시므로 ⓒa banker로 고쳐야 내용상 적절하다.

04 과거의 어느 시점에서부터 현재까지 어떤 일이 계속되고 있음을 나타내는 현재완료(have+p.p.)의 계속적 용법을 쓸 수 있다.

05 (b)는 현재완료의 경험적 용법이 사용된 문장이다. 따라서 이와 같은 경험적 용법으로 사용된 문장은 '현규는 개미를 먹어본 적이 있다.'는 문장이다.

06 (1) 경험의 유무를 나타내는 현재완료의 경험적 용법을 사용해 문장을 만들 수 있다. (2) 과거의 어느 시점부터 현재까지 이어지는 일에 대해 나타낼 때 현재완료의 계속적 용법을 이용해 문장을 만들 수 있다.

07 ⓒ에는 What이, 나머지 빈칸들에는 how[How]가 들어가는 것이 어법상 자연스럽다.

08 위 대화에서 Sue와 두 친구 Rosa, Mike는 영어를 좋아해서 같은 동아리에 있다(We all love English. We are also in the same club.)고 언급되어 있다.

09 Sue와 두 친구들이 속한 동아리의 이름은 대화 중에 언급되지 않았다.

10 (1) Sue와 두 친구들은 모두 영어를 좋아한다(We all love English.)고 언급되어 있다. (2) Mike는 외향적(He is outgoing.)이라고 대화에 언급되어 있다.

11 A가 Amy는 매우 빨리 달린다고 말했을 때 B가 Amy가 참을성이 있고 친절하다고 말하는 것은 대화 흐름상 자연스럽지 않다.

12 worried 걱정하는 / practice 연습하다, promise 약속하다 / nervous 긴장한, relaxed 느긋한

13 위 대화에서 Minsu는 시험 볼 때 선생님 앞에서는 긴장이 된다고 언급했다.

14 B의 대답으로 미루어 볼 때, A는 Jenny가 어떤 성격이냐?(What is she like?)고 물어봤다고 유추할 수 있다.

15 위 대화의 흐름상 5시 이전에 도착할 수 있다고 확신하는 문장이 들어가야 적절하다.

16 ② have you visited → did you visit
④ have left → left

17 ① Junho는 Hojin의 같은 반 친구이며 ② Junho는 노래를 아름답게 부른다고 Hojin이 말했다. ③ Junho는 지난주에 전학을 왔으며 ⑤ Hojin이 Junho의 전화번호를 주고 싶어 하는지 않은지는 언급되어 있지 않다.

18 M이 그들의 성격은 어떠냐?(What are they like?)고 물어봤으므로 G의 대답으로는 성격을 묘사하는 ④ They are outgoing and helpful.이 가장 적절하다.

19 아버지가 가족들에게 빵을 건네달라고 요청한 것이므로 ③ My father asked us to pass him the bread.가 가장 적절하다.

20 ⓐ는 so로, ⓒ는 was jumping으로 고쳐야 한다. ⓓ는 disappeared로, ⓔ는 are로 고쳐야 적절하다.

21 (B) right는 '바로, 꼭'이라는 뜻으로 사용되었다. ① 맞는, ② 꼭 맞는, ④ 오른쪽의, ⑤ 옳은, 올바른

22 어떤 일에 대해 확신할 때 "I'm sure ~"라는 표현을 쓸 수 있다.

23 울 때 눈에서 나오는 물(a drop of liquid that comes out of your eyes when you cry)은 ⓒ tear(눈물)를 가리킨다.

24 위 글에서는 아빠가 가족들 눈에 보이지 않게 되었다가 다시 보이게 되는 내용을 담고 있으므로 ① 집으로 돌아온 아빠(Father Returning Home)라는 제목이 가장 적절하다.

25 그가 무얼 좋아하는지에 대해 물어보는 A의 질문에 B는 그의 새로운 머리가 마음에 든다고 했으므로 대화의 흐름상 어색하다.

26 ① have kept는 과거의 어느 시점부터 현재까지 계속되는 일에 대해서 나타내는 현재완료의 계속적 용법이다. 나머지는 모두 현재완료의 경험적 용법이 사용된 문장들이다.

27 in a few moments는 '곧'이라는 뜻을 가진 숙어이다.

28 ask A to B A에게 B를 요청하다 / has been invisible 현재완료의 계속적 용법

29 빈칸 (가)가 포함된 문장에서 시제가 현재완료의 계속적 용법이 사용되었으므로 since(이래로)가 들어가는 것이 가장 적절하다.

30 (C)는 현재완료의 경험적 용법이다. 따라서 이와 같은 용법으로 사용된 문장은 ④ 우리 부모님은 전에 영국에 가 보신 적이 있다.(My parents have been to England before.)이다.

Lesson 2 (중간) 2회

01 ② **02** ⑤
03 (Jane) has studied English for (6) years.
04 ① **05** ② **06** ③ **07** ① **08** ④ **09** ③
10 She has known them for a long time.
11 ③ **12** ① **13** ② **14** ⑤ **15** ② **16** ⑤
17 how do you like your school these days?
18 ③ **19** ④ **20** ① **21** ④ **22** ② **23** ⑤
24 ⓐ bank ⓑ teacher ⓒ younger ⓓ eighth ⓔ dog
25 ④ **26** ② **27** ④ **28** ① **29** ③ **30** ④

01 ① promise, ③ yell, ④ shake, ⑤ secret을 의미하는

영영 풀이이다.

02 these days 최근에

03 주어진 문장들은 Jane이 6년 전부터 영어를 공부해 오고 있다는 의미의 문장들이다. 따라서 현재완료의 계속적 용법을 이용해 Jane has studied English for 6 years.라고 표현할 수 있다.

04 A가 그의 성격이 어떠냐고 물어봤으므로 B의 대답은 그의 외모에 대한 대답이 아니라 성격에 대한 묘사여야 한다.

05 주어진 문장의 밑줄 친 부분은 현재완료의 경험적 용법이다. 따라서 이와 같이 현재완료의 경험적 용법이 사용되지 않은 문장은 현재완료의 계속적 용법이 사용된 ② 그는 10년 동안 이곳에서 살아 왔다.(He has lived here for 10 years.)이다.

06 '학생들이 배우기 위해 가는 장소'라는 영영 풀이가 가리키는 단어는 school(학교)이다.

07 Hojin의 대답으로 유추해 볼 때, Judy는 Junho의 성격에 대해 물어보았다고 볼 수 있다.

08 위 대화에 나와 있듯이, Junho는 지난 주에 전학을 왔고 아직 밴드 동아리에 가입되어 있지 않다.

09 위 대화에 언급되어 있듯이, Judy의 학교로 전학을 온 것은 Hojin이 아니라 Junho이다.

10 현재 완료의 계속적 용법을 사용해서 오랫동안 알아 왔다는 의미로 has known for a long time이라는 표현을 쓸 수 있다.

11 글의 흐름상 ⓒ는 시험을 앞두고 긴장한 B에게 G가 격려하는 문장이 되어야 한다. 따라서 "Everyone doesn't." 가 아니라 "Everyone does."가 되어야 한다.

12 위 대화는 Minsu가 영어 말하기 시험을 앞두고 긴장하고 있다는 내용이다. 따라서 ① Minsu에게 무슨 일이 일어났는지(What happened to Minsu?)에 대해서 답할 수 있다.

13 A는 Mina의 성격에 대해 물어봤으므로 B는 Mina의 외모가 아니라 성격에 대해 대답해야 하지만 외모에 대해 설명하고 있으므로 대화의 흐름상 적절하지 않다.

14 A는 Jack이 하루 종일 공부를 한다고 말했으므로, 보기 중 B의 대답으로 가장 적절한 것은 ⑤ 그가 시험에서 좋은 성적을 받을 것을 확신한다(I'm sure he will get a good grade on the test.)이다.

15 아빠는 딸에게 친구들의 성격을 물어보고 있으므로 ⓑ do 가 아니라 are가 되어야 한다.

16 위 대화에서 어떻게 친구가 됐느냐는 아빠의 물음에 (e) 모두 영어를 좋아해서 같은 동아리에 들게 되었고, (a) 아빠는 친구들의 성격이 어떤지 묻는다. 그에 대한 대답으로

(c) Rosa는 친절하다고 대답한다. 또한 (d) 아빠는 Mike의 성격에 대해 묻고 (b) 딸은 Mike가 외향적이라고 대답하는 순서로 이어지는 것이 대화 흐름상 가장 적절하다.

17 "How do you like ~?"은 어떤 사람이나 사물에 대해 마음에 드는지 묻는 표현이다.

18 Sue는 이미 영어 동아리에 친구들과 함께 가입했다.

19 빵을 매일 건네주겠다고 약속한 것은 딸 Hope가 아빠에게 약속한 것이다.

20 ⓐ 주절과 동일하게 과거 시제 came이 되어야 한다.
ⓑ 과거 시제 appeared가 되어야 한다.
ⓒ 과거 시제 hugged가 되어야 한다.

21 대화 흐름상 극장에 늦게 도착할까봐 걱정하는 A에게 B가 할 말로 가장 적절한 것은 ④ 우린 분명히 7시 전에 도착할 거야.(I'm sure we'll get there before 7.)이다.

22 ⓑ '아버지가 우리와 주말마다 놀아주신다'라는 문장이나 ⓓ '엄마가 딸 Hope에게 그러라고 말하고 계셨다'라는 문장은 모두 글의 흐름과 반대되는 문장들이다.

23 아빠가 식사 자리에서 무엇을 했는지(What did my father do at the table?)는 위 대화에서 아직 언급되어 있지 않다.

24 위 글에서 Jimmy의 아빠는 은행원이며, 엄마는 선생님이라고 언급되어 있다. 또한 Hope는 Jimmy의 여동생이고 Jimmy는 8학년이며 Smiley라는 개를 키우고 있다.

25 (A)pretty는 '꽤, 아주'라는 뜻으로 쓰였다. (ㄷ)의 pretty는 '예쁜'이라는 의미이다.

26 위 글에 직접적으로 지난 주 금요일 저녁 아빠가 집에 일찍 오셔서 다같이 저녁 식사를 했다(But last Friday, he came home early for dinner. At the table, we were all doing our own thing.)고 언급되어 있다.

27 (D)는 딸 Hope를 가리킨다. 나머지는 모두 Hope의 아빠를 가리킨다.

28 위 글에서 금요일의 저녁 식사 자리에서는 가족들이 각자의 할 일을 하면서 아빠의 말소리도 안 들릴 정도로 산만하다.

29 ⓐlike는 '~처럼'이라는 뜻으로 사용되었다. ①, ②, ④, ⑤는 모두 '좋아하다'라는 뜻으로 사용되었다.

30 아빠가 저녁 식사 자리에서 가족들에게 빵을 달라고 소리쳤다고 직접적으로 언급되어 있다(My father shouted, "Am I invisible? Pass me the bread!").

Lesson 3 (기말)

> **01** ⑤ **02** ② **03** ①
>
> **04** If he breaks the rule, he will be punished.
>
> **05** ② **06** ④ **07** ③ **08** ④ **09** ③ **10** ④
>
> **11** If it rains this afternoon, I will bring you the umbrella.
>
> **12** ③ **13** ⑤ **14** ④ **15** ③ **16** ③ **17** ①, ②, ④
>
> **18** ⑤ **19** ③ **20** ① **21** ⑤ **22** ③, ④ **23** ②
>
> **24** ① **25** ②, ⑤ **26** ③ **27** ②
>
> **28** The concert hall goes wild. **29** ④ **30** ⑤

01 end 끝내다, 끝나다 / pianist 피아니스트 / invent 발명하다 / powerful 힘 있는

02 '폐로 들이쉬고 다시 내쉬는 공기'라는 영영 풀이가 가리키는 것은 ② breath(숨)이다.

03 위 글에서 공연을 보는 관객 일부는 공연에서 열광하여 소리를 지르고, 다른 일부의 관객들은 그 스타를 보고 사진 찍기 위해 몇 시간씩 기다린다는 내용이 나온다. 따라서 빈칸에 들어갈 말로 가장 적절한 것은 일부는(some), 다른 일부는 (others)이다.

04 '만약 ~이라면'이라는 뜻으로 현재에 일어날 법한 일을 가정하는 단순 조건절에서 if를 쓸 수 있다. 이때 접속사 if가 포함되는 조건절에서는 미래를 의미하더라도 현재형 동사를 쓴다. / break a rule 규칙을 깨다

05 글의 문맥상 (A)에는 종이꽃이 많은 이유를 묻는 질문이, (B)에는 어떻게 그것들을 얻었는지 묻는 질문이 들어가는 것이 가장 적절하다.

06 ④ 대화의 소녀가 어느 종이 꽃을 가장 좋아하는지 (Which paper flower does the girl like best?)에 대해서는 언급되지 않았다.

07 위 글은 왜 오래된 옷을 갖고 있냐는 A의 질문에 벼룩시장에서 그것을 팔 것이라는 B의 대답으로 시작한다. 이에 A 자신도 오래된 옷을 갖고 있다고 말하자, B가 자신과 함께 벼룩시장에서 오래된 옷을 판매할 것이냐고 묻는 순서로 가는 것이 대화의 흐름상 가장 적절하다.

08 ④는 Why로 시작하는 질문이므로 giving이 아니라 동사원형 give가 들어가는 것이 어법상 적절하다.

09 ③ Amy는 Blue Sky라는 밴드를 정말 좋아한다(I'm also a big fan of the band.)고 언급되어 있다.

10 '~을 가장 좋아한다'고 표현할 때 '주어+like+목적어+best[most]'라고 쓸 수 있다.

11 '만약 ~이라면'이라는 뜻으로 현재에 일어날 법한 일을 가정하는 단순 조건절에서 if를 쓸 수 있다. 이때 접속사 if가 포함되는 조건절에서는 미래를 의미하더라도 현재형 동사를 쓴다.

12 대화 흐름상 위에서부터 순서대로 ⑤-②-④-①이 들어간다.

13 이야기가 흥미롭다는 내용이므로 ⑤interested가 아니라 interesting이 들어가는 것이 어법상 적절하다.

14 ④ loved를 were loved로 고쳐야 어법상 적절한 문장이 된다.

15 to ~로 / in+장소 ~에 / in+연도 ~(연도)에

16 위 글에서 ③ Elvis Presley는 최초의 아이돌이 아니며 (How about Elvis Presley in the 1950's? Not even close.) 그 이전에 최초의 아이돌이 있었다고 언급되어 있다.

17 위 글에서 공연장에서 소리를 지르거나 스타와 사진을 찍기 위해 몇 시간을 기다리거나 심지어는 스타를 보기 위해 다른 도시로 이동을 한다(Some scream madly at concerts. Others wait hours to take pictures of their stars. Some students even travel to another city to see their favorite stars.)라고 직접적으로 언급되어 있다.

18 행위의 대상이 주어인 수동태 문장이므로 빈칸에는 과거분사형인 ⑤ written이 들어가야 어법상 적절하다.

19 ③selled를 sell의 올바른 과거분사형인 sold로 고쳐야 어법상 적절하다.

20 독서 동아리가 어떻게 되어가느냐는 A의 질문에 33번 버스를 타라는 B의 대답은 대화 흐름상 자연스럽지 않다.

21 빈칸 (A)에 들어갈 말로 적절한 것은 recent(최근에, 최근의)이다. ⑤에 들어갈 말로 적절한 것은 recent이다.

22 (B)는 to부정사의 부사적 용법으로 사용되었다. ①는 형용사적 용법, ②는 명사적, ⑤는 형용사적 용법으로 사용되었다.

23 위 글에 언급된 것처럼, 비틀즈나 엘비스 프레슬리가 최초의 아이돌이 아니며 그 이전에 최초의 아이돌이 있었다.

24 위 글의 마지막 문장에 최초의 아이돌이 누군지 알기 위해 타임머신을 타고 과거로 돌아가 보자고 했으므로 위 글에 이어질 내용은 최초의 아이돌에 대한 것이다.

25 ⓐ face → faces / ⓒ pays → pay / ⓓ was born → he was born으로 고쳐야 어법상 적절한 문장이 된다.

26 위 글에서 Liszt는 긴 손가락으로 건반을 동시에 여러 개 누른다(his long fingers press down on many keys at once)고 언급되었다.

27 from memory 기억을 더듬어, 외워서

28 go wild 열광의 도가니가 되다

29 위 글의 마지막 문단의 마지막 문장에 Liszt의 음악을 들어보는 건 어떨까요?(Why don't you give his music a listen now?)라고 제안하고 있으므로 ④ Franz Liszt의 음악 듣기가 가장 적절하다.

30 아마존 강이 브라질에 위치해 있는 것이므로 locate(위치시키다)라는 동사의 수동형 is located in이 빈칸에 가장 적절하다.

Lesson 3 (기말)

01 ①	**02** ③	**03** ②	**04** ②	**05** ⑤	**06** ②	**07** ③
08 ①	**09** ③	**10** ②	**11** ⑤	**12** ②	**13** ④	**14** ④

15 To find the answer, let's take a time machine to a concert hall in Vienna in 1845.

16 ②	**17** ⑤	**18** ②	**19** ②	**20** ③	**21** ②	**22** ③
23 ①						

24 Because they didn't want to miss a single note.

25 ⑤	**26** ③	**27** ①	**28** ①	**29** ①	**30** ③

01 순서대로 cheer, breath, single, successfully, person이 들어간다.

02 순서대로 some, others, to, even, another가 들어간다.

03 테이블이 엄마에 의해 만들어졌다는 내용이므로 동사 자리에는 수동형 was made가 적절하다.

04 어느 나라를 가장 방문해 보고 싶냐는 A의 물음에 인도의 타지마할에 가고 싶기 때문이라는 B의 대답은 대화의 흐름상 적절하지 않다.

05 '만약 ~이라면'이라는 뜻으로 현재에 일어날 법한 일을 가정하는 단순 조건절에서 if를 쓸 수 있다. 이때 접속사 if가 포함되는 조건절에서는 미래를 의미하더라도 현재형 동사를 쓴다.

06 위 대화에서 B가 자신이 만드는 종이꽃이 엄마의 생신 선물이라고 말하자 G는 그것들이 멋지다고 이야기한다. 그러자 B는 자신이 직접 만들었다고 대답하자 A는 B가 잘 만든다고 칭찬을 한다. 이에 B는 자신이 종이접기 수업을 들었다고 설명하고 A는 엄마를 위한 완벽한 생신 선물이라고 말하는 순서로 이어지는 것이 흐름상 가장 자연스럽다.

07 상대방이 Tom의 종이꽃이 엄마를 위한 완벽한 생신 선물이 될 것이라고 이야기하자 이에 대한 Tom의 마지막 말(I hope so, too)로 미루어 볼 때, ③ Tom은 엄마가 그의 선물을 마음에 들어 하기를 원한다(Tom hopes that his mom will like his gift.)는 문장이 내용상 적절하다.

08 위 대화에서 오래된 옷을 중고 시장에 팔려는 Amy에게 Mike가 자신도 오래된 옷이 있다고 하였으므로 이에 대한 Amy의 반응으로 적절한 것은 ①나랑 같이 벼룩시장에서 판매할래?(why don't you join me?)이다.

09 주어진 ⓐfaces는 동사 '마주보다', '향하다'라는 뜻으로 사용되었다. 따라서 이와 같은 뜻으로 사용된 문장은 ③ 내 집은 호수의 옆에 남쪽을 향하고 있다(My house faces the south by the lake.)라는 문장이다.

10 ⓑ그 말을 들어서 유감이다.(I'm sorry to hear that.)라는 문장은 위 글의 흐름상 적절하지 않다.

11 ⑤Jiho가 지난주 토요일에 친구와 함께 팬미팅에 갔던 것이 아니라 이번주 토요일에 가기로 했으므로 (F)는 옳은 대답이다. 나머지는 ① (T) ② (F) ③ (T) ④ (F)이다.

12 위 대화에서는 두 사람이 주말에 함께 팬미팅을 가기로 한 내용까지만 언급되어 있지 어디서 팬미팅이 개최되는지는 언급되어 있지 않다.

13 '아이돌이란 개념이 1960년대에 비틀즈와 함께 시작되었나?'라는 질문은 '많은 사람들이 비틀즈를 사랑했지만 최초의 아이돌은 아니다'(Many people loved them, but they were not the first.)라는 문장 앞에 위치하는 것이 가장 적절하다.

14 위 글의 흐름상 많은 사람들이 사랑했지만 최초의 아이돌은 아니었던 The Beatles를 가리킨다.

15 take a time machine 타임머신을 타다 / find an answer 해답을 찾다

16 ⓐ definite 확실한, definitely 분명히, 절대로 / ⓑ '어느 노래를 가장 좋아하니?'라고 묻는 내용이었으므로 Which가 적절하다 / ⓒ 접속사 when(~할 때)가 어법상 적절하다

17 ⑤ 라디오 방송이 끝난 후 그들을 무엇을 할 것인가?(What are they going to do after this show is over?)에 대한 대답은 위 대화에서 언급되어 있지 않다.

18 '만약 ~이라면'이라는 뜻으로 현재에 일어날 법한 일을 가정하는 단순 조건절에서 if를 쓸 수 있다. 이때 접속사 if가 포함되는 조건절에서는 미래를 의미하더라도 현재형 동사를 쓴다.

19 여러 개 혹은 여러 명 중에 일부를 some, 그리고 다른 일부를 others라고 표현한다. 만약 남은 것이 한 개 혹은 한 명일 경우엔 the other라고 표현한다. 따라서 ② Others가 들어가는 것이 어법상 적절하다.

20 ⓐ, ⓑ, ⓓ는 to부정사의 부사적 용법으로 쓰였으며, ⓒ, ⓔ는 전치사 to로 '~으로'라는 뜻으로 사용되었다.

21 몇몇 학생들은 심지어 그들이 가장 좋아하는 스타를 보기 위해 다른 도시로 이동하기도 한다.(Some students even travel to another city to see their favorite stars.)라고 언급되어 있다.

22 ⓐ 마주하다, 향하다/ ⓑ 숨을 참다/ ⓓ 동시에, 한번에/ ⓔ 열광의 도가니가 되다

23 (A) 모든 좌석들이 차 있는 상태이므로 are filled가 적절하다. (B) 사람들이 하나의 음정이라도 놓치기 싫어했다는 뜻이므로 to miss가 적절하다. (C) 전치사 like 뒤에는 동명사 watching이 적절하다.

24 '왜 사람들이 공연장에서 숨을 참았는가?'라는 질문에 대한 답은 두 번째 문단에 하나의 음정이라도 놓치지 않기 위해(because they didn't want to miss a single note.)라고 언급되어 있다.

25 청중들이 음정을 하나라도 놓치지 않기 위해 피아니스트가 건반을 누르기 시작했을 때 숨을 참았다(The audience holds the breath when the pianist starts to touch the keys.)고 언급되어 있다.

26 '이 놀라운 스타는 누구였는가?'라는 질문이 들어가기에 가장 적절한 곳은 그가 누구인지 설명하는 부분 바로 앞이다.

27 사람들이 Liszt를 최초의 아이돌로 여긴 이유는 바로 ① 그의 연주(his performance) 때문이었다.

28 '만약 ~이라면'이라는 뜻으로 현재에 일어날 법한 일을 가정하는 단순 조건절에서 if를 쓸 수 있다. 이때 접속사 if가 포함되는 조건절에서는 미래를 의미하더라도 현재형 동사를 쓴다.

29 ⓐat once는 '동시에', '한번에'라는 뜻으로 ① at the same time(동시에)이라는 숙어와 동일한 뜻을 지닌다.

30 위 세 질문 모두 대화 상대방의 선호를 묻는 질문이므로 ③ Which가 들어가는 것이 어법상 적절하다.

Lesson 4 (기말)   1회

01 ⑤ **02** ③ **03** ② **04** ① **05** ③ **06** ⑤ **07** ⑤
08 ① **09** ④
10 (1) break the rules, will be punished
    (2) was sung by
11 The police saved the man whose boat was sunk.
12 ⑤ **13** ① **14** ③ **15** ④ **16** ④ **17** ③
18 She often goes rock climbing (with her dad).
19 ③ **20** Have you ever heard of flying yoga?
21 ① **22** ④ **23** ④ **24** ① **25** ① **26** ② **27** ⑤
28 ② **29** ② **30** ②
31 Salt is one of the most important things in the world.

01 temperature는 '기온', '온도'를 의미한다.

02 위에서부터 순서대로 tough, ordinary, limit, participants, burn이 들어가야 한다.

03 out of ~는 '~이 떨어진, 바닥난'이라는 뜻이다.

04 위 글의 흐름상 한계를 시험해 보고(test my limits) 자신만의 역사를 만들고 싶다(make my own history)는 내용이 들어가는 것이 적절하다.

05 scary는 '무섭게 하는,' scared는 '무서워하는'이라는 뜻을 갖는다. 따라서 ③ scary - scared - scary가 빈칸에 가장 적절하다.

06 ⓔhave been을 are나 were로 바꿔야 어법상 적절한 문장이 된다.

07 ⓕ를 Why did you take part in the race?라는 문장으로 영작할 수 있다.

08 위에서부터 순서대로 jogged, ridden, run, swum이 들어가야 내용상 자연스럽다.

09 '가장 ~하다'는 최상급 표현을 사용해 Which class got the highest score?라고 표현할 수 있다.

10 (1) '만약 ~이라면'이라는 뜻으로 현재에 일어날 법한 일을 가정하는 단순 조건절에서 if를 쓸 수 있다. 이때 접속사 if가 포함되는 조건절에서는 미래를 의미하더라도 현재형 동사를 쓴다.
(2) 수동태 문장을 만들 때는 본래의 동사를 be+p.p.(과거분사형)으로 고치는 것 뿐만 아니라 시제를 본래 문장과 일치시켜 표현해야 한다. 또한 본래 문장에서 주어 자리에 있던 행위의 주체는 by를 붙여 문장 뒤에 쓴다.

11 위 문장은 The police saved the man.과 His boat was sunk.라는 두 문장으로 이루어져 있다. 따라서 소유격 관계대명사 whose를 이용해 The police saved the man whose boat was sunk.라고 표현할 수 있다.

12 ⑤에서 are를 is로 고쳐야 어법상 적절한 문장이 된다.

13 head to ~로 향하다 / up to ~까지 / travel to ~로 이동하다

14 아타카마 사막은 가장 건조한 사막이고 사막의 일부 지역은 400년 동안 비가 온 적이 없다(It is the driest desert in the world. In fact, it hasn't rained in some parts of the Atacama Desert for 400 years!)고 언급되어 있다.

15 위 글 (a)If는 '만약 ~이라면'이라는 뜻으로 현재에 일어날 법한 일을 가정하는 단순 조건절에서 쓰였다. ④에는 unless가 들어가야 어법상 적절하다.

16 위 대화의 빈칸에는 Judy에게 여가 시간 혹은 자유 시간에 무엇을 하냐고 물어보는 질문이 들어가야 흐름상 자연

스럽다.

17 대화 후반부에 Judy는 Hojin이가 암벽 등반을 좋아할 것 (You're going to love it!)이라고 언급했다.

18 Judy는 아빠와 함께 암벽 등반을 종종 가곤 해(I often go rock climbing with my dad.)라고 말했다.

19 위 대화에서 Jessy와 Mike는 플라잉 요가에 대해서 이야기하고 있는데, Jessy는 요즘 자신이 플라잉 요가를 배우고 있다(I'm learning it these days.)고 말했다.

20 '~해 본 적이 있냐'고 물을 때는 현재완료의 경험적 용법을 사용해 "Have you ever ~?"라는 문장으로 표현할 수 있다.

21 (A)에는 아타카마 사막이 얼마나 건조한지 부연 설명하고 있으므로 In fact(사실은)가, (B)에는 당신과 나처럼 평범한 사람들도 4대 사막 경주를 할 수 있다고 말한 후 그래서 왜 참가자들이 경주를 하느냐는 문장이므로, So(그래서)가 들어가는 것이 글의 흐름상 적절하다.

22 ⓓ는 Adrianna에 대한 부연 설명이므로 librarian으로 바꿔야 적절하다.

23 Adrianna는 4대 사막 경주에 참가하는 것이 자신의 한계를 시험하고 자신만의 역사를 쓸 수 있는 기회(It's a chance to test your limits and make your own history.)라고 말했다.

24 왜 경주에 참여했냐고 묻는 질문이므로 의문사 Why를 이용해 Why did you take part in the race?라는 문장을 만들 수 있다. ① take place는 '개최하다', '일어나다'라는 뜻으로 쓰인다.

25 Adrianna의 직업이 무엇인지는 위 대화에서 언급되지 않았다.

26 <보기>의 who는 접속사이자 대명사로 쓰인 관계대명사이다. 이와 같이 관계대명사로 쓰인 문장은 ②Did you meet the girl who has blonde hair?이다. ①, ③, ④, ⑤는 모두 의문사로 쓰였다.

27 tough는 '힘든', '고된'이라는 뜻을 가진 단어이므로, '고난으로 가득 차고, 이루기 쉬운'이라는 영영 풀이와는 맞지 않다.

28 (A) keep ~ing 계속해서 ~하다 (B) 선행사가 the participants로 사람이므로 which가 아니라 who나 that을 쓰는 것이 어법상 적절하다. (C) each race라는 단수 주어이므로 takes를 쓰는 것이 어법상 적절하다.

29 몇 명의 사람들이 이 경주에 참여하는지(How many people participate in this race?)는 위 글에서 언급되어 있지 않다.

30 위 글은 4대 사막 경주에 대해서 설명하기 위해 쓰인 소개

글이자 서론이므로 ② The Introduction of the Four Deserts Race(4대 사막 경주의 소개)가 제목으로 가장 적절하다.

31 최상급 표현 중 하나인 'one of the 최상급'을 이용해 'Salt is one of the most important things in the world.'라는 문장을 만들 수 있다. 이때 of 뒤의 최상급 표현에서는 복수형을 써야 한다.

Lesson 4 (기말) 2회

01 ③	**02** ④	**03** ②	**04** ③	**05** ④	**06** ③	**07** ④
08 ①						

09 I lost the books which were written by my mom.

10 ④	**11** ②	**12** ⑤	**13** ②

14 I don't like stories which have unhappy endings.

15 The black car is the slowest **16** ⑤ **17** ①

18 ① **19** ④ **20** ② **21** ⑤ **22** ①

23 Each race is 250 kilometers long and takes seven days.

24 ④ **25** ⑤ **26** ① **27** ③ **28** ① **29** ③

01 ① boils → freezes / ② tough → pleasant / ④ dry → humid / ⑤ am out of → am not out of

02 어떤 장소나 사물이 얼마나 더운지 혹은 추운지에 대한 정도(a measure of how hot or cold a place or thing is)라는 영영풀이가 가리키는 것은 temperature(기온, 온도)이다.

03 athlete은 운동선수라는 뜻으로, ② 스포츠에서 경쟁하는 사람(a person who competes in sports)을 가리킨다.

04 그녀는 직업이 무엇이냐는 A의 질문에 그녀는 서울에 살고 있다는 B의 대답은 흐름상 자연스럽지 않다.

05 ⓓ는 Judy가 다니는 the gym을 가리킨다. 나머지는 모두 암벽 등반을 가리킨다.

06 Judy는 주로 집 근처 헬스장에서 여가 활동인 암벽 등반을 한다(I usually do it at a gym near my house.)고 말했다.

07 대화 초반에 Judy의 대답으로 미루어 볼 때 Hojin은 Judy에게 여가 시간에 뭘 하냐고 물어봤다(What do you do in your free time?). 또한 Hojin이가 진짜 산에서 암벽 등반을 해봤냐고 묻자 Judy는 아직 아니라고 (Not yet.) 대답하면서 나중에 해보고 싶다고 말한다. 마지막으로 Hojin이가 다음에 자신도 같이 가서 암벽 등반을 해봐도 되냐고 묻자 Judy는 좋다고 말한다(Can I come and join you next time?). 따라서 ④ (B) - (E) - (D)가 정답이 된다.

08 '가장 ~하다'는 최상급 표현을 사용해서 This is the largest department in Asia.라고 쓸 수 있다.

09 주어진 우리말은 I lost the books.와 They were written by my mom.이라는 두 문장으로 이루어져 있는 문장이다. 따라서 두 문장을 관계대명사 which 또는 that으로 연결할 수 있다. 이때 관계대명사는 접속사이자 대명사 역할을 한다.

10 good의 최상급은 best, famous의 최상급은 most famous이다.

11 ② What do you do for a living?은 직업이 무엇이냐고 묻는 질문이다.

12 위 글에서 A가 하기를 좋아하는 것은 헬스장에서 할 수 있는 것이므로 ⑤ rock climbing(암벽 등반)이 가장 적절하다.

13 ② who live를 who lives로 고쳐야 어법상 적절한 문장이 된다.

14 두 문장에서 공통되는 부분이 stories와 They이므로 관계대명사 which나 that을 이용할 수 있다.

15 slow라는 단어가 주어졌을 때, 세 자동차 중에 가장 느린 것은 검은색 차이므로 The black car is the slowest라고 쓸 수 있다.

16 각각 (A)hanging(달려 있는)과 (B) scary(무섭게 하는)가 어법상 적절하다.

17 Mike는 플라잉 요가가 무섭다고 말하면서 자신은 농구를 하겠다(that's too scary for me. I'll just play basketball.)고 말했다.

18 ① 요가 수업을 어디서 하는지(Where is the yoga class?)는 위 대화에서 언급되지 않았다.

19 ④take place(발생하다)가 아니라 take part in(~에 참가하다)이 되어야 한다.

20 위 글의 흐름상 한 방울의 물로 목을 축인다(wet)라는 의미가 되어야 한다.

21 ⑤ 경주 참가자의 수가 얼마인지는 위 글에서 언급되지 않았다.

22 위 글은 전반에 걸쳐 네 개의 대륙에 있는 네 가지 사막을 달리는 4대 사막 경주에 대해서 소개하고 설명하고 있다. 따라서 위 글의 목적으로는 ① 4 Deserts Race 소개가 가장 적절하다.

23 each 각각의 / take (시간이) 걸리다

24 '난 네가 더 운동해야 한다고 생각해'(I think you should exercise more, too.)라는 문장은 위 대화의 흐

름상 적절하지 않다.

25 '50도를 넘는 것은 이 지역에서는 매우 흔하다'라는 주어진 문장이 들어가기에 가장 적절한 곳은 가장 더운 사막이라고 하는 사하라 사막에 대한 설명 뒤에 들어가는 것이 적절하다.

26 글의 흐름상 ⓐ에는 비가 400년 동안 오지 않았다고 했으므로 driest가, ⓑ에는 가장 추운 사막인 남극 대륙에서 끓는 물을 뿌리면 언다는 내용의 freezes가, ⓒ에는 많은 참가자들이 평범하다는 내용의 ordinary가 들어가는 것이 적절하다.

27 pessimistic(회의적인)은 위 글에 나타난 4대 사막 경주의 정신과는 상반된다.

28 위 글에서는 4대 사막 경주에 대해서 소개하고 있으므로 주제로 ① 4 Deserts Race가 가장 적절하다.

29 중국의 고비 사막은 가장 바람이 많이 분다고 했으므로 스포츠 고글을 쓰면 먼지로부터 눈을 보호해줄 것이라는 박예송의 말이 가장 적절하다.

MEMO

MEMO